P9-CNC-079

Cabell's Directory
of Publishing Opportunities in
Educational Psychology and Administration

Eight Edition
Volume I
A through J of B

David W. E. Cabell, Editor-in-Chief

Deborah L. English, Executive Editor
Twyla J. George, Executive Managing Editor
Lacey E. Earle, Editor

www.cabells.com

P O Box 5428, Beaumont, Texas 77726-5428
409/898-0575 / Fax: 409/866-9554

$174.95 U.S. for addresses in the United States
Price includes shipping and handling for the U.S.
Add $60 for surface mail to countries outside the U.S.
Add $150 for airmail to countries outside the U.S.

ISBN: 978-0-911753-37-0

WITHDRAWAL

University Libraries, University of Memphis

©2007 by Cabell Publishing, Inc., Box 5428, Beaumont, Texas 77726-5428.

All rights reserved. No part of this publication may be reproduced, stored in a retrieval system, or transmitted in any form or by any means, electronic, mechanical, photocopying, recording, or otherwise without the prior written permission of the publisher.

Although every reasonable effort has been made to ensure the accuracy of the information contained in this directory, the author cautions the reader that there may be mistakes in the information provided. Thus, the reader is responsible for his or her actions resulting from the use of this information.

Printed by McNaughton & Gunn, Inc.:
    960 Woodland Drive; Saline, MI 48176; www.bookprinters.com.

Cover Design by *Wayne Hale / Alphabet Soup, Inc.*:
    2494 Broadway, Beaumont, TX 77702

University Libraries, University of Memphis

TABLE OF CONTENTS

i REF
Z
286
.E3
C37
8th ed.
2007/08
v.1

iv

Preface

The objective of *Cabell's Directory of Publishing Opportunities in Educational Psychology and Administration* is to help you publish your ideas.

The *Directory* contains the editor's name(s), address(es), phone number(s), e-mail and web address(es) for over 350 journals.

To help you in selecting those journals that are most likely to publish your manuscripts the **Index** classifies the journals into twenty-eight (**28**) different topic areas. In addition, the Index provides information on the journal's type of review process, number of external reviewers and acceptance rate.

To further assist you in organizing and preparing your manuscripts, the *Directory* includes extensive information on the style and format of most journals. If a journal has its own set of manuscript guidelines, a copy of these guidelines is published in the *Directory*. Also, each entry indicates the use of a standard set of publication guidelines by a journal. For example, some journals use the *Chicago Manual of Style* or the *Publication Manual of the American Psychological Association*.

Furthermore, the *Directory* describes the type of review process used by the editor(s) of a journal, type of review, number of reviewers, acceptance rate, time required for review, availability of reviewers comments, fees charged to review or publish the manuscript, copies required and manuscript topics. Information on the journal's readership is also provided.

Although this *Directory* focuses on journals in the specialized areas of **Educational Psychology and Administration**, other directories focus on **Educational Curriculum and Methods**, **Educational Technology and Library Science** and **Psychology and Psychiatry**. The division of journals into these four directories more appropriately meets the researcher's need for publishing in his area of specialization.

The decision to place journals in their respective directory is based on the manuscript topics selected by the editor as well as the journals' guidelines for authors. If you wish to find the most current information on the *Directory*, visit **www.cabells.com**. Please contact us for the login registration procedure.

Also, the *Directory* includes a section titled "**What is a Refereed Article?**" which tends to emphasize the value of a blind review process and use of external reviewers. However, this section cautions individuals using these criteria to also consider a journal's reputation for quality. Additionally, it indicates that differences in acceptance rates may be the result of different methods used to calculate these percentages and the number of people associated with a particular area of specialization.

How to Use the Directory

TABLE OF CONTENTS
Table of Contents provides over 350 journals to help you locate a publication.

INDEX
Index classifies the journals according to twenty-eight (28) different manuscript topics. It also includes information on the type of review, number of external reviewers, acceptance rate and page number of each journal.

SUBMISSION PROCESS
Submission Process indicates the preferred method of manuscript submission for each journal.

CONTACT INFORMATION
Contact Information provides: the Editor's name(s), Mailing address(es), Telephone number(s), E-mail and Web address(es).

PUBLICATION GUIDELINES
Manuscript Style refers to the overall style guide the journal uses for text, references within the text and the bibliography. This is usually either the *Chicago Manual of Style* or the *Publication Manual of the American Psychological Association (APA).*

Manuscript Length refers to the length of the manuscript in terms of the number of double-spaced typescript pages.

Copies Required indicates the number of manuscript copies you should submit to the editor.

REVIEW PROCESS
Type of Review specifies blind, editorial, or optional review methods. A blind review indicates the reviewer(s) does not know who wrote the manuscript. An editorial review indicates the reviewer knows who wrote the manuscript. The term "optional" indicates the author may choose either one of these types of review.

No. of External Reviewers and *No. of In House Reviewers*
These two items refer to the number of reviewers who review the manuscript prior to making a decision regarding the publication of the manuscript. Although the editor attempted to determine whether the reviewers were on the staff of the journal or were outside reviewers, many of the respondents had trouble distinguishing between internal and external reviewers. Thus it may be more accurate to add these two categories and determine the total number of reviewers.

Acceptance Rate refers to the number of manuscripts accepted for publication relative to the number of manuscripts submitted within the last year. The method of calculating acceptance rates varies among journals.

Time to Review indicates the amount of time that passes between the submission of a manuscript and notification to the author regarding the results of the review process.

Reviewer's Comments indicates whether the author can obtain a copy of the reviewer's comments. In some cases, the author needs to request that the editor send these remarks.

Invited Articles indicates the percentage of articles for which the editor requests an individual to write specifically for publication in the journal. The percentage is the number of invited articles relative to the total number of articles that appeared in a journal within the past year.

Fees to Publish refers to whether the journal charges a fee to publish the manuscript. Knowing this item assists the author in his decision to place the manuscript into the review process.

Fees to Review refers to whether the journal charges a fee to review the manuscript. Knowing this item permits the author to send the required funds with the manuscript.

CIRCULATION DATA
Reader indicates the predominant type of reader the publication seeks to attract. These are classified into academics, practitioners, administrators and counselors.

Frequency of Issue indicates the number of times a journal will be published in a year.

Sponsor/Publisher indicates the journal's affiliation with a professional association, educational institution, governmental agency, and/or publishing company.

MANUSCRIPT TOPICS
Manuscript Topics indicates those subjects the journal emphasizes.

MANUSCRIPT GUIDELINES/COMMENTS
Manuscript Guidelines/Comments provides information on the journal's objectives, style and format for references and footnotes that the editor expects the author to follow in preparing his manuscript for submission.

How the Directory Helps You Publish

Although individuals must communicate their ideas in writing, the *Directory* helps the author determine which journal will most likely accept the manuscript. In making this decision, it is important to compare the characteristics of your manuscript and the needs of each journal. The following table provides a framework for making this comparison.

Information Provided by the Directory for Each Journal	Manuscript Characteristics
Topic(s) of Articles Manuscript Guidelines	Theme
Acceptance Rate Percentage of Invited Articles	Significance of Theme
Type of Reader	Methodology and Style
Circulation Review Process	Prestige
Number of Reviewers Availability of Reviewers Comments Time Required for Reviewer	Results of Review

This framework will help the author determine a small number of journals that will be interested in publishing the manuscript. The *Directory* can assist the author in determining these journals, yet a set of unwritten and written laws prevent simultaneous submission of a manuscript to more than one journal. However, a manuscript can be sent to another journal in the event of a rejection by any one publication.

Furthermore, copyright laws and editorial policy of a given publication often require the author to choose only one journal. Consequently, some journals will require the author to sign a statement indicating the manuscript is not presently under review by another publication.

Publication of the manuscript in the proceedings of a professional association does not prevent the author from sending it to a journal, however there usually are some restrictions attached. Most professional associations require that the author acknowledge the presentation of the manuscript at the associate meeting.

Since the author is limited to submission of a manuscript to only one journal and the review process for each journal requires a long period of time, contacting the editors of the journals may help the author determine the journal most likely to publish the manuscript.

To interest the editor the author should provide the following information:

- Topic, major idea or conclusion of the manuscript
- The subject sample, research setting conceptual framework, methodology type of organization or location
- The reasons why the author thinks the journal's readers would be interested in your proposed article
- Asks the editor to make comments or suggestions on the usefulness of this type of article to the journal

While contacting the editor is helpful in selecting a journal that will be likely to publish the manuscript, the author could use the *Directory* and the framework presented to develop a set of journals which would be likely to publish the manuscript.

Relating the Theme of the Manuscript to the Topics of Articles Published by Each Journal

To begin the processes of choosing editors to contact and/or submitting a manuscript, the author needs to examine the similarity between the theme of the manuscript and the editor's needs. The *Directory* describes these needs by listing the topics each publication considers important and the manuscript guidelines. To find those journals that publish manuscripts in any particular area, refer to the topic index.

In attempting to classify the theme, the author should limit his choice to a single discipline. With the increasing specialization in the academic world, it is unlikely that reviewers, editors, or readers will understand an article that requires knowledge of two different disciplines. If these groups do not understand a manuscript, the journal will reject it.

If a manuscript emphasizes an interdisciplinary approach, it is important to decide who will be reading the article. The approach should be to explain the theoretical concepts of one discipline to the specialist in another discipline. The author should not attempt to resolve theoretical issues present in his discipline and explain their implications for specialists in another discipline.

Although the discipline classifications indicate the number of journals interested in your manuscript topic, the manuscript guidelines help the author determine the journals that will most likely have the greatest interest in the manuscript. The manuscript guidelines provide a detailed statement of the criteria for judging manuscripts, the editorial objectives, the readership and the journal's content and approach. This information makes it possible to determine more precisely the congruence between the manuscript and the type of articles the journal publishes. **The *Directory* contains the manuscript guidelines for a large number of journals.**

The Relationship Between the Journal's Acceptance Rate and Significance of the Theme of the Manuscript

In addition to determining the similarity between the topic of the manuscript and the topic of articles published by the journal, an examination of the significance of the theme to the discipline is also an important criterion in selecting a journal. The journals with the lowest acceptance rate will tend to publish those manuscripts that make the most significant contributions to the advancement of the discipline. Since these journals receive a large number of manuscripts, the editors distinguish those manuscripts likely to make a significant contribution to the reader's knowledge.

Defining newness or the contribution of any one study to the understanding of a discipline is difficult. However, it is possible to gain some insights into this definition by asking the following questions:

1. Is the author stating the existence of a variable, trend or problem, not previously recognized by the literature?

2. Is the author testing the interactions of a different set of variables or events?

3. Is the author presenting a new technique to cope with a problem or test an idea not previously presented in the literature?

4. Is the author using a subject sample with different characteristics than previously presented in the literature?

If the manuscript does not satisfy one of the first two categories, it is unlikely that a journal with a low acceptance rate will accept it for publication. Thus, the author should send the manuscript to those journals where the acceptance rate is higher.

Although the *Directory* provides the acceptance rates of manuscripts for many different journals, it is important to examine the data on percentage of invited articles for each journal. A high acceptance rate may result because the editor has asked leaders in the discipline to write articles on a particular subject. These invited articles are usually accepted. Since the author of an unsolicited manuscript competes with the leaders in the discipline, the manuscript will have to make a significant contribution to receive the editor's approval.

The Relationship of the Manuscript's Style and
Methodology to the Journal's Readership

Another factor in selecting the journal to receive the manuscript is the journal's readership. The readers of each journal include practitioners, academics, administrators and counselors or a combination of these groups.

Since the most important goal for an author is to publish the manuscript, the author should consider the prestige of the journal only after the manuscript has a relatively high probability of being published by more than one journal. This probability is determined by the responses the author received from contact with the editors and the similarity between the finished manuscript and the needs of the journal.

The method of determining the prestige of a journal varies depending on its readership, review process and acceptance rate. If the readership is primarily administrators or practicing professionals, the author should request the editor provide a media package that would contain the journal's circulation and an average reader profile.

In contrast, the prestige of journals whose readership is primarily academic is determined by the review process, the acceptance rate and the journal's reputation. The review process should be a blind review with two or three reviewers and the acceptance rate should be low. In addition, the journal should posses a reputation for quality.

The Possible Results of the Review Process and the
Selection of a Journal to Receive the Manuscript

Despite the fact that a journal with lower prestige would most likely publish the article, the author might be willing to take a chance on a journal with a greater amount of prestige. Since this will decrease the chances of manuscript acceptance, the author should also consider the consequences of rejection. The consequences include the knowledge the author will gain from having his manuscript rejected.

To determine the amount of knowledge the author is likely to gain requires consideration of the number of reviewers the journal uses in the review process, the availability of the reviewer's comments and the time required for the review process. If the journal makes the reviewer's comments available to the author, this provides a great learning opportunity. Also, the more people that review the manuscript, the greater the author's knowledge will be concerning how to improve the present manuscript. Hopefully, the author will transfer the knowledge gained from writing this manuscript to future manuscripts.

Should the review process take a small amount of time relative to a long period of time, the author is provided with a greater opportunity to use this knowledge to revise the manuscript. To assist the author in determining those journals that provide a suitable learning opportunity, each journal in the *Directory* includes information on the number of reviewers, availability of reviewer's comments to the author and time required for review.

Sending the Manuscript

Before sending the manuscript to an editor, the author should write a cover letter, make sure the manuscript is correctly typed, the format conforms to the journal's guidelines and the necessary copies have been included. **The author should always keep a copy of the manuscript.**

The cover letter that is sent with the manuscript makes it easy for the editor to select reviewers and monitor the manuscript while it is in the review process. This letter should include the title of the manuscript, the author name(s), mailing address(es) phone and fax number(s) and e-mail addresses. In addition, this letter should provide a brief description of the manuscript theme, its applicability and significance to the journal's readership. Finally it should request a copy of the reviewer's comments regardless of whether the manuscript is accepted or rejected.

Receipt of the Reviewer's Comments

The reviewers may still reject the article although the author may have followed this procedure and taken every precaution to avoid rejection. When this occurs, the author's attitude should be focused on making those changes that would make the manuscript more understandable to the next editor, and/or reviewer. These changes may include providing additional information and/or presenting the topic in a more concise manner. Also, the author needs to determine whether some error occurred in selecting the journal to receive the manuscript. Regardless of the source of the errors, the author needs to make those changes that will improve the manuscript's chances of being accepted by the next journal to receive it.

Unless the journal specifically requests the author to revise the manuscript for publication, the author should not send the manuscript to the journal that first rejected it. In rejecting the manuscript, the reviewers implied that it could not be revised to meet their standards for publication. Thus, sending it back to them would not improve the likelihood that the manuscript will be accepted.

If your manuscript is accepted, go out and celebrate but write another one very quickly. When you find you're doing something right, keep doing it so you won't forget.

"What is a Refereed Article?"

With some exceptions a refereed article is one that is blind reviewed and has two external reviewers. The blind review requirement and the use of external reviewers are consistent with the research criteria of objectivity and of knowledge.

The use of a blind review process means that the author of the manuscript is not made known to the reviewer. With the large number of reviewers and journals, it is also likely that the name of the reviewers for a particular manuscript is not made known to the author. Thus, creating a double blind review process. Since the author and reviewers are frequently unknown, the manuscript is judged on its merits rather than on the reputation of the author and/or the author's influence on the reviewers.

The use of two (2) reviewers permits specialists familiar with research similar to that presented in the paper to judge whether the paper makes a contribution to the advancement of knowledge. When two reviewers are used it provides a broader perspective for evaluating the research. This perspective is further widened by the discussion between the editor and reviewers in seeking to reconcile these perspectives.

In addition to these criteria, some researchers include the journal's acceptance rate in their definition of a refereed journal. However, the method of calculating acceptance rates varies among journals. Some journals use all manuscripts received as a base for computing this rate. Other journals allow the editor to choose which papers are sent to reviewers and calculate the acceptance rate on those that are reviewed that is less than the total manuscripts received. Also, many editors do not maintain accurate records on this data and provide only a rough estimate.

Furthermore, the number of people associated with a particular area of specialization influences the acceptance rate. If only a few people can write papers in an area, it tends to increase the journal's acceptance rate.

Although the type of review process and use of external reviewers is one possible definition of a refereed article, it is not the only criteria. Judging the usefulness of a journal to the advancement of knowledge requires the reader to be familiar with many journals in their specialization and make their own evaluation.

AASA Journal of Scholarship and Practice, The

SUBMISSION PROCESS:

Postal & Electronic Submission Required via EMail

frederick.dembowski@selu.edu

CONTACT INFORMATION:

Frederick Dembowski, Editor
Southeastern Louisiana University
Department of Educational Leadership
  and Technology
SLU 10549
Hammond, LA 70402 USA

Phone:
  985-549-5713

Email:
  fdembowski@selu.edu
  jessica.kastner@selu.edu

Website:

REVIEW PROCESS:

Type of Review:	Blind Review
No. External Reviewers:	3
No. InHouse Reviewers:	2
Acceptance Rate:	50%
Time to Review:	3-4 Months
Reviewer's Comments:	Yes
Invited Articles:	0-5%
Fees to Publish:	$0.00 US$
Fees to Review:	$0.00 US$

PUBLICATION GUIDELINES:

Manuscript Style:
  American Psychological Association

Manuscript Length:
  6-10

Copies Required:
  Electronic Only

CIRCULATION DATA:

Reader:
  Administrators, Academics

Frequency of Issue:
  Quarterly

Sponsor/Publisher:
  The American Association of School
Administrators (AASA)

MANUSCRIPT TOPICS:
Education Management / Administration

MANUSCRIPT GUIDELINES/COMMENTS:

Contact the Editor. Editor, AASA Journal Of Scholarship and Practice, Dr. Frederick Dembowski, Hibernia Endowed Professor & Head, Department of Educational Leadership & Technology, Southeastern Louisiana University, SLU 10549, Hammond, LA 70402 Phone: 985-549-5713; Fax: 985-549-5712; E-mail: **frederick.dembowski@selu.edu**

The AASA Journal of Scholarship and Practice invites Articles, Commentaries, Book Reviews News and Notes.

Author Guidelines
The AASA Journal of Scholarship and Practice is a refereed, blind-reviewed, quarterly journal with a focus on research and best practices that advance the profession of educational administration. Articles that express a point of view, shed light on a contemporary issue or report findings and

conclusions from a field of interest to educational administration professors will be given preference. AASA members are also invited to submit news, notices and announcements relevant to administrators and faculty in higher education. Reactions to previously published articles are also welcome.

Length of manuscripts should be as follows: Research and best practice articles between 1,200 and 1,800 words; columns and book and media reviews between 600 and 1,000 words; and commentaries between 400 and 500 words. Citations and references are to follow the *Publication Manual of the American Psychological Association*, latest edition. Permission to use previously copyrighted materials is the responsibility of the author, not the *AASA Journal of Scholarship and Practice*. For review purposes, the title of the article, contributor's name, address, title, affiliation (for inclusion on the title page and in the author note), telephone and fax number, and e-mail address should appear on a detachable cover page. The contributor must indicate whether the submission is to be considered as a research or best practice article, book or media review or commentary. The type of submission must be indicated on the cover sheet in order to be considered. Four paper copies and one electronic version written in Microsoft Word are required. All figures and diagrams must be printed with 300 dpi or greater.

Submissions should be mailed to: Dr. Frederick L. Dembowski, Editor, AASA Journal of Scholarship and Practice, Department of Educational Leadership and Technology, Southeastern Louisiana University, SLU 10549, Hammond, LA 70402.

Contributors will be notified of board decisions within 90 days of receipt of their papers at the editorial office. Articles to be returned must be accompanied by a postage-paid, self-addressed envelope.

Academe: Bulletin of AAUP

<table>
<tr><td colspan="2" align="center">SUBMISSION PROCESS:

Electronic Submission Preferred
via EMail

academe@aaup.org</td></tr>
</table>

CONTACT INFORMATION:	REVIEW PROCESS:
Editor American Assn. of University Professors Suite 500 1012 14th Street N.W. Washington, DC 20005 USA	**Type of Review:** Editorial Review **No. External Reviewers:** 0 **No. InHouse Reviewers:** 2 **Acceptance Rate:** 0-5%
Phone: 202-737-5900 ext. 114	**Time to Review:** 2 - 3 Months **Reviewer's Comments:** Yes **Invited Articles:** 50% +
Email: academe@aaup.org **Website:** www.aaup.org	**Fees to Publish:** $0.00 US$ **Fees to Review:** $0.00 US$
PUBLICATION GUIDELINES:	**CIRCULATION DATA:**
Manuscript Style: Chicago Manual of Style	**Reader:** Academics
Manuscript Length: 8-12	**Frequency of Issue:** Bi-Monthly
Copies Required: Electronic Only	**Sponsor/Publisher:** American Association of University Professors

MANUSCRIPT TOPICS:
Higher Education

MANUSCRIPT GUIDELINES/COMMENTS:

Manuscript Submissions
Academe explores topics in higher education from the perspective of faculty members. Because *Academe*'s readership includes faculty members from many different disciplines, *Academe* seeks to publish thoughtful articles written in a lively, nontechnical style. The editors of *Academe* edit articles with such a style in mind. They also aim to break up long sentences, clarify confusing points, and remove any repetitions. Articles are first reviewed for content and substantive changes by *Academe*'s faculty editor, after which they are sent to the managing editor for copyediting.

Style. *Academe* uses the *Chicago Manual of Style* (14th ed.) and the *Merriam Webster Collegiate Dictionary* (10th ed.).

Preparation. Authors are asked to submit articles to *Academe*'s faculty editor, Paula Krebs (see address below). We can accept manuscripts in hard copy or by fax, but the editing process will require an electronic text, either as an e-mail submission or on disk.

Length. Most features run between 2,000 and 3,000 words.

Biographical Statement. Include a brief biographical statement describing academic or other affiliation.

Notes. Avoid bibliographies, endnotes, and lengthy parenthetical references. Work any necessary citations into the text.

Illustrations. We welcome illustratons and other graphic materials.

Contact Information. Please submit home and office addresses, telephone numbers, and e-mail addresses.

Note. We encourage you to contact *Academe*'s faculty editor before submitting a manuscript to determine if the manuscript's topic is compatible with *Academe*'s editorial program. An invitation to submit an article does not guarantee publication.

Letters to the Editor
Acdaeme welcomes letters to the editor of three hundred words or fewer. Submit letters by mail to the address above or by e-mail to **academe@aaup.org**. *Academe* reserves the right to edit letters. In order to be considered for publication, submissions must include the writer's name and telephone number.

For further information, contact Paula Krebs. E-mail: **pkrebs@wheatoncollege.edu**. You may also contact Wendi Maloney, Managing Editor, *Academe*, AAUP, 1012 Fourteenth St., NW, Suite 500, Washington DC 20005-3465. (202) 737-5900, ext. 114. E-mail: **wmaloney@aaup.org**.

Academic Leadership Journal

SUBMISSION PROCESS:	
Electronic Submission Preferred via EMail **kdale@fhsu.edu**	

CONTACT INFORMATION:	REVIEW PROCESS:	
Kathy Dale, Editor Fort Hays State University	**Type of Review:**	Blind Review
	No. External Reviewers:	3+
Phone: 785-628-4547	**No. InHouse Reviewers:**	2
	Acceptance Rate:	21-30%
Email: kdale@fhsu.edu	**Time to Review:**	1 - 2 Months
	Reviewer's Comments:	No
Website: www.academicleadership.org	**Invited Articles:**	0-5%
	Fees to Publish:	$0.00 US$
	Fees to Review:	$0.00 US$

PUBLICATION GUIDELINES:	CIRCULATION DATA:
Manuscript Style: American Psychological Association	**Reader:** Academics, Administrators
Manuscript Length: 1-5	**Frequency of Issue:** 3 Times/Year
Copies Required: Electronic Only	**Sponsor/Publisher:** Fort Hays State University, College of Education & Technology

MANUSCRIPT TOPICS:
Higher Education; Leadership

MANUSCRIPT GUIDELINES/COMMENTS:

About this Journal
Academic Leadership is a quarterly, peer-reviewed online periodical focusing on all aspects of academic leadership including research reports and interpretive articles, essays and critical reviews of books and teaching materials, and rural academic leadership perspectives. We welcome submissions from a wide community of practitioners—from professors, teachers, trainers, and support specialists to program administrators and leaders in K-12 educational leadership positions. Please read the following material and review our style sheet before submitting a manuscript for publication consideration.

Deadlines
First edition: January, February, March & April
Deadline for submission: Nov. 15
Nov. 15-Dec. 10--The Review Board reviews the submissions.
Dec. 11-16--The editors make final preparations for the articles to be published in the first issue of the year.

Second edition: May, June, July & August
Deadline for submission: March 15
Mar. 15-April 10--The Review Board reviews the submissions
April 11-16--The editors make final preparations for the articles to be published in the second issue of the year.

Third edition: Sept., Oct. Nov. & Dec.
Deadline for submission: July 15
July 15-Aug. 10--The Review Board reviews submissions
Aug. 10-16--The editors make final preparations for the articles to be published in the third issue of the year.

Manuscript Submissions. Send submissions to the editor-in-chief, Kathy Dale (**kdale@fhsu.edu**). Save each of the following items in its own, separate file:

- Single-spaced manuscript in a Word or HTML file. Please include the full name, job title, organizational affiliation, and e-mail address of each author. (Personal information will be removed before the manuscript is subjected to peer review.)
- Brief abstract (200 words or fewer).
- Biographical note and high-quality JPEG photo for each author (see our style guidelines for author biographies).
- Any supplementary files, labeled as requested in our guidelines for article supplements.
- Manuscript should be in Times New Roman font and 12 point type.

Article Length. We seek articles that are substantive but concise (1,800 to 2,500 words). We encourage authors to expand and illuminate key concepts by linking to supplementary files (e.g., graphic images, tables, exhibits, audio clips, video clips, and embedded flash files) from the article proper. Such materials take full advantage of the Web's multimedia capacities, thereby enhancing the interactive educational experience for readers. Article supplements do not count toward the word limit stated above. They must, however, add meaning to the main text rather than simply repeat information within it. For more information and related policies, see our guidelines for article supplements.

Conference Presentations. We will consider a manuscript that has been presented at a conference or even published in conference proceedings. Disclose conference information at the end of the manuscript, imitating this example: [This article was modified from a presentation at the NCPEA annual conference in Branson , MO , August 2004.] If possible, provide hyperlinks for the presentation file (if available in Web conference proceedings), the sponsoring organization, and the conference home page.

Required Style. *Academic Leadership* employs Chicago style and uses the author-date system for reference citations; please consult our style sheet for examples of correct usage. Submissions that do not conform to Chicago style will not be reviewed and will be returned to the author for revision.

The Review and Revision Process
Promising manuscripts enter a double-blind review process involving at least three members of the *Academic Leadership* editorial board. Reviewers comment on an article's strengths and weaknesses, provide suggestions to authors, and make general recommendations about publication. The editor-in-chief reviews these comments and posts them online, at the end of the original manuscript. She then directs the authors to the article URL and provides overall revision guidance.

Authors are free to respectfully disagree with any element of the critiques, but they should provide justification for not complying with major revision requests. Productive, collegial interaction among authors, reviewers, and editors ultimately allows us to produce the most professional and readable articles in the field of educational leadership. The majority of articles submitted to *Academic Leadership* undergo multiple revisions and copyedits before they are ready for publication. After the editor approves an article for publication, it is assigned to a future issue. We retain an electronic copy of every original submission and subsequent reviewed and revised drafts; we encourage authors to do the same. These documents become useful references as the manuscript evolves.

STYLE SHEET
Formatting and Typeface
- Put all text (except indented block quotations and bulleted lists) flush with the left margin.
- Insert only one space between sentences. Insert no spaces around dashes.
- Use italics instead of bold or capitals to emphasize words or ideas.
- Italicize (rather than underline) all book and journal titles. Enclose article titles mentioned in the text in quotation marks.

Punctuation
- In a list separated by commas, place a comma before the coordinating conjunction (e.g., "*Academic Leadership* is accessible, lively, and widely read.").
- Use double quotation marks when quoting someone else. Use single quotation marks only when quoting someone else's quote.
- Use parentheses rather than brackets for citations or additional commentary. Use brackets only when adding an extra citation or comment within a parenthetical sequence.
- Use periods in the abbreviation for United States when it is used as an adjective (e.g., "U.S. Army" or "U.S. Department of Education"). When it appears as a noun, use the full term " United States ."
- Avoid contractions unless they appear within the language of a quoted source.
- Use spaced ellipsis points (. . .) within a sentence to indicate that you have omitted material from the original source. Three dots indicate an omission within a quoted sentence, whereas four mark the omission of one or more sentences. Please do not to use ellipsis points at the beginning of any quotation unless, to prevent misinterpretation, you need to emphasize that the quotation begins or ends in mid-sentence.

Capitalization
- When referring to specific computer commands, capitalize and use quotation marks (e.g., "Insert File" or "Draw Table").
- In general, do not capitalize titles such as "director," "manager," "president," and "professor."
- Capitalize the title of an academic course, but do not put it in quotation marks or italics (e.g., Educational Finance 854).
- Do not capitalize seasonal names such as "spring" or "summer" unless they are designations for the volume or issue of a publication.
- Use sentence-style capitalization for the titles of supplementary files (exhibits, figures, tables, and the like). Capitalize only the first word, any proper nouns, and the first word of the subtitle if present (e.g., "Framework for effective teaching, 2000").

Headings and Subheadings
- Put section headings in bold (e.g., Contemporary Challenges for the Elementary Educator) and subheadings within major sections in italics (e.g., Rise in Youth Violence).
- Capitalize the first word of section headings and subheadings, as well as all other words within the heading except definite and indefinite articles, conjunctions, and prepositions.

Numbers
- Adhere to the alternative rule outlined in section 9.6 of the Chicago Manual: In general, spell out only single-digit numbers; use numerals for all others (e.g., "Susan bought nine computers to accommodate 18 new students").
- When multiple items in the same category are mentioned in the same sentence, maintain consistency (e.g., "Of the students in Susan's classroom, only 2 were from single parent families").

- Treat ordinal numbers as you would cardinal numbers (e.g. "the first item on the 10th survey," "21st-century characteristics of effective leaders," "data in the 5th and 15th rows of the table"). Note that the ordinal suffix should not be in superscript.
- Use numerals for a sequential list of steps, procedures, or supplementary materials (e.g., Step1, Step 2; Test 1, Test 2; Table 1, Table 2).
- Unless it begins a sentence, always state a percentage in numerals and use the percent sign (e.g., 5%, 45%).
- Except at the beginning of a sentence, state amounts of money with numerals and the appropriate currency sign (e.g., $15).
- Express years in numerals (e.g., 1996). For decades, use numerals and add a final -s, without an apostrophe (e.g., 1990s).
- Denote times of day with numerals (e.g., "To attend the seminar, arrive by 10:30 a.m. ").
- When providing inclusive page numbers, always give the full form of each number (e.g., 114-119 rather than 114-19).

Acronyms
- Upon first use, spell out the full term in question and enclose the acronym in parentheses. Thereafter, use only the acronym.
- Even technology, state and national school improvement acronyms (such as IT, NCLB, NCA) that are well-known and accepted must be spelled out upon first use.

Internet Terminology and Spelling
- Type these common terms as they appear below, using the spelling and capitalization provided. An obvious exception: Any term used at the beginning of a sentence should be capitalized: e-mail; online; home page; Internet; Web, Web site, World Wide Web; webmaster, webcast; log in, log off, log out (verbs); login, logout, logoff (nouns/adjectives)

In-Text Parenthetical Citations
- To cite references in the text proper, enclose the surname of the author and year of publication in parentheses; this information will point readers to the expanded bibliographic entry at the end of the document. When referring to the entirety of a source, do not provide page numbers. When referring to a specific part of the work or quoting it directly, include a page number or span.
- Basic examples can be found on the web site.

The References Section
- Place the list of references at the end of your manuscript. Title this list "References" rather than "Works Cited" or "Bibliography." Include only those references cited in the article proper.
- Place the entries in alphabetical order by name. For two or more works by the same author, editor, or organization, alphabetize by title (ignoring the articles "A," "An," and "The").
- The essential information contained in a reference entry is as follows: author name(s), year of publication, title of publication, publisher location and/or name, and page numbers (for book chapters, journal articles, and the like). A reference entry for an electronic source should also include the URL and the date on which you last accessed the material in question.
- Do not spell out the full names of authors; used spaced initials for the first and, if present, middle names. Invert the first author's name, but transcribe any co-authors' names normally.
- In general, use sentence-style capitalization for the titles of books, articles, Web site sections, listserv messages, etc. Capitalize only the first word of the title, the first word of the subtitle (if present), and any proper nouns. Note that *Academic Leadership* treats "Web" and "Internet" as proper nouns.
- Italicize book titles and journal names; use regular text for most everything else.
- Basic examples can be found on the web site.

Academy of Educational Leadership Journal

SUBMISSION PROCESS:
Electronic Submission Only **via Online Portal** **www.alliedacademics.org**

CONTACT INFORMATION:	REVIEW PROCESS:	
Current Editor / Check Web Page Submission Address: Digital submission through website only Address other Questions to: Jim or JoAnn Carland at # below USA	**Type of Review:**	Blind Review
	No. External Reviewers:	3
	No. InHouse Reviewers:	0
	Acceptance Rate:	21-30%
	Time to Review:	2 - 3 Months
Phone: 828-293-9151	**Reviewer's Comments:**	Yes
	Invited Articles:	0-5%
Email: info@alliedacademies.org	**Fees to Publish:**	$75.00 US$ Membership
Website: www.alliedacademics.org	**Fees to Review:**	$0.00 US$

PUBLICATION GUIDELINES:	CIRCULATION DATA:
Manuscript Style: American Psychological Association	**Reader:** Academics
Manuscript Length: 16-20	**Frequency of Issue:** 3 Times/Year
Copies Required: Electronic Only	**Sponsor/Publisher:** Allied Academies, Inc.

MANUSCRIPT TOPICS:
Business Education; Curriculum Studies; Education Management / Administration; Educational Psychology; Higher Education

MANUSCRIPT GUIDELINES/COMMENTS:

The Editorial Board accepts theoretical, empirical, educational or pedagogic manuscripts for review. The primary criterion upon which manuscripts are judged is whether the research advances the education discipline or the teaching profession. Key points include currency, interest, and relevancy.

Theoretical manuscripts are particularly vulnerable to problems in literature review. In order for theoretical research to advance a discipline, it must address the literature which exists in the discipline to support conclusions or models which extend knowledge and understanding. Consequently, referees for theoretical manuscripts pay particular attention to completeness of literature review and appropriateness of conclusions drawn from that review.

Empirical manuscripts are particularly vulnerable to methodological problems. In order to advance the literature, empirical manuscripts must employ appropriate and effective sampling and statistical analysis techniques. However, empirical papers must also incorporate thorough literature reviews in order to advance the literature. Referees will pay close attention to the conclusions which are drawn from statistical analyses and their consistency with the literature.

In order for educational or pedagogic manuscripts to be useful to educators, they must address appropriate literature to support conclusions, teaching methodologies or pedagogies. Consequently, referees pay particular attention to completeness of literature review and appropriateness of conclusions drawn from that review.

Pedagogies or teaching methodologies must be well described with sound foundations in order to be useful to educators. Referees will pay particular attention to such issues in judging manuscripts.

In every case, educational or pedagogic manuscripts must embody well developed and well documented ideas in order to be useful to educators. Referees will pay close attention to the ideas presented in the manuscript and how well they are presented and supported.

We ask referees to be as specific as possible in indicating what must be done to make a manuscript acceptable for journal publication. This embodies a primary objective of the Academy: to assist authors in the research process.

Our Editorial Policy is one which is supportive, rather than critical. We encourage all authors who are not successful in a first attempt to rewrite the manuscript in accordance with the suggestions of the referees. We will be pleased to referee future versions and rewrites of manuscripts and work with authors in achieving their research goals.

Adult Education Quarterly

SUBMISSION PROCESS:	

**Electronic Submission Preferred
via EMail**

adultedquarterly@psu.edu

CONTACT INFORMATION:	**REVIEW PROCESS:**	
Edward Taylor, Co-Editor Penn State University	**Type of Review:**	Blind Review
School of Behavioral Science & Education W351 Olmsted Building	**No. External Reviewers:** **No. InHouse Reviewers:**	3 0
777 W. Harrisburg Pike Middletown, PA 17057 USA	**Acceptance Rate:**	11-20%
	Time to Review:	2 - 3 Months
Patricia Cranton, Co-Editor	**Reviewer's Comments:**	Yes
Daniele Flannery, Co-Editor	**Invited Articles:**	0-5%
Elizabeth Tisdell, Co-Editor		
	Fees to Publish:	$0.00 US$
Phone:	**Fees to Review:**	$0.00 US$
717-948-6364		
Email:		
ewt1@psu.edu pac23@psu.edu ddf3@psu.edu ejt11@psu.edu		
Website: http://aeq.sagepub.com		

PUBLICATION GUIDELINES:	**CIRCULATION DATA:**
Manuscript Style: American Psychological Association	**Reader:** Academics, Practicing Teachers
Manuscript Length: 26-30	**Frequency of Issue:** Quarterly
Copies Required: One	**Sponsor/Publisher:** American Association of Adult & Continuing Education (AAACE) / Sage Publications

MANUSCRIPT TOPICS:
Adult Career & Vocational; Higher Education

MANUSCRIPT GUIDELINES/COMMENTS:

AEQ **Mission Statement**
The *Adult Education Quarterly (AEQ)* is a scholarly refereed journal committed to advancing the understanding and practice of adult and continuing education. The journal strives to be inclusive in scope, addressing topics and issues of significance to scholars and practitioners concerned with diverse aspects of adult and continuing education. *AEQ* publishes research employing a variety of

methods and approaches, including (but not limited to) survey research, experimental designs, case studies, ethnographic observations and interviews, grounded theory, phenomenology, historical investigations, and narrative inquiry as well as articles that address theoretical and philosophical issues pertinent to adult and continuing education. Innovative and provocative scholarship informed by diverse orientations is encouraged, including (but not limited to) positivism, post-positivism, constructivism, critical theory, feminism, race-based / Africentric, gay/lesbian, and poststructural / postmodern theories. *AEQ* aims to stimulate a problem-oriented, critical approach to research and practice, with an increasing emphasis on inter-disciplinary and international perspectives. The audience includes researchers, students, and adult and continuing education practitioners of many orientations including teachers, trainers, facilitators, resource persons, organizational developers, community organizers, and policy designers.

Guidelines for Contributors
The *Adult Education Quarterly* is committed to the dissemination of knowledge produced by disciplined inquiry in the field of adult and continuing education. Three criteria are used in the review and selection process. First, articles must significantly advance knowledge and practice. Second, all material must be accurate and technically correct. Finally, articles must be well-crafted and well-written. To facilitate the preparation and submission of manuscripts, we offer the following information, guidelines, and procedures.

General Information
Journal Address. Adult Education Quarterly, Penn State University, School of Behavioral Sciences and Education, W351 Olmsted Building, 777 W. Harrisburg Pike, Middletown, PA 17057.E-Mail: **adultedquarterly@psu.edu**

Editorial Staff
Editors. Patricia Cranton, Penn State Harrisburg, Daniele D. Flannery, Penn State Harrisburg, Edward W. Taylor, Penn State Harrisburg, Elizabeth J. Tisdell, Penn State Harrisburg

Book Review Editor. Daniele Flannery, Penn State Harrisburg

Editorial Associates. Patricia Thompson, Penn State Harrisburg, Karen Milheim, Penn State Harrisburg

Organizational Sponsorship
American Association for Adult and Continuing Education (AAACE), Commission of Professors of Adult Education (CPAE), 4380 Forbes Blvd., Lanham, MD 20706 USA; Phone: 301-918-1913; Fax: 301-918-1846

Scope
AEQ is a blind-review scholarly journal committed to the dissemination of research and theory that advances the understanding and practice of adult and continuing education.

Types of Articles Published
- Research approaches including (but not limited to): survey research, experimental designs, case studies, ethnographic observations and interviews, grounded theory, phenomenology, historical investigations, and narrative inquiry
- Inquiry orientations including (but not limited to): positivism, post-positivism, constructivism, critical theory, feminism, race-based/Africentric, gay/lesbian, and poststructural/postmodern theories
- Theory building and philosophical analysis
- Critical integrative reviews of adult and continuing education literature
- Forum (position statements or reasoned critiques of articles previously printed in AEQ)
- Essay reviews (commissioned by the editors)
- Book reviews (contact the book review editor; see the book review section)
- "To the Editor" comments and contributions

Editorial Style
Publication Manual of the American Psychological Association (fourth edition).

Preparation for Submission
Prospective authors might consider the following strategies in preparing manuscripts for *AEQ:*
- Study the Editorial Policy and its sections on guidelines to ensure that your manuscript falls within the scope of the journal and will meet stylistic requirements.
- Consider the "Review Criteria" (see that section of the Editorial Policy) in developing and crafting your manuscript.
- Study back issues of *AEQ* and its predecessor, *Adult Education*, focusing especially on articles of purpose and form similar to your manuscript.
- Ask at least two colleagues who are insightful and constructive in their appraisals to critically review the manuscript before submitting it to *AEQ*.

Technical and Stylistic Requirements
For the editorial process to begin, all submissions must meet the following technical and stylistic requirements:

Typed Copy
Submit typed, **double-spaced** copy with numbered pages, using one inch margins on all sides.

Number of Copies
Submit one paper copy and one electronic as an email attachment sent to: **adultedquarterly@ psu.edu**. Authors should retain a copy of their manuscripts. The editors are not responsible for returning copies to authors.

Article Length
Articles generally should not exceed 7500 words, including charts, tables, and bibliography.

Title Page
On the title page, indicate the following: title of paper; full name(s) of author(s), author titles and institutional affiliations, postal addresses, phone numbers, fax numbers, and email addresses; brief acknowledgement of the contribution of colleagues or students, if warranted; statement of place and date of previous oral presentation, if any; and date of submission.

Abstract
In 150 words or less, summarize the purpose, approach, and conclusions of the paper in an abstract immediately following the title pg. Include only the title of the paper on this and subsequent pages.

Text
Repeat a shortened version of the title of the manuscript (a running head) on the top of each page of the text. The name of the author(s) must not appear on any page, other than through standard reference usage.

Stylistic Requirements
Manuscripts submitted to *AEQ* must be grammatically correct and stylistically consistent. *AEQ* uses the *Publication Manual of the American Psychological Association*, fourth edition. Consult this publication for rules governing references and citations as well as other elements of grammar and style.

Warrant Statement
Any submission must include a typed, dated, and signed warrant statement assigning first publication rights to AAACE effective if and when it is accepted for publication by the editors. Manuscripts cannot be processed for publication until the editors of *AEQ* have received this signed statement, worded as follows:

I hereby confirm the assignment of first publication rights only in and to the manuscript named above in all forms and media to AAACE effective if and when it is accepted for publication by the *AEQ* editorial board. I warrant that my manuscript is original work and has not bee accepted for publication by another periodical. I further warrant that my work (including tables, figures, photographs, and other illustrative material) does not infringe on the copyright or statutory rights of others, does not contain libelous statements, and that the editorial board members, staff, and officers of AAACE are indemnified against costs, expenses, and damages arising from any breach of the foregoing in regard to the manuscript. Finally, I acknowledge that *AEQ* is relying on this statement in any publishing of this manuscript's information.

Manuscripts submitted to *AEQ* should not be under consideration for publication by any other journals, nor should they have been published previously in any form. A paper may, however, have been presented at a meeting or conference. In such cases, the author should state where and when such a paper was presented. After acceptance, a paper may not be published elsewhere without written permission from AAACE and/or CPAE.

Letter of Transmittal
Attach a letter addressed to the editors indicating the title of the manuscript, date of submission, and all authors with their institutional affiliations.

Editorial Procedure
AEQ editorial staff initially reviews all manuscript submissions for compliance with *AEQ* editorial policy. If the manuscript fails to fall within the scope and stylistic guidelines of the journal, it is returned to the authors. If a manuscript is in accord with the scope of the journal and meets submission guidelines, all references to the author name and institution are removed from the manuscript, and it is submitted for blind reviews to three *AEQ* consulting editors. Each consulting editor is a professional scholar judged competent to appraise such manuscripts.

In compliance with advice of consulting editors, the editors make one of four decisions: *accept*; conditional accept, contingent upon major revisions; reject and encourage revision; or reject. In the case of conditional acceptance, the editors will specify necessary revisions in writing to the author. When revisions are completed and the editors accept a manuscript, the editors will then notify and inform the author(s) about the next steps in the publication process.

Review Criteria
In seeking to advance the understanding and practice of adult and continuing education, the journal strives to be inclusive in scope and aims to stimulate a problem-oriented, critical approach to research and practice, with an increasing emphasis on inter-disciplinary and international perspectives. The following are used to review scholarly papers submitted to *AEQ*:

Importance of the Problem
A problem or subject addressed by a manuscript should contribute to knowledge or theory pertinent to adult and continuing education. Importance is enhanced when a paper promotes understanding or improvement of practice.

Background
Through the abstract and a brief introduction, readers should be provided with sufficient background information to understand the problem being addressed.

Problem/Purpose
The purpose of the paper should be clearly and unambiguously stated. This typically requires a clearly described research problem.

Literature Review
Research and scholarship should be linked to relevant empirical and theoretical literature. The applicability of the research and the quality of the discussion are more important than the length of the literature review.

Methodology
The approach and procedures must be appropriate for addressing the stated research problem(s) and purpose(s).

Findings
Findings must be presented and documented to show clear relationships to the purpose(s) and research question(s). Evidence needed to support conclusions must be clearly identified and amply arrayed, including (but not limited to) the presentation of statistics, charts, and graphs; use of quotations; observational data; references; and citations.

Conclusions
Conclusions and logical inferences should be pertinent, clearly drawn, and convincingly supported by evidence.

Readability
All manuscripts must be well organized, well written, and readable.

Book Reviews
The book review editor solicits, edits, and manages the book review process. Suggestions for books to be reviewed or nominations to review books should be submitted to: Book Review Editors, Daniele Flannery, Penn State Harrisburg, School of Behavioral Sciences and Education, W351 Olmsted Building, 777 W. Harrisburg Pike, Middletown, PA 17057.E-Mail: **ddf3@psu.edu**

Subscription Prices
Individual (Print Only) $67.00 US / £45.00 GBP
Institution: Combined (Print & E-access) $229.00 US / £153.00 GBP
Electronic only & Print only subscriptions are available at a discounted rate.

Adult Learning

SUBMISSION PROCESS:

**Postal & Electronic Submission Required
via EMail**

**episaac@umsl.edu
malfred@tamu.edu**

CONTACT INFORMATION:

Mary V. Alfred, Co- Editor
Educational Administration and Human
  Resource Development
Texas A&M University
559 Harrington, 4226
College Station, TX 77843-4226 USA

E. Paulette Isaac-Savage, Co-Editor
Educational Leadership & Policy Studies
269 Marillac Hall
University of Missouri - St. Louis
One University Blvd., St. Louis, MO 63121
  USA

Phone:
  979-854-2788
  314-516-5941

Email:
  malfred@tamu.edu
  episaac@umsl.edu

Website:
  http://www.aaace.org/publications/index.
  html

REVIEW PROCESS:

Type of Review:	Blind Review
No. External Reviewers:	3
No. InHouse Reviewers:	1
Acceptance Rate:	21-30%
Time to Review:	2 - 3 Months
Reviewer's Comments:	No
Invited Articles:	21-30%
Fees to Publish:	$0.00 US$
Fees to Review:	$0.00 US$

PUBLICATION GUIDELINES:

Manuscript Style:
  American Psychological Association

Manuscript Length:
  2500 words

Copies Required:
  Three + 1 Electronic

CIRCULATION DATA:

Reader:
  Practicing Teachers, Adult Educators

Frequency of Issue:
  Quarterly

Sponsor/Publisher:
  American Association for Adult and
Continuing Education

MANUSCRIPT TOPICS:
Adult Career & Vocational; Adult Education; Adult Learning

MANUSCRIPT GUIDELINES/COMMENTS:

Adult Learning is a magazine for adult educators designed to provide short, well-written, professionally oriented articles with a problem-solving emphasis. The audience for *Adult Learning* includes all individuals who design, manage, teach, conduct, and evaluate programs of adult and continuing education broadly defined.

Address of the Magazine
American Association for Adult and Continuing Education (AAACE), 10111 Martin Luther King, Jr. Highway, Suite 200C, Bowie, MD, 20720

Suggested Length
Feature Articles: 2000-2500 words
Department Articles: 700-1,000 words

Format
Send two copies of the manuscript—one electronically and the other by regular mail. The manuscript should be typed, double-spaced (keep a personal copy). Include a brief biography (current position and title) and a separate title page. Include the address and telephone number where you can be reached. Include the titled if the article on the actual manuscript page.

Where to Submit
All manuscripts should be sent to the Editors at the **Address for Submission** address listed.

Photos
Photos to illustrate the article are accepted. Black and white glossy prints are preferred over color prints.

Editorial Procedure
Three members of the editorial board review articles. Authors receive a decision within three months of article submission. Reviewers make one of the following four recommendations: Accept/Publish, Conditional Accept/Revise, Reject & Rewrite, or Reject.

The magazine uses articles receiving recommendations to publish first. Articles receiving recommendations to Revise are published on a space available basis. It is the policy of *Adult Learning* to receive for review a second draft of articles that initially receive recommendations to Revise. These authors are given comments and suggestions on how substantive, content changes could be made successfully. Suggestions for organization and readability may also be offered. The same member of the editorial board who reviewed the first draft generally reviews second drafts. Second drafts that are acceptable in terms of content may be subject to further revision for organization and readability.

Types of Articles Published
1. Refereed or Non-themed Articles
The current editors are interested in publishing more non-theme articles in the future and are actively soliciting manuscripts.

Editorial procedure for non-theme manuscripts. Three members of the editorial board review manuscripts. Authors generally receive a decision within three to four months of article submission.

Reviewers make one of the following four recommendations:
- Accept for Publication;
- Conditional Accept (conditional upon revisions);
- Reject, Encourage Rewrite and Submission;
- and Reject.

For refereed manuscripts, the journal gives first priority to manuscripts receiving recommendations to publish. Articles receiving recommendations to Revise are published on a space available basis after revisions have been made and the manuscript is deemed acceptable for publication. It is the policy of *Adult Learning* to review a second draft of articles that initially received recommendations to Revise. These authors are given comments and suggestions on how substantive, content changes could be made successfully. Suggestions for organization and readability may also be offered. The same member of the editorial board who reviewed the first draft generally reviews second drafts. Second drafts that are acceptable in terms of content may be subject to further revision for organization and readability.

2. Theme (Non-Refereed) Articles

Theme articles are solicited by theme editors for each issue's theme. Topics selected for themes have included the following: workforce education, mentoring, older adult learners, adult literacy, staff development, adult learners with disabilities, instructional technology, intercultural education, learning to learn, and the philosophy of adult education. The editors of *Adult Learning* welcome your suggestions for future themes. Theme editors will work with authors on the content and form of manuscript. Theme proposals should be sent to Mary Alfred. For more details, see Author Guidelines for theme issues.

The article guidelines, editorial review procedures, and other specifications are the same for both refereed and theme articles. Theme and refereed articles should be approximately **2000-2500** words. Please submit two copies (one electronic version and one hard copy) of the manuscript. The manuscript should be typed and double-spaced with one-inch margins. Times Roman 12 pt. or Arial 11 pt. font are preferred. APA (5th edition) formatting should be used. Include a brief biography (one to two sentences that contain the author's name and current position) and a separate title page. Include your address, telephone number(s), and e-mail address on the title page, but not in the manuscript itself. Place the title of the article on the first manuscript page.

3. Personal Reflections

This section publishes short articles on topics that usually relate to the theme of the issue or current events, if possible. Other theme articles will also be published. Reflections articles need to demonstrate the author's personal thoughts about the issue s/he is writing about and should be no more than **1200** words. These articles should be submitted directly to the Personal Reflections Editor, Molly Robertson, at **gedontv@iquest.net**.

4. Resources

This section is for book, video, and other material reviews. Full reviews should be no more than **500** words in length; shorter treatments ("notices") should be no more than 200 words. Reviews of materials less than three years old are preferred. Reviews and inquiries should be submitted directly to the Resource Editor, Kathleen B. Rager, at **Kbrager@ou.edu**.

5. Futures

This section contains articles that articulate a vision of future directions for the broad field of adult and continuing education . Articles should be no more than **1200** words. Judy Adrian and Meg Wise edit the manuscripts for this section. They can be reached at **Adrian50@charter.net** and **mewise@wisc.edu**, respectively.

Where to Submit

E. Paulette Isaac-Savage is Co-Editor of *Adult Learning* and manages the editorial process. Please send your refereed manuscript to her at University of Missouri-St. Louis, College of Education, One University Blvd., St. Louis, MO 63121, and **EPIsaac@umsl.edu**. She can also be reached by phone at (314) 516-5941.

Mary V. Alfred of Texas A&M University is Co-Editor of Adult Learning and manages the publication process. Please send your theme manuscripts to her at **malfred@tamu.edu**. She can also be reached by phone at (979) 845-2788.

One copy of your manuscripts should be sent and one by regular mail. Be sure to include your address, telephone number(s), e-mail address, and brief biography as described above. The copyright release form should also be included with your submission.

Photos and Illustrations
Photos to illustrate the article are accepted. Black and white glossy prints are preferred over color prints. Illustrations should be camera-ready unless they have been created in Microsoft Word.

Copy Editing
Manuscripts accepted for publication will be edited for grammar and punctuation.

Exclusivity
Manuscripts should not be under consideration for publication by other periodicals, nor should they have been published previously (except as a part of a presentation at a meeting.) Articles should be submitted with a typed, dated, and signed copyright form that reads as follows:

> I(we) hereby confirm the assignment of first publications rights only in and to the manuscript named above in all forms and media to AAACE effective if and when it is accepted for publication by *Adult Learning* . I(we) warrant that the manuscript is original work and has not been accepted for publication by another periodical. I(we) further warrant that my(our) work (including tables, figures, photographs, and other illustrative material) does not infringe copyright or statutory rights of others, does not contain libelous statements, and that the editorial board members, staff, and officers of AAACE are indemnified against costs, expenses, and damages arising from any breach of the foregoing in regards to the manuscript. Finally, I acknowledge that *Adult Learning* is relying on this statement in any publishing of the manuscript's information.

Please include the title of the manuscript at the top of this page, and print the author(s)' names after the warrant statement followed by the relevant signatures.

Advancing Women in Leadership

SUBMISSION PROCESS:
Postal or Electronic Submission Accepted via EMail **edu_bid@shsu.edu**

CONTACT INFORMATION:	REVIEW PROCESS:	
Beverly Irby & Genevieve Brown, Co-Eds Sam Houston State University	**Type of Review:**	Blind Review
P.O. Box 2119 Huntsville, TX 77341-2119 USA	**No. External Reviewers:** **No. InHouse Reviewers:**	3 1-2
Phone: 936-294-1147	**Acceptance Rate:** **Time to Review:** **Reviewer's Comments:** **Invited Articles:**	15% 2 - 3 Months Yes 0-5%
Email: irby@shsu.edu advancingwomen@shsu.edu	**Fees to Publish:** **Fees to Review:**	$0.00 US$ $0.00 US$
Website: http://www.advancingwomen.com/awl/awl.html		

PUBLICATION GUIDELINES:	CIRCULATION DATA:
Manuscript Style: American Psychological Association **Manuscript Length:** 11-30 **Copies Required:** Electronic Only	**Reader:** Academics, Administrators, Counselors, Professionals, PreK-12 Educators **Frequency of Issue:** 3 Times/Year **Sponsor/Publisher:** Gretchen Glassock, publisher

MANUSCRIPT TOPICS:
Adult Career & Vocational; Art / Music; Bilingual / E.S.L.; Counseling & Personnel Services; Curriculum Studies; Education Management / Administration; Educational Psychology; Educational Technology Systems; Elementary / Early Childhood; English Literature; Foreign Language; Gifted Children; Global Business; Health & Physical Education; Medicine; Multicultural Education; Reading; Religious Education; Rural Education & Small Schools; School Law; Science Math & Environment; Secondary / Adolescent Studies; Social Studies / Social Science; Special Education; Teacher Education; Tests, Measurement & Evaluation; Urban Education, Cultural / Non-Traditional

MANUSCRIPT GUIDELINES/COMMENTS:

Manuscripts should meet the following requirements:
1. All articles should follow *The Publication Manual of the American Psychological Association* (APA) Fifth Edition format. If an individual is from a country other than the United States and is unfamiliar with this publication style, the editors will assist the author in formatting the manuscript in APA style if the manuscript is accepted for publication. (There are some internet web sites dealing with APA that may be helpful.) Because html formatting is slightly different from that of

regular paper publishing, the APA style will be followed as closely as possible. Indentions, spacing, and footnoting may vary in this journal.

2. Manuscripts, in MS Word, should be typed, double-spaced, titled, and should be preferably no more than a total of 30 pages in length. Do not put any identification of the author(s) within the text of the manuscript. Pertinent photographs, charts, or graphs need to accompany the manuscript.

3. Manuscripts submitted should be previously unpublished and not under consideration by another publication venue.

4. A cover page needs to be included containing such itmes as the title of the manuscript, all authors and their complete contact information such as address, telephone number, fax number, and e-mail addresses. Give a brief biography of each author stating affiliation, position, degree received, etc.

5. Submit manuscript by e-mail.

E-mail to the Editors at: **irby@shsu.edu** and **advancingwomen@shsu.edu**

Postal Mail. Dr. Genevieve Brown/Dr. Beverly J. Irby, Editors, Advancing Women in Leadership On-line Journal, Sam Houston State University, P.O. Box 2119, Huntsville, Texas 77341-2119; Telephone: 936-294-1147; Fax: 936-294-3886

Manuscript Deadline. On a continuous basis

American Educational Research Journal: Social and Institutional Analysis

SUBMISSION PROCESS:
Electronic Submission Only **via Online Portal** **http://ojs.aera.net/journals/index.php/aerj-sia**

CONTACT INFORMATION:	REVIEW PROCESS:	
Margie Gallego & Craig Bevan, Editors NE-162-F, Mail Code 1183 San Diego State University 5500 Campanile Drive San Diego, CA 92182-1183 USA	**Type of Review:**	Blind Review
	No. External Reviewers: **No. InHouse Reviewers:**	3+ 1
	Acceptance Rate: **Time to Review:** **Reviewer's Comments:** **Invited Articles:**	7-13% 2 - 3 Months Yes 0-5%
Phone: 619-594-6436		
Email: aerj.sia@mail.sdsu.edu	**Fees to Publish:** **Fees to Review:**	$0.00 US$ $0.00 US$
Website: www.aera.net		

PUBLICATION GUIDELINES:	CIRCULATION DATA:
Manuscript Style: See Manuscript Guidelines	**Reader:** Academics
Manuscript Length: 50-75 not incl. Refs	**Frequency of Issue:** Quarterly
Copies Required: Electronic Only	**Sponsor/Publisher:** American Educational Research Association (AERA)

MANUSCRIPT TOPICS:
Education Management / Administration; Higher Education; School Law; Social & Institutional Analysis in Education; Tests, Measurement & Evaluation; Urban Education, Cultural / Non-Traditional

MANUSCRIPT GUIDELINES/COMMENTS:

Focus and Scope
The *American Educational Research Journal* has as its purpose to carry original empirical and theoretical studies and analyses in education. The editors seek to publish articles from a wide variety of academic disciplines and substantive fields; they are looking for clear and significant contributions to the understanding and/or improvement of educational processes and outcomes. Manuscripts not appropriate for submission to this journal include essays, reviews, course evaluations, and brief reports of studies to address a narrow question.

Section on Social and Institutional Analysis (SIA)
The Social and Institutional Analysis section of *AERJ* publishes scholarly research that addresses significant political, cultural, social, economic, and organizational issues in education. This section

publishes research analyzing the broader contextual and organizational factors affecting teaching and learning, the links between those factors and the nature and processes of schooling, and the ways that such "external" domains are conceptualized in research, policy, and practice. The section invites manuscripts that advance the theoretical understandings of the social and institutional contexts of education and that encompass the diverse communities of schooling and educational research to achieve social justice in education. The Social and Institutional Analysis section welcomes research across a wide range of methodological paradigms, including ethnographic, historical, narrative, legal, experimental/quantitative, critical, and interpretive approaches; the section also invites studies that make the nature and uses of educational research itself the subject of social and cultural inquiry.

The review process is conducted electronically. To submit manuscripts for the SIA section, go to: **http://ojs.aera.net/journals/index.php/aerj-sia/information/authors**

All editorial correspondence and inquiries relating to this section should be sent to: AERJ/SIA, College of Education, Margie Gallego/Craig Bevan, NE-162-F, Mail Code 1183, San Diego State University, 5500 Campanile Drive, San Diego, CA 92182-1183; Phone: (619) 594-6436; Fax: (619) 594-6438; E-mail: **aerj.sia@mail.sdsu.edu**

Author Guidelines
Submit all manuscripts electronically to the editorial team at **http://ojs.aera.net/journals/index. php/aerj-sia**

For specific questions or inquiries, send e-mail to editors at the following addresses: Sandra Hollingsworth at (**samholl@ssctv.net**) with a copy to Margaret A. Gallego (**mgallego@mail. sdsu.edu**)

Submission Preparation Checklist
As part of the submission process, authors are required to check off their submission's compliance with all of the following items, and submissions may be returned to authors that do not adhere to these guidelines.

1. **Style manuals**. Submissions must follow the styles outlined in either of these two guides. Preferred: the *Chicago Manual of Style* (2003, 15th edition) – available from the University of Chicago Press, 1467 E. 60th St., Chicago, IL 60637). This is our preferred style manual [IMPORTANT: Authors who follow Chicago must use the author-date citation system]. Alternative: the *Publication Manual of the American Psychological Association* (2001, 5th edition)—available from the American Psychological Association, Order Department, P.O. Box 2710, Hyattsville, MD 20784. The submission file is in Microsoft Word, RTF, or WordPerfect document file format. Any supplemental files are in Microsoft Word, RTF, WordPerfect, or Excel format. PDFs are NOT acceptable.

2. **Contact information**. Supply complete contact information for all authors on the title page: Name, affiliation, complete street address, e-mail address, fax, phone numbers (the more, the better). Indicate which is the corresponding author.

3. **Abstract**. All manuscripts should include an abstract of 100–120 words.

4. **Author Identification**. The complete title of the article and the name of the author(s) should be typed only on the first sheet to ensure anonymity in the review process. Subsequent pages should have no author names, but may carry a short title at the top. Information in text or references that would identify the author should be deleted from the manuscript including both text citations and the reference list. These may be reinserted in the final draft. The first-named author or the coauthor who will be handling the correspondence with the editor, clearing galleys, and working with the association's publications should be clearly indicated, along with telephone numbers. fax numbers, and e-mail addresses.

5. The author's name should be removed from the document's Properties, which in Microsoft Word is found in the File menu.

6. **Typescript**. Manuscripts should be typed for 8½" x 11" paper, in upper and lower case, double-spaced, with 1½" margins on all sides. They should be in IBM-compatible MS Word, WordPerfect or RTF format. Subheads should be used at reasonable intervals to break the monotony of text. Words and symbols to be italicized must be clearly indicated, by either italic type or underlining. Abbreviations and acronyms should be spelled out at first mention unless found as entries in their abbreviated form in *Merriam-Webster's Tenth Collegiate Dictionary* (e.g., "IQ" needs no explanation). Pages should be numbered consecutively.

7. **Length**. Manuscripts for the SIA section should typically run between 50 and 75 pages in typed form, not including the reference list. Manuscripts for the TLHD section should typically run between 35 and 60 pages in typed form, including the reference list.

8. **Notes and references**. Notes are for explanations or amplifications of textual material. They are distracting to readers and expensive to set and should be avoided whenever possible. They should be typed as normal text at the end of the text section of the manuscript rather than as part of the footnote or endnote feature of a computer program and should be numbered consecutively throughout the article.

A reference list contains only references that are cited in the text. Its accuracy and completeness are the responsibility of the author(s). Personal communications (letters, memos, telephone conversations) are cited in the text after the name with as exact a date as possible.

9. **Tables, Figures, and Illustrations**. The purpose of tables and figures is to present data to the reader in a clear and unambiguous manner. The author should not describe the data in the text in such detail that illustration or text is redundant.

Figures and tables should be keyed to the text. Tables should each be typed on a separate sheet and attached at the end of the manuscript (after the references). Tables will be typeset.

Figure captions should be typed on a separate sheet (and should not appear in full on the original figures). One high-quality, camera-ready version or final electronic version of each figure must be submitted with the manuscript that is to be typeset, and photocopies may be submitted with the additional copies of the manuscript.

Once an article has been accepted, all tables and figures should be e-mailed to the editors along with the manuscript.

10. As you prepare your paper, you might take a look at the criteria under which it will be reviewed. See Reviewer Guidelines at: **http://ojs.aera.net/journals/index.php/aerj-sia/about/editorialPolicies#custom1**

Copyright Notice
© 2005 by the American Educational Research Association. No written or oral permission is necessary to reproduce a table, a figure, or an excerpt of fewer than 500 words from this journal, or to make photocopies for classroom use. Authors are granted permission, without fee, to photocopy their own material. Copies must include a full and accurate bibliographic citation and the following credit line: "Copyright [year] by the American Educational Research Association; reproduced with permission from the publisher." Written permission must be obtained to reproduce or reprint material in circumstances other than those just described. Please direct all requests for permission or for further information on policies and fees to the AERA Central Office.

AERA Publications Department, 1230 17th Street, N.W., Washington, DC 20036-3078; Telephone: 202.223.9485; Fax. 202.775.1824

Privacy Statement
The names and email addresses entered in this journal site will be used exclusively for the stated purposes of this journal and will not be made available for any other purpose or to any other party.

American Educational Research Journal: Teaching, Learning and Human Development

SUBMISSION PROCESS:

Electronic Submission Only
via EMail

AERJ-TLHDeditors@aera.net

CONTACT INFORMATION:	REVIEW PROCESS:
B. Thompson, S. Knight, Y. Lincoln, Eds. Department of Educational Psychology Texas A&M University 704 Harrington College Station, TX 77843-4225 USA	**Type of Review:** Blind Review **No. External Reviewers:** 3+ **No. InHouse Reviewers:** **Acceptance Rate:** 7-13% **Time to Review:** 3-4 Months **Reviewer's Comments:** Yes **Invited Articles:** 0-5% **Fees to Publish:** $0.00 US$ **Fees to Review:** $0.00 US$

Phone:
   979-845-1335
Email:
   bruce-thompson@tamu.edu
   s-knight@tamu.edu
   ysl@tamu.edu
Website:
   http://www.aera.net/	

PUBLICATION GUIDELINES:	CIRCULATION DATA:

Manuscript Style:
   American Psychological Association
   Chicago Manual of Style
Manuscript Length:
   No set length
Copies Required:
   Five
	Reader:
	   Academics
	Frequency of Issue:
	   Quarterly
	Sponsor/Publisher:
	   American Educational Research Association (AERA)

MANUSCRIPT TOPICS:
Educational Psychology; Elementary / Early Childhood; Gifted Children; Higher Education; Reading; Science Math & Environment; Secondary / Adolescent Studies; Social Studies / Social Science; Special Education

MANUSCRIPT GUIDELINES/COMMENTS:

Statement of Purpose
The Section on Teaching, Learning, and Human Development (TLHD) publishes research articles that explore the processes and outcomes of teaching, learning, and human development at all educational levels and in both formal and informal settings. This section also welcomes policy research related to teaching, learning, and learning to teach. It publishes articles that represent a wide range of academic disciplines and use a variety of research methods. All editorial correspondence and manuscripts should be sent to **AERJ-TLHDeditors@aera.net**.

General Information for Contributors to AERA Journals
AERA has a general set of standards that apply to submissions for all journals. Please review the General Information for Contributors to AERA Journals prior to submitting your article (**http://www.aera.net/publications/?id=503**)

Specifications for Manuscripts
The preferred style guide for all AERA journals is the *Publication Manual of the American Psychological Association*, 5th ed., 2001. The only exception is the Social and Institutional Analysis section of the American Educational Research Journal. Contributors to that section may, if they wish, use *The Chicago Manual of Style*, 15th ed., 2003. If a manuscript that is accepted for that section does not use author-date citation, the author will need to reformat it for publication in author-date style, following either the *APA* or *Chicago Manual*.

Manuscripts should be typed on 8 ½ x 11-inch white paper, upper and lower case, double spaced in entirety, with 1-inch margins on all sides. The type size should be at least 10 pitch (CPI) or 12 point. Subheads should be at reasonable intervals to break the monotony of lengthy text. Words to be set in italics (contrary to the rules of the style manual) should be set in italics, not underlined; sentence structure should be used to create emphasis. Abbreviations and acronyms should be spelled out at first mention unless they are found as entries in their abbreviated form in the *Merriam-Webster's Collegiate Dictionary*, 11th ed., 2003 (e.g., IQ needs no explanation).

Pages should be numbered consecutively, beginning with the page after the title page. Mathematical symbols and Greek letters should be clearly marked to indicate italics, boldface, superscript, and subscript.

Requirements for Computer Disks
A 3.5-inch computer disk should be sent to the editor once an article has been accepted. (The disk may accompany the manuscript for book reviews.) The computer file must contain all revisions and must agree with the final version of the manuscript. We prefer a file in Microsoft Word for Windows, but can convert from RTF and WordPerfect. Tables and figures should be included on disk and hard copy.

It would be most helpful if you would use the following practices in typing your manuscript on disk:
- Continue to follow the APA Manual to differentiate among subhead levels; the managing editor will convert these to the proper codes.
- Type only one space after a period or other punctuation.
- Begin each paragraph with a tab, not the space bar.
- In text, use hard returns only at the ends of paragraphs, heads, and subheads. Do not use hard returns in block quotations.
- Despite the instructions in the APA Manual, do not use indents or margin changes in the References. Just type straight copy and use one hard return at the end of each entry.
- Type footnotes in as normal text at the end of the text section of the manuscript rather than as part of the footnote or endnote feature of a computer program.

Submit all Features and Research News and Comment manuscripts electronically to the editorial team at **http://ojs.aera.net/journals/er**. For specific questions or inquiries, send e-mail to editors at the following addresses: Features (**EREditors@aera.net**) Research News and Comment (**ERResearchNews@aera.net**). Do not send manuscripts to these email addresses.

Author Identification
The complete title of the article and the name of the author(s) should be typed only on the first sheet to ensure anonymity in the review process. Subsequent pages should have no author names, but may carry a short title at the top. Information in text or references that would identify the author should be deleted from the manuscript (e.g., text citations of "my previous work," especially when accompanied by a self-citation; a preponderance of the author's own work in the reference list).

These may be reinserted in the final draft. The first-named author or the coauthor who will be handling the correspondence with the editor, clearing galleys, and working with the association's publications department should submit a complete address and telephone number; fax numbers and e-mail addresses are also helpful.

Footnotes and References
Footnotes are explanations or amplifications of textual material. Because footnotes are distracting to readers and expensive to set, the information should be incorporated into the text whenever possible. When they must occur, they should be typed on a separate sheet (to be inserted at the end of the manuscript before tables and figures). Footnotes must be numbered consecutively throughout the article.

The accuracy and completeness of all references are the responsibility of the author(s). A reference list should contain only those references that are cited in the text. Examples of references to a book, a chapter in a book, and a journal article follow:

Garner, R. (1987). Metacognition and reading comprehension. New York: Ablex.

Tatsuoka, M., & Silver, P. (1988). Quantitative research methods in educational administration. In N. J. Boyan (Ed.), Handbook of research on educational administration (pp. 677-701). New York: Longman.

Tyack, D. B., & Hansot, E. (1988). Silence and policy talk: Historical puzzles about gender and education. Educational Researcher, 17(3), 33-41.

Reference notes referring to material that is not readily available to the public (e.g., reports of limited circulation, unpublished works, personal communications, papers presented at meetings, some technical reports, and works in progress) should include as much information as possible to make them retrievable.

Tables, Figures, and Illustrations
The purpose of tables and figures is to present data to the reader in a clear and unambiguous manner. The author should not describe the data in the text in such detail that illustration or text is redundant.

Figures and tables should be keyed to the text. Tables should each be typed on a separate sheet and attached at the end of the manuscript (after the references). Tables will be typeset.

Figure captions should be typed on a separate sheet (and should not appear in full on the original figures). One high-quality, camera-ready version of each figure must be submitted with the manuscript that is to be typeset, and photocopies may be submitted with the additional copies of the manuscript.

Photographs should have a resolution of no less than 150 DPI and preferably 300 DPI.

Once an article has been accepted, all tables and figures should be included on disk with the manuscript and sent to the editors.

Review Process
Manuscripts will be acknowledged by the editor upon receipt. After a preliminary editorial review, articles will be sent to reviewers who have expertise in the subject of the article. The review process takes anywhere from 3 to 6 months, depending on the individual journal. Authors should expect to hear from editors within that time regarding the status of their manuscripts. AERA publications use the blind review system. The names of referees are published annually in the various journals.

Originality of Manuscript
Manuscripts are accepted for consideration with the understanding that they are original material and are not under consideration for publication elsewhere.

Copyright
To protect the works of authors and the association, AERA copyrights all of its publications. Rights and permissions regarding the uses of AERA-copyrighted materials are handled by the AERA Publications Department. Authors who wish to use material, such as figures or tables, for which they do not own the copyright must obtain written permission from the copyright holder (usually the publisher) and submit it to AERA with their manuscripts.

Comments
The Publications Committee welcomes comments and suggestions from authors. Please send these to the Publications Committee in care of the AERA central office.

Right of Reply
The right-of-reply policy encourages comments on articles recently published in an AERA publication. Such comments are subject to editorial review and decision. If the comment is accepted for publication, the editor shall inform the author of the original article. If the author submits a reply to the comment, the reply is also subject to editorial review and decision. The editor may allot a specific amount of journal space for the comment (ordinarily about 1,500 words) and for the reply (ordinarily about 750 words). The reply may appear in the same issue as the comment or in a later one.

Grievances
Authors who believe that their manuscripts were not reviewed in a careful or timely manner and in accordance with the American Educational Research Association's procedures should call the matter to the attention of the association's executive officer or president.

American Indian Culture and Research

SUBMISSION PROCESS:
Postal Submission Only

CONTACT INFORMATION:	REVIEW PROCESS:
Editor American Indian Studies Center UCLA 3220 Campbell Hall, Box 951548 Los Angeles, CA 90095-1548 USA	**Type of Review:** Blind Review
	No. External Reviewers: 3+ **No. InHouse Reviewers:** 1
	Acceptance Rate: 21-30%
Phone: 310-825-7315	**Time to Review:** 2 - 3 Months **Reviewer's Comments:** Yes **Invited Articles:** 6-10%
Email: editor@aisc.ucla.edu	**Fees to Publish:** $0.00 US$ **Fees to Review:** $0.00 US$
Website: www.books.aisc.ucla.edu	

PUBLICATION GUIDELINES:	CIRCULATION DATA:
Manuscript Style: Chicago Manual of Style	**Reader:** Academics
Manuscript Length: 26-30	**Frequency of Issue:** Quarterly
Copies Required: Four	**Sponsor/Publisher:** UCLA American Indian Studies Center

MANUSCRIPT TOPICS:

American Indian Studies; American Literature; Art / Music; Educational Psychology; History, Anthropology; Languages & Linguistics; Multicultural Education; Social Studies / Social Science; Urban Education, Cultural / Non-Traditional

MANUSCRIPT GUIDELINES/COMMENTS:

About us

The foremost referred research journal of American Indian Studies is released quarterly by the UCLA American Indian Studies Center Publications Unit. Each issue is packed with timely, well-researched articles, haunting lyrical literature, and the latest reviews of the academic literature available--in short, a vista on the world of American Indian Studies.

Manuscript Submission

1. Submit four (4) copies of the manuscript to: Editor, American Indian Culture and Research Journal, American Indian Studies Center, UCLA, 3220 Campbell Hall, Box 951548, Los Angeles, CA 90095-1548. Include your email address, phone number, and mailing address.

2. Since all manuscripts are evaluated by at least three anonymous referees, please keep identifying material out of the manuscript. Attach a cover page giving authorship, institutional affiliation, and acknowledgments.

3. All copy must be typed, double-spaced (including indented material and endnotes) on 8 ½ - by 11-inch white paper. All margins must be at least one inch. After an article is accepted, the author will be asked to submit a 3-1/2-inch computer disk containing the article. Manuscripts should be on Macintosh-formatted disks with the text written in Microsoft Word. Disks will not be returned to authors.

4. The *Journal* requires that tables, endnotes, and format conform to *The Chicago Manual of Style*, 15th edition (Chicago and London: University of Chicago Press, 2003). Special attention should be given to chapter 17. Do not use footnotes or any variation of the author date system. Submissions that do not conform to our style format may be returned for retyping.

5. Copies of manuscripts submitted for review will not be returned to authors. Do not submit original artwork for review. Original artwork will be requested upon acceptance for publication.

6. The review process is ordinarily completed within three months. If processing is delayed beyond that point, authors will be notified.

7. Manuscripts accepted for publication in the *American Indian Culture and Research Journal* are subject to stylistic editing. Page proofs are sent to authors. All authors and reviewers are required to assign copyright to the Regents of the University of California.

Multiple Submission Policy. The *American Indian Culture and Research Journal* regards submission of a manuscript to one professional journal while that manuscript is under review by any other journal as unacceptable. It is further assumed by the *American Indian Culture and Research Journal* that work submitted for review has not been previously published and is not scheduled for publication elsewhere. If other published or submitted papers exist that are based on the same or closely related data sets, such papers should be noted and referenced in a cover letter to the editor, and their relation to the submitted paper should be explained briefly.

Style Sheet for Copyeditors and Authors
We follow *Chicago Manual of Style strictly,* using documentation one style and capitalizing titles in bibliographies.

Heads. In heads and subheads of all *AICRJ* articles, all nouns, pronouns, adjectives, verbs, and adverbs, and subordinating conjunctions (if, because, since, that, etc.) are capitalized in titles; all coordinating conjunctions (and, but, or, for, nor) and prepositions (behind, among) are not. No endnotes are allowed on heads.

Epigraphs. All epigraphs appear with the author's name and the title of the book (not the date or any other information). No endnotes are allowed on epigraphs. The author's name should be preceded by an em-dash. Please visit the web site for examples.

Subheads. With few exceptions, all articles should have subheads (this is our house style, Chicago has no comment on subheads either way) for ease of reading. Please query authors for subheads if they are missing. Feel free to suggest possible subheads. Please check heads and subheads for levels and query authors if unclear. The first paragraph after a subhead is not indented. Unless the article is in social science style (with an abstract, methodology, etc.), the article should never start with a subhead (e.g., no Introduction).

Punctuation. *AICRJ* uses a serial comma and punctuation appears before the final quotation mark. A colon is used to introduce a formal statement, a speech in dialogue, or an extract. Please visit the web site for examples.

Plurals. One can omit the possessive apostrophe from organizations like city government or carpenters union, but be sure to include it in other proper nouns (e.g., Kansas's). Plurals of acronyms appear with lower cases (e.g., NGOs). Plurals of titles: two Chicago Tribunes, three New York Times.

Non-English Words. If a word can be found in an English dictionary, it should not be italicized. Proper nouns are not. italicized. We italicize each instance of a foreign word, not just the first mention.

Special Words. Use *more than* in front of numbers or quantities; use over in front of terms such as *the course of*, *the next few years*, etc. Some words are treated specially:
- United States is spelled out as a noun, but is spelled US as an adjective.
- Robert Jones Jr. and E. F. Hutton III
- worldwide web, website
- Internet (uppercase)

Compound Words. Remember *Chicago*'s rules concerning hyphenated and closed compounds. Do not use a hyphen before compound words including an adverb. Please visit the web site for examples.

Capitalization of Words in Text. Remember that *Chicago* prefers lowercase job titles unless they appear in front of a name. *AICRJ* house style includes capitalizing "Native" in reference to Native peoples. Please visit the web site for examples.

Italics. Use italics for titles and for foreign words. Authors should not be allowed to use italics for emphasis except rarely. If the word can be found in an English dictionary, it should not be italicized. Special terminology being introduced is set in italics on first appearance. Words used as words are set in italics as well.

Numbers. Whole numbers from one through ninety-nine are spelled out and round numbers above that (e.g. two thousand years) are also spelled out, unless in a percentage (e.g., 45 percent voted). We show dates with the day first and the month second (e.g., 6 October 1924). We use the full decade in numerals (e.g., 1920s not twenties). The year should never appear abbreviated (always 1990, not '90). Use commas in all numbers over three digits (e.g., 1,000) except dates (1920). We use *Chicago*'s crazy abbreviated number style (e.g., 343–45) with an en-dash; see *Chicago*. We discourage in-text superscript numbers in headlines or subheads. Move them to the body of the text whenever feasible.

Quotations. When a quotation is used as part of a sentence, it is okay to begin it with a lowercase letter even thought the original begins with a capital letter or vice versa.

Figures. References to figures are spelled out in text, but abbreviated in parenthetical references (e.g., see fig. 1).

Layout. First paragraphs after a head are not indented. Subsequent paragraphs are.

Acknowledgments. If there are several acknowledgments, they should be listed under the heading "Acknowledgments" just before the Notes.

Documentation: **Endnotes**
AICRJ uses the endnote documentation system. If the first note is about previous publication or acknowledgments, it should be unnumbered. Note numbers appear at the end of a sentence, *outside* punctuation.

1. For a discussion on the first animal in the Midewiwin ritual, see Michael M. Pomedli, "The Otter: Laughter and Treaty Three," *Trente-deuxième Congrès des Algonquinistes* (Winnipeg: Université de Manitoba, 2001), 359–73.

2. Robert E. and Pat Ritzenthaler, *The Woodland Indians of the Western Great Lakes* (Garden City, NY: Natural History Press, 1970), 87.

3. Fred K. Blessing, *The Ojibway Indians Observed* (St. Paul: Minnesota Archaeological Society, 1977), 111; Julia Harrison, "'He Heard Something Laugh': Otter Imagery in the Midewiwin," in David W. Penney, ed., *Bulletin of the Detroit Institute of Arts* 62 (1986): 51.

Subsequent notes should include author's name, shortened title, and page number. If the note immediately follows the same citation, use "Ibid." and the page number.
4. Blessing, *Ojibway Indians Observed*, 121.

5. Ibid., 133.

To Cite Information from the Internet:
Author's First and Last Name/Name of organization hosting site, "Title of Internet Site," http://www.addaddresshere.org (accessed which date).

Electronic Image Guidelines for the *American Indian Culture and Research Journal*
1. Images should be scanned in grayscale between 266 and 300 dpi. They should be approximately the print size (e.g., a 8x10 print should be scanned at 4x5). Typically, with popular scan software, large images are scanned at 72 dpi at actual size; while it is possible for us to reduce the dimensions and increase the dpi, it produces an inferior result.

2. File formats should be .tif or .eps. Acrobat (.pdf) can be used, but usually incorporates some compression and therefore is not as sharp. Acrobat also must be processed by the typesetter before placing in a Quark (publishing software) file, so it is less efficient. If a contributor must use .pdf format, she or he should be sure that all compression is off or set to minimal values and that the dpi is not greatly reduced (it should be between 266 and 300). If using .tif format, do not use LZW compression.

3. Following the above guidelines will result in large files, probably 2.5 MB, but this is the standard for print production (as opposed to laser or inkjet). Files can be compressed using WinZip or StuffIt if being sent via email.

4. We will make adjustments to the highlight and shadow values for optimal print quality, so just leave scan software at default settings, or "auto."

5. We can also make decent desktop scans ourselves if necessary. Originals are best. Inkjet prints, while sometimes usable, tend to "band" and create more patterns. Scans from printed material also cause those patterns because of the halftone dots, so original prints are best.

6. For computer-generated images created in Illustrator, Draw, or other vector programs, save as .eps. We can make any changes to these files as necessary. For images created in Photoshop or other raster-image programs, follow above guidelines as to format and resolution, and save as grayscale (not RGB). For images created and/or embedded in Word, Excel, etc., save as .eps if possible, or .pcx if necessary. These images are highly problematic and should be avoided, but pie charts, etc. are often created this way. Often they must be recreated by us in Illustrator, but as they sometimes import successfully in the native format, we can try to work with them if necessary. However, these images are often captured screen shots that are embedded in Word, and therefore are extremely low-resolution. Check with your editor before attempting to incorporate these in your article

American Journal of Evaluation

SUBMISSION PROCESS:

**Electronic Submission Preferred
via Online Portal**

http://mc.manuscriptcentral.com/ajeval

CONTACT INFORMATION:	REVIEW PROCESS:	
Robin Lin Miller, Editor Michigan State University Department of Psychology 316 Psychology Building East Lansing, MI 48824-1116 USA	**Type of Review:**	Blind Review
	No. External Reviewers:	3+
	No. InHouse Reviewers:	1
	Acceptance Rate:	21-30%
Phone: 517-432-5640	**Time to Review:**	3 Months
	Reviewer's Comments:	Yes
	Invited Articles:	20%
Email: aje@eval.org	**Fees to Publish:**	$0.00 US$
	Fees to Review:	$0.00 US$
Website: www.sagepub.com		

PUBLICATION GUIDELINES:	CIRCULATION DATA:
Manuscript Style: American Psychological Association	**Reader:** Academics, Practitioners
Manuscript Length: 26-40	**Frequency of Issue:** Quarterly
Copies Required: Six (4 w/out ID, 2 w/ID)	**Sponsor/Publisher:** American Evaluation Association (AEA) / Elsevier Inc.

MANUSCRIPT TOPICS:
Program and Policy Evaluation; Tests, Measurement & Evaluation

MANUSCRIPT GUIDELINES/COMMENTS:

The *American Journal of Evaluation (AJE)* publishes original papers about the methods, theory, practice, and findings of evaluation. The general goal of *AJE* is to present the best work in and about evaluation, in order to improve the knowledge base and practice of its readers. Because the field of evaluation is diverse, with different intellectual traditions, approaches to practice, and domains of application, the papers published in *AJE* will reflect this diversity. Nevertheless, preference is given to papers that are likely to be of interest to a wide range of evaluators and that are written to be accessible to most readers.

Individuals interested in contributing to the Ethical Challenges, Exemplars, Teaching Evaluation, and Book Reviews sections should contact the relevant section editor (see Contribution Categories). All other manuscripts should be addressed to: Dr. Robin Lin Miller, Editor, AJE, Michigan State University, Department of Psychology, 316 Psychology Building, East Lansing, MI 48824-1116. Submission letters should specify that the manuscript is not currently under consideration elsewhere and has not been published elsewhere in the same or a substantially similar form.

A total of six double-spaced typewritten copies should be submitted. On two copies, each author's name, title, full mailing address, telephone number(s), and e-mail address should be listed. Author information should be omitted on four copies (for blind review).

Manuscripts should be prepared following the style of the *Publication Manual of the American Psychological Association*, 4th Edition. References, citations in text, tables, and figures should all conform to the APA style. Any figures should be camera-ready.

Authors whose works have been accepted for publication will be asked to submit the final manuscript on a disk prepared with an IBM-compatible word processor. WordPerfect or Word formats are preferred, but others can be used. (Please contact Robin Miller for specific guidelines.)

If prospective contributors have questions or are uncertain about the appropriateness of possible submissions, they are welcome to contact Robin Miller via email at **aje@eval.org** or by phone at (517) 353-5010.

American Journal of Orthopsychiatry

SUBMISSION PROCESS:	
Electronic Submission Only via Online Portal http://www.jbo.com/jbo3/submissions	

CONTACT INFORMATION:	REVIEW PROCESS:	
Nancy Felipe Russo, Editor Arizona State University Department of Psychology Box 1104 Tempe, AZ 85287-1104 USA	**Type of Review:**	Blind Review
	No. External Reviewers:	2
	No. InHouse Reviewers:	Varies
Phone:	**Acceptance Rate:**	6-10%
	Time to Review:	2-5 Months
	Reviewer's Comments:	Yes
	Invited Articles:	0-5%
Email: nancy.russo@asu.edu	**Fees to Publish:**	$0.00 US$
Website: www.amerortho.org	**Fees to Review:**	$0.00 US$

PUBLICATION GUIDELINES:	CIRCULATION DATA:
Manuscript Style: American Psychological Association	**Reader:** Academics, Practitioners, Agency Staff
Manuscript Length: 26-30	**Frequency of Issue:** Quarterly
Copies Required: Electronic Only	**Sponsor/Publisher:** American Orthopsychiatric Association / American Psychological Association

MANUSCRIPT TOPICS:

Mental Health & Social Justice; Minority, Refugee & Family Mental Health; Public Policy & Professional Practice; Urban Education, Cultural / Non-Traditional

MANUSCRIPT GUIDELINES/COMMENTS:

Journal Description

The *Journal* is dedicated to informing public policy and professional practice and to the expansion of knowledge relating to mental health and human development from a multidisciplinary and interprofessional perspective. Especially welcome are research, clinical, theoretical, or policy papers that are directed at development of concepts or theory, reconceptualization of major issues and/or previous findings, or policy applications related to human rights and social justice.

Instructions to Authors

Submission. Submit manuscripts electronically (**http://www.jbo.com/jbo3/submissions/dsp_jbo. cfm?journal_code=ort**) (.rtf, PDF, or .doc files; .doc files preferred). General correspondence may be directed to: **amerortho@gmail.com**.

Manuscript preparation. Manuscripts should be in final form, with consistent headings and subheadings in roman typeface (i.e., no boldface, italics, etc.). Manuscripts are limited to 30 pages, inclusive of references, tables, and figures. The abstract should be 125–180 words.

Footnotes should be worked back into the text or deleted, if possible. Where essential, they should appear on a page by themselves following the references and be indicated by superscript Arabic numerals.

References should conform with the style set forth in *the Publication Manual of the American Psychological Association* (5th ed.).

The entire manuscript, including quotations, footnotes, references, and tables, must be double-spaced.

The *Journal* is dedicated to informing public policy and professional practice and to the expansion of knowledge relating to mental health and human development from a multidisciplinary and interprofessional perspective. Especially welcome for editorial consideration are clinical, theoretical, research, or expository papers that are essentially synergistic and directed at development of concept or theory, reconceptualization of major issues, explanation, and interpretation. Selection of articles for publication is based on originality, adequacy of method, significance of findings, contribution to theory, relevance to service delivery and public policy, and clarity and brevity of presentation.

Masked review policy. Articles published in the *Journal* are selected from unsolicited submissions, papers invited by the Editor, and manuscripts of presentations at the American Orthopsychiatric Association's meetings. Whatever their source, all articles considered for publication in the *Journal* are subject to a process of masked peer review.

Publication policies. Manuscripts of papers presented at Ortho meetings must be submitted in timely fashion to the Journal in accordance with submission guidelines. Publication elsewhere than in the *Journal* or by the Association is prohibited prior to release by the Editor. Manuscripts must be submitted exclusively for publication in the *American Journal of Orthopsychiatry*. Papers previously published or now under consideration elsewhere are not eligible for editorial review. Authors of accepted manuscripts will be required to transfer copyright to APA.

Figures. Graphics files should be supplied as Tiff, EPS, or PowerPoint. High-quality printouts or glossies are needed for all figures. The minimum line weight for line art is 0.5 point for optimal printing. When possible, please place symbol legends below the figure image instead of to the side. Original color figures can be printed in color at the editor's and publisher's discretion and provided the author agrees to pay $255 for one figure, $425 for two figures, $575 for three figures, $675 for four figures, and $55 for each additional figure.

Permissions. Authors are required to obtain and provide to the editor on final acceptance all necessary permissions to reproduce in print and electronic form any copyrighted work, including, for example, test materials (or portions thereof) and photographs of people.

Preparing files for production. If your manuscript is accepted for publication, please follow the guidelines for file formats and naming provided at Preparing Your Accepted Manuscript for Production. Please ensure that the final version for production includes a byline and full author note for typesetting.

The American Orthopsychiatric Association assumes no responsibility for any statements of fact or opinion in the papers printed. Nor does acceptance of advertising in the *Journal* imply endorsement by the Association of any products or services advertised. The Editorial Board reserves the right to reject any manuscript, to suggest modifications prior to publication, and to edit accepted manuscripts in conformance with *Journal* style and standards.

American Journal of Pharmaceutical Education

SUBMISSION PROCESS:
Electronic Submission Only **via Online Portal** **http://ajpe.edmgr.com**

CONTACT INFORMATION:	REVIEW PROCESS:	
Joseph T. DiPiro, Editor Medical University of South Carolina University of South Carolina - Columbia	**Type of Review:**	Blind Review
	No. External Reviewers:	2
Karen Shipp, Assistant Editor	**No. InHouse Reviewers:**	1
Coker Life Science Bldg., Room 109 715 Sumter St.	**Acceptance Rate:**	60%
Columbia, SC 29208 USA	**Time to Review:**	1 - 2 Months
	Reviewer's Comments:	Yes
	Invited Articles:	0-5%
Phone:		
	Fees to Publish:	$0.00 US$
	Fees to Review:	$0.00 US$
Email:		
ajpe@cop.sc.edu		
Website: www.ajpe.org		

PUBLICATION GUIDELINES:	CIRCULATION DATA:
Manuscript Style: See Manuscript Guidelines	**Reader:** Academics
Manuscript Length: 10-20	**Frequency of Issue:** Bi-Monthly
Copies Required: Electronic Only	**Sponsor/Publisher:** American Association of Colleges of Pharmacy

MANUSCRIPT TOPICS:
Book Reviews; Curriculum Studies; Educational Technology Systems; Instructional Design and Assessment; Research Articles; Statements and Reviews; Tests, Measurement & Evaluation

MANUSCRIPT GUIDELINES/COMMENTS:

Introduction
The *Journal* is devoted to providing relevant information for pharmaceutical educators and all others interested in the advancement of pharmaceutical education. The *Journal* provides a forum for communication among pharmaceutical educators. To be considered, manuscripts must provide useful information for the national or international audience of the *Journal*. If a submission has only local or regional relevance, its usefulness to the majority of our readers is limited. To assure that only accurate and substantive articles are included, all manuscripts undergo a peer review process and editorial approval prior to acceptance.

Manuscript Categories

- **Viewpoints**. Viewpoints are short editorials and commentaries on educational policy, philosophical issues, or other pertinent subjects authored by the Editor, Editorial Board, AACP officers, or invited authors.
- **Statements**. Statements are papers that present fully developed ideas, concepts, or recommendations on a topic of widespread interest to pharmacy education.
- **Reviews**. Reviews are comprehensive, well-referenced descriptive papers on teaching or research topics directly related to pharmacy and graduate or post-graduate education and training. This section includes papers on the history of pharmacy education.
- **Research Articles**. Research articles describe experimental or observational investigations that used formal methods for data collection and reporting of results.
- **Instructional Design and Assessment**. Instructional Design and Assessment papers describe novel methods for professional and graduate student instruction (lectures, laboratories, practice experiences, or courses), or informational manuscripts on programmatic and curriculum development.
- **Teachers' Topics**. Teachers' Topics are invited manuscripts from the "Teachers of the Year" at AACP member institutions.
- **Innovations in Teaching**. Innovations in Teaching are invited manuscripts from recipients of the AACP Innovations in Teaching Award.
- **AACP Reports**. AACP Reports are summaries of activity of officers, delegates, and committee chairpersons within AACP.
- **Letters to the Editor**. Letters to the Editor serve as a forum for the expression of ideas or for commenting on matters of interest. It is also an avenue for critiquing or expanding on the information presented in a previously published manuscript. Authors are required to identify themselves. The Editor reserves the right to reject, shorten, excerpt, or edit letters for publication.
- **Book and Software Reviews**. Book and Software Reviews are brief documents that provide the reader with a clear understanding of content in a book or software program, as well as the product structure, scope, and limitations. The reviewer should state the value or utility of the product for instruction, research, or other academic activities.

Stylistic Considerations

The style specifications for the *Journal* must be followed. Below are general guidelines for manuscript format and style. If in doubt about style, authors should refer to the *American Medical Association Manual of Style*, 9th ed., or consult a recent issue of the *Journal*.

Text. The text should be scholarly, readable, clear and concise. Standard nomenclature should be used. Unfamiliar terms and acronyms should be defined at first mention. Manuscripts that were prepared for oral presentation must be rewritten for print. Authors of research papers are discouraged from writing excessively long introduction or discussion sections.

Word style. Consult a current edition of *Webster's* dictionary for guidance on spelling, compounding, and word separation. Foreign words, not in general use, should be italicized. For proper use of chemical and biochemical terms, mathematical equations, mathematical expressions, special symbols, subscripts, superscripts, or Greek letters, please refer to the *AMA Manual of Style*.

Capitalization. The word "association" must be capitalized when referring to the American Association of Colleges of Pharmacy. When the word "journal" is capitalized and italicized as *Journal*, it can refer only to the *American Journal of Pharmaceutical Education*. In scientific writing, always capitalize the following: major words in titles and headings of manuscripts, designators (eg, Table 3), eponyms (but not the noun that follows them, eg, Gram stain, Babinski sign), names of tests (eg, Beck Depression Inventory), genus names of organisms (but not the name of species, varieties or subspecies), acts of legislation (eg, Medicare), awards (eg, Nobel Prize), proprietary names (eg, Xerox copier), the title of a person when followed by the person's name (eg, Chair John W. Jones), official names of organizations and institutions (eg, Centers for Disease

Control and Prevention), geographic places (eg, United States of America), sociocultural designations (eg, Republicans, French people), historical events (eg, Vietnam War).

Abbreviations. In instances where repeated use of an organization or chemical name would become awkward, an official or accepted abbreviation may be substituted. The abbreviation should be placed in parentheses immediately following the first use of the name in the main body of the text. Abbreviations of common pharmaceutical organizations do not require periods or spaces between letters (eg, AMA). Abbreviations of "eg," "ie," and "viz" should not be seperated by periods. The names of US states and countries should be spelled out when they stand alone (eg, "…pharmacists throughout the United States…"). When the name of a state follows the name of a city or town, it should be abbreviated and periods should not be used (eg, Boston, Mass). Postal abbreviations for states are not used. Refer to the *AMA Manual of Style* for a list of proper abbreviations. The abbreviation "US" may be used as a modifier only when it directly precedes the word it modifies (eg, US health policies). Otherwise, it should be spelled out (eg, "…the population of the United States"). The names of all other cities, states, provinces, and countries should be spelled out when they occur within the text of the article.

Numbers. Numbers must be written as Arabic numerals unless they occur at the beginning of a sentence, in which case the number should be spelled out. The exception to this rule is when the number "one" is used in isolation within the text and substituting an Arabic number would seem awkward (eg, "there was only one logical solution to the problem"). A number containing a decimal must be styled as an Arabic number. All fractions must be written as decimal equivalents.

Measurements. The metric system will be used for all measurements; however, conventional units should be used instead of SI units. Do not use periods when abbreviating units of measure.

Reference numbers. These numbers should be superscript Arabic numerals placed at the end of the sentence, outside the final period or other punctuation. Subsequent citations to the same reference must be indicated by the same number originally assigned to that reference. Do not place parentheses around the reference numbers.

Personal Communications. If the source of material referred to in an article is from a personal communications, it should be referenced as such in parentheses immediately following reference to the material, followed by the date (eg, written communication, October 2, 2002).

Hypertext Links. Authors may identify uniform resource locators (URLs) for Internet web sites that provide the reader with additional information on the topic addressed in the manuscript. Although URLs are an important feature of electronic publishing, authors are encouraged to be selective in their choice of sites to include. Do not include URLs for web pages with newspaper or journal articles that will be removed or archived to another web page. Links to pharmaceutical manufacturers or other sources of product information are acceptable; however, providing a URL to the reader should not be substituted for adequate discussion within the manuscript itself. Do not include links to sites that are not accessible without a password.

Manuscript Organization
Within the document, each page of the manuscript should be arranged and numbered consecutively in the following order: title page, abstract, footnotes, text, references, tables, figure legends, and illustrations.

Title Page. The title page should have the following information: a concise title, name of each author, terminal degree, academic/professional title and affiliation, and city and state where located. If an author has relocated to another institution, please include his/her affiliation during the time the author worked on the manuscript. At the lower left of the page, indicate the name of the corresponding author and provide his/her mailing address, telephone number, facsimile number, and e-mail address. At the bottom of the title page, indicate 3 to 5 keywords.

Abstract. Each manuscript must include an abstract of 100 to 150 words. For Research Articles, the abstract should include a brief (1 to 3 sentences) statement for each of the following sections: Objectives, Methods, Results, and Conclusions. For Instructional Design and Assessment papers, the abstract should include a statement for the following sections: Objectives, Design, Assessment, and Conclusion. Each section within the abstract should be flushed left, followed by a period and the statements summarizing that section.

Main Body of Text. The use of subheadings to divide the text is encouraged. Primary headings should be in bold capital letters and should contain no more than 35 characters or spaces. Secondary headings should be in bold title case and appear above the paragraph. Tertiary headings should be in bold with only the initial letter capitalized. Tertiary headings should end with a period and should appear before the beginning of the first sentence in that section.

Acknowledgments. Any special funding received for research that is the subject of the manuscript should be included under a section entitled "Acknowledgments" at the end of the text. If the authors wish to thank colleagues or others who provided assistance with their research or manuscript preparation, those acknowledgments also should be included under this section. Any statements concerning liability for the content of the manuscript may be included here as well (eg, "the ideas expressed in this manuscript are those of the author and in no way are intended to represent the position of…").

Reference Section. References to a published source should be provided for all information in the manuscript that contains dates, facts, or opinions other than those of the author. Authors are responsible for the accuracy and completeness of all citations. References should be numbered consecutively in the order in which the information contained in the referenced publication appears or is referred to in the manuscript. Do not create a second abbreviated reference or use "ibid" to refer to information cited in a previous reference. Instead, if information from the same source is referred to a second time in the manuscript, cite the same reference number originally assigned to that source. For detailed information on reference style, refer to the section on Stylistic Concerns.

Each journal citation must include the surnames and complete initials of all authors. For manuscripts with 7 or more authors, the first 3 authors should be listed, followed by "et al." The names of all periodicals cited must be abbreviated in accordance with abbreviations adopted by the National Library of Medicine and used in *Index Medicus*. An example and special instructions for specific types of references are provided below. For additional guidance, please refer to the *American Medical Association Manual* of Style, 9th ed., or to a recent issue of the *Journal*.

Journal articles. For references to journal articles, first list the names of the authors beginning with the last name of the first author, followed by his/her initials. The authors' names are followed by the title of the article. The first letter of the title is capitalized, but the remainder of the title should be in lower case letters, except for the first letter of proper names. A period should be placed after the title. Next, give the properly abbreviated title of the journal being referenced. The title of the journal should be in italics followed by a period. One space should be left between the journal and the year of publication. A semicolon should be placed after the year of publication, followed by the volume number in which the article appeared. After the volume number, place a colon followed by the number of the first page of the article, then a dash, then the number of the last page of the article, followed by a period. If the article does not appear on consecutive pages, use a semicolon between each segment of pages (eg, 172-175;179-183;199.) Example: Stratton TP, Cochran GA. A rural geriatric experience. *Am J Pharm Educ*. 1990;62:151-5.

Reference to a book. List the last name of the first author of the book, followed by the first and middle initial if given, just as in a journal reference. The names of all authors of the book must be listed. Place a period after the last author's initials. Next, state the title of the book using standard rules for capitalization within titles. A period should be placed at the end of the title. If more than one edition of the book has been published, then the edition number must be given. An ordinal number should be used to indicate the edition number (eg, 9th), followed by a space and "ed." Next, provide the city and state where the publisher is located. Use the abbreviations for states provided in the *AMA Style Manual* rather than postal abbreviations. A colon should separate the city and state from the name of the publisher. The full name of the publisher should be given, followed by a semicolon. Next, provide the year of publication, followed by a colon and the page or page numbers referenced. Example: Martin AN. *Physical Pharmacy*. 4th ed. Philadelphia, Penn: Lea & Febiger; 1993:268.

Reference to a chapter in a book. To reference a single chapter in a book, first list the authors and state the title as you would if citing a journal article. The chapter title should be followed by the word "In" followed by a colon. Next, list the name(s) and initials of the editors of the book, followed by a comma and the abbreviation "ed" or "eds" if more than one editor, followed by a period. Next include the title of the book, location of the publisher, publisher's name, year of publication and page numbers in the same format as for a reference to an entire book (see previous example). Example: Lyon RA, Titeler M. Pharmacology and biochemistry of the 5-HT2 receptor. In: Sanders-Bush E, ed. *The Serotonin Receptors*. Clifton, NJ: Humana Press;1989: 59-88.

For further detailed examples, please visit the web site.

Tables and Figures

Tables. Table should be created in Microsoft Word table format. Data must be placed in separate cells of the table to prevent text and numbers from shifting when the table is converted for publication on the Internet. You can insert empty cells to create spacing. Footnotes should be placed at the bottom of the table inside a single row or cell and should be indented. The following symbols are used to indicate footnotes: first footnote should be indicated by an asterisk (*); second, by a dagger (†); third, double dagger (‡); fourth, section mark (§); fifth, parallel mark (||), etc. Refer to a current issue of the *Journal* for more examples of table style.

Tables should not duplicate information provided in the text. Instead, tables should be used to provide additional information that illustrates or expands on a specific point the author wishes to make. Each table should be self-explanatory and begin on a separate page in the document. Tables should be numbered using Arabic numbers according to the order in which they are referred to in the text. The table number and a concise title should be placed above the body of the table.

Figures. Figures should be numbered using Arabic numbers, based on the order in which they are presented in the text. Figure legends should be concise and self-explanatory. All illustrative materials for the figures should be submitted as high-resolution gif or jpg files. The key to any symbols in a graph or chart should be included as part of the illustration itself, rather than in the legend. If figures contain illustrations that have been published elsewhere, a letter of permission to reprint from the original publisher must accompany the manuscript.

A graphic image embedded into a MS Word file has a resolution of only 72 dpi (computer screen resolution). As a result, when printed, the graphics will look fuzzy. If possible, send graphics with a resolution of at least 300 dpi. Preferably, save the original image at a high resolution (ie, 1200 dpi or higher) and with the image quality set at maximum. Each high-resolution graphic image should be saved and submitted in a separate file from the manuscript text.

Original (first generation) graphics are the preferred files to work with because they have the highest resolution (ie, at this point the image has not been compressed to reduce its size). If necessary, high-resolution graphics can be reduced to a lower resolution for use on the web and within the .pdf files. However, low-resolution graphics cannot be improved and may result in poor online and printed images.

In general, an image can be categorized as either a photograph or a graphic (eg, line drawing of a chemical process, a map depicting pharmacy sites, a bar graph). Always save photographs in "RGB" mode. For optimum conversion results, save all color **graphics** in "CMYK" mode and all black-and-white **graphics** in "grayscale" mode.

Use the chart available on the web site to choose an appropriate file format. **Caution**: never save a JPEG file in CMYK mode; use RGB (computer monitor display) mode. If a graphic image has been saved in RGB mode and must be converted back to CMYK mode for printing, there may be a change to the color resulting in less than satisfactory final graphics.

Use Arial font for any lettering within the graphic images. Figures, symbols, lettering and numbering should be clear and large enough to be legible when reduced. The minimum font size that should be used is 10 pt and the maximum is 14 pt. As a general rule, the original graphic should be 8 inches in width, large enough to span both columns of a *Journal* page. (Note: high-resolution graphics will appear larger on a computer screen than they actually are. Refer to the "image size" dialog box in the graphic software program to determine the graphic's actual size.)

Use a professional graphics program such as Adobe *PhotoShop* to edit and/or save photographs and graphics. Because of difficulties with exporting graphics from Microsoft *PowerPoint*, please send the original graphic (the one imported into *PowerPoint*), saved in an acceptable file format, such as jpg or eps (see chart for more options). However, if the graphic was created in PowerPoint, send it as a *PowerPoint* file.

Manuscript Submission
Please submit your manuscript using *AJPE*'s Editorial Manager online tracking system at **http://ajpe.edmgr.com**. Log in using your user name and password, and then follow the step-by-step on-screen instructions for uploading your files. If you do not know your user name and password or need us to create an account for you, please send an e-mail to **ajpe@cop.sc.edu** and we will respond as quickly as possible.

If for any reason it is not possible for you to submit your paper using *AJPE*'s Editorial Manager site as outlined above, send your manuscript as an e-mail attachment to **ajpe@cop.sc.edu** and we will assist you. If you do not have e-mail access, you may send manuscripts and related files, such as graphics, on a floppy disk, CD-ROM, or Zip disk, to the following address: Karen Shipp, Assistant Editor, American *Journal* of Pharmaceutical Education, Coker Life Sciences Bldg., Room 109, 715 Sumter St., Columbia, SC 29208.

American Journal of Play

SUBMISSION PROCESS:
Postal & Electronic Submission Required **via EMail** **sasbury@museumofplay.org**

CONTACT INFORMATION:	REVIEW PROCESS:	
Jon-Paul Dyson, Editor American Journal of Play Strong National Museum of Play One Manhattan Square Rochester, NY 14607 USA	**Type of Review:**	Blind Review
	No. External Reviewers:	3
	No. InHouse Reviewers:	3+
	Acceptance Rate:	New J
Phone: 585-410-6341	**Time to Review:**	4 - 6 Months
	Reviewer's Comments:	Yes
	Invited Articles:	New J

Email:
  jpdyson@museumofplay.org
  sasbury@museumofplay.org
	Fees to Publish:	$0.00 US$

	Fees to Review:	$0.00 US$
Website:		

PUBLICATION GUIDELINES:	CIRCULATION DATA:

Manuscript Style:
  See Manuscript Guidelines
 	
Manuscript Length:
  16-20
 	
Copies Required:
  Five
	Reader:
	  Academics, Administrators, Counselors,
	  Practicing Teachers
	
	Frequency of Issue:
	  Quarterly
	
	Sponsor/Publisher:
	  Strong Museum of Play

MANUSCRIPT TOPICS:
Adult Career & Vocational; Art / Music; Counseling & Personnel Services; Curriculum Studies; Educational Psychology; Educational Technology Systems; Elementary / Early Childhood; Gifted Children; Health & Physical Education; Higher Education; Reading; Rural Education & Small Schools; School Law; Science Math & Environment; Secondary / Adolescent Studies; Social Studies / Social Science; Special Education; Teacher Education; Tests, Measurement & Evaluation; Urban Education, Cultural / Non-Traditional

MANUSCRIPT GUIDELINES/COMMENTS:

Aims and Scope
The *American Journal of Play* is a new national publication about the history, culture, and psychology of play issued four times a year by Strong National Museum of Play. The Journal features articles in such disciplines as child development, education, psychology, sociology, anthropology, history, communications, and museology and is aimed at a general audience of educators, psychologists, play therapists, sociologists, anthropologists, historians, museum professionals, and others interested in children and the importance of play.

Written in a clear, straightforward style suitable for such a wide readership, work appearing in the *American Journal of Play* is intended to increase national awareness and understanding of the critical role of play in learning and human development and the way in which play illuminates the cultural history of the United States. To these ends, the *American Journal of Play* seeks articles that present significant new research about the nature of play; synthesize and put into perspective major themes of play scholarship; summarize emerging areas of research regarding play; illuminate the important role of play in learning and human development throughout the life cycle; examine the interrelationship of play to other aspects of endeavor; explicate social, cultural, educational, and public policy issues related to play; and explore American cultural history through the window of play.

The *American Journal of Play* also publishes reviews of books and, from time to time, reviews of other media related to the above areas of interest.

Guidelines for Authors

All submissions should include a cover sheet, a one-paragraph summary of about 150 words, and a complete manuscript. Query letters are also welcome. Both paper and electronic versions of the cover letter, summary, and manuscript are required. Five paper copies should be sent to Jon-Paul Dyson, Editor, American Journal of Play, Strong National Museum of Play, One Manhattan Square, Rochester, NY, 14607. The electronic version should be in Word, WordPerfect, or Rich Text Format and may be submitted on a disk or as an email attachment. Disks should be mailed to the editor. Emails should be sent to **sasbury@museumofplay.org**. All text, including quotations, bibliography, and endnotes, should be prepared in double-spaced, 12-point typescript preferably according to the most recent edition of *The Chicago Manual of Style* (University of Chicago Press). See the style section below for further details. Manuscripts, including endnotes, must not exceed 20,000 words. Most articles are 2,500 to 7,500 words. Because submissions are evaluated by blind review, the author's name (and the names of coauthors) should appear only on the cover sheet. Please provide complete addresses for each author, including e-mail, along with academic titles and institutional affiliations. The *American Journal of Play* does not accept manuscripts previously published elsewhere or currently under consideration for publication elsewhere as either an article or part of a book. Articles that are accepted become the property of Strong National Museum of Play. The museum allows authors the free use of their materials as long as a decent interval elapses between publication in the *American Journal of Play* and subsequent publication.

Style

General. Because play spans a number of academic disciplines, the *American Journal of Play* strives to accommodate contrasting scholarly methods and at the same time ensure easy readability for a wide and diverse audience. In general follow the rules for style, spelling, and capitalization established in the latest edition of *The Chicago Manual of Style*; *Webster's Third New International Dictionary*; and Strunk and White, *The Elements of Style*.

Writing for the *Journal* should be addressed to interested and educated readers as well as to immediate peers in the author's specialty. Whenever possible, avoid professional jargon and currently fashionable buzzwords and define any necessary difficult terms. Also, do not use acronyms without providing the full name upon first usage.

Normally use the active voice, and omit needless phrases, such as "the question as to whether," "the fact that," and "along these lines." Use "that" for restrictive clauses, "which" for nonrestrictive.

The *Journal* prefers complete citations with page numbers. Authors who document their work with notes should use endnotes, not footnotes, and should follow *The Chicago Manual of Style*. Authors who do not use endnotes should include a bibliography. Authors who normally write in the American Psychological Association style and wish to include sources in the text should attempt to weave them into the prose. For example, "In 1997, psychologists John Jones and Sue Smith found that children…," or "In her classic book on toddler play, Jane Doe suggested that…," or "James

Doe, whose ground-breaking research on early childhood spanned two decades, argued in 1985 that…," or "According to John Jones and Sue Smith, writing in the *Journal of North American Scholarship* in 2001, the…."

People should be fully identified by first and last names when they are first mentioned in the text. Names of authors mentioned in text should usually correspond exactly to their names as given in endnotes. The *Journal* discourages the use of titles such as Dr., Rev., Gen., Mrs., and Miss in the body of an article.

As a matter of conviction and policy, the editors and publisher of the *Journal* urge authors to use inclusive language, that is, language that does not exclude or disparage people on the basis of gender, age, race, class, or disability.

Text abbreviations, quotations, and illustrations. In general, avoid abbreviations in the text. For organizations that have long names and are frequently referred to by their acronyms, spell out the name of the organization the first time it appears. For example: "American Association for State and Local History (AASLH)."

Quotations should correspond exactly with the originals in wording, spelling, interior capitalization, and internal punctuation. The *Journal* will not typically use *sic* in a published article, but it encourages authors to use it in the manuscripts they submit to indicate errors or idiosyncrasies present in the original source.

If tables are included, each should be identified by both a number and a descriptive title. Each must have its sources indicated, and the author should clearly indicate where each table should be placed in the text. They may not be clustered together at the end of an article.

Figures and illustrations must be numbered separately from tables and also identified by descriptive captions (including a date). The source for each figure should be given, and the author should clearly indicate where each figure should be placed in the text.

When an article is accepted for publication, the author is responsible for obtaining permission to reprint the images and for supplying camera ready or digital copies of figures.

Endnotes and bibliography. Avoid excessive endnotes and make each note complete in itself. Even if the title or author of a work appears in the text, that information should be included in the note.

Keep "see also" references and general bibliographical discussion to a minimum. Once a source of information is given, citation of other sources that treat the same subject is rarely needed. A citation should usually mention specific pages in the cited work that are directly relevant to the article. Also keep discursive material to a minimum. Notes should not be used to "save" material cut from the text.

Combine notes when possible. Endnote numbers should appear at the end of text sentences, never in mid sentence. In general, there should be no more than one note per paragraph.

When a note combines citations with discursive material, the citations should follow the discursion and not be inserted within it. Use the form "For a good discussion of the problem, see Joe L. Frost, *Play and Playscapes* (Albany, 1992), 230–45" rather than "Joe L. Frost, *Play and Playscapes* (Albany, 1992), 230–45 contains a good discussion of this problem."

Scholarly abbreviations. The *Journal* accepts some scholarly abbreviations but not others. The use of *ibid.* is acceptable. *Ibid.* refers to the item preceding and takes the place of as much of the succeeding material as is identical. If more than one work is cited in a note, ibid. should not be used for the first citation of the following note.

Op. cit., loc. cit., idem, and "hereafter cited as" are not part of the *Journal*'s style. Instead, for second references to books and articles, use the author's last name, the short title, and pages. (See endnote samples below.) In assigning short titles, do not change the order of words in the title. Form a short title by dropping any initial article (i.e., A, An, or The) and anything after a colon. The *Journal* also does not encourage the use of and *ff.* and *passim.* Specific pages should be cited whenever possible; otherwise cite the whole title.

Sample endnote citations. In the following examples, samples of full references are followed by samples of second references. Unlike *The Chicago Manual of Style*, the *Journal* does not include the names of publishers in book citations.

Books: Author, *Book Title* (Place of publication, year of publication), page numbers.
1. Joe L. Frost, *Play and Playscapes* (Albany, 1992), 230–45.

2. Frost, *Play and Playscapes*, 250–56.

Edited or translated works: Editor and Editor, eds., *Book Title* (Place of publication, year of publication), page numbers.
3. Doris P. Fromberg and Doris Bergen, eds., *Play from Birth to Twelve and Beyond: Contexts, Perspectives, and Meanings* (New York, 1998), 71.

4. Fromberg and Bergen eds., *Play from Birth to Twelve and Beyond*, 75.

Author, *Book Title*, trans. Translator (Place of publication, year of publication), page numbers.
5. Friedrich Froebel, *Education of a Man*, trans. W. N. Hailmann (New York, 1902), 110–15.

6. Froebel, *Education of a Man*, trans. W. N. Hailmann, 121.

Books with multiple authors or editors: Author, Author, Author, et al. *Book Title* (Place of publication, year of publication), page number.
7. Joseph E. Zins, Roger P. Weissberg, and Margaret C. Wang, et al., eds. *Building Academic Success on Social and Emotional Learning: What Does the Research Say?* (New York, 2004), 63.

8. Zins et al., *Building Academic Success on Social and Emotional Learning*, 63.

Government publications: Publishing Agency, *Book Title* (Place of publication, year of publication), page number.
9. U.S. Department of Education, *America 2000: An Education Strategy* (Washington, 1991), 3.

10. Department of Education, *America 2000*, 14.

(When in doubt, the *Journal* treats published government documents as books. Note that U.S. is abbreviated in endnote references to government agencies [an exception to the general rule against abbreviation.)

Articles or chapters in books: Author, "Article/Chapter Title," in *Periodical Title*, ed. Editor (Place of publication, year of publication), page number.
11. Tom Reed, "Rough and Tumble Play during Recess: Pathways to Successful Social Development," in *Elementary School Recess*, ed. Rhonda Clements (Lake Charles, La., 2000), 45.

12. Reed, "Rough and Tumble Play during Recess," 47.

Articles in journals: Author, "Article Title," *Periodical Title*, volume number (Month/Season of publication [no comma] year of publication), page numbers.

13. David Elkind, "School and Family in the Postmodern World," *Phi Delta Kappan*, 77 (Fall 1995), 8–14.

14. Elkind, "School and Family in the Postmodern World," 9.

(Note that a comma is used between the journal title and the volume number, and there is no comma between the month or season and the year.)

Dissertations: Author, "Dissertation Title" (Degree, diss., University, year of completion), page numbers.

15. Karen L. Hutchison, "A Case Study of Classroom Change in Three Texas Schools: Third-Grade Recess Policy and Practice in a Context of High-Stakes Testing" (Ed.D. diss., University of Texas at San Antonio, 2005), 69–80.

16. Hutchison, "Case Study of Classroom Change in Three Texas Schools," 93.

Web sites: Author, *Entry Title*, Web address (date accessed).

17. Council for Physical Education and Children, *Recess in Elementary Schools: A Position Paper from the National Association for Sports and Physical Education*, http://www.aahperd.org/naspe/pdf_files/pos_papers/current_res.pdf (October 21, 2002).

18. Council for Physical Education and Children, *Recess in Elementary Schools*.

American Journal of Sexuality Education

SUBMISSION PROCESS:
Electronic Submission Only **via EMail** **sexedjournal@hotmail.com**

CONTACT INFORMATION:	REVIEW PROCESS:	
William J. Traverner, Co-Editor 4248 Shadowstone Drive Easton, PA 18040 USA Elizabeth Schroeder, Co-Editor 120 Willowdale Ave Montclair, NJ 07042 USA **Phone:** 610-258-0168 973-655-1172 **Email:** traverner@pdt.net elizschroe@comcast.net **Website:** www.haworthpress.com	**Type of Review:**	Blind Review
	No. External Reviewers:	3+
	No. InHouse Reviewers:	2
	Acceptance Rate:	40-50%
	Time to Review:	2 - 3 Months
	Reviewer's Comments:	Yes
	Invited Articles:	6-10%
	Fees to Publish:	$0.00 US$
	Fees to Review:	$0.00 US$

PUBLICATION GUIDELINES:	CIRCULATION DATA:
Manuscript Style: American Psychological Association **Manuscript Length:** 20-40 **Copies Required:** Electronic Only	**Reader:** Academics, Administrators, Counselors, Practicing Teachers, Trainers **Frequency of Issue:** Quarterly **Sponsor/Publisher:** American Assn. of Sexuality Educators, Counselors & Therapists (AASECT) / Haworth Press, Inc.

MANUSCRIPT TOPICS:
Health & Physical Education; Teacher Education

MANUSCRIPT GUIDELINES/COMMENTS:

About the Journal
Unlike previous journals that have tried (and failed) to be all things to all sexuality professionals, the *American Journal of Sexuality Education* speaks directly to the distinct, individual professional needs of sexuality educators and trainers. This peer-reviewed journal provides sexuality educators and trainers at all skill levels with current research about sexuality education programming and "best practices," sample lesson plans, reports on curriculum development and assessment, literature reviews, scholarly commentary, educational program reports, media reviews (books, videos, Internet resources, and curricula), and letters to the editor.

Each issue of the *American Journal of Sexuality Education* addresses a variety of sexuality topics and audiences, presenting up-to-date theory and practice, lessons, and evaluations. The lessons include: target age group; learning objectives; description of the materials needed; step-by-step procedures; handouts and worksheets; commentary on using and, if applicable, adapting the lesson.

Since sexuality encompasses so many different topics, content for the journal will always be diverse, including but certainly not limited to teaching about: pregnancy prevention, sexually transmitted infections, sexual coercion, healthy versus unhealthy relationships, sexual orientation and identity, sexual response, sexual decision-making, gender identity, and more.

Instructions for Authors
Journal Co-Editors. William J Taverner, MA, Director, 4248 Shadowstone Drive, Easton, PA 18040; Email: **taverner@ptd.net**

Elizabeth Schroeder, EdD(c), MSW, 120 Willowdale Ave, Montclair, NJ 07042; Email: **elizschroe @comcast.net**

Special Notes
1. ORIGINAL ARTICLES ONLY
Submission of a manuscript to this journal represents a certification on the part of the author(s) that it is an original work, and that neither this manuscript nor a version of it has been published elsewhere nor is being considered for publication elsewhere.

2. MANUSCRIPT LENGTH
A. **Articles**. Your article manuscript may be approximately 5–50 typed pages double-spaced (including references and abstract). Lengthier manuscripts may be considered, but only at the discretion of the editors. Sometimes, lengthier manuscripts may be considered if they can be divided up into sections for publication in successive journal issues.

B. **Lesson Plans**. Lesson plans may be 5 or more typed pages double-spaced, and must include the following:
   a. Title
   b. Author(s) or citation
   c. Goals and Objectives
   d. Timing
   e. Description of Intended Audience(s)
   f. Materials needed
   g. Detailed, numbered procedural steps
   h. Worksheets, handouts, and other educational resources needed for the lesson
   i. Commentary on experiences using the activity, suggestions for adaptation, circumstances under which the activity is best used (or not used), and any other relevant information the author thinks would be useful to readers.

C. **Resource Reviews**. Reviews of sexuality education books, curricula, videos, and any other educational materials may be 4 or more typed pages double-spaced.

3. MANUSCRIPT STYLE
References, citations, and general style of manuscripts for this Journal should follow the APA style (as outlined in the latest edition of the *Publication Manual of the American Psychological Association*). References should be double-spaced and placed in alphabetical order. The use of footnotes within the text is discouraged. Words should be underlined only when it is intended that they be typeset in italics.

If an author wishes to submit a paper that has been already prepared in another style, he or she may do so. However, if the paper is accepted (with or without reviewer's alterations), the author is fully responsible for retyping the manuscript in the correct style as indicated above. Neither the editors nor the publisher is responsible for revising manuscript copy to adhere to the journal's style.

4. MANUSCRIPT PREPARATION

Margins: leave a one-inch margin on all four sides.
Title page:
Include the title, plus:

- full authorship
- an ABSTRACT of about 100 words. (Below the abstract, provide 3–10 key words for index purposes).
- a header or footer on each page with abbreviated title and pg number of total (e.g., pg 2 of 7)
- an introductory footnote with authors' academic degrees, professional titles, affiliations, mailing and e-mail addresses, and any desired acknowledgment of research support or other credit.
- a bio for each author, not to exceed 100 words.

Electronic Submission. Required submission is via e-mail **only** directly to the Editors (**sexedjournal@hotmail.com**) as an attached MS Word or Rich Text Format document. In the e-mail subject line, the author(s) should indicate that this is a submission for the *American Journal of Sexuality Education*. The body of the e-mail should contain your cover letter indicating names and affiliations for all authors. Authors must complete a manuscript submission form (See 14. Copyright below).

5. REFERENCE LINKING

The Haworth Press is participating in reference linking for journal articles. (For more information on reference linking initiatives, please consult the CrossRef Web site at www.crossref.org.) When citing a journal article, include the article's Digital Object Identifier (DOI), when available, as the last item in the reference. A Digital Object Identifier is a persistent, authoritative, and unique indentifier that a publisher assigns to each article. Because of its persistence, DOIs will enable The Haworth Press and other publishers to link to the article referenced, and the link will not break over time. This will be a great resource in scholarly research.

An example of a reference to a journal article which includes a DOI:
Vizine-Goetz, Diane (2002).

Classification Schemes for Internet Resources Revisited.
Journal of Internet Cataloging 5(4): 5:18. doi: 10.1300/J141v05n04_02

6. SPELLING, GRAMMAR, AND PUNCTUATION

You are responsible for preparing manuscript copy which is clearly written in acceptable, scholarly English and which contains no errors of spelling, grammar, or punctuation. Neither the editors nor the publisher is responsible for correcting errors of spelling and grammar. The manuscript, after acceptance by the editors, must be immediately ready for typesetting as it is finally submitted by the author(s).

Check your paper for the following common errors:
- dangling modifiers
- misplaced modifiers
- unclear antecedents
- incorrect or inconsistent abbreviations
- coffee stains

Also, check the accuracy of all arithmetic calculations, statistics, numerical data, text citations, and references.

7. INCONSISTENCIES MUST BE AVOIDED

Be sure you are consistent in your use of abbreviations, terminology, and in citing references, from one part of your paper to another.

8. PREPARATION OF TABLES, FIGURES, AND ILLUSTRATIONS

Any material that is not textual is considered artwork. This includes tables, figures, diagrams, charts, graphs, illustrations, appendices, screen captures, and photos. Tables and figures (including legend, notes, and sources) should be no larger than 4 ½ x 6 ½ inches. Type styles should be Helvetica (or Helvetica narrow if necessary) and no smaller than 12 point for the main text, and 10 point for footnotes and references. We request that computer-generated figures be in black and white and/or shades of gray (preferably no color, for it does not reproduce well).

Camera-ready art must contain no grammatical, typographical, or format errors and must reproduce sharply and clearly in the dimensions of the final printed page (4 ½ x 6 ½ inches). Photos and screen captures must be on disk as a TIFF file, or other graphic file format such as JPEG, BMP, or GIF. For rapid publication we must receive black-and-white glossy or matte positives (white background with black images and/or wording) in addition to files on disk. Tables should be created in the text document file using the software's Table feature.

9. SUBMITTING ART

An electronic copy of the art must be provided. We request that each piece of art be sent in its own file, separate from the manuscript text file(s), and be clearly labeled. We reserve the right (if necessary) to request new art, alter art, or if all else has failed in achieving art that is presentable, delete art. If submitted art cannot be used, the publisher reserves the right to redo the art and to change the author for a fee of $55.00 per hour for this service. The Haworth Press, Inc. is not responsible for errors incurred in the preparation of new artwork. Camera-ready artwork must be prepared on separate sheets of paper. Always use black ink and professional drawing instruments. On the back of these items, write your article title and the journal title lightly in soft-lead pencil (please do not write on the face of art). In the text file, skip extra lines and indicate where these figures are placed. Photos are considered part of the acceptable manuscript and remain with the publisher for use in additional printings.

10. ELECTRONIC MEDIA

Haworth's in-house typesetting unit is able to utilize your final manuscript material as prepared on most personal computers and word processors. This will minimize typographical errors and decrease overall production time.

NOTE: Authors are advised that no revisions of the manuscript can be made after acceptance by the editors for publication. The benefits of this procedure are many with speed and accuracy being the most obvious. We look forward to working with your electronic submission which will allow us to serve you more efficiently.

11. ALTERATIONS REQUIRED BY REFEREES AND REVIEWERS

Many times a paper is accepted by the editors contingent upon changes that are mandated by anonymous specialist referees and members of the editorial board. If the editors return your manuscript for revisions, you are responsible for retyping any sections of the paper to incorporate these revisions. Revisions should also be submitted electronically to **sexedjournal@hotmail.com.**

12. TYPESETTING

You will not be receiving galley proofs of your article. Editorial revisions, if any, must therefore be made while your article is still in manuscript. The final version of the manuscript will be the version you see published. Typesetter errors will be corrected by the production staff of The Haworth Press. Authors are expected to submit manuscripts, disks, and/or art that are free from error.

13. REPRINTS

The senior author will receive two copies of the journal issue as well as complimentary reprints of his or her article. The junior author will receive two copies of the journal issue. These are sent several weeks after the journal issue is published and in circulation. An order form for the purchase of additional reprints will also be sent to all authors at this time. (Approximately 8 weeks is necessary for the preparation of reprints.) Please do not query the journal's editors about reprints. All such questions should be sent directly to The Haworth Press, Inc., Production Department, 37 West Broad Street, West Hazleton, PA 18202. To order additional reprints (minimum: 50 copies), please contact The Haworth Document Delivery Center, 10 Alice Street, Binghamton, NY 13904–1580; 1–800–342–9678 or Fax (607) 722–6362.

14. COPYRIGHT

Copyright ownership of your manuscript must be transferred officially to The Haworth Press, Inc. before we can begin the peer-review process. The editors' letter acknowledging receipt of the manuscript will be accompanied by a form fully explaining this. All authors must sign the form and return the original to the editors as soon as possible. Failure to return the copyright form in a timely fashion will result in a delay in review and subsequent publication.

American Psychologist

SUBMISSION PROCESS:

**Electronic Submission Only
via Online Portal**

www.apa.org/journals/amp

CONTACT INFORMATION:	REVIEW PROCESS:	
Norman B. Anderson, Editor-in-Chief 750 First Street N.E. Washington, DC 20002-4242 USA	**Type of Review:**	Blind Review
	No. External Reviewers:	3
	No. InHouse Reviewers:	0
Phone: 202-336-5500	**Acceptance Rate:**	12%
	Time to Review:	6 Months
Email: Apeditor@apa.org	**Reviewer's Comments:**	Yes
	Invited Articles:	31-50%
Website: www.apa.org/amp	**Fees to Publish:**	$0.00 US$
	Fees to Review:	$0.00 US$

PUBLICATION GUIDELINES:	CIRCULATION DATA:
Manuscript Style: American Psychological Association	**Reader:** Academics
Manuscript Length: 35 Max, dble-spaced	**Frequency of Issue:** Monthly
Copies Required: Electronic Only	**Sponsor/Publisher:** American Psychological Association

MANUSCRIPT TOPICS:
Educational Psychology; Psychology

MANUSCRIPT GUIDELINES/COMMENTS:

Topics Include. Current issues, empirical, theoretical, and practical articles on broad aspects of psychology.

Manuscript Preparation. Authors should prepare manuscripts according to the *Publication Manual of the American Psychological Association* (5th ed.). Manuscripts should be no more than 35 double-spaced pages, including references. All manuscripts must include an abstract containing a maximum of 180 words. Formatting instructions, including instructions on preparing tables, figures, references, metrics, and abstracts, appear in the *Manual*. All manuscripts are copyedited for bias-free language. Comments should be submitted no later than two months from the date of the issue containing the article to which they respond. (Comments on comments are rarely considered.) Comments on matters of APA policy are also considered. Comments must be limited to 1,000 words (about five pages) and should contain no more than nine references. As in all manuscripts, authors should include page numbers and references for quotes. APA can now place supplementary materials online, which will be available via the journal's Web page as noted above. To submit such materials, please see **www.apa.org/journals/supplementalmaterial.html** for details.

Publication Policy. APA policy prohibits an author from submitting the same manuscript for concurrent consideration by two or more publications. APA policy prohibits as well publication of any manuscript that has already been published in whole or substantial part elsewhere. Authors have an obligation to consult journal editors if there is any question concerning prior publication of part or all of their submitted manuscripts. Authors are required to obtain and provide to APA prior to production all necessary permissions to reproduce in print and electronic form any copyrighted work, including, for example, test materials (or portions thereof) and photographs of people. Also, authors of research reports submitted to APA journals are expected to have their data available throughout the editorial review process and for at least five years after the date of publication. Of course, APA expects authors submitting to this journal to adhere to the APA ethical standards regarding previous publication of data (Standard 8.13) and making research data available (Standard 8.14). Authors of research reports will be required to state in writing that they have complied with APA ethical standards in the treatment of their sample, human or animal, or to describe the details of treatment. A copy of the APA Ethical Principles may be obtained at www.apa.org/ethics/ or by writing the APA Ethics Office, 750 First Street, NE, Washington, DC 20002-4242. APA requires authors to reveal any possible conflict of interest in the conduct and reporting of research (e.g., financial interests in a test or procedure, funding by pharmaceutical companies for drug research).

Review Policy. The first step in the *AP* editorial review process is performed by the *AP* Editor-in-Chief/APA, CEO. Approximately 70% of author-submitted manuscripts are returned without review within 30 days for a host of reasons: Empirical manuscripts are more appropriate for one of the APA primary journals; topic of the manuscript or style of the writing is too specialized for the broad *AP* readership; the same topic was recently covered in the journal; inappropriate content or style; or other, more typical reasons such as the paper does not offer a major contribution to the field or is simply not written well enough. As a matter of policy, the identities of authors and reviewers are masked. Manuscripts that are peer reviewed are circulated without their title pages to mask the identity of the authors. Each copy of a manuscript should include a separate title page with authors' names and affiliations, and these should not appear anywhere else on the manuscript. Footnotes that identify the authors should be typed on a separate page. Authors should make every effort to see that the manuscript itself contains no clue to their identity.

Manuscript Submission. Submit manuscripts electronically via the Manuscript Submission Portal at **www.apa.org/journals/amp**. In addition to addresses and phone numbers, authors should supply electronic mail addresses and fax numbers, if available. Authors should keep a copy of the manuscript to guard against loss. General correspondence may be directed to Norman B. Anderson, Editor-in-Chief, American Psychologist, 750 First Street, NE, Washington, DC 20002-4242. **E-Mail Address**. To contact the editorial office of the *American Psychologist* via electronic mail (Internet), contact **APeditor@apa.org**.

American Scholar

SUBMISSION PROCESS:

Postal Submission Only

CONTACT INFORMATION:	REVIEW PROCESS:
Robert Wilson, Editor	**Type of Review:** Editorial Review
The Phi Beta Kappa Society	
1606 New Hampshire Avenue, NW	**No. External Reviewers:**
Washington, DC 20009 USA	**No. InHouse Reviewers:** 2
	Acceptance Rate: 0-5%
Phone:	**Time to Review:** 2-4 Months
202-265-3808	**Reviewer's Comments:** No
Email:	**Invited Articles:** 50% +
scholar@pbk.org	
Website:	**Fees to Publish:** $0.00 US$
www.pbk.org/pubs/amscholar.htm	**Fees to Review:** $0.00 US$

PUBLICATION GUIDELINES:	CIRCULATION DATA:
Manuscript Style:	**Reader:**
Chicago Manual of Style	, General, college educated
Manuscript Length:	**Frequency of Issue:**
	Quarterly
Copies Required:	**Sponsor/Publisher:**
One	Phi Beta Kappa Society

MANUSCRIPT TOPICS:
Art / Music; English Literature; General Issues in Education; Languages & Linguistics; Science Math & Environment; Secondary / Adolescent Studies; Social Studies / Social Science

MANUSCRIPT GUIDELINES/COMMENTS:

Articles. *The Scholar* is a quarterly journal published by Phi Beta Kappa for general circulation. Our intent is to have articles by scholars and experts but written in nontechnical language for an intelligent audience. We prefer articles between 3,500 and 4,000 words, and we pay up to $500. Manuscripts may be submitted by e-mail attachment or by mail (for return of hard copy, send SASE).

Poetry. We do not consider poetry.

Sample Copies. We do not have arrangements for sending sample copies of the *Scholar* to prospective contributors. It would be possible, of course, for you to purchase the latest issue for the regular price of $7.95. If you do not care to purchase a copy, your library would probably have copies you could see.

American School Board Journal

<table>
<tr><td colspan="2" align="center">**SUBMISSION PROCESS:**

Postal Submission Only</td></tr>
<tr>
<td>

CONTACT INFORMATION:

Glenn Cook, Editor-in-Chief
National School Boards Association
1680 Duke Street
Alexandria, VA 22314 USA

Phone:
   703-838-6739

Email:
   editorial@asbj.com

Website:
   www.asbj.com

</td>
<td>

REVIEW PROCESS:

Type of Review:	Editorial Review
No. External Reviewers:	0
No. InHouse Reviewers:	3
Acceptance Rate:	11-20%
Time to Review:	1 - 2 Months
Reviewer's Comments:	No
Invited Articles:	11-20%
Fees to Publish:	$0.00 US$
Fees to Review:	$0.00 US$

</td>
</tr>
<tr>
<td>

PUBLICATION GUIDELINES:

Manuscript Style:
   See Manuscript Guidelines

Manuscript Length:
   10-20

Copies Required:
   Two

</td>
<td>

CIRCULATION DATA:

Reader:
   Administrators, School Board Members

Frequency of Issue:
   Monthly

Sponsor/Publisher:
   National School Boards Association

</td>
</tr>
</table>

MANUSCRIPT TOPICS:
Education Management / Administration; Education Trends

MANUSCRIPT GUIDELINES/COMMENTS:

About
Welcome to *American School Board Journal*, an award-winning, editorially independent education magazine published monthly by the National School Boards Association. Founded in 1891, *American School Board Journal* chronicles change, interprets issues, and offers readers -- some 40,000 school board members and school administrators -- practical advice on a broad range of topics pertinent to school governance and management, policy making, student achievement, and the art of school leadership. In addition, regular departments cover education news, school law, research, and new books.

The mission of *American School Board Journal* is to meet the informational needs of school board members, professional educators, and the educational policy community by chronicling change, interpreting issues, and providing practical advice on a broad range of topics pertinent to school governance and management, policy making, student achievement, and the art of school leadership. An editorially independent publication of the National School Boards Association, *American School Board Journal* serves as a free marketplace of ideas and an open forum of opinions on the issues and developments affecting education.

Writer's Guidelines

As the nation's oldest education publication, founded in 1891, *American School Board Journal* has a reputation for independence, professionalism, and accuracy. Although *ASBJ* is published by the National School Boards Association, it is editorially independent and does not reflect the positions of the association.

These writer's guidelines are designed to lead you through the process we use to add outside writers to our mix of staff-written news and features.

We are not 'scholarly.' Although we are *American School Board Journal*, we are not a peer-reviewed journal. And, as a news and feature magazine, we generally do not publish footnotes and references.

What do we want? We strive to give the best, most comprehensive accounts of emerging education trends and solutions available. We are looking for good writing and good ideas, intelligently presented, aimed at our audience of school board members, superintendents, and other administrators. We don't publish theme issues; instead, we're always looking for a mix of practical, thought-provoking, and timely articles. We cover just about every educational topic, with special emphasis on district-level leadership.

What we *don't* want. Few teachers read our magazine, so articles aimed specifically at classroom educators aren't right for us. And we don't publish articles that push a particular product or service.

Getting Started

We feature two kinds of writers in *ASBJ*. One is the professional writer or journalist who researches and writes articles that are objective and present different viewpoints. The other kind of writer is the school board member, administrator, teacher, or professor who writes about what's going on in a local school, district, or community.

If you're a professional writer or journalist, query us with story ideas. Include clips that show you can handle education subjects and that you can write magazine-length articles. Your best chance of getting in the magazine is through our on-assignment stories, so if you have a controversy or interesting education story brewing in your backyard, let us know. Payment varies with the length and nature of the article. Also, we sometimes make assignments to journalists, so let us know you're out there.

If you're a school board member, administrator, teacher, professor, or anyone else who doesn't write for a living, send us your completed manuscripts. What we want from you is your experience and expertise. Did your board save your taxpayers $1 million this year? Write about it. Did your district raise achievement scores 10 points? Write about it. Did your university work with a local district to offer standards-based professional development? Write about it.

Before submitting a manuscript, LOOK AT OUR MAGAZINE. Check to see what subjects we've covered. Read the articles for subject matter, style, tone, and length. We can provide you with sample copies, or you can check out selected articles on the web site.

Our readers are school board members and administrators. Focus your article on how your subject might interest or affect them. For example, if you're a professor writing about a professional development program at your university, include information about how much the program will cost a district or school or how it can be tailored to fit local or state standards.

Forget the jargon. Educators probably will know what you're talking about, but not all of our readers have education backgrounds. Avoid passive voice when you can. **Not good**: "A decision was made to effect paradigm shifts in educational teaming, in order to promote the impacting of educational outcomes." **Better**: "We formed teams to help students achieve."

Be specific. Provide facts, figures, and examples. **Not good**: "Few people in our community have children in school, and few citizens vote in bond elections." **Better**: "Only 20 percent of the people in our community have children in school, and well under half of our citizens voted in each of the last two bond elections."

Write from personal experience. Use the pronouns "I" or "we." Write as though you're having a conversation with a friend. When you make a point, give specifics. **Not good**: "The board made suggestions on how to change the program." **Better**: "The board suggested we lengthen the school day by seven minutes and give each ninth-grade teacher a laptop computer." If you don't know details, talk to people who do and include what they say in your article.

A lead is not a thesis statement. Instead of thinking back to your papers in English 101, pattern your manuscript after an interesting newspaper article or magazine story. Begin your article with an anecdote or a statement that focuses on your subject. **Not good**: "I'm writing this article to explain how education can be improved." **Better**: "Our principal issued a challenge to her teachers: Bring more parents into their classrooms."

A magazine article is not a graduate school paper. Leave out the "review of the literature" and the footnotes. If the topic warrants, include a short list of suggested readings. If you want to quote another author, include the citation in the text. **Example**: As John Smith pointed out in his 1998 book Raising Student Achievement, ...

Don't worry. If your writing skills are rusty, but you have a great story to tell, we'll work with you.

Expect to be edited. If you believe every word in your manuscript is a jewel, don't send it to us. We edit everyone, in varying degrees, for length, style, clarity, even content.

After You Write
When preparing your manuscript, whether by typewriter or word processor:
- Double-space on white paper. Put your name on each page and number the pages.
- Include brief biographical information, including a daytime telephone number, a fax number, and your e-mail address.

Your manuscript should be approximately five to 10 double-spaced pages, or 1,250 to 2,500 words.

If you want to submit your manuscript on a computer disk, please send it to us using Word 97. We cannot return disks. You also may send your manuscript as an e-mail attachment to articles (**articles@asbj.com**). Either way, please keep the formatting of the document simple.

Do not send your manuscript to multiple magazines at the same time. We do not accept simultaneous submissions. Also, we accept articles only when all copyrights -- including electronic ones -- are offered to our magazine.

We cannot return manuscripts submitted to us for review.

Acceptance and Publication
We will acknowledge your manuscript when we receive it. We make decisions to accept or reject articles as quickly as possible. The review process usually takes between six to eight weeks, but sometimes longer when we receive large volumes of manuscripts. As a monthly magazine, we plan months in advance for each issue, so expect several months between acceptance and publication. Once your article has been accepted, our editors will be in touch with you. We'll send you a copy of the edited manuscript before it goes to press, and we'll send you copies of the magazine in which it appears. Send your manuscripts to: American School Board Journal, 1680 Duke St., Alexandria, VA 22314; Phone: (703) 838-6739; Fax: (703) 549-6719; E-mail: **editorial@asbj.com**; Editor-in-Chief, Glenn Cook

American Sociological Review

SUBMISSION PROCESS:
Postal Submission Only

CONTACT INFORMATION:	REVIEW PROCESS:	
Vincent J. Roscigno & Randy Hodson, Eds. American Sociological Review The Ohio State University Department of Sociology 300 Bricker Hall 190 North Oval Mall Columbus, OH 43210-1321 USA	**Type of Review:**	Blind Review
	No. External Reviewers:	2-3+
	No. InHouse Reviewers:	0-1
	Acceptance Rate:	6-10%
	Time to Review:	2 - 3 Months
	Reviewer's Comments:	Yes
	Invited Articles:	0-5%
Phone: 614-292-9972	**Fees to Publish:**	$0.00 US$
	Fees to Review:	$25.00 US$
Email: asr@osu.edu		
Website: www.asanet.org/journals/asr/		

PUBLICATION GUIDELINES:	CIRCULATION DATA:
Manuscript Style: See Manuscript Guidelines	**Reader:** Academics
Manuscript Length: 11-30+	**Frequency of Issue:** Bi-Monthly
Copies Required: Four	**Sponsor/Publisher:** American Sociological Association

MANUSCRIPT TOPICS:
All Areas of Sociology/Not Social Studies; Social Studies / Social Science

MANUSCRIPT GUIDELINES/COMMENTS:

Scope and Mission
The *American Sociological Review* publishes original (not previously published) works of interest to the discipline in general, new theoretical developments, results of qualitative or quantitative research that advance our understanding of fundamental social processes, and important methodological innovations. All areas of sociology are welcome. Emphasis is on exceptional quality and general interest.

Ethics. Submission of a manuscript to another professional journal while it is under review by the *ASR* is regarded by the ASA as unethical. Significant findings or contributions that have already appeared (or will appear) elsewhere must be clearly identified. All persons who publish in ASA journals are required to abide by ASA guidelines and ethics codes regarding plagiarism and other ethical issues. This requirement includes adhering to ASA's stated policy on data-sharing: "Sociologists make their data available after completion of the project or its major publications, except where proprietary agreements with employers, contractors, or clients preclude such accessibility or when it is impossible to share data and protect the confidentiality of the data or the anonymity of research participants (e.g., raw field notes or detailed information from ethnographic interviews)" (ASA *Code of Ethics*, 1997).

Manuscript format. Manuscripts should meet the format guidelines specified in the *Notice to Contributors* published in the February and August issues of each volume. The electronic files should be composed in MS Word, WordPerfect, and/or Excel. All text must be printed *double-spaced* on 8-1/2 by 11 inch white paper. Use Times New Roman, 12-point size font. Margins must be at least 1 inch on all four sides. On the title page, note the manuscript's total word count (include all text, references, and footnotes; do not include word counts for tables or figures). You may cite your own work, but do not use wording that identifies you as the author.

Submission requirements. Submit *four (4) print copies* of your manuscript and an *abstract* of 150 to 200 words. Include all *electronic files* on floppy disk or CD. Enclose a *$25.00 manuscript processing fee* in the form of a check or money order payable to the American Sociological Association. Provide *e-mail address* and *ASR* will acknowledge the receipt of your manuscript. In your *cover letter*, you may recommend specific reviewers (or identify individuals *ASR* should not use). Do not recommend colleagues, collaborators, or friends. *ASR* may choose to disregard your recommendation. Manuscripts are not returned after review.

Address for submission. *American Sociological Review*, The Ohio State University, Department of Sociology, 300 Bricker Hall, 190 North Oval Mall, Columbus, OH 43210-1321

Editorial decisions. Median time between submission and decision is approximately twelve weeks. Please see the *ASR* journal web site for more information (**http://www.asanet.org/journals/asr/**).

Advertisements. Submit to Publications Department, American Sociological Association, 1307 New York Avenue NW, Suite 700, Washington, DC 20005-4701; (202) 383-9005 ext. 303; e-mail publications@asanet.org.

Subscription rates. ASA members, $40; ASA student member, $25; nonmembers, $90; institutions, $196. *Add $20 for postage outside the U.S./Canada*. To subscribe to *ASR* or to request single issues, contact the ASA Subscriptions Department (subscriptions@asanet.org).

Address change. Subscribers must notify the ASA Executive Office (customer@asanet.org) six weeks in advance of an address change. Include both old and new addresses. Claims for undelivered copies must be made within the month following the regular month of publication. When the reserve stock permits, ASA will replace copies of *ASR* that are lost because of an address change.

Copyright. Copyright © 2005, American Sociological Association. Copying beyond fair use: Copies of articles in this journal may be made for teaching and research purposes free of charge and without securing permission, as permitted by Sections 107 and 108 of the United States Copyright Law. For all other purposes, permission must be obtained from the ASA Executive Office. (Articles in the American Sociological Review are indexed in *the Abstracts for Social Workers, Ayer's Guide, Current Index to Journals in Education, International Political Science Abstracts, Psychological Abstracts, Social Sciences Index, Sociological Abstracts, SRM Database of Social Research Methodology, United States Political Science Documents,* and *University Microfilms.*)

The American Sociological Association acknowledges with appreciation the facilities and assistance provided by the University of Pennsylvania.

MANUSCRIPT SUBMISSION

Package your manuscript securely and include the following:

- **Cover Letter**. Please provide complete contact information for the corresponding author (name, address, phone/fax, e-mail), the complete manuscript title, total word count (include all text, footnotes, and references; do not include word counts for tables or figures), and any other important and relevant information.
- **Biography Page**. On a separate page, provide short biography (less than 100 words) for each author. See previous issues for examples.
- **One (1) original manuscript**. Manuscript must be complete and typed double-spaced with 1 inch margins (see below).
- **Three (3) blinded copies**. Blinded copies start with the Abstract page headed by the full article title; but **do not include** the title page or the biography page (or any self identifying information—see below). Copies may be printed or photocopied.
- **Disk**. All manuscript materials must be included as electronic files on disk or CD. Standard word processing files are preferred (MS Word, etc.) for text and tables.
- **$25.00 manuscript processing fee**. Please make check payable to the American Sociological Association. All manuscripts (new and revised) require a fee. No fee is required for *Comments* and *Replies* or for submissions by ASA student members.

Send your manuscript to the *ASR* editorial office at the following address:

American Sociological Review, The Ohio State University, Department of Sociology, 300 Bricker Hall, 190 North Oval Mall, Columbus, OH 43210-1321. The *ASR* editorial office will acknowledge the receipt of your manuscript via e-mail.

NOTE. Additional details on preparing and submitting manuscripts to *ASR* are published in the *ASA Style Guide* (2nd ed., 1997) available from the American Sociological Association.

Preparation

All pages must be typed, double-spaced (including notes and references), on 8-1/2 by 11 inch white paper. Margins must be at least 1 inch (i.e., line length must not exceed 6-1/2 inches). Please use 12-point Times New Roman font.

ASR **Articles** may be any length, from short reports (e.g., 10 to 20 pages) to full-length articles (e.g., 30 to 40 pages) as well as qualitative and historical papers, which may need more space (e.g., 50 to 60 pages). *ASR Comments/Replies* should not exceed 10 pages. Send *Comments* and *Replies* directly to the *ASR* office—*ASR* does not require that *Comments* first be sent to article authors.

Sections in a manuscript may include the following: (1) Title page, (2) Biography Page, (3) Abstract, (4) Text, (5) Notes, (6) References, (7) Tables, (8) Figures, and (9) Appendices.

1. **Title page**. Please include the following:
- Full article title
- Each author's complete name and institutional affiliation(s)
- Total word count
- Running head (short title, less than 55 characters w/spaces)
- Acknowledgments and credits
- Grant numbers and/or funding information
- Corresponding author (name, address, phone/fax, e-mail)

2. **Biography page**. On a separate page, provide short biography (less than 100 words) for each author. See previous issues for examples.

3. **Abstract page**. On a separate page headed by the full article title, print the abstract (150 to 200 words). *Omit author(s)'s name(s).*

4. Text. Begin article text on a new page headed by the full article title. Omit author(s)'s names. *ASR* uses anonymous peer review for manuscript evaluation. Delete or rewrite any text that identifies you as the author: when citing your own work, please write "Smith (1992) concluded . . .," but do not write "I concluded (Smith 1992). . . ."

a. *Headings* and *subheadings*. Generally, three heading levels are sufficient to organize text. See recent issues for examples.

b. *Citations* in the text should provide the last name of the author(s) and year of publication. Include page numbers for direct quotes or specific passages. Cite only those works needed to provide evidence for your assertions and to refer to important sources on the topic. In the following examples of text citations, ellipses (. . .) indicate manuscript text:

- When author's name is in the text, follow it with the year in parentheses— . . . Duncan (1959).
- When author's name is not in the text, enclose the last name and year in parentheses— . . . (Gouldner 1963).
- Pages cited follow the year of publication after a colon— . . . (Ramirez and Weiss 1979:239–40).
- Provide last uthors, list all three last names in the first citation in the text— . . . (Carr, Smith, and names for joint authors— . . . (Martin and Bailey 1988).
- For three a Jones 1962). For all subsequent citations use "et al."— . . . (Carr et al. 1962). For works with four or more authors, use "et al." throughout.
- For institutional authorship, supply minimal identification from the complete citation— . . . (U.S. Bureau of the Census 1963:117).
- List a series of citations in alphabetical order or date order separated by semicolons— . . . (Burgess 1968; Marwell et al. 1971).
- Use "forthcoming" to cite sources scheduled for publication. For dissertations and unpublished papers, cite the date. If no date, use "n.d." in place of the date— . . . Smith (forthcoming) and Oropesa (n.d.).
- For machine-readable data files, cite authorship and date— . . . (Institute for Survey Research 1976).

c. *Notes* should be numbered in the text consecutively using superscript Arabic numerals. When referring to a note later in the text, use a parenthetical note— . . . (see note 3).

d. *Equations* in the text should be typed or printed. Use consecutive Arabic numerals in parentheses at the right margin to identify important equations. Align all expressions and clearly mark compound subscripts and superscripts. Clarify all unusual characters or symbols with notes circled in the margin.

5. Notes (footnotes or e t pages or in a separate "Endnotes" section. Begin each note with the superscript numeral to ndnotes) should be typed or printed, double-spaced, either as footnotes at the bottom of the tex which it is keyed in the text (e.g., "1 After 1981, there were . . ."). Notes can (a) explain or amplify text, (b) cite materials of limited availability, or (c) append information presented in a table or figure. *Avoid long notes*: consider (a) stating in the text that information is available from the author, (b) depositing the information in a national retrieval center and inserting a short footnote or a citation in the text, or (c) adding an appendix.

6. References are presented in a separate section headed "References." All references cited in the text must be listed in the reference section, and vice versa. Publication information for each must be complete and correct. List the references in alphabetical order by authors' last names; include first names and middle initials for all authors when available. List two or more entries by the same as been accepted for publication, use "Forthcoming" in place of the date and give the journal author(s) in order of the year of publication. When the cited material is not yet published but h name or publishing house. For dissertations and unpublished papers, cite the date and place the paper was presented and/or where it is available. If no date is available, use "N.d." in place of the date. If two or more cited works are by the same author(s) within the same year, list them in alphabetical order by title and distinguish them by adding the letters a, b, c, etc., to the year (or to "Forthcoming"). For works with more than one author, only the name of the first author is inverted (e.g., "Jones, Arthur B., Colin D. Smith, and James Petersen"). List all authors; using "et al." in the reference list is not acceptable. Refer to the *ASA Style Guide* (2d ed., 1997) for additional examples:

Books
Bernard, Claude. [1865] 1957. *An Introduction to the Study of Experimental Medicine*. Translated by H. C. Greene. New York: Dover.

Periodicals
Goodman, Leo A. Are Unobservable. Part I—A Modified Latent Structure Approach." *American Journal* 1947a. "The Analysis of Systems of Qualitative Variables When Some of the Variables *of Sociology* 79:1179–1259.

Collections
Clausen, John A. 1972. "The Life Course of Individuals." Pp. 457–514 in *Aging and Society*, vol. 3, *A Sociology of Age Stratification*, edited by M.W. Riley, M. Johnson, and A. Foner. New York: Russell Sage.

7. **Tables** should be numbered consecutively in the order in which they appear in the text and must include table titles. Tables will appear in the published article in the order in which they are numbered initially. Each table must include a descriptive title and headings for all columns and rows. Gather general notes to tables as "*Note:*" or "*Notes:*"; use a, b, c, etc., for table footnotes. Use asterisks *, **, and/or *** to indicate significance at the $p < .05$, $p < .01$, and $p < .001$ levels, respectively, and *always* specify one-tailed or two-tailed tests.

8. **Figures** should be numbered consecutively in the order in which they appear in the text and must include figure captions. Figures will appear in the published article in the order in which they are numbered initially. All artwork must be submitted as computer files on disk. All figures must be black and white, no color. Contact the *ASR* office for further details regarding preferred file formats for computer-generated figures.

IMPORTANT: All figures (including all type) must be legible when resized to fit one or two column widths, 2-9/16 and 5-5/16 inches wide, respectively. **PERMISSION**: *The author(s) are responsible for securing permission to reproduce all copyrighted figures or any other materials before they are published by* ASR. *A copy of the written permission must be included with the manuscript submission.*

9. **Appendices** should be lettered to distinguish them from numbered tables and figures. Include a descriptive title for each appendix (e.g., "Appendix A. Variable Names and Definitions").

Applied Measurement in Education

SUBMISSION PROCESS:
Postal Submission Only

CONTACT INFORMATION:	REVIEW PROCESS:	
Kurt F. Geisinger, Editor	**Type of Review:**	Blind Review
University of Nebraska, Lincoln		
Buros Center for Testing	**No. External Reviewers:**	3
21 Teachers College Hall	**No. InHouse Reviewers:**	1
Lincoln, NE 68588-0352 USA		
	Acceptance Rate:	21-30%
	Time to Review:	2 - 3 Months
Phone:	**Reviewer's Comments:**	Yes
402-472-6203	**Invited Articles:**	6-10%
Email:		
kgeisinger2@unl.edu	**Fees to Publish:**	$0.00 US$
	Fees to Review:	$0.00 US$
Website:		

PUBLICATION GUIDELINES:	CIRCULATION DATA:
Manuscript Style:	**Reader:**
American Psychological Association	Academics, Practitioners
Manuscript Length:	**Frequency of Issue:**
20-40 pages	Quarterly
Copies Required:	**Sponsor/Publisher:**
Four	Lawrence Erlbaum Associates, Inc.

MANUSCRIPT TOPICS:
Educational Psychology; Tests, Measurement & Evaluation

MANUSCRIPT GUIDELINES/COMMENTS:

Applied Measurement In Education, sponsored by the Buros Center for Testing, is a scholarly journal dedicated to the application of educational and psychological measurement research to the educational process. Its intended audience consists of researchers and practitioners who are interested in research likely to have an impact on educational measurement practice. A major aim of the journal is to provide both a greater understanding of educational measurement issues and an improved use of measurement techniques in education.

Types of manuscripts that will be considered for publication in *Applied Measurement In Education* include (a) reports of original applied research focusing on measurement issues in educational contexts, (b) presentations of innovative strategies for solving existing educational measurement problems, and (c) integrative reviews of research pertaining to contemporary measurement issues. An additional section of the journal will be dedicated to providing comparative reviews of tests and methods currently used in addressing specific educational measurement needs. The editors also welcome proposals for special issues dealing with a focused treatment of a particular area of applied educational measurement. Manuscripts dealing exclusively with the validation of specific measures are not considered.

Manuscript Submission

Submit four manuscript copies to Applied Measurement In Education, 21 Teachers College Hall, University of Nebraska-Lincoln, Lincoln, NE 68588-0352. Only original manuscripts submitted to *Applied Measurement In Education* will be considered for publication. The cover letter should include a statement that the manuscript is not being simultaneously submitted elsewhere. Manuscripts will not be returned.

Format and Organization

Manuscripts should be prepared according to the guidelines in the *Publication Manual of the American Psychological Association* (5th ed.). Double-space all text. On the first page, indicate the title of the manuscript, the names and affiliations of authors, and the name and address of the person to whom reprint requests are to be sent; suggest a shortened version of the title of the manuscript for use as a running head (40 characters or fewer, including spaces). On the second page, provide a 100 to 175-word abstract. On the third page (the first text page), type the title of the manuscript.

Permissions

Authors are responsible for all statements made in their work and for obtaining permission from copyright owners to use a lengthy quotation (100 words or more) or to reprint or adapt a table or figure published elsewhere. Authors should write to both author(s) and publisher of such material to request nonexclusive world rights in all languages for use in the article and in future editions of it.

Content

Do not use new technical words, psychological jargon or slang, or terminology not consistent with the style guidelines in the *Publication Manual of the APA*. Define any abbreviations or acronyms the first time they are used.

Figures and Tables

All figures and tables should be numbered separately using Arabic numerals and should be grouped at the end of the manuscript. Clearly visible notes within the text should indicate approximate placement of figures and tables. Figures must be professionally prepared and must be camera-ready. Type figure captions on a separate sheet. Write the article title and figure number lightly in pencil on the back of each piece of artwork. Refer to the *Publication Manual of the APA* for format of tables. Double-space.

References

Double-space. Compile references alphabetically (see the *Publication Manual of the APA* for multiple-author citations and references). Spell out names of journals. Provide page numbers of chapters in edited books. Text citations must correspond accurately to the references in the reference list.

Page Proofs

Authors are sent page proofs of their manuscripts and are asked to proofread them for printers errors and other defects. Correction of typographical errors will be made without charge; other alterations will be charged to the author.

Reprints

Authors may order article reprints of their articles when they receive page proofs. Printing considerations do not permit the ordering of reprints after authors have returned proofs.

Dear Journal Contributor

Now that your manuscript has been accepted for publication, we at Lawrence Erlbaum Associates, Inc. (LEA) would like to open the communication lines-offer our preproduction assistance, inform you of your responsibilities, and introduce you to our journal production process. We believe this early dialogue will get our collaboration off on the right foot.

This letter is divided into five sections: Keeping in Touch; Understanding the Publication Process; Preparing a Manuscript; Preparing the Word-Processed, Electronic File and Disk; and Taking Action.

Keeping in Touch

The Editor of the journal is your primary source of information and advice. However, if you have a question the Editor is unable to answer, feel free to contact the LEA Production Editor or Electronic Publishing Manager. (The Editor can put you in touch with these individuals.) The journal is on a tight production schedule, so . . .

1. If you move or are away for an extended period during the time your manuscript is in production, please let the Editor and Production Editor know where you can be reached (address and phone number). You can imagine the delays that occur when the Production Editor (a) mails typeset page proofs to an old address or (b) phones a contributor with an important question, only to learn that the contributor is on overseas sabbatical and did not leave a forwarding number.
2. Call the Production Editor if you are unable to return page proofs within two days of receipt.

Understanding the Publication Process

1. You return a finalized, complete, correctly formatted manuscript – printout and disk – to the Editor.
2. The Editor compiles an issue of manuscripts and disks from several contributors and forwards the issue to the Production Editor.
3. The Production Editor reviews the manuscripts and disks. If your manuscript is not prepared correctly – see Preparing a Manuscript – the Production Editor returns it to the Editor so you can revise it. (Production on the issue is suspended until all manuscripts are ready.)
4. When all manuscripts are ready, the Production Editor copyedits and typesets the issue and sends each contributor (a) two sets of page proofs of the respective article, (b) a list of queries concerning the article, and (c) a reprint request form.
5. You proofread your typeset pages, indicate corrections on both sets, keep one set for your records, and return to the Production Editor (a) the other set, (b) answers to the queries and (c) the reprint request form (with payment if ordering reprints).
6. The Production Editor finalizes the issue and sends it to the printer.

Preparing the Manuscript

Take a few moments now to make certain that your manuscript is complete and that it complies with the editorial guidelines appearing in the *Publication Manual of the American Psychological Association* (5th ed.). (The manual is available from the APA Order Department, P.O. Box 92984, Washington, DC 20090-2984; phone: 800-374-2721; fax: 202-336-5502; e-mail: order@apa.org; online: www.apa.org/books/) You may find it helpful to consult "Appendix A: Checklist for Manuscript Submission" and "Appendix B: Checklist for Transmitting Accepted Manuscripts for Electronic Production" appearing on pages 379 through 386 of the *APA Manual*, the contributor information appearing in the journal, and/or the following summary of requirements for acceptable manuscripts. If you have any questions whatsoever, please ask for clarification.

Typing. Use 8½ - x 11-in. nonsmear paper. Set all margins at 1 in. Type all components double-spaced, including title page, abstract, text, acknowledgments, references, appendices, tables, figure captions, and footnotes. Indent all paragraphs and make sure the entire manuscript is neat and readable. Use superscript numbers to cite footnotes; type all footnotes on a separate page (not at the bottom of the pages on which they are cited). Indicate in the manuscript approximately where each figure or table is to be positioned; type all figure captions on a separate page.

Abstract. If an abstract is required, consult the Editor or the journal for the limit on length. Provide key words or phrases if required.

References. Provide complete, APA-formatted references and text citations and make sure the two correspond exactly. Pages 207 through 281 of the *APA Manual* provide (a) detailed guidelines on preparing references and citations and (b) many excellent sample references and citations. When typing a reference for a chapter in an edited book, be sure to add the inclusive page numbers of the chapter.

Tests, Scales, Subscales, Factors, Variables, Effects. See *APA Manual* regarding capitalization. *Statistics.* See *APA Manual* regarding presentation. *Acronyms.* Define on first mention.

Figures. Submit (a) high-quality laser prints, professionally prepared black-and-white originals or camera-ready glossy reproductions and (b) photocopies of all figures. (c) as many computer files for these figures as you have (see Preparing the Word-Processed, Electronic File and Disk). Please note that figures appearing in the journal will look only as good as what you provide. Make sure lettering and details are crisp, clear, and large enough so that they will be legible upon reduction. (Figures are reduced in size in order to conserve space on the printed page.)

All hard copies for which we do not have computer files will be scanned electronically, so please avoid using gray shading or dot screens in graphs. Use solid black or white or diagonal lines to distinguish columns instead (for further examples and guidelines, see *APA Manual*, pp. 176-201).

Make sure each figure is identified. Assess whether textual information appearing on a piece of artwork might be best presented as part of the caption; alter artwork and caption accordingly.

Permissions. You are responsible for all statements made in your work and for obtaining permission from the copyright owner(s) to reprint or adapt a table or figure or to reprint quotes from one source totaling 500 words or more. Write to original author(s) and publisher to request nonexclusive world rights in all languages for use of the material in the article and in future print and nonprint editions. Please note that you must obtain permission for any lines of poetry or song lyrics you quote as well as for prose, and that you will be liable for any licensing fees required for such use. Provide copies of all permissions and credit lines obtained. Attached to this letter are (a) a sample permission request form you can copy/adapt and use in order to secure permissions and (b) sample credit lines from the *APA Manual.*

*Concordance of Elements. M*ake sure your manuscript is complete and internally consistent. Each reference must be cited in text at least once; each citation must have a corresponding reference. Likewise, each figure, table, and footnote must be cited; if a figure, table, or footnote is cited in text, the corresponding element must be included with the manuscript.

Preparing the Word-Processed, Electronic File and Disk
Now is the time to submit the word-processed, electronic file (as well as an ASCII version) and a disk for copyediting and typesetting. Working with an electronic manuscript allows us to capture your keystrokes-thereby maintaining the accuracy of your article and reducing the time between research and publication.

Shortening the production schedule involves combining the stages of author review of copyedited articles and subsequent review of typeset page proofs into a single review of proofs made from copyedited disk files via desktop publishing. With timely publication the concern of all involved, we assume you will (a) accept minor editorial changes that do not alter intended meanings and (b) alter page proofs only to correct errors, update publication information, and respond to editors, queries. As substantial alterations will not be made after manuscripts have been typeset, please take the time now to make sure that your manuscript and its file are complete and identical and that they represent your 'final say."

Our first choice for format is WordPerfect or Word on an IBM-formatted disk. Other formats are acceptable.

IBM-Compatible Users. Submit a PC disk containing two files: (a) the file produced with your word processor and (b) the same file saved as ASCII DOS text or MS-DOS text. If we are unable to read the native file produced by your word processor, we can try the ASCII or MS-DOS file.

Macintosh Users. Submit a high-density Mac disk containing two files: (a) the file produced with your word processor and (b) the same file saved as ASCII DOS text or MS-DOS text. If we are unable to read the native file produced by your word processor, we can try the ASCII or MS-DOS file.

Other Computer Users. Please try to convert and transfer your file to an IBM-compatible or Mac disk; then follow directions for IBM-compatible or Mac users. If unable to do so, please contact the Electronic Publishing Manager. However you submit your electronic manuscript, please (a) let us know computer type (IBM-compatible, Macintosh), word processor (including version number), and file name; and (b) make sure the content of the files exactly matches that of the printed, accepted, finalized manuscript. In addition, if your figures were prepared using a computer and you can obtain files from which the hard copies were printed, please include these on your disk (or on additional disks if they are too large). If you have any questions regarding disk preparation, please contact the LEA Electronic Journal Publishing Manager.

Taking Action
In a nutshell, now is the time for you to (a) make sure your manuscript is formatted correctly, (b) check on permissions, and (c) send the finalized manuscript--printout and disk--to the Editor. We hope this letter has been informative, and we look forward to working with you. If you think of any way we can improve the production process, by all means let us know. We're here to help: Journal Production Office, Lawrence Erlbaum Associates, Inc., 10 Industrial Avenue, Mahwah, New Jersey 07430-3362; Voice: (201) 236-9500; FAX: (201) 236-0072; Production Fax: (201) 236-6396

Sample Credit Lines from *APA Manual*
3.73 Tables from Another Source
Authors must obtain permission to reproduce or adapt all or part of a table (or figure) from a copyrighted source. It is not necessary to obtain permission from APA to reproduce one table (or figure) from an APA article provided you obtain the author's permission and give full credit to APA as copyright holder and to the author through a complete and accurate citation. When you wish to reproduce material from sources not copyrighted by APA, contact the copyright holders to determine their requirements for both print and electronic reuse. If you have any doubt about the policy of the copyright holder, you should request permission. Always enclose the letter of permission when transmitting the final version of the accepted manuscript for production.

Any reproduced table (or figure) must be accompanied by a note at the bottom of the reprinted table (or in the figure caption) giving credit to the original author and to the copyright holder. If the table (or figure) contains test items, see the cautionary note in section 3.93. Use the following form for tables or figures. (For copyright permission footnotes in text [see section 3.41 for permission to quote], use the following form, but substitute the indented superscript footnote number for the word Note.)

Material reprinted from a journal article
Note. From [or The data in column 1 are from] "Title of Article," by A. N. Author and C. O. Author, 2000, Title of Journal, 50, p. 22. Copyright 2000 by the Name of Copyright Holder. Reprinted [or Adapted] with permission.

Material reprinted from a book
Note. From [or The data in column 1 are from] Title of Book (p. 103), by A. N. Author and C. O. Author, 1999, Place of Publication: Publisher. Copyright 1999 by the Name of Copyright Holder. Reprinted [**or** Adapted] with permission.

Art Therapy: Journal of the American Art Therapy Association

SUBMISSION PROCESS: **Electronic Submission Only** **via EMail** **atj@mtmary.edu**	

CONTACT INFORMATION:	REVIEW PROCESS:
Lynn Kapitan, Editor Editorial Office Mount Mary College 2900 N. Menomonee R. Parkway Milwaukee, WI 53222 USA **Phone:** 414-256-1215 **Email:** atj@mtmary.edu kapitanl@mtmary.edu info@arttherapy.org **Website:** www.arttherapy.org	**Type of Review:** Blind Review **No. External Reviewers:** 2 **No. InHouse Reviewers:** 1 **Acceptance Rate:** 21-30% **Time to Review:** 2 - 3 Months **Reviewer's Comments:** Yes **Invited Articles:** 6-10% **Fees to Publish:** $0.00 US$ **Fees to Review:** $0.00 US$

PUBLICATION GUIDELINES:	CIRCULATION DATA:
Manuscript Style: American Psychological Association **Manuscript Length:** 21-25 **Copies Required:** Electronic Only	**Reader:** Academics, Art Therapists, Counselors **Frequency of Issue:** Quarterly **Sponsor/Publisher:** American Art Therapy Association

MANUSCRIPT TOPICS:

Art / Music; Counseling & Personnel Services; Educational Psychology; Secondary / Adolescent Studies; Special Education; Urban Education, Cultural / Non-Traditional

MANUSCRIPT GUIDELINES/COMMENTS:

The above mentioned topics as they relate to the therapeutic use of art.

All submissions will be acknowledged upon receipt by the AATA National Office. *Art Therapy: Journal of the American Art Therapy Association* uses a blind peer review procedure for articles, brief reports, and viewpoints. Final decisions regarding publication in these categories are made by the Editor. Decisions regarding submissions to other sections are made by the Editor, Associate Editor, and special section editors.

The following are guidelines for submissions. Submissions that do not conform to these guidelines will be returned to the author without review.

Submission Categories

1. **Articles**. Full-length articles may focus on the theory, practice, and research in art therapy or related areas. Articles must include an abstract of no more than 150 words summarizing the major points of the article. Submissions may not exceed 5,500 words including references.

2. **Brief Reports**. Short articles that focus on art therapy practice or the results of research are appropriate for this section. Research reports require a short introduction, methodology, results, and conclusions, and must include an abstract of no more than 150 words. Submissions may not exceed 3,500 words including references.

3. **Viewpoints**. Short articles with focus on personal experiences, opinions, or informed responses that may implications for the field.. No abstract is required. Submissions may not exceed 2,500 words including references.

4. **Cover Art**. Artwork by AATA members in vertical format. High resolution copy on CD plus one glossy print, one photocopy, and a brief description of the artwork are required for consideration; send by post to the Editorial Office.

5. **Book Reviews**. Reviews of books of interest to art therapists may be submitted; may not exceed 1,500 words including references. Books which authors wish to have considered for review may be sent directly to the Editorial Office.

6. **Video Reviews**. Reviews of media may be submitted; may not exceed 1,500 words including references. Media which producers wish to have considered for review may be sent by post to the Editorial Office.

7. **Commentaries**. Brief comments on submissions published in *Art Therapy*, issues critical to the profession and practice of art therapy, or Letters to the Editor may be submitted. Submission must conform to APA style and may not exceed 500 words.

Other Requirements

1 Only original submissions that are not under consideration by another periodical or publisher are acceptable.

2. Submissions must be prepared in APA style; refer to the *Publication Manual of the American Psychological Association* (Fifth Edition) for information on how to romat and prepare a manuscript for submission.

3. Include a cover sheet with the following: full name and degree(s) of the author, affiliations, email address and return mainling address to whom correspondence can be sent, additional information to include in an Editor's note (e.g. how to contact the author for more informaiton, whether material was presented at a conference, acknowledgements, etc.).

4. Author's name, position, and places of employment should not appear in the body of the text to facilitate the blind review.

5. Use tables and figures (graphs, charts, diagrams, and illustrations/artwork) sparingly and type them on separate pages with figure number/caption; refer to the APA publication for style of tabular presentations. All tables and figures must be legible and able to withstand reduction. The total number of tables and figures must not exceed eight (8).

6. Lengthy quotations (300 words or more from one source) or reproduction of works of art (except client art addressed below) require written permission from the copyright holder. Adaptation of tables or figures from copyrighted sources also requires approval. It is the author's responsibility to secure such permissions and be provided to the Editor upon acceptance of the article for publication.

7. Client/patient confidentiality must be protected in all components of the submission and accompanying material. Proper releases for use of client art expressions and other client information must be obtained and kept on file by the author.

8. The author bears full responsibility for the accuracy of all references, quotations, and materials accompanying their submissions.

To Send Submission

1. Send submission as an electronic document via email attachment in either Microsoft Word of Rich Text Format (rtf) to: **atj@mtmary.edu** (subject line: Art Therapy submission). Neither AATA nor the Editorial Office can be responsible for submissions sent to any other address, or addressed properly but undeliverable.

2. Send illustrations/artwork with the submission as a jpeg file at 72 dpi (600 pixels). This size allows for ease of electronic transfer to reviewers. Do not embed images in the text. Note: If the submission is accepted for publication, authors will be asked to send to the Editorial Office a final copy of illustrations on CD at high quality resolution (300 dpi jpegs at actual reproduction size).

3. Direct correspondence and questions to: Lynn Kapitan, Ph.D., ATR-BC, Editor, Art Therapy Editorial Office, Mount Mary College, 2900 N. Menomonee River Parkway, Milwaukee, WI 53222. Email: **atj@mtmary.edu**; Phone: 414-256-1215; FAX: 414-256-1205.

Assessing Writing

<table>
<tr><td colspan="2" align="center">SUBMISSION PROCESS:

Electronic Submission Only
via EMail

lhamplyons@hkucc.hku.hk</td></tr>
<tr>
<td valign="top">

CONTACT INFORMATION:

Liz Hamp-Lyons, Editor
University of Hong Kong
Faculty of Education
Pokfulam, Hong Kong

Phone:

Email:
lhamplyons@hkucc.hku.hk
Website:
www.elsevier.com/locate/asw

</td>
<td valign="top">

REVIEW PROCESS:

Type of Review:
No. External Reviewers:
No. InHouse Reviewers:

Acceptance Rate:
Time to Review:
Reviewer's Comments:
Invited Articles:

Fees to Publish:	$0.00 US$
Fees to Review:	$0.00 US$

</td>
</tr>
<tr>
<td valign="top">

PUBLICATION GUIDELINES:

Manuscript Style:
American Psychological Association

Manuscript Length:
21-25

Copies Required:
Electronic Only

</td>
<td valign="top">

CIRCULATION DATA:

Reader:
Administrators, Educators, Researchers,
Writing Assessment Professionals

Frequency of Issue:
3 Times/Year

Sponsor/Publisher:
British Assn. of Lecturers in English for
Academic Purposes / Elsevier Inc.

</td>
</tr>
</table>

MANUSCRIPT TOPICS:
Languages & Linguistics; Writing

MANUSCRIPT GUIDELINES/COMMENTS:

Submission requirements
Submission of a paper requires the assurance that the manuscript is an original work which has not been published previously and is not currently being considered for publication elsewhere. Article submissions should not normally exceed 20 pages excluding tables. All articles should have abstracts which summarize the scope and Purpose of the article and, if applicable, the results of the study. The abstracts should be between 100 and 200 words in length. Articles must be written in English. Manuscript pages should be consecutively numbered in the upper right hand corner. All artwork must be suitable for publication and need no further work. Submit your manuscript by email to the editor: Professor Liz Hamp-Lyons: **lhamplyons@hkucc.hku.hk**.

In a separate electronic file, please supply the senior author's telephone number, fax number and e-mail address along with a brief biographical sketch of about fifty words. The manuscript pages themselves must not indicate authorship. Receipt of manuscripts will be acknowledged, but they cannot be returned; therefore, authors should retain a copy of the paper exactly as it was submitted.

Author's unable to submit by e-mail should send three hard copies of their manuscript and a separate sheet of contact details to either editor at their address listed on the masterhead.

Style
Manuscripts must be typed double-spaced with wide margins on only one side of A4 or letter-size paper, and should follow the style of the APA. Grammatical, lexical, and orthographic features may conform to either British or American norms. Citations may be given of lexical material from languages other than English; however, citations from languages not employing a Roman alphabet must be given in a Romanized transliteration or in a transcription which uses standard symbols available in the International Phonetic Alphabet.

References and footnotes
In the text, references are cited using author's last name, publication date (Wilkins, 1976). If quotations are cited, these should additionally have page numbers (Wilkins, 1976: 21-22). The reference list should be arranged in alphabetical order following the style sheet of the American Psychological Association and should appear on a separate page at the end of the article. The reference list should include only those items specifically cited in the body of the text. Generally speaking, comments and references should be incorporated into the text; but when necessary, footnotes should be typed at the bottom of the page on which the reference appears and should be set off from text with a horizontal line.

Keywords
Authors should provide up to six keywords, to appear just underneath the abstract. These keywords will be used to help provide efficient indexing,search and retrieval mechanisms as articles become available through electronic systems.

Tables and Illustrations
Prepare each table, figure, graph or illustration on its own page and number all such material clearly. Make sure that the text refers to the figures and tables in consecutive order. Tables should be numbered consecutively and titled, and should be referred to in the text and submitted on separate pages at the end of the manuscript. Please keep lines and frames to a minimum.

Submit colour illustrations as original photographs, high-quality computer prints or transparencies, close to the size expected in publication, or as 35 mm slides. Polaroid colour prints are not suitable. If, together with your accepted article, you submit usable colour figures then Elsevier will ensure, at no additional charge, that these figures will appear in colour on the web (e.g., ScienceDirect and other sites) regardless of whether or not these illustrations are reproduced in colour in the printed version. For further information on the preparation of electronic artwork, please see **http://authors.elsevier.com/artwork**

Electronic submission
Authors should submit an electronic copy of their paper with the final version of the manuscript. The electronic copy should match the hardcopy exactly. Always keep a backup copy of the electronic file for reference and safety. Full details of electronic submission and formats can be obtained from **http://authors.elsevier.com** and from Author Support at Elsevier.

Proofs
Proofs will be sent to the author (first named author if no corresponding author is identified of multi-authored papers) and should be returned within 48 hours of receipt. Corrections should be restricted to typesetting errors; any others may be charged to the author. Any queries should be answered in full. Please note that authors are urged to check their proofs carefully before return, since the inclusion of late corrections cannot be guaranteed. Proofs are to be returned to the Log-in Department, Elsevier Ltd, Stover Court, Bampfylde Street, Exeter EX1 2AH, UK.

Offprints

Authors will receive 25 offprints of their own contributions. Writers of reviews will receive 10 offprints. If extra prints are desired, authors must request them with the offprint order form that the editorial office sends before publication of the journal. Additional offprints and copies of the issue can be ordered at a specially reduced rate using the order form sent to the corresponding author after the manuscript has been accepted. Orders for reprints (produced after publication of an article) will incur a 50% surcharge.

Copyright

All authors must sign the "Transfer of Copyright" agreement before the article can be published. This transfer agreement enables Elsevier Ltd to protect the copyrighted material for the authors, without the author relinquishing his/her proprietary rights. The copyright transfer covers the exclusive rights to reproduce and distribute the article, including reprints, photographic reproductions, microfilm or any other reproductions of a similar nature, and translations. It also includes the right to adapt the article for use in conjunction with computer systems and programs, including reproduction or publication in machine-readable form and incorporation in retrieval systems. Authors are responsible for obtaining from the copyright holder permission to reproduce any material for which copyright already exists.

Author Support

For queries relating to the general submission of manuscripts (including electronic text and artwork) and the status of accepted manuscripts, please contact Author Support at **author support@elsevier.ie**

Authors can also keep track of progress of their accepted article, and set up e-mail alerts informing them of changes to their manuscript's status, by using the "Track a Paper" feature of Elsevier's Author Gateway (**http://authors.elsevier.com**).

Assessment & Evaluation in Higher Education

SUBMISSION PROCESS:
Electronic Submission Only via EMail **aehe@bath.ac.uk**

CONTACT INFORMATION:	REVIEW PROCESS:	
William Scott, Editor University of Bath Department of Education Bath, BA2 7AY UK	**Type of Review:**	Blind Review
	No. External Reviewers:	2
	No. InHouse Reviewers:	1
Phone:	**Acceptance Rate:**	21-30%
	Time to Review:	2 - 3 Months
	Reviewer's Comments:	Yes
Email: aehe@bath.ac.uk	**Invited Articles:**	0-5%
Website: http://www.tandf.co.uk/journals/titles/ 02602938.asp	**Fees to Publish:**	$0.00 US$
	Fees to Review:	$0.00 US$

PUBLICATION GUIDELINES:	CIRCULATION DATA:
Manuscript Style: See Manuscript Guidelines	**Reader:** Academics, Practicing Teachers
Manuscript Length: 16-20	**Frequency of Issue:** Bi-Monthly
Copies Required: Electronic Only	**Sponsor/Publisher:** Routledge, Taylor & Francis, Ltd.

MANUSCRIPT TOPICS:
Higher Education; Tests, Measurement & Evaluation

MANUSCRIPT GUIDELINES/COMMENTS:

Aims & Scope
Assessment & Evaluation in Higher Education is an established international peer-reviewed journal which publishes papers and reports on all aspects of assessment and evaluation within higher education. Its purpose is to advance understanding of assessment and evaluation practices and processes, particularly the contribution that these make to student learning and to course, staff and institutional development.

Assessment & Evaluation in Higher Education welcomes research-based, reflective or theoretical studies which help to illuminate the practice of assessment and evaluation in higher education. The journal is aimed at all higher education practitioners, irrespective of discipline. It sets out to provide readily accessible, up-to-date information about significant developments within the field, with a view to the sharing and extension of evaluated, innovative practice and the development of ideas. Suggestions for special issues are welcomed.

Instructions for Authors

Note to Authors. Please make sure your contact address information is clearly visible on the **outside** of <u>all</u> packages you are sending to Editors.

Manuscripts, ideally between 3000 and 5000 words, or 1500 to 2500 words for research or fieldwork, should be sent electronically to the Editor at **aehe@bath.ac.uk**. Please send two files: one should contain the full paper (including abstract and references) with NO details of the author(s). Pages should be numbered; the other should only contain the title of the paper, author name(s), post and email address(es), and short professional biographies of each author. Where this is not possible, 3 copies of the article, with any illustrations, should be submitted to: Professor William Scott, *Assessment & Evaluation in Higher Education*, Department of Education, University of Bath, Bath, BA2 7AY, UK.

Manuscripts should be typed on one side of A4 paper with double spacing and a wide margin to the left. All articles should be written in a clear and straightforward style, and be free from technical jargon. Detailed statistical evidence should be summarised in the text, though a limited amount of tabulated data may be included if they aid understanding, and will be comprehensible to lay readers. Footnotes to the text should normally be avoided. All papers should be original, but if there is overlap with material published elsewhere, details should be given.

To download a Word template for this journal, see our website.

For further information on electronic submission, including information on accepted file types, please see our website at **http://www.tandf.co.uk/journals/authors/electronic_edu.asp**.

Tables and captions to illustrations. Tables must be typed out on separate sheets and not included as part of the text. The captions to illustrations should be gathered together and also typed out on a separate sheet. Tables and Figures should be numbered consecutively by Arabic numerals. The approximate position of tables and figures should be indicated in the manuscript. Captions should include keys to any symbols used.

Figures. Please supply one set of artwork in a finished form, suitable for reproduction. Figures will not normally be redrawn by the publisher.

Citations of other work should be limited to those strictly necessary for the argument. Any quotations should be brief, and accompanied by precise references.

References should be indicated in the typescript by giving the author's name, with the year of publication in parentheses. If several papers by the same author and from the same year are cited, a, b, c, etc. should be put after the year of publication. The references should be listed in full, including pages, at the end of the paper in the following standard form:

For books
Norton, P. & Wiberg, K. (1998) *Teaching with technology* (Orlando, FL, Harcourt Brace).

For articles
Loughran, J. & Corrigan, D. (1995) Teaching portfolios: a strategy for developing learning and teaching in preservice education, *Teaching and Teacher Education*, 11(6), 565-577.

For chapters within books
Marzano, R. J. (1994) Commentary on literacy portfolios: windows on potential, in: S. H. Valencia, E. H. Hiebert & P. P. E. Afflerbach (Eds) *Authentic reading assessment: practices and possibilities* (Newark, NJ, International Reading Association), 41-56.

78

For online documents

Standler, R. (2000) *Plagiarism in colleges in the USA*. Available online at: www.rbs2.com/plag.htm (accessed 6 August 2004).

Titles of journals and names of publishers, etc. should not be abbreviated. Acronyms for the names of organisations, examinations, etc. should be preceded by the title in full.

Proofs will be sent to authors if there is sufficient time to do so. They should be corrected and returned to the Publisher within three days. Major alterations to the text cannot be accepted.

Early Electronic Offprints. Corresponding authors can now receive their article by e-mail as a complete PDF. This allows the author to print up to 50 copies, free of charge, and disseminate them to colleagues. In many cases this facility will be available up to two weeks prior to publication. Or, alternatively, corresponding authors will receive the traditional 50 offprints. A copy of the journal will be sent by post to all corresponding authors after publication. Additional copies of the journal can be purchased at the author's preferential rate of £15.00/$25.00 per copy.

Copyright. It is a condition of publication that authors assign copyright or licence the publication rights in their articles, including abstracts, to Taylor & Francis. This enables us to ensure full copyright protection and to disseminate the article, and of course the Journal, to the widest possible readership in print and electronic formats as appropriate. Authors may, of course, use the article elsewhere *after* publication without prior permission from Taylor & Francis, provided that acknowledgement is given to the Journal as the original source of publication, and that Taylor & Francis is notified so that our records show that its use is properly authorised. Authors retain a number of other rights under the Taylor & Francis rights policies documents. These policies are referred to at **www.tandf.co.uk/journals/authorrights.pdf** for full details. Authors are themselves responsible for obtaining permission to reproduce copyright material from other sources.

Assessment for Effective Intervention

SUBMISSION PROCESS:
Electronic Submission Only **via Online Portal** **https://mc.manuscriptcentral.com/PROED/aei**

CONTACT INFORMATION:	REVIEW PROCESS:	
Nick Elksnin & Linda K. Elksnin, Co-Eds Assessment for Effective Intervention 37 Stocker Drive Charleston, SC 29407 USA	**Type of Review:**	Blind Review
	No. External Reviewers:	3
	No. InHouse Reviewers:	2
Phone: 843-573-4725	**Acceptance Rate:**	40%
	Time to Review:	2 - 3 Months
	Reviewer's Comments:	Yes
Email: assessmentei@citadel.edu	**Invited Articles:**	0-5%
Website: www.proedinc.com	**Fees to Publish:**	$0.00 US$
	Fees to Review:	$0.00 US$

PUBLICATION GUIDELINES:	CIRCULATION DATA:
Manuscript Style: American Psychological Association **Manuscript Length:** 15-30 **Copies Required:** Electronic Only	**Reader:** Practicing Teachers, School Psychologists, Eductional Diagnosticians, Academics **Frequency of Issue:** Quarterly **Sponsor/Publisher:** PRO-ED, Inc.

MANUSCRIPT TOPICS:
Curriculum Studies; Gifted Children; Special Education; Tests, Measurement & Evaluation

MANUSCRIPT GUIDELINES/COMMENTS:

Manuscript Topics. Assessment of children and adolescents who are disabled and/or gifted and talented; Tests, measurement & evaluation; Curriculum-based assessment.

Assessment for Effective Intervention (*AEI*) is the official journal of the Council for Educational Diagnostic Services, a division of the Council for Exceptional Children. The editorial board of *AEI* will review manuscripts relevant for practicing educational diagnosticians, special educators, school psychologists, academic trainers, and others interested in psychoeducational assessment. The primary purpose of the journal is to publish empirically sound manuscripts that have implications for practitioners.

Types of Articles
The co-editors welcome manuscripts that center on practitioner developed assessment procedures, as well as papers that focus on published tests. Manuscripts that describe the relationship between assessment and instruction, innovative assessment strategies, diagnostic procedures, relationships between existing instruments, and review articles of assessment techniques, strategies, and

instrumentation are particularly desirable. Implications for the practitioner should be clearly communicated. Manuscripts should be no more than 30 typed, double-spaced pages, and should be accompanied by an abstract of 100 to 150 words.

Special Series. Special series are thematic issues composed of articles by different authors. A special series is conceptualized, coordinated, and guest edited by an author with recognized expertise in a particular area. Authors who wish to guest edit a special series should first submit a vita and a proposal that includes the following: overview, article-by-article content with abstract, and proposed authors. The co-editors should be consulted prior to submission concerning the appropriateness of the proposed topic.

Book and Test Reviews. *AEI* will accept unsolicited test and book reviews. Only reviews of recently published tests and books will be considered. When writing a test review, the author should address relevant test construction guidelines described in the most recent edition of Standards for Educational and Psychological Tests, published by the American Educational Research Association, the American Psychological Association, and the National Council on Measurement in Education. Test and book reviews should be written with the practitioner's needs in mind. Test and book review manuscripts should be no more than 10 typed, double-spaced pages.

Manuscript Submission
AEI prefers to receive all manuscript submissions electronically at: **https://mc.manuscriptcentral. com/PROED/aei**.

Acceptance Criteria
The co-editors will screen each manuscript for appropriateness of content, as well as adherence to publication guidelines. A manuscript that meets criteria will be sent to three consulting or guest editors for blind peer review. The co-editors will consider reviewers' comments when making an editorial decision. All reviewers' comments are sent to the author and reviewers of the manuscript. Authors are typically notified about the status of the manuscript within 8 weeks of submission. Individuals who wish to serve as guest reviewers should send a letter of interest highlighting areas of expertise and a curriculum vitae to the co-editors.

Manuscript Preparation
In preparing manuscripts, authors should adhere to the guidelines specified in the *Publication Manual of the American Psychological Association* (5th ed., 2001). Copies may be ordered from: APA Order Department, PO Box 2710, Hyattsville, MD 20784. When preparing the manuscript, please adhere to the following guidelines:
1. Set all margins to 1 inch.
2. Use left alignment, a nonproportional font, and 12-pt. type.
3. Format for 8 1/2 in. 11 in. paper. Do not format for A4 paper.
4. Please type all copy upper and lower case—do not use all capitals or small capitals.
5. Indicate correct location of tables and figures in text in boldface, enclosed in angle brackets. Example: **<Fig. 1 here>**
6. Please use your tab key and centering functions to do head alignment, paragraph indents, etc. DO NOT USE THE SPACE BAR.
7. **Double space** all text and tables.

Artwork
Figures must be provided as production-ready. Do not use rules or tick marks smaller than 1 point in size. Acceptable electronic formats for figures or other art are: TIFF, EPS, Word, or Excel. If you have trouble loading Excel files, copy and paste them into a Word document. Scans must be at least 300 dpi (also sometimes called lpi). Scans done at lower resolutions will have a very poor print quality, even if they look crisp and clear on a laser printout. Contact the PRO-ED Journals design editor (**lhattersley@proedinc.com**) if you have any questions.

Permissions

Obtaining **written permissions** for material such as figures, tables, art, and extensive quotes taken directly—or adapted in minor ways—from another source **is the author's responsibility, as is payment of any fees the copyright holder may require**. Because permissions often take a considerable amount of time to be granted, authors should start the request process as soon as possible. Authors should never assume that material taken from software or downloaded from the Internet may be used without obtaining permission. Each source must be investigated on a case-by-case basis. In addition, because JSE is available online to subscribers and in other formats as well, such as Braille and large print, authors must ensure that any written permissions specifically allow for publication in these formats. The best way to ensure this is to use PRO-ED's permission request form, which has been written to cover these areas; however, copyright holders may require use of their own form. In these cases, the author should read any forms carefully to make sure that the language is broad enough to allow publication in all formats. Failure to obtain permission will result in either removal of the particular item or the article being pulled from the journal issue. To obtain a copy of our permission request form, you may download it from the Manuscript Central Web site: **https://mc.manuscriptcentral.com/PROED/aei** at the Instructions & Forms link in the grey "Resources" box or contact PRO-ED Journals, 8700 Shoal Creek Blvd., Austin, TX 78757; 512/451-3246; fax: 512/302-9129; e-mail: **journals@proedinc.com**

Copyright

After your article has been accepted for publication, please go to the journal's Manuscript Central Web site; **https://mc.manuscriptcentral.com/PROED/aei** At the Instructions and Forms link in the grey "Resources" box you may obtain the Author Information Form and Copyright Release. Please download and fill out these forms. The Author Information Form may be sent as an e-mail attachment to the *AEI* editorial office (**assessmentei@citadel.edu**). Please make sure all authors sign the Copyright Release and then fax it to the *AEI* editorial office (843/573-4725or 828/297-6961).

Ordering Reprints

Information regarding reprints will be sent with the complimentary printed copy of the journal issue in which your article appears.

Journal Contact Information. Nick Elksnin, PhD, NCSP or Linda K. Elksnin, PhD, Co-Editors, Assessment for Effective Intervention, 37 Stocker Drive, Charleston, SC 29407

Assessment in Education: Principles, Policy & Practice

SUBMISSION PROCESS:
Postal Submission Only

CONTACT INFORMATION:	REVIEW PROCESS:	
Editorial Office University of Bristol Graduate School of Education Helen Wodehouse Bldg 35 Berkeley Square Bristol, BS8 1JA UK **Phone:** +44 (0) 117 9287033 **Email:** brigid.walker@bristol.ac.uk **Website:** www.tandf.co.uk/journals/0969594X	**Type of Review:** **No. External Reviewers:** **No. InHouse Reviewers:** **Acceptance Rate:** **Time to Review:** **Reviewer's Comments:** **Invited Articles:** **Fees to Publish:** **Fees to Review:**	Blind Review 2 1 11-20% 3-9 months Yes 30% $0.00 US$ $0.00 US$
PUBLICATION GUIDELINES:	**CIRCULATION DATA:**	
Manuscript Style: See Manuscript Guidelines **Manuscript Length:** 26-30 (5,000-7,000 Words) **Copies Required:** Four	**Reader:** Academics, Administrators, Policy Makers, Examination Bodies **Frequency of Issue:** 3 Times/Year **Sponsor/Publisher:** Taylor & Francis, Ltd.	

MANUSCRIPT TOPICS:
Curriculum Studies; Educational Psychology; Educational Technology Systems; Elementary / Early Childhood; Higher Education; Secondary / Adolescent Studies; Teacher Education; Tests, Measurement & Evaluation

MANUSCRIPT GUIDELINES/COMMENTS:

Topics Also Include. Assessment Developments; Early Childhood Assessment; Higher Education Assessment; Secondary Assessment; Educational Policy; Institutional Development; Education Innovation and Practice; Examination Systems and Practices; Formative Assessment; International Comparisons of Educational Standards; Test Development

Note to Authors. Please make sure your contact address information is clearly visible on the outside of all packages you are sending to Editors.

Papers accepted become the copyright of the journal, unless otherwise specifically agreed.

Manuscripts should be sent to The Editorial Office, Graduate School of Education, University of Bristol, Helen Wodehouse Building, 35 Berkeley Square, Bristol BS8 1JA, UK. **brigid.walker@ bristol.ac.uk**. Articles can be considered only if four complete copies of each manuscript are submitted. (We prefer to receive disks in Microsoft Word PC format.) Articles should be typed on one side of the paper, double spaced, with ample margins, and bear the title of the contribution, name(s) of the author(s) and the address where the work was carried out. An abstract of 100-150 words should be included and a short note of bibliographical details for the 'Notes on Contributors' section. The full postal and email addresses of the author who will check proofs and receive correspondence and offprints should also be included. All pages should be numbered.

Footnotes to the text should be avoided wherever this is reasonably possible.

Profiles should be 3000-6000 words in length (including bibliography) and should be submitted to the journal as detailed above, indicating clearly that they are to be considered for publication within the section **Profiles of Educational Assessment Systems World-wide**.

Rejected manuscripts will not normally be returned to contributors unless sufficient international postal coupons have been sent.

Tables and captions to illustrations. Tables must be typed out on separate sheets and not included as part of the text. The captions to illustrations should be gathered together and also typed out on a separate sheet. Tables should be numbered by Arabic numerals. The approximate position of tables and figures should be indicated in the manuscript. Captions should include keys to symbols.

Figures. Please supply one set of artwork in a finished form, suitable for reproduction. Figures will not normally be redrawn by the publisher.

Citations of other work should be limited to those strictly necessary for the argument. Any quotations should be brief, and accompanied by precise references.

References should be indicated in the typescript by giving the author's name, with the year of publication in parentheses. If several papers by the same author and from the same year are cited, a, b, c, etc. should be put after the year of publication. The references should be listed in full, including pages, at the end of the paper in the following standard form:

For books
Kress, G. (2003) *Literacy in the new media age* (London, Routledge).

For articles
Cremin, L. A. (1983) The problematics of education in the 1980s: some reflections on the Oxford Workshop, *Oxford Review of Education*, 9, pp. 33-40.

For chapters within books
Willis, P. (1983) Cultural production and theories of reproduction, in: L. Barton & S. Walker (Eds) *Race, class and education* (London, Croom Helm), 25-50.

Titles of journals and names of publishers, etc. should **not** be abbreviated. Acronyms for the names of organisations, examinations, etc. should be preceded by the title in full.

If you have any further questions about the style for this journal, please submit your questions using the Style Queries form at **www.tandf.co.uk/journals/authors/stylequeries.asp**.

Proofs will be sent to authors if there is sufficient time to do so. They should be corrected and returned to the Publisher within three days. Major alterations to the text cannot be accepted.

Offprints. Fifty offprints of each paper are supplied free. Additional copies may be purchased and should be ordered when the proofs are returned. Offprints, together with a complete copy of the relevant journal issue, are sent by accelerated surface post about three weeks after publication.

84

Early Electronic Offprints. Corresponding authors can now receive their article by e-mail as a complete PDF. This allows the author to print up to 50 copies, free of charge, and disseminate them to colleagues. In many cases this facility will be available up to two weeks prior to publication. Or, alternatively, corresponding authors will receive the traditional 50 offprints. A copy of the journal will be sent by post to all corresponding authors after publication. Additional copies of the journal can be purchased at the author's preferential rate of £15.00/$25.00per copy.

Copyright. It is a condition of publication that authors vest copyright in their articles, including abstracts, in Taylor & Francis Ltd. This enables us to ensure full copyright protection and to disseminate the article, and the journal, to the widest possible readership in print and electronic formats as appropriate. Authors may, of course, use the article elsewhere after publication without prior permission from Taylor & Francis, provided that acknowledgement is given to the *Journal* as the original source of publication, and that Taylor & Francis is notified so that our records show that its use is properly authorized. Authors retain a number of other rights under the Taylor & Francis rights policies documents. These policies are referred to at **www.tandf.co.uk/journals/ authorrights.pdf** for full details. Authors are themselves responsible for obtaining permission to reproduce copyright material from other sources.

Athletics Administration

SUBMISSION PROCESS:

Postal Submission Only

CONTACT INFORMATION:	REVIEW PROCESS:
Julie Work, Editor NACDA PO Box 16428 Cleveland, OH 44116 USA	**Type of Review:** Editorial Review **No. External Reviewers:** 1 **No. InHouse Reviewers:** 1
Phone: 440-892-4000 **Email:** jwork@nacda.com **Website:** www.nacda.com	**Acceptance Rate:** 50% **Time to Review:** 1 Month or Less **Reviewer's Comments:** No **Invited Articles:** 50% + **Fees to Publish:** $0.00 US$ **Fees to Review:** $0.00 US$
PUBLICATION GUIDELINES:	**CIRCULATION DATA:**
Manuscript Style: See Manuscript Guidelines **Manuscript Length:** 6-10 **Copies Required:** One	**Reader:** Administrators **Frequency of Issue:** Bi-Monthly **Sponsor/Publisher:** National Association of Collegiate Directors of Athletics (NACDA) / Host Communications, Inc.

MANUSCRIPT TOPICS:
Administration of Intercollegiate Athletics; Education Management / Administration

MANUSCRIPT GUIDELINES/COMMENTS:

Athletics Administration is the official publication of the National Association of Collegiate Directors of Athletics (NACDA). It is published six times annually and distributed to every athletics director at four-year and two-year colleges and universities in the United States and Canada. It is also distributed to all other individuals who are NACDA members, and to those who subscribe annually ($15).

Athletics Administration is primarily written by athletics directors for athletics directors. Manuscripts are carefully reviewed and printed under the following priority structure:
1. NACDA members who are athletics directors
2. NACDA members who are not athletics directors
3. Athletics directors who are not NACDA members
4. All others

Articles should contain in the neighborhood of 1,000 to 1,200 words, typed double-spaced, and preferably be broken with three to five sub-headings throughout the text. The contents should include bottom-line results of a study rather than explaining study design, variables, correlation coefficients, etc.

Our goal is to provide information to our members that they don't already know, and need to know. The best articles are the ones dealing with the most specific topics. Generic material dwelling on obvious management principles (planning, communicating, establishing goals and objectives, evaluating, etc. do not really tell anyone anything. On the other hand, a step-by-step outline for a ticket plan promoting women's basketball would be an ideal topic that can be very helpful to those who read the article.

Finally, articles should include a short, "catchy" title, and be submitted with a photo of the author and a 75-word (approx.) biography.

Behavior Research Methods

SUBMISSION PROCESS:
Electronic Submission Only **via Online Portal** http://mc.manuscriptcentral.com/psychonomic/brmic

CONTACT INFORMATION:	REVIEW PROCESS:	
John H. Krantz, Editor Hanover College P. O. Box 890 Hanover, IN 47243 USA	**Type of Review:**	Editorial Review
	No. External Reviewers: **No. InHouse Reviewers:**	2 1
Phone: 812-866-7316	**Acceptance Rate:** **Time to Review:** **Reviewer's Comments:**	21-30% 1 - 2 Months Yes
Email: krantzj@hanover.edu	**Invited Articles:**	0-5%
Website: http://www.psychonomic.org/ BRMIC/	**Fees to Publish:** **Fees to Review:**	$0.00 US$ $0.00 US$

PUBLICATION GUIDELINES:	CIRCULATION DATA:
Manuscript Style: American Psychological Association	**Reader:** Academics
Manuscript Length: 11-30+	**Frequency of Issue:** Quarterly
Copies Required: Electronic Only	**Sponsor/Publisher:** Psychonomic Society

MANUSCRIPT TOPICS:
Educational Technology Systems; Instrument & Research Techniques; Operations Research / Statistics; Program Abstracts

MANUSCRIPT GUIDELINES/COMMENTS:

About the Journal
Behavior Research Methods is the psychologist's primary source for information on the methods, techniques, and instrumentation of research in experimental psychology. The journal focuses particularly on the use of computer technology in psychological research, including the latest hardware and software developments. An annual special issue is also devoted to this field.

Guidelines for Authors
New Submissions. Submissions should be sent to the Editor of the relevant journal. Note, however, that submission procedures vary among the journals. For specific requirements and addresses, see the inside cover of the journal or click on the journal's title above.

Accepted Submissions. Manuscripts should, in general, adhere to the conventions described in the *Publication Manual of the American Psychological Association* (5th ed.). When in doubt, consult a recent issue of a Psychonomic Society journal. See also the Psychonomic Society Publications Guidelines for References (**http://www.psychonomic.org/ref.htm**).

Printed Manuscript. The printed manuscript, including the abstract, references, and notes, must be double-spaced throughout (2.5-3 lines per inch), with 1.5-in. margins.

In addition to the main text, manuscripts (whether hard copy or electronic file) should include: Title page-with (a) title, author name(s) and affiliation(s), (b) mailing address, telephone number, and e-mail address of the author contact, and (c) a suggested running head; abstract of 100–150 words; author's note; list of figure captions; references-complete and correct (with all journal names written out); note(s)-if needed; table(s)-if needed; appendix(es) and listing(s)-if needed. These sections should begin on separate pages, and the pages should be numbered consecutively from the abstract on. Approximate locations of the figures should be noted within the text (e.g. "Figure 1 about here"). The figures themselves should be on separate pages.

Manuscript Tracking. Once a manuscript has been submitted, it is assigned a manuscript number, used by the editor of the journal while the manuscript is under review. When a manuscript is accepted for publication, however, it is assigned a production number (e.g., C325, for *Memory & Cognition*; P436, for *Perception & Psychophysics*; etc.). From that time on, authors must identify their manuscripts by referring to this production number in any correspondence with the Publications Office or the editor of the journal. The running head on the final copy of the accepted manuscript (both printed and electronic versions) sent to the Publications Office should include this production number.

Permissions. It is the author's responsibility to determine from the copyright owner whether or not permission is required for quoting text or for reproducing or adapting all or part of a table or figure from a copyrighted source. Authors must obtain any necessary written permission and enclose a copy with the submitted or revised manuscript.

Please note that authors who cite personal communications must obtain permission from their source. This may be done via e-mail, and the permission may be sent to the Managing Editor at the Publications Office: **jbellquist@ psychonomic.org**.

Proofs. Proofs are sent to authors via e-mail as pdf attachments. It is incumbent upon authors to check the proof carefully. Authors' responses to the copy editor's queries, as well as any additional corrections, should be sent via e-mail to the managing editor: **jbellquist@psychonomic.org**.

Reprints. Reprint order requests are sent via e-mail with the proofs. Reprints should be ordered or rejected at that time using the link provided.

For general questions regarding publication, call or e-mail the Publications Office at (512) 462-2442; **frank@psychonomic.org** or **jbellquist@psychonomic.org**. For questions regarding electronic files and figures, see below.

Electronic Files. After a manuscript has been accepted, authors must also submit electronic files containing the text that agrees exactly with the latest printed revision approved by the editor. The printed manuscript must be sent to the Publications Office and, if required, to the journal editor. The electronic files can be sent as e-mailed attachments to **newms@ psychonomic.org** or on CD or disk with the printed copy. If any further changes or additions are to be made, please send to the Publications Office a letter that lists the further changes, or, if the changes are extensive, revised electronic and printed versions of the manuscript with the changes indicated. Such changes must be cleared with the Editor of the journal of course.

Electronic File Requirements
Please note: Electronic files prepared in TEX or LATEX **will not** be accepted.
1. All files must contain the production number at the beginning of the file name.

2. **A Microsoft Word document** or other word processing document. Files with the extension .doc for MS Word are preferable, but most others are acceptable.
3. **An ASCII or text only document of the manuscript**. From this document, all printing/formatting commands other than paragraph breaks will have been deleted. (Note: Many word processing programs define ASCII as "text only"; e.g., in Microsoft Word, simply save the document as "text only.")
4. **Graphics**. Please provide documents for all figures and illustrations composed on computers, in addition to camera-ready versions. Do not embed graphic boxes within text lines. Please refer to FIGURES section.

Call or e-mail the Publications Office if you have questions regarding typesetting or electronic files (512-462-2442; **kat@psychonomic.org**).

Tables

The *Publication Manual of the American Psychological Association* (5th ed., pp. 147–175) gives excellent instructions for constructing tables. The following will emphasize areas that are particularly important and will explain some Psychonomic journal departures from APA style.

Table Software. Tables should be created with your word processing or spreadsheet program. They should never be submitted as graphics files.

General. Make sure the table is necessary. Small tables with few entries can often be dealt with just as effectively in a line or two of text. Do not combine two tables of dissimilar format into one table (e.g., if sections A and B of Table 1 are not of similar format, section A should be Table 1 and section B, Table 2). However, do combine small tables of identical format with few entries (i.e., provide one table with, say, four columns and four rows, one for each experiment, rather than four tables of four columns and one row giving data for each of four experiments).

Keep the material as simple and straightforward as possible. Double-space all tables for easy editing and typesetting. Number all tables in the order in which they are mentioned in the text. Make sure all tables are mentioned in the text.

Table Arrangement. Instead of a column of 0.00 plus or minus .00 entries, use two columns with separate appropriate headings (e.g., M and SE or SD). Arrange tables so that similar numbers fall into separate columns. That is, if possible, do not mix, in one column, such numbers as 0000, 00.00, .0000.

Avoid unnecessary repetitions throughout the table. Columns with the same numerical entries throughout the table or throughout sections of the table can be put in footnotes (e.g., "In Condition 1, n = 20 for each group; in Condition 2, n = 30 for each group"). Units of measurement can simply be abbreviated in headings-"RTs (in msec)"- or explained in footnotes ("RTs are given in milliseconds").

Other Requirements. Define all measurements used for values in the table (e.g., "Thresholds are given in decibels"). Define (or avoid using) all abbreviations. Do not use material in tables that should normally be placed in figures (e.g., graphic objects, photographic reproductions).

Define, in the table footnotes, all asterisks, daggers, and other symbols used. General footnotes (denoted by "Note-...") qualify, explain, or provide information relating to the table as a whole or to a major section of the table (e.g., a column or a group of columns). Specific footnotes (denoted by *, †, ‡, etc.) relate to individual entries or give probability levels. Do not use asterisks, daggers, and other symbols to denote anything other than footnotes pertaining to particular entries in the body of the table. Psychonomic journals do not normally use superscripted footnotes (raised a, b, c, etc.) in tables.

All major words of table titles and column headings should be capitalized. Column headings refer only to entries in the column(s) below them. A column heading may never refer to other column headings to its right across the top of the table.

Do not print a table in a visible "cellular" format: Vertical rules are never used in Psychonomic journals; horizontal rules are never used within the body of the table.

Figures

High-quality hard copies must be provided for all figures.

Please ensure that your hard copies match your digital files exactly.

Authors must obtain permission from the copyright holder to reproduce or adapt any figure from a copyrighted source, and a permission statement must accompany the figure. Please refer to the *Publication Manual of the American Psychological Association* (5th ed., p. 175) for models of permission statements. The copyright holder's letter of permission must be submitted to the publications office along with the final copy of the accepted manuscript for production.

Label each figure with the figure number, the manuscript's production number, and the author's name. The top of each figure should be clearly indicated.

Figures should be from 3 in. (18 picas) to 6.5 in. (39 picas) wide.

Our house style is for panels within figures to be labeled and read from left to right and then down, rather than vice versa.

Legends and captions should explain the contents of figures as they appear from top down, not from the bottom up.

Type should be proportional to the figure. Type should vary by no more than 4 points within a figure. Helvetica and Times are the preferred fonts.

Graph fills or symbols should be easy to distinguish from one another. Do not use similar shades of gray in graphs.

Avoid hairlines or even thin lines in any type of figure.

Please check that legends (if any) match the figure—that is, that lines and colors in the legend look like the ones they correspond to within the figure.

Digital figures should be high resolution (at least 300 dpi), submitted via emailed attachment with your manuscript files or on 3.5-in. disk or CD.

PDFs or EPS files with the fonts embedded are the preferable formats. Hi res (300 dpi or more) Photoshop files, TIFFs, or JPEGs (at maximum quality) are also acceptable.

Since figures in PowerPoint, Excel, and Word can be problematic, we suggest instead submitting a PDF created from these programs.

Hand drawn originals (except when appropriate) are not acceptable.

With specific exceptions approved by the editor of the journal, figures are printed in black and white. Any color figures converted to grayscale or black and white must be checked for clarity and contrast before they are submitted.

Color figures approved for publication must be high resolution (at least 300 dpi). RGB or CMYK files are acceptable.

Refer to the *Publication Manual of the American Psychological Association* (5th ed., pp. 176-201) for additional guidelines on the preparation of figures.

E-mail **molly@psychonomic.org** with figure questions or concerns.

For detailed Guidelines for References please visit: **http://www.psychonomic.org/ref.htm**

Behavioral & Social Sciences Librarian

SUBMISSION PROCESS:
Postal or Electronic Submission Accepted **via EMail** **neciap@uark.edu**

CONTACT INFORMATION:	REVIEW PROCESS:	

Necia Parker-Gibson, Editor
Mullins Library
University of Arkansas
365 N. McIlroy Ave.
Fayetteville, AR 72701 USA
 	
Phone:
  479-575-8421
 	
Email:
  neciap@uark.edu
Website:
  http://www.haworthpressinc.com/store/product.asp?sku=J103
	Type of Review:
	
	No. External Reviewers:
	No. InHouse Reviewers:
	
	Acceptance Rate:
	Time to Review:
	Reviewer's Comments:
	Invited Articles:
	
	Fees to Publish:
	Fees to Review:
		Blind Review
		
		1
		1
		
		80%
		1-3 Months
		Yes
		21-30%
		
		$0.00 US$
		$0.00 US$

PUBLICATION GUIDELINES:	**CIRCULATION DATA:**	

Manuscript Style:
  Chicago Manual of Style
 	
Manuscript Length:
  5-50
 	
Copies Required:
  Two
	Reader:
	  Academics, Academic Librarians,
	  Researchers
	
	Frequency of Issue:
	  2 Times/Year
	
	Sponsor/Publisher:
	  Haworth Press, Inc.	

MANUSCRIPT TOPICS:
Educational Psychology; Library Science / Information Resources; Social Studies / Social Science

MANUSCRIPT GUIDELINES/COMMENTS:

About the Journal
For more than 25 years, scholars, educators, and professional information specialists have turned to *Behavioral & Social Sciences Librarian*. This landmark publication is the only journal that provides both professional information specialists and scholars with the latest research on the production, collection, organization, dissemination, and retrieval of the vital information they need in the social and behavioral sciences. Since its first printing, *Behavioral & Social Sciences Librarian* has presented a unique range of material to a readership that includes librarians and information specialists, collection development administrators, library educators, and scholars, teachers, policymakers, publishers, and database producers. The journal focuses on the core fields of anthropology, sociology, economics, psychology, education, political science, communication, language and area studies, and population-specific studies such as Latin American, ethnic, and women's studies, but in particular on the interaction of those fields with library and information science.

Behavioral & Social Sciences Librarian is built on a foundation of unusual and interesting biographies and checklists, descriptions of collections or institutional resources, and evaluations of resources. The *Journal* also seeks articles that study characteristics of social sciences literatures and studies of user behavior. The wide range of material includes:

- reference and bibliographic instruction
- publishing trends
- bibliographic and numeric databases
- descriptive and critical analyses of information resources
- indexing, abstracting, thesaurus building, and database construction

Behavioral & Social Sciences Librarian features regular columns such as "The Internet Connection" and "Electronic Roundup" that present up-to-date information on the capacity and accessibility of electronic resources. Recent topics have included innovations in useful Web tools, electronic publishing, fair use, copyright law and digitized works, the impact of the Internet on research strategies, reviews of popular search engines, and ERIC (Educational Resources Information Center) resources online. The journal also offers tips and tutorials on searching online databases and reviews of available Web content.

Behavioral & Social Sciences Librarian is a fundamental source of information on the resources for librarians, archivists and information seekers in the social sciences, and has been since 1979.

Instructions for Authors

1. **Original Articles Only**. Submission of a manuscript to this journal represents a certification on the part of the author(s) that it is an original work, and that neither this manuscript nor a version of it has been published elsewhere nor is being considered for publication elsewhere.

2. **Manuscript Length**. Your manuscript may be approximately 5-50 typed pages double-spaced (including references and abstract). Lengthier manuscripts may be considered, but only at the discretion of the Editor. Sometimes, lengthier manuscripts may be considered if they can be divided up into sections for publication in successive *Journal* issues.

3. **Manuscript Style**. References, citations, and general style of manuscripts for this *Journal* should follow the Chicago style (as outlined in the latest edition of the *Manual of Style* of the *University of Chicago Press*). References should be double-spaced and placed in alphabetical order.

If an author wishes to submit a paper that has been already prepared in another style, he or she may do so. However, if the paper is accepted (with or without reviewer's alterations), the author is fully responsible for retyping the manuscript in the correct style as indicated above. Neither the Editor nor the Publisher is responsible for re-preparing manuscript copy to adhere to the *Journal*'s style.

4. **Manuscript Preparation** (Note: electronic submission by attachment to e-mail is highly encouraged. Microsoft Word is the preferred software.)
Margins. Leave at least a one-inch margin on all four sides.
Paper. Use clean white, 8 ½" x 11" bond paper. If submitting electronically, submit as a e-mail attachment or on disk or CD.
Number of Copies. Four (the original plus three photocopies) in print. Two copies if submitting electronically—the anonyous review copy and the "title page" copy.
Cover Page. Important--staple (or include in the file) a cover page to the manuscript, indicating only the article title (this is used for anonymous refereeing).
Second "Title Page." Enclose (or include) a regular title page but do not staple it to the manuscript. Include the title again, plus:

- full authorship
- a header or footer on each page with abbreviated title and pg number of total (e.g., pg2 of 7)
- an introductory footnote with authors' academic degrees, professional titles, affiliations, mailing addresses, and any desired acknowledgment of research support or other credit.

5. **Return Envelopes**. When you submit your four manuscript copies, if in hard copy, also include:

- a 9" x 12" envelope, self-addressed and stamped with sufficient postage to ensure return of your manuscript;
- a regular envelope, stamped and self-addressed. This is for the Editor to send you an "acknowledgement of receipt" letter.
- Acknowledgement of receipt may be by e-mail, especially if the manuscript is submitted electronically, at the editor's discretion. Electronic submission is tacit agreement to electronic correspondence.

6. **Spelling, Grammar, and Punctuation**. You are responsible for preparing manuscript copy which is clearly written in acceptable scholarly English, and which contains no errors of spelling, grammar, or punctuation. Neither the Editor nor the Publisher is responsible for correcting errors of spelling and grammar: the manuscript, after acceptance by the Editor, must be immediately ready for typesetting as it is finally submitted by the author(s). Check your paper for the following common errors:

- dangling modifiers
- misplaced modifiers
- unclear antecedents
- incorrect or inconsistent abbreviations
- misuse of homonyms.

Check the accuracy of all arithmetic calculations, statistics, numerical data, text citations, and references. If you include graphics, attach them or send them as separate files, but clearly mark the place to include them (see futher instructions below).

7. **Be consistent.** Be uniform and correct in your use of abbreviations, terminology, and in citing references, throughout your paper. In most cases, for abbreviations or acronyms include the full name or phrase in the first use, with the acronym following in parentheses, e.g., American Psychological Association (APA), and use the acronym thereafter.

8. **Preparation of Tables, Figures, and Illustrations**. Any material that is not textual is considered artwork. This includes tables, figures, diagrams, charts, graphs, illustrations, appendices, screen captures, and photos. Tables and figures (including legend, notes, and sources) should be no larger than 4 ½ x 6 ½ inches. Type styles should be Helvetica (or Helvetica narrow if necessary) and no smaller than 8 point. We request that computer-generated figures be in black and white and/or shades of gray (preferably not color, for it does not reproduce well). Camera-ready art must contain no grammatical, typographical, or format errors and must reproduce sharply and clearly in the dimensions of the final printed page (4 ½ x 6 ½ inches). Photos and screen captures must be on disk as a TIF file, or other graphic files format such as JPEG or BMP. For rapid publication we must receive black-and-white glossy or matte positives (white background with black images and/or wording) in addition to files on disk. Tables should be created in the text document file using the software's *Table* feature.

9. **Submitting Art**. Both a printed hard copy and a disk copy of the art must be provided. We request that each piece of art be sent in its own file, on a disk separate from the disk containing the manuscript text file(s), and be clearly labeled. We reserve the right to (if necessary) request new art, alter art, or if all else has failed in achieving art that is presentable, delete art. If submitted art cannot be used, the Publisher reserves the right to redo the art and to charge the author a fee of $35.00 per hour for this service. The Haworth Press, Inc. is not responsible for errors incurred in the preparation of new artwork. Camera-ready artwork must be prepared on separate sheets of paper. Always use black ink and professional drawing instruments. On the back of these items, write your article title and the journal title lightly in soft-lead pencil (please do not write on the face of art). In the text file, skip extra lines and indicate where these figures are placed. Photos are considered part of the acceptable manuscript and remain with the Publisher for use in additional printings.

10. **Electronic Media**. Haworth's in-house type-setting unit is able to utilize your final manuscript material as prepared on most personal computers and word processors. This will minimize typographical errors and decrease overall production time. Please send the first draft and final draft copies of your manuscript to the journal Editor in print format for his/her final review and approval. After approval of your final manuscript, please submit the final approved version both on printed format ("hard copy") and diskette. On the outside of the diskette package write:

- the brand name of your computer or word processor
- the word-processing program that you used; Microsoft Word is preferred.
- the title of your article, and
- file name

Note: Disk and hard copy must agree. In case of discrepancies, it is The Haworth Press' policy to follow hard copy. Authors are advised that **No Revisions** of the manuscript can be made after acceptance by the Editor for publication. The benefits of this procedure are many with speed and accuracy being the most obvious.

11. **Alterations Required By Referees and Reviewers**. Many times a paper is accepted by the Editor contingent upon changes that are mandated by anonymous specialist referees and members of the Editorial Board. If the Editor returns your manuscript for revisions, you are responsible for retyping any sections of the paper to incorporate these revisions (if applicable, revisions should also be put on disk).

12. **Typesetting**. You will not receive galley proofs of your article. Editorial revisions, if any, must therefore be made while your article is still in manuscript. The final version of the manuscript will be the version you see published. Typesetter's errors will be corrected by the production staff of The Haworth Press. Authors are expected to submit manuscripts, disks, and art that are free from error.

13. **Reprints**. The senior author will receive two copies of the journal issue and 25 complimentary reprints of his or her article. The junior author(s) will receive two copies of the journal issue. These are sent several weeks after the journal issue is published and in circulation. An order form for the purchase of additional reprints will also be sent to all authors at this time (approximately 4-6 weeks is necessary for the preparation of reprints). **Please do not ask the Journal's Editor about reprints**. Send all such questions directly to The Haworth Press, Inc. Production Department, 21 East Broad Street, West Hazleton, PA 18201 USA. To order additional reprints (minimum: 50 copies), please contact The Haworth Document Delivery Center, 10 Alice Street, Binghamton, NY 13904-1580 USA; 1-800-342-9678 or Fax (607) 722-6362.

14. **Copyright**. Copyright ownership of your manuscript must be transferred officially to The Haworth Press, Inc. before we can begin the peer-review process. The Editor's letter or e-mail acknowledging receipt of the manuscript will be accompanied by a form(or a link to the form) fully explaining this. All authors must sign the form and return the original to the Editor as soon as possible. Failure to return the copyright form in a timely fashion will result in delay in review and subsequent publication.

Bilingual Family Newsletter, The

SUBMISSION PROCESS:

**Postal or Electronic Submission Accepted
via EMail**

info@multilingualmatters.com

CONTACT INFORMATION:	REVIEW PROCESS:
Sami Grover, Editor	**Type of Review:**
Multilingual Matters	**No. External Reviewers:** 0
Frankfurt Lodge	**No. InHouse Reviewers:** 1
Clevedon Hall	
Victoria Road	**Acceptance Rate:** 70%
Clevedon, England, BS21 7HH	**Time to Review:** 1 - 2 Months
	Reviewer's Comments:
Phone:	**Invited Articles:** 11-20%
+44 (0) 1275 876519	
	Fees to Publish: $0.00 US$
Email:	**Fees to Review:** $0.00 US$
info@multilingualmatters.com	
Website:	
http://multilingual-matters.com	

PUBLICATION GUIDELINES:	CIRCULATION DATA:
Manuscript Style:	**Reader:**
American Psychological Association	Practicing Teachers, Parents
Manuscript Length:	**Frequency of Issue:**
1-5	Quarterly
Copies Required:	**Sponsor/Publisher:**
Two	Multilingual Matters Ltd.

MANUSCRIPT TOPICS:
Bilingual / E.S.L.; Educational Psychology; Elementary / Early Childhood; Foreign Language; Gifted Children; Languages & Linguistics; Reading

MANUSCRIPT GUIDELINES/COMMENTS:

Aims of the Journal
The *Newsletter* publishes short, informative articles on current thoughts and research on language learning, bilingualism, biculturalism, mother tongue schools, cross-cultural marriage, intercultural living, etc. It publishes descriptions of how particular families have managed their situation, problems encountered and how these were overcome. The *Newsletter* also acts as a means of communication between similar families all over the world by providing answers to readers" queries, not only from experts, but also from other readers.

Guidelines
Main articles are usually 1,500 to 2000 words long, although we are also interested in shorter pieces and anecdotes. The language of submission is English. Submissions should preferably include at least one photograph in a digital format, either of an image that illustrates the article, or

of the author. We reserve the right to edit submissions for length and content and we cannot guarantee inclusion in any particular issue. Entries in the "Contacts" section should be limited to name, telephone number/email, geographical area, age of any children, languages spoken in the family, and whom you are seeking to contact.

Unfortunately the *BFN* does not make a profit so we are unable to pay for contributions, but we do provide some free copies of the issue in which an article appears, so contributors can share it with family and friends.

Bottom Line: Managing Library Finances, The

SUBMISSION PROCESS:
Electronic Submission Preferred **via EMail** **eden@library.ucsb.edu**

CONTACT INFORMATION:	REVIEW PROCESS:	
Bradford Lee Eden, Editor University of California, Santa Barbara Santa Barbara, CA 93106-9010 USA	**Type of Review:**	Editorial Review
	No. External Reviewers:	1
	No. InHouse Reviewers:	1
Phone:	**Acceptance Rate:**	
	Time to Review:	
Email: eden@library.ucsb.edu	**Reviewer's Comments:**	
	Invited Articles:	
Website: http://iris.emeraldinsight.com/info/journals/bl/bl.jsp	**Fees to Publish:**	$0.00 US$
	Fees to Review:	$0.00 US$

PUBLICATION GUIDELINES:	CIRCULATION DATA:
Manuscript Style: USC - Harvard Blue Book	**Reader:** Academics, Administrators
Manuscript Length: 11-15	**Frequency of Issue:** Quarterly
Copies Required: Electronic Only	**Sponsor/Publisher:** Emerald Group Publishing Limited

MANUSCRIPT TOPICS:
Education Management / Administration; Higher Education; Library Science / Information Resources

MANUSCRIPT GUIDELINES/COMMENTS:

About the Journal
If you require current information on the financial aspects of library operations, whether you are a librarian, library trustee or anyone concerned with library management, then you can enhance your understanding of all aspects of managing library finances through *The Bottom Line*. This innovative journal provides examples of genuinely practical initiatives that can help librarians deal with financial constraints. If you wish to access examples of applied economic strategies that will enable you to make your budgets go further and expand your collections *The Bottom Line* will ensure that you can meet ever-increasing service demands and keep to a tight budget - essential reading for anyone committed to their library as a respected resource serving contemporary information needs.

Notes for Contributors
Copyright. Articles submitted to the journal should be original contributions and should not be under consideration for any other publication at the same time. Authors submitting articles for publication warrant that the work is not an infringement of any existing copyright and will

indemnify the publisher against any breach of such warranty. For ease of dissemination and to ensure proper policing of use, papers and contributions become the legal copyright of the publisher unless otherwise agreed.

For details of Emerald's editorial policy on plagiarism please view the Plagiarism in depth information.

Submissions should be sent to: The Editor, Bradford Lee Eden, Ph.D., Associate University Librarian for Technical Services and Scholarly Communication, University of California, Santa Barbara, Santa Barbara, CA 93106-9010 USA; E-mail:**eden@library.ucsb.edu**

Editorial objectives. *The Bottom Line: Managing Library Finances* provides librarians, library trustees, and others concerned with library management, with current information related to the financial aspects of library operations. The journal focuses on cost measurement and containment, fundraising, development, fiscal policies and procedures, and the financial implications of technological change. The journal seeks to provide current, practical information that can be applied in all types of libraries.

The editor welcomes submissions which discuss budgeting, economic trends affecting libraries, endowments, leasing, outsourcing, insurance, grantsmanship, resource allocation, cost analysis, funding, technological innovation and alternative sources of revenue.

Authors should:
- prepare articles that are specific enough for readers to apply to their local situations;
- report on experiences or the results of research;
- include facts and pertinent examples;
- employ a simple, readable style, even when the subject matter is complex.

The reviewing process. Each paper submitted is reviewed by the editor for general suitability for publication and the decision whether or not to publish is made in consultation with members of the editorial board.

Emerald Literati Editing Service
The Literati Club can recommend the services of a number of freelance copy editors, all themselves experienced authors, to contributors who wish to improve the standard of English in their paper before submission. This is particularly useful for those whose first language is not English. **www.emeraldinsight.com/editingservice**

Article Features and Formats Required of Authors
There are a number of specific requirements with regard to article features and formats which authors should note carefully:
1. **Word length**. Articles should be between 1,000 and 3,000 words in length.

2. **Methodology**. In papers reporting upon surveys and case studies, methodology should be clearly described under a separate heading. Particularly for survey-based articles full details should be given, i.e. type and size of sample, data instruments used including, for mailed surveys, the final percentage response and the treatment of bias.

3. **Title**. A title, ideally, of not more than eight words in length should be provided.

4. **Autobiographical note**. A brief autobiographical note should be supplied including full name, appointment, name of organization and e-mail address.

5. **Word processing**. Please submit to the Editor three copies of the manuscript in double line spacing with wide margins.

6. **Headings and sub-headings**. These should be short and to-the-point, appearing approximately every 750 words. Headings should be typed in capitals and underlined; sub-headings should be typed in upper and lower case and underlined. Headings should not be numbered.

7. **References**. References to other publications should be complete and in Harvard style. They should contain full bibliographical details and journal titles should not be abbreviated. For multiple citations in the same year use a, b, c immediately following the year of publication. References should be shown within the text by giving the author's last name followed by a comma and year of publication all in round brackets, e.g. (Fox, 1994). At the end of the article should be a reference list in alphabetical order as follows:

For books
surname, initials and year of publication, title, publisher, place of publication, e.g. Casson, M. (1979), Alternatives to the Multinational Enterprise, Macmillan, London.

For chapter in edited book
surname, initials and year, "title", editor's surname, initials, title, publisher, place, pages, e.g. Bessley, M. and Wilson, P. (1984), "Public policy and small firms in Britain", in Levicki, C. (Ed.), Small Business Theory and Policy, Croom Helm, London, pp.111-26. Please note that the chapter title must be underlined.

For articles
surname, initials, year "title", journal, volume, number, pages, e.g. Fox, S.(1994) "Empowerment as a catalyst for change: an example from the food industry", Supply Chain Management, Vol 2 No 3, pp. 29-33

If there is more than one author list surnames followed by initials. All authors should be shown.

Electronic sources should include the URL of the electronic site at which they may be found, as follows:
Neuman, B.C.(1995), "Security, payment, and privacy for network commerce", IEEE Journal on Selected Areas in Communications, Vol. 13 No.8, October,pp.1523-31. Available (IEEE SEPTEMBER) http://www.research.att.com/jsac/

Notes/Endnotes should be used only if absolutely necessary. They should, however, always be used for citing Web sites. They should be identified in the text by consecutive numbers enclosed in square brackets and listed at the end of the article. Please then provide full Web site addresses in the end list.

8. **Figures, charts and diagrams** should be kept to a minimum. They should be provided both electronically and as good quality originals. They must be black and white with minimum shading and numbered consecutively using Arabic numerals.

Artwork should be either copied or pasted from the origination software into a blank Microsoft Word document, or saved and imported into a blank Microsoft Word document. Artwork created in MS Powerpoint is also acceptable. Artwork may be submitted in the following standard image formats: .eps - Postscript, .pdf - Adobe Acrobat portable document, .ai - Adobe Acrobat portable document, .wmf - Windows Metafile. If it is not possible to supply graphics in the formats listed above, authors should ensure that figures supplied as .tif, .gif, .jpeg, .bmp, .pcx, .pic, .pct are supplied as files of at least 300 dpi and at least 10cm wide.

In the text the position of a figure should be shown by typing on a separate line the words "take in Figure 2". Authors should supply succinct captions.

For photographic images good quality original photographs should be submitted. If submitted electronically they should be saved as tif files of at least 300dpi and at least 10cm wide. Their position in the text should be shown by typing on a separate line the words "take in Plate 2".

9. **Tables**. Use of tables should be kept to a minimum. Where essential, these should be typed on a separate sheet of paper and numbered consecutively and independently of any figures included in the article. Each table should have a number in roman numerals, a brief title, and vertical and horizontal headings. In the text, the position of the table should be shown by typing on a separate line the words "take in Table I". Tables should not repeat data available elsewhere in the paper.

10. **Photos, illustrations**. Half-tone illustrations should be restricted in number to the minimum necessary. Good glossy bromide prints should accompany the manuscripts but not be attached to manuscript pages. Illustrations unsuitable for reproduction, e.g. computer-screen capture will not be used. Any computer programs should be supplied as clear and sharp print-outs on plain paper. They will be reproduced photographically to avoid errors.

11. **Emphasis**. Words to be emphasized should be limited in number and italicized. Capital letters should be used only at the start of sentences or in the case of proper names.

12. **Abstracts**. Authors must supply a structured abstract set out under 4-6 sub-headings: Purpose; Methodology/Approach; Findings; Research limitations/implications (if applicable); Practical implications (if applicable); and, the Originality/value of paper. Maximum is 250 words in total. In addition provide up to six keywords which encapsulate the principal topics of the paper and categorise your paper under one of these classifications: Research paper, Viewpoint, Technical paper, Conceptual paper, Case study, Literature review or General review. For more information and guidance on structured abstracts visit: **www.emeraldinsight.com/structuredabstracts**

13. **Keywords**. Up to six keywords should be included which encapsulate the principal subjects covered by the article. Minor facets of an article should not be keyworded. These keywords will be used by readers to select the material they wish to read and should therefore be truly representative of the article's main content.

Brigham Young University Education and Law Journal

SUBMISSION PROCESS:

**Electronic Submission Preferred
via EMail**

lawed@lawgate.byu.edu

CONTACT INFORMATION:	REVIEW PROCESS:	
Kassie Campbell, Editor	**Type of Review:**	Editorial Review
Brigham Young University		
J. Reuben Clark Law School	**No. External Reviewers:**	0
4716 JRCB	**No. InHouse Reviewers:**	2
Provo, UT 84602-8000		
	Acceptance Rate:	
	Time to Review:	1 Month or Less
Phone:	**Reviewer's Comments:**	Yes
801-422-3671	**Invited Articles:**	0-5%
Email:		
lawed@lawgate.byu.edu	**Fees to Publish:**	$0.00 US$
Website:	**Fees to Review:**	$0.00 US$

PUBLICATION GUIDELINES:	CIRCULATION DATA:
Manuscript Style:	**Reader:**
USC - Harvard Blue Book	Academics
Manuscript Length:	**Frequency of Issue:**
26-30	2 Times/Year
Copies Required:	**Sponsor/Publisher:**
Two	

MANUSCRIPT TOPICS:
School Law

MANUSCRIPT GUIDELINES/COMMENTS:

As is often the case with law reviews, the editor and editorial board are for the most part, law students. The editor-in-chief serves for one year. The faculty advisor is a more constant conduit of information year to year. Permanent Faculty Advisor: Scott Ferrin, J.D., Ed.D., 310-D MCKB, Brigham Young University, Provo, UT 84602-5002; 801-422-4804, fax 801-422-7740; email: **ferrin@byu.edu**

The *Brigham Young University Education and Law Journal* is a unique publication in that both the J. Reuben Clark Law School and the BYU Department of Educational Leadership work jointly towards its publication. The *Journal* is published twice yearly in April and in January of each academic year. This collaboration is vital to the *Journal*'s mission, which is to discuss issues concerning education and the Law. These discussions range from issues affecting formative education, beginning with kindergarten, to those affecting higher education institutions. The *Journal* addresses controversial issues, examining the problems from both an educational and a Legal standpoint, and will help you remain in touch.

Submission Guidelines

We use *The Blue Book: A Uniform System of Citation.* We consider the following things crucial for publication and would ask all contributors to review their submissions for the following:

- The paper must have a clear thesis statement on an educational issue.
- The topic sentence of every paragraph must relate back to the thesis statement.
- The conclusion must appropriately summarize the arguments of the paper and not add any new information.
- The paper must be written on a timely and current issue in the world of education and law.

All articles for the Fall edition of the *Journal* need to be submitted to the Solicitations Editor of the *Journal* no later than August 1, of each year (The submission deadline for the Spring Edition of the *Journal* is set for November 15, of each year) They will be reviewed by the Solicitations Editor initially for appropriateness of topic, duplication of articles, and consistency with theme and values of the *Journal*. Articles are then passed on the by the Solicitations Editor to the Editor-In-Chief who, with the help advise and counsel of the Management Committee, has the final decision as to publish-ability.

Each article is reviewed in a timely manner as they come in to the *Journal* staff. Authors of articles will be contacted by a member of the Committee upon receipt of the piece and a time frame for review will be set up with the author at that time, according to the necessities of the *Journal* as well as those of the author. All selections for the *Journal* will be made on a space-available basis. It is anticipated by the *Journal* staff that 5-6 professionals written works will be accepted in each edition, with an additional 4-5 student-written pieces accepted. Articles received and reviewed by the Committee early on in the solicitations period will have a better chance of publication, simply due to the rolling admission policy of the *Journal*.

All articles submitted for consideration must meet the following requirements:

- One hard copy of the article
- One computer diskette of the article, saved in WordPerfect 6.0 or MSWord 95 higher format

OR

- Electronic copy of the article submitted to the Solicitations Editor via e-mail at **lawed@lawgate.byu.edu**
- Articles should be approximately 20-40 pages in length
- Double spaced
- Articles may be submitted by faculty, students, educators or other professionals with an interest in educational legal issues so Long as the writing is of publishable quality.

All articles published by the *Journal* will require a signed agreement by the author and the Solicitations Editor of the *Journal* waiving compensation and the right to publish the paper in any other form. All rights to the article will remain the property of the author. Also in the agreement the author will have to agree to allow Lexis-Nexis, WestLaw and other electronic services to publish the article as per the *Journal*'s agreement with such services.

Please submit all articles to: BYU Education and Law Journal, J. Reuben Clark Law School 4716 JRCB, Provo, Utah 84602-8000

British Educational Research Journal

SUBMISSION PROCESS:
Electronic Submission Only **via EMail** **berj@mmu.ac.uk**

CONTACT INFORMATION:	REVIEW PROCESS:
The Editors Manchester Metropolitan University Institute of Education 799 Wilmslow Road Manchester, M20 2RR UK **Phone:** +44 161 247 2318 **Email:** berj@mmu.ac.uk **Website:** www.tandf.co.uk/journals/titles/01411926	**Type of Review:** Blind Review **No. External Reviewers:** 2-3 **No. InHouse Reviewers:** 1 **Acceptance Rate:** 11-20% **Time to Review:** 1 - 2 Months **Reviewer's Comments:** Yes **Invited Articles:** 0-5% **Fees to Publish:** $0.00 US$ **Fees to Review:** $0.00 US$

PUBLICATION GUIDELINES:	CIRCULATION DATA:
Manuscript Style: See Manuscript Guidelines **Manuscript Length:** 21-30 **Copies Required:** Three	**Reader:** Academics **Frequency of Issue:** 6 Times/Year **Sponsor/Publisher:** Carfax Publishing, Taylor and Francis, Ltd.

MANUSCRIPT TOPICS:

Curriculum Studies; Education Management / Administration; Education Policy; Educational Psychology; Educational Research; Educational Technology Systems; Elementary / Early Childhood; Gender / Education; Gifted Children; Health & Physical Education; Higher Education; Interdisciplinary; Languages & Linguistics; Literacy Education; Reading; Religious Education; Rural Education & Small Schools; Science Math & Environment; Secondary / Adolescent Studies; Special Education; Teacher Education; Tests, Measurement & Evaluation

MANUSCRIPT GUIDELINES/COMMENTS:

Aims and Scope

The *British Educational Research Journal* is an international medium for the publication of articles of interest to researchers in education and has rapidly become a major focal point for the publication of educational research from throughout the world.

For further information on the association please connect directly to the British Educational Research Association web site: **www.bera.ac.uk**

The journal is interdisciplinary in approach, and includes reports of experiments and surveys, discussions of conceptual and methodological issues and of underlying assumptions in educational research, accounts of research in progress, and book reviews. The journal is the major publication of the British Educational Research Association, an organisation which aims to promote interest in education and to disseminate findings and discussions of educational research.

Notes for Contributors

Note to Authors. Please make sure your contact address information is clearly visible on the **outside** of all packages you are sending to Editors. Papers accepted become the copyright of the British Educational Research Association, unless otherwise specifically agreed.

Manuscripts should be sent to The Editors, BERJ, Institute of Education, Manchester Metropolitan University, 799 Wilmslow Road, Manchester M20 2RR UK. Email: **berj@mmu.ac.uk**. Articles should normally be between 5000 and 7000 words and can only be considered if three complete copies of each manuscript are submitted along with an electronic disk. Drafts of papers which can be accessed on individual/personal websites will be regarded as unpublished. However 'working papers' or 'formal reports' on institutional or quasi-institutional websites which are specifically designed to publicise findings and act as dissemination vehicles will be regarded as 'previously published'. Authors should ensure that papers submitted to the journal are substantially different from such working papers and reports, summarising and referring to them as appropriate, but not repeating them verbatim.

Manuscripts should be typed on one side of the paper, double spaced, with ample margins, and bear the title of the contribution, name(s) of the author(s) and the address where the work was carried out. Each article should be accompanied by an abstract of 100-150 words on a separate sheet. Abstracts should be accurate summaries including the rationale for the article, methods employed (if relevant in empirical reports) and conclusions drawn. The full postal and email address of the author who will check proofs and receive correspondence and offprints should also be included. All pages should be numbered. Footnotes to the text should be avoided. Sponsorship of the research reported (e.g. by research councils, government departments and agencies, etc.) should be declared.

Non-discriminatory writing. Please ensure that writing is free from bias, for instance by substituting 'he' or 'his' by 'he or she' or 's/he' or 'his/her' and by using non-racist language. Authors might wish to note the BERA Ethical Guidelines for Educational Research.

Contributors will normally receive a decision on their article within **12** weeks of its receipt by the Editor. Rejected manuscripts will not normally be returned to contributors unless sufficient stamps/international postal coupons have been sent.

To download a Word template for this journal, please visit our website at: **http://www.tandf.co.uk/ journals/authors/edstylea.dot**

For further information on electronic submission, including information on accepted file types, please visit our website at: **http://www.tandf.co.uk/journals/authors/electronic_edu.asp**.

Tables and captions to illustrations. Tables must be typed out on separate sheets and not included as part of the text. The captions to illustrations should be gathered together and also typed out on a separate sheet. Tables and figures should be numbered by Arabic numerals. The approximate position of tables and figures should be indicated in the manuscript. Captions should include keys to symbols.

Figures. Please supply one set of artwork in a finished form, suitable for reproduction. Figures will not normally be redrawn by the publisher.

References should be indicated in the typescript by giving the author's name, with the year of publication in parentheses. If several papers by the same author and from the same year are cited, a, b, c, etc. should be put after the year of publication. The references should be listed in full at the end of the paper in the following standard form:

Journal
Smyth, J. & Hattam, R. (2002) Early school leaving and the cultural geography of high schools, *British Educational Research Journal*, 28(3), 375–398.

Book
Whitty, G.(2002) *Making sense of education policy: studies in the sociology and politics of education* (London,Paul Chapman).

Chapters in a book
Zukas, M. & Malcolm, J. (2002) Pedagogies for lifelong learning: building bridges or building walls?, in: R.Harrison, F. Reeve, A. Hanson & J. Clarke (Eds) Supporting *lifelong learning. Vol. One: Perspectives on learning* (London, Routledge).

For online documents
Standler, R. (2000) *Plagiarism in colleges in the USA*. Available online at: www.rbs2.com/plag.htm (accessed 6 August 2004).

Titles of journals should **not** be abbreviated.

Proofs will be sent to authors if there is sufficient time to do so. They should be corrected and returned to the Editor within three days. Major alterations to the text cannot be accepted.

Early Electronic Offprints. Corresponding authors can now receive their article by email as a complete PDF. This allows the author to print up to 50 copies, free of charge, and disseminate them to colleagues. In many cases this facility will be available up to two weeks prior to publication. Or, alternatively, corresponding authors will receive the traditional 50 offprints. A copy of the journal will be sent by post to all corresponding authors after publication. Additional copies of the journal can be purchased at the authors' preferential rate of £15.00/$25.00 per copy.

Copyright. It is a condition of publication that authors vest copyright in their articles, including abstracts, in the British Educational Research Association. This enables us to ensure full copyright protection and to disseminate the article, and the journal, to the widest possible readership in print and electronic formats as appropriate. Authors may, of course, use the article elsewhere **after** publication without prior permission from Carfax Publishing, Taylor & Francis Limited is notified so that our records show that its use is properly authorized. Authors are themselves responsible for obtaining permission to reproduce copyright material from other sources.

Notes for Referees
Referees are asked to bear the following in mind when assessing papers for inclusion.

We want *BERJ* to represent the best of educational research and so it is important that referees are rigorous and demanding, taking into account the status of the journal as a premier international publication.

Articles are welcomed on all kinds and aspects of educational research, and addressing any form of education, formal or informal.

It is the policy of the journal that articles should offer original insight in terms of theory, methodology, or interpretation, arid not be restricted to the mere reporting of results. Submitted work should be substantially original, recent in reference, and unpublished.

It is important that referees pay particular attention to the appropriateness, accuracy, consistency and accessibility of tabular data, arid the specified referencing protocols.

We welcome original ways of presenting research findings, and support accessible, well written accounts.

It is important that referees are decisive in their judgments of submissions.

In writing up their comments on articles submitted to the journal, referees are asked, in a minimum of 250 words, or so, to address whatever is relevant in the following:

- offer a brief critical resume of theoretical, methodological, or substantive issues raised by the author;
- assess how adequately the research is located in terms of previous relevant research;
- make a reasoned appraisal of the overall quality of the submission in terms of its excellence, contribution to knowledge, or originality;
- provide feedback useful to the author (a) for resubmission (b) more generally in terms of the further development of the research. It is helpful in the resubmission process if specific numbered points are made by referees and addressed by authors;
- indicate where appropriate any limitations on their ability to comment.

We also expect referees to be able to report on submissions within a three week period. It is important that these deadlines are respected. Articles published in *BERJ* include information, on. 'date received' / 'date resubmitted' / 'date finally accepted' and we do not wish to exhibit unprofessional delays between receipt and acceptance/resubmission/rejection.

British Journal of Educational Psychology

SUBMISSION PROCESS:
Electronic Submission Only via Online Portal **http://bjep.edmgr.com**

CONTACT INFORMATION:	REVIEW PROCESS:
Andrew Tolmie, Editor British Psychological Society Journals Department St. Andrews House 48 Princess Road East Leicester, LE1 7DR UK **Phone:** +44 116 254 9568 **Email:** bjep@bpsjournals.co.uk **Website:** www.bpsjournals.co.uk/bjep	**Type of Review:** Blind Review **No. External Reviewers:** 2 **No. InHouse Reviewers:** 0 **Acceptance Rate:** 11-20% **Time to Review:** 2 - 3 Months **Reviewer's Comments:** Yes **Invited Articles:** 0-5% **Fees to Publish:** $0.00 US$ **Fees to Review:** $0.00 US$

PUBLICATION GUIDELINES:	CIRCULATION DATA:
Manuscript Style: American Psychological Association See Manuscript Guidelines **Manuscript Length:** 26-30 **Copies Required:** Electronic Only	**Reader:** Academics **Frequency of Issue:** Quarterly **Sponsor/Publisher:** British Psychological Society

MANUSCRIPT TOPICS:
Educational Psychology

MANUSCRIPT GUIDELINES/COMMENTS:

The *British Journal of Educational Psychology* seeks to publish psychological research that makes a significant contribution to the understanding and practice of education. The aims are to give access to research to a broad, international readership including researchers, practitioners and students in education. Empirical, theoretical and methodological papers are welcomed, including action research, case studies, critical reviews of the literature, experimental studies and surveys. Important criteria in the selection process are quality of argument and execution, clarity in presentation and educational significance.

1. Circulation
The circulation of the *Journal* is worldwide. Papers are invited and encouraged from authors throughout the world.

2. Length
Papers should normally be no more than 5,000 words, although the Editor retains discretion to publish papers beyond this length in cases where the clear and concise expression of the scientific content requires greater length.

3. Reviewing
The journal operates a policy of anonymous peer review. Papers will normally be scrutinised and commented on by at least two independent expert referees (in addition to the Editor) although the Editor may process a paper at his or her discretion. The referees will not be aware of the identity of the author. All information about authorship including personal acknowledgements and institutional affiliations should be confined to the title page (and the text should be free of such clues as identifiable self-citations e.g. 'In our earlier work...').

4. Online submission process
1.   All manuscripts must be submitted online at **http://bjep.edmgr.com**.
2.   Follow the step-by-step instructions to submit your manuscript.

Authors can log on at any time to check the status of the manuscript.

5. Manuscript requirements
*   Contributions must be typed in double spacing with wide margins. All sheets must be numbered.
*   Tables should be typed in double spacing, each on a separate page with a self-explanatory title. Tables should be comprehensible without reference to the text. They should be placed at the end of the manuscript with their approximate locations indicated in the text.
*   Figures can be included at the end of the document or attached as separate files, carefully labelled in initial capital/lower case lettering with symbols in a form consistent with text use. Unnecessary background patterns, lines and shading should be avoided. Captions should be listed on a separate page. The resolution of digital images must be at least 300 dpi.
*   All articles should be preceded by a Structured Abstract of not more than 250 words using six required headings: Background, Aims, Sample(s), Methods, Results and Conclusions, with Comment as optional. These headings may need some adaptation in the case of theoretical papers and reviews.
*   For reference citations, please use APA style. Particular care should be taken to ensure that references are accurate and complete. Give all journal titles in full.
*   SI units must be used for all measurements, rounded off to practical values if appropriate, with the Imperial equivalent in parentheses.
*   In normal circumstances, effect size should be incorporated.
*   Authors are requested to avoid the use of sexist language.
*   Authors are responsible for acquiring written permission to publish lengthy quotations, illustrations etc for which they do not own copyright.

For Guidelines on editorial style, please consult the *APA Publication Manual* published by the American Psychological Association, Washington DC, USA (http://www.apastyle.org).

6. Supplementary data
Supplementary data too extensive for publication may be deposited with the British Library Document Supply Centre. Such material includes numerical data, computer programs, fuller details of case studies and experimental techniques. The material should be submitted to the Editor together with the article, for simultaneous refereeing.

7. Post acceptance
PDF page proofs are sent to authors via email for correction of print but not for rewriting or the introduction of new material. Authors will be provided with a PDF file of their article prior to publication for easy and cost-effective dissemination to colleagues.

8. Copyright

To protect authors and journals against unauthorised reproduction of articles, The British Psychological Society requires copyright to be assigned to itself as publisher, on the express condition that authors may use their own material at any time without permission. On acceptance of a paper submitted to a journal, authors will be requested to sign an appropriate assignment of copyright form.

9. Checklist of requirements

- Abstract (100-200 words)
- Title page (include title, authors' names, affiliations, full contact details)
- Full article text (double-spaced with numbered pages and anonymised)
- References (APA style). Authors are responsible for bibliographic accuracy and must check every reference in the manuscript and proofread again in the page proofs.
- Tables, figures, captions placed at the end of the article or attached as separate files.

British Journal of Sociology of Education

SUBMISSION PROCESS:
Postal Submission Only

CONTACT INFORMATION:	REVIEW PROCESS:	
Len Barton, Editor	**Type of Review:**	Blind Review
c/o Helen Oliver		
University of Sheffield	**No. External Reviewers:**	0
School of Education	**No. InHouse Reviewers:**	2
388 Glossop Road		
Sheffield, S10 2JA UK	**Acceptance Rate:**	50%
	Time to Review:	1 - 2 Months
Phone:	**Reviewer's Comments:**	Yes
0114 222 8090	**Invited Articles:**	0-5%
Email:	**Fees to Publish:**	$0.00 US$
h.j.oliver@sheffield.ac.uk	**Fees to Review:**	$0.00 US$
Website:		
http://www.tandf.co.uk/journals/journal.asp?issn=0142-5692&link type=5		

PUBLICATION GUIDELINES:	CIRCULATION DATA:
Manuscript Style:	**Reader:**
See Manuscript Guidelines	Academics, Administrators, Practicing Teachers, Counselors
Manuscript Length:	**Frequency of Issue:**
26-30	6 Times/Year
Copies Required:	**Sponsor/Publisher:**
Three	Routledge, Taylor & Francis, Ltd.

MANUSCRIPT TOPICS:
Education Management / Administration; Higher Education; Teacher Education

MANUSCRIPT GUIDELINES/COMMENTS:

Aims & Scope
British Journal of Sociology of Education publishes academic articles from throughout the world which contribute to both theory and empirical research in the sociology of education. The journal attempts to reflect the variety of perspectives current in the field. In order to ensure that all articles are of the highest quality, all contributions are submitted to at least two referees before acceptance for publication. Apart from the main articles each issue will normally contain a review essay, an extended review and a review symposium on a major book or collection of books.

Instructions for Authors
Note to Authors. Please make sure your contact address information is clearly visible on the outside of all packages you are sending to Editors.

Papers accepted become the copyright of the *Journal*, unless otherwise specifically agreed.

112

Contributors should bear in mind that they are addressing an international audience.

Manuscripts that do not conform to the requirements listed below will not be considered for publication or returned to their authors.

Manuscripts, between 3000 and 7000 words **maximum** (including the bibliography), should be sent to Mrs. Helen Oliver, British Journal of Sociology of Education, School of Education, University of Sheffield, 388 Glossop Road, Sheffield S10 2JA, UK. Articles can only be considered if **three complete copies of each manuscript** are submitted. They should be typed on one side of the paper, double spaced, with ample margins, and bear the title of the contribution, name(s) of the author(s) and the address where the work was carried out. Each article should be accompanied by a summary of 100-150 words on a separate sheet, and a short note of biographical details. The full postal address, telephone, fax and email numbers (where possible) of the author who will check proofs and receive correspondence and offprints should also be included. All pages should be numbered.

Footnotes to the text should be avoided wherever this is reasonably possible.

Tables and captions to illustrations. Tables must be typed out on separate sheets and not included as part of the text. The captions to illustrations should be gathered together and also typed out on a separate sheet. Tables should be numbered by Roman numerals, and figures by Arabic numerals. The approximate position of tables and figures should be indicated in the manuscript. Captions should include keys to symbols.

Figures. Please supply one set of artwork in a finished form, suitable for reproduction. If this is not possible, figures can be redrawn by the publisher.

References should be indicated in the typescript by giving the author's name, with the year of publication in parentheses. If several papers by the same author and from the same year are cited, a, b, c, etc. should be put after the year of publication. The references should be listed in full at the end of the paper in the following standard form:

For books
Scott, P. (1984) *The crisis of the university* (London, Croom Helm).

For articles
Cremin, L. A. (1983) The problematics of education in the 1980s: some reflections on the Oxford Workshop, *Oxford Review of Education*, 9, 33-40.

For chapters within books
Willis, P. (1983) Cultural production and theories of reproduction, in: L. Barton & S. Walker (Eds) *Race, class and education* (London, Croom Helm).

Titles of journals should not be abbreviated.

Proofs will be sent to authors if there is sufficient time to do so. They should be corrected and returned to the Editor within three days. Major alterations to the text cannot be accepted.

Early Electronic Offprints. Corresponding authors can now receive their article by e-mail as a complete PDF. This allows the author to print up to 50 copies, free of charge, and disseminate them to colleagues. In many cases this facility will be available up to two weeks prior to publication. Or, alternatively, corresponding authors will receive the traditional 50 offprints. A copy of the journal will be sent by post to all corresponding authors after publication. Additional copies of the journal can be purchased at the author's preferential rate of £15.00/$25.00 per copy.

Copyright. It is a condition of publication that authors assign copyright or licence the publication rights in their articles, including abstracts, to Taylor & Francis. This enables us to ensure full copyright protection and to disseminate the article, and of course the *Journal*, to the widest possible readership in print and electronic formats as appropriate. Authors may, of course, use the article elsewhere after publication without prior permission from Taylor & Francis, provided that acknowledgement is given to the Journal as the original source of publication, and that Taylor & Francis is notified so that our records show that its use is properly authorised. Authors retain a number of other rights under the Taylor & Francis rights policies documents. These policies are referred to at **www.tandf.co.uk/journals/author rights.pdf** for full details. Authors are themselves responsible for obtaining permission to reproduce copyright material from other sources.

Processing your article electronically
We strongly encourage you to send the final, revised version of your article electronically, by email. This will ensure that it can be dealt with quickly and will reduce errors at the typesetting stage. This guide sets out the procedures which will allow us to process your article efficiently.

Please note: This guide does not apply to authors who are submitting an article for consideration and peer review; they apply only to authors whose articles have been reviewed, revised, and accepted for publication.

You should save the files as Word documents, although figures can also be supplied as eps, tif, pdf, or word files (see below).

Tables and figures should be saved as separate files, and a separate list of figure captions should also be provided. Give the files clear names such as Smith_text.doc, Smith_tables.doc, Smith_figures.doc, Smith_figurecaptions.doc.

The approximate position of tables and figures should be indicated in the text file, and they must be mentioned in the text.

Ensure that the files are not saved as read only.

Please see the journal Instructions for Authors page for a Word template to help you style your article correctly. Please pay particular attention to the references. Please also supply the running heads for your article in the style of the journal (this will usually be the authors' initials and surname plus a short title).

Please make sure that the full postal and email address of the author who will check proofs and receive correspondence and offprints is clearly marked.

Guidance on supplying figures
Avoid the use of colour and tints. Line figures will normally be reproduced in black and white. Subtle variations in grey tones which are distinguishable on screen may not be distinct when printed, and should be avoided. Strong contrasts such as black/white and cross-hatched patterns give a better printed result.

Figures should be produced as near to the finished size as possible. If the figure is to be reduced to fit the final printed page, allow for this reduction when selecting lettering size and line weight.

Half-tones, scans, photographs and transparencies should be saved at a minimum of 1200 dpi. They will not normally be reproduced in colour unless first agreed by the journal editor. In some cases it may be possible to present figures in black and white in the printed journal, but in colour in the online journal, if the originals are suitable.

All figures must be numbered in the order in which they occur (e.g. Figure 1, Figure 2 etc.). In multi-part figures, each part should be labelled (e.g. Figure 1 (a), Figure 1 (b) etc.).The figure captions must be saved as a separate file with the text and numbered correspondingly.

Files should be saved as TIFF (tagged image file format), PostScript or EPS (encapsulated PostScript), containing all the necessary font information and the source file of the application (e.g., CorelDraw/Mac, CorelDraw/PC).

Career Development for Exceptional Individuals

SUBMISSION PROCESS:

Electronic Submission Only
via Online Portal

http://mc.manuscriptcentral.com/cdei

CONTACT INFORMATION:	REVIEW PROCESS:

CONTACT INFORMATION:

David W. Test & Bob Algozzine, Co-Eds.
University of North Carolina - Charlotte
Special Education Program
9201 University City Blvd.
Charlotte, NC 28223 USA

Moira Konrad, Managing Editor
The Ohio State University

Phone:
  704-687-8853

Email:
  dwtest@email.uncc.edu
  rfalgozz@email.uncc.edu
  konrad.14@osu.edu

Website:
  http://www.dcdt.org/publications/

REVIEW PROCESS:

Type of Review:	Blind Review
No. External Reviewers:	3
No. InHouse Reviewers:	1
Acceptance Rate:	36%
Time to Review:	1 - 2 Months
Reviewer's Comments:	Yes
Invited Articles:	21-30%
Fees to Publish:	$0.00 US$
Fees to Review:	$0.00 US$

PUBLICATION GUIDELINES:

Manuscript Style:
  American Psychological Association

Manuscript Length:
  16-20

Copies Required:
  Electronic Only

CIRCULATION DATA:

Reader:
  Academics

Frequency of Issue:
  3 Times/Year

Sponsor/Publisher:
  Council for Exceptional Children's Division on Career Development and Transition / Pro-Ed

MANUSCRIPT TOPICS:
Adult Career & Vocational; Secondary / Adolescent Studies; Special Education

MANUSCRIPT GUIDELINES/COMMENTS:

Career Development for Exceptional Individuals (*CDEI*) is the official journal of the Division on Career Development and Transition (DCDT) of The Council for Exceptional Children (CEC). The journal is published three times each year and specializes in the fields of secondary education, transition, and career development of persons with documented disabilities and/or special needs. Articles published in *CDEI* include original quantitative and qualitative research, scholarly reviews, and program descriptions and evaluations.

Manuscripts submitted for publication to *CDEI* should be prepared according to the *Publication Manual of the American Psychological Association*: Fifth Edition (2001). All manuscripts should be written as clearly and simply as possible, have a 75 to 120 word abstract, and have a narrative between 15 and 20 pages of typed, doubled spaced text in 12-point font, excluding references, figures, and tables. Authors should use nonsexist language and person first terminology (e.g., adolescents with disabilities instead of disabled adolescents). CDEI prefers that manuscripts be written in the active voice, which usually can be achieved by writing in first person (e.g., We selected participants . . .). When submitting a manuscript describing a research or evaluation study, authors should ensure that (a) the research or evaluation method is connected closely to the question(s) being addressed; and (b) the setting, participants, and procedures are described in sufficient detail to allow for possible replication. All manuscripts should include recommendations for secondary education and transition practice that could be applied at the system, program, or individual level.

Manuscripts submitted to *CDEI* should be accompanied by a letter from the principal author that includes the names, degrees, titles, and affiliations of all authors, and contact information for the principal author (telephone, email, and mailing address).

Additional information may be obtained on the following websites:
http://www.dcdt.org/publications/
http://www.proedinc.com (click on "Journals")
http://mc.manuscriptcentral.com/cdei

Career Development Quarterly

SUBMISSION PROCESS:

**Electronic Submission Only
via EMail**

cdq@ncda.org

CONTACT INFORMATION:	REVIEW PROCESS:	
Mark Pope, Editor University of Missouri - Saint Louis 415 Marillac Hall One University Boulevard Saint Louis, MO 63121-4400 USA	**Type of Review:**	Blind Review
	No. External Reviewers:	3
	No. InHouse Reviewers:	0
	Acceptance Rate:	21-30%
Phone: 314-516-7121	**Time to Review:**	2 - 3 Months
	Reviewer's Comments:	Yes
	Invited Articles:	0-5%
Email: cdq@ncda.org	**Fees to Publish:**	$0.00 US$
Website: www.ncda.org	**Fees to Review:**	$0.00 US$

PUBLICATION GUIDELINES:	CIRCULATION DATA:
Manuscript Style: American Psychological Association	**Reader:** Counselors
Manuscript Length: 11-15	**Frequency of Issue:** Quarterly
Copies Required: Three	**Sponsor/Publisher:** National Career Development Association

MANUSCRIPT TOPICS:
Adult Career & Vocational; Counseling & Personnel Services; Higher Education; Secondary / Adolescent Studies; Tests, Measurement & Evaluation

MANUSCRIPT GUIDELINES/COMMENTS:

Topics Also Include. All topics as related to Career Counseling; Individual and Organizational Career Development; Work and Leisure; Career Education; Career Coaching; Career Management

Information for Authors
The *Career Development Quarterly* (*CDQ*) invites articles regarding career counseling, individual and organizational career development, work and leisure, career education, career coaching, and career management. Methodologies can include but are not limited to literature reviews that make research accessible to practitioners, case studies, history and public policy analyses, qualitative research, and quantitative research that is of specific relevance to the practice of career development. Each article should include implications for practice because *CDQ* is concerned with fostering career development through the design and use of career interventions.

Regular manuscripts must be double-spaced throughout (including references) and must not exceed 26,700 characters (including spaces), 3,750 words, or 15 pages. Occasionally, a longer manuscript may be considered. Provide, but do not count, a cover page with each author's name, position, and place of employment, and a clear abstract of essential information of up to 100 words. Authors should not place their names or other identifying information on the manuscript itself, as all manuscripts are peer-reviewed with a blind reviewing system. Manuscripts should be submitted electronically via email as an attachment to **cdq@ncda.org**. Manuscripts will be acknowledged by email when they are received.

Reports of demonstrably effective career counseling methods or programs are featured in the section "Effective Techniques." Articles in this section describe theoretically based techniques that advance career development for people of all ages. Qualitative or quantitative data providing evidence of the techniques' effectiveness will be included in these articles. Manuscripts submitted to the "Effective Techniques" section should be double-spaced throughout (including references) and should not exceed 21,360 characters (including spaces), 3,000 words, or 12 pages. Such articles should contain (a) a brief review of the literature related to the theoretically based intervention, (b) a clear description of the intervention, (c) a brief report of data supporting the techniques' effectiveness, and (d) a summary.

The "Personal Perspectives" section contains analyses of personal career development experiences and short editorials about critical issues in research or practice. Articles prepared for this section should be double-spaced throughout (including references) and should not exceed 12,460 characters (including spaces), 1,750 words, or 7 pages.

Responses to previously published articles appear in the "Reader Reactions" section. These responses should be double-spaced throughout (including references) and should not exceed 8,900 characters (including spaces), 1,250 words, or 5 pages.

"Brief Reports" manuscripts should be double-spaced throughout (including references) and should not exceed 8,900 characters (including spaces), 1,250 words, or 5 pages (excluding title page, an abstract of no more than 80 words, references, and no more than one table or figure) and should contain a clear and concise summary of the study (including rationale, objectives, design, instruments, sample, analyses, results, and implications for research and practice).

Manuscripts must be prepared carefully, such that ideas flow coherently and writing is clear and concise. Avoid jargon, acronyms, and sexist terminology. Headings and subheadings should be used to structure the content. Article titles and headings in the articles should be as short as possible. Use tables sparingly, include only essential data, and combine tables wherever possible. Authors should submit no more than three tables or two figures with each manuscript. The *Publication Manual of the American Psychological Association* (5th edition) serves as the style manual for *CDQ*. Authors are encouraged to reduce bias in language against persons on the basis of gender, sexual orientation, racial or ethnic group, disability, or age by referring to the guidelines in the fifth edition of the APA manual. Authors must address the clinical significance of their results using effect size indicators, narrative analyses, or both.

Authors who use lengthy quotations or adapt tables and figures from another source must secure written permission to do so from the copyrighted source. Manuscripts that include copyrighted material will not be accepted for publication in *CDQ* until the author provides the editor with written permission from the copyright holder.

Submit all manuscripts electronically through email to Dr. Mark Pope, Editor, Career Development Quarterly at **cdq@ncda.org**. If you do not have access to electronic mail services, please send an original and three photocopies of the manuscript to Dr. Mark Pope, Editor, Career Development Quarterly, Division of Counseling & Family Therapy, College of Education, University of Missouri - Saint Louis, 415 Marillac Hall, One University Boulevard, Saint Louis, Missouri 63121-4400, USA, voice 1.314.516.7121. Be sure to include your e-mail address on the title page of the manuscript. Never submit material that is under consideration by another journal or that has been previously published. About 10 weeks will elapse between acknowledgment of the manuscript's receipt and notification of its disposition. After the final acceptance of an article, authors should expect minor editing for style consistency. Authors of manuscripts accepted for publication will be asked to provide the final article electronically via email, specifying word processing software that was used to prepare the manuscript (MS Word is preferred). After an article's publication, all authors of articles and senior contributors to sections will receive a complimentary copy of *CDQ* from ACA Publications.

Catalyst, The

SUBMISSION PROCESS:

Electronic Submission Preferred
via EMail

nccet@earthlink.net

CONTACT INFORMATION:	REVIEW PROCESS:	
William J. Flynn, Editor National Council for Continuing 　Education & Training PO Box 820062 Portland, OR 97282-1062 USA	**Type of Review:**	Editorial Review
	No. External Reviewers:	0-2
	No. InHouse Reviewers:	2
	Acceptance Rate:	60%
Phone: 　503-233-1842	**Time to Review:**	1 - 2 Months
	Reviewer's Comments:	No
	Invited Articles:	31-50%
Email: 　nccet@earthlink.net	**Fees to Publish:**	$0.00 US$
	Fees to Review:	$0.00 US$
Website: 　www.nccet.org		

PUBLICATION GUIDELINES:	CIRCULATION DATA:
Manuscript Style: 　American Psychological Association	**Reader:** 　Administrators
Manuscript Length: 　11-15	**Frequency of Issue:** 　3 Times/Year
Copies Required: 　Two	**Sponsor/Publisher:** 　Ellen Long

MANUSCRIPT TOPICS:
Adult Career & Vocational; Education Management / Administration; Higher Education

MANUSCRIPT GUIDELINES/COMMENTS:

Manuscript Submission Guidelines
To be considered for publication in *The Catalyst*, your manuscript should follow these guidelines:

Manuscripts should be typed on white bond, 8.5 x 11.0 inches. Submit one original and two copies.

Use DOUBLE SPACE throughout, including indented quotations, footnotes, and bibliography.

Manuscripts may be submitted on 3.5 inch double sided disk (whether high density or double density). Acceptable operating systems are DOS, Windows or Macintosh. Please use an industry standard word processing application (i.e., WordPerfect, Word for Windows, etc.). In addition to the manuscript in application format, please include on the disk a copy of the document in ASCII format. Also include a hard copy of the article with your submission. E-mail submissions are acceptable.

Types of submissions:

- Length of feature articles should be 1,500 to 2,500 words.
- Catalyst Exchange articles (shorter pieces which share information on successful, innovative practices in the profession) may be from 500 to 1,000 words in length.
- Opinion pieces or editorial submissions should not exceed 500 words.

Footnotes and bibliographical entries should follow *The Publication Manual of the American Psychological Association*, 4th ed.

Manuscript topics should be related to the fields of Community Services, Continuing Education, Workforce Training, Lifelong Learning or Economic Development.

Authors should include the following information: author's name, title, institution, address, telephone and/or fax number, email address.

Please identify if the submission has been previously published or if it is being considered for publication.

Manuscripts submitted are subject to editing. Wherever possible the author will be consulted during the editing process.

If you wish your manuscript or disk returned, please enclose a stamped, self-addressed envelope at the time of submission.

No material, other than questions and routine correspondence, may be submitted by fax.

Please submit all materials to: William J. Flynn, Editor, PO Box 820062 Portland, Oregon 97282-1062; **nccet@earthlink.net**; (503) 233-1842; FAX (503) 232-1073

Change: The Magazine of Higher Learning

SUBMISSION PROCESS:
Electronic Submission Only **via EMail** **ch@heldref.org**

CONTACT INFORMATION:	REVIEW PROCESS:	
Cheryl Fields, Managing Editor Heldref Publications, Inc. 1319 Eighteenth St., NW Washington, DC 20036 USA	**Type of Review:**	Editorial Review
	No. External Reviewers:	3+
	No. InHouse Reviewers:	2
Phone: 202-296-6267 ext. 1248	**Acceptance Rate:**	6-10%
	Time to Review:	2 - 3 Months
	Reviewer's Comments:	Yes
Email: ch@heldref.org	**Invited Articles:**	50% +
Website: www.heldref.org	**Fees to Publish:**	$0.00 US$
	Fees to Review:	$0.00 US$

PUBLICATION GUIDELINES:	CIRCULATION DATA:
Manuscript Style: Associated Press Stylebook and Washington Post	**Reader:** Academics, Administrators, Academic Libraries
Manuscript Length: 16-20	**Frequency of Issue:** Bi-Monthly
Copies Required: Three	**Sponsor/Publisher:** American Association For Higher Education / Heldref Publications, Inc.

MANUSCRIPT TOPICS:

College Costs; Curriculum Studies; Education Management / Administration; Educational Technology Systems; Higher Education; Library Science / Information Resources; Policy; Teaching & Learning; Technological Developments on Campuses; Urban Education, Cultural / Non-Traditional

MANUSCRIPT GUIDELINES/COMMENTS:

Topics Include. Trend-setting institutions and individuals, innovative teaching methods, technology, liberal learning, the curriculum, the financing and management of higher education, for-profit and entrepreneurial higher education, faculty, the changing needs and nature of students, the undergraduate experience, administrative practice and governance, public policy, accountability, the social role of higher education, and other topics related to changes in higher education. Those that have been exhausted (the culture wars) or that are too broad (the history of universities in 2,000 words or less) or too specific for our broad audience (preventing dormitory theft) will not be published.

Scope

Change is a magazine dealing with contemporary issues in higher learning. It is intended to stimulate and inform reflective practitioners in colleges, universities, corporations, government, and elsewhere. Using a magazine format rather than that of an academic journal, *Change* spotlights trends, provides new insights and ideas, and analyzes the implications of educational programs, policies, and practices.

The topics of the coming year's issues can be found on the Heldref Website, at **http://www. heldref.org/**. Since several articles in each issue on not on the issue's theme, we also invite articles on other topics. But even the best manuscripts compete for limited space: We publish just six times a year, and given that many of the articles are solicited, we can use but 20 or so of the hundreds of manuscripts submitted each year.

Audience

Change is intended for individuals responsible for higher learning in college, university, and other settings, including faculty, administrators, trustees, state and federal officials, and students, as well as corporation, union, and foundation officers.

Manuscripts

Owned by Heldref Publications, a division of the nonprofit Helen Dwight Reid Education Foundation in Washington, *Change* is one of the 43 journals and magazines published by Heldref. The magazine staff at Heldref includes a full-time managing editor, Cheryl Fields, and an associate editor, Rachel Adams. It is to Heldref that you direct all manuscripts, letters to the editor, and queries about guidelines for writers, as well as questions about advertising and subscriptions. (See below for relevant contact information.)

Because *Change* is a magazine rather than a journal, footnotes should not be included. References can be worked into the text or given parenthetically when necessary. A short list of "Related Readings" or "Resources" can be provided with the article where appropriate, and URLs can be provided for Web sites containing more extensive documentation.

A separate title page should provide short biographical information (up to four or five lines) and contact information, including the complete address, telephone, and fax number, and e-mail of the author(s). The first-named author of a multi-authored article will receive the notification of acceptance, rejection, or need for revision. The cover page should also indicate the word count of the article.

Review Process

When we receive your manuscript, we will send you a postcard verifying that your article has entered the review process. By agreement with Heldref, AAHE is responsible for all editorial judgments about the magazine: its themes, articles, and editorial voice. AAHE exercises that judgment through its executive editor, Margaret Miller, or the guest editor of a particular issue. All manuscripts are read first by Margaret Miller to determine their suitability for *Change*. If the fit is not good, you will hear within six weeks. Those that are promising she sends to two consulting editors for review. Those that are returned with positive reviews she or the guest editor considers for publication. This process takes from two to three months to complete. (Should the manuscript be held for longer than usual, you will be notified and offered the option of withdrawing the manuscript from consideration.)

If the article is accepted, you will be contacted to discuss editing procedures and the production schedule for the issue of the magazine in which your article will appear. Each author receives six complimentary copies of the issue in which the article is included. Authors may also order additional copies or reprints (minimum order of 100) at their expense.

Manuscripts should be submitted exclusively to this publication.

Contributing To *Change*

Change is a magazine, and the magazine article is a genre unto itself. A good article compels attention to an important matter. It shows a mind at work, one that reaches judgment and takes a stance. It is credible: it knows its subject and the context. And it is concrete: It names people, places, dates, and events. Articles written in the style of a journal—heavy on jargon and footnotes, light on analysis and point of view—will not be accepted. For a good idea of the kind of writing that works for *Change*, we encourage you to read a few past issues.

Change doesn't start with an ideological predisposition; we court good ideas from all sides. But tracts, broadsides, and grand plans seldom impress reviewers (or readers), who prefer real, usable ideas that someone has actually tried out and evaluated.

Send manuscripts to: Managing Editor, Change magazine, Heldref Publications, 1319 Eighteenth Street, NW, Washington, DC 20036-1802; Telephone: 202/296-6267, Extension 222; Fax: 202/296-5149, Email: **ch@heldref.org**

Chemical Engineering Education

SUBMISSION PROCESS:
Postal & Electronic Submission Required via EMail **cee@che.ufl.edu**

CONTACT INFORMATION:	REVIEW PROCESS:	
Tim Anderson, Editor Chemical Engineering Education c/o Chemical Engineering Department University of Florida Gainesville, FL 32611-6005 USA	**Type of Review:**	Editorial Review
	No. External Reviewers:	3
	No. InHouse Reviewers:	1
	Acceptance Rate:	48%
Phone:	**Time to Review:**	2 - 3 Months
	Reviewer's Comments:	Yes
	Invited Articles:	0-5%
Email: cee@che.ufl.edu	**Fees to Publish:**	$0.00 US$
Website:	**Fees to Review:**	$0.00 US$
http://cee.che.ufl.edu/		

PUBLICATION GUIDELINES:	CIRCULATION DATA:
Manuscript Style: See Manuscript Guidelines	**Reader:** Academics
Manuscript Length: 11-15	**Frequency of Issue:** Quarterly
Copies Required: Three + 1 Electronic	**Sponsor/Publisher:** Chemical Engineering Division of the American Society for Engineering Education (ASEE)

MANUSCRIPT TOPICS:
Chemical Engineering; Higher Education

MANUSCRIPT GUIDELINES/COMMENTS:

CEE publishes papers in the broad field of chemical engineering education. Papers generally describe a course, a laboratory, a ChE department, a ChE educator, a ChE curriculum, research program, machine computation, special instructional programs, or give views and opinions on various topics of interest to the profession.

Title
Use specific and informative titles. They should be as brief as possible, consistent with the need for defining the subject area covered by the paper.

Authorship
Be consistent in authorship designation. Use first name, second initial, and surname. Give complete mailing address of place where work was conducted. If current address is different, include it in a footnote on title page.

Abstract: Key Words
Include an abstract of 75 words or less and up to four keywords for use in literature searches.

Text
We request that manuscripts not exceed twelve double-spaced type written pages in length. Longer manuscripts may be returned to the author(s) for revision/shortening before being reviewed. Assume your reader is not a novice in the field. Include only as much history as is needed to provide background for the particular material covered in your paper. Sectionalize the article and insert brief appropriate headings.

Tables
Avoid tables and graphs which involve duplication or superfluous data. If you can use a graph, do not include a table. If the reader needs the table, omit the graph. Substitute a few typical results for lengthy tables when practical. Avoid computer printouts.

Nomenclature
Follow nomenclature style of Chemical Abstracts; avoid trivial names. If trade names are used, define at point of first use. Trade names should carry an initial capital only, with no accompanying footnote. Use consistent units of measurement and give dimensions for all terms. Write all equations and formulas clearly, and number important equations consecutively.

Acknowledgment
Include in acknowledgment only such credits as are essential.

Literature Cited
References should be numbered and listed on a separate sheet in the order occurring in the text.

Copy Requirements
Submit the manuscript electronically as a pdf file that includes all graphical material as well as tables and diagrams. Label ordinates and abscissas of graphs along the axes and outside the graph proper. Number all illustrations consecutively. Send an additional copy of the manuscript on standard letter-size paper through regular mail channels. Authors should also include brief biographical sketches. Send your electronic manuscript to **cee@che.ufl.edu** and your hard copy to Chemical Engineering Education, c/o Chemical Engineering Department University of Florida, Gainesville, FL 32611-6005.

Child & Family Behavior Therapy

SUBMISSION PROCESS:
Postal Submission Only

CONTACT INFORMATION:	REVIEW PROCESS:	
Cyril M. Franks, Editor	**Type of Review:**	Blind Review
c/o Charles Diament, Co-Editor		
41 Reckless Place	**No. External Reviewers:**	3+
Red Bank, NJ 07701 USA	**No. InHouse Reviewers:**	2
	Acceptance Rate:	40-50%
Phone:	**Time to Review:**	2 - 3 Months
609-924-0117	**Reviewer's Comments:**	Yes
Email:	**Invited Articles:**	6-10%
vfranks@patmedia.net		
drcdiament@home.com	**Fees to Publish:**	$0.00 US$
Website:	**Fees to Review:**	$0.00 US$
www.haworthpress.com		

PUBLICATION GUIDELINES:	CIRCULATION DATA:
Manuscript Style:	**Reader:**
American Psychological Association	Counselors
Manuscript Length:	**Frequency of Issue:**
21-25	Quarterly
Copies Required:	**Sponsor/Publisher:**
One	Haworth Press, Inc.

MANUSCRIPT TOPICS:
Counseling & Personnel Services

MANUSCRIPT GUIDELINES/COMMENTS:

About the Journal
Child & Family Behavior Therapy is the ideal supplement to today's growing psychological literature on children, adults, and their families. This peer reviewed/peer refereed journal offers original research, examples, and behavioral techniques for parents, teachers, mental health professionals, and counselors. Dr. Cyril Franks, Editor and founder of the Association for Advancement of Behavior Therapy, along with Co-editor Charles Diament and Associate Editors Howard Paul and Raymond Romanczyk, bring together leading internationally known experts on behavior therapy to review developments in the field and highlight implications for clinical practice.

This journal focuses on the practical applications of behavior therapy, sharing the latest developments, extensive case studies, and step-by-step instructions for using these methods in your own practice. These proven interventions from around the world will facilitate the work of teachers, child psychologists, psychiatrists, social workers, school counselors, family therapists, researchers, and other special educators. Regular features include extensive book reviews, case studies, and technique innovations.

128

In addition, *Child & Family Behavior Therapy* examines such issues as:
- interventions for parents as well as children
- classroom behavior and homework issues
- social skills development for emotionally disturbed children
- behavioral interventions for children with ADHD, conduct disorders, and other presenting problems

Instructions for Authors
Journal Co-Editors. Cyril M Franks, PhD, Princeton, NJ 08540-5330; Email: **vfranks@pat media.net**. Charles Diament, PhD, 41 Reckless Place, Redbank, NJ 07701; Email: **DrCDiament@ home.com**

Associate Editors. Howard A Paul, PhD, ABPP, 1 Wedgewood Drive, North Brunswick, NJ 08902; Email: **paulha@umdnj.edu**. Raymond Romancyzk, PhD, Psychology Dept, Binghamton University

Special Notes. All manuscripts should be submitted to the Co-Editor: Charles Diament, Co-Editor, 41 Reckless Place, Red Bank, NJ 07701. Authors must complete a Manuscript Submission & Limited Copyright Transfer Form (See "2. Copyright"). Download the Manuscript Submission & Limited Copyright Transfer Form from the web site.

1. **Original Articles Only**. Submission of a manuscript to this journal represents a certification on the part of the author(s) that it is an original work, and that neither this manuscript nor a version of it has been published elsewhere nor is being considered for publication elsewhere.

2. **Copyright**. Copyright ownership of your manuscript must be transferred officially to The Haworth Press, Inc., before we can begin the peer-review process. All authors must sign the form and return the original to the editor as soon as possible. Failure to return the copyright form in a timely fashion will result in a delay in review and subsequent publication.

3. **Manuscript Length**. 25 typed pages. Lengthier manuscripts may be considered, but only at the discretion of the editor. There is no specific manuscript length. The abstract should precede the text on a separate piece of paper. The entire manuscript, including abstract, quotations, tables, and references, must be double-spaced.

4. **Manuscript Style**. *APA Style Publication Manual of the American Psychological Association.* References should be double-spaced and placed in alphabetical order. The use of footnotes within the text is discouraged. Words should be underlined only when it is intended that they be typeset in italics. If an author wishes to submit a paper that has been already prepared in another style, he or she may do so. However, if the paper is accepted (with or without reviewer's alterations), the author is fully responsible for retyping the manuscript in the correct style as indicated above. Neither the Editor nor the Publisher is responsible for re-preparing the manuscript copy to adhere to the journal's style.

5. **Manuscript Preparation**. Double-spaced, including endnotes and references; 12-point font
Margins. Leave at least a one inch margin on all four sides; set all notes as endnotes.
Cover page. Important -- Submit a cover page with the manuscript, indicating only the article title (this is used for anonymous refereeing).
Second "title page". Include a regular title page as a separate document. Include the title again, plus:
- full authorship
- an ABSTRACT of about 100 words (below the abstract provide 3-10 key words for indexing purposes)
- a header or footer on each page with abbreviated title and page number of total (e.g., pg 2 of 7)
- an introductory note with authors' academic degrees, professional titles, affiliations, mailing and e-mail addresses, and any desired acknowledgement of research support or other credit

6. **Preparation of Tables, Figures, and Illustrations**. Any material that is not textual is considered artwork. This includes tables, figures, diagrams, charts, graphs, illustrations, appendices, screen captures, and photos. Tables and figures (including legend, notes, and sources) should be no larger than 4 ½ x 6 ½ inches. Type style should be Helvetica (or Helvetica narrow if necessary) and no smaller than 8 point. We request that computer-generated figures be in black and white and/or shades of gray (preferably no color; for it does not reproduce well). Camera-ready art must contain no grammatical, typographical, or format errors and must reproduce sharply and clearly in the dimensions of the final printed page (4 ½ x 6 ½ inches). Photos and screen captures must be saved as a TIFF file or other graphic file format such as JPEG or BMP. For final hardcopy submission, these should be on disk or CD-ROM accompanying your manuscript. For rapid publication we must receive black-and-white glossy or matte positives (white background with black images and/or wording) in addition to files on disk. Tables should be created in the text document file using the software's Table feature.

7. **Submitting Art**. Both a printed hard copy and an electronic copy of the art must be provided. We request that each piece of art be sent in its own file or on a disk separate from the disk containing the manuscript text file(s); disks should be clearly labeled. We reserve the right to (if necessary) request new art, alter art, or if all else has failed in achieving art that is presentable, delete art. If submitted art cannot be used, the publisher reserves the right to redo the art and to charge the author a fee of $55.00 per hour for this service. The Haworth Press, Inc. is not responsible for errors incurred in the preparation of new artwork. Camera-ready artwork must be prepared on separate sheets of paper. Always use black ink and professional drawing instruments. On the back of these items, write your article title and the journal title lightly in soft-lead pencil (please do not write on the face of art). In the text file, skip extra lines and indicate where these figures are placed. Photos are considered part of the acceptable manuscript and remain with the publisher for use in additional printings.

8. **Typesetting**. You will not be receiving galley proofs of your article. Editorial revisions, if any, must therefore be made while your article is still in manuscript form. The final version of the manuscript will be the version you see published. Typesetter's errors will be corrected by the production staff of The Haworth Press, Inc. Authors are expected to submit manuscripts, disks, and art that are free from error.

9. **Disk Media**. (For Hardcopy Submissions) Haworth's in-house typesetting unit is able to utilize your final manuscript material as prepared on most personal computers and word processors. This will minimize typographical errors and decrease overall production time. Please send the first draft and final draft copies of your manuscript to the journal editor in print format for his/her final review and approval. After approval of your final manuscript, please submit the final approved version both in printed format ("hard copy") and floppy diskette or CD-ROM. On the outside of the diskette package write: 1) the brand name of your computer or word processor 2) the word processing program and version that you used 3) the title of your article, and 4) the file name. NOTE: Disk and hard copy must agree. In case of discrepancies, it is The Haworth Press' policy to follow hard copy. Authors are advised that no revisions of the manuscript can be made after acceptance by the editor for publication. The benefits of this procedure are many with speed and accuracy being the most obvious. We look forward to working with your disk submission which will allow us to serve you more efficiently.

10. **Spelling, Grammar, and Punctuation**. You are responsible for preparing manuscript copy which is clearly written in acceptable, scholarly English and which contains no errors of spelling, grammar, or punctuation. Neither the editor nor the publisher is responsible for correcting errors of spelling and grammar. The manuscript, after acceptance by the editor, must be immediately ready for typesetting as it is finally submitted by the author(s). Check your paper for the following common errors:
- dangling modifiers
- misplaced modifiers

- unclear antecedents
- incorrect or inconsistent abbreviations

Also, check the accuracy of all arithmetic calculations, statistics, numerical data, text citations, and references. INCONSISTENCIES MUST BE AVOIDED. Be sure you are consistent in your use of abbreviations, terminology, and in citing references, from one part of your paper to another.

11. **Acknowledgment of Receipt**. Please allow 10-15 weeks for the review process. Postage inquiries regarding submissions made from outside of the U.S. should be directed to the editor of this journal.

12. **Reference Linking**. The Haworth Press, Inc. is participating in reference linking for journal articles. (To obtain information on reference linking initiatives, please consult the CrossRef Web site at **www.crossref.org**.) When citing a journal article include the article's Digital Object Identifier (DOI), when available, as the last item in the reference. A Digital Object Identifier is a persistent, authoritative, and unique identifier that a publisher assigns to each article. Because of its persistence, DOIs will enable The Haworth Press, Inc., and other publishers to link to the article referenced, and the link will not break over time. This will be a great resource in scholarly research.

An example of a reference to a journal article which includes a DOI:
Vizine-Goetz, Diane (2002). Classification Schemes for Internet Resources Revisited. Journal of Internet Cataloging 5(4): 5:18. doi:10.1300/J141v05n04_02

13. **Alterations Required by Referees and Reviewers**. Many times a paper is accepted by the editor contingent upon changes that are mandated by anonymous specialist referees and/or members of the editorial board. If the editor returns your manuscript for revisions, you are responsible for retyping any sections of the paper to incorporate these revisions (if applicable, revisions should also be put on disk).

Child & Youth Services

SUBMISSION PROCESS:
Postal Submission Only

CONTACT INFORMATION:	REVIEW PROCESS:	
Doug Magnuson, Editor University of Victoria School of Child & Youth Care Box 1700, STN CSC Victoria, BC V9C 2T6 Canada	**Type of Review:**	Blind Review
	No. External Reviewers:	3+
	No. InHouse Reviewers:	2
	Acceptance Rate:	40-50%
Phone:	**Time to Review:**	2 - 3 Months
250-721-6479	**Reviewer's Comments:**	Yes
	Invited Articles:	6-10%
Email:		
dougm@uvic.ca	**Fees to Publish:**	$0.00 US$
Website:	**Fees to Review:**	$0.00 US$
www.haworthpress.com		

PUBLICATION GUIDELINES:	CIRCULATION DATA:
Manuscript Style: See Manuscript Guidelines	**Reader:** Academics, Administrators, Counselors
Manuscript Length: 30+	**Frequency of Issue:** Biannually
Copies Required: One	**Sponsor/Publisher:** Haworth Press, Inc.

MANUSCRIPT TOPICS:
Counseling & Personnel Services; Education Management / Administration

MANUSCRIPT GUIDELINES/COMMENTS:

About the Journal
Child & Youth Services is a unique journal devoted exclusively to the development and treatment of children and adolescents. The journal covers a variety of relevant topics, including current concerns, topics of long-range importance, and concepts that can generally enrich youth services. The valuable information you'll find in *Child & Youth Services* is designed to further the academic literature on the subject and provide practical applications and interventions for day-to-day youth contact at home, in school, or in other environments.

Child & Youth Services provides a forum for both scholars and youth service providers. Each issue, with its own unique thematic approach, provides in-depth coverage of a particular area of interest in the field. As such, the journal provides text material for use in relevant courses where such a resource is not otherwise readily available. In practice, *Child & Youth Services* is widely used to update those already working in the areas covered, and to illuminate new perspectives for colleagues throughout the field.

Themes that have been covered by the journal include:

- Pain, Normality, and Struggle for Congruence: Reinterpreting Residential Care for Children and Youth
- Residential Child Care Staff Selection: Choose with Care
- Innovative Approaches in Working with Children and Youth: New Lessons from the Kibbutz
- We Are in the Streets Because They Are in the Streets: Street Social Education in Brazil
- Assaultive Youth: Responding to Physical Assaultiveness in Residential, Community, and Health Care Settings
- Transitioning Exceptional Children and Youth Into the Community: Research and Practice
- Family Perspectives in Child and Youth Services
- Helping the Youthful Offender: Individual and Group Therapies That Work
- Specialist Foster Family Care: A Normalizing Experience
- Perspectives in Professional Child and Youth Care
- The Watchers and the Waiters: America's Homeless Children
- Being in Child Care: A Journey Into Self

Instructions for Authors
Journal Co-Editor. Doug Magnuson, PhD, Associate Professor, School of Child & Youth care, University of Victoria, Box 1700, STN CSC, Victoria, BC V9C 2T6; Email: **dougm@uvic.ca**

Special Notes. Manuscript Length Notes: Individual Submissions--10-50 typed pages Book Length Submissions--175-325 typed pages. Authors must complete a Manuscript Submission & Limited Copyright Transfer Form (See "2. Copyright"). Download the Manuscript Submission & Limited Copyright Transfer Form from the web site.

1. **Original Articles Only**. Submission of a manuscript to this journal represents a certification on the part of the author(s) that it is an original work, and that neither this manuscript nor a version of it has been published elsewhere nor is being considered for publication elsewhere.

2. **Copyright**. Copyright ownership of your manuscript must be transferred officially to The Haworth Press, Inc., before we can begin the peer-review process. All authors must sign the form and return the original to the editor as soon as possible. Failure to return the copyright form in a timely fashion will result in a delay in review and subsequent publication.

3. **Manuscript Length**. 10–50 typed pages. Lengthier manuscripts may be considered, but only at the discretion of the editor. There is no specific manuscript length. The abstract should precede the text on a separate piece of paper. The entire manuscript, including abstract, quotations, tables, and references, must be double-spaced.

4. **Manuscript Style**. References should be double-spaced and placed in alphabetical order. The use of footnotes within the text is discouraged. Words should be underlined only when it is intended that they be typeset in italics.

5. **Manuscript Preparation**. Double-spaced, including endnotes and references; 12-point font
Margins. Leave at least a one inch margin on all four sides; set all notes as endnotes.
Cover page. Important -- Submit a cover page with the manuscript, indicating only the article title (this is used for anonymous refereeing).
Second "title page". Include a regular title page as a separate document. Include the title again, plus:

- full authorship
- an ABSTRACT of about 100 words (below the abstract provide 3-10 key words for indexing purposes)
- a header or footer on each page with abbreviated title and page number of total (e.g., pg 2 of 7)
- an introductory note with authors' academic degrees, professional titles, affiliations, mailing and e-mail addresses, and any desired acknowledgement of research support or other credit

6. **Preparation of Tables, Figures, and Illustrations**. Any material that is not textual is considered artwork. This includes tables, figures, diagrams, charts, graphs, illustrations, appendices, screen captures, and photos. Tables and figures (including legend, notes, and sources) should be no larger than 4 ½ x 6 ½ inches. Type style should be Helvetica (or Helvetica narrow if necessary) and no smaller than 8 point. We request that computer-generated figures be in black and white and/or shades of gray (preferably no color; for it does not reproduce well). Camera-ready art must contain no grammatical, typographical, or format errors and must reproduce sharply and clearly in the dimensions of the final printed page (4 ½ x 6 ½ inches). Photos and screen captures must be saved as a TIFF file or other graphic file format such as JPEG or BMP. For final hardcopy submission, these should be on disk or CD-ROM accompanying your manuscript. For rapid publication we must receive black-and-white glossy or matte positives (white background with black images and/or wording) in addition to files on disk. Tables should be created in the text document file using the software's Table feature.

7. **Submitting Art**. Both a printed hard copy and an electronic copy of the art must be provided. We request that each piece of art be sent in its own file or on a disk separate from the disk containing the manuscript text file(s); disks should be clearly labeled. We reserve the right to (if necessary) request new art, alter art, or if all else has failed in achieving art that is presentable, delete art. If submitted art cannot be used, the publisher reserves the right to redo the art and to charge the author a fee of $55.00 per hour for this service. The Haworth Press, Inc. is not responsible for errors incurred in the preparation of new artwork. Camera-ready artwork must be prepared on separate sheets of paper. Always use black ink and professional drawing instruments. On the back of these items, write your article title and the journal title lightly in soft-lead pencil (please do not write on the face of art). In the text file, skip extra lines and indicate where these figures are placed. Photos are considered part of the acceptable manuscript and remain with the publisher for use in additional printings.

8. **Typesetting**. You will not be receiving galley proofs of your article. Editorial revisions, if any, must therefore be made while your article is still in manuscript form. The final version of the manuscript will be the version you see published. Typesetter's errors will be corrected by the production staff of The Haworth Press, Inc. Authors are expected to submit manuscripts, disks, and art that are free from error.

9. **Disk Media**. (For Hardcopy Submissions) Haworth's in-house typesetting unit is able to utilize your final manuscript material as prepared on most personal computers and word processors. This will minimize typographical errors and decrease overall production time. Please send the first draft and final draft copies of your manuscript to the journal editor in print format for his/her final review and approval. After approval of your final manuscript, please submit the final approved version both in printed format ("hard copy") and floppy diskette or CD-ROM. On the outside of the diskette package write: 1) the brand name of your computer or word processor 2) the word processing program and version that you used 3) the title of your article, and 4) the file name. NOTE: Disk and hard copy must agree. In case of discrepancies, it is The Haworth Press' policy to follow hard copy. Authors are advised that no revisions of the manuscript can be made after acceptance by the editor for publication. The benefits of this procedure are many with speed and accuracy being the most obvious. We look forward to working with your disk submission which will allow us to serve you more efficiently.

10. **Spelling, Grammar, and Punctuation**. You are responsible for preparing manuscript copy which is clearly written in acceptable, scholarly English and which contains no errors of spelling, grammar, or punctuation. Neither the editor nor the publisher is responsible for correcting errors of spelling and grammar. The manuscript, after acceptance by the editor, must be immediately ready for typesetting as it is finally submitted by the author(s). Check your paper for the following common errors:
- dangling modifiers
- misplaced modifiers

- unclear antecedents
- incorrect or inconsistent abbreviations

Also, check the accuracy of all arithmetic calculations, statistics, numerical data, text citations, and references. INCONSISTENCIES MUST BE AVOIDED. Be sure you are consistent in your use of abbreviations, terminology, and in citing references, from one part of your paper to another.

11. **Acknowledgment of Receipt**. Please allow 10-15 weeks for the review process. Postage inquiries regarding submissions made from outside of the U.S. should be directed to the editor of this journal.

12. **Reference Linking**. The Haworth Press, Inc. is participating in reference linking for journal articles. (To obtain information on reference linking initiatives, please consult the CrossRef Web site at **www.crossref.org**.) When citing a journal article include the article's Digital Object Identifier (DOI), when available, as the last item in the reference. A Digital Object Identifier is a persistent, authoritative, and unique identifier that a publisher assigns to each article. Because of its persistence, DOIs will enable The Haworth Press, Inc., and other publishers to link to the article referenced, and the link will not break over time. This will be a great resource in scholarly research.

An example of a reference to a journal article which includes a DOI:
Vizine-Goetz, Diane (2002). Classification Schemes for Internet Resources Revisited. Journal of Internet Cataloging 5(4): 5:18. doi:10.1300/J141v05n04_02

13. **Alterations Required by Referees and Reviewers**. Many times a paper is accepted by the editor contingent upon changes that are mandated by anonymous specialist referees and/or members of the editorial board. If the editor returns your manuscript for revisions, you are responsible for retyping any sections of the paper to incorporate these revisions (if applicable, revisions should also be put on disk).

Child Development

SUBMISSION PROCESS:
Electronic Submission Only **via Online Portal** **www.srcd.org/cdsubmit**

CONTACT INFORMATION:	REVIEW PROCESS:	
Lynn S. Liben, Editor University of Michigan 3131 S. State St. Suite 302 Ann Arbor, MI 48108-1623 USA	**Type of Review:**	Blind Review
	No. External Reviewers:	2-4
	No. InHouse Reviewers:	0
Phone: 734-998-7310	**Acceptance Rate:**	26%
	Time to Review:	2-4 Months
	Reviewer's Comments:	Yes
Email: cdev@srcd.org	**Invited Articles:**	0-5%
Website: www.srcd.org/cd.html	**Fees to Publish:**	$0.00 US$
	Fees to Review:	$0.00 US$

PUBLICATION GUIDELINES:	CIRCULATION DATA:
Manuscript Style: American Psychological Association	**Reader:** Academics
Manuscript Length: 25-40	**Frequency of Issue:** Bi-Monthly
Copies Required: Electronic Only	**Sponsor/Publisher:** Society for Research in Child Development / Blackwell Publishing, Inc.

MANUSCRIPT TOPICS:
Educational Psychology; Elementary / Early Childhood; Interdisciplinary; International; School Law

MANUSCRIPT GUIDELINES/COMMENTS:

Child Development publishes empirical, theoretical, review, applied, and policy articles reporting research on child development. Published by the interdisciplinary Society for Research in Child Development (SRCD), the journal welcomes relevant submissions from all disciplines.

Types of Articles
Child Development considers manuscripts in formats described below. Inquiries concerning alternative formats should be addressed to the Editor prior to submission. All submissions are expected to be no more than 40 manuscript pages, including tables, references, and figures (but excluding appendices). Authors should provide a justification if the submission is substantially longer. Unless the editor finds that justification compelling, the submission will be returned to the author for shortening prior to editorial review.

Empirical articles comprise the major portion of the journal. To be accepted, empirical articles must be judged as being high in scientific quality, contributing to the empirical base of child development, and having important theoretical, practical, or interdisciplinary implications. Reports of multiple studies, methods, or settings are encouraged, but single-study reports are also considered. Empirical articles will thus vary considerably in length (approximately 8 to 40 manuscript pages); text and graphics should be as concise as material permits. All modes of empirical research are welcome.

Reviews focus on past empirical and/or on conceptual and theoretical work. They are expected to synthesize or evaluate a topic or issue relevant to child development, should appeal to a broad audience, and may be followed by a small number of solicited commentaries.

Essays describe original concepts, methods, trends, applications, and theories; these may also be accompanied by solicited commentaries.

Child Development and ... are articles that provide readers with tutorials about some new concept or academic specialty pertinent to research in child development. These papers should review the major definitions, methods, and findings of the concept or specialty and discuss past or potential links to child development.

From another perspective is a format in which papers on a focal topic, written by different authors, are published simultaneously. Papers represent diverse perspectives (e.g., authors whose work represents different populations; different disciplines; different theories, methods, or analytic tools). In some cases, calls for submissions on particular topics will be disseminated through SRCD (via e-mail or SRCD publications), and submissions will undergo normal editorial review. In some cases, a submitted manuscript (e.g., an empirical article) may be selected as a lead article for this format, with invited commentaries providing additional perspectives. The editors also welcome suggestions from readers for topics for this format.

Manuscript Submission
Child Development invites for consideration manuscripts that are neither identical to nor substantially similar to work published or under review elsewhere. In the submission cover letter, please provide details about other published or submitted papers having substantial overlap (including data sets) with the new CD submission to enable editors to judge whether the new submission is sufficiently distinct from other work to warrant consideration. Please note if the paper is posted on a website, see **http://www.srcd.org/webposting.html**. Editors retain the right to reject manuscripts that do not meet established ethical standards for research or dissemination.

Manuscripts should be submitted electronically to the Child Development Online Submission Site at www.srcd.org/CDsubmit/ as a Word or WordPerfect file. Please also submit a cover letter that contains the name(s) of the author(s) and affiliation(s), and the street address, telephone, fax, and electronic mail address of the corresponding author. A corresponding author's submission to Child Development implies that all co-authors have agreed to the content and form of the manuscript and that the ethical standards of SRCD have been followed (see the Child Development website or pp. 283-284 of the 2000 SRCD Directory). Any financial interest or conflict of interest must be explained to the Editor in the cover letter. The corresponding author is responsible for informing all co-authors, in a timely manner, of manuscript submission, editorial decisions, reviews, and revisions.

The manuscript file should be formatted with double spaced, 12-point type, and should include a single paragraph abstract of 100-120 words. Please follow all guidelines on format, style, and ethics provided in the *Publication Manual of the American Psychological Association* (5th ed.). Figures included with initial submissions will not be returned. Therefore, please submit only electronic files or copies of figures. Authors should keep a copy of all correspondence, files, and figures to guard against loss.

Manuscript Review

If you have any questions about your submission, please inquire at **cdev@srcd.org** or call (734) 998-7310. Each manuscript is handled by the Editor or an Associate Editor who consults with one or more Consulting Editors and/or ad hoc reviewers who have relevant expertise. To ensure blind review, cover sheets are removed before review; authors should avoid including any other information about identity or affiliation in submissions. Copies of the submission and associated correspondence are retained in the SRCD archives. For accepted manuscripts, authors are required to prepare a 300-500 layperson's summary for public dissemination purposes. Details are provided to authors as part of final processing.

There is no charge for publication in *Child Development* unless tabular or graphic materials exceed 10% of the total number of pages. Charges are also levied for changes in proofs other than correction of printer's errors. Any inquiries relating to charges or business matters (including reprint orders) should be addressed to Blackwell Publishers, Child Development, Production Coordinator, 350 Main Street, Malden, MA 02148, (781) 388-8200.

Inquiries and suggestions regarding editorial policy may be addressed to: Dr. Lynn S. Liben, Editor, Child Development, Department of Psychology, The Pennsylvania State University, University Park, PA 16802, **liben@psu.edu**. *Please do not send electronic or paper manuscripts to the above address.* Doing so will delay the processing of your manuscript.

Children & Schools

SUBMISSION PROCESS:
Postal Submission Only

CONTACT INFORMATION:	REVIEW PROCESS:	
Melissa Jonson-Reid, Editor-in-Chief NASW Press 750 First Street NE, Suite 700 Washington, DC 20002-4241 USA	**Type of Review:**	Blind Review
	No. External Reviewers:	3
	No. InHouse Reviewers:	1
Phone: 202-408-8600	**Acceptance Rate:**	21-30%
	Time to Review:	2 - 3 Months
	Reviewer's Comments:	Yes
Email: jonsonrd@wustl.edu mroman@naswdc.org	**Invited Articles:**	6-10%
	Fees to Publish:	$0.00 US$
	Fees to Review:	$0.00 US$
Website: www.naswpress.org		
PUBLICATION GUIDELINES:	**CIRCULATION DATA:**	
Manuscript Style: See Manuscript Guidelines	**Reader:** Academics, School Social Workers, Child Welfare Workers	
Manuscript Length: 16-20	**Frequency of Issue:** Quarterly	
Copies Required: Five	**Sponsor/Publisher:** National Association of Social Workers / NASW Press	

MANUSCRIPT TOPICS:

Counseling & Personnel Services; Elementary / Early Childhood; Health & Physical Education; Social Studies / Social Science; Special Education; Tests, Measurement & Evaluation

MANUSCRIPT GUIDELINES/COMMENTS:

Children & Schools (formerly *Social Work In Education*, established in 1978) publishes professional materials relevant to social work services in education. The journal addresses school social workers, health and mental health agencies, educational institutions, the juvenile justice system, and others concerned about education.

Authors are invited to submit manuscripts related to early intervention programs; preschool, elementary, and secondary education; and transitions to adulthood. The editorial board particularly encourages practitioners to share their practice knowledge. The board welcomes articles on innovations in practice, interdisciplinary efforts, legislation, policy, planning, and administration. The journal seeks research articles including quantitative studies, such as single-subject designs, group designs, and program evaluation, and qualitative studies, such as case studies, ethnographic interviews, and focus groups.

As a practice-oriented journal *Children & Schools* seeks to represent the broad spectrum of activities related to schools, children, and families; controversial manuscripts that will encourage dialogue are welcomed. The editorial board particularly invites manuscripts that emphasize practice and cultural diversity. Because the journal represents the breadth of social work practice in education, the preference is to vary the content within a single issue. From time to time, however, the journal publishes special issues on themes of importance to the field.

Articles. Manuscripts for full-length articles should not exceed 20 pages, including all references and tables. The entire review process is anonymous. At Least three reviewers critique each manuscript; then the editor-in-chief makes a decision, taking those reviews into account.

Note: All submissions must be typed double-spaced, including references and tables, with one-inch margins on all sides.

COLUMNS
Trends & Issues provides program and policy updates on local, regional, or national developments. Authors are encouraged to address programmatic responses to social trends, changes in policy, innovative programs, reforms in the field, and other events that have generalizable implications for practice. Manuscripts should be short - no more than eight pages. The Trends & Issues editor may assist authors in developing potential articles for this column.

Practice Highlights describes exemplary social work services in educational settings. Authors are encouraged to submit descriptive case studies of their direct work with individuals and families. The editorial board encourages a strong emphasis on interdisciplinary collaboration. Intended as a practitioner-to-practitioner resource, the column is more relaxed in style than are the regular articles. Manuscripts should be short – up to six pages. The Practice Highlights editor may assist authors in developing potential articles for this column.

Resources for Practice provides reviews of books, films, videotapes, software, and other professional resources of interest to school social workers and their colleagues. The editor of this column selects materials for review, solicits reviews, and accepts or rejects the review. Although every effort is made to publish solicited reviews, reviews are not guaranteed publication. Unsolicited reviews are not accepted.

As Readers See It provides a forum for letters and comments from readers. The editorial board welcomes opinions of interest to the field as well as comments on articles published in the journal.

This section describes how to assemble and submit a manuscript. Adhering to NASW Press format and style will improve the chances of acceptance if the substance of a manuscript has merit.

MANUSCRIPT PREPARATION
Appropriate Content
To determine which journal is most appropriate for your manuscript, please refer to chapter 3 in this booklet. You also should be aware that the following submissions will be rejected automatically without peer review:
- Obituaries, biographical sketches, or testimonials
- Organizational reports
- Speeches that have not been recast in article format.

If the content is related to the mission of the journal and the manuscript is a scholarly article with utility for social work practice, the editorial boards generally will be interested in reviewing it. Editorial boards do not screen query letters.

Appropriate Length
Manuscripts submitted to any NASW Press journal should be no longer than 20 pages. You should be aware of the following information when you consider the length of your manuscript:

You should type the entire manuscript double-spaced with one-inch margins on all four sides.

- Every component of the manuscript (text, references, tables, figures) is included in the total page count.
- Editorial boards welcome short articles, and they do not equate length with quality.
- The NASW Press will return manuscripts in excess of 25 pages unreviewed.

Overwriting and excessive length for the subject at hand often result in rejection, even if the manuscript meets page limits. Consequently, you should review your manuscript carefully with an eye to tightening and condensing.

MANUSCRIPT COMPONENTS

Cover Sheet

The cover sheet should contain the following:

- The full title of the article
- Information on all authors: name; highest degree, credentials, and title; full address; telephone and fax numbers, and e-mail address if available
- The date of submission.

If there is more than one author, names should be listed in the order you would prefer for the byline of a published article. Designate one author as the corresponding author. The cover sheet is the only component of the manuscript that should identify the authors in any way.

Title Page

The title page will be circulated for review with the manuscript. An effective title expresses the essence of a manuscript in as few words as possible. Conciseness and precision, the hallmarks of good writing, are particularly important for titles. Try to use key words, without resorting to jargon, so that a title will attract readers and provide an accurate picture of the article. Do not attempt to communicate all of the article's content in the title.

Abstract

The abstract should provide a distillation of the key concepts in the manuscript. Whenever possible, the abstract should be informative, and it should include theoretical concepts, major hypotheses, and conclusions. Abstracts for research papers should include the purpose of the research, the study sample size and characteristics, the measurement instruments used, and the conclusions. You should present the value of the contribution without exaggerating the results.

A comprehensive yet concise abstract is important because readers and researchers often decide to read an article on the basis of the abstract. Write the abstract as a single paragraph of about 150 words. Do not include any tables or references.

If your manuscript is accepted, the abstract will be published at the beginning of the article. Following publication of the full article, the abstract will be entered into the *Social Work Abstracts* database and will appear in the print version, as well as in SWAB+, available on CD-ROM and on Internet.

Key Words

List up to five key words that describe the content of the manuscript on the abstract page.

Example: Key words: administration, health, Hispanic, people of color, women

The NASW Press uses authors' designations of key words to develop data on manuscript submissions. In addition, if the article is accepted, the key words will appear in the journal with the abstract and in the *Social Work Abstracts* database. Key words are not necessarily used for indexing.

Text

Reviewers are looking for new work that extends the knowledge base and builds on the contribution of others. There is, however, no one formula for a successful article. You may want to keep the following in mind.

State your purpose. You should state your purpose clearly within the first few paragraphs of the article. If the reader cannot recognize what you hoped to accomplish in writing the article easily, the manuscript is likely to be rejected.

Organize. Establish a clear framework for the article and organize the manuscript so that it flows coherently. Use subheadings judiciously to help the reader track the flow of the article. If the article is organized properly, it will proceed logically and directly from the opening statements to your conclusions.

Relate your work to existing knowledge. You must relate your work to existing knowledge on the subject. However, you should not be tempted to run voluminous electronic searches and incorporate every related reference you find. Instead, use those references that demonstrate best how the new information will fill gaps in the knowledge base.

Review and rewrite. Reviewing and rewriting are basic steps in developing a manuscript for publication. As you review your work, eliminate redundancies and superfluous language. The use of pretentious jargon interferes with communication and can conceal the importance of your work. Write precisely in the active voice, use jargon only when absolutely necessary to convey specialized knowledge, and eliminate any language that might convey the perception of bias or any kind of stereotyping of people and behavior (see chapter 7). Finally, review your manuscript for spelling, punctuation, and grammatical errors. Use electronic tools, such as spell-check and a thesaurus, to assure that you have used words correctly.

References

Authors are responsible for the completeness and accuracy of the references in their manuscripts. Generally, take reference data for published material from the title page of a book or pamphlet, first page of an article, or contents page of a periodical. Take dates from the copyright page. For additional information on formatting references, please see the Authors Guidelines on the NASW Press Web site: **www.naswpress.org**

Christian Higher Education: An Int'l Journal of Applied Research & Practice

SUBMISSION PROCESS:
Postal Submission Only

CONTACT INFORMATION:	REVIEW PROCESS:	
D. Barry Lumsden, Editor Senior Research Fellow	**Type of Review:**	Blind Review
University of Alabama Educational Policy Center	**No. External Reviewers:** **No. InHouse Reviewers:**	3 0
Box 870231 Tuscaloosa, AL 35487-0231 USA	**Acceptance Rate:**	21-30%
	Time to Review:	1 - 2 Months
	Reviewer's Comments:	Yes
Phone:	**Invited Articles:**	0-5%
940-597-7923		
Email:	**Fees to Publish:**	$0.00 US$
blumsden@bamaed.ua.edu	**Fees to Review:**	$0.00 US$
Website: www.tandf.co.uk/journals/titles/15363759 .asp		

PUBLICATION GUIDELINES:	CIRCULATION DATA:
Manuscript Style: American Psychological Association	**Reader:** Practicing Teachers, Academics, Administrators, Counselors
Manuscript Length: 16-20	**Frequency of Issue:** 5 Times/Year
Copies Required: Three	**Sponsor/Publisher:** Taylor and Francis, Ltd.

MANUSCRIPT TOPICS:

Adult Career & Vocational; Counseling & Personnel Services; Curriculum Studies; Education Management / Administration; Educational Psychology; Educational Technology Systems; English Literature; Higher Education; Library Science / Information Resources; Professional Development; Religious Education; School Law; Social Studies / Social Science; Teacher Education; Tests, Measurement & Evaluation; Urban Education, Cultural / Non-Traditional

MANUSCRIPT GUIDELINES/COMMENTS:

Aims and Scope

Christian Higher Education is a peer reviewed archival journal that features articles on developments being created and tested by those engaged in the study and practice of Christian higher education. This journal addresses issues in finance, enrollment management, innovative teaching methods, higher education administration, program assessment, faculty development, curriculum development, and student services. Each issue offers a balance of essays on current research as well as programs and methods at the cutting edge of progress. *Christian Higher Education* is the only journal to be international, interdenominational, interdisciplinary, and to focus exclusively on Christian higher education.

Readership
Professors, scholars, administrators, practitioners, and scholarly societies throughout the world involved in the research, development, and practice of Christian higher education.

Instructions to Authors
Note to Authors. Please make sure your contact address information is clearly visible on the outside of all packages you are sending to Editors.

Manuscripts should be concise yet sufficiently detailed to permit critical review. All papers should contain an abstract, which should not exceed 250 words. Manuscripts should conclude with a section on Implications for Practice stating what the implications of the research findings are to practitioners in the field and including any recommendations for change indicated by the research results.

Manuscripts should be submitted to the Editor-in-Chief, D. Barry Lumsden, Senior Research Fellow, University of Alabama, Education Policy Center, Box 870231, Tuscaloosa, AL 35487-0232, Email: **blumsden@bamaed.ua.edu**.

Submission of Manuscripts
Original and two copies of each manuscript should be submitted to the editor. Authors are strongly encouraged to submit manuscripts on disk. The disk should be prepared using MS Word or WordPerfect and should be clearly labeled with the authors' names, file name, and software program. All parts of the manuscript should be typewritten, double-spaced, with margins of at least one inch on all sides. Number manuscript pages consecutively throughout the paper. Authors should also supply a shortened version of the title suitable for the running head, not exceeding 50 character spaces. Each article should be summarized in an abstract of 150-250 words, which should be typed, double-spaced, on a separate page. Avoid abbreviations, diagrams, and reference to the text within the abstract.

All papers, including figures, tables, and references, must conform to the specifications described in the *Publication Manual of the American Psychological Association* (5th ed., 2001). Any papers that do not adhere to this style will be returned for revision.

Each manuscript must be accompanied by a statement that it has not been published elsewhere and that it has not been submitted simultaneously for publication elsewhere. Authors are responsible for obtaining permission to reproduce copyrighted material from other sources and are required to sign an agreement for the transfer of copyright to the publisher. All accepted manuscripts, artwork, and photographs become the property of the publisher.

For further information on electronic submission, including information on accepted file types, please visit **http://www.tandf.co.uk/journals/authors/electronic_edu.asp**.

Tables and Figures
Tables and figures should not be embedded in the text, but should be included as separate sheets or files. A short descriptive title should appear above each table with a clear legend and any footnotes suitably identified below. All units must be included. Figures should be completely labeled, taking into account necessary size reduction. Captions should be typed, double-spaced, on a separate sheet. All original figures should be clearly marked in pencil on the reverse side with the number, author's name, and top edge indicated.

Illustrations
Illustrations submitted (line drawings, halftones, photos, photomicrographs, etc.) should be clean originals or digital files. Digital files are recommended for highest quality reproduction and should follow these guidelines:
- 300 dpi or higher

- sized to fit on journal page
- EPS, TIFF, or PSD format only
- submitted as separate files, not embedded in text files

Color illustrations will be considered for publication; however, the author will be required to bear the full cost involved in their printing and publication. The charge for the first page with color is $900.00. The next three pages with color are $450.00 each. A custom quote will be provided for color art totaling more than 4 journal pages. Good-quality color prints should be provided in their final size. The publisher has the right to refuse publication of color prints deemed unacceptable.

Reprints
The corresponding author of each article will receive one complete copy of the issue in which the article appears. Reprints of an individual article may be ordered from Taylor & Francis by using the reprint order form included with the page proofs.

Clinical Supervisor, The

SUBMISSION PROCESS:
Postal Submission Only

CONTACT INFORMATION:	REVIEW PROCESS:	
Lawrence Sulman, Editor 27 Hunt Club Circle E. Amherst, NY 14051 USA	**Type of Review:**	Blind Review
	No. External Reviewers:	3+
	No. InHouse Reviewers:	2
Phone: 716-645-3381 ext. 257	**Acceptance Rate:**	40-50%
	Time to Review:	2 - 3 Months
Email: shulman@acsu.buffalo.edu	**Reviewer's Comments:**	Yes
	Invited Articles:	6-10%
Website: www.haworthpress.com	**Fees to Publish:**	$0.00 US$
	Fees to Review:	$0.00 US$

PUBLICATION GUIDELINES:	CIRCULATION DATA:
Manuscript Style: American Psychological Association	**Reader:** Academics, Counselors
Manuscript Length: 16-20	**Frequency of Issue:** Biannually
Copies Required: One	**Sponsor/Publisher:** Haworth Press, Inc.

MANUSCRIPT TOPICS:
Counseling & Personnel Services; Educational Psychology

MANUSCRIPT GUIDELINES/COMMENTS:

About the Journal

The Clinical Supervisor is the premier journal in the United States devoted exclusively to the art and science of clinical supervision. An interdisciplinary, refereed publication of the highest standards, the journal communicates the ideas, experiences, skills, techniques, concerns, and needs of supervisors in psychotherapy and mental health. You will find what you need to know about supervision to effectively supervise students and trainees.

The Clinical Supervisor provides a unique forum for debate, historical analysis, new techniques, program description, theory, managed care and clinical practice issues, and other topics of vital interest to today's supervisors. The journal maintains high standards, with recent articles covering: the usefulness of developmental stage models for clinical social work students; the effects of therapist self-monitoring on therapeutic alliance and subsequent therapeutic outcome; becoming a supervisor in family therapy; the inter-subjective approach in supervision; legal and ethical issues for supervisors; mentoring in clinical psychology doctoral programs (a national survey of directors-in-training); unexpected challenges faced by psychotherapy trainees; and much more!

146

Instructions for Authors
Journal Co-Editors. Lawrence Shulman, EdD, MSW, BA, 27 Hunt Club Circle, E Amherst, NY 14051, Email: **shulman@acsu.buffalo.edu**

Andrew Safyer, PhD, Dean and Professor, School of Social Work, Adelphi University, 1 South Avenue, Garden City, NY 11530; Email: **asafyer@adelphi.edu**

Managerial Assistant. Denise Finnan, School of Social Work, University at Buffalo, 219 Parker Hall, Buffalo, NY 14214; Email: **dfinnan@buffalo.edu**

Authors must complete a Manuscript Submission & Limited Copyright Transfer Form (See "2. Copyright"). Download the Manuscript Submission & Limited Copyright Transfer Form from the web site.

1. **Original Articles Only**. Submission of a manuscript to this journal represents a certification on the part of the author(s) that it is an original work, and that neither this manuscript nor a version of it has been published elsewhere nor is being considered for publication elsewhere.

2. **Copyright**. Copyright ownership of your manuscript must be transferred officially to The Haworth Press, Inc., before we can begin the peer-review process. All authors must sign the form and return the original to the editor as soon as possible. Failure to return the copyright form in a timely fashion will result in a delay in review and subsequent publication.

3. **Manuscript Length**. 20 typed pages. Lengthier manuscripts may be considered, but only at the discretion of the editor. There is no specific manuscript length. The abstract should precede the text on a separate piece of paper. The entire manuscript, including abstract, quotations, tables, and references, must be double-spaced.

4. **Manuscript Style**. *APA Style Publication Manual of the American Psychological Association*. References should be double-spaced and placed in alphabetical order. The use of footnotes within the text is discouraged. Words should be underlined only when it is intended that they be typeset in italics. If an author wishes to submit a paper that has been already prepared in another style, he or she may do so. However, if the paper is accepted (with or without reviewer's alterations), the author is fully responsible for retyping the manuscript in the correct style as indicated above. Neither the Editor nor the Publisher is responsible for re-preparing the manuscript copy to adhere to the journal's style.

5. **Manuscript Preparation**. Double-spaced, including endnotes and references; 12-point font
Margins. Leave at least a one inch margin on all four sides; set all notes as endnotes.
Cover page. Important -- Submit a cover page with the manuscript, indicating only the article title (this is used for anonymous refereeing).
Second "title page". Include a regular title page as a separate document. Include the title again, plus:
- full authorship
- an ABSTRACT of about 100 words (below the abstract provide 3-10 key words for indexing purposes)
- a header or footer on each page with abbreviated title and page number of total (e.g., pg 2 of 7)
- an introductory note with authors' academic degrees, professional titles, affiliations, mailing and e-mail addresses, and any desired acknowledgement of research support or other credit

6. **Preparation of Tables, Figures, and Illustrations**. Any material that is not textual is considered artwork. This includes tables, figures, diagrams, charts, graphs, illustrations, appendices, screen captures, and photos. Tables and figures (including legend, notes, and sources) should be no larger than 4 ½ x 6 ½ inches. Type style should be Helvetica (or Helvetica narrow if necessary) and no smaller than 8 point. We request that computer-generated figures be in black and white and/or shades of gray (preferably no color; for it does not reproduce well). Camera-ready art

must contain no grammatical, typographical, or format errors and must reproduce sharply and clearly in the dimensions of the final printed page (4 ½ x 6 ½ inches). Photos and screen captures must be saved as a TIFF file or other graphic file format such as JPEG or BMP. For final hardcopy submission, these should be on disk or CD-ROM accompanying your manuscript. For rapid publication we must receive black-and-white glossy or matte positives (white background with black images and/or wording) in addition to files on disk. Tables should be created in the text document file using the software's Table feature.

7. **Submitting Art**. Both a printed hard copy and an electronic copy of the art must be provided. We request that each piece of art be sent in its own file or on a disk separate from the disk containing the manuscript text file(s); disks should be clearly labeled. We reserve the right to (if necessary) request new art, alter art, or if all else has failed in achieving art that is presentable, delete art. If submitted art cannot be used, the publisher reserves the right to redo the art and to charge the author a fee of $55.00 per hour for this service. The Haworth Press, Inc. is not responsible for errors incurred in the preparation of new artwork. Camera-ready artwork must be prepared on separate sheets of paper. Always use black ink and professional drawing instruments. On the back of these items, write your article title and the journal title lightly in soft-lead pencil (please do not write on the face of art). In the text file, skip extra lines and indicate where these figures are placed. Photos are considered part of the acceptable manuscript and remain with the publisher for use in additional printings.

8. **Typesetting**. You will not be receiving galley proofs of your article. Editorial revisions, if any, must therefore be made while your article is still in manuscript form. The final version of the manuscript will be the version you see published. Typesetter's errors will be corrected by the production staff of The Haworth Press, Inc. Authors are expected to submit manuscripts, disks, and art that are free from error.

9. **Disk Media**. (For Hardcopy Submissions) Haworth's in-house typesetting unit is able to utilize your final manuscript material as prepared on most personal computers and word processors. This will minimize typographical errors and decrease overall production time. Please send the first draft and final draft copies of your manuscript to the journal editor in print format for his/her final review and approval. After approval of your final manuscript, please submit the final approved version both in printed format ("hard copy") and floppy diskette or CD-ROM. On the outside of the diskette package write: 1) the brand name of your computer or word processor 2) the word processing program and version that you used 3) the title of your article, and 4) the file name. NOTE: Disk and hard copy must agree. In case of discrepancies, it is The Haworth Press' policy to follow hard copy. Authors are advised that no revisions of the manuscript can be made after acceptance by the editor for publication. The benefits of this procedure are many with speed and accuracy being the most obvious. We look forward to working with your disk submission which will allow us to serve you more efficiently.

10. **Spelling, Grammar, and Punctuation**. You are responsible for preparing manuscript copy which is clearly written in acceptable, scholarly English and which contains no errors of spelling, grammar, or punctuation. Neither the editor nor the publisher is responsible for correcting errors of spelling and grammar. The manuscript, after acceptance by the editor, must be immediately ready for typesetting as it is finally submitted by the author(s). Check your paper for the following common errors:
- dangling modifiers
- misplaced modifiers
- unclear antecedents
- incorrect or inconsistent abbreviations

Also, check the accuracy of all arithmetic calculations, statistics, numerical data, text citations, and references. INCONSISTENCIES MUST BE AVOIDED. Be sure you are consistent in your use of abbreviations, terminology, and in citing references, from one part of your paper to another.

11. **Acknowledgment of Receipt**. Please allow 10-15 weeks for the review process. Postage inquiries regarding submissions made from outside of the U.S. should be directed to the editor of this journal.

12. **Reference Linking**. The Haworth Press, Inc. is participating in reference linking for journal articles. (To obtain information on reference linking initiatives, please consult the CrossRef Web site at **www.crossref.org**.) When citing a journal article include the article's Digital Object Identifier (DOI), when available, as the last item in the reference. A Digital Object Identifier is a persistent, authoritative, and unique identifier that a publisher assigns to each article. Because of its persistence, DOIs will enable The Haworth Press, Inc., and other publishers to link to the article referenced, and the link will not break over time. This will be a great resource in scholarly research.

An example of a reference to a journal article which includes a DOI:
Vizine-Goetz, Diane (2002). Classification Schemes for Internet Resources Revisited. Journal of Internet Cataloging 5(4): 5:18. doi:10.1300/J141v05n04_02

13. **Alterations Required by Referees and Reviewers**. Many times a paper is accepted by the editor contingent upon changes that are mandated by anonymous specialist referees and/or members of the editorial board. If the editor returns your manuscript for revisions, you are responsible for retyping any sections of the paper to incorporate these revisions (if applicable, revisions should also be put on disk).

Cognition & Instruction

SUBMISSION PROCESS:

Electronic Submission Preferred
via EMail

ci@vanderbilt.edu

CONTACT INFORMATION:	REVIEW PROCESS:	
R. Lehrer & A. S. Palincsar, Co-Editors Vanderbilt University 1930 South Drive Box 330, GPC Nashville, TN 37203 USA	**Type of Review:**	Blind Review
	No. External Reviewers:	2
	No. InHouse Reviewers:	1
	Acceptance Rate:	11-20%
Phone: 615-322-1745 734-647-0622	**Time to Review:**	4 - 6 Months
	Reviewer's Comments:	Yes
	Invited Articles:	0%
Email: ci@vanderbilt.edu	**Fees to Publish:**	$0.00 US$
	Fees to Review:	$0.00 US$
Website: http://www.leaonline.com/loi/ci		

PUBLICATION GUIDELINES:	CIRCULATION DATA:
Manuscript Style: American Psychological Association	**Reader:** Academics
Manuscript Length: Any	**Frequency of Issue:** Quarterly
Copies Required: Two	**Sponsor/Publisher:** Lawrence Erlbaum Associates, Inc.

MANUSCRIPT TOPICS:

Educational Psychology; Elementary / Early Childhood; Higher Education; Intersection of Instruction & Reasoning; Reading; Science Math & Environment; Secondary / Adolescent Studies; Social Studies / Social Science; Teacher Education; Tests, Measurement & Evaluation

MANUSCRIPT GUIDELINES/COMMENTS:

Editorial Statement

The editors and editorial board of *Cognition and Instruction* recall an admonition of a historian of science, deSolla Price, to consider scientific reasoning as "thinking creatively about anything with no holds barred." We invite work that imaginatively considers problems in cognition and instruction, along with the evidence that would allow others to participate in the exercise of such imagination. Given that methodologies are tools of theory, we invite careful consideration of how methods and theories are reflexively constituted in accounts of teaching and learning. Mindful that education has long been regarded as a design profession, we are most interested in the development of pragmatic theories that offer empirically well-grounded accounts of cognition in designed contexts such as schools, museums, and workplaces.

We invite manuscripts that:

- systematically investigate the design, generation, functioning, and support of innovative contexts for learning;
- examine the growth and development of interest and identity in these contexts;
- explore how social practices, especially in professions, shape cognition;
- describe the activity of teaching in support of learning;
- advance our understanding of cognitive processes and their development as they occur in subject matter domains and across contexts, such as laboratories, schools, professions, and/or informal sites of learning;
- analyze the nature of fluent and skilled cognition, including professional expertise, in important domains of knowledge and work;
- examine learners in interaction with innovative tools designed to support new forms of literacy;
- and contribute to theory building and educational innovation.

Research investigating cognition and instruction at multiple grain sizes and through the use of mixed methods is welcomed. In addition, proposals for topic specific special issues will be considered.

Cognition and Instruction has instituted a policy of blind review. Moreover, we will not identify reviewers to the authors unless the reviewer wishes us to do so.

Cognition and Instruction is published by Lawrence Erlbaum Associates. Manuscripts for review should be sent submitted by e-mail to **ci@vanderbilt.edu** as well as submitted in duplicate hard copy to Richard Lehrer at the address noted above. Proposals for edited collections of papers should be discussed in advance with one of the editors.

Cognitive Psychology

SUBMISSION PROCESS:
Electronic Submission Only via Online Portal
http://www.ees.elsevier.com/cogpsy/

CONTACT INFORMATION:	REVIEW PROCESS:	
Gordon Logan, Editor Editorial Office 525 B Street, Suite 1900 San Diego, CA 92101-4495 USA	**Type of Review:**	Editorial Review
	No. External Reviewers:	3
	No. InHouse Reviewers:	0
Phone: 619-669-6417	**Acceptance Rate:**	11-20%
	Time to Review:	4 - 6 Months
	Reviewer's Comments:	Yes
Email: cogpsy@elsevier.com	**Invited Articles:**	0-5%
Website: http://www.elsevier.com/	**Fees to Publish:**	$0.00 US$
	Fees to Review:	$0.00 US$

PUBLICATION GUIDELINES:	CIRCULATION DATA:
Manuscript Style: See Manuscript Guidelines	**Reader:** Academics
Manuscript Length: 30+	**Frequency of Issue:** 8 Times/Year
Copies Required: Electronic Only	**Sponsor/Publisher:** Elsevier Inc.

MANUSCRIPT TOPICS:
Languages & Linguistics; Reading; Thinking, Reasoning, Memory, Attention, Perception

MANUSCRIPT GUIDELINES/COMMENTS:

Description
Cognitive Psychology is concerned with advances in the study of memory, language processing, perception, problem solving, and thinking. The journal presents original empirical, theoretical, and tutorial papers, methodological articles, and critical reviews. *Cognitive Psychology* specializes in extensive articles that have a major impact on cognitive theory and/or provide new theoretical advances.

Research Areas include:
- Artificial intelligence
- Developmental psychology
- Linguistics
- Neurophysiology
- Social psychology

Guide for Authors

Cognitive Psychology publishes original empirical, theoretical, and tutorial papers, methodological articles, and critical reviews dealing with memory, language processing, perception, problem solving, and thinking. This journal emphasizes work on human cognition. Papers dealing with relevant problems in such related areas as social psychology, developmental psychology, linguistics, artificial intelligence, and neurophysiology also are welcomed provided that they are of direct interest to cognitive psychologists and are written to be understandable by such readers. Minor or very specialized studies are seldom accepted.

Submission of Manuscripts

Authors are requested to submit their papers electronically by using online manuscript submission available at **http://www.ees.elsevier.com/cogpsy**. This site will guide authors stepwise through the submission process. Authors should upload the source files of their articles in the preferred format of Microsoft (MS) Word, RTF, WordPerfect, or LaTeX for text and TIFF or EPS for figures. The system automatically converts source files to a single Adobe Acrobat PDF version of the article, which is used in the peer-review process. Please note that even though manuscript source files are converted to PDF at submission for the review process, these source files are needed for further processing after acceptance. Authors, reviewers, and editors send and receive all correspondence by e-mail and no paper correspondence is necessary. Should you be unable to provide an electronic version, please contact the Editorial Office prior to submission at: Cognitive Psychology, 525 B Street, Suite 1900, San Diego, CA 92101-4495, USA; E-mail: **cogpsy@elsevier.com**; Telephone: (619) 699-6517; Fax: (619) 699-6211

Manuscripts must be written in English. A manuscript submitted for publication is judged by three main criteria: (a) appropriateness of the subject matter for this journal; (b) significance of its contribution to knowledge; and (c) clarity and conciseness of writing. No changes in a manuscript may be made once it has been accepted and is in press.

Manuscripts are accepted for review with the understanding that no substantial portion of the study has been published or is under consideration for publication elsewhere and that its submission for publication has been approved by all the authors and by the institution where the work was carried out. Manuscripts that do not meet the general criteria or standards for publication in *Cognitive Psychology* will be immediately returned to the author(s), without detailed review.

Upon acceptance of an article, authors will be asked to transfer copyright (for more information on copyright, see **http://Authors.elsevier.com**). This transfer will ensure the widest possible dissemination of information. A letter will be sent to the corresponding author confirming receipt of the manuscript. A form facilitating transfer of copyright will be provided after acceptance.

If material from the other copyrighted works is included, the author(s) must obtain written permission from the copyright owners and credit the source(s) in the article. Elsevier has preprinted forms for use by authors in these cases: contact Elsevier Global Rights Department, P.O. Box 800, Oxford OX5 1DX, UK; phone: (+44) 1865 843830, fax: (+44) 1865 853333, e-mail: **permissions@elsevier.com**.

Preparation of a Manuscripts

Format and style of manuscript should conform to the conventions specified in the latest edition of *Publication Manual of the American Psychological Association* with the exceptions listed below. Please note that it is the responsibility of the author that manuscripts for *Cognitive Psychology* conform to the requirements of this journal. Manuscripts should be double-spaced throughout. Pages should be numbered consecutively and organized as follows:

The **title page** (p. 1) should contain the article title, authors' names and affiliations, footnotes to the title, and the address for manuscript correspondence (including e-mail address and telephone and fax numbers).

The **abstract** (p. 2) must be a single paragraph that summarizes the main findings of the paper in less than 150 words. After the abstract a list of up to 10 keywords that will be useful for indexing or searching should be included.

The **introduction** should be concise as possible, without subheadings.

Materials and methods should be sufficiently detailed to enable the experiments to be reproduced.

Results and Discussion may be combined and may be organized into subheadings.

References should be cited in the text by surname of the author, followed by the year of publication. Only articles that have been published or are in press should be included in the references. Unpublished results or personal communications should be cited as such in the text. Please use the following style.

Biggs, J. B., & Collis, K. F. (1982). *Evaluating the quality of learning: The SOLO taxonomy*. New York: Academic Press.

Mattys, S. L., Jusczyk, P. W., Luce, P. A., & Morgan, J. L. (1999). Phonotactic and prosodic effects on word segmentation in infants. *Cognitive Psychology*, 38 465-494.

Ross, B. H. (1996). Category learning as problem solving. In D. L. Medin (Ed.), *The psychology of learning and motivation* (Vol. 35, pp. 165-192, San Diego: Academic Press.

Figures should be in a finished form suitable for publication. Please visit our Web site at **http://authors.elsevier.com/artwork** for detailed instructions on preparing electronic artwork.

Color figures in the printed issue can be accepted only if the authors defray the cost. However, if, together with your accepted article, you submit usable color figures, then Elsevier will ensure, at no additional charge, that these figures will appear in color on the Web (e.g., ScienceDirect and other sites) regardless of whether these illustrations are reproduced in color in the printed version. For color reproduction in print, you will receive information regarding the costs from Elsevier after receipt of your accepted article. For further information on the preparation of electronic artwork, please see **http://authors.elsevier.com/artwork**. Please note: Because of technical complications that can arise in converting color figures to "gray scale" (for the printed version should you not opt for color in print), please submit in addition usable black-and-white files corresponding to all the color illustrations.

Tables should be numbered consecutively with Arabic numerals in order of appearance in the text. Type each table double-spaced on a separate page with a short descriptive title typed directly above and with essential footnotes below.

Preparation of Supplementary Material

Elsevier now accepts electronic supplementary material to support and enhance your scientific research. Supplementary files offer additional possibilities for publishing supporting applications, movies, animation sequences, high-resolution images, background datasets, sound clips, and more. Supplementary files supplied will be published online alongside the electronic version of your article in Elsevier Web products, including ScienceDirect (**http://www.sciencedirect.com**). To ensure that your submitted material is directly usable, please provide the data in one of our recommended file formats. Authors should submit the material in electronic format together with the article and supply a concise and descriptive caption for each file. Please note, however, that supplementary material will not appear in the printed journal. For more detailed instructions, please visit our Author Gateway at **http://authors.elsevier.com**, click on "Artwork instructions," and then click on "Multimedia files."

154

Proofs

PDF proofs will be sent by e-mail to the corresponding author. To avoid delay in publication, only necessary changes should be made, and corrections should be returned promptly. Authors will be charged for alterations that exceed 10% of the total cost of composition.

Reprints

Twenty-five (25) reprints will be provided free of charge. Additional reprints may be ordered.

Author Inquiries

For inquiries relating to the submission of articles (including electronic submission where available) please visit the Elsevier Author Gateway at **http://authors.elsevier.com**. The Author Gateway also provides the facility to track accepted articles and set up e-mail alerts to inform you of when an article's status has changed, as well as detailed artwork guidelines, copyright information, frequently asked questions, and more. Contact details for questions arising after acceptance of an article, especially those relating to proofs, are provided after registration of an article for publication.

Cognitive Science

SUBMISSION PROCESS:
Electronic Submission Only via Online Portal http://www.editorialmanager.com/cogsci/

CONTACT INFORMATION:	REVIEW PROCESS:	
Arthur B. Markman, Executive Editor University of Texas, Austin Austin, TX USA	**Type of Review:**	Editorial Review
	No. External Reviewers:	3
	No. InHouse Reviewers:	0
Phone:	**Acceptance Rate:**	11-20%
	Time to Review:	2 - 3 Months
Email:	**Reviewer's Comments:**	Yes
cogscij@indiana.edu	**Invited Articles:**	6-10%
Website:	**Fees to Publish:**	$0.00 US$
www.cognitivesciencesociety.org	**Fees to Review:**	$0.00 US$

PUBLICATION GUIDELINES:	CIRCULATION DATA:
Manuscript Style: American Psychological Association	**Reader:** Academics
Manuscript Length: 30+	**Frequency of Issue:** Bi-Monthly
Copies Required: Electronic Only	**Sponsor/Publisher:** Cognitive Science Society / Lawrence Erlbaum Associates, Inc.

MANUSCRIPT TOPICS:
Artificial Intelligence; Computer Science; Education; Educational Psychology; Languages & Linguistics; Reading; Science Math & Environment

MANUSCRIPT GUIDELINES/COMMENTS:

Topics Also Include. Anthropology, Artificial Intelligence, Biology, Computer Science, Education, Linguistics, Neuroscience, Philosophy and Psychology

Submission Information for Authors
Cognitive Science is a bimonthly journal for the multidisciplinary study of minds and other intelligent systems. It publishes articles on cognition from perspective in artificial intelligence, education, linguistics, neuroscience, philosophy, psychology, and anthropology of multidisciplinary concern. Editorial decisions are made on the basis of content, rather than discipline or author, and papers in all areas of cognitive science are welcome. Research reports which are specifically written for a multidisciplinary audience are given the highest priority. Papers which are very general or speculative, which constitute parametric refinements of well-known ideas, or which are accessible to only a narrow or discipline-specific audience, will be given very low priority and may be returned to authors without formal review.

The following kinds of articles are appropriate for the journal: (a) theories or theoretical analyses of knowledge representation, cognitive processes, and brain theory; (b) experimental or ethnographic studies relevant to theoretical issues in cognitive science; (c) descriptions of intelligent programs that exhibit or model some human ability; (d) design proposals for cognitive models; (e) protocol or discourse analysis of human cognitive processing; (f) discussions of new problem areas or methodological issues in cognitive science; and (g) short theoretical notes or rebuttals. The journal will publish four categories of articles. *Regular articles* are approximately 30 published pages (12,000 words). *Extended articles* have a target length of approximately 45 pages (18,000 words), and are expected to present particularly noteworthy research that cannot be adequately described within the constraints of a regular article. *Brief reports* have a target length of about 10 pages (4,000 words). *Letters to the editor* will typically consist of approximately 2-3 page (1,000 words) commentaries to articles, responses to commentaries, and discussion items of general relevance to the cognitive science community.

Original articles only will be considered. Submission of an article is understood to imply that the article is original and unpublished, is not being considered for publication elsewhere, and will not be submitted elsewhere while it is under review by *Cognitive Science.* Distribution of a prepublication draft in paper or electronic form is not considered as prior publication, as long as the distributed article is clearly identified as a prepublication draft. Following publication, authors are entitled to distribute copies of their article for personal use, either on paper or electronically, through their own personal mailing or website, or through mailing or the website of an agency by which they are employed, but permission of the Cognitive Science Society is required to reproduce published papers in other sources, including electronic archives.

Cognitive Science uses a web-based submission and review process, Editorial Manager. Authors should log onto **http://www.editorialmanager.com/cogsci/** for instructions on how to register and submit manuscripts online. Paper copies of submissions are no longer acceptable. When submitting their manuscripts to Editorial Manager, authors will need to provide an electronic version of their manuscript and abstract, a set of keywords chosen from a set of classifications, and a category designation for their manuscript (letter to the editor, brief report, regular article, or extended article). Authors may send queries concerning the submission process, manuscript status, or journal procedures to the editorial office at **cogscij@indiana.edu**.

Illustrations. Color figures can now be reproduced on **www.leaonline.com** at no additional charge, regardless of whether or not these illustrations are reproduced in color in the printed version. In situations where figures make essential use of color, the journal also has the capacity to publish a limited number of color figures in the printed version. In these cases, costs incurred will be the author's responsibility. For further information on the preparation of electronic artwork, please see: **https://www.erlbaum.com/shop/tek9.asp?pg=products&specific=0364-0213**

Please note: Because of technical complications that can arise by converting color figures to 'gray scale' (for printed version should you not opt for color in print) please also submit usable black and white prints corresponding to all the color illustrations. For manuscripts submitted online, a file of a black and white version of each color should be uploaded, in addition to the color figure file.

Manuscripts should conform to APA 5th edition as specified in the *Publication Manual of the American Psychological Association* with the exceptions and considerations listed below. Authors may be asked to re-format manuscripts that do not conform to the following guidelines prior to editorial evaluation.

Preparation of Manuscript

Please double-space all material. Manuscripts should have 1-in. margins on all sides. Number pages consecutively with the title page as page 1 and include a brief abstract of 100 to 150 words as page 2. In departure from APA format, we accept and encourage submissions in which tables, figures, and figure captions are integrated into the text body rather than separated into sections. However, if authors choose to integrate these materials, they will still need to separate them for the version of the manuscript sent to the publisher. All tables and other end-of-paper matter except art should be numbered.

Figures

Figures must be supplied in electronic format and should be of sufficiently high resolution to appear sharp and artifact-free when printed. All figures must be in a form suitable for reproduction. Ideally, we would like authors to submit their figures in the actual final size. The maximum size allowed for this journal is 5½ by 7¼ inches (to allow room for the legend). Color illustrations are only available for the printed version of the journal. Figures captions should appear on a list separate from the text or on the figures themselves. The word "Figure" should always appear as Fig. in text and in legends.

Numbering of Figures and Tables

Each figure and table must be mentioned in the text and must be numbered consecutively using Arabic numerals in the order of its appearance in the text. On the reverse side of every figure write the name of the author and the figure number, unless figures are integrated with the text. A brief title should be typed directly above each table. Tables do not need any legends, and any explanations or clarifications of tabular material should be indicated as a footnote to the table by means of lower case letters.

References

Contributors should refer to the *APA Publication Manual* for the correct listing of references in the text and reference list. All references must be closely checked in text and lists to determine that dates and spellings are consistent. Please note that the names of all authors should be given in the list of references, and "et al." used only in the text. Examples for books, journals, and conference proceedings follow:

Reisen, A.H. (1966). Sensory deprivation. In E. Stellar & J.M. Sprague (Eds.), *Progress in physiological psychology* (Vol. 1). New York: Academic Press.

Atkinson, R.C., & Shiffrin, R.M. (1971). The control of short-term memory. *Scientific American,* 225, 82-90.

Keane, M.T.(1995). On order effects in analogical mapping: Predicting human error using IAM. In J.D. Moore & J.F. Lehman (Eds.), *Proceedings of the Seventeenth Annual Conference of the Cognitive Science Society* (pp. 449-454). Mahwah, NJ:Erlbaum.

Spelling, Terminology, and Abbreviations

American spelling, rather than British, is preferred. The Third Edition of *Webster's Unabridged Dictionary* is the standard reference work when in doubt. Please try to avoid jargon and, wherever possible, abbreviations that are not commonly accepted.

Permissions

Contributors are responsible for obtaining permission from copyright owners if they use an illustration, table, or lengthy quote from material that has been published elsewhere. Contributors should write to both the publisher and author of material they are seeking permission to reproduce.

Reprints

The only opportunity contributors have to order offprints is when page proofs are returned.

Please submit to **http://cogsci.edmgr.com**

Acceptable Formats

Word, WordPerfect, TXT, RTF, LaTeX2e, AMSTeX, TIFF, GIF, JPEG, EPS, Postscript, PICT, Excel and Powerpoint

College and University

SUBMISSION PROCESS:
Electronic Submission Only **via EMail** **louise@bc.edu**

CONTACT INFORMATION:	REVIEW PROCESS:	
Louise Lonabocker, Editor Boston College 102 Lyons Hall Chestnut Hill, MA 02467 USA	**Type of Review:**	Blind Review
	No. External Reviewers:	3+
	No. InHouse Reviewers:	1
Phone: 617-552-3318	**Acceptance Rate:**	21-30%
	Time to Review:	1 Month
	Reviewer's Comments:	Yes
Email: louise@bc.edu	**Invited Articles:**	0-5%
Website: www.aacrao.org/publications/candu/write.cfm	**Fees to Publish:**	$0.00 US$
	Fees to Review:	$0.00 US$

PUBLICATION GUIDELINES:	CIRCULATION DATA:
Manuscript Style: Chicago Manual of Style **Manuscript Length:** 11-15 **Copies Required:** One	**Reader:** Administrators, Higher Education Administrators **Frequency of Issue:** Quarterly **Sponsor/Publisher:** American Association of Collegiate Registrars and Admissions Officers

MANUSCRIPT TOPICS:
Higher Education

MANUSCRIPT GUIDELINES/COMMENTS:

Topics Also Include. Enrolment Management; Financial Aid; Registration and Records; Student Record Systems; Student Recruitment & Retention

Write for *College and University*
What's the best way to share your ideas, innovations, and opinions with registrars, admissions officers, and enrollment managers nationwide? Contribute to AACRAO's prestigious *College and University* (*C&U*) quarterly journal.

Give your research and experience a voice by writing for the "Feature" section, or address best practices, how-tos, new technologies, the latest books, and other pertinent topics in "The Forum" section. With a substantial circulation base, *C&U* is an excellent vehicle for shaping the profession and gaining recognition.

AACRAO members are especially encouraged to submit articles, but non-members, faculty, graduate students, and members of the corporate sector are also welcome to share their work. Authors will receive copies of the issue in which their article appears, and will be issued an author honorarium.

MANUSCRIPT PREPARATION FOR *C&U*
Feature Articles (refereed articles)
The editor will acknowledge receipt of manuscripts and will forward them to the Editorial Board for review. The Committee will consider the appropriateness of the article for AACRAO's membership, the usefulness of the information, the nature and logic of the research methodology, clarity, and the style of presentation. This review may take as long as three months, after which the *C&U* editor will inform the author of the manuscript's acceptance or rejection.

- Manuscripts for **feature articles** should be no longer than 4,500 words.
- All submissions must be sent as an attachment via e-mail.
- Because the Editorial Board has a blind review policy, the author's name should not appear on any text page. *A separate cover sheet should be sent via e-mail and include the title of the manuscript and the author's name, address, phone, fax, and e-mail, if applicable.*
- References should be formatted in author-date style and follow guidelines provided on page 526 of *The Chicago Manual of Style*, 14th edition, published by the University of Chicago Press. A list of references should appear at the end of the article. Text citations also follow the author-date format; examples may be found on page 641 of the *Manual*. For more information or for samples, please contact the editor.
- In addition to being placed in the manuscript, the data for essential tables and charts should also be included in a separate Microsoft Excel (spreadsheet) file.
- Articles are accepted for publication with the understanding that the editors and Editorial Board reserve the right to edit for clarity and style.
- Authors whose manuscripts are selected for submission will be asked to submit a short biographical statement and an abstract of their article, both no more than 35 words.
- Do not submit articles that are under consideration for publication in another periodical.
- Submit manuscripts, letters, and direct inquiries to: Louise Lonabocker, *C&U* Editor-in-Chief, Director, Student Services, Boston College, Lyons 102, Chestnut Hill, MA 02467; Tel: (617) 552-3318; E-mail: **louise@bc.edu**

Forum Articles (commentary, analysis, book reviews, international resources)
College & University also welcomes comments on articles, timely issues in higher education, new technologies, and other topics of interest to the journal's readers in the form of commentary, policy analysis, international observations, and book reviews. This is an excellent venue for individuals to share their knowledge and experience, and for companies to share corporate know-how and the latest techniques and technologies.

- Manuscripts for "The Forum" should not exceed 2,000 words.
- Companies submitting articles should not have a sales-oriented focus to the article, but rather, provide a general overview.
- All other guidelines follow as above.
- Submit commentary, book reviews, and other non-refereed pieces to: Heather Zimar, *C&U* Managing Editor, AACRAO, One Dupont Circle, NW, Suite 520, Washington, DC 20036; Tel: (607) 273-3337; E-mail: **zimarh@aacrao.org**

College Language Association Journal

SUBMISSION PROCESS:
Postal Submission Only

CONTACT INFORMATION:	REVIEW PROCESS:	
Cason L. Hill, Editor Morehouse College Atlanta, GA 30314 USA	**Type of Review:**	Editorial Review
	No. External Reviewers:	1
	No. InHouse Reviewers:	3
Phone: 404-681-2800 ext. 2160	**Acceptance Rate:**	75%
	Time to Review:	4 - 6 Months
Email: chill@morehouse.edu	**Reviewer's Comments:**	Yes
	Invited Articles:	0-5%
Website: www.clascholars.org	**Fees to Publish:**	$0.00 US$
	Fees to Review:	$0.00 US$
PUBLICATION GUIDELINES:	**CIRCULATION DATA:**	
Manuscript Style: MLA Handbook, Latest Edition	**Reader:** Academics	
Manuscript Length: 11-15	**Frequency of Issue:** Quarterly	
Copies Required: Two	**Sponsor/Publisher:** Professional Association & University	

MANUSCRIPT TOPICS:
Adult Career & Vocational; African - American Literature; American Literature; Curriculum Studies; English Literature; Foreign Language; Foreign Literature; Languages & Linguistics

MANUSCRIPT GUIDELINES/COMMENTS:

Manuscripts sought on the following:
- Language and Literature* (criticism)
- Book Reviews

*English, American, Foreign (In English Translation)

Manuscripts submitted for consideration and possible publication should conform to the *MLA Handbook*, latest edition, in all matters of form.

The *CLA Journal* primarily publishes:
1. Articles on language and literature (all periods and all countries)
2. Literary criticism and book reviews (all periods and all countries)

College Quarterly, The

SUBMISSION PROCESS:

**Electronic Submission Preferred
via EMail**

katharine.janzen@senecac.on.ca

CONTACT INFORMATION:	REVIEW PROCESS:	
Katharine Janzen, Editor Seneca College of Applied Arts and Technology 70 The Pond Road Toronto, Ontario, M3J 3M6 Canada	**Type of Review:**	Blind Review
	No. External Reviewers:	3
	No. InHouse Reviewers:	3
	Acceptance Rate:	50-75%
Phone:	**Time to Review:**	2 - 3 Months
416-491-5050 ext. 3461	**Reviewer's Comments:**	Yes
	Invited Articles:	6-10%
Email:		
katharine.janzen@senecac.on.ca	**Fees to Publish:**	$0.00 US$
Website:	**Fees to Review:**	$0.00 US$
www.collegequarterly.ca		

PUBLICATION GUIDELINES:	CIRCULATION DATA:
Manuscript Style: American Psychological Association	**Reader:** Academics, Administrators, Practicing Teachers in Colleges
Manuscript Length: 26-30	**Frequency of Issue:** Quarterly
Copies Required: Five or 1 Electronic	**Sponsor/Publisher:** Seneca College of Applied Arts & Technology

MANUSCRIPT TOPICS:
Curriculum Studies; Education Management / Administration; Educational Psychology; Educational Technology Systems; Higher Education

MANUSCRIPT GUIDELINES/COMMENTS:

About the Journal
The College Quarterly is an academic journal devoted to the improvement of college education and the professional development of college educators. Focused on colleges in Canada but developed to serve the common needs of college educators in North America and worldwide, *CQ* is a resource for teaching and learning and provides an opportunity for research publication, information about developments of significance to college educators, and commentary on policy issues of concern to the educational community and its attentive publics.

Information for Authors
The College Quarterly (*CQ*) is an independent journal of research and discussion published by Seneca College. It is directed primarily to college educators, and others interested in post-secondary college education relevant to the Canadian context.

Submissions should be original manuscripts; electronic format, Canadian spelling and APA style are required. Work most likely to be published will address one or more of the following themes as they relate to education and Canadian colleges. The journal publishes both peer reviewed and editor only reviewed articles; peer reviewed articles will be clearly identified as such with the symbol P.

1. Teaching and Learning
- scholarly discussions related to teaching and learning issues
- approximately 2,000 – 2,500 words in length
- discussion on technology enhanced learning
- discussion of teaching/learning strategies
- case studies may be included

2. Applied Research
- both peer reviewed and non-peer reviewed
- applied research – examples, findings, announcements of calls for proposals, links to resources and funding sources

3. Governance issues
- issues related to administration and governance of the colleges
- legislative and political issues e.g., New Charter for Ontario CAATs
- announcements, news

4. Reviews
- book reviews approximately 500-750 words in length
- new technology related to college context

5. The colleges and the community
- relationships between colleges & universities
- relationships with the private sector, business and industry and non-government organizations
- relevant social issues

6. Commentary
- commentary/guest viewpoint
- commentaries no more than 400 words
- letters to the editors
- editorial page

The content of manuscripts accepted for publication, including titles, text, tables, diagrams and graphics, are subject, without consultation with the author(s), to such reformatting and modification as is deemed necessary for publication and to those minor editorial changes which, in the Editors' judgement, do not substantially alter the intent of the original manuscript.

The copyright for all content published in the *CQ* belongs to *The College Quarterly*, Seneca College of Applied Arts and Technology, Toronto, Ontario.

Publication Schedule

Issue	Publication Date	Article Submission Deadline (digital form)
Spring	March 31	February 15
Summer	June 30	May 15
Fall	September 30	August 15
Winter	December 31	November 15

Submissions to *CQ*
Authors are requested to submit work in electronic format (e.g., within an e-mail or as an attachment to an e-mail, on diskette or CD) using any software (e.g., Rich Text Format or MS

WORD for PC or MAC computers) and in APA style with as little formatting as possible. We would prefer not to receive printed text manuscripts.

All submissions must be accompanied by an abstract of no more than 100 words, and a byline about the author(s). *CQ* accepts no responsibility for the return of contributors' media if submitted in a format other than e-mail, and authors are reminded to retain current copies of all work submitted.

Manuscripts may be submitted at any time. Authors will normally be notified within 2 to 3 weeks that the manuscript has been received and whether or not the article is accepted for review. Manuscripts submitted for peer review will be blinded and reviewed by a panel of experts in the relevant field. It may take up to three months for a peer review to be completed. General interest articles accepted for publication may be published in the next edition of the *CQ* or held for later publication as appropriate.

All correspondence should be addressed Katharine Janzen, Ed.D., Senior Editor, The College Quarterly, at Seneca College of Applied Arts and Technology, 70 The Pond Road, Toronto, Ontario, Canada M3J 3M6.

The Senior Editor also can be reached by telephone at (416) 491–5050, extension 2080, by fax at (416) 491–7745 or by e-mail at **katharine.janzen@senecac.on.ca**.

College Student Affairs Journal

SUBMISSION PROCESS:
Electronic Submission Only **via EMail** dgregory@odu.edu

CONTACT INFORMATION:	REVIEW PROCESS:	
Dennis Gregory, Editor Old Dominion University 110 Education Bldg. Norfolk, VA 23529 USA	**Type of Review:**	Blind Review
	No. External Reviewers:	0
	No. InHouse Reviewers:	3+
Phone: 757-683-3702	**Acceptance Rate:**	21-30%
	Time to Review:	2 - 3 Months
	Reviewer's Comments:	Yes
Email: dgregory@odu.edu	**Invited Articles:**	0-5%
	Fees to Publish:	$0.00 US$
Website: www.sacsa.org	**Fees to Review:**	$0.00 US$

PUBLICATION GUIDELINES:	CIRCULATION DATA:
Manuscript Style: American Psychological Association	**Reader:** Academics, Administrators
Manuscript Length: 16-20	**Frequency of Issue:** 2 Times/Year
Copies Required: Electronic Only	**Sponsor/Publisher:** Southern Association for College Student Affairs

MANUSCRIPT TOPICS:
College Student Issues; Education Management / Administration; Higher Education; Student Affairs

MANUSCRIPT GUIDELINES/COMMENTS:

Purpose. The *College Student Affairs Journal* publishes articles related to research, concepts, and practices that have implications for both practitioners and scholars in college student affairs work.

Types of Manuscripts Accepted. General articles may be research reports, updates on professional issues, examinations of legislative issues, dialogues and debates, historical articles, literature reviews, opinion pieces, or projections of future trends. Authors may also submit reviews of works in any medium, such as books or films.

Publication Schedule. Twice yearly, fall and spring.

Circulation. 1,200.

Index. Current Index to Journals in Education and Higher Education Abstracts.

Concurrent Submissions to Other Publications. Not accepted.

Style Guide. Manuscripts should follow the style of the fifth edition of the *Publication Manual of the American Psychological Association* (APA). Authors should particularly note this manual's recommendation to use active voice and first person narration. All copy should be typed, double-spaced in Times New Roman 12-point font with notes, references, tables, and figures appearing at the end of the manuscript per APA style.

Special Format Guidelines. The first page of the manuscript should include the article title; the name, position, and institutional affiliation of each author; and appropriate contact information for editorial response. The article's first text page should include the manuscript title, but no information that would identify any author.

Recommended Length. Manuscripts submitted for the Articles section generally range between 3,000 and 6,500 words including abstract, tables, figures, and references. Reviews may be between 1,000 and 2,000 words.

Figures and Graphs. Supply camera-ready art.

Manuscript Submission. The *College Student Affairs Journal* uses an electronic submission and review process. Authors should submit by e-mail an electronic copy of the manuscript/review in Microsoft Word format (for PC) to the Journal editor, Dr. Dennis Gregory, Associate Professor, Old Dominion University at **dgregory@odu.edu**.

Review Process. All submissions are refereed using a blind review system. Evaluative criteria include significance of topic, clarity of presentation, style of writing, usefulness to practitioners and/or importance for scholarship, contribution to the student affairs profession, and quality of methodology or program. Notification of acceptance or rejection of all manuscripts will be made by the editor. All manuscripts received and approved for publication become the property of the association. All others will be returned on request. The editor reserves the right to edit or rewrite accepted articles to meet the *Journal*'s standards.

College Student Journal

SUBMISSION PROCESS:
Postal Submission Only

CONTACT INFORMATION:	REVIEW PROCESS:	
George E. Uhlig, Editor c/o Project Innovation of Mobile PO Box 8508 Spring Hill Station Mobile, AL 36689-8508 USA	**Type of Review:**	Editorial Review
	No. External Reviewers:	2
	No. InHouse Reviewers:	1
	Acceptance Rate:	60%
Phone: 251-343-1878	**Time to Review:**	1 - 2 Months
	Reviewer's Comments:	Yes
	Invited Articles:	0-5%
Email: guhlig007@yahoo.com	**Fees to Publish:**	$30.00 US$ per Pg
	Fees to Review:	$0.00 US$
Website: www.projectinnovation.biz		

PUBLICATION GUIDELINES:	CIRCULATION DATA:
Manuscript Style: American Psychological Association	**Reader:** Academics, Administrators
Manuscript Length: 11-15	**Frequency of Issue:** Quarterly
Copies Required: Two	**Sponsor/Publisher:** Project Innovation, Inc.

MANUSCRIPT TOPICS:
Curriculum Studies; Education Management / Administration; Higher Education; Urban Education, Cultural / Non-Traditional

MANUSCRIPT GUIDELINES/COMMENTS:

College Student Journal publishes original investigations and theoretical papers dealing with college student values, attitudes, opinions, and learning. This includes the areas of undergraduate, graduate, and professional schools, and may include selected contributions dealing with college preparation.

Manuscript Submission
Manuscripts must be submitted in duplicate and should be prepared to conform to the style and procedures described in the *Publication Manual of the American Psychological Association*. Manuscripts must be accompanied by an abstract of 100 to 200 words typed on a separate sheet of paper. The abstract should contain statements of the (a) problem, (b).method, (c) results, (d) conclusions when appropriate.

The abstract should provide the reader with an idea of the theme and scope of the article.

At least one copy of the manuscript and the abstract must be original with clear, clean typing or printing. We prefer disk-based manuscripts in either Macintosh or MS-Dos format. However, at least one printed copy of the manuscript must be included with the disk.

Review Process
Manuscripts are reviewed by at least two reviewers knowledgeable in the field of study. An attempt is made to review manuscripts within two weeks of receipt when possible.

Fees to Publish
This *Journal* is not supported by either membership or association dues, or advertising. Authors or their institutions share the cost of publication. Except for invited articles, authors will be invoiced for their share of publication costs at the time the manuscript is accepted for publication. The article will be scheduled for publication after payment or an institutional purchase order is received.

Reprints
Information concerning reprints and reprint policy is disseminated with page proofs/galleys.

College Teaching

SUBMISSION PROCESS:
Electronic Submission Only **via Online Portal** **http://mc.manuscriptcentral.com/ct**

CONTACT INFORMATION:

Katy Lindenmuth, Editor
Heldref Publications
1319 Eighteenth St. NW
Washington, DC 20036 USA

Phone:
202-296-6267 etx. 1298

Email:
ct@heldref.org

Website:
http://www.heldref.org/ct.php

REVIEW PROCESS:

Type of Review:	Blind Review
No. External Reviewers:	2
No. InHouse Reviewers:	0
Acceptance Rate:	21-30%
Time to Review:	4 - 6 Months
Reviewer's Comments:	Yes
Invited Articles:	0-5%
Fees to Publish:	$0.00 US$
Fees to Review:	$0.00 US$

PUBLICATION GUIDELINES:

Manuscript Style:
Chicago Manual of Style

Manuscript Length:
16-20

Copies Required:
Electronic Only

CIRCULATION DATA:

Reader:
Academics

Frequency of Issue:
Quarterly

Sponsor/Publisher:
Heldref Publications, Inc.

MANUSCRIPT TOPICS:
Curriculum Studies; Higher Education; Library Science / Information Resources; Teacher Education

MANUSCRIPT GUIDELINES/COMMENTS:

College Teaching provides an interdisciplinary forum on issues related to teaching at the undergraduate and graduate levels. This journal is interested in articles that explore (1) aims and outcomes of teaching philosophy and practices that have significance beyond a specific discipline (these may include teaching techniques, new classroom procedures, evaluations of innovative programs, and examination of contemporary developments); (2) teachers' roles, education, professional development, preparation to teach, and evaluation; and (3) incentives that encourage good teaching and ways good teaching is evaluated and rewarded. The editors welcome thoughtful reactions to articles appearing in the journal.

The journal welcomes articles on research in one field as long as it has applications to others as well. However, the journal cannot use: (1) articles that are purely descriptive without any critical evaluation or analysis; (2) those that are limited to one specific discipline; or (3) those that show no awareness of current work and literature in the field.

Articles range from 750 to 5,000 words, depending on the nature of the topic. Discussion of promising practices should be short, while articles on research material may be longer. Commentaries, of no more than 850 words, will be considered. The journal is refereed. Each article is read by two reviewers, with a total review time of three to five months. Accepted manuscripts usually are published within one year; however, there is no guarantee.

Manuscripts must be submitted exclusively to *College Teaching*. We cannot review or publish duplicate submissions.

Contributors should submit both blind and nonblind Microsoft Word documents of their manuscript at **http://mc.manuscriptcentral.com/ct**. The author(s) should keep an exact copy so the editors can refer to specific pages and lines if a question arises. The manuscript should be double spaced.

The *Chicago Manual of Style*, 15th ed., University of Chicago Press, 2003, should be used as a style reference in preparation of manuscripts. REFERENCES at the end of the manuscript should be unnumbered and listed alphabetically according to the author's last name, followed by the year of publication, as in Smith, J. 1989. Citation in the text should list author and date, as in (Smith 1989).

Reproductions of figures (graphs and charts) may be submitted for review purposes, but the originals must be supplied if the manuscript is accepted for publication. Tables should be prepared exactly or adapted as they are to appear in the journal. For tables reproduced or adapted from another publication, permission must be obtained by the author and noted on the ms.

Avoid explanatory notes whenever possible by incorporating their content in the text. For essential notes, identify them with consecutive superscripts and list them in a section entitled NOTES at the end of the text.

We reserve the right to make editorial changes in style and format.

Authors receive two complimentary copies of the issue in which their article appears and permission to reproduce additional copies of that article. Reprints are available through the journal.

Submit manuscripts at **http://mc.manuscriptcentral.com/ct**. Authors must create a free Manuscript Central user account to do so. If a manuscript has multiple contributing authors, one must be selected as its corresponding author. If an author submits other manuscripts in the future, the same user account should be used.

Community & Junior College Libraries

SUBMISSION PROCESS:	
Postal Submission Only	

CONTACT INFORMATION:	REVIEW PROCESS:	
Susan Anderson, Editor St. Petersburg College PO Box 13489 St. Petersburg, FL 33733 USA	**Type of Review:**	Blind Review
	No. External Reviewers:	3+
	No. InHouse Reviewers:	2
Phone: 727-341-3719	**Acceptance Rate:**	40-50%
	Time to Review:	2 - 3 Months
	Reviewer's Comments:	Yes
Email: andersons@spcollege.edu	**Invited Articles:**	6-10%
	Fees to Publish:	$0.00 US$
Website: www.haworthpressinc.com	**Fees to Review:**	$0.00 US$

PUBLICATION GUIDELINES:	CIRCULATION DATA:
Manuscript Style: See Manuscript Guidelines	**Reader:** Academics
Manuscript Length: 30+	**Frequency of Issue:** Quarterly
Copies Required: One	**Sponsor/Publisher:** Haworth Press, Inc.

MANUSCRIPT TOPICS:

Educational Technology Systems; Information Literacy; Library Management; Library Science / Information Resources

MANUSCRIPT GUIDELINES/COMMENTS:

About the Journal

Community & Junior College Libraries is a refereed journal especially for professionals working in academic and technical libraries, learning or media centers, library training programs, and library organizations. The journal's focus is on the distinctive, dynamic nature of learning resources centers in two-year colleges. The professional contributions being made by these colleges are highlighted. Contributors to this fundamental resource present profiles of LRCs around the country and address news of special relevance—legislation, systems development, and various concerns faced by professionals in the libraries and information centers of two-year colleges. *Community & Junior College Libraries* also features several noteworthy regular features that serve to inform readers about the people and the programs making headlines in the profession. The journal contains informative recurring features that include book reviews by David Voros as well as:

- "Nothing But Net," edited by Julie Todaro—a review of Web sites by topic
- "A Librarian Abroad," edited by Luella Teuton—descriptions of various libraries (community college and other libraries as well) highlighting the accomplishments of libraries around the world

Through research and interviews with professionals in the field, *Community & Junior College Libraries* provides a coherent voice for community college librarians. It addresses the need to define and enhance the leading edge of LRC planning and practice in the United States and abroad. Readers receive information on pertinent topics such as the Internet in the LRC, LRC standards, proven policies, conference reports, and networks and consortia. This savvy journal offers comprehensive and authoritative information that will benefit any community or junior college librarian.

Instructions for Authors
Journal Editor. Susan Anderson, DSc, MLIS, St. Petersburg College, PO Box 13489, St Petersburg, FL 33733; Email: **andersons@spcollege.edu**

Authors must complete a Manuscript Submission & Limited Copyright Transfer Form (See "2. Copyright") **www.haworthpress.com**.

1. **Original Articles Only**. Submission of a manuscript to this journal represents a certification on the part of the author(s) that it is an original work, and that neither this manuscript nor a version of it has been published elsewhere nor is being considered for publication elsewhere.

2. **Copyright**. Copyright ownership of your manuscript must be transferred officially to The Haworth Press, Inc., before we can begin the peer-review process. All authors must sign the form and return the original to the editor as soon as possible. Failure to return the copyright form in a timely fashion will result in a delay in review and subsequent publication.

3. **Manuscript Length**. 5-50 typed pages. Lengthier manuscripts may be considered, but only at the discretion of the editor. The abstract should precede the text on a separate piece of paper. The entire manuscript, including abstract, quotations, tables, and references, must be double-spaced.

4. **Manuscript Style**. References should be double-spaced and placed in alphabetical order. The use of footnotes within the text is discouraged. Words should be underlined only when it is intended that they be typeset in italics.

5. **Manuscript Preparation**. Double-spaced, including endnotes and references; 12-point font
Margins. Leave at least a one inch margin on all four sides; set all notes as endnotes.
Cover page. Important -- Submit a cover page with the manuscript, indicating only the article title (this is used for anonymous refereeing).
Second "title page". Include a regular title page as a separate document. Include the title again, plus:
- full authorship
- an ABSTRACT of about 100 words (below the abstract provide 3-10 key words for indexing purposes)
- a header or footer on each page with abbreviated title and page number of total (e.g., pg 2 of 7)
- an introductory note with authors' academic degrees, professional titles, affiliations, mailing and e-mail addresses, and any desired acknowledgement of research support or other credit

6. **Preparation of Tables, Figures, and Illustrations**. Any material that is not textual is considered artwork. This includes tables, figures, diagrams, charts, graphs, illustrations, appendices, screen captures, and photos. Tables and figures (including legend, notes, and sources) should be no larger than 4 ½ x 6 ½ inches. Type style should be Helvetica (or Helvetica narrow if necessary) and no smaller than 8 point. We request that computer-generated figures be in black and white and/or shades of gray (preferably no color; for it does not reproduce well). Camera-ready art must contain no grammatical, typographical, or format errors and must reproduce sharply and clearly in the dimensions of the final printed page (4 ½ x 6 ½ inches). Photos and screen captures must be saved as a TIFF file or other graphic file format such as JPEG or BMP. For final hardcopy submission, these should be on disk or CD-ROM accompanying your manuscript. For rapid publication we must receive black-and-white glossy or matte positives (white background with

black images and/or wording) in addition to files on disk. Tables should be created in the text document file using the software's Table feature.

7. **Submitting Art**. Both a printed hard copy and an electronic copy of the art must be provided. We request that each piece of art be sent in its own file or on a disk separate from the disk containing the manuscript text file(s); disks should be clearly labeled. We reserve the right to (if necessary) request new art, alter art, or if all else has failed in achieving art that is presentable, delete art. If submitted art cannot be used, the publisher reserves the right to redo the art and to charge the author a fee of $55.00 per hour for this service. The Haworth Press, Inc. is not responsible for errors incurred in the preparation of new artwork. Camera-ready artwork must be prepared on separate sheets of paper. Always use black ink and professional drawing instruments. On the back of these items, write your article title and the journal title lightly in soft-lead pencil (please do not write on the face of art). In the text file, skip extra lines and indicate where these figures are placed. Photos are considered part of the acceptable manuscript and remain with the publisher for use in additional printings.

8. **Typesetting**. You will not be receiving galley proofs of your article. Editorial revisions, if any, must therefore be made while your article is still in manuscript form. The final version of the manuscript will be the version you see published. Typesetter's errors will be corrected by the production staff of The Haworth Press, Inc. Authors are expected to submit manuscripts, disks, and art that are free from error.

9. **Disk Media**. (For Hardcopy Submissions) Haworth's in-house typesetting unit is able to utilize your final manuscript material as prepared on most personal computers and word processors. This will minimize typographical errors and decrease overall production time. Please send the first draft and final draft copies of your manuscript to the journal editor in print format for his/her final review and approval. After approval of your final manuscript, please submit the final approved version both in printed format ("hard copy") and floppy diskette or CD-ROM. On the outside of the diskette package write: 1) the brand name of your computer or word processor 2) the word processing program and version that you used 3) the title of your article, and 4) the file name. NOTE: Disk and hard copy must agree. In case of discrepancies, it is The Haworth Press' policy to follow hard copy. Authors are advised that no revisions of the manuscript can be made after acceptance by the editor for publication. The benefits of this procedure are many with speed and accuracy being the most obvious. We look forward to working with your disk submission which will allow us to serve you more efficiently.

10. **Spelling, Grammar, and Punctuation**. You are responsible for preparing manuscript copy which is clearly written in acceptable, scholarly English and which contains no errors of spelling, grammar, or punctuation. Neither the editor nor the publisher is responsible for correcting errors of spelling and grammar. The manuscript, after acceptance by the editor, must be immediately ready for typesetting as it is finally submitted by the author(s). Check your paper for the following common errors:
- dangling modifiers
- misplaced modifiers
- unclear antecedents
- incorrect or inconsistent abbreviations

Also, check the accuracy of all arithmetic calculations, statistics, numerical data, text citations, and references. INCONSISTENCIES MUST BE AVOIDED. Be sure you are consistent in your use of abbreviations, terminology, and in citing references, from one part of your paper to another.

11. **Acknowledgment of Receipt**. Please allow 10-15 weeks for the review process. Postage inquiries regarding submissions made from outside of the U.S. should be directed to the editor of this journal.

12. **Reference Linking**. The Haworth Press, Inc. is participating in reference linking for journal articles. (To obtain information on reference linking initiatives, please consult the CrossRef Web site at **www.crossref.org**.) When citing a journal article include the article's Digital Object Identifier (DOI), when available, as the last item in the reference. A Digital Object Identifier is a persistent, authoritative, and unique identifier that a publisher assigns to each article. Because of its persistence, DOIs will enable The Haworth Press, Inc., and other publishers to link to the article referenced, and the link will not break over time. This will be a great resource in scholarly research.

An example of a reference to a journal article which includes a DOI:
Vizine-Goetz, Diane (2002). Classification Schemes for Internet Resources Revisited. Journal of Internet Cataloging 5(4): 5:18. doi:10.1300/J141v05n04_02

13. **Alterations Required by Referees and Reviewers**. Many times a paper is accepted by the editor contingent upon changes that are mandated by anonymous specialist referees and/or members of the editorial board. If the editor returns your manuscript for revisions, you are responsible for retyping any sections of the paper to incorporate these revisions (if applicable, revisions should also be put on disk).

14. **Reprints**. The senior author will receive two copies of the journal issue as well as ten complimentary reprints of his or her article. The junior author(s) will receive two copies of the journal issue. These are sent several weeks after the journal issue is published and in circulation. An order form for the purchase of additional reprints will also be sent to all authors at this time. (Approximately 8 weeks is necessary for the preparation of reprints.) Please do not query the journal's editor about reprints. All such questions should be sent directly to The Haworth Press, Inc., Production Department, 37 West Broad Street, West Hazleton, PA 18202. To order additional reprints (minimum: 50 copies), please contact The Haworth Document Delivery Service, 10 Alice Street, Binghamton, NY 13904-1580; Tel: 1-800-429-6784 or Fax: (607) 722-6362.

Please remember to include the Manuscript Submission & Limited Copyright Transfer Form along with your submission. These instructions for authors in no way reflect how manuscripts are to be submitted to the Publisher. The Editor should follow Haworth's guidelines when making journal issue submissions.

Community College Enterprise: A Journal of Research and Practice, The

SUBMISSION PROCESS:

**Electronic Submission Preferred
via EMail**

gwilson@schoolcraft.edu

CONTACT INFORMATION:

Louis A. Reibling, Editor
c/o Gordon L. Wilson, Manging Editor
The Community College Enterprise
Schoolcraft College
18600 Haggerty Rd.
Livonia, MI 48152-2696

Phone:
734-462-4400

Email:
lreiblin@schoolcraft.edu
gwilson@schoolcraft.edu
nkhan@schoolcraft.edu

Website:
www.schoolcraft.edu/cce

REVIEW PROCESS:

Type of Review:	Blind Review
No. External Reviewers:	3
No. InHouse Reviewers:	1
Acceptance Rate:	70%
Time to Review:	1 - 2 Months
Reviewer's Comments:	Yes
Invited Articles:	0-5%
Fees to Publish:	$0.00 US$
Fees to Review:	$0.00 US$

PUBLICATION GUIDELINES:

Manuscript Style:
American Psychological Association
See Manuscript Guidelines

Manuscript Length:
11-15

Copies Required:
One

CIRCULATION DATA:

Reader:
Academics, Administrators, Practicing
Teachers, Counselors, Grad Stu.

Frequency of Issue:
2 Times/Year

Sponsor/Publisher:
Schoolcraft College

MANUSCRIPT TOPICS:
Adult Career & Vocational; Counseling & Personnel Services; Curriculum Studies; Education Management / Administration; Higher Education; Urban Education, Cultural / Non-Traditional

MANUSCRIPT GUIDELINES/COMMENTS:

Mission
The Community College Enterprise (formerly *Michigan Community College Journal*), published by and for community college practitioners, fosters and shares sound educational practices based upon scholarship and research.

Purpose
- Create a community college dialogue to support positive change based on research and exemplary practices.

- Stimulate awareness of future trends in educational leadership, technology and learning theory.
- Encourage unpublished authors by providing mentoring, writing workshops, and a forum for small sample research.
- Utilize a national editorial board to foster a research agenda based on the evolving mission of the community college.

The Community College Enterprise (formerly *Michigan Community College Journal*) publishes research and educational articles for community college educators. The *Journal* is indexed in the ERIC database.

Comments or questions can be emailed to: Gordon Wilson, The Community College Enterprise, Schoolcraft College, 18600 Haggerty Rd., Livonia, MI 48152-2696; Email: **gwilson@schoolcraft.edu**

Information About the Journal
The Community College Enterprise (formerly *Michigan Community College Journal*) is a refereed journal that encourages work primarily from community college educators. Issues are published in Fall and Spring. The journal publishes models of exemplary practice, case studies, research articles, analysis of public policy, innovative strategies, commissioned articles, and visioning practices for the next century. Each piece must define the context, a concern, an approach, and a solution.

The journal seeks to publish newer writers, as well as established authors, individuals, as well as co-authors. To encourage new writers, the editorial staff hopes to establish a dialogue with them. Contact the managing editor with questions: Gordon Wilson (**gwilson@schoolcraft.edu**)

Manuscript Preparation
Language and format, including headings, figures, citations and references, should conform to the Publications Manual of the American Psychological Association, 5th edition, 2001.

Manuscripts should be eight to fifteen, double-spaced, 8½" x 11" pages.

Include the following hard copy:
- a four to six line author biography
- an abstract of up to ten lines
- the article

Also include the copy in electronic form as an email attachment to Gordon Wilson (**gwilson@schoolcraft.edu**)or on a 3½" diskette in any of the following formats:
- IBM compatible PC - WordPerfect or Microsoft Word
- Macintosh - Microsoft Word, or
- a standard text file

Manuscripts and diskettes cannot be returned.

Community College Journal

SUBMISSION PROCESS:
Electronic Submission Preferred **via EMail** **nkent@aacc.nche.edu**

CONTACT INFORMATION:	REVIEW PROCESS:	
Norma Kent, VP, Communications Amer Association of Community Colleges One Dupont Circle, Suite 410 Washington, DC 20036 USA	**Type of Review:**	Editorial Review
	No. External Reviewers:	0
	No. InHouse Reviewers:	2
Phone: 202-728-0200 ext. 209	**Acceptance Rate:**	21-30%
	Time to Review:	2 - 3 Months
	Reviewer's Comments:	No
Email: nkent@aacc.nche.edu	**Invited Articles:**	50% +
Website: www.aacc.nche.edu	**Fees to Publish:**	$0.00 US$
	Fees to Review:	$0.00 US$

PUBLICATION GUIDELINES:	CIRCULATION DATA:
Manuscript Style: Chicago Manual of Style	**Reader:** Administrators
Manuscript Length: 6-10	**Frequency of Issue:** Bi-Monthly
Copies Required: One	**Sponsor/Publisher:** American Association of Community Colleges

MANUSCRIPT TOPICS:
Adult Career & Vocational; Curriculum Studies; Higher Education; Urban Education, Cultural / Non-Traditional

MANUSCRIPT GUIDELINES/COMMENTS:

The *Community College Journal* is published six times yearly, on the first day of every other month: August/September, October/November, December/January, February/March, April/May, and June/July. AACC welcomes *Journal* submissions. All manuscripts, solicited or unsolicited, are subject to review by the editorial board and **may be published or not according to the editors' discretion**. AACC assumes no responsibility for the receipt, return, or publication of unsolicited manuscripts. AACC reserves the right to edit all articles for length, style, and accuracy. All articles published in the *Journal* become the property of AACC.

A. **Topics**
1. Each issue of the *Journal* focuses on a theme. See Section E for 2004-2006 themes and deadlines.

2. Journal articles examine in-depth trends, problems and solutions, innovations, new technologies, and new ideas in higher education. The *Journal* avoids articles on empirical research and favors essays offering an objective look at problems and solutions of contemporary community colleges.

3. Articles should involve community and junior colleges, technical institutes, and independent schools. Issues should be of current interest to presidents, board members, administrators, faculty, and staff at two-year institutions. The *Journal* does not accept articles on K–12 or four-year education and rarely accepts articles about general higher education unless they are germane to the two-year college audience.

4. Book reviews should describe the book's scope, content, arguments, and structure.

5. For a guest editorial, write an opinion piece on a topic of concern to community colleges. The topic should be controversial, not a statement with which everyone obviously agrees. Query the *Journal* editor for topics of interest.

B. Length

1. Features: **1,100 – 1,200 words** on national perspectives, long-term trends, analysis.

2. News in Brief: approximately **200-300 words** on exemplary programs at individual campuses or current news items of pertinence to community colleges. News should be national in scope. Candid, publication-quality photographs required.

3. New in Print: approximately **500-1,000 words**; book reviews should describe the scope, content, basic arguments, and structure of the book.

4. Feedback: (Guest Editorial) **500-1,000 words**; opinion pieces on a topic of concern to community colleges; be controversial.

C. Style

1. *Chicago Manual of Style*. For references, refer to chapter 16 (reference style 2, author-date style).

2. *American Heritage Dictionary*

D. Tips for Writers

1. Add to the current literature or research. Original, even controversial articles are more desirable than well-written pieces on outworn issues. Discuss cutting-edge trends, not programs that have already been implemented on community college campuses.

2. Provide a nuts-and-bolts look at how to implement programs in the real world.

3. Present a national perspective, long-term trends, or analysis.

4. Submit well-written, coherent, and logical articles.

5. Avoid self-promotional articles. The *Journal* does not run public relations pieces for colleges, outside organizations, or companies that provide products or services to colleges. The only exceptions to this rule are paid advertising and house ads.

6. Include appropriate, complete bibliographical references. Articles that contain incomplete citations will be rejected. Do not cite your own previous publications, however. Readers will assume that the ideas are the author's unless otherwise noted. Rewrite the material rather than quote your own previous publications. Articles that are otherwise excellent but do not follow *Chicago*

Manual of Style for references may be accepted, but the author will be asked to rewrite the reference section.

7. Include candid, publication-quality photographs illustrating the article. For News in Brief, photographs are required for the article to be considered. Avoid posed photographs, "grip and grin," etc. **All photos must have an accompanying caption identifying its subject**. With feature articles, accompanying charts, graphs and tables are a definite plus. Submitted graphic elements **should not be embedded** in the article copy. Please send graphics as separate electronic files. Consult *Journal* editor first if you wish to send photographs or other art electronically.

E. **Deadlines**
To be considered for publication, manuscripts must be received at least two and a half months before the issue date, **no later than** the following:

Writer's Due Date	Issue Date	Theme
October 20, 2006	December/January 2007	Economic & Workforce Development
December 20, 2006	February/March 2007	Legislative Advocacy
February 19, 2007	April/May 2007	A New Vision for Community Colleges
April 18, 2007	June/July 2007	Resource Development
June 20, 2007	August/September, 2007	The Community College Student
August 20, 2007	October/November 2007	Technology

F. **Submission**
1. Electronic files sent as an e-mail attachment are the preferred method of delivery. Submissions sent by snail mail must include hard copy and electronic file. Microsoft Word for PC platform preferred. Send art by fast, traceable service. Consult the *Journal* editor if you wish to send photographs or other art electronically. Photographs must be high resolution tagged image file format (TIFF) or encapsulated postscript (EPS) file of at least **300 dpi**.

2. Insert a running header in the text that includes filename, article name, your name, date, and page numbers. Double-space text.

3. LABEL ALL DISKS with filename, name of program, and your name.

4. Address for Submissions: Cheryl Gamble, Editor, Community College Journal, One Dupont Circle, NW, Suite 410, Washington, DC 20036-1176; Phone: (202) 728-0200, ext 215; Fax: 202) 223-9390; E-mail: **cgamble@aacc.nche.edu**

Community College Journal of Research and Practice

SUBMISSION PROCESS:	
Postal Submission Only	

CONTACT INFORMATION:	REVIEW PROCESS:	
D. Barry Lumsden, Editor		
Seniro Research Fellow	**Type of Review:**	Blind Review
University of Alabama		
Education Policy Center	**No. External Reviewers:**	3
Box 870231	**No. InHouse Reviewers:**	0
Tuscaloosa, AL 35487-1960 USA	**Acceptance Rate:**	21-30%
	Time to Review:	1 - 2 Months
Phone:	**Reviewer's Comments:**	Yes
940-597-7923	**Invited Articles:**	0-5%
Email:	**Fees to Publish:**	$0.00 US$
blumsden@bamaed.ua.edu	**Fees to Review:**	$0.00 US$
Website:		
http://www.tandf.co.uk/journals/titles/106 68926.asp		

PUBLICATION GUIDELINES:	CIRCULATION DATA:
Manuscript Style:	**Reader:**
American Psychological Association	Academics, Administrators, Practicing Teachers
Manuscript Length:	
15-20	**Frequency of Issue:**
	12 Times/Year
Copies Required:	
Three	**Sponsor/Publisher:**
	Higher Education Program, University of North Texas / Taylor & Francis, Ltd.

MANUSCRIPT TOPICS:
Adult Career & Vocational; Counseling & Personnel Services; Curriculum Studies; Education Management / Administration; Educational Psychology; Educational Technology Systems; Health & Physical Education; Higher Education; Professional Development; School Law

MANUSCRIPT GUIDELINES/COMMENTS:

Aims and Scope
The only two-year college journal that is international in scope and purpose, *Community College Journal of Research and Practice* is published twelve times per volume year. The journal is a multidisciplinary forum for researchers and practitioners in higher education and the behavioral and social sciences. It promotes an increased awareness of community college issues by providing an exchange of ideas, research, and empirically tested educational innovations.

Readership
Community college educators, curriculum specialists, teachers, counselors, behavioral and social scientists, and researchers studying the broad field of higher education.

Instructions for Authors

Note to Authors. Please make sure your contact address information is clearly visible on the outside of all packages you are sending to Editors.

Timely reviews of subjects and books of interest to community and junior college administrators, teachers, counselors, researchers, and scholars in the social and behavioral sciences will be considered for publication. Letters to the editor will be published on approval by the editorial board. Announcements of general interest to the journal's readership will also be accepted for publication.

Manuscripts should be concise yet sufficiently detailed to permit critical review. All papers should contain an abstract, which should not exceed 250 words. Manuscripts should conclude with a section on Implications for Practice stating what the implications of the research findings are to practitioners in the field and including any recommendations for change indicated by the research results.

Submission of Manuscripts

Original and two copies of each manuscript should be submitted to the Editor, D. Barry Lumsden, Senior Research Fellow, University of Alabama, Education Policy Center, Box 870231, Tuscaloosa, AL 35487-0232, Tel: 940-597-7923. Email: **blumsden@bamaed.ua.edu**.

Authors are strongly encouraged to submit manuscripts on disk. The disk should be prepared using MS Word or WordPerfect and should be clearly labeled with the authors' names, file name, and software program.

All parts of the manuscript should be typewritten, double-spaced, with margins of at least one inch on all sides. Number manuscript pages consecutively throughout the paper. The length must not exceed 20 pages. All titles should be as brief as possible, 6 to 12 words. Authors should also supply a short-ended version of the title suitable for the running head, not exceeding 50 character spaces. Each article should be summarized in an abstract of not more that 100 words. Avoid abbreviations, diagrams, and reference to the text.

All papers, including figures, tables, and references, must conform to the specifications described in the *Publication Manual of the American Psychological Association* (4th ed., 1994). Any papers that do not adhere to this style will be returned for revision. Copies of the Manual can be obtained from the Publication Department of the American Psychological Association, 750 First Street, N.E., Washington, D.C. 20002-4242. Phone: (202) 336-5500.

Each manuscript must be accompanied by a statement that it has not been published elsewhere and that it has not been submitted simultaneously for publication elsewhere. Authors are responsible for obtaining permission to reproduce copyrighted material from other sources and are required to sign an agreement for the transfer of copyright to the publisher. All accepted manuscripts, artwork, and photographs become the property of the publisher.

A Microsoft Word author template file, which also includes more detailed instructions in its "Read Me" file, can be downloaded from **http://www.tandf.co.uk/journals/authors/mstemplate/T&F_Manuscript_Template.dot**.

For further information on electronic submission, including information on accepted file types, please visit **http://www.tandf.co.uk/journals/authors/electronic_edu.asp**.

Tables and Figures

Tables and figures should not be embedded in the text, but should be included as separate sheets or files. A short descriptive title should appear above each table with a clear legend, and any footnotes suitably identified below. All units must be included. Figures should be completely labeled, taking into account necessary size reduction. Captions should be typed, double spaced, on a separate sheet.

All original figures should be clearly marked in pencil on the reverse side with the number, author's name, and top edge indicated.

Illustrations

Illustrations submitted (line drawings, halftones, photos, photomicrographs, etc.) should be clean originals or digital files. Digital files are recommended for highest quality reproduction and should follow these guidelines:

- 300 dpi or higher
- sized to fit on journal page
- EPS, TIFF, or PSD format only
- submitted as separate files, not embedded in text files

Four-color illustrations will be considered for publication; however, the author will be required to bear the full cost involved in their printing and publication. The charge for the first figure is $1,200. Subsequent figures, totaling no more than 4 text pages, are $500.00 each. Good quality color prints should be provided, in their final size. Figures needing reduction or enlargement will be charged an additional 25 percent. The publisher has the right to refuse publication of color prints deemed unacceptable.

Reprints

The corresponding author of each article will receive one complete copy of the issue in which the article appears. Reprints of an individual article may be ordered from Taylor & Francis. Use the reprint order form included with the page proofs.

Community College Review

SUBMISSION PROCESS:
Postal Submission Only

CONTACT INFORMATION:	REVIEW PROCESS:	
Managing Editor	**Type of Review:**	Blind Review
Community College Review		
North Carolina State University	**No. External Reviewers:**	2
Dept. of Adult & Higher Education	**No. InHouse Reviewers:**	3
Box 7801		
Raleigh, NC 27695-7801 USA	**Acceptance Rate:**	21-30%
	Time to Review:	1 - 2 Months
Phone:	**Reviewer's Comments:**	Yes
919-515-6248	**Invited Articles:**	0-5%
Email:	**Fees to Publish:**	$0.00 US$
community_college_review@ncsu.edu	**Fees to Review:**	$0.00 US$
Website:		
http://crw.sagepub.com/		

PUBLICATION GUIDELINES:	CIRCULATION DATA:
Manuscript Style:	**Reader:**
American Psychological Association	Academics
Manuscript Length:	**Frequency of Issue:**
12-20	Quarterly
Copies Required:	**Sponsor/Publisher:**
Three	University / Sage Publications

MANUSCRIPT TOPICS:

Adult Career & Vocational; Bilingual / E.S.L.; Educational Technology Systems; Scheduling; Serving Unique Popluations w/the Community College; Tests, Measurement & Evaluation; Transfer & Articulation

MANUSCRIPT GUIDELINES/COMMENTS:

Managing Editor (address, phone, fax, email same as above.) The *Community College Review* (circulation 1,000), a quarterly academic journal dedicated to community college education, publishes manuscripts from scholars and practitioners who would like to present their research and experiences in community college education to readers. One way to become familiar with the kinds of articles published in the *Review* is to study recent issues.

As a fully refereed journal, the *Review* relies on a nine-member editorial board composed of community college educators and scholars to evaluate manuscripts. Submissions to the *Review*'s editorial office are reviewed initially by the editorial staff. The staff assigns those manuscripts that meet style and topic guidelines to at least two reviewers for evaluation. Reviewers include members of the editorial board and researchers who are interested in the topic being presented.

Decisions to publish a manuscript are based on the reviewers recommendations. Exceptions to this policy occasionally are made for manuscripts based on personal experiences or opinion rather than on research or literature reviews.

The editor selects such essays for publication, and they are designated as editor's selections when they are published.

Content

The *Review*'s readers include a broad national audience of community college presidents, administrators, and faculty, as well as university faculty and graduate students involved in community college education. Thus, the most important criteria for evaluating a manuscript are the timeliness and relevance of its topic for community colleges in general.

Most manuscripts accepted for publication describe original qualitative or quantitative research that involves community colleges. Essays that combine authors' personal experiences with their knowledge of the existing literature on specific topics or issues constitute a small percentage of accepted submissions.

Authors of acceptable research reports document design and methodology before presenting results and conclusions. They interpret findings in the context of existing theory and research, and they discuss implications for community colleges in general as part of the manuscript's conclusion.

Style

The *Review*'s editorial staff generally uses the most recent edition of the *Publication Manual of the American Psychological Association* as a style guide. The following brief instructions summarize some basic guidelines.

Provide three copies of the manuscript for evaluation. Limit manuscripts to 20 typed (double-spaced) pages with one-inch margins, indented paragraphs, and pages clearly numbered.

Include a cover page that lists the manuscript's title along with each author's name, position, affiliation, complete mailing address, email address and phone number below it. A second page should bear the title of the manuscript only with an abstract of approximately 50 words.

Do not use footnotes. Cite material from other sources in the text, and list the sources in a reference list at the end of the manuscript. Citations within the text should be in parentheses with the last name(s) of the author(s) cited and the publication year. Citations for quotations and statistics must include page numbers (for example, Jones, 1987, pp. 2-4).

Alphabetize the reference list of cited sources by authors' last names according to American Psychological Association style. Entries for journals and edited volumes should include article or chapter page numbers, and entries for edited anthologies should include editors' names.

Declined manuscripts will be returned if stamped, self-addressed envelopes are enclosed with submissions. Requests for detailed guidelines for submitting manuscripts and questions about what is required should be directed to the managing editor at the following location: Community College Review, N. C. State University, Box 7801, Raleigh, NC 27695-7801; **http://crw.sagepub.com/**; Telephone (919) 515-6248; Facsimile (919) 515-4039; Telephone (919) 515-6248; Email **community_college_review@ncsu.edu**

Community Development: Journal of Community Development Society

SUBMISSION PROCESS:
Postal & Electronic Submission Required via EMail
jcds@ucdavis.edu

CONTACT INFORMATION:	REVIEW PROCESS:	
Norm Walzer & Ron Hustedde, Int Co-Eds Human & Community Development Dept. University of California, Davis Davis, CA 95616 USA	**Type of Review:**	Blind Review
	No. External Reviewers:	3+
	No. InHouse Reviewers:	1
Phone: 530-752-1353	**Acceptance Rate:**	6-10%
	Time to Review:	2 - 3 Months
	Reviewer's Comments:	Yes
Email: jcds@ucdavis.edu	**Invited Articles:**	6-10%
	Fees to Publish:	$35.00 US$ per page
Website: http://www.comm-dev.org	**Fees to Review:**	$0.00 US$

PUBLICATION GUIDELINES:	CIRCULATION DATA:
Manuscript Style: American Psychological Association	**Reader:** Academics, Practitioners, Urban & Rural Development Specialists
Manuscript Length: 26-30	**Frequency of Issue:** Quarterly
Copies Required: One + 1 Electronic	**Sponsor/Publisher:** University of California, Davis / Allen Press

MANUSCRIPT TOPICS:

Community Development & Studies; Economic Development; Human Development; Rural Education & Small Schools; Social Studies / Social Science; Teacher Education; Tests, Measurement & Evaluation; Urban Education, Cultural / Non-Traditional

MANUSCRIPT GUIDELINES/COMMENTS:

Community Development: Journal of Community Development Society is devoted to improving knowledge and practice in the field of purposive community change. The purpose of the *Journal* is to disseminate information on theory, research, and practice. The Editors welcome manuscripts that report research; evaluate theory, techniques, and methods; examine community problems; or analyze, critically, the profession itself.

Instructions to Authors. Address submissions to the Editors (See address above.)

Submission Requirements
Submit one printed copy of the manuscript on 8½" by 11 inch bond in near-letter quality type. Double space **all** material, including indented passages, end-notes, and references, with ragged

right margins and no hyphenation. The *Journal* requests that an electronic copy be submitted by electronic mail. Manuscripts without author identification will be submitted to referees for review.

Printed Manuscript
Cover Page. Show article title, institutional affiliation(s), professional position(s) of author(s), and contact information (including email address). Omit author name(s) and affiliation(s) from the manuscript itself and from the end section listing references.

Abstract. Include on a separate page the article title and a summary of 100 to 150 words.

Keywords. Authors must supply from three (3) to five (5) alphabetized key words, or phrases that identify the most important subjects covered by the paper. Place key words on the bottom of the **Abstract** page.

Tables and Figures. Append tables and figures on separate pages at the end of the manuscript. The format of tables and figures should be consistent with tables published in recent issues of the Journal. Include location notes, e.g., "Table 1 about here," "Fig. 1 near here," at appropriate places within the text. Tables and figures must be included in the electronic file, sized to fit within the *Journal*'s 7" by 10" page format. Art for figures must be camera-ready copy and sized to fit within the Journal's 7" by 10" page format.

References within the Text. References within the body of the text should include the name of the author(s) cited and date of reference in parentheses within the manuscript, e.g., (Walzer, 2006). Do not use ibid., *op. sit.*, *loc. sit.*, etc. If reference is a direct quote, include page number also, e.g., (Walzer, 2006, p. 3). For repeat citations, continue to use name of author(s) and date. In case of multiple works with the same author(s) and publication year, use 1991a," "1991b," etc.

References at End of the Text. Complete data on all references should follow standard APA (American Psychological Association) Research Style (Crib Sheet) guidelines. At the end of the manuscript, submit a double spaced listing of all references alphabetically, including page numbers, volume and issue numbers of journals, and all authors' names. The format for articles, books, and articles in books is shown as follows:

Hustedde, R. J., & Ganowicz, J. (2002). The basics: what's essential about theory for community development practice? *COMMUNITY DEVELOPMENT: Journal of the Community Development Society*, 33(1), 1-19.

Putnam, R. D. (2000). *Bowling Alone: The Collapse and Revival of American Community*. New York: Simon and Schuster.

Pigg, K. E., & Bradshaw, T. K. (2003). Catalytic Community Development: A Theory of Practice for Changing Rural Society. In D. L. Brown & L. E. Swanson (Eds.), *Challenges for rural America in the twenty-first century*. University Park: Pennsylvania State University Press.

U.S. Census. (2000). *State and Country QuickFacts*. Washington, D.C.: United States Bureau of the Census. Retrieved November 7, 2006, from http://quickfacts.census.gov/qfd/

Endnotes. Use notes sparingly in the text for *substantive comments only*, not for bibliographic references. Notes should be numbered consecutively and appear at the end of the text, before the reference section. Mark location of notes at the appropriate places within the text of the manuscript. You may use the note function of word processing software in MicroSoft Word.

Community Development: Journal of Community Development Society regards submission of a manuscript as a commitment by the author(s) that is not to be breached by submission to another journal while the manuscript is under review.

Computers and Composition

SUBMISSION PROCESS:
Electronic Submission Preferred **via Online Portal** http://ees.elsevier.com/cocomp/

CONTACT INFORMATION:	REVIEW PROCESS:
G. Hawisher & C. Selfe, Co-Editors Department of English The Ohio State University 365 Denney Hall 164 W. 17th Avenue Columbus, OH 43210 USA **Phone:** **Email:** 　candc@osu.edu **Website:** 　http://computersandcomposition.osu.edu 　http://www.elsevier.com	**Type of Review:**　　Blind Review **No. External Reviewers:**　3 **No. InHouse Reviewers:**　3 **Acceptance Rate:**　　30% **Time to Review:**　　3 Months **Reviewer's Comments:**　Yes **Invited Articles:**　　Occasional **Fees to Publish:**　　$0.00 US$ **Fees to Review:**　　$0.00 US$

PUBLICATION GUIDELINES:	CIRCULATION DATA:
Manuscript Style: 　American Psychological Association **Manuscript Length:** 　15-30 **Copies Required:** 　Five　or 1 Electronic	**Reader:** 　Academics, Practicing Teachers **Frequency of Issue:** 　Quarterly **Sponsor/Publisher:** 　Elsevier Inc.

MANUSCRIPT TOPICS:
Higher Education; Languages & Linguistics; Tests, Measurement & Evaluation; Writing

MANUSCRIPT GUIDELINES/COMMENTS:

Topics Include. Information Technologies and New Media as they relate to the impact they are making on writing, teaching, academics, and everyday lives

Guidelines for Submission
Authors are requested to submit their manuscripts electronically by using our online submission system, the Elsevier Editorial System (EES) <**http://ees.elsevier.com/cocomp/**>. This site provides guidelines for Authors throughout the submission process. Authors should upload all source files for each manuscript in the preferred formats as detailed below, and the system will convert source files into a single Adobe Acrobat PDF version that is then used in the peer-review process. Please note that even as manuscript source files are converted into a PDF at submission for the review process, these files are needed for further processing after acceptance. Authors, Reviewers, and Editors will send and receive all correspondence by email.

Should you be unable to provide an electronic version, please contact **candc@osu.edu** or one of the Editors, Cynthia L. Selfe, The Ohio State University, USA, or Gail E. Hawisher, University of Illinois, Urbana-Champaign, USA.

Manuscripts are accepted for review with the understanding that the same work has not been and will not be published nor is presently submitted elsewhere, that all persons listed as Authors have given their approval for the submission of the paper, and that any person cited as a source of personal communication has approved such citation.

Authors submitting a manuscript do so with the understanding that if it is accepted for publication, copyright of the article, including the right to reproduce that article in all forms of media, shall be assigned to the Publisher. The Publisher will not refuse any reasonable request by the Author for permission to reproduce any of his or her contributions to Computers and Composition. See below for more information on copyright.

Manuscript Preparation and Submission
Manuscripts should be submitted and tracked electronically through the EES. Authors will need to submit at least three separate files: the manuscript in a Word document or RTF file that includes a 200-word abstract, 5-10 relevant key words, and no author identifiers; a cover letter; and a title page with a short (50-100 words) biographical statement. Manuscripts should be between 15 and 30 pages in length, double-spaced, and formatted for an 8 ½ x 11-inch document with 1-inch margins on all sides.

Registration is required for new users, and instructions for submission are provided online. Log in or register as an author and upload all files. Processing may take up to four weeks, and once all required reviews are submitted, manuscripts are forwarded to the editorial office for evaluation and processing. Queries about possible submissions can be directed to Cynthia L. Selfe, Humanities Distinguished Professor, Department of English, The Ohio State University, 365 Denny Hall, 164 West 17th Ave, Columbus, OH 43210, USA, e-mail: **candc@osu.edu**.

Style
The guidelines of the most recent edition of the *Publication Manual of the American Psychological Association* (5th ed., 2001) should be followed apart from these exceptions: Authors must provide first and middle names or first names and middle initials of authors upon first mention within the text (but not in parenthetical citations) and also in the references section (see below). Additionally, specific tenses are used for in-text references to works: descriptions or reporting of results are made in the past or present perfect tenses (the author argued or has argued) while discussions or analyses of results are made in the present tense (the author's argument indicates). See the *Computers and Composition Style Manual* <**http://computersandcomposition.osu.edu/manuals/StyleManual. pdf**> for more details on the journal house style.

Review
Since manuscripts are submitted for blind review, all identifying information must be removed from the body of the paper. Once files are converted into PDFs, all metadata is automatically removed from files, and the manuscripts remain anonymous. The same applies to responses composed by Reviewers for Authors.

Tables and Figures
Tables and figures should be completely understandable independent of the text. Each table and figure must be mentioned in the text, given titles, and consecutively numbered with Arabic numerals. Authors must provide appropriately formatted files for all figures to be directly reproduced for publication. Detailed instructions can be found in Elsevier's Artwork Guidelines page linked to the EES main page.

Elsevier also accepts electronic supplementary material to support and enhance your research. Supplementary files offer additional possibilities to publish supporting applications, movies, animation sequences, high-resolution images, background datasets, sound clips, and more. Supplementary files are published online alongside the electronic version of articles in Elsevier Web products, including ScienceDirect <**http://www.sciencedirect.com/**>. In order to ensure that the submitted material is directly usable, data should be provided in one of the recommended file formats. Authors should submit the material in electronic format together with the article and supply a concise and descriptive caption for each file. More detailed instructions are located in the Artwork Guidelines page.

Notes
Notes should be used sparingly and indicated by consecutive numbers in the text. Acknowledgments, grant numbers, or other credits should be given in separate footnotes.

References
All sources cited in the text must be included alphabetically in the reference list, and all reference items must appear within the text. Computers and Composition varies from the APA style by including first names in all references. Below are examples of entries:

- Flinn, Jane Zeni & Madigan, Chris (1989). The gateway writing project: Staff development and computers in St. Louis . In Cynthia L. Selfe, Dawn Rodrigues & William R. Oates (Eds.) Computers in English and the language arts: The challenge of teacher education (pp. 55-68). Urbana , IL : National Council of Teachers of English.
- McDaid, John. (1990, March). The shape of texts to come: Response and the ecology of hypertext. Paper presented at the convention of the Conference on College Composition and Communication, Chicago , IL .
- Strenski, Ellen. (1995). Electronic tutor training with a local e-mail LISTSERV discussion group. Computers and Composition, 12, 246-256.
- Guyer, Carolyn & Petry, Martha (1991) IZME PASS [Computer program] Boston : Eastgate Systems.

Additionally, a digital object identifier (DOI) may be used to cite and link to electronic documents. The DOI consists of a unique alpha-numeric character string that is assigned to a document by the publisher upon the initial electronic publication. The assigned DOI never changes. Therefore, it is an ideal medium for citing a document, particularly 'Articles in press' because they have not yet received their full bibliographic information. The correct format for citing a DOI is shown as follows (example taken from a document in the journal, Physics Letters B):

doi:10.1016/j.physletb.2003.10.071

The DOIs used to create URL hyperlinks to documents on the Web are guaranteed never to change.

Permissions
If excerpts from other copyrighted works are included, the Author(s) must obtain written permission from the copyright owners and credit the source(s) in the article. Elsevier has preprinted forms for use by Authors. In these cases, and in cases of any other copyright queries, contact Elsevier's Rights Department, Oxford , UK : phone (+44) 1865 843830, fax (+44) 1865 853333, e-mail permissions@elsevier.com. Further information can be found and copyright requests may be completed online via Elsevier's permissions page. Copies of any letters granting permission to reproduce illustrations, tables, or lengthy quotations should be included with the manuscript file.

Copyright
Upon acceptance of an article, Authors will be asked to transfer copyright. (For more information on copyright, visit the "copyright" link at Elsevier's Author Gateway. This transfer will ensure the widest possible dissemination of information. A letter will be sent to the corresponding Author confirming receipt of the manuscript. A form facilitating transfer of copyright will be provided.

Authors' rights

Authors (or employers or institutions) may do the following within the standard Elsevier Copyright agreement without the need for further or special permissions:

- make copies (print or electronic) of the article for your own personal use, including for your own classroom teaching use
- make copies and distribute such copies (including through e-mail) of the article to research colleagues for the personal use by such colleagues (but not commercially or systematically, e.g., via an e-mail list or list server)
- post a pre-print version of the article on Internet Web sites including electronic pre-print servers and retain indefinitely such a version on such servers or sites
- post a revised personal version of the final text of the article (to reflect changes made in the peer review and editing process) on your personal or institutional website or server with a link to the journal homepage (at elsevier.com)
- present the article at a meeting or conference and to distribute copies of the article to the delegates attending such a meeting
- for employers if the article is a "work for hire" made within the scope of your employment; your employer may use all or parts of the information in the article for other intra-company use (e.g., training)
- retain patent and trademark rights and rights to any processes or procedure described in the article
- include the article in full or in part in a thesis or dissertation (provided that it is not to be published commercially)
- use the article or any part thereof in a printed compilation of works, such as collected writings or lecture notes (subsequent to publication of your article in the journal)
- prepare other derivative works, to extend the article into book-length form, or to otherwise re-use portions or excerpts in other works, with full acknowledgement of its original publication in the journal

Author Inquiries

Authors can also track the progress of their accepted article and set up e-mail alerts informing them of changes to their manuscript's status by using the "Track a Paper" feature in Elsevier's Author Gateway.

Offprints

Each lead Author will receive 25 free offprints.

Computers in the Schools

SUBMISSION PROCESS:
Postal Submission Only

CONTACT INFORMATION:	REVIEW PROCESS:	
D. LaMont Johnson, Editor University of Nevada - Reno Dept. of Counseling & Educational Psychology	**Type of Review:**	Blind Review
	No. External Reviewers:	3+
	No. InHouse Reviewers:	2
Phone: 775-784-6327	**Acceptance Rate:**	40-50%
	Time to Review:	2 - 3 Months
	Reviewer's Comments:	Yes
Email: ljohnson@unr.edu	**Invited Articles:**	6-10%
Website: www.haworthpress.com	**Fees to Publish:**	$0.00 US$
	Fees to Review:	$0.00 US$

PUBLICATION GUIDELINES:	CIRCULATION DATA:

Manuscript Style:
  See Manuscript Guidelines
	Reader:
	  Academics, Administrators

Manuscript Length:
  16-20
	Frequency of Issue:
	  Quarterly

Copies Required:
  One
	Sponsor/Publisher:
	  Haworth Press, Inc.

MANUSCRIPT TOPICS:
Educational Technology Systems

MANUSCRIPT GUIDELINES/COMMENTS:

About the Journal
Under the editorship of D. LaMont Johnson, PhD, a nationally recognized leader in the field of educational computing, *Computers in the Schools* is supported by an editorial review board of prominent specialists in the school and educational setting. Material presented in this highly acclaimed journal goes beyond the "how we did it" magazine article or handbook by offering a rich source of serious discussion for educators, administrators, computer center directors, and special service providers in the school setting. Articles emphasize the practical aspect of any application, but also tie theory to practice, relate present accomplishments to past efforts and future trends, identify conclusions and their implications, and discuss the theoretical and philosophical basis for the application.

Instructions for Authors
Journal Editor. D. Lamont Johnson, PhD, Professor, Dept of Counseling & Educational Psychology, University of Nevada – Reno

Authors must complete a Manuscript Submission & Limited Copyright Transfer Form (See "2. Copyright"). Download the Manuscript Submission & Limited Copyright Transfer Form from the web site.

1. **Original Articles Only**. Submission of a manuscript to this journal represents a certification on the part of the author(s) that it is an original work, and that neither this manuscript nor a version of it has been published elsewhere nor is being considered for publication elsewhere.

2. **Copyright**. Copyright ownership of your manuscript must be transferred officially to The Haworth Press, Inc., before we can begin the peer-review process. All authors must sign the form and return the original to the editor as soon as possible. Failure to return the copyright form in a timely fashion will result in a delay in review and subsequent publication.

3. **Manuscript Length**. 10–20 typed pages. Lengthier manuscripts may be considered, but only at the discretion of the editor. There is no specific manuscript length. The abstract should precede the text on a separate piece of paper. The entire manuscript, including abstract, quotations, tables, and references, must be double-spaced.

4. **Manuscript Style**. References should be double-spaced and placed in alphabetical order. The use of footnotes within the text is discouraged. Words should be underlined only when it is intended that they be typeset in italics.

5. **Manuscript Preparation**. Double-spaced, including endnotes and references; 12-point font
Margins. Leave at least a one inch margin on all four sides; set all notes as endnotes.
Cover page. Important -- Submit a cover page with the manuscript, indicating only the article title (this is used for anonymous refereeing).
Second "title page". Include a regular title page as a separate document. Include the title again, plus:
- full authorship
- an ABSTRACT of about 100 words (below the abstract provide 3-10 key words for indexing purposes)
- a header or footer on each page with abbreviated title and page number of total (e.g., pg 2 of 7)
- an introductory note with authors' academic degrees, professional titles, affiliations, mailing and e-mail addresses, and any desired acknowledgement of research support or other credit

6. **Preparation of Tables, Figures, and Illustrations**. Any material that is not textual is considered artwork. This includes tables, figures, diagrams, charts, graphs, illustrations, appendices, screen captures, and photos. Tables and figures (including legend, notes, and sources) should be no larger than 4 ½ x 6 ½ inches. Type style should be Helvetica (or Helvetica narrow if necessary) and no smaller than 8 point. We request that computer-generated figures be in black and white and/or shades of gray (preferably no color; for it does not reproduce well). Camera-ready art must contain no grammatical, typographical, or format errors and must reproduce sharply and clearly in the dimensions of the final printed page (4 ½ x 6 ½ inches). Photos and screen captures must be saved as a TIFF file or other graphic file format such as JPEG or BMP. For final hardcopy submission, these should be on disk or CD-ROM accompanying your manuscript. For rapid publication we must receive black-and-white glossy or matte positives (white background with black images and/or wording) in addition to files on disk. Tables should be created in the text document file using the software's Table feature.

7. **Submitting Art**. Both a printed hard copy and an electronic copy of the art must be provided. We request that each piece of art be sent in its own file or on a disk separate from the disk containing the manuscript text file(s); disks should be clearly labeled. We reserve the right to (if necessary) request new art, alter art, or if all else has failed in achieving art that is presentable, delete art. If submitted art cannot be used, the publisher reserves the right to redo the art and to charge the author a fee of $55.00 per hour for this service. The Haworth Press, Inc. is not responsible for errors incurred in the preparation of new artwork. Camera-ready artwork must be

prepared on separate sheets of paper. Always use black ink and professional drawing instruments. On the back of these items, write your article title and the journal title lightly in soft-lead pencil (please do not write on the face of art). In the text file, skip extra lines and indicate where these figures are placed. Photos are considered part of the acceptable manuscript and remain with the publisher for use in additional printings.

8. **Typesetting**. You will not be receiving galley proofs of your article. Editorial revisions, if any, must therefore be made while your article is still in manuscript form. The final version of the manuscript will be the version you see published. Typesetter's errors will be corrected by the production staff of The Haworth Press, Inc. Authors are expected to submit manuscripts, disks, and art that are free from error.

9. **Disk Media**. (For Hardcopy Submissions) Haworth's in-house typesetting unit is able to utilize your final manuscript material as prepared on most personal computers and word processors. This will minimize typographical errors and decrease overall production time. Please send the first draft and final draft copies of your manuscript to the journal editor in print format for his/her final review and approval. After approval of your final manuscript, please submit the final approved version both in printed format ("hard copy") and floppy diskette or CD-ROM. On the outside of the diskette package write: 1) the brand name of your computer or word processor 2) the word processing program and version that you used 3) the title of your article, and 4) the file name. NOTE: Disk and hard copy must agree. In case of discrepancies, it is The Haworth Press' policy to follow hard copy. Authors are advised that no revisions of the manuscript can be made after acceptance by the editor for publication. The benefits of this procedure are many with speed and accuracy being the most obvious. We look forward to working with your disk submission which will allow us to serve you more efficiently.

10. **Spelling, Grammar, and Punctuation**. You are responsible for preparing manuscript copy which is clearly written in acceptable, scholarly English and which contains no errors of spelling, grammar, or punctuation. Neither the editor nor the publisher is responsible for correcting errors of spelling and grammar. The manuscript, after acceptance by the editor, must be immediately ready for typesetting as it is finally submitted by the author(s). Check your paper for the following common errors:

- dangling modifiers
- misplaced modifiers
- unclear antecedents
- incorrect or inconsistent abbreviations

Also, check the accuracy of all arithmetic calculations, statistics, numerical data, text citations, and references. INCONSISTENCIES MUST BE AVOIDED. Be sure you are consistent in your use of abbreviations, terminology, and in citing references, from one part of your paper to another.

11. **Acknowledgment of Receipt**. Please allow 10-15 weeks for the review process. Postage inquiries regarding submissions made from outside of the U.S. should be directed to the editor of this journal.

12. **Reference Linking**. The Haworth Press, Inc. is participating in reference linking for journal articles. (To obtain information on reference linking initiatives, please consult the CrossRef Web site at **www.crossref.org**.) When citing a journal article include the article's Digital Object Identifier (DOI), when available, as the last item in the reference. A Digital Object Identifier is a persistent, authoritative, and unique identifier that a publisher assigns to each article. Because of its persistence, DOIs will enable The Haworth Press, Inc., and other publishers to link to the article referenced, and the link will not break over time. This will be a great resource in scholarly research.

An example of a reference to a journal article which includes a DOI:
Vizine-Goetz, Diane (2002). Classification Schemes for Internet Resources Revisited. Journal of Internet Cataloging 5(4): 5:18. doi:10.1300/J141v05n04_02

13. **Alterations Required by Referees and Reviewers**. Many times a paper is accepted by the editor contingent upon changes that are mandated by anonymous specialist referees and/or members of the editorial board. If the editor returns your manuscript for revisions, you are responsible for retyping any sections of the paper to incorporate these revisions (if applicable, revisions should also be put on disk).

Contemporary Educational Psychology

SUBMISSION PROCESS:

Electronic Submission Only
via Online Portal

http://ees.elsevier.com/cedpsych

CONTACT INFORMATION:	REVIEW PROCESS:	
Patricia Alexander, Editor	**Type of Review:**	Blind Review
University of Maryland		
Dept. of Human Development	**No. External Reviewers:**	3
Benjamin Bldg.	**No. InHouse Reviewers:**	0
College Park, MD 20742 USA		
	Acceptance Rate:	11-20%
	Time to Review:	2 - 3 Months
Phone:	**Reviewer's Comments:**	Yes
301-405-2821	**Invited Articles:**	0-5%
Email:	**Fees to Publish:**	$0.00 US$
palexand@umd.edu	**Fees to Review:**	$0.00 US$
cep@umd.edu		
Website:		
http://ees.elsevier.com/cedpsych		

PUBLICATION GUIDELINES:	CIRCULATION DATA:
Manuscript Style:	**Reader:**
American Psychological Association	Academics
Manuscript Length:	**Frequency of Issue:**
30+	Quarterly
Copies Required:	**Sponsor/Publisher:**
Electronic Only	Elsevier Inc.

MANUSCRIPT TOPICS:
Bilingual / E.S.L.; Educational Psychology; Gifted Children; Languages & Linguistics; Reading; Science Math & Environment; Social Studies / Social Science; Special Education; Tests, Measurement & Evaluation

MANUSCRIPT GUIDELINES/COMMENTS:

Description
Contemporary Educational Psychology publishes articles that involve the application of psychological theory and science to the educational process. Of particular relevance are descriptions of empirical research and the presentation of theory designed to either explicate or enhance the educational process. In addition, reviews of educational research are encouraged if the research being reviewed involves the application of psychological science to an important educational issue.

Features

- Original research articles - covering both classroom and laboratory experiments as they emphasize problem solving
- Theoretical contributions - relating issues, comparisons, and analyses to the application of psychological methods and skills to the educational process
- Instructional techniques - reports on instructional techniques when the use of adequate controls demonstrates the validity of the findings
- Research critiques - reviews on selected educational topics reflecting implications for the field of educational psychology.

Guide for Authors

Contemporary Educational Psychology publishes articles that involve the application of psychological theory and science to the educational process. Of particular relevance are descriptions of, research reviews of, and the presentation of theory designed to either explicate or enhance the educational process. The journal publishes quantitative, qualitative, and single-subject design studies that involve the application of psychological science to an important educational process, issue, or problem.

The journal does not limit its scope to any age range. Articles dealing with the education of preschoolers, K-12 children, adults, and the elderly are all relevant if they apply psychological theory and science to the process of education. Likewise, articles that make a substantial contribution to the understanding of individual differences in the process of learning are also appropriate. The journal does not focus on a particular educational setting. Articles applying psychological theory and research methods in school settings, industry, or other formal or informal settings involving adults or children are relevant, assuming they are judged in the review process to advance the science of education.

Type of Articles Published in *CEP*

The journal publishes three types of articles: Research Studies, Brief Research Reports, and Reviews.

Research Studies report a quantitative, qualitative, or single-subject design study. Articles that contain multiple studies are seen as particularly desirable contributions. For quantitative studies, authors should report effect sizes. Methods for calculating and interpreting effect sizes are presented in *Contemporary Educational Psychology* in Volume 25 (Number 3) on pages 241-286.

Review Articles are primarily based on other published work and include reviews of existing literature, methodological reviews of research in a particular area, or theoretical presentations that advance or clarify psychological theory or science as it applies to education.

Electronic Submission

Authors should submit their articles electronically via the Elsevier Editorial System (EES) page of this journal (**http://ees.elsevier.com/cedpsych**). The system automatically converts source files to a single Adobe Acrobat PDF version of the article, which is used in the peer-review process. Please note that even though manuscript source files are converted to PDF at submission for the review process, these source files are needed for further processing after acceptance. All correspondence, including notification of the Editor's decision and requests for revision, takes place by e-mail and via the Author's EES homepage, removing the need for a hard-copy paper trail.

Submission Requirements

Manuscripts are accepted for review with the understanding that the same work has not been and is not currently submitted elsewhere, and that it will not be submitted elsewhere prior to the journal's making an editorial decision. At the time of submission, authors must notify the Editor if any part of the data on which their article depends has been published elsewhere. Moreover, it must be the case that submission of the article for publication has been approved by all of the authors and by the institution where the work was carried out; further, that any person cited as a source of personal communications has approved such citation. Written authorization may be required at the Editor's discretion. Articles and an other material published in *Contemporary Educational Psychology* represent the opinions of the author(s) and should not be construed to reflect the opinions of the Editor or the Publisher.

Upon acceptance of an article, authors will be asked to transfer copyright (for more information on copyright, see **http://authors.elsevier.com**). This transfer will ensure the widest possible dissemination of information. A letter will be sent to the corresponding author confirming receipt of the manuscript. A form facilitating transfer of copyright will be provided after acceptance.

If excerpts from other copyrighted works are included, the author(s) must obtain written permission from the copyright owners and credit the source(s) in the article. Elsevier has preprinted forms for use by authors in these cases: contact Elsevier Global Rights Department, P.O. Box 800, Oxford OX5 1DX, UK; phone: (+44) 1865 843830, fax: (+44) 1865 853333, e-mail: permissions@ elsevier.com.

Preparation of the Manuscript
Allow ample margins and type double spaced throughout. Authors are requested to follow the instructions given in the most recent edition of the *Publication Manual of the American Psychological Association*. Each page of the manuscript should be numbered consecutively.

The **title page** (p. 1) should contain the article title, authors' names and complete affiliations, footnotes to the title, and the address for manuscript correspondence (including e-mail address and telephone and fax numbers). This data should appear on the title page only as manuscripts are sent out for blind review.

The **second page** (p. 2) should contain only the article title and footnotes to the title. These items should be placed in the same position as they were on the title page.

The **abstract** (p. 3) must be a single paragraph that summarizes the main findings of the paper in less than 150 words. After the abstract a list of up to 10 keywords that will be useful for indexing or searching should be included.

References in the text should be cited by author's surname and the year of publication, e.g., Hum (1994); Hum et al. (1993); Hum and St. Clair (1993, p. 128) (for references to a specific page); Hum & St. Clair (1993) (ampersand for references in parentheses). If more than one paper was published by the same author in a given year, the correct style is Smith (1985a) and Smith (1985b). References cited in the text should be listed alphabetically and typed double-spaced at the end of the article. Journal titles should be written out in full according to the form followed in the most recent edition of the *Publication Manual of the American Psychological Association*. Personal communications should be cited as such in the text and should not be included in the reference list. Please note the following examples:

Gagne, R. M., & Driscoll, M. P. (1988). Essentials of learning for instruction. Englewood Cliffs, NJ: Prentice-Hall.

Griffin, M. M., & Griffin, B. W. (1995, April). An investigation of the effects of reciprocal peer tutoring on achievement, self-efficacy, and test anxiety. Paper presented at the Annual Meeting of the National Consortium for Instruction and Cognition, San Francisco, CA.

Kulhavy, R. W., Schwartz, N. H., & Peterson, S. (1986). Working memory: The encoding process. In G. D. Phye & T. Andre (Eds.), Cognitive classroom learning: Understanding, thinking, and problem solving (pp. 115-140). Orlando, FL: Academic Press.

Zeidner, M., & Schleyer, E. J. (1999). The big-fish-little-pond effect for academic self-concept, test anxiety, and school grades in gifted children. Contemporary Educational Psychology, 24, 305-329.

Figures and Tables

All tables and figures should be grouped together at the end of the manuscript and numbered separately using Arabic numerals. Clearly visible notes within the text should indicate their approximate placement. The appropriate format for figures is described at the Author Gateway page mentioned above. Please see the EES web page (**http://ees.elsevier.com/cedpsych**) for full detailed instructions. If, together with your accepted article, you submit usable color figures, then Elsevier will ensure, at no additional charge, that these figures will appear in color on the Web (e.g., ScienceDirect and other sites) regardless of whether these illustrations are reproduced in color in the printed version. For color reproduction in print, you will receive information regarding the costs from Elsevier after receipt of your accepted article. For further information on the preparation of electronic artwork, please see http://authors.elsevier.com/artwork.

Preparation of Supplementary Material

Elsevier now accepts electronic supplementary material to support and enhance your scientific research. Supplementary files offer additional possibilities for publishing supporting applications, movies, animation sequences, high-resolution images, background datasets, sound clips, and more. Supplementary files supplied will be published online alongside the electronic version of your article in Elsevier Web products, including ScienceDirect (http://www.sciencedirect.com). To ensure that your submitted material is directly usable, please provide the data in one of our recommended file formats. Authors should submit the material in electronic format together with the article and supply a concise and descriptive caption for each file. Please note, however, that supplementary material will not appear in the printed journal. For more detailed instructions, please visit our Author Gateway at http://authors.elsevier.com, click on "Artwork instructions", and then click on "Multimedia files".

Proofs

Proofs will be sent to the corresponding author. To avoid delay in publication, only necessary changes should be made, and proofs should be returned promptly. Authors will be charged for alterations that exceed 10% of the total cost of composition.

Reprints

Twenty-five reprints will be provided to the corresponding author free of charge. Additional reprints may be ordered. A reprint order form will accompany your proofs.

Author Inquiries

For inquiries relating to the submission of articles please visit the Elsevier Author Gateway at **http://authors.elsevier.com**. The Author Gateway also provides the facility to track accepted articles and set up e-mail alerts to inform you of when an article's status has changed, as well as detailed artwork guidelines, copyright information, frequently asked questions, and more.

Continuing Higher Education Review

SUBMISSION PROCESS:

**Electronic Submission Preferred
via EMail**

ishikawa@hudce.harvard.edu

CONTACT INFORMATION:	REVIEW PROCESS:
Wayne Ishikawa, Associate Editor Harvard University Division of Continuing Education 51 Brattle Street Cambridge, MA 02138-3722 USA **Phone:** 617-495-2478 **Email:** ishikawa@hudce.harvard.edu **Website:**	**Type of Review:** **No. External Reviewers:** **No. InHouse Reviewers:** 2 **Acceptance Rate:** 10% **Time to Review:** 1 Month **Reviewer's Comments:** Yes **Invited Articles:** 90% **Fees to Publish:** $0.00 US$ **Fees to Review:** $0.00 US$
PUBLICATION GUIDELINES:	CIRCULATION DATA:

Manuscript Style:
    See Manuscript Guidelines
 	
Manuscript Length:
    6-10 1500 Words
 	
Copies Required:
    One
	Reader:
	    Academics, Administrators
	
	Frequency of Issue:
	    Yearly
	
	Sponsor/Publisher:
	    Professional Association & University

MANUSCRIPT TOPICS:
Higher Education

MANUSCRIPT GUIDELINES/COMMENTS:

Continuing Higher Education Review (ISSN 0893-0384) Published once a year by Harvard University, in affiliation with the University Continuing Education Association (UCEA). Michael Shinagel, Editor.

Guidelines for Contributors
The *Continuing Higher Education Review,* a journal that supports the mission of the University Continuing Education Association (UCEA), is intended for leaders in higher education nationally and internationally as well as continuing education professionals. The *Review* solicits articles for publication and also considers unsolicited articles and program case studies to ensure a broad range of essays on topics of relevance to the profession. Editorial criteria include the article's relevance to issues of national and international importance in continuing education, its potential for stimulating the readership to engage not only in further scholarly discourse but also in meaningful institutional action, and its substantive content and clarity of exposition. Solicited articles will contain 4,000–6,000 words. Other articles will range from 1,500–4,000 words. Book reviews will generally not

exceed 1,500 words. In all cases, manuscripts must conform to the style guidelines contained in the latest edition of the *Publication Manual of the American Psychological Association*. An electronic version should be sent to **ishikawa@hudce.harvard.edu**. All submitted articles will be acknowledged upon receipt of the manuscript, and every effort will be made to ensure timely review. Once a decision has been reached, a notification will be sent out immediately.

Continuous Improvement Monitor

SUBMISSION PROCESS: **Electronic Submission Only via EMail** **jrllanes@auburn.edu**	

<table>
<tr>
<td>

CONTACT INFORMATION:

J.R. Llanes, Managing Editor
Auburn University
4036 Haley Center
Auburn, AL 36849 USA

Phone:
   334-844-4460

Email:
   jrllanes@auburn.edu

Website:
   http://llanes.auburn.edu/journal/cim1

</td>
<td>

REVIEW PROCESS:

Type of Review:	Blind Review
No. External Reviewers:	3
No. InHouse Reviewers:	1
Acceptance Rate:	11-20%
Time to Review:	1 - 2 Months
Reviewer's Comments:	Yes
Invited Articles:	6-10%
Fees to Publish:	$0.00 US$
Fees to Review:	$0.00 US$

</td>
</tr>
<tr>
<td>

PUBLICATION GUIDELINES:

Manuscript Style:
   American Psychological Association
      Chicago Manual of Style

Manuscript Length:
   11-15

Copies Required:
   Electronic Only

</td>
<td>

CIRCULATION DATA:

Reader:
   Academics, Administrators

Frequency of Issue:
   Continuously

Sponsor/Publisher:
   Educational Foundations, Leadership
and Technology / Auburn University

</td>
</tr>
</table>

MANUSCRIPT TOPICS:
Education Management / Administration; Higher Education

MANUSCRIPT GUIDELINES/COMMENTS:

General Information
Contributions are solicited world-wide from scholars and practitioners of educational quality improvement for the current Edition of the International Journal: *Continuous Improvement Monitor*, which is published continuously, as articles are reviewed and approved for publication

The *Continuous Improvement Monitor* is a peer-reviewed, electronic journal published by the Department of Educational Leadership at the University of Texas Pan American

The Journal is interested in research, theory and analysis of practice. It is mainly interested in restructuring of public education, reorganization of schools and school curricula, school-reform networks and their effectiveness, and the transformation of educational institutions to quality systems at the K-12 and Post-secondary levels.

Quality improvement systems are better known in industry and global trade, but hundreds of applications have been noted in K-16 education. It is the vision of the Journal to help educators and those involved in human services understand the dynamics of quality systems within their own practice, and it will be the mission of the Journal to act as a communications link between research and experiences with quality systems in global organizations and educational institutions, educational researchers and educators worldwide.

Journal Objectives
1. To serve as a Forum for exchange of opinion, information, theses, research findings, and qualitative or quantitative analysis of quality in education, such as:
- Quality Standards in education
- Restructuring and reform of public education
- Leadership of school-based teams
- Management of Change

2. To relate the new findings and the fresh understandings of quality in education to what has been previously attempted and to draw parallels between quality efforts in business and industry to those being attempted in public-sector agencies.

3. To serve as a source of impartial research-based data on school reform programs, projects and practices.

Article Submission Process
Before submitting an article for publication, the author is encouraged to contact the journal's Managing Editor via e-mail or regular mail, or fax and to submit a one-page outline of the article's main idea.

We accept articles continuously and send them to editors for review without regard as to which may be published first. The speed of the individual editors and our own internal editorial process would determine in which issue your article will appear. In order to speed up the process articles must be submitted in Microsoft Word format, or as part of an e-mail format, or as a text file in ASCII format or as an html file and addressed to: **jrllanes@auburn.edu**.

Peer-Review Process
Articles will be received by the Managing Editor and if they meet the Journal's criteria will be forwarded anonymously to at least three reviewers (Associate Editors) whose educational background, experiences, research and/or training has enabled them to evaluate the significance, adequacy and completeness of scholarly contributions to the field. A current list of the Associate Editors may be found at http://llanes.panam.edu/journal/aeinfo . Please do not contact Associate Editors directly regarding your article. All reviews must remain anonymous or be judged invalid.

Features and Limitations
There's no page limit for the articles, but in every case, the author will be asked to complete a one-page summary.

Because the articles will be available through the World Wide Web, the publishers have added a feature, which will enable the Journal reader to access the full text (or the relevant portion) of the references used by the authors in the article. A hyperlink is made between each citation and either the full text of the article quoted, or the relevant portion of that article or book, will be stored in our server and made available to the reader. In order to enable us to include this feature, and after the article has been approved for publication, authors should submit scanned or camera-ready copies of the references cited. We will obtain necessary permission to post the article in the Web from the copyright holder.

We will also furnish to the readers, the back-up data authors utilize in the articles. If the author's article is based upon a database which was collected by the author(s), the publishers would like to make the database available to readers who may want to replicate the study. We will accept these data in any widely used spreadsheet or statistical program, such as SPSS, Excel, 1-2-3, or any other similar program. The Web server will make available these data via a hyperlink to the writer's text.

The above features will enable the Journal to be more useful to scholars in small institutions lacking reference materials, to researchers in foreign universities who may not subscribe to U.S. journals, and to of those wanting a more thorough reading of your contribution.

Editorial Policy
The current Editorial Policy is very inclusive, and the following guidelines are only suggestive. The journal will publish mainly two types of articles:

Scholarly articles in either *APA*, *Chicago* or *MLA* format which may be based upon research studies, meta-analysis of research and/or evaluation data, qualitative review of programs in place, theoretical pieces on quality systems, and program descriptions of quality systems. These may also be historical articles on the evolution of school management theories, humanistic assessments of quality systems, reviews of literature on quality or quality systems, or theoretical analyses of quality programs or philosophies. We have accepted several opinion pieces by recognized experts in their fields and also welcome future submission in this area.

The Journal will also publish Program Reviews which involve an in-depth analysis of a school reform or quality improvement program which promises to improve the quality of instruction in K-16. These program reviews should be in a specific format which is available upon request from the Managing Editor. There are 60 School Reform Networks nationwide which qualify for Program Review. A list of those Networks is contained here. If you are interested in preparing a review of one of these, please contact the Managing Editor, via e-mail, via fax or phone.

News and Comments. From time to time we will also publish a Reader's Forum, which will consist of items contributed by readers and likely to be of interest to other readers, commentaries on previous articles, and whatever happens to be in the minds of our readers. Your contributions are solicited.

Deadlines
We accept articles on a continuous basis and publish (electronically) as soon as the editorial team concludes its review, usually 60 days after original submission if there are no major corrections to be made.

Electronic Journal editions are available on the World Wide Web as soon as they are edited and placed on-line. As a result, we can publish your article 9-12 months before it can appear in any paper-bound edition.

Article Review Process
Articles may be reviewed in three categories
1.   accepted for publication as is
2.   accepted with changes
3.   rejected.

If accepted as is, the article will be published in the current edition immediately. If the article is accepted with changes, the author will be informed and formal changes requested. The author then has 30 days to resubmit the article. Resubmissions are sent back to the reviewers for comments and approval.

Advantages of Publishing in Our Journal
Fast. We expect that most articles will be reviewed and if approved be ready for publishing within 60 days.

Peer-Review. To support the author, our team of associate editors, a multi-national group (8 countries), collaborate to improve the quality of each article submitted.

Widely Distributed. The journal's web pages have been accessed by over 1,500,000 visitors in the past ten years. The current number of accesses is contained in the Journal's Home Page. You may link your author's name with your own web page or an e-mail feature which allows feedback. If there's something in the article for which you require feedback, we would flag that section inviting comments from readers and often our authors get them.

International Scope. The 1,500,000 visitors come from over 65 countries and our contributions come from 19 countries. Our ability to serve reference material makes us 1) a truly accessible source of information in other nations where US reference materials are not as common as in the United States and 2) cross-disciplinary, insofar as no technical expertise in one or another of the disciplines of quality is required to read and understand our articles. We are listed and abstracted in web servers in Spanish, Japanese, Chinese, Dutch and German.

Flexible Copyrights. The Journal accepts for electronic publication articles which have been previously published in hardbound journals (particularly those of limited --less than 1,000-- distribution), providing the subject of the article meets the guidelines for significance and the author holds intellectual property rights. The Journal also grants the author the right to republish in other journals or magazines. For additional information you may contact: J. R. Llanes Ph. D. Professor, Auburn University 4036 Haley Center Auburn, AL 36849 (334) 844-4460 e-mail: **jrllanes@auburn.edu**; web: **http://llanes.auburn.edu/journal/cim1**

Counseling and Values

<table>
<tr><td colspan="2" align="center">

SUBMISSION PROCESS:

Electronic Submission Preferred
via EMail

csink@spu.edu

</td></tr>
<tr><td>

CONTACT INFORMATION:

Christopher Sink, Editor
Counseling and Values
Seattle Pacific University
School of Education
3307 3rd Avenue West
Seattle, WA 98119 USA

Phone:
  206-281-2453

Email:
  csink@spu.edu

Website:
  www.aservic.org

</td><td>

REVIEW PROCESS:

Type of Review:	Blind Review
No. External Reviewers:	2+
No. InHouse Reviewers:	0
Acceptance Rate:	20%
Time to Review:	2 - 3 Months
Reviewer's Comments:	Yes
Invited Articles:	5-10%
Fees to Publish:	$0.00 US$
Fees to Review:	$0.00 US$

</td></tr>
<tr><td>

PUBLICATION GUIDELINES:

Manuscript Style:
  American Psychological Association

Manuscript Length:
  10-25

Copies Required:
  Electronic Only

</td><td>

CIRCULATION DATA:

Reader:
  Academics, Counselors, Practitioners

Frequency of Issue:
  3 Times/Year

Sponsor/Publisher:
  ASERVIC / American Counseling Association

</td></tr>
</table>

MANUSCRIPT TOPICS:
Higher Education; Religious Education; Social Studies / Social Science

MANUSCRIPT GUIDELINES/COMMENTS:

Topics Also Include. Spiritual, Ethical, Religious and Values Issues as these relate to Counseling Practice, Counseling Theory/Philosophy, and Counselor Preparation

Additional topics as they relate to spirituality, ethics, religion, and/or values in counseling: Abnormal Psychology; Adolescent Psychology; Adulthood; Alcoholism & Drug Addiction/ Addictive Disorders; Child Psychology; Counseling Process/Psychoanalysis & Psychotherapy; Culture/Ethnicity; Developmental Psychology; Educational Psychology; Family Counseling & Therapy; Gerontology; Personality; Psychological Testing; Research Methods & Statistics; Social Psychology; Philosophical considerations

The Association for Spiritual, Ethical and Religious Values in Counseling (ASERVIC) is one of 17 divisions of the American Counseling Association. Originally the National Catholic Guidance Conference, ASERVIC was chartered in 1974. ASERVIC is devoted to professionals who believe that spiritual, ethical, religious, and other human values are essential to the full development of the person and to the discipline of counseling.

To Contact ASERVIC: ASERVIC, A Division of the American Counseling Association, 5999 Stevenson Avenue, Alexandria, VA 22304-3300, 1-800-347-6647

ASERVIC's Journal is *Counseling and Values*.

Counseling and Values is a professional journal of theory, research and informed opinion concerned with relationships among counseling, ethics, philosophy, psychology, religion, personal and social values and spirituality. Its mission is to promote free intellectual inquiry across these domains. Its vision is to attract a diverse readership reflective of a growing diversity in the membership of ASERVIC and to effect change leading to the continuing growth and development of a more genuinely civil society. *Counseling and Values* welcomes theoretical, philosophical, empirical or methodological manuscripts dealing with significant moral, ethical, religious, spiritual and values issues as these relate to counseling and related mental health work. Manuscripts must be initially submitted as an e-copy attachment as well as in the original and two clear copies. Manuscripts must be submitted in accordance with the guidelines that follow. Manuscripts that do not meet these specifications may be returned to the authors before any review for publication formally takes place.

Journal Editor. Christopher Sink, Ph.D., LMHC, NCC, Professor and Chair, Department of School Counseling, School of Education, Seattle Pacific University, 3307 3rd Ave West, Seattle, WA 98119; Phone: 206 281-2453 (W), Fax: 206 281-2756; Email: **csink@spu.edu**

Guidelines for Authors

Articles. Manuscripts should be well organized and concise so that the development of ideas is clear. Avoid dull, clichéd writing and use of jargon.

- Manuscripts must be initially submitted as an e-copy attachment.
- Authors are required to submit a disk of the latest revised copy in MS Word.
- Provide an abstract of the article of approximately 100 words. Do not use footnotes. Most footnote material can be incorporated into the body of the manuscript.
- Manuscripts are typically between 10 and 25 APA pages, typewritten, and double spaced. This does not include title page, abstract, and references.
- Double space all material, including direct quotations and references.
- Authors' names, positions, and places of employment should appear only on the title page. Authors' names should not appear on the manuscript.
- Manuscript style is that of the fifth edition of the *Publication Manual of the American Psychological Association* (available from APA, 750 First St. N.E., Washington, DC 20002-4242). All items cited in articles should be listed as references. Reference notes are not used. Provide page numbers for direct quotations.
- Authors should not submit more than three tables or two figures with each manuscript. Include only essential data and combine tables where possible. Tables should be typed on separate pages. Figures (graphs, illustrations, line drawings) should be supplied as camera-ready art (prepared by a commercial artist). Figure captions should be attached to the art and will be set in the appropriate type.
- Authors should reduce bias in language against persons on the basis of gender, sexual orientation, racial or ethnic group, disability, or age by referring to the guidelines in the fifth edition of the *APA Publication Manual*.
- If you wish to have your manuscript returned, you must include a stamped, self-addressed envelope.
- Never submit material for concurrent consideration by another periodical. Manuscripts that meet the guidelines and are appropriate for the focus of the journal are ordinarily submitted to a blind review by the Editorial Board members. Two or 3 months may elapse between acknowledgment of receipt of a manuscript and notification of its disposition. After publication of an article, each author receives a copy of the journal.

Forum

- Forum articles will be published in concert with preannounced special topic(s) subject headings. Please consult ACA's newspaper *Counseling Today* for special topic(s) to be addressed in future issues.
- Reactions to editorials, articles, and other Forum subjects will be considered for publication in this section as space is available. The editor reserves the right to edit and abridge responses published as reactions to original articles.
- All other guidelines for articles apply to Forum.

Issues and Insights

- Philosophical and practical applications of first person narratives that are written in accordance with *APA Publication Manual* standards for publication will be featured.
- Manuscripts must be clearly referenced and represent an author's attempt to offer fresh information.
- "New" counseling interventions and accompanying "techniques that work" will be considered for publication in this section.
- All other guidelines for articles apply to Issues and Insights.

Send all manuscripts and correspondence to: Christopher Sink, Ph.D., LMHC, NCC, Professor and Chair, Department of School Counseling, School of Education, Seattle Pacific University, 3307 3rd Ave West, Seattle, WA 98119, Phone: 206 281-2453 (W), FAX: 206 281-2756, Email: **csink@ spu.edu**

Counselor Education and Supervision

SUBMISSION PROCESS:
Electronic Submission Only **via EMail** **ces@kent.edu**

CONTACT INFORMATION:	REVIEW PROCESS:	
John D. West & Cynthia J. Osborn, Eds. 310 White Hall Kent State University PO Box 5190 Kent, OH 44242-0001 USA	**Type of Review:**	Blind Review
	No. External Reviewers:	3
	No. InHouse Reviewers:	2
	Acceptance Rate:	11-20%
Phone:	**Time to Review:**	4 - 6 Months
330-672-0691	**Reviewer's Comments:**	Yes
	Invited Articles:	0-5%
Email:		
ces@kent.edu	**Fees to Publish:**	$0.00 US$
Website:	**Fees to Review:**	$0.00 US$
http://chdsw.educ.kent.edu/ces		

PUBLICATION GUIDELINES:	CIRCULATION DATA:
Manuscript Style: American Psychological Association	**Reader:** Academics
Manuscript Length: 21-25	**Frequency of Issue:** Quarterly
Copies Required: Electronic Only	**Sponsor/Publisher:** Association for Counselor Education and Supervision / American Counseling Association

MANUSCRIPT TOPICS:

Adult Career & Vocational; Counseling & Personnel Services; Curriculum Studies; Education Management / Administration; Higher Education; Tests, Measurement & Evaluation

MANUSCRIPT GUIDELINES/COMMENTS:

Topics Also Include. Research, theory development, or program applications related to counselor education and supervision. Preparation and supervision of counselors in agency or school settings, in colleges and universities, or at local, state, or federal level.

Counselor Education and Supervision is dedicated to publishing manuscripts concerned with research, theory development, or program applications related to counselor education and supervision. The journal is concerned with the preparation and supervision of counselors in agency or school settings, in colleges and universities, or at local, state, or federal levels.

Manuscripts are acknowledged on receipt by the Editor, who then sends them out for review. The journal uses an anonymous review procedure. Final decisions regarding publication are made by the Co-Editors. Generally, authors can expect a decision regarding a manuscript within 3 to 5 months of being sent out for review.

Following are guidelines for developing and submitting a manuscript. Manuscripts that do not conform to these guidelines will be returned to the author without review.

Manuscript Categories

1. **Counselor Preparation**. Research and theory articles on counseling curriculum and counselor training.

2. **Supervision**. Research and theory articles on counseling supervision.

3. **Professional Development**. Research articles and position papers related to ongoing professional development for counselors by counselor educators and supervisors.

4. **Current Issues**. Research articles and position papers relevant to counselor education and supervision. Relevant areas include diversity, accreditation, licensure, counselor function, supervision issues, and other timely topics.

5. **Innovative Methods**. Clearly delineated and substantiated descriptions of new methods, ideas, and innovations in counselor education and supervision. Manuscripts must include a review of the literature establishing a basis for the methods, a description of the methods including the context in which the methods are used, and a qualitative or quantitative evaluation of the method.

Manuscript Requirements

1. Manuscripts are not to exceed 25 pages total, including all references, tables, etc. Manuscripts should include a 50-100 word Abstract. All manuscripts are to be double-spaced including references and extensive quotes. Allow 1" margins on all sides.

2. Manuscript files should be submitted in Microsoft Word or WordPerfect for Windows. We do not accept Macintosh formats. For re-submissions only, please combine the cover letter and manuscript into one complete file, which is prepared for blind review. Files must be submitted in a 12-point Times Roman Font.

3. Use the *Publication Manual for the American Psychological Association* (5th edition) as a manual for style and manuscript format, including style for all figures, tables, and references. Figures that are not camera-ready will be returned to the author and may cause a delay in publication. Authors bear responsibility for the accuracy of references tables and figures.

4. Authors are encouraged to use guidelines to reduce bias in language against persons based on gender, sexual orientation, racial or ethnic group, disability, or age by referring to the 5th edition of the *Publication Manual for the American Psychological Association*.

5. Do not submit previously published or in press material or a manuscript that is under consideration for publication in another periodical.

6. Lengthy quotations (300-500 words) require written permission from the copyright holder for reproduction. Adaptation of tables and figures also requires reproduction approval. It is the author's responsibility to secure such permission. A copy of the publisher's permission must be provided to the journal Co-Editors immediately on acceptance of the article for publication.

7. Submission Procedures. Submit your manuscript and cover by email attachment. Please be sure the manuscript is prepared for blind review. Send your manuscript to **ces@kent.edu**. All tables and figures must be included and properly formatted within the electronic file (i.e., they will not be accepted separately). For additional information regarding submission requirements, please refer to our website: **http://chdsw.educ.kent.edu/ces**

Creativity Research Journal

SUBMISSION PROCESS:
Postal Submission Only

CONTACT INFORMATION:	REVIEW PROCESS:	
Mark A. Runco, Editor California State University EC 105 PO Box 6868 Fullerton, CA 92834 USA	Type of Review:	Blind Review
	No. External Reviewers:	2
	No. InHouse Reviewers:	2
	Acceptance Rate:	11-20%
	Time to Review:	2 - 3 Months
Phone: 714-278-3376	Reviewer's Comments:	Yes
	Invited Articles:	6-10%
Email: runco@fullerton.edu	Fees to Publish:	$0.00 US$
	Fees to Review:	$0.00 US$
Website: www.erlbaum.com		

PUBLICATION GUIDELINES:	CIRCULATION DATA:
Manuscript Style: American Psychological Association **Manuscript Length:** 15-40 **Copies Required:** Five	**Reader:** Academics, Organizational, Social, and Experimental Psychologists **Frequency of Issue:** Quarterly **Sponsor/Publisher:** Lawrence Erlbaum Associates, Inc.

MANUSCRIPT TOPICS:

Art / Music; Creativitiy, High Achievement; Educational Psychology; Educational Technology Systems; Gifted Children; Special Education; Tests, Measurement & Evaluation

MANUSCRIPT GUIDELINES/COMMENTS:

Topics Also Include. Behavioral, clinical, cognitive, developmental, educational, historical, personality or psychometric research on Creativity and related topics (e.g., Innovation, Originality, the Arts, Aesthetics, Entrepreneurship, Problem solving, Brainstorming, Giftedness).

Editorial Scope

This well-established journal publishes high quality, scholarly research capturing the full range of approaches to the study of creativity – behavioral, clinical, cognitive, cross-cultural, developmental, educational, genetic, organizational, psychoanalytic, psychometric, and social. Interdisciplinary research is also published, as is research within specific domains such as art and science, as well as on critical issues such as aesthetics, genius, imagery, imagination, incubation, insight, intuition, metaphor, play, and problem finding and solving. Integrative literature reviews and theoretical pieces that appreciate empirical work are welcome, but purely speculative articles will not be published.

Audience. Behavioral, clinical, cognitive, developmental, and educational psychologists, and others interested in the study of creativity.

Instructions to Contributors

Manuscript Preparation. Prepare manuscripts according to the *Publication Manual of the American Psychological Association* (5th ed., 1994; American Psychological Association, P.O. Box 2710, Hyattsville, MD 20784), especially with regard to reference lists and text citations. Follow "Guidelines to Reduce Bias in Language" (*APA Manual*, pp. 46-60). Report exact probabilities (e.g., $p = .03$) and effect sizes. Using 8½ x 11-in. non-smear paper and 1-in. margins, type all components double-spaced and in the following order: title page (p. 1), abstract (p. 2), text (including quotations), references, appendices, footnotes, tables, and figure captions. On page 1, type article title, author name(s) and affiliation(s), running head (abbreviated title, no more than 45 characters and spaces), author notes and acknowledgments, submission date (month, day, and year on original manuscript and on any revisions), and name and address of the person to whom requests for reprints should be addressed; on page 2, type an abstract of 150 to 200 words. Indent all paragraphs. Use footnotes sparingly. Attach photocopies of all figures. Number all manuscript pages (including photocopies of figures). Cover Letter, Permissions, Credit Lines:

In a cover letter, include the contact author's complete mailing address, e-mail address, and telephone and fax numbers. State that the manuscript includes only original material that has not been published and that is not under review for publication elsewhere. Authors are responsible for all statements made in their work and for obtaining permission to reprint or adapt a copyrighted table or figure or to quote at length from a copyrighted work. Authors should write to original author(s) and original publisher to see if permission is required and to request nonexclusive world rights in all languages to use the material in the current article and in future editions. Include copies of all permissions and credit lines with the manuscript. (See p. 140 of the *APA Manual* for samples of credit lines.)

Manuscript Submission. Prepare manuscript on a word processor and submit five (5) high quality printouts to the Editor, Mark A. Runco, EC 105, Calif State Univ, PO Box 6868, Fullerton, CA 92834, USA. E-mail: **runco@fullerton.edu**. Manuscripts are not returned.

Accepted Manuscripts and Computer Disk Submission. After manuscripts are accepted, authors are asked to sign and return copyright-transfer agreements and submit uniquely labeled, highly legible, camera-ready figures (use Times Roman font for text appearing in figures). It is the responsibility of the contact author to ascertain that all co-authors approve the accepted manuscript and concur with its publication in the journal. Submit a disk containing two files: word-processor and ASCII versions of the manuscript. File content must match the printed manuscript exactly, or there will be a delay in publication. Disks are not returned. Production Notes: Files are copyedited and typeset into page proofs. Authors read proofs to correct errors and answer editors' queries. Authors may order reprints at that time.

Culture, Health and Sexuality

SUBMISSION PROCESS:
Electronic Submission Preferred via EMail
chs@ioe.ac.uk

CONTACT INFORMATION:	REVIEW PROCESS:	
Peter Aggleton, Editor Thomas Coram Research Unit Institute of Education University of London 27/28 Woburn Square London, WC1H 0AA UK	**Type of Review:**	Blind Review
	No. External Reviewers:	2
	No. InHouse Reviewers:	1
	Acceptance Rate:	21-30%
	Time to Review:	2 - 3 Months
Phone:	**Reviewer's Comments:**	Yes
	Invited Articles:	0-5%
Email: chs@ioe.ac.uk	**Fees to Publish:**	$0.00 US$
	Fees to Review:	$0.00 US$
Website: www.culturehealthsexuality.com		

PUBLICATION GUIDELINES:	CIRCULATION DATA:

Manuscript Style:
  See Manuscript Guidelines
	Reader:
	  Academics

Manuscript Length:
  21-25
	Frequency of Issue:
	  Bi-Monthly

Copies Required:
  Electronic Only
	Sponsor/Publisher:
	  Routledge, Taylor & Francis, Ltd.

MANUSCRIPT TOPICS:
Health & Physical Education

MANUSCRIPT GUIDELINES/COMMENTS:

Aims & Scope
Culture, Health & Sexuality is a leading international environment for the publication of scholarly papers in the fields of culture, health and sexuality. The journal is broad and multi-disciplinary in focus, publishing papers that deal with methodological concerns as well as those that are empirical and conceptual in nature. It offers a forum for debates on policy and practice, and adopts a practitioner focus where appropriate. Culture, Health and Sexuality takes a genuinely international stance in its consideration of key issues and concerns, as reflected by the composition of the editorial board.

Instructions for Authors
Please read these Guidelines carefully. Failure to follow them may result in consideration of your paper being delayed.

Submitting a Paper to *Culture, Health & Sexuality*. Authors are encouraged to submit manuscripts by e-mail to **chs@ioe.ac.uk**. Please prepare your manuscript in MSWORD or Rich Text format. Alternatively one paper copy may be sent to the Editor-in-Chief, Peter Aggleton at: Thomas Coram Research Unit, Institute of Education, University of London, 27/28 Woburn Square, London WC1H 0AA, United Kingdom; fax: +44 (0) 20 7612 6927; E-mail: **chs@ioe.ac.uk**

Please ensure your full postal address and e-mail details are provided at the time of submission.

Queries concerning the preparation of manuscripts may be directed to the Editor-in-Chief by e-mail at the above address in advance of submission.

General Guidelines. *Culture, Health & Sexuality* considers all manuscripts on the strict condition that they have been submitted only to *Culture, Health & Sexuality*, and that they have not been published already nor are they under consideration for publication or in press elsewhere. Authors who fail to adhere to this condition will be charged with all costs which *Culture, Health & Sexuality* incurs and their papers will not be published.

Contributions to *Culture, Health & Sexuality* must report original research and will be subjected to peer review.

There are a limited number of colour pages within the annual page allowance. Authors should restrict their use of colour to situations where it is necessary on scientific, and not merely cosmetic, grounds. In addition, authors may pay to publish colour illustrations, but please consult the publisher regarding cost before submission.

Writing your paper
- For all manuscripts non-discriminatory language is mandatory. Sexist, heterosexist, and racist terms should not be used.
- A typical article will not exceed 7,500 words in total (including all references and notes). Papers that greatly exceed this will not be eligible for entry into the peer review process.
- Each paper should include three to six keywords on its title page.
- Papers are accepted only in English.
- Manuscripts should be typed on single sides of good quality white A4 or 8 x 11 inch paper, double-spaced throughout including the reference section, with wide (3 cm) margins.
- All the authors of a paper should include their full names, affiliations, postal and email addresses, telephone and fax numbers on the cover page of manuscripts.
- Abstracts of 150 - 200 words are required for all papers submitted and should precede the text of a paper.
- Manuscripts should be compiled in the following order: title page; abstract; keywords; main text; acknowledgments; appendixes (as appropriate); references; table(s) with caption(s) (on individual sheets); figure caption(s) (as a list).
- When using a word which is or is asserted to be a proprietary term or trade mark authors must use the symbol ® or TM or alternatively a footnote can be inserted using the wording below:
  This article includes a word that is or is asserted to be a proprietary term or trade mark. Its inclusion does not imply it has acquired for legal purposes a non-proprietary or general significance, nor is any other judgement implied concerning its legal status.

Copyright. It is a condition of publication that authors vest or license copyright in their articles, including abstracts, in Taylor & Francis Group Ltd. This enables us to ensure full copyright protection and to disseminate the article, and the Journal, to the widest possible readership in print and electronic formats as appropriate. Authors may, of course, use the material elsewhere after publication providing that prior permission is obtained from Taylor & Francis Group Ltd. Authors are themselves responsible for obtaining permission to reproduce copyright material from other sources.

For details on copyright permission please visit the web site. Copies of the permission letters should be sent with the manuscript to the Editors.

Notes on Style. For a full description of the Journal's style (including referencing) please visit the web site.

Page Charges. There are no page charges to individuals or institutions.

SUBMISSION PROCESS:

Electronic Submission Preferred
via EMail

communications@cupahr.org

CONTACT INFORMATION:	REVIEW PROCESS:

Missy Kline, Editor
CUPA-HR
Tyson Place
2607 Kingston Pike, Suite 250
Knoxville, TN 37919 USA
 	
Phone:
  865-637-7673
 	
Email:
  communications@cupahr.org
Website:
  www.cupahr.org
	Type of Review: Peer Review
	
	No. External Reviewers: 10
	No. InHouse Reviewers: 2
	
	Acceptance Rate: 70%
	Time to Review: 3 Months
	Reviewer's Comments: Yes
	Invited Articles: 20%
	
	Fees to Publish: $0.00 US$
	Fees to Review: $0.00 US$

PUBLICATION GUIDELINES:	**CIRCULATION DATA:**

Manuscript Style:
  See Manuscript Guidelines
 	
Manuscript Length:
  1,500 - 3,500 Words
 	
Copies Required:
  One
	Reader:
	  Administrators, Higher Education HR
	  Professionals
	
	Frequency of Issue:
	  2 Times/Year
	
	Sponsor/Publisher:
	  College and University Professional
	  Association for Human Resources (CUPA-
	  HR)

MANUSCRIPT TOPICS:
Higher Education; Higher Education Human Resources

MANUSCRIPT GUIDELINES/COMMENTS:

Two types of articles are of interest to our readers. The first type of article is on an HR topic from a practical approach. This kind of how-to article describes an innovative program that has been put in place at a member institution and that could be implemented on other campuses as well. Senior practitioners in HR management are encouraged to submit articles of this nature. The second type of article presents information or observations of universal importance to higher education HR professionals. Rather than focusing on a practice at a particular university, this type of article addresses a recently emerging trend in human resource management; a technical area in need of clarification, such as immigration law; or an issue that just won't go away, such as sexual harassment or merit pay. This type of article is written by experts in a particular area of HR management or by attorneys, compensation specialists and the like. Send articles as a Word attachment via e-mail to **communications@cupahr.org**. Include all author names, professional titles, addresses (including e-mail addresses) and telephone numbers on the cover page. Also include a brief, one-paragraph biography of all authors on a separate page. Include current title, place of employment, academic degrees and the names of institutions conferring them.

Decision Sciences Journal of Innovative Education

SUBMISSION PROCESS: **Electronic Submission Only via Online Portal** **http://mc.manuscriptcentral.com/dsjie**	

CONTACT INFORMATION:	**REVIEW PROCESS:**
Barbara B. Flynn, Editor Indiana University Kelley School of Business 801 W. Michigan St., BS 4010 Indianapolis, IN 46202 USA **Phone:** 317-278-8586 **Email:** bbflynn@iupui.edu **Website:** http://kelley.iupui.edu/dsjie/	**Type of Review:** Blind Review **No. External Reviewers:** 2 **No. InHouse Reviewers:** 0 **Acceptance Rate:** 21-30% **Time to Review:** 2 - 3 Months **Reviewer's Comments:** Yes **Invited Articles:** 0-5% **Fees to Publish:** $0.00 US$ **Fees to Review:** $0.00 US$
PUBLICATION GUIDELINES:	**CIRCULATION DATA:**

Manuscript Style:
   See Manuscript Guidelines
 	
Manuscript Length:
   26-30
 	
Copies Required:
   Electronic Only
	Reader:
	   Academics
	
	Frequency of Issue:
	   2 Times/Year
	
	Sponsor/Publisher:
	   Decision Sciences Institute / Blackwell Publishing, Inc.

MANUSCRIPT TOPICS:
Education Management / Administration; Educational Psychology; Educational Technology Systems; Higher Education; Tests, Measurement & Evaluation

MANUSCRIPT GUIDELINES/COMMENTS:

The *Decision Sciences Journal of Innovative Education* is a peer-reviewed journal published by the Decision Sciences Institute. Its mission is to publish significant research relevant to teaching and learning issues in the decision sciences. The decision sciences is the union of the quantitative and behavioral approaches to managerial decision making, encompassing all of the functional areas of business, including (but not limited to) accounting, business strategy and entrepreneurship, economics, finance, international business and globalization, marketing, MIS/DSS and computer systems, organizational behavior/organizational design, operations and logistics management, quantitative methods and statistics. Types of articles suitable for publication in the *Decision Sciences Journal of Innovative Education* include the following:

Empirical Research Articles
An empirical research article describes high quality empirical research related to innovative education in the decision sciences. It should begin with an in-depth review of the literature and

development of hypotheses, drawing upon theory in the functional area to support details of the innovative approach, as well as upon educational and psychological theory to support the intended learning effects of the innovation. The hypotheses will typically refer to the effect of the innovation, in terms of measures of student learning, measures of course effectiveness, etc. Empirical research articles should include a description of the innovative approach and its rationale, a description of the methodology used for gathering data to test the effectiveness of the approach, description of the statistical analysis of the data and a discussion of the findings, including suggestions for readers who would like to implement the approach in their classroom.

Case Study Research Articles

A case study research article describes high quality research related to innovative education in the decision sciences that employs a class as a case. This approach allows in-depth study of a single class or several classes and is based on careful and detailed documentation of the use and impact of an educational innovation in the decision sciences. The multiple case study, which contains detailed information on several classes or several sections of a class, is preferred. In analyzing the data, similarities and differences between the classes should be noted and documented, to the extent possible. The following article provides a good guide to case study research:

Eisenhardt, K.M. "Building Theories from Case Study Research." *Academy of Management Review*, vol. 14., no. 4, 532-550.

A case study research article should begin with an in-depth review of the literature, drawing upon theory in the functional area to support details of the innovative approach, as well as upon educational and psychological theory to support the intended learning effects of the innovation. It should include a structured approach for analyzing the data and should lead to a set of propositions providing a foundation for future research. Either quantitative or qualitative analysis of the data may be appropriate. A case study research article should include a description of the innovative approach and a description of the cases (classes), highlighting their similarities and differences. Tables should be used to present summaries of the quantitative or qualitative comparisons. It should also include a thorough discussion of the findings, including suggestions for readers who would like to implement the innovative approach in their classrooms.

A good example of a case study research article is provided by McLachlin, Ron, "Management Initiatives and Just-in-Time Manufacturing." *Journal of Operations Management*, vol. 15, no 4 (1997), 271-292., although it doesn't deal with teaching or learning issues.

The *Decision Sciences Journal of Innovative Education* does not publish case studies designed for classroom use.

Conceptual/Theoretical Articles

A conceptual/theoretical article describes an approach to innovative education or a learning issue relevant to the decision sciences. A conceptual/theoretical article should be strongly grounded in the relevant theoretical literature in an area such as education, organizational behavior or psychology, as well as in the literature specific to the innovative approach or learning issue being described. It may focus on a single approach or issue, or it may be based on a comparison and contrast of alternative approaches or issues. Because it should lay the groundwork for future research in the area, a conceptual/theoretical article should develop a set of propositions about the effectiveness of the innovative approach or learning issue. It is important that conceptual/ theoretical articles focus on cutting-edge topics and present significant new insight.

Teaching Briefs

A teaching brief *briefly* describes an innovative approach for teaching in the decision sciences. Limited to five double-spaced pages (12-pt. font) of text, it should describe the innovative approach in sufficient detail so that it could be replicated in the reader's classroom. It should also provide a brief summary of the evidence of the effectiveness of the innovative approach. Teaching briefs should focus on the innovative approach itself, and do not need to include a literature review or statistical analysis of the data. They should have more of a "how to" flavor than the empirical or case study research articles. Teaching briefs may refer readers to the authors' website for additional detail about how to use the innovative approach.

Submission
Manuscripts should be submitted electronically via **http://mc.manuscriptcentral.com/dsjie**.

Your submission certifies that none of the contents are copyrighted, published or accepted for publication by another journal, under review by another journal or submitted to another journal while under review by the *Decision Sciences Journal of Innovative Education*. All manuscripts should be accompanied by an abstract of not more than 180 words (except for teaching briefs, which do not require an abstract) and an author's vita of not more than 150 words. The author's name and affiliation should appear on a separate page.

Figures, charts and tables should be consecutively numbered in Arabic. *Decision Sciences Journal of Innovative Education* does not allow the use of footnotes or endnotes. References should be listed alphabetically by author at the end of the paper and referred to in the body of the text by Name (date).

Should the manuscript be accepted for publication, the author will be asked to submit a copy on a disk containing the final post-review version of the paper. The word processing file (or ASCII text file) will be used in the typesetting process.

Authors will be required to assign copyright in their paper to the Decision Sciences Institute. Copyright assignment is a condition of publication, and papers will not be passed to the publisher for production unless copyright has been assigned. (Papers subject to government or Crown copyright are exempt from this requirement). To assist authors, an appropriate copyright form will be supplied by the editorial office.

Website – http://kelley.iupui.edu/dsjie/
The *Decision Sciences Journal of Innovative Education* website contains abstracts of all empirical research, case study research and conceptual/theoretical articles, as well as teaching briefs in their entirety. It contains information for contributors and a site where authors can check on the status of articles in process. The website also contains announcements about upcoming events related to innovative education in the decision sciences and a section for personal news about DSI members, such as news about winners of teaching awards. Please send your news and announcements to the Editor, at the address listed above.

Review Process
Each manuscript submitted to the *Decision Sciences Journal of Innovative Education* is subjected to the following review process:
1. An initial screening by the Editor to determine the suitability of the article for the journal. Suitable articles are assigned to two or three referees, according to their functional and methodological content. If the manuscript is deemed inappropriate for the journal because it is not a match for the *Decision Sciences Journal of Innovative Education*'s audience or mission, it will be promptly returned to the author.
2. A careful review by the referees, each of whom makes a recommendation to the Editor and provides comments for authors.
3. An appraisal of the reviews by the Editor. If the Editor feels the paper has potential for publication, the author is invited to make revisions, following the suggestions of the reviewers.
4. Upon receipt of the revisions, the Editor will make a final decision. The Editor will appraise the entire review process, making sure that all revisions suggested by the referees have been addressed.

The Editor reserves the right to deviate from the above procedures when the situation warrants and as it is deemed appropriate.

Delta Pi Epsilon Journal

SUBMISSION PROCESS:
Electronic Submission Preferred via EMail **mcewenb@ncat.edu**

CONTACT INFORMATION:	REVIEW PROCESS:	
Beryl C. McEwen, Editor North Carolina A&T State University School of Business and Economics Greensboro, NC 27411 USA	**Type of Review:**	Blind Review
	No. External Reviewers:	3
	No. InHouse Reviewers:	1
Phone: 336-334-7657 ext. 4001	**Acceptance Rate:** **Time to Review:** **Reviewer's Comments:**	21-30% 2 - 3 Months Yes
Email: mcewenb@ncat.edu	**Invited Articles:**	0-5%
Website: http://dpe.org/core/DPEJournals.htm	**Fees to Publish:** **Fees to Review:**	$0.00 US$ $0.00 US$

PUBLICATION GUIDELINES:	CIRCULATION DATA:
Manuscript Style: American Psychological Association	**Reader:** Academics, Practicing Teachers
Manuscript Length: 21-25	**Frequency of Issue:** Quarterly
Copies Required: One	**Sponsor/Publisher:** Delta Pi Epsilon

MANUSCRIPT TOPICS:
Business Teacher Education; Educational Technology Systems; Higher Education; Teacher Education

MANUSCRIPT GUIDELINES/COMMENTS:

The Delta Pi Epsilon Journal publishes articles that build the knowledge base for both business and education and that relay ways the two reinforce each other. Articles reporting sound quantitative or qualitative research are selected for publication.

Manuscript reviews for this refereed publication occur on a continual basis, so you are welcome to submit them at any time.

All manuscripts must:
1. Be research based and contain actual research data to support findings and conclusions.
2. Be reliable, generalizable, and adequate.
3. Be sufficiently well written to require minimal editing and revision.
4. Be 2,000 to 5,000 words in length.

Specific Procedures for Preparing a Manuscript for *The Delta Pi Epsilon Journal*

a. Use the *Publication Manual for the American Psychological Association*, 5th Edition, to prepare the manuscript. Obtain this manual at most bookstores, or order it from the American Psychological Association, 1200 Seventeenth Street, N.W., Washington, DC 20036.

b. Include a title page *and* abstract (maximum 150 words) with the manuscript.

c. Include a brief biographical statement for each author. Include titles (e.g., Dr., Mr., Mrs., Ms., or Miss); full names; position titles; phone numbers; places of employment; and cities, states, and zip codes. If appropriate, include an acknowledgment statement for agencies that assisted with authorship or research funding.

d. Conclude research manuscripts with a section that elaborates on the findings and how they contribute to the body of knowledge in the area being investigated. Also, provide recommendations for further research that would build upon and complement this study.

e. Send *ONE* hard copy and one electronic copy, in MS Word, of the manuscript, including the title page and abstract to the editor: Dr. Beryl C. McEwen, Editor, The Delta Pi Epsilon Journal, 324 Merrick Hall, North Carolina A&T State University, Greensboro, NC 27411; Phone: (336) 334-7657, ext. 4001, E-mail: **mcewenb@ncat.edu**

Developmental Review

SUBMISSION PROCESS:
Electronic Submission Preferred via Online Portal **http://ees.elsevier.com/dr**

CONTACT INFORMATION:	REVIEW PROCESS:	
C.J. Brainerd, Editor Department of Human Development Cornell University	**Type of Review:**	Editorial Review
	No. External Reviewers:	3
	No. InHouse Reviewers:	1
Phone:	**Acceptance Rate:**	11-20%
	Time to Review:	2 - 3 Months
Email:	**Reviewer's Comments:**	Yes
	Invited Articles:	11-20%
Website: http://www.elsevier.com/	**Fees to Publish:**	$0.00 US$
	Fees to Review:	$0.00 US$

PUBLICATION GUIDELINES:	CIRCULATION DATA:
Manuscript Style: American Psychological Association	**Reader:** Academics
Manuscript Length: 30+	**Frequency of Issue:** Quarterly
Copies Required: Electronic Only	**Sponsor/Publisher:** Elsevier Inc.

MANUSCRIPT TOPICS:
Developmental Psychology; Educational Psychology

MANUSCRIPT GUIDELINES/COMMENTS:

Description
Presenting research that bears on important conceptual issues in developmental psychology, *Developmental Review: Perspectives in Behavior and Cognition* provides child and developmental, child clinical, and educational psychologists with authoritative articles that reflect current thinking and cover significant scientific developments. The journal emphasizes human developmental processes and gives particular attention to issues relevant to child developmental psychology. The research concerns issues with important implications for the fields of pediatrics, psychiatry, and education, and increases the understanding of socialization processes.

Guide for Authors
Developmental Review (*DR*), an international and interdisciplinary journal, publishes original articles that bear on conceptual issues in psychological development. Appropriate papers include (1) theoretical statements, (2) reviews of literature, (3) summaries of programmatic research, (4) empirical findings that are provocative and of particular relevance for developmental theory, (5) integrated collections of papers on a single theme, (6) analyses of social policy as it affects human development, (7) historical analyses, (8) essays on major books, and (9) analyses of method and

design. Discussions and commentaries are welcomed. Subject matter may be from the disciplines of psychology, sociology, education, or pediatrics, may be basic or applied, and may be drawn from any species or age range as long as it speaks to issues of psychological development.

Submission of Manuscripts

Authors should submit their articles electronically via the Elsevier Editorial System (EES) page for this journal (**http://ees.elsevier.com/dr**). The system automatically converts source files to a single Adobe Acrobat PDF version of the article, which is used in the peer-review process. Please note that even though manuscript source files are converted to PDF at submission for the review process, these source files are needed for further processing after acceptance. All correspondence, including notification of the Editor's decision and requests for revision, takes place by e-mail and via the Author's EES homepage, removing the need for a hard-copy paper trail.

There are no submission fees or page charges. Each manuscript should be accompanied by a letter outlining the basic findings of the paper and their significance.

Original papers only will be considered. Manuscripts are accepted for review with the understanding that the same work has not been and is not currently submitted elsewhere, and that it will not be submitted elsewhere prior to the journal making an editorial decision. Moreover, submission of the article for publication has been approved by all of the authors and by the institution where the work was carried out, and any person cited as a source of personal communications has approved such citation. Written authorization may be required at the Editor's discretion. Articles and any other material published in *Developmental Review* represent the opinions of the author(s) and should not be construed to reflect the opinions of the Editor(s) and the Publisher.

Manuscripts fitting the objectives of *Developmental Review* will ordinarily be submitted to at least two reviewers for comments. Authors are invited to suggest potential reviewers with the understanding that present or former students or collaborators should not be suggested and that these recommendations are subject to the Editor's discretion. Authors wishing blind review should specifically request it and should remove identifying material from the abstract and the body of the manuscript. Persons interested in organizing a thematic collection of papers, submitting a book review, or preparing a commentary on previously published material are invited to make a preliminary inquiry to the Editor.

Upon acceptance of an article, authors will be asked to transfer copyright (for more information on copyright, see **http://authors.elsevier.com**). This transfer will ensure the widest possible dissemination of information. A letter will be sent to the corresponding author confirming receipt of the manuscript. A form facilitating transfer of copyright will be provided.

If excerpts or material from other copyrighted works are included, the author(s) must obtain written permission from the copyright owners and credit the source(s) in the article. Elsevier has preprinted forms for use by authors in these cases: contact Elsevier Global Rights Department, P.O. Box 800, Oxford OX5 1DX, UK; phone: (+44) 1865 843830, fax: (+44) 1865 853333, e-mail: permissions@elsevier.com.

Preparation of Manuscript

Manuscripts should be double-spaced throughout. Authors are requested to follow the instructions given in the most recent edition of the *Publication Manual of the American Psychological Association*. Pages should be numbered consecutively and organized as follows:

The **title page** (p. 1) should contain the article title, authors' names and complete affiliations, footnotes to the title, and the address for manuscript correspondence (including e-mail address and telephone and fax numbers).

The **abstract** (p. 2) must be a single paragraph that summarizes the main findings of the paper in less than 150 words. After the abstract a list of up to 10 keywords that will be useful for indexing or searching should be included.

The **Introduction** should be as concise as possible, without subheadings. Other sections should begin with appropriate headings and contain subheadings that follow the methods of subordination in the *Publication Manual of the American Psychological Association.*

Materials and **methods** should be sufficiently detailed to enable the experiments to be reproduced.

Results and **Discussion** may be combined and may be organized into subheadings.

Acknowledgments should be brief.

References. Literature references in the text should be cited by author's surname and the year of publication, e.g., Smith (1980); Smith et al. (1981); Smith and Jones (1982, p. 250) (for references to a specific page); (Smith & Jones, 1983) (ampersand for references in parentheses). If a reference has more than two authors, the citation includes the surnames of all authors at the first mention, but later citations of the same reference include only the surname of the first author and the abbreviation "et al." Suffixes a, b, etc., should be used following the date to distinguish two or more works by the same author(s) in the same year, e.g., Smith (1984a, 1984b). References cited in the text should be listed alphabetically and type double-spaced at the end of the article. Journal titles should be written out in full. Personal communication should be cited as such in the text and should not be included in the reference list. Please note the following examples:

Cohen, J. (1977). *Statistical power analysis for the behavioral sciences.* New York: Academic Press.

Treiman, R., & Baron, J. (1981). Segmental analysis ability: Development and relation to reading ability. In G. Waller & T. MacKinnon (Eds.), *Reading research: Advances in theory and practice* (Vol. 3, pp. 159-198). New York: Academic Press.

Waterman, A.S. (1999). Issues of identity formation revisited: United States and The Netherlands. *Developmental Review, 19,* 462-479.

Figures. Number figures consecutively with Arabic numeral. Please visit our Web site at **http://authors.elsevier.com/artwork** for detailed instruction on preparing electronic artwork.

Free color on the Web. If, together with your accepted article, you submit usable color figures, then Elsevier will ensure, at no additional charge, that these figures will appear in color on the Web (e.g., ScienceDirect and other sites) regardless of whether these illustrations are reproduced in color in the printed version. For color reproduction in print, you will receive information regarding the costs from Elsevier after receipt of your accepted article.

Please note. Because of technical complications that can arise in converting color figures to "gray scale" (for the printed version should you not opt for color in print), please submit in addition usable black-and-white files corresponding to all the color illustrations.

Tables should be numbered consecutively with Arabic numerals in order of appearance in the text. Type each table double-spaced on a separate page with a short descriptive title typed directly above and with essential footnotes below.

Preparation of Supplementary Material
Elsevier now accepts electronic supplementary material to support and enhance your scientific research. Supplementary files offer additional possibilities for publishing supporting applications, movies, animation sequences, high-resolution images, background datasets, sound clips, and more.

Supplementary files supplied will be published online alongside the electronic version of your article in Elsevier Web products, including ScienceDirect (**http://www.sciencedirect.com**). To ensure that your submitted material is directly usable, please provide the data in one of our recommended file formats. Authors should submit the material in electronic format together with the article and supply a concise and descriptive caption for each file. Please note, however, that supplementary material will not appear in the printed journal. For more detailed instructions, please visit our Author Gateway at **http://authors.elsevier.com**, click on "Artwork instructions," and then click on "Multimedia files."

Proofs

PDF proofs will be sent by e-mail to the corresponding author. To avoid delay in publication, only necessary changes should be made, and corrections should be returned promptly. Authors will be charged for alterations that exceed 10% of the total cost of composition.

Reprints

Twenty-five reprints will be provided to the corresponding author free of charge. Additional reprints may be ordered. A reprint order form will accompany your proofs.

Disability and Society

SUBMISSION PROCESS:
Postal Submission Only

CONTACT INFORMATION:	REVIEW PROCESS:	
Len Barton, Editor c/o Helen Oliver University of Sheffield School of Education 388 Glossop Road Sheffield, S10 2JA UK	**Type of Review:**	Blind Review
	No. External Reviewers:	0
	No. InHouse Reviewers:	2
	Acceptance Rate:	50%
	Time to Review:	1 - 2 Months
Phone:	**Reviewer's Comments:**	Yes
	Invited Articles:	0-5%
Email: h.j.oliver@sheffield.ac.uk	**Fees to Publish:**	$0.00 US$
	Fees to Review:	$0.00 US$
Website: http://www.tandf.co.uk/journals/titles/096 87599.asp		
PUBLICATION GUIDELINES:	**CIRCULATION DATA:**	

Manuscript Style:
    See Manuscript Guidelines
	Reader:
	    Academics, Administrators, Practicing
	    Teachers, Counselors	

Manuscript Length:
    11-15
	Frequency of Issue:
	    7 Times/Year	

Copies Required:
    Three
	Sponsor/Publisher:
	    Routledge, Taylor & Francis, Ltd.	

MANUSCRIPT TOPICS:
Counseling & Personnel Services; Educational Psychology; Health & Physical Education; Secondary / Adolescent Studies; Social Studies / Social Science; Special Education; Teacher Education; Urban Education, Cultural / Non-Traditional

MANUSCRIPT GUIDELINES/COMMENTS:

Aims & Scope
Disability & Society is an international journal providing a focus for debate about such issues as human rights, discrimination, definitions, policy and practices. It appears against a background of change in the ways in which disability is viewed and managed.

Definitions of disability are more readily acknowledged to be relative; custodial approaches are seen as inadequate and unacceptable - placing greater emphasis on community care and integration. However, policy intentions may not have the desired effects on the realities of everyday practice and policy changes themselves may be merely cosmetic, or appropriate but unfounded.

While publishing articles that represent all the professional perspectives, the journal also provides an opportunity for the consumers of the services to speak for themselves.

As well as main articles there is a Current Issues section that is intended to give people the opportunity to write about things that concern them in a less formal and academic way. The pieces should be interesting, controversial or even polemical and may encourage others to respond. They do not need to meet the conventional academic criteria but they should not be personal attacks or libellous. The word limit is 2000. If you wish to submit, articles can be sent direct to Michelle Moore, University of Sheffield, School of Education, 388 Glossop Road, Sheffield S10 2JA, UK or if you wish to discuss ideas for articles contact her direct on 0114 222 8131 E-mail: **m.p.moore@sheffield.ac.uk**

Instructions for Authors
Contributors should bear in mind that they are addressing an international audience. Manuscripts that do not conform to the requirements listed below will not be considered for publication or returned to their authors. Submissions will be seen anonymously by two referees.

Manuscripts, between 3000 and 7000 words maximum (including the bibliography), should be sent to, should be sent to Mrs Helen Oliver, Disability & Society, School of Education, University of Sheffield, 388 Glossop Road, Sheffield S10 2JA, UK. Articles can be considered if three complete copies of each manuscript are submitted. They should be typed on one side of the paper, double spaced, with ample margins, and bear the title of the contribution, name(s) of the author(s) and the address where the work was carried out. Each article should be accompanied by an abstract of 100-150 words on a separate sheet, and a short note of biographical details. The full postal address, telephone, fax and email numbers (where possible) of the author who will check proofs and receive correspondence and offprints should also be included. All pages should be numbered.

Proofs will be sent to authors if there is sufficient time to do so. They should be corrected and returned to the Editor within three days. Major alterations to the text cannot be accepted.

Early Electronic Offprints. Corresponding authors can now receive their article by e-mail as a complete PDF. This allows the author to print up to 50 copies, free of charge, and disseminate them to colleagues. In many cases this facility will be available up to two weeks prior to publication. Or, alternatively, corresponding authors will receive the traditional 50 offprints. A copy of the journal will be sent by post to all corresponding authors after publication. Additional copies of the journal can be purchased at the author's preferential rate of £15.00/$25.00 per copy.

Copyright. It is a condition of publication that authors assign copyright or licence the publication rights in their articles, including abstracts, to Taylor & Francis. This enables us to ensure full copyright protection and to disseminate the article, and of course the Journal, to the widest possible readership in print and electronic formats as appropriate. Authors may, of course, use the article elsewhere after publication without prior permission from Taylor & Francis, provided that acknowledgement is given to the Journal as the original source of publication, and that Taylor & Francis is notified so that our records show that its use is properly authorised. Authors retain a number of other rights under the Taylor & Francis rights policies documents. These policies are referred to at **www.tandf.co.uk/journals/author rights.pdf** for full details. Authors are themselves responsible for obtaining permission to reproduce copyright material from other sources.

Processing your article electronically
We strongly encourage you to send the final, revised version of your article electronically, by email. This will ensure that it can be dealt with quickly and will reduce errors at the typesetting stage. This guide sets out the procedures which will allow us to process your article efficiently.

Please note: This guide does not apply to authors who are submitting an article for consideration and peer review; they apply only to authors whose articles have been reviewed, revised, and accepted for publication.

You should save the files as Word documents, although figures can also be supplied as eps, tif, pdf, or word files (see below).

Tables and figures should be saved as separate files, and a separate list of figure captions should also be provided. Give the files clear names such as Smith_text.doc, Smith_tables.doc, Smith_figures.doc, Smith_figurecaptions.doc.

The approximate position of tables and figures should be indicated in the text file, and they must be mentioned in the text.

Ensure that the files are not saved as read only.

Please see the journal Instructions for Authors page for a Word template to help you style your article correctly. Please pay particular attention to the references. Please also supply the running heads for your article in the style of the journal (this will usually be the authors' initials and surname plus a short title).

Please make sure that the full postal and email address of the author who will check proofs and receive correspondence and offprints is clearly marked.

Discourse

SUBMISSION PROCESS:

**Electronic Submission Preferred
via EMail**

discourse@uq.edu.au

CONTACT INFORMATION:	REVIEW PROCESS:	
B Lingard, M Mills & V Carrington, Eds. c/o Dawn Butler, Production Manager School of Education University of Queensland Brisbane Queensland 4072, Australia	**Type of Review:**	Blind Review
	No. External Reviewers:	2-3
	No. InHouse Reviewers:	3
	Acceptance Rate:	63%
	Time to Review:	1 - 2 Months
Phone:	**Reviewer's Comments:**	Yes
	Invited Articles:	31-50%
Email: discourse@uq.edu.au	**Fees to Publish:**	$0.00 US$
	Fees to Review:	$0.00 US$
Website: http://www.tandf.co.uk/journals/titles/015 96306.asp		

PUBLICATION GUIDELINES:	CIRCULATION DATA:
Manuscript Style: See Manuscript Guidelines	**Reader:** Academics, Practicing Teachers, Counselors
Manuscript Length: 11-15	**Frequency of Issue:** Quarterly
Copies Required: Electronic Only	**Sponsor/Publisher:** Routledge, Taylor & Francis, Ltd.

MANUSCRIPT TOPICS:
Cultural Politics of Education; Urban Education, Cultural / Non-Traditional

MANUSCRIPT GUIDELINES/COMMENTS:

Aims & Scope
Discourse is an international, fully peer-reviewed journal publishing contemporary research and theorising in the cultural politics of education. The journal publishes academic articles from throughout the world which contribute to contemporary debates on the new social, cultural and political configurations that now mark education as a highly contested but important cultural site.

Discourse adopts a broadly critical orientation, but is not tied to any particular ideological, disciplinary or methodological position. It encourages interdisciplinary approaches to the analysis of educational theory, policy and practice. It welcomes papers which explore speculative ideas in education, are written in innovative ways, or are presented in experimental ways.

228

Apart from articles and book reviews, *Discourse* also contains, from time to time, review essays, symposia on emerging issues, as well as interviews and policy debates.

Instructions for Authors
Note to Authors. Please make sure your contact address information is clearly visible on the outside of all packages you are sending to Editors.

Papers accepted become the copyright of the Journal, unless otherwise specifically agreed.

Contributors should bear in mind that they are addressing an international audience.

Manuscripts that do not conform to the requirements listed below will not be considered for publication or returned to their author.

Manuscripts should be submitted in electronic format to Dr Dawn Butler, Production Manager, at **discourse@uq.edu.au**. All printed correspondence can be sent to Discourse: studies in the cultural politics of education, School of Education, The University of Queensland, Brisbane, Queensland 4072, Australia. Articles should contain no more than 6,000 words and should adhere strictly to the style guide of the American Psychological Association (APA). Each article should contain the title of the contribution, name(s) and email address(es) of the author(s), the address where the work was carried out, short note of biographical details, and should begin with an Abstract of 100-150 words. All pages should be numbered. The full postal and email address of the author who will receive correspondence and offprints should also be included.

Articles are prepared by *Discourse* editorial staff at the University of Queensland for submission to the publishers, Taylor & Francis. First-level queries are dealt with at this stage.

Tables and captions to illustrations. Tables must be typed out on separate sheets and not included as part of the text. The captions to illustrations should be gathered together and printed on a separate sheet. Tables and figures should be with Arabic numerals. The approximate position of tables and figures should be indicated in the manuscript. Captions should include keys to symbols.

Figures. Please supply one set of artwork in a finished form, suitable for reproduction. Figures will not normally be redrawn by the publisher.

References should be indicated in the typescript by giving the author's name, with the year of publication in parentheses, as detailed in the APA style guide. If several papers by the same author and from the same year are cited, a, b, c, etc. should be put after the year of publication. The references should be listed in full at the end of the paper in standard APA format. For example:

Adams, M. J. (1990). Beginning to Read: *Thinking and learning about print*. Cambridge, MA: MIT Press.

Kameenui, E. J., Simmons, D. C., Baker, S., Chard, D. J., Dickson, S. V., Gunn, B., Smith, S. B., Sprick, M., & Lin, S-J. (1998). Effective strategies in teaching beginning reading. In E. J. Kameenui, & D. C. Simmons (Eds.), *Effective teaching strategies that accommodate diverse learners* (pp. 45-70; 194-196). New Jersey: Prentice Hall.

Stanovich, K. E. (1986). Metthew effects in reading: Some consequences of individual differences in the acquisition of literacy. *Reading Research Quarterly*, 21, 360-407.

Titles of journals should not be abbreviated.

Proofs will be sent by the publishers to authors in electronic form. There is usually a turn-around time of three days for authors to answer queries and directly to the publishers.

Early Electronic Offprints. Corresponding authors can now receive their article by e-mail as a complete PDF. This allows the author to print up to 50 copies, free of charge, and disseminate them to colleagues. In many cases this facility will be available up to two weeks prior to publication. Or, alternatively, corresponding authors will receive the traditional 50 offprints. A copy of the journal will be sent by post to all corresponding authors after publication. Additional copies of the journal can be purchased at the author's preferential rate of £15.00/$25.00 per copy.

Copyright. It is a condition of publication that authors assign copyright or licence the publication rights in their articles, including abstracts, to Taylor & Francis. This enables us to ensure full copyright protection and to disseminate the article, and of course the journal, to the widest possible readership in print and electronic formats as appropriate. Authors may, of course, use the article elsewhere after publication without prior permission from Taylor & Francis, provided that acknowledgement is given to the Journal as the original source of publication, and that Taylor & Francis is notified so that our records show that its use is properly authorised. Authors retain a number of other rights under the Taylor & Francis rights policies documents. These policies are referred to at **www.tandf.co.uk/journals/author rights.pdf** for full details. Authors are themselves responsible for obtaining permission to reproduce copyright material from other sources.

Processing your article electronically

We strongly encourage you to send the final, revised version of your article electronically, by email. This will ensure that it can be dealt with quickly and will reduce errors at the typesetting stage. This guide sets out the procedures which will allow us to process your article efficiently.

Please note: This guide does not apply to authors who are submitting an article for consideration and peer review; they apply only to authors whose articles have been reviewed, revised, and accepted for publication.

You should save the files as Word documents, although figures can also be supplied as eps, tif, pdf, or word files (see below).

Tables and figures should be saved as separate files, and a separate list of figure captions should also be provided. Give the files clear names such as Smith_text.doc, Smith_tables.doc, Smith_figures.doc, Smith_figurecaptions.doc.

The approximate position of tables and figures should be indicated in the text file, and they must be mentioned in the text.

Ensure that the files are not saved as read only.

Please see the journal Instructions for Authors page for a Word template to help you style your article correctly. Please pay particular attention to the references. Please also supply the running heads for your article in the style of the journal (this will usually be the authors' initials and surname plus a short title).

Please make sure that the full postal and email address of the author who will check proofs and receive correspondence and offprints is clearly marked.

Guidance on supplying figures

Avoid the use of colour and tints. Line figures will normally be reproduced in black and white. Subtle variations in grey tones which are distinguishable on screen may not be distinct when printed, and should be avoided. Strong contrasts such as black/white and cross-hatched patterns give a better printed result.

Figures should be produced as near to the finished size as possible. If the figure is to be reduced to fit the final printed page, allow for this reduction when selecting lettering size and line weight.

Half-tones, scans, photographs and transparencies should be saved at a minimum of 1200 dpi. They will not normally be reproduced in colour unless first agreed by the journal editor. In some cases it may be possible to present figures in black and white in the printed journal, but in colour in the online journal, if the originals are suitable.

All figures must be numbered in the order in which they occur (e.g. Figure 1, Figure 2 etc.). In multi-part figures, each part should be labelled (e.g. Figure 1 (a), Figure 1 (b) etc.).The figure captions must be saved as a separate file with the text and numbered correspondingly.

Files should be saved as TIFF (tagged image file format), PostScript or EPS (encapsulated PostScript), containing all the necessary font information and the source file of the application (e.g., CorelDraw/Mac, CorelDraw/PC).

Economics of Education Review

SUBMISSION PROCESS:
Postal Submission Only

CONTACT INFORMATION:	REVIEW PROCESS:	
Elchanan Cohn, Editor University of South Carolina The Moore School of Business Department of Economics 1705 College Street Columbia, SC 29208 USA	**Type of Review:**	Blind Review
	No. External Reviewers:	2
	No. InHouse Reviewers:	0
	Acceptance Rate:	21-30%
	Time to Review:	4 - 6 Months
Phone: 803-777-2714	**Reviewer's Comments:**	Yes
	Invited Articles:	0-5%
Email: feu00004@moore.sc.edu	**Fees to Publish:**	$0.00 US$
	Fees to Review:	$0.00 US$
Website: http://elsevier.com/locate/econedurev		

PUBLICATION GUIDELINES:	CIRCULATION DATA:
Manuscript Style: 　See Manuscript Guidelines	**Reader:** 　Academics
Manuscript Length: 　Reasonable	**Frequency of Issue:** 　Bi-Monthly
Copies Required: 　One	**Sponsor/Publisher:** 　Elsevier Inc.

MANUSCRIPT TOPICS:
Economics and Finance of Education; Education Management / Administration

MANUSCRIPT GUIDELINES/COMMENTS:

Notes for Contributors
Authors are requested to submit one copy of their manuscript along with two electronic files (one for the full text, one anonymous, with all identifying information removed, submitted in Word on a CD) to the Editor, Elchanan Cohn, Department of Economics, The Moore School of Business, University of South Carolina, 1705 College Street, Columbia, SC 29208, USA.

Submission of a paper implies that it has not been published previously, that it is not under consideration for publication elsewhere, and that if accepted it will not be published elsewhere in the same form, in English or in any other language, without the written consent of the publisher.

Manuscript Preparation
General. Manuscripts must be typewritten, double-spaced with wide margins on one side of white paper. Good quality printouts with a font size of 12 or 10 pt are required. The corresponding author should be identified (include a Fax number and E-mail address). Full postal addresses must be given for all co-authors. Authors should consult a recent issue of the journal for style if possible.

An electronic copy of the paper should accompany the **final** version. The Editors reserve the right to adjust style to certain standards of uniformity. Authors should retain a copy of their manuscript since we cannot accept responsibility for damage or loss of papers. Original manuscripts are discarded one month after publication unless the Publisher is asked to return original material after use.

Abstracts. Manuscripts must contain an abstract briefly summarizing the essential contents, followed by the relevant *JEL* classification. This should not exceed 150 words.

Keywords. Authors should select 2-6 keywords to describe their paper from the following list: costs, demand for schooling, economic development, economic impact, economics of scale, educational economics, educational finance, educational vouchers, efficiency, expenditures, grants, human capital, input output analysis, privatization, productivity, rate of return, resource allocation, salary wage differentials, school choice, state and federal aid, student financial aid, teacher salaries.

Text. Follow this order when typing manuscripts: Title, Authors, Affiliations, Abstract, Keywords, Main text, Acknowledgements, Appendix, References, Figure Captions and then Tables. Do not import the Figures or Tables into your text. The corresponding author should be identified with an asterisk and footnote.

Footnotes. All other footnotes (except for table footnotes) should be identified with superscript Arabic numbers. Short footnotes may be included at the foot of a manuscript page. Longer notes should be numbered and grouped together in a "Notes" section at the end of the text.

References. All publications cited in the text should be present in a list of references following the text of the manuscript. In the text refer to the author's name (without initials) and year of publication, e.g. "Since Peterson (1993) has shown that..." or "This is in agreement with results obtained later (Kramer, 1994)". For 2-6 authors, all authors are to be listed at first citation, with "&" separating the last two authors. For more than six authors, use the first six authors followed by et al. In subsequent citations for three or more authors, use author et al. in the text. The list of references should be arranged alphabetically by authors' names. The manuscript should be carefully checked to ensure that the spelling of authors names and dates are exactly the same in the text as in the reference list.

References should be given in the following form:

Becker, G.S. (1964). *Human capital.* New York, National Bureau of Economic Research.

Hansen, W.L., & King, M.A. (1971). A new approach to higher education finance. In: M.O. Orwig, *Financing higher education: Alternatives for the Federal Government* (pp. 206-236). Iowa City: American College Testing Program.

Stanovnik, T. (1997). The returns to education in Slovenia. *Economics of Education Review 16* (4) , 443-449.

Illustrations. All illustrations should be provided in camera-ready form, suitable for reproduction (which may include reduction) without retouching. Photographs, charts and diagrams are all to be referred to as "Figure(s)" and should be numbered consecutively in the order to which they are referred. They should accompany the manuscript, but should not be included within the text. All illustrations should be clearly marked on the back with the figure number and the author's name. All figures are to have a caption. Captions should be supplied on a separate sheet.

Line drawings. Good quality printouts on white paper produced in black ink are required. All lettering, graph lines and points on graphs should be sufficiently large and bold to permit reproduction when the diagram has been reduced to a size suitable for inclusion in the journal. Dyeline prints or photocopies are not suitable for reproduction. Do not use any type of shading on computer-generated illustrations.

Photographs. Original photographs must be supplied as they are to be reproduced (e.g. black and white or colour). If necessary, a scale should be marked on the photograph. Please note that photocopies of photographs are not acceptable.

Colour. Authors will be charged for colour at current printing costs.

Tables. Tables should be numbered consecutively and given a suitable caption and each table typed on a separate sheet. Footnotes to tables should be typed below the table and should be referred to by superscript lowercase letters. No vertical rules should be used. Tables should not duplicate results presented elsewhere in the manuscript, (e.g. in graphs).

Electronic Submission
Authors should submit an electronic copy of their paper when requested after the final version of the manuscript. The electronic copy should match the hardcopy exactly.

Always keep a backup copy of the electronic file for reference and safety. Full details of electronic submission and formats can be obtained from http://www.elsevier.nl/locate/disksub or from Author Services at Elsevier Science.

Proofs
Proofs will be sent to the author (first named author if no corresponding author is identified of multi-authored papers) and should be returned within 48 hours of receipt. Corrections should be restricted to typesetting errors; any others may be charged to the author. Any queries should be answered in full. Please note that authors are urged to check their proofs carefully before return, since the inclusion of late corrections cannot be guaranteed. Proofs are to be returned to the Log-in Department, Elsevier Science, Stover Court, Bampfylde Street, Exeter, Devon EX1 2AH, UK.

Offprints
Twenty-five offprints will be supplied free of charge. Additional offprints and copies of the issue can be ordered at a specially reduced rate using the order form sent to the corresponding author after the manuscript has been accepted. Orders for reprints (produced after publication of an article) will incur a 50% surcharge.

Copyright
All authors must sign the "Transfer of Copyright" agreement before the article can be published. This transfer agreement enables Elsevier Science Ltd to protect the copyrighted material for the authors, without the author relinquishing his/her proprietary rights. The copyright transfer covers the exclusive rights to reproduce and distribute the article, including reprints, photographic reproductions, microfilm or any other reproductions of a similar nature, and translations. It also includes the right to adapt the article for use in conjunction with computer systems and programs, including reproduction or publication in machine-readable form and incorporation in retrieval systems. Authors are responsible for obtaining from the copyright holder permission to reproduce any material for which copyright already exists.

Author Services
For queries relating to the general submission of manuscripts (including electronic text and artwork) and the status of accepted manuscripts, please contact Author Services, Log-in Department, Elsevier Science, The Boulevard, Langford Lane, Kidlington, Oxford OX5 1GB, UK. E-mail: authors@elsevier.co.uk, Fax: +44 (0) 1865 843905, Phone: +44 (0) 1865 843900. Authors can also keep a track of the progress of their accepted article through our OASIS system on the Internet. For information on an article go to this Internet page and key in the corresponding author's name and the Elsevier reference number.

Education + Training

SUBMISSION PROCESS:
Postal Submission Only

<table>
<tr><td colspan="3">CONTACT INFORMATION:</td></tr>
<tr><td colspan="3">Richard Holden, Editor
Leeds Metropolitan University
Leeds Business School
Cavendish Hall, Beckett Park
Leeds, LS6 3QS UK</td></tr>
</table>

CONTACT INFORMATION:

Richard Holden, Editor
Leeds Metropolitan University
Leeds Business School
Cavendish Hall, Beckett Park
Leeds, LS6 3QS UK

Phone:
1113-283-2600 ext. 4883

Email:
r.holden@lmu.ac.uk

Website:
www.emeraldinsight.com

REVIEW PROCESS:

Type of Review:	Editorial Review
No. External Reviewers:	1
No. InHouse Reviewers:	1
Acceptance Rate:	30-40%
Time to Review:	1 - 2 Months
Reviewer's Comments:	Yes
Invited Articles:	21-30%
Fees to Publish:	$0.00 US$
Fees to Review:	$0.00 US$

PUBLICATION GUIDELINES:

Manuscript Style:
See Manuscript Guidelines

Manuscript Length:
21-25

Copies Required:
Three

CIRCULATION DATA:

Reader:
Academics, Business Persons

Frequency of Issue:
9 Times/Year

Sponsor/Publisher:
Emerald Group Publishing Limited

MANUSCRIPT TOPICS:
Business Education; Higher Education; Small Business Entrepreneurship

MANUSCRIPT GUIDELINES/COMMENTS:

Are we witnessing a fundamental shift in the way we view institutional learning, away from education and towards training? Without a clear conceptual distinction between education and training are we in danger of losing something of importance? The growing understanding of the critical relationship between what is taught in schools, colleges and universities and how what is learnt there prepares the individual for the training received in industry and for a career involving lifelong learning, provides the focus of this major journal.

Coverage
- Education-business partnership
- Managing the transition from school/college to work
- The recruitment of school leavers and graduates
- Graduate training and development
- Expectations/aspiration of school leavers and graduates
- Initiation, implementation and evaluation of "youth training schemes"
- Covers all aspects of vocational education and training; graduates, graduate training and utilization; young person training; transition, graduate recruitment and development.

NOTES FOR CONTRIBUTORS

Copyright

Articles submitted to the journal should be original contributions and should not be under consideration for any other publication at the same time. Authors submitting articles for publication warrant that the work is not an infringement of any existing copyright and will indemnify the publisher against any breach of such warranty. For ease of dissemination and to ensure proper policing of use, papers and contributions become the legal copyright of the publisher unless otherwise agreed. Submissions should be sent to:

Editorial Objectives

To focus on the increasingly complex relationship between education and training, particularly relating to the 16-24 age group. To address vocationalism in learning, reporting on innovative themes within vocational education and training and highlighting the changing nature of partnership between the worlds of work and education.

General Principles

- To maintain a sound balance between theory and practice.
- Contributors are encouraged to identify issues and questions raised by their work and to develop the practical implications for those involved in education and training.
- Articles based on experience and case material—rather than just philosophical speculation—are preferred.
- A series of short articles on a linked theme appearing in successive issues is particularly welcome.

Reviewing Process

Each paper is reviewed by the Editor and, if it is judged suitable for publication, it is then sent to at least two referees from Peernet for electronic double-blind peer review. Based on their recommendations, the Editor then decides whether the paper should be accepted as is, revised or rejected. Further information on Peernet can be found at http://www.peer-net.com.

Manuscript Requirements

Three copies of the manuscript should be submitted in double line spacing with wide margins. All authors should be shown and author's details must be printed on a separate sheet and the author should not be identified anywhere else in the article.

As a guide, articles should be between 3,000 and 4,000 words in length. A title of not more than eight words should be provided. A brief **autobiographical note** should be supplied including full name, affiliation, e-mail address and full international contact details. Authors must supply an **abstract** of 100-150 words. Up to six **key words** should be included which encapsulate the principal subjects covered by the article.

Where there is a **methodology**, it should be clearly described under a separate heading. **Headings** must be short, clearly defined and not numbered.

Notes or **endnotes** should be used only if absolutely necessary. They should, however, always be used for citing Web sites. They should be identified in the text by consecutive numbers enclosed in square brackets and listed at the end of the article. Please then provide full Web site addresses in the end list.

Figures, charts and **diagrams** should be kept to a minimum. They must be black and white with minimum shading and numbered consecutively using Arabic numerals with a brief title and labelled axes. In the text, the position of the figure should be shown by typing on a separate line the words "take in Figure 2". Good quality originals must be provided.

Tables should be kept to a minimum. They must be numbered consecutively with roman numerals and a brief title. In the text, the position of the table should be shown by typing on a separate line the words "take in Table IV".

Photos and **illustrations** must be supplied as good quality black and white original half tones with captions. Their position should be shown in the text by typing on a separate line the words "take in Plate 2".

References to other publications should be complete and in Harvard style. They should contain full bibliographical details and journal titles should not be abbreviated. For multiple citations in the same year use a, b, c immediately following the year of publication. References should be shown within the text by giving the author's last name followed by a comma and year of publication all in round brackets, e.g. (Fox, 1994). At the end of the article should be a reference list in alphabetical order as follows:

For Books
Surname, initials and year of publication, title, publisher, place of publication, e.g. Casson, M. (1979), Alternatives to the Multinational Enterprise, Macmillan, London.

For Chapter in Edited Book
Surname, initials and year, "title", editor's surname, initials, title, publisher, place, pages, e.g. Bessley, M. and Wilson, P. (1984), "Public policy and small firms in Britain", in Levicki, C. (Ed.), Small Business Theory and Policy, Croom Helm, London, pp. 111-26. Please note that the chapter title must be underlined.

For Articles
Surname, initials, year "title", journal, volume, number, pages, e.g. Fox, S. (1994) "Empowerment as a catalyst for change: an example from the food industry", Supply Chain Management, Vol 2 No 3, pp. 29-33

If there is more than one author list surnames followed by initials. All authors should be shown.

Electronic sources should include the URL of the electronic site at which they may be found, as follows:
Neuman, B.C.(1995), "Security, payment, and privacy for network commerce", IEEE Journal on Selected Areas in Communications, Vol. 13 No.8, October, pp. 1523-31. Available (IEEE SEPTEMBER) http://www.research.att.com/jsac/

Final Submission of the Article
Once accepted for publication, the final version of the manuscript must be provided, accompanied by a 3.5" **disk** of the same version labelled with: disk format; author name(s); title of article; journal title; file name.

Each article must be accompanied by a completed and signed **Journal Article Record Form** available from the Editor or on http://www.literaticlub.co.uk/

The manuscript will be considered to be the definitive version of the article. The author must ensure that it is complete, grammatically correct and without spelling or typographical errors. In preparing the disk, please use one of the following formats: Word, WordPerfect, Rich Text Format or TeX/LaTeX. Figures which are provided electronically must be in tif, gif or pic file extensions. All figures and graphics must also be supplied as good quality originals.

Final Submission Requirements
Manuscripts must be
• Clean, good quality hard copy
• Include an abstract and key words

- Have Harvard style references
- Include any figures, photos and graphics as good quality originals
- Be accompanied by a labelled disk
- Be accompanied by a completed Journal Article Record Form

Technical assistance is available from MCB's World Wide Web Literati Club on **http://www.literaticlub.co.uk/** or contact Mike Massey at MCB, e-mail **mmassey@mcb.co.uk**.

Education and Information Technologies

<table>
<tr><td colspan="2" align="center">

SUBMISSION PROCESS:

**Electronic Submission Only
via Online Portal**

www.edmgr.com/eait
</td></tr>
<tr><td>

CONTACT INFORMATION:

Ian Selwood, Editor
University of Birmingham
UK

Phone:

Email:

Website:
   http://www.springerlink.com/
</td><td>

REVIEW PROCESS:

Type of Review:	Blind Review
No. External Reviewers:	3
No. InHouse Reviewers:	0
Acceptance Rate:	
Time to Review:	4 - 6 Months
Reviewer's Comments:	Yes
Invited Articles:	11-20%
Fees to Publish:	$0.00 US$
Fees to Review:	$0.00 US$

</td></tr>
<tr><td>

PUBLICATION GUIDELINES:

Manuscript Style:
   See Manuscript Guidelines

Manuscript Length:
   11-15

Copies Required:
   Electronic Only
</td><td>

CIRCULATION DATA:

Reader:
   Academics, Practicing Teachers

Frequency of Issue:
   Quarterly

Sponsor/Publisher:
   International Federation for Information
Processing / Springer
</td></tr>
</table>

MANUSCRIPT TOPICS:
Educational Technology Systems; Elementary / Early Childhood; Higher Education; Secondary / Adolescent Studies; Social Studies / Social Science

MANUSCRIPT GUIDELINES/COMMENTS:

Aims of the Editors
It is our determination to develop this journal into a key international voice in the growing and significant field of education and information technologies.

This journal is a platform for the range of debates and issues that are current in our field. It is a broad field; we aim to provide perspectives at all levels, from the micro of specific applications or instances of use in classrooms to macro concerns of national policies and major projects; from classes of five year olds to adults in tertiary institutions; from teachers and administrators, to researchers and designers; from institutions to open, distance and lifelong learning. The strength of this breadth lies in the opportunity to raise and debate fundamental issues at all levels, to discuss specific instances and cases, draw inference and probe theory. This journal is embedded in the research and practice of professionals. It will not proselytise on behalf of the technologies but rather provoke debate on all the complex relationships between information and communication technologies and education.

As editors we are determined to maintain and expand the international standing of *Education and Information Technologies* by careful selection on merit of the papers submitted to us. Our goal is that we should provide an ongoing forum for debate. We shall occasionally produce special editions to enable us to cover particular issues at depth. We invite you, our readers, to send us papers on your work for consideration for inclusion, but also to comment and reflect upon the argument and opinions that we shall be publishing.

Online Manuscript Submission

Springer now offers authors, editors and reviewers of *Education and Information Technologies* the use of our fully web-enabled online manuscript submission and review system. To keep the review time as short as possible, we request authors to submit manuscripts online to the journal's editorial office. Our online manuscript submission and review system offers authors the option to track the progress of the review process of manuscripts in real time.

The online manuscript submission and review system for Education and Information Technologies offers easy and straightforward log-in and submission procedures. This system supports a wide range of submission file formats: for manuscripts - Word, WordPerfect, RTF, TXT and LaTex; for figures - TIFF, GIF, JPEG, EPS, PPT, and Postscript. It also accepts Postscript and Adobe PDF, but if your submission is done using a Postscript or PDF file we will need to contact you for the source files if your article is accepted.

Note. In case you encounter any difficulties while submitting your manuscript online, please get in touch with the responsible Editorial Assistant by clicking on "CONTACT US" from the tool bar.

Authors are requested to download the Consent to Publish and Transfer of Copyright form from the journal's online submission system (see the URL provided below). Please send a completed and duly signed form either by mail or fax to the Editorial Office of Education and Information Technologies as instructed on the form. Authors should still follow the regular instructions for authors when preparing their manuscripts (see below).

Manuscripts should be submitted to: **http://eait.edmgr.com**

Manuscript Style

- Typeset, double or 1 1/2 space.
- Use an informative title for the paper and include an abstract of 100 to 250 words at the head of the manuscript. The abstract should be a carefully worded description of the problem addressed, the key ideas introduced, and the results. Abstracts will be printed with the article.
- Provide a separate double–spaced page listing all footnotes, beginning with "affiliation of author" and continuing with numbered footnotes.
- Acknowledgment of financial support may be given if appropriate.
- Regarding units, symbols and displayed equations, use only recommended SI units. Numerals should be used for all numbers of two or more digits, and for single digits when attached to units of measure. Abbreviations should be defined in brackets after their first mention in the text in accordance with internationally agreed rules. Equations should be presented as simply as possible. Numerical subscripts and superscripts should be used wherever possible, and the root sign should be avoided. Vector quantities should be presented in bold type. Displayed equations should be numbered consecutively, using parenthesized Arabic numerals.

References

References in the text should be cited as follows: one or two authors — Smith (1993) or (Smith, 1993) or Smith and Brown (1993) etc. Three or more authors — Smith et al. (1993) or (Smith et al., 1993) Papers by the same author(s) in the same year should be distinguished by the letters a, b, etc. References should be listed at the end of the paper giving the year of publication, title of paper, journal titles in full, volume number and first and last page numbers. References to books should include their edition, editor(s), publisher and place of publication. Names of journals must be given in full, with abbreviations. Please adhere closely to the following format in the list of references.

Journal
Billiam, A. T. (1986) Effect of surface runoff on water quality measurements. Journal of Environmental Science, 84, 161—175.

Book
Jones, A. B. and Smith, W. (1984) Statistical Methods for Scientists. Wiley, New York.

Excerpt in Book
Lawson, W. (1987) A survey of soil remediation methods. In Advances in Soil Science, A. Hall and B. West (eds), Cambridge University Press, Cambridge, pp. 104—106.

Illustration Style
- Originals for illustrations should be sharp, noise-free, and of good contrast. We regret that we cannot provide drafting or art service.
- Each figure should be mentioned in the text and numbered consecutively using Arabic numerals. Specify the desired location of each figure in the text. Each figure must have a caption. Proper style for captions, e.g., "Figure 1. Buffer occupancy for various bit rates."
- Number each table consecutively using Arabic numerals. Please label any material that can be typeset as a table, reserving the term "figure" for material that has been drawn. Specify the desired location of each table in the text. Type a brief title above each table.
- All lettering should be large enough to permit legible reduction.
- Suggested figure formats: TIFF, GIF, EPS, PPT, and Postscript. Files should be at least 300 dpi.

Proofing
Please be sure to include your e-mail address on your paper. If your paper is accepted, we will provide proofs electronically. Your cooperation is appreciated. The proofread copy should be returned to the Publisher within 72 hours.

Copyright
Authors will be asked, upon acceptance of an article, to transfer copyright of the article to the Publisher. This will ensure the widest possible dissemination of information under copyright laws. Open access articles (an option available for authors, against payment of an Article Processing Fee via the Springer Open Choice program) do not require transfer of copyright as the copyright remains with the author. In opting for open access, they agree to the Springer Open Access Licence. Details about the program and a link to the Open Access Licence can be found on the Springer Open Choice web pages: **www.springer.com/openchoice**

Education and the Law

SUBMISSION PROCESS:
Postal Submission Only

CONTACT INFORMATION:	REVIEW PROCESS:	
Geoffrey J. Bennett, Editor	**Type of Review:**	
Notre Dame University	**No. External Reviewers:**	1
London Law Centre	**No. InHouse Reviewers:**	2
One Suffolk Street		
London, SW1Y 4HG UK	**Acceptance Rate:**	
	Time to Review:	1 Month or Less
Phone:	**Reviewer's Comments:**	No
+44 (0) 20 7484 7822	**Invited Articles:**	31-50%
Email:	**Fees to Publish:**	$0.00 US$
bennett.24@nd.edu	**Fees to Review:**	$0.00 US$
Website:		
www.tandf.co.uk/journals/09539964.asp		

PUBLICATION GUIDELINES:	CIRCULATION DATA:
Manuscript Style:	**Reader:**
See Manuscript Guidelines	Academics, Administrators, Lawyers
Manuscript Length:	**Frequency of Issue:**
4-20	Quarterly
Copies Required:	**Sponsor/Publisher:**
One	Routledge, Taylor & Francis, Ltd.

MANUSCRIPT TOPICS:
Education Management / Administration; Higher Education; School Law; Special Education

MANUSCRIPT GUIDELINES/COMMENTS:

Editor's Comments
We are flexible about length. A rough average might be 5,000 words but many of our articles are shorter and some being considerably longer, have been spread over several issues.

Education and the Law is an academic journal addressing all aspects of the law relating to primary, secondary, tertiary and higher education. Papers accepted become the copyright of the journal unless otherwise agreed.

Author's Guidelines
Manuscripts should be sent to: Professor Geoffrey Bennett, Editor. All submissions will normally be sent anonymously for the observations of referees. Submissions should be typed, double-spaced, on one side of the paper only. Each paper should be accompanied by an abstract of 100-150 words on one page together with the title of the article and the names of the authors. The full postal address of the author who will check proofs and receive correspondence and offprints should also be included. All pages should be numbered. Papers will, be considered provided that they are nor

submitted simultaneously elsewhere for publication, and have not previously been published elsewhere.

Tables and Captions should be typed out on separate sheets and not included as part of the text. Tables should be numbered by roman numerals and figures by Arabic numerals. The approximate position of tables and figures should be indicated in the manuscript. Captions should include keys to any symbols.

Figures and any line drawings should be of a quality suitable for printing and will not normally be redrawn by the publishers.

References should follow the Harvard system, i.e. they should be indicated in the typescript by giving the author's name, with the year of publication in parentheses, e.g. smith (1994); or if there are more than two authors--Smith et al. (1994). If several papers from the same author(s) and from the same year are cited, (s), (b), (c), etc. should be put after the year of publication. The references should then be listed in full alphabetically at the end of the paper on a separate sheet in the following standard form:

HARRIS, N. S. (1993) Local complaints procedures under the Education Reform Act 1988, Journal of Social Welfare and Family Law, pp. 19-39.

JACKSON, B. S. (1993) Piaget, Kohlberg and Habermas: psychological and comunicational approaches to legal theory, in: V. FERRARI & C. FARALLI (eds), laws and Rights; pp. 571-592 (Milan; Giuffre).

LYON, C. M. (1993) The Law Relating to Children (London, Buterworths).

Titles of Journals should not be abbreviated.

Cases should be cited in the usual English law form with the name of the case and its date in the text and a list of cases in alphabetical order at the end of the article.

Proofs will be sent to authors, if there is sufficient time to do so. they should be corrected and returned within three days. Proofs are supplied for checking and making essential corrections, not for general revision or alteration.

Offprints. Fifty offprints of each paper are supplied free of charge. Additional copies may be purchased an should be ordered when the proofs are returned. Offprints, together with a complete copy of the relevant journal issue, are sent about three weeks after publication.

Printed and bound in Great Britain by Wace Journals, Abingdon, Oxfordshire, England.

Copyright. It is a condition of publication that authors assign copyright or licence the publication rights in their articles, including abstracts, to Taylor & Francis. This enables us to ensure full copyright protection and to disseminate the article, and of course the Journal, to the widest possible readership in print and electronic formats as appropriate. Authors may, of course, use the article elsewhere *after* publication without prior permission from Taylor & Francis, provided that acknowledgement is given to the Journal as the original source of publication, and that Taylor & Francis is notified so that our records show that its use is properly authorised. Authors retain a number of other rights under the Taylor & Francis rights policies documents. These policies are referred to at **www.tandf.co.uk/journals/authorrights.pdf** for full details. Authors are themselves responsible for obtaining permission to reproduce copyright material from other sources.

Education and Urban Society

SUBMISSION PROCESS:	
Electronic Submission Preferred **via EMail** **charles.russo@notes.udayton.edu**	

CONTACT INFORMATION:	REVIEW PROCESS:	
Charles J. Russo, Editor University of Dayton School of Education & Allied Professions Department of Educational Administration 324 Chaminade Hall Dayton, OH 45469-0534 USA	**Type of Review:**	Blind Review
	No. External Reviewers: **No. InHouse Reviewers:**	3 0
	Acceptance Rate: **Time to Review:** **Reviewer's Comments:** **Invited Articles:**	21-30% 2 - 3 Months Yes 6-10%
Phone: 937-229-3722		
Email: charles.russo@notes.udayton.edu elizabeth.pearn@notes.udayton.edu charles_j_russo@hotmail.com	**Fees to Publish:** **Fees to Review:**	$0.00 US$ $0.00 US$
Website: www.sagepublications.com		

PUBLICATION GUIDELINES:	CIRCULATION DATA:
Manuscript Style: American Psychological Association	**Reader:** Academics, Administrators
Manuscript Length: 21-25	**Frequency of Issue:** Quarterly
Copies Required: Three	**Sponsor/Publisher:** Sage Publications

MANUSCRIPT TOPICS:
Education Management / Administration; Elementary / Early Childhood; Secondary / Adolescent Studies; Teacher Education; Urban Education, Cultural / Non-Traditional

MANUSCRIPT GUIDELINES/COMMENTS:

Manuscripts should be sent to Charles J. Russo, Editor, Education and Urban Society, and Panzer Chair in Education in the Department of Educational Leadership, 324 Chaminade Hall, Department of Educational Administration, University of Dayton, Dayton, OH 45469-0534, or submitted electronically to **charles.russo@notes.udayton.edu**. Only submit one manuscript at a time for consideration; multiple submission (of different articles) will not be accepted. Manuscript style should adhere to guidelines of the *Publication Manual of the American Psychological Association* (5th edition). Please use double spacing, with tables and figures placed at the end of the article. An electronic copy must also be provided.

Education Economics

SUBMISSION PROCESS:
Postal Submission Only

CONTACT INFORMATION:	REVIEW PROCESS:	
Steve Bradley, Editor	**Type of Review:**	Editorial Review
Lancaster University		
The Management School	**No. External Reviewers:**	2
Department of Economics	**No. InHouse Reviewers:**	0
Lancaster, LA1 4YX UK		
	Acceptance Rate:	21-30%
	Time to Review:	3-6 Months
Phone:	**Reviewer's Comments:**	Yes
+44 1524 593880	**Invited Articles:**	10%
Email:		
s.bradley@lancaster.ac.uk	**Fees to Publish:**	$0.00 US$
Website:	**Fees to Review:**	$0.00 US$
http://www.tandf.co.uk/journals		

PUBLICATION GUIDELINES:	CIRCULATION DATA:
Manuscript Style:	**Reader:**
See Manuscript Guidelines	Academics
Manuscript Length:	**Frequency of Issue:**
26-30	4Times/Year
Copies Required:	**Sponsor/Publisher:**
Three	Routledge, Taylor and Francis, Ltd.

MANUSCRIPT TOPICS:
Economics and Finance of Education; Education Management / Administration

MANUSCRIPT GUIDELINES/COMMENTS:

Aims and Scope
Education Economics serves as a forum for debate in all areas of the economics and management of education. Particular emphasis is given to the 'quantitative' aspects of educational management which involve numerate disciplines such as economics and operational research. The content is of international appeal and is not limited to material of a technical nature. Applied work with clear policy implications is especially encouraged.

Readership of the journal includes academics in the field of education, economics and management; civil servants and local government officials responsible for education and manpower planning; educational managers at the level of the individual school or college.

Manuscripts to be considered for publication should be emailed or mailed to the Editor. In the latter case, three complete copies of each manuscript should be submitted. They should be typed on one side of the paper, double-spaced, with ample margins, and bear the title of the contribution and name(s) of the author(s). The full postal address of the author who will check proofs and receive correspondence and offprints should also be included. All papers should be numbered.

Contributions should not normally be more than 5000 words in length and should be written in the English Language. They should also include an abstract of 100 words. Footnotes to the text should be avoided wherever this is reasonably possible.

Rejected manuscripts will not normally be returned unless a self-addressed envelope and international postal coupons have been sent.

Tables and Captions to Illustrations. Tables must be typed out on separate sheets and not included as part of the text. The captions to illustrations should be gathered together and also typed out on a separate sheet. Tables and figures should be numbered by Arabic numerals. The approximate position of tables and figures shouts be indicated in the manuscript. Captions should include keys to symbols.

Figures. Artwork must be submitted in suitable condition for publication.

References. These should be indicated in the typescript by giving the author's name and the year of publication, as follows: Weaver (1978) or (Weaver, 1978). If several papers by the same author and from the same year are cited, a, b, c, etc. should be put after the year of publication. The references should be listed in full at the end of the paper in the following standard form:

Blaug, M. (Ed.) (1992) **The Economic Value of Education: Studies in the Economics of Education** (Aldershot, Edward Elgar).

Grubel, H. G. (1987) The economics of the brain drain, in Psacharopoulos, G. (Ed.) **Economics of Education: Research and Studies** (Oxford, Pergamon).

Halsey, A. H. (1991) **The Decline of Donnish Dominion** (Oxford, Oxford University Press).

Murnane, R. J. & Olsen, R. J. (1989) Will there be enough teachers? **American Economic Review**, 79, pp. 242-246.

Titles of journals should not be abbreviated.

Proofs. These will be sent to authors if there is sufficient time to do so. They should be corrected and returned to the publishers within three days. Major alterations to the text cannot be accepted.

Offprints. Fifty offprints of each paper are supplied free. Additional copies may be purchased and should be ordered when the proofs are returned. Offprints, together with a complete copy of the relevant journal issue are sent about three weeks after publication.

Copyright. It is a condition of publication that authors vest copyright in their articles, including abstracts, in Taylor & Francis Ltd. This enables us to ensure full copyright protection and to disseminate the article, and the journal, to the widest possible readership in print and electronic formats as appropriate. Authors may, of course, use the article elsewhere **after** publication without prior permission from Taylor & Francis, provided that acknowledgement is given to the Journal as the original source of publication, and that Taylor & Francis is notified so that our records show that its use is properly authorised. Authors are themselves responsible for obtaining permission to reproduce copyright material from other sources.

Education for Information

SUBMISSION PROCESS:
Postal Submission Only

CONTACT INFORMATION:	REVIEW PROCESS:	
Andrew Large, Editor McGill University GSLIS 3459 McTavish Montreal Quebec, H3A 1Y1 Canada	**Type of Review:**	Blind Review
	No. External Reviewers:	2
	No. InHouse Reviewers:	0
Dick Hartley, Editor Manchester Metropolitan University Dept of Information & Communications Geoffrey Manton Building, Rosamund Street Manchester, M15 6LL UK	**Acceptance Rate:**	20%
	Time to Review:	1 - 2 Months
	Reviewer's Comments:	Yes
	Invited Articles:	0-5%
	Fees to Publish:	$0.00 US$
	Fees to Review:	$0.00 US$
Phone: 514-398-3360 0161 247 6144		
Email: andrew.large@mcgill.ca r.j.hartley@mmu.ac.uk		
Website: http://www.iospress.nl		

PUBLICATION GUIDELINES:	CIRCULATION DATA:

Manuscript Style:
   See Manuscript Guidelines
	Reader:
	   Academics

Manuscript Length:
   16-20
	Frequency of Issue:
	   Quarterly

Copies Required:
   Two
	Sponsor/Publisher:
	   IOS Press

MANUSCRIPT TOPICS:
Curriculum Studies

MANUSCRIPT GUIDELINES/COMMENTS:

Aims and Scope
Information is widely recognized as a vital resource in economic development. The skills of information handling, traditionally associated with libraries are now in great demand in all sectors, including government, business and commerce. The education and training of information professionals is, therefore, an issue of growing significance. *Education for Information* has established itself as a forum for debate and discussion on education and training issues in the sphere of information handling. It includes full-length articles, an occasional section on computer software applications for education and training and short communications on matters of current concern. Its

News section reports on significant activities and events in the international arena. In-depth book reviews complete each issue of this quarterly publication, essential reading for those involved and interested in education and training for information handling.

SUBMISSION OF MANUSCRIPTS

Submit to: Dick Hartley, Department of Information and Communications, Manchester Metropolitan University, Geoffrey Manton Building, Rosamund Street, Manchester M15 6LL United Kingdom Tel.: +44 161 247 6144; Fax: +44 161 247 6351; E-mail: **r.j.hartley@mmu. ac.uk** or: Andrew Large, Graduate School of Library and Informations Studies, McGill University, McLennan Library Building, 3459 McTavish Street, Montreal, Quebec, H3A 1Y1 Canada Tel.: +1 514 398 4204; Fax: +1 514 398 7193; E-mail: **andrew.large @mcgill.ca**

Required files
The following electronic files are required:
- a word processor file of the text, such as Word, WordPerfect, LateX (If using LaTeX, please use the standard article.sty as a style file also send a pdf version of the LaTeX file)
- separate files of all figures (if any); see "Preparation of manuscripts" for the required file formats.

Colour figures
It is possible to have figures printed in colour, provided the cost of their reproduction is paid for by the author. See Preparation of Manuscripts for the required file formats.

PREPARATION OF MANUSCRIPTS
Organization of the paper and style of presentation
Manuscripts must be written in English. Authors whose native language is not English are recommended to seek the advice of a native English speaker, if possible, before submitting their manuscripts.

You can also visit **www.internationalscienceediting.com**. International Science Editing offers a language and copyediting service to all scientists who want to publish their manuscript in scientific peer-reviewed periodicals and books.

Manuscripts should be prepared with wide margins and double spacing throughout, including the abstract, footnotes and references. Every page of the manuscript, including the title page, references, tables, etc., should be numbered. However, in the text no reference should be made to page numbers; if necessary, one may refer to sections. Try to avoid the excessive use of italics and bold face.

Manuscripts should be organized in the following order:
- Title page
- Body of text (divided by subheadings)
- Acknowledgements
- References
- Tables
- Figure captions
- Figures
- Headings and subheadings should be numbered and typed on a separate line, without indentation.

SI units should be used, i.e., the units based on the metre, kilogramme, second, etc.

Title page
- The title page should provide the following information:
- Title (should be clear, descriptive and not too long)

- Name(s) of author(s); please indicate who is the corresponding author
- Full affiliation(s)
- Present address of author(s), if different from affiliation
- Complete address of corresponding author, including tel. no., fax no. and e-mail address
- Abstract; should be clear, descriptive, self-explanatory and not longer than 200 words, it should also be suitable for publication in abstracting services
- Keywords

Tables

- Number as Table 1, Table 2 etc, and refer to all of them in the text
- Each table should be provided on a separate page of the manuscript. Tables should not be included in the text.
- Each table should have a brief and self-explanatory title.
- Column headings should be brief, but sufficiently explanatory. Standard abbreviations of units of measurement should be added between parentheses.
- Vertical lines should not be used to separate columns. Leave some extra space between the columns instead.
- Any explanations essential to the understanding of the table should be given in footnotes at the bottom of the table.

Figures

- Number figures as Fig. 1, Fig. 2, etc and refer to all of them in the text.
- Each figure should be provided on a separate sheet. Figures should not be included in the text.
- Colour figures can be included, provided the cost of their reproduction is paid by the author.
- For the file formats of the figures please take the following into account:
  o line art should be have a minimum resolution of 600 dpi, save as EPS or TIFF
  o grayscales (incl photos) should have a minimum resolution of 300 dpi (no lettering), or 500 dpi (when there is lettering); save as tiff
  o do not save figures as JPEG, this format may lose information in the process
  o do not use figures taken from the Internet, the resolution will be too low for printing
  o do not use colour in your figures if they are to be printed in black & white, as this will reduce the print quality (note that in software often the default is colour, you should change the settings)
  o for figures that should be printed in colour, please send a CMYK encoded EPS or TIFF
- Figures should be designed with the format of the page of the journal in mind. They should be of such a size as to allow a reduction of 50%.
- On maps and other figures where a scale is needed, use bar scales rather than numerical ones, i.e., do not use scales of the type 1:10,000. This avoids problems if figures need to be reduced.
- Each figure should have a self-explanatory caption. The captions to all figures should be typed on a separate sheet of the manuscript.
- Photographs are only acceptable if they have good contrast and intensity.

Reference

For citations in the text, numbers between square brackets should be used. All publications cited in the text should be presented in a list of references following the text of the manuscript.
References should be listed alphabetically in the following style:
[1] B. Newman and E.T. Liu, Perspective on BRCA1, Breast Disease 10 (1998), 3-10.
[2] D.F. Pilkey, Happy conservation laws, in: Neural Stresses, J. Frost, ed., Controlled Press, Georgia, 1995, pp. 332-391.
[3] E. Wilson, Active vibration analysis of thin-walled beams, Ph.D. Dissertation, University of Virginia, 1991.

Footnotes

Footnotes should only be used if absolutely essential. In most cases it is possible to incorporate the information in the text.

- If used, they should be numbered in the text, indicated by superscript numbers and kept as short as possible.

COPYRIGHT
Copyright of your article

Authors submitting a manuscript do so on the understanding that they have read and agreed to the terms of the IOS Press Author Copyright Agreement.

Quoting from other publications

An author, when quoting from someone else's work or when considering reproducing figures or table from a book or journal article, should make sure that he is not infringing a copyright. Although in general an author may quote from other published works, he should obtain permission from the holder of the copyright if he wishes to make substantial extracts or to reproduce tables, plates or other figures. If the copyright holder is not the author of the quoted or reproduced material, it is recommended that the permission of the author should also be sought. Material in unpublished letters and manuscripts is also protected and must not be published unless permission has been obtained. Submission of a paper will be interpreted as a statement that the author has obtained all the necessary permission. A suitable acknowledgement of any borrowed material must always be made.

PROOFS & PURCHASES
PDF Proofs

The corresponding author will receive a pdf proof and is asked to check this proof carefully (the publisher will execute a cursory check only). Corrections other than printer's errors, however, should be avoided. Costs arising from such corrections will be charged to the authors.

How to order reprints, a pdf file, journals, or IOS Press books

The corresponding author of a contribution to the journal is entitled to receive 1 copy of the journal free of charge, unless otherwise stated. Free copies will not be provided for conference proceedings and abstract issues. An order form for reprints, additional journal copies or a pdf file will be provided along with the pdf proof.

If you wish to order reprints of an earlier published article, please contact the publisher for a quotation. IOS Press, Fax: +31 20 6870039. E-mail: **editorial@iospress.nl**.

An author is entitled to 25 % discount on IOS Press books. See Author's discount (25%) on all IOS Press book publications.

IOS Press
Nieuwe Hemweg 6B, 1013 BG Amsterdam, The Netherlands Tel.: +31 20 688 3355, Fax: +31 20 687 0039; E-mail: **info@iospress.nl**

Education Leadership Review

SUBMISSION PROCESS:

**Electronic Submission Only
via EMail**

sandra.harris@lamar.edu

CONTACT INFORMATION:	REVIEW PROCESS:	
Sandra Harris, Editor	**Type of Review:**	Blind Review
Lamar University		
	No. External Reviewers:	3
Phone:	**No. InHouse Reviewers:**	0
409-880-8689		
	Acceptance Rate:	15-25%
Email:	**Time to Review:**	2 - 3 Months
sandra.harris@lamar.edu	**Reviewer's Comments:**	Yes
Website:	**Invited Articles:**	11-20%
www.ncpea.net		
	Fees to Publish:	$0.00 US$
	Fees to Review:	$0.00 US$

PUBLICATION GUIDELINES:	CIRCULATION DATA:
Manuscript Style:	**Reader:**
American Psychological Association	Academics, Administrators
Manuscript Length:	**Frequency of Issue:**
21-25	2 Times/Year
Copies Required:	**Sponsor/Publisher:**
One	National Council of Professors of Educational Administration

MANUSCRIPT TOPICS:
Education Management / Administration; Higher Education; Teacher Education

MANUSCRIPT GUIDELINES/COMMENTS:

We now have digital versions of the NCPEA *Education Leadership Review* posted in Hyperion (the library's web-based program for providing access to digital files). Following is the link to the main directory: **http://webcat.shsu.edu/uhtbin/hyperion.exe/SHSUPublications/NCPEAEducationLeadershipReview**

Submission Guidelines
Submissions should be 2000 to 3000 words in length (approximately 20 pages including references). Articles, including references, must follow the guidelines in the 5th Edition of the *APA Manual*. Submissions in different formats will be automatically rejected. Limit the use of tables, figures, and appendices as they are difficult to import into the journal text layout. Submissions may be submitted electronically in Word to: Sandy Harris, **drsandy@flash.net** or **Sandra.harris@ lamar.edu**. All manuscripts must include a cover page with complete contact information (name, position, institution, mailing address, phone, e-mail and fax). Manuscripts may be submitted at any time, with publication dates in February and August. Non-theme manuscripts will be considered when appropriate.

Education Policy Analysis Archives

SUBMISSION PROCESS:
See Manuscript Guidelines

CONTACT INFORMATION:	REVIEW PROCESS:	
Sherman Dorn, Editor University of South Florida EDU 162 4202 E. Fowler Ave. Tampa, FL 33620-7750 USA	**Type of Review:**	Blind Review
	No. External Reviewers:	3
	No. InHouse Reviewers:	1
Phone: 813-974-9482	**Acceptance Rate:**	21-30%
	Time to Review:	2-6 Months
	Reviewer's Comments:	Yes
Email: epaa-editor@shermandorn.com	**Invited Articles:**	0-5%
Website: http://epaa.asu.edu	**Fees to Publish:**	$0.00 US$
	Fees to Review:	$0.00 US$

PUBLICATION GUIDELINES:	CIRCULATION DATA:
Manuscript Style: American Psychological Association	**Reader:** Academics
Manuscript Length: 26-30+	**Frequency of Issue:** 30 Times/Year
Copies Required: Electronic Only	**Sponsor/Publisher:** Mary Lou Fulton College of Ed, Arizona State University / College of Ed, Univ of South Florida

MANUSCRIPT TOPICS:
Curriculum Studies; Elementary / Early Childhood; Higher Education; Rural Education & Small Schools; School Law; Science Math & Environment; Secondary / Adolescent Studies; Special Education; Urban Education, Cultural / Non-Traditional

MANUSCRIPT GUIDELINES/COMMENTS:

How to Submit an Article to *EPAA*
EPAA welcomes submitted articles for consideration for publication. Articles should deal with education policy in any of its many aspects, and may focus at any level of the education system in any nation. Articles may be written in either English or Spanish or both languages.

Please prepare manuscripts in accord with the format recommended in the *Publication Manual of the American Psychological Association*. Articles may be of any length, though contributions of fewer than 1,500 words are discouraged.

Please submit *English-language* manuscripts at **http://www.epaa.info/english/**, where there is more complete information on manuscript preparation. Manuscripts submitted through postal mail will not be considered. If there are technical problems submitting an English-language manuscript, please contact *EPAA*'s main editor, Sherman Dorn, at **epaa-editor@shermandorn.com**.

Articles written in *Spanish* may be submitted to the Associate Editors for Spanish & Portuguese, Gustavo E. Fischman, Arizona State University, and Pablo Gentili of the Laboratório de Políticas Públicas, Universidade do Estado do Rio de Janeiro. Articles in Spanish or Portuguese can be submitted to either Associate Editor at either Fischman at **fischman@asu.edu**, or Gentili at **pablo@lpp-uerj.net**.

Authors are normally informed of the publication decision within twelve to sixteen weeks.

Education Research and Perspectives

SUBMISSION PROCESS:
Postal Submission Only

CONTACT INFORMATION:	REVIEW PROCESS:
Clive Whitehead & Marnie O'Neill, Eds. The University of Western Australia Graduate School of Education Nedlands, WA 6907 Australia	**Type of Review:** Blind Review **No. External Reviewers:** 1 **No. InHouse Reviewers:** 1
Phone: +61 8 6488 2388 **Email:** clive.whitehead@uwa.edu.au **Website:** http://www.education.uwa.edu.au	**Acceptance Rate:** 50-60% **Time to Review:** 2 - 3 Months **Reviewer's Comments:** Yes **Invited Articles:** 0-5% **Fees to Publish:** $0.00 US$ **Fees to Review:** $0.00 US$

PUBLICATION GUIDELINES:	CIRCULATION DATA:
Manuscript Style: See Manuscript Guidelines **Manuscript Length:** 16-30 **Copies Required:** Three	**Reader:** Academics **Frequency of Issue:** 2 Times/Year **Sponsor/Publisher:** Graduate School of Education

MANUSCRIPT TOPICS:

Adult Career & Vocational; Art / Music; Audiology / Speech Pathology; Bilingual / E.S.L.; Counseling & Personnel Services; Curriculum Studies; Education Management / Administration; Educational Psychology; Educational Technology Systems; Elementary / Early Childhood; English Literature; Foreign Language; Gifted Children; Health & Physical Education; Higher Education; Languages & Linguistics; Library Science / Information Resources; Reading; Religious Education; Rural Education & Small Schools; School Law; Science Math & Environment; Secondary / Adolescent Studies; Social Studies / Social Science; Special Education; Teacher Education; Tests, Measurement & Evaluation; Urban Education, Cultural / Non-Traditional

MANUSCRIPT GUIDELINES/COMMENTS:

General Topics. In recent years subjects have included history and philosophy of education, curriculum history and theory, teaching, school effectiveness, educational mentoring, female academics, participant observation, and education as a university subject. In recent years two post-graduate theses have been published in full as separate issues.

This journal has been published continuously by the Department of Education/Graduate School of Education since December 1950. Initially it was published as *The Educand*.

In 1961 the title was changed to *The Australian journal of Higher Education*. The present title was adopted in 1974. Throughout its history, the journal has been multi-disciplinary in outlook, with a mixture of general issues and issues devoted to special topics. The range of authors is worldwide. The journal includes articles, review essays and book reviews. Since 1991 the journal has been free of charge on the internet at: **http://www.education.uwa.edu.au**

The journal is published on a bi-annual basis (in June and December) and all articles are subject to external review and report. The present joint editors and their email addresses are as follows: A/Prof. Clive Whitehead (**Clive.Whitehead@uwa.edu.au**) and Dr. Marnie O'Neill (**Marnie. O'Neill@uwa.edu.au**)

For information about subscriptions to the hard copy edition of the journal or contributing articles see the end pages of any issue or contact one of the joint editors by email or by addressing correspondence to: The Editors, Education Research and Perspectives, Graduate School of Education, The University of Western Australia, 35 Stirling Highway, Crawley, WA 6009

Notes for Contributors
1. Each article should be less than 10,000 words in length.

2. Manuscripts should be submitted in both soft and hard copy.
- The soft copy to be submitted preferably in the word processing program Microsoft Word or WordPerfect in IBM or Macintosh version
- The hard copy should be an original printout in double-spaced typescript on one side only of opaque, white paper, leaving ample top and left-hand margins.

3. Tables and/or figures should be presented on separate sheets and only when essential. The position in the text should be clearly indicated.

4. The title of the article, author's name and affiliation should be set on a separate title page.

5. A mini-abstract, of not more than 100 words, should be provided at the head of the article.

6. Please also supply a three to four line autobiography (stating current academic position, institution, previous education and main research interests) for the 'Contributor's to this Issue' page.

7. Referencing: Due to the multi-disciplinary nature of the journal a variety of established forms of annotation are accepted. In each case it is imperative that authors remain *consistent* in their use of a reference style.

8. All articles submitted are subject to review and report.

Contributions should be addressed to: The Editors, Education Research and Perspectives, Graduate School of Education, The University of Western Australia, 35 Stirling Highway, Crawley, WA 6009 Australia

Further information on editorial matters will be supplied on application to the Editors.

Education Review

SUBMISSION PROCESS:	
Electronic Submission Only **via EMail** **glass@asu.edu**	
CONTACT INFORMATION:	**REVIEW PROCESS:**
Gene V. Glass, Editor Arizona State University College of Education Tempe, AZ 85287-2411 USA	**Type of Review:** Blind Review **No. External Reviewers:** 0 **No. InHouse Reviewers:** 2 **Acceptance Rate:** 90% **Time to Review:** 1 Month or Less **Reviewer's Comments:** Yes **Invited Articles:** 50% +
Phone: 480-965-2692 **Email:** glass@asu.edu **Website:** http://edrev.asu.edu	**Fees to Publish:** $0.00 US$ **Fees to Review:** $0.00 US$
PUBLICATION GUIDELINES:	**CIRCULATION DATA:**
Manuscript Style: American Psychological Association **Manuscript Length:** 6-10 **Copies Required:** Electronic Only	**Reader:** Academics **Frequency of Issue:** 100 Times/Year **Sponsor/Publisher:** Arizona State University

MANUSCRIPT TOPICS:
Adult Career & Vocational; Bilingual / E.S.L.; Counseling & Personnel Services; Curriculum Studies; Education Management / Administration; Educational Psychology; Educational Technology Systems; Elementary / Early Childhood; Gifted Children; Higher Education; Reading; Religious Education; Rural Education & Small Schools; School Law; Science Math & Environment; Secondary / Adolescent Studies; Social Studies / Social Science; Special Education; Teacher Education; Tests, Measurement & Evaluation; Urban Education, Cultural / Non-Traditional

MANUSCRIPT GUIDELINES/COMMENTS:

Education Review publishes reviews of recent books in education, covering the entire range of education scholarship and practice. Reviews are archived and their publication announced by means of a listserv (**EDREV@asu.edu**). The *Education Review* is made available to the public without cost as a service of the College of Education at Arizona State University.

Procedures
All review articles must be submitted in electronic format (either on a floppy disk or transmitted over the Internet as an attachment to an email letter to the appropriate Editor).

Long reviews. Gene V Glass, Editor **glass@asu.edu**

Brief reviews. Kate Corby, Brief Reviews Editor **corby@msu.edu**

Reviews in Spanish or Portuguese. Gustavo E. Fischman, Editor for Spanish & Portugese **fischman@asu.edu**

Reviews should be submitted in a standard word-processing format (such as Microsoft Word or WordPerfect) or, preferably, in "Rich Text Format." Long review articles should be between 2,500 and 5,000 words. Reviews outside these limits may be considered at the Editor's discretion. Brief Reviews call attention to current practical books for teachers and administrators. The Brief Reviews section publishes brief evaluative summaries of books from the current and previous year.

Every review article should begin by citing the book or books to be reviewed, with full bibliographic information including authors (please include first names), copyright date, full title including any subtitle, place of publication, publisher, number of pages, ISBN Number, and price if available. For example,

> Hunt, Morton. (1997). How Science Takes Stock: The Story of Meta-Analysis. N.Y: Russell Sage Foundation. Pp. xii + 210. ISBN 0-87154-389-3. $38.95

References and all other citations of published work in the review itself should follow the form specified in the *Publication Manual of the American Psychological Association* (4th Edition). See http://www.apa.org/journals/faq.html. For example,

> ... as argued by Hedges (1982) in his investigation into the reliability of observations in the physical sciences."

And then in the References at the end of the review, the citation of Hedges (1982) would appear as follows:

References

Hedges, L.V. (1982). How hard is hard science, how soft is soft science? The empirical cumulativeness of research. American Psychologist, 42, 443-455.

Footnotes are not permitted; auxiliary information normally included in footnotes should be included in Endnotes that appear directly before any References at the end of the review.

Submitted articles should be accompanied by a paragraph describing the review author's institutional affiliation and areas of interest.

Editorial Policy
All accepted articles are subject to copyediting by the Editor, including editing for length and format consistency, as well as editing for content. All changes will be submitted to authors for final approval before publication.

Copyright Policy
Copyright for all articles published in *ER* will be retained by the authors. Permission to use any copyrighted material in review articles, or permission to republish reviews also being published elsewhere, must be obtained by the author prior to publication in *ER*.

Criteria by Which Submitted Reviews Will Be Judged
Submitted reviews will be judged for possible publication according to the following:

Review Procedures and Criteria

Review articles are either solicited by the Editor, or offered unsolicited by reviewers. In either case, decisions on acceptance for publication are made by the Editor, who may on occasion solicit assistance from other readers in helping them make a decision. However, the articles are not typically refereed by any standard anonymous review process. In making his decision, the Editor will be guided by the following criteria:

- Does the review help readers form a clear idea of the contents of the book under consideration?
- Is the review fair and accurate in its presentation of the evidence, arguments, and methodology of the book?
- Does the review present a reasoned evaluation of the book and its conclusions?
- Is the article written in a manner that will promote understanding and further discussion? Is it respectful in tone?
- Does the article satisfy editorial standards of clarity of presentation, organization of ideas, and quality of writing?
- Does the article fit within the specific format and length requirements of this journal?

If you are interested in writing a review for *ER*, please contact the Editor at **glass@asu.edu**. *Education Review* discourages unsolicited submissions of book reviews conducted by students, advisees, colleagues, spouses, or personal friends of a book's author. Such relations place the reviewer's credibility into question and could, in certain situations, make a reviewer vulnerable to an untenable conflict of interest.

Publication of commissioned articles is presumed, but only when in the Editor's judgment the criteria listed above are satisfied. In addition, *ER* is committed to prompt turnaround times on its reviews, and commissioned articles should be completed by the agreed upon deadline. Failure to meet such deadlines removes any obligation to publish the article, although this decision remains at the Editor's discretion.

Education, Citizenship and Social Justice

SUBMISSION PROCESS:	
Electronic Submission Only via EMail **am.gallagher@qub.ac.uk**	

CONTACT INFORMATION:	REVIEW PROCESS:	
Tony Gallagher, Editor Queen's University Belfast, UK	**Type of Review:**	Blind Review
	No. External Reviewers:	2
	No. InHouse Reviewers:	1
Phone: +44 28 9097 5929	**Acceptance Rate:**	50%
	Time to Review:	4 - 6 Months
Email: am.gallagher@qub.ac.uk	**Reviewer's Comments:**	Yes
	Invited Articles:	0-5%
Website: www.qub.ac.uk/edu	**Fees to Publish:**	$0.00 US$
	Fees to Review:	$0.00 US$

PUBLICATION GUIDELINES:	CIRCULATION DATA:
Manuscript Style: See Manuscript Guidelines	**Reader:** Academics
Manuscript Length: 21-25	**Frequency of Issue:** 3 Times/Year
Copies Required: Two	**Sponsor/Publisher:** Sage Publications

MANUSCRIPT TOPICS:
Bilingual / E.S.L.; Curriculum Studies; Higher Education; Languages & Linguistics; Religious Education; Secondary / Adolescent Studies; Social Studies / Social Science; Special Education; Urban Education, Cultural / Non-Traditional

MANUSCRIPT GUIDELINES/COMMENTS:

About the Journal
Education, Citizenship and Social Justice launched in 2006 to provide a strategic forum for international and multi-disciplinary dialogue for all academic educators and educational policy-makers concerned with the meanings and form of citizenship and social justice as these are realised throughout the time spent in educational institutions.

Manuscript Submission Guidelines
Authors should retain one copy of their manuscript and send two identical copies (plus a Word version of the paper by email), each fully numbered and typed in double spacing throughout, on one side only of white A4 or US standard size paper to Tony Gallagher, School of education, Queen's University, Belfast BT7 1GL, United Kingdom [email: **am.gallagher@qub.ac.uk**].

Books for review should be sent to Ruth Leitch, Graduate School of Education, Queen's University Belfast, BT7 1HL, United Kingdom.

When submitting your article please confirm, in your email, that all authors have agreed to the submission and that the article is not currently being considered for publication by any other journal. (You will be asked to sign a formal printed agreement once your article is accepted).

Style. Papers must be typed, written in English and avoid discriminatory language. They should be aimed at an international audience, using a clear style, avoiding jargon. You must therefore explain points that might only be understood within your own education system. Acronyms, abbreviations and technical terms should be defined when they are first used. UK spellings are preferred. If notes are essential only use endnotes. Do not indent at the start of a new paragraph; instead, leave one line between each paragraph; and at least two lines between each (sub)section and the next.

Each manuscript should contain:
- A title page with full title and subtitle (if any). For the purposes of blind refereeing, full name of each author with current affiliation and full address/phone/fax/email details should be supplied on a separate sheet.
- An abstract of 100-150 words.
- Up to 6 keywords.
- Papers should normally be between 4000-7000 words, excluding references. The text should be clearly organized, with a clear hierarchy of heading and subheading.

Tables. Tables should be types (double-line spaced) on separate sheets and their positions indicated by a marginal note in the text. All tables should have short descriptive captions with footnotes and their source(s) typed below the tables.

Illustrations. All line diagrams are termed 'Figures' and should be referred to as such in the manuscript. They should be numbered consecutively. Line diagrams should be presented in a form suitable for immediate reproduction (i.e. not requiring redrawing), each on a separate A4 sheet, or if possible, on disk as either EPS (all fonts embedded) or TIFF files with a minimum resolution of 600 dpi (b/w only).

Authors are responsible for obtaining permissions from copyright holders for reproduction of any illustrations, tables, or lengthy quotations previously published elsewhere.

References. The styles indicated below must be followed exactly by authors:
- Every citation should have a reference and every reference should be cited.
- Use ampersands in multiple references (e.g. Smith, Brown, & Jones), but in the text put first author et al. (e.g. Smith et al.).
- Do not use bold, underlining or quotation marks in references
- Provide translations for non-English titles in the references

Journal article
Smith, J. R. (2003) Choosing your style for references. Journal of Guidelines, 4(1), 24-9.

Books
Smith, J. R. (2003) Reference Style Guidelines. London: Sage.

Smith, J. R. & Brown, A. P. (2003) References for All: Choosing an Appropriate Style. London: Sage.

Chapter in a book
Smith, J. R. (2003) The importance of matching disk and hard copy. In R. Brown (ed.) Guidelines for References, pp. 55-8. London: Sage.

For more detailed examples please visit the web site.

Copyright. Before publication authors are requested to assign copyright to SAGE publications, subject to retaining their right to reuse the material in other publications written or edited by themselves and due to be publisher preferably at least one year after initial publication in the journal.

Offprints. Authors receive a proof of their article for checking and correction, and are given controlled access to a pdf of their article and a complimentary copy of the issue after publication.

Education, Knowledge and Economy

SUBMISSION PROCESS:
Postal Submission Only

CONTACT INFORMATION:	REVIEW PROCESS:	
Anthony Kelly, Editor University of Southhampton School of Education Highfield, SO17 1BJ UK	**Type of Review:**	Blind Review
	No. External Reviewers:	2
	No. InHouse Reviewers:	1
Phone: 0044 2380 593351	**Acceptance Rate:**	11-20%
	Time to Review:	1 - 2 Months
	Reviewer's Comments:	Yes
Email: edknowec@soton.ac.uk	**Invited Articles:**	0-5%
Website: http://www.tandf.co.uk/journals/titles/174 96896.asp	**Fees to Publish:**	$0.00 US$
	Fees to Review:	$0.00 US$

PUBLICATION GUIDELINES:	CIRCULATION DATA:
Manuscript Style: See Manuscript Guidelines	**Reader:** Academics, Administrators, Practicing Teachers, Counselors
Manuscript Length: 16-20	**Frequency of Issue:** 3 Times/Year
Copies Required: Three	**Sponsor/Publisher:** Routledge, Taylor & Francis

MANUSCRIPT TOPICS:

MANUSCRIPT GUIDELINES/COMMENTS:

Coverage. All areas of education, business, economics and management, with particular emphasis on education policy and social enterprise/entrepreneurship.

Aims & Scope
The relationship between education, social enterprise, business and the economy is a rapidly growing one, the importance of which is widely recognised by government, academics and practitioners. It is especially important in today's knowledge/learning society.

Education, Knowledge & Economy is an international, peer-reviewed journal which aims to facilitate the dissemination of high quality theoretical advances and empirical research, and to serve as a forum for debate in all areas of education, business, economics and management, with particular emphasis on education policy and social enterprise/entrepreneurship.

The journal consciously promotes an interdisciplinary approach to intellectual endeavour in these related areas, and is research-focused and critically orientated.

Papers in the following areas are especially welcome: government policy as it relates to education, social enterprise and the knowledge economy; ethical dimensions of social entrepreneurship; customer and market relationships in education; citizenship, globalisation and fair trade as they relate to education; skills development; organisational theory in not-for-profit sectors; psycho-social aspects of organizations; entrepreneurial learning; agent-centred perspectives on education and social enterprise; the role of education and social entrepreneurship in regional development; SME (small and medium-sized enterprise) and school-to-school networks; and community enterprise as a basis for corporate citizenship.

Instructions for Authors
Note to Authors. Please make sure your contact address information is clearly visible on the outside of all packages you are sending to Editors.

Unless agreed otherwise all accepted papers become the copyright of Taylor & Francis. All contributors should be aware they are addressing an international audience.

Manuscripts, (3 copies), typed on A4 size (or equivalent) double-spaced, of between 5,000 and 8,000 words, plus a disk or e-mail version, should be sent to the Editor, Professor A E Kelly, School of Education, University of Southampton, Highfield, SO17 1BJ, UK; E-mail: **edknowec @soton.ac.uk**

Manuscripts submitted should be original, not under review by any other publication and not published elsewhere.

All pages should be numbered. Footnotes to the text should be avoided. Sponsorship of research reported (e.g. by research councils, government departments and agencies, etc.) should be declared. To allow refereeing, all submissions must be properly formatted for anonymous reviewing. Authors' names and institutions should be typed on a separate sheet and submitted with the manuscript. The full postal and email address of the author who will check proofs and receive correspondence and offprints should be included also.

Each paper should be accompanied on separate sheets by an abstract of 100 to 150 words.

For further guidance on the journal style, please visit: **http://www.tandf.co.uk/journals/authors/ edstylea.dot**

Tables and captions to illustrations. Tables must be typed out on separate sheets and not included as part of the text. The captions to illustrations should be gathered together and also typed out on a separate sheet. Tables and Figures should be numbered consecutively by Arabic numerals. The approximate position of tables and figures should be indicated in the manuscript. Captions should include keys to any symbols used.

Figures. Please supply one set of artwork in a finished form, suitable for reproduction. Figures will not normally be redrawn by the publisher.

References should be indicated in the typescript by giving the author's name, with the year of publication in parentheses. If several papers by the same author and from the same year are cited, a, b, c, etc. should be put after the year of publication. The references should be listed in full, including pages, at the end of the paper in the following standard form:

For books
Rhodes, J. (2005) The crisis in vocational training (New York, Routledge).

For articles
Brown, W., Smith, J. & Jones, B. (2005) The study of vocational education in universities: some reflections, Journal of Education, 8, 38-44.

For chapters within books
White, S. & Morley, J. (2004) Teaching of adults, in: F. Green (Ed.) Vocational training (Maidenhead, Open University Press), pp. 174-194.

For online documents
Standler, R. (2000) Plagarism in college in the USA. Available online at: www.rb2.com/plag.htm (accessed 6 August 2004).

Titles of journals and names of publishers, etc. should not be abbreviated. Acronyms for the names of organisations, examinations, etc. should be preceded by the title in full.

Proofs will be sent to authors by email if there is sufficient time to do so. They should be corrected and returned to the Publisher within seven days. Major alterations to the text cannot be accepted.

Early Electronic Offprints. Corresponding authors can now receive their article by email as a complete PDF. This allows the author to print up to 50 copies, free of charge, and disseminate them to colleagues. In many cases this facility will be available up to two weeks prior to publication. Alternatively, corresponding authors will receive the traditional 50 offprints. A copy of the journal will be sent by post to all corresponding authors after publication. Additional copies of the journal can be purchased at the author's preferential rate of £15.00/$25.00 per copy.

Copyright. It is a condition of publication that authors assign copyright or licence the publication rights in their articles, including abstracts in Taylor & Francis. This enables the Publisher to ensure full copyright protection and to disseminate the article, and of course the Journal, to the widest possible readership in print and electronic formats as appropriate. Authors may, of course, use the article elsewhere after publication without prior permission from Taylor & Francis, provided that acknowledgement is given to the Journal as the original source of publication, and that Taylor & Francis is notified so that our records show that its use is properly authorised. Authors retain a number of other rights under the Taylor & Francis rights policies documents. These policies are referred to at **http://www.tandf.co.uk/journals/authorrights.pdf** for full details. Authors are themselves responsible for obtaining permission to reproduce copyright material from other sources.

For further information on electronic submission, including information on accepted file types, please see: **http://www.tandf.co.uk/journals/authors/electronic.asp**

Educational Administration Quarterly

<table>
<tr><td colspan="2" align="center">

SUBMISSION PROCESS:

**Electronic Submission Only
via EMail**

eaq@ed.utah.edu
</td></tr>
<tr><td valign="top">

CONTACT INFORMATION:

Diana G. Pounder, Editor
University of Utah
Dept. of Educational Leadership & Policy
1750 Campus Center Drive, Room 339
Salt Lake City, UT 84112-9254 USA

Phone:
  801-581-6714

Email:
  eaq@ed.utah.edu

Website:
  www.sagepub.com
</td><td valign="top">

REVIEW PROCESS:

Type of Review:	Blind Review
No. External Reviewers:	3
No. InHouse Reviewers:	3
Acceptance Rate:	6-10%
Time to Review:	3 Months
Reviewer's Comments:	Yes
Invited Articles:	6-10%
Fees to Publish:	$0.00 US$
Fees to Review:	$0.00 US$
</td></tr>
<tr><td valign="top">

PUBLICATION GUIDELINES:

Manuscript Style:
  American Psychological Association

Manuscript Length:
  25-40

Copies Required:
  Electronic Only
</td><td valign="top">

CIRCULATION DATA:

Reader:
  Academics

Frequency of Issue:
  5 Times/Year

Sponsor/Publisher:
  Sage Publications
</td></tr>
</table>

MANUSCRIPT TOPICS:
Education Management / Administration; Educational Leadership; Educational Organizations; Higher Education; Schools; Social Studies / Social Science

MANUSCRIPT GUIDELINES/COMMENTS:

About the Journal & Editorial Policy
EAQ presents prominent empirical and conceptual articles focused on timely and critical leadership and policy issues of educational organizations. As an editorial team, we embrace traditional and emergent research paradigms, methods, and issues. We particularly promote the publication of rigorous and relevant scholarly work that enhances linkages among and utility for educational policy, practice, and research arenas, including work that examines:
a. the relationship among educational leadership structures and processes and valued organizational outcomes in educational institutions from pre-school to higher education, most notably improved teaching processes and learning outcomes;
b. improved leadership preparation and development structures and processes and assesses the relationship between leadership preparation & development & valued organizational outcomes;
c. educational environments that promote equity and social justice for students and faculty; and
d. theoretical frameworks that advance and have utility for issues such as those outlined above.

Author Submission Guidelines and Manuscript Specifications

EAQ uses an electronic submission and review process. Authors should submit by e-mail an electronic copy of the manuscript in Microsoft Word format (for PC) to **eaq@ed.utah.edu**. If electronic files cannot be e-mailed, a copy on floppy disk or CD may be mailed here: EAQ Editor, Professor Diana G. Pounder, Ph.D., Department of Educational Leadership & Policy, University of Utah, 1705 Campus Center Drive, Room 339, Salt Lake City, UT 84112-9254

Ordinarily, manuscripts should be 25 to 40 pages in length. All tables should be included in the electronic file. Figures may be submitted in separate electronic files, preferably as TIFF or JPEG images, although we can accept with most other formats. Figures must be of sufficient resolution for high-end printing: 1200 dpi for line art, 300 dpi for grayscale, and 600 dpi for color.

Manuscripts should follow the style of the fifth edition of the *Publication Manual of the American Psychological Association* (APA). All copy should be typed, double-spaced in Times New Roman 12-point font with notes, references, tables, and figures appearing at the end of the manuscript per APA style.

Structured Abstract

Each manuscript should include a structured abstract, similar to those described by Mosteller, Nave, and Miech in the January/February 2004 *Educational Researcher* Commentary, "Why We Need a Structured Abstract in Education Research." The structured abstract for empirical manuscripts should include very brief subheaded sections such as *Purpose, Conceptual or Theoretical Framework, Research Methods/Approach (e.g. Setting, Participants, Research Design, Data Collection and Analysis), Findings*, and *Implications for Research and for Practice*. Non-empirical or conceptual manuscripts should use sub-heads appropriate to the conceptual argument or position promoted or discussed. Including section heads, abstracts should not exceed 250 words. Additionally, five key words or phrases should appear after the abstract, including an indication of the type of article (e.g. empirical paper, conceptual paper).

Author Identification

Manuscripts should include a cover sheet with the title, author's name, address, phone number, fax number, and e-mail address, along with a brief biographical statement (2-3 sentences). If the article was authored by more than one person, coauthors' names, e-mail addresses, phone numbers, and biographical statements should also be included. However, to assure appropriate blind review, the author's name or identifying information should NOT appear in headers, footers, reference list, or other portions of the manuscript text; instead, information in text or references that would identify the author should be replaced with the word "Author" in lieu of the author's name or identifying information.

Originality of Manuscript

Manuscripts are accepted for consideration with the understanding that they are original material and are not under consideration for publication elsewhere. Referees evaluate submitted manuscripts anonymously.

"From the Field" Submissions. In addition to its regular blind refereed empirical or conceptual manuscripts, the *EAQ* editorial staff reviews and accepts other work for inclusion in the "From the Field" section of the journal. These works may include highlights of award-winning dissertations, book reviews, policy commentaries or updates, brief updates on longitudinal research in progress, and other shorter pieces that highlight timely issues in the field.

Open Disclosure of Review Statistics. At the completion of each volume year, the *EAQ* editorial staff will compute review statistics such as average review time for original and revised manuscripts, average time from manuscript acceptance to "in print" publication, and acceptance rate (excluding special issues). These data will be posted on the *EAQ* Website, **http://www.sage pub.com** OR **http://www.ed.utah.edu/ELP/**

Educational and Psychological Measurement

<table>
<tr><td colspan="2" align="center">SUBMISSION PROCESS:

Electronic Submission Only
via EMail

emp_uva@virginia.edu</td></tr>
</table>

CONTACT INFORMATION:	REVIEW PROCESS:
Xitao Fan, Editor University of Virginia Curry School of Education 405 Emmet Street South Charlottesville, VA 22903-2495 USA	**Type of Review:** Blind Review **No. External Reviewers:** 2-3 **No. InHouse Reviewers:** 1-2 **Acceptance Rate:** 21-30%
Phone: 434-243-8906	**Time to Review:** 2-6 Months **Reviewer's Comments:** Yes **Invited Articles:** 0-5%
Email: epm_uva@virginia.edu	**Fees to Publish:** $0.00 US$ **Fees to Review:** $0.00 US$
Website: http://epm.sage.com/	

PUBLICATION GUIDELINES:	CIRCULATION DATA:
Manuscript Style: American Psychological Association	**Reader:** Academics
Manuscript Length: 26-30	**Frequency of Issue:** Bi-Monthly
Copies Required: Electronic Only	**Sponsor/Publisher:** Sage Publications

MANUSCRIPT TOPICS:
Tests, Measurement & Evaluation

MANUSCRIPT GUIDELINES/COMMENTS:

Educational and Psychological Measurement (*EPM*) publishes a wide range of articles dealing with the measurement of individual differences, including, but not limited to, classical test theory, item response theory, "reliability generalization" (RG) studies, and validity studies for new and existing measures. *EPM* also publishes articles on quantitative methods dealing with issues relevant for quantitative researchers in the field of measurement.

Manuscript Submission
All manuscripts should be submitted electronically to the editor (Xitao Fan, EPM Editor, Curry School of Education, University of Virginia, U.S.A.; telephone: (434) 243-8906; fax: (434) 924-1384; e-mail: **epm_uva@virginia.edu**). Send submission letter and manuscript as attachments to the above e-mail address. Microsoft Word or Acrobat PDF file formats are preferred. There should be only one electronic file for each manuscript, and multiple files for one manuscript must be consolidated before submission. The corresponding author must provide both the postal mailing address and e-mail address.

Manuscripts should follow the general guidelines of the *Publication Manual of the American Psychological Association* (5th edition). Manuscripts should comply with the author guidelines presented in the lead of issue 4, volume 54 of the journal (Winter 1994, pp. 837-847) and in supplementary "guidelines editorials" published on an occasional basis (e.g., August 1995, pp. 525-534; April 1996, pp. 197-208; and August 2001, pp. 517-531). Copies of these guideline editorials are available online at **http://www.people.virginia.edu/~xf8d**. The editor strongly encourages authors to review the recommendations of the American Psychological Association's Task Force on Statistical Inference, published in the August 1999 issue of *American Psychologist* (http://content.apa.org/journals/amp/54/8/594.html).

Educational Assessment

SUBMISSION PROCESS:
Postal & Electronic Submission Required via EMail **herman@cse.ucla.edu**

CONTACT INFORMATION:	REVIEW PROCESS:	
Joan Herman, Editor Nat'l Center for Research on Evaluation, Standards, and Student Testing GSE&IS Bldg., 3rd Fl, Box 951522 300 Charles E. Young Drive North Los Angeles, CA 90095-1522 USA	**Type of Review:**	Blind Review
	No. External Reviewers:	3
	No. InHouse Reviewers:	1
	Acceptance Rate:	21-30%
	Time to Review:	4 - 6 Months
Phone: 310-794-9157	**Reviewer's Comments:**	Yes
	Invited Articles:	11-20%
Email: herman@cse.ucla.edu	**Fees to Publish:** **Fees to Review:**	$0.00 US$ $0.00 US$
Website: www.erlbaum.com		

PUBLICATION GUIDELINES:	CIRCULATION DATA:

Manuscript Style:
  American Psychological Association
	Reader:
	  Academics

Manuscript Length:
  26-30+
	Frequency of Issue:
	  Quarterly

Copies Required:
  One + 2 Electronic
	Sponsor/Publisher:
	  Lawrence Erlbaum Associates, Inc.

MANUSCRIPT TOPICS:
Educational Psychology; Tests, Measurement & Evaluation

MANUSCRIPT GUIDELINES/COMMENTS:

Editorial Scope
This journal publishes original research and scholarship on the assessment of individuals, groups, and programs in educational settings. Its coverage encompasses a broad range of issues related to theory, empirical research, and practice in the appraisal of educational achievements by students and teachers, young children and adults, and novices and experts. The journal also reports on studies of conventional testing practices, discusses alternative approaches, presents scholarship on classroom practice, and debates on national assessment issues. *Educational Assessment*'s stated purpose is to provide a forum for integrating conceptual and technical domains with the arenas of practice and policy, and for unifying a literature that is presently scattered over a variety of disciplines and outlets.

Audience. Educational researchers, test developers, administrators, and policy makers.

INSTRUCTIONS TO CONTRIBUTORS
Manuscript Submission
Only articles written in English will be considered. Submit one paper copy and two electronic copies (one with author identified; one prepared for blind review) of your manuscript to the Editor: Joan Herman, National Center for Research on Evaluation, Standards, and Student Testing (CRESST), 300 Charles E. Young Drive North GSE&IS Building, 3rd Floor, Mailbox 951522, Los Angeles, CA 90095-1522 Phone: 310-794-9157, E-mail: **herman@cse.ucla.edu**

Prepare manuscripts according to the *Publication Manual of the American Psychological Association* (4th ed.). Type all components of the manuscript double-sided, including title page, abstract, text, quotes, acknowledgements, references, appendices, tables, figure captions, and footnotes. An abstract of 100 to 150 words should be typed on a separate page. Authors must follow the "Guidelines to Reduce Bias in Language," on pages 46-60 of the *APA Manual*. Four photocopies of the illustrations and the original illustrations should accompany the manuscript. All manuscripts submitted will be acknowledged promptly. Authors should keep a copy of their manuscripts to guard against loss.

Blind Review
To facilitate anonymous review, only the article title should appear on the first page of the manuscript. An attached cover page must contain the title; authorship; authors' affiliations; any statements of credit or research support; and authors; mailing addresses, phone and fax numbers, and e-mail addresses. Every effort should be made by the authors to see that the manuscript itself contains no clues to their identities.

Permissions
Authors are responsible for all statements made in their work and for obtaining permission from copyright owners to reprint or adapt a table or figure or to reprint a quotation of 500 words or more. Authors should write to original author(s) and publisher to request nonexclusive world rights in all languages to use the material in the article and in future editions. Provide copies of all permissions and credit lines obtained.

Regulations
In a cover letter, authors should state that the findings reported in the manuscript are original and have not been published previously and that the manuscript is not being simultaneously submitted elsewhere. Authors should also state that they have complied with American Psychological Association ethical standards in the treatment of their samples.

Production Notes
After a manuscript is accepted for publication, its author is asked to provide a computer disk containing the manuscript file. Files are copyedited and typeset into page proofs. Authors read proofs to correct errors and answer editors' queries.

Educational Evaluation & Policy Analysis

SUBMISSION PROCESS:
Electronic Submission Only **via Online Portal** http://ojs.aera.net/journals/index.php/eepa/about/submissions#onlineSubmissions

CONTACT INFORMATION:	REVIEW PROCESS:	
Evelyn Fisch, Editorial Associate Policy Evaluation and Research Center Educational Testing Service Rosedale Road, Mail Stop 19-R Princeton, NJ 08541 USA	**Type of Review:**	Blind Review
	No. External Reviewers:	3
	No. InHouse Reviewers:	0
	Acceptance Rate:	11-20%
Phone: 609-734-5287	**Time to Review:**	4 - 6 Months
	Reviewer's Comments:	Yes
	Invited Articles:	0-5%
Email: eepaeditors-ef@aera.net	**Fees to Publish:**	$0.00 US$
Website: www.aera.net	**Fees to Review:**	$0.00 US$

PUBLICATION GUIDELINES:	CIRCULATION DATA:
Manuscript Style: American Psychological Association	**Reader:** Academics, Administrators
Manuscript Length: 30+	**Frequency of Issue:** Quarterly
Copies Required: Electronic Only	**Sponsor/Publisher:** American Educational Research Association (AERA)

MANUSCRIPT TOPICS:
Education Management / Administration; Educational Psychology; Elementary / Early Childhood; Higher Education; Secondary / Adolescent Studies; Social Studies / Social Science; Teacher Education; Tests, Measurement & Evaluation; Urban Education, Cultural / Non-Traditional

MANUSCRIPT GUIDELINES/COMMENTS:

Focus and Scope
EEPA publishes scholarly manuscripts of theoretical, methodological, or policy interest to those engaged in educational policy analysis, evaluation, and decision making. *EEPA* is a multidisciplinary policy journal, and considers original research from multiple disciplines, theoretical orientations, and methodologies.

Author Guidelines
The preferred style guide for all AERA journals is the *Publication Manual of the American Psychological Association*, 5th ed., 2001 (available from Order Department, American Psychological Association, P.O. Box 2710, Hyattsville, MD 20784). *The Chicago Manual of Style*, 15th ed., 2003, is also acceptable for all AERA journals.

Manuscripts should be double spaced in entirety, with 1-inch margins on all sides. The type size should be at least 10 pitch (CPI) or 12 point. Subheads should be at reasonable intervals to break the monotony of lengthy text. Words to be set in italics (contrary to the rules of the style manual) should be set in italics, not underlined; sentence structure should be used to create emphasis. Abbreviations and acronyms should be spelled out at first mention unless they are found as entries in their abbreviated form in the *Merriam-Webster's Collegiate Dictionary*, 11th ed., 2003 (e.g., IQ needs no explanation).

Manuscripts should not exceed 40 pages total, including all tables, appendices, notes and references.

Pages should be numbered consecutively, beginning with the page after the title page. Mathematical symbols and Greek letters should be clearly marked to indicate italics, boldface, superscript, and subscript.

All manuscripts must be blind. Please do not include any identifying information -- even on the title page -- in your manuscript. Please do not use headers or footers.

Submission Preparation Checklist
As part of the submission process, authors are required to check off their submission's compliance with all of the following items, and submissions may be returned to authors that do not adhere to these guidelines.

1. The submission has not been previously published nor is it before another journal for consideration; or an explanation has been provided in Comments to the Editor.

2. The submission file is in Microsoft Word, RTF, or WordPerfect document file format. Any supplemental files are in Microsoft Word, RTF, WordPerfect, or Excel format. Please do not upload PDF files.

3. All URL addresses in the text (e.g., http://www.aera.net) are activated and ready to click.

4. The text is double-spaced; uses a 12-point font; employs italics, rather than underlining (except with URL addresses); with figures and tables placed within the text, rather than at the end. Keywords and an abstract of no more than 120 words.

5. The text meets this journal's formatting requirements outlined in the Author Guidelines found in About the Journal on the web site.

6. All manuscripts must be blind. Please do not include any identifying information -- even on the title page -- in your manuscript.

Before submitting your manuscript, please ensure that:
1. All Author identification has been removed, from all pages, including the title page.
2. "Author" and year have been used in the bibliography and footnotes, instead of authors' names, titles, etc.
3. The author's name has been removed from the document's Properties, which in Microsoft Word is found in the File menu (Select "File," "Properties," "Summary" and remove the Author's name. Select "OK" to save).

If you have submitted a manuscript with identifying information you will need to replace the submitted file with a new, blind, copy before your submission can proceed.

Copyright Notice
© 2005 by the American Educational Research Association. No written or oral permission is necessary to reproduce a table, a figure, or an excerpt of fewer than 500 words from this journal, or

to make photocopies for classroom use. Authors are granted permission, without fee, to photocopy their own material. Copies must include a full and accurate bibliographic citation and the following credit line: "Copyright [year] by the American Educational Research Association; reproduced with permission from the publisher." Written permission must be obtained to reproduce or reprint material in circumstances other than those just described. Please direct all requests for permission or for further information on policies and fees to the AERA Central Office.

AERA Publications Department, 1230 17th Street, N.W., Washington, DC 20036-3078; Telephone: 202.223.9485; Fax. 202.775.1824

Privacy Statement
The names and email addresses entered in this journal site will be used exclusively for the stated purposes of this journal and will not be made available for any other purpose or to any other party.

Educational Forum

<table>
<tr><td colspan="2" align="center">SUBMISSION PROCESS:

Electronic Submission Only
via EMail

pubs@kdp.org</td></tr>
<tr>
<td valign="top">

CONTACT INFORMATION:

Helen McCarthy, Managing Editor
Kappa Delta Pi Publications
3707 Woodview Trace
Indianapolis, IN 46268-1158 USA

Phone:
  317-871-4900
  800-284-3167

Email:
  pubs@kdp.org

Website:
  www.kdp.org

</td>
<td valign="top">

REVIEW PROCESS:

Type of Review:	Blind Review
No. External Reviewers:	4+
No. InHouse Reviewers:	2
Acceptance Rate:	35%
Time to Review:	2 Months
Reviewer's Comments:	Yes
Invited Articles:	5%
Fees to Publish:	$0.00 US$
Fees to Review:	$0.00 US$

</td>
</tr>
<tr>
<td valign="top">

PUBLICATION GUIDELINES:

Manuscript Style:
  Chicago Manual of Style

Manuscript Length:
  10

Copies Required:
  Four

</td>
<td valign="top">

CIRCULATION DATA:

Reader:
  Academics, Practicing Teachers

Frequency of Issue:
  Quarterly

Sponsor/Publisher:
  Kappa Delta Pi, International Honor
Society in Education

</td>
</tr>
</table>

MANUSCRIPT TOPICS:

Adult Career & Vocational; Art / Music; Audiology / Speech Pathology; Bilingual / E.S.L.; Counseling & Personnel Services; Curriculum Studies; Education Management / Administration; Educational Psychology; Educational Technology Systems; Elementary / Early Childhood; English Literature; Foreign Language; Gifted Children; Health & Physical Education; Higher Education; Languages & Linguistics; Library Science / Information Resources; Reading; Religious Education; Rural Education & Small Schools; School Law; Science Math & Environment; Secondary / Adolescent Studies; Social Studies / Social Science; Special Education; Teacher Education; Tests, Measurement & Evaluation; Urban Education, Cultural / Non-Traditional

MANUSCRIPT GUIDELINES/COMMENTS:

Manuscripts submitted to *The Educational Forum* should not be submitted simultaneously to another publication, nor be under consideration by other publishers at the time of submission. Manuscripts should be original material and not published previously.

To help facilitate the review and communication process, electronic submissions are encouraged. They should be in IBM-compatible Microsoft Word format and sent as an e-mail attachment or on a floppy disk. The e-mail address for submissions is **pubs@kdp.org**. Manuscripts may be sent by

274

postal mail as long as five hard copies are enclosed; but electronic submissions are ultimately required.

All manuscripts must be formatted for blind reviewing. A separate title page with the author's name, affiliation, preferred mailing address, telephone number, fax number, and e-mail address should be provided to ensure anonymity in the review process. If more than one person has authored the manuscript, please provide contact information for all authors and indicate which person is the corresponding author.

An abstract of no more than 75 words must accompany the manuscript. Submissions should be typed double-spaced for 8½" x 11" paper. Article length should not exceed 7,000 words, including quotations and references. Pages should be numbered. *The Chicago Manual of Style*, 15th edition, should be used as a guide for formatting manuscripts and reference style. To preserve the advantages of blind reviewing, authors should avoid identifying themselves in the manuscript.

It is the author's responsibility to quote accurately and provide complete reference information, as well as secure necessary permissions. Authors of accepted papers will be requested to assign all rights to copyright to *The Forum* by means of a standard form.

Deadlines for Submissions
The Educational Forum is published the first week of January, April, July, and October. For consideration in specific issues, manuscripts should be received six months prior to the publication date.

Book Reviews
The Educational Forum also accepts unsolicited reviews on recent books. Submissions should include a brief summary of the content of the book, provide its bibliographic information (including ISBN number and total page count), and discuss its strengths and weaknesses and its contribution to the field of education.

All submissions should be addressed to: Managing Editor, *The Educational Forum,* Kappa Delta Pi, 3707 Woodview Trace, Indianapolis, IN 46268-1158; E-mail: **pubs@kdp.org**

Educational Gerontology

SUBMISSION PROCESS:
Postal Submission Only

CONTACT INFORMATION:	REVIEW PROCESS:	
D. Barry Lumsden, Editor Senior Research Fellow	**Type of Review:**	Blind Review
University of Alabama Education Policy Center	**No. External Reviewers:**	3
Box 870231	**No. InHouse Reviewers:**	0
Tuscaloosa, AL 35487-0231 USA	**Acceptance Rate:**	21-30%
	Time to Review:	1 - 2 Months
Phone:	**Reviewer's Comments:**	Yes
940-579-7923	**Invited Articles:**	0-5%
Email:	**Fees to Publish:**	$0.00 US$
blumsden@bamaed.ua.edu	**Fees to Review:**	$0.00 US$
Website: http://www.tandf.co.uk/journals/titles/036 01277.asp		

PUBLICATION GUIDELINES:	CIRCULATION DATA:
Manuscript Style: American Psychological Association	**Reader:** Academics
Manuscript Length: 15-20	**Frequency of Issue:** 12 Times/Year
Copies Required: Three	**Sponsor/Publisher:** Taylor & Francis, Ltd.

MANUSCRIPT TOPICS:

Adult Career & Vocational; Aging In General; Art / Music; Audiology / Speech Pathology; Counseling & Personnel Services; Curriculum Studies; Health & Physical Education; Higher Education; Reading; Religious Education

MANUSCRIPT GUIDELINES/COMMENTS:

Aims and Scope

This well-respected journal offers up-to-date original research in the fields of gerontology, adult education, and the social and behavioral sciences. Researchers from around the world will benefit from the exchange of ideas for both the study and practice of educational gerontology. Papers published in the journal will also serve as authoritative contributions to the growing literature in this burgeoning field. *Educational Gerontology* is the only international journal of its kind to publish twelve issues per volume year. 2005 Impact Factor: 0.425 Ranking: 17/24 (Gerontology), 52/98 (Education & Educational Research) Thomson Scientific, Journal Citation Reports 2006

Readership

Gerontologists, adult educators, behavioral and social scientists, and geriatricians.

Instructions for Authors

Note to Authors. Please make sure your contact address information is clearly visible on the outside of all packages you are sending to Editors.

Submission of Manuscripts

Educational Gerontology: An International Journal publishes refereed materials in the fields of gerontology, adult education, and the social and behavioral sciences. According to the double-blind procedures established for critiquing papers, copies of materials received by the Editor-in-Chief are reviewed by panels appointed by the Editor-in-Chief. The peer review process consists of three or more persons knowledgeable in the areas covered by the materials.

Original and two copies of each manuscript should be submitted to the editor, D. Barry Lumsden, Senior Research Fellow, University of Alabama, Education Policy Center, Box 870231, Tuscaloosa, AL 35487-0232, Tel: 940-597-7923. Email: **blumsden@bamaed.ua.edu**.

Authors are required to submit manuscripts on disk. The disk should be prepared using MS Word or WordPerfect and should be clearly labeled with the authors' names, file name, and software program. Each manuscript must be accompanied by a statement that it has not been published elsewhere and that it has not been submitted simultaneously for publication elsewhere. Authors are responsible for obtaining permission to reproduce copyrighted material from other sources and are required to sign an agreement for the transfer of copyright to the publisher. All accepted manuscripts, artwork, and photographs become the property of the publisher.

All parts of the manuscript should be typewritten, double-spaced, with margins of at least one inch on all sides. Number manuscript pages consecutively throughout the paper. Authors should also supply a shortened version of the title suitable for the running head, not exceeding 50 character spaces. Each article should be summarized in an abstract of no more that 100 words. Avoid abbreviations, diagrams, and reference to the text.

Manuscripts, including figures, tables, and references, must conform to the specifications described in the *Publication Manual of the American Psychological Association* (5th ed., 2001). Manuscripts that do not adhere to this style will be returned for revision.

For further information on electronic submission, including information on accepted file types, please visit **http://www.tandf.co.uk/journals/authors/electronic_edu.asp**.

Tables and Figures / Illustrations

Illustrations submitted (line drawings, halftones, photos, photomicrographs, etc.) should be clean originals or digital files. Digital files are recommended for highest quality reproduction and should follow these guidelines:

- 300 dpi or higher
- sized to fit on journal page
- EPS, TIFF, or PSD format only
- submitted as separate files, not embedded in text files

Color illustrations will be considered for publication; however, the author will be required to bear the full cost involved in their printing and publication. The charge for the first page with color is $900.00. The next three pages with color are $450.00 each. A custom quote will be provided for color art totaling more than 4 journal pages. Good-quality color prints or files should be provided in their final size. The publisher has the right to refuse publication of color prints deemed unacceptable.

Tables and Figures

Tables and figures should not be embedded in the text, but should be included as separate sheets or files. A short descriptive title should appear above each table with a clear legend and any footnotes suitably identified below. All units must be included. Figures should be completely labeled, taking into account necessary size reduction. Captions should be typed, double-spaced, on a separate sheet. All original figures should be clearly marked in pencil on the reverse side with the number, author's name, and top edge indicated.

Proofs

One set of page proofs is sent to the designated corresponding author. Proofs should be checked and returned promptly.

Reprints

The corresponding author of each article will receive one complete copy of the issue in which the article appears. Reprints of an individual article may be ordered from Taylor & Francis by using the reprint order form included with page proofs.

Educational Leadership

SUBMISSION PROCESS:
Postal Submission Only

CONTACT INFORMATION:	REVIEW PROCESS:	

Margaret M. Scherer, Editor
Association for Supervision and
  Curriculum Development
1703 North Beauregard Street
Alexandria, VA 22311 USA
 	
Phone:
  703-575-5691
 	
Email:
  el@ascd.org
 	
Website:
  www.ascd.org
	Type of Review:	Editorial Review

	No. External Reviewers:	0
	No. InHouse Reviewers:	3
	Acceptance Rate:	6-10%
	Time to Review:	1 - 2 Months
	Reviewer's Comments:	No
	Invited Articles:	31-50%
	Fees to Publish:	$0.00 US$
	Fees to Review:	$0.00 US$

PUBLICATION GUIDELINES:	CIRCULATION DATA:

Manuscript Style:
  Chicago Manual of Style
 	
Manuscript Length:
  10-12
 	
Copies Required:
  Two
	Reader:
	  Academics, Administrators, Practicing
	  Teachers
	
	Frequency of Issue:
	  8 Times/Year
	
	Sponsor/Publisher:
	  ASCD Association

MANUSCRIPT TOPICS:

Assessment; Counseling & Personnel Services; Curriculum Studies; Education Management / Administration; Educational Technology Systems; Elementary / Early Childhood; Gifted Children; Multicultural Education; National Standards; Reading; Rural Education & Small Schools; Scheduling; Science Math & Environment; Social Studies / Social Science; Special Education; Tests, Measurement & Evaluation; Urban Education, Cultural / Non-Traditional

MANUSCRIPT GUIDELINES/COMMENTS:

Educational Leadership, the flagship journal of the Association for Supervision and Curriculum Development (ASCD), is intended for everyone interested in curriculum, instruction, supervision, and leadership in education. Each issue contains articles by leading educators, reports of effective programs and practices, interpretations of research, book reviews, and columns.

Issues are organized around themes (see "Themes"). In general, the more appropriate an article is for a theme issue, the more likely we will be able to publish it. We also accept articles on special topics if the subject is not related to a theme but is of great interest.

Other important information

Decisions regarding publication are made by the *EL* editorial staff. ASCD reserves the right to reject material, whether solicited or otherwise, if it lacks quality or timeliness. ASCD offers no remuneration for articles.

What We Look for

- Brief (1,500-2,500 words) manuscripts that are helpful to practicing K-12 educators.
- Articles in which the writer speaks directly to the reader in an informal, conversational style.
- Treatments of the theme that are interesting and insightful.
- Practical examples that illustrate key points.
- Program descriptions (school, district, or state).
- Features describing research-based solutions to current problems in education.
- An emphasis on explaining and interpreting research results rather than on methodology.
- Opinion pieces that interweave experiences and ideas and debate on controversial subjects.
- International contributions.

We are not looking for term papers or reviews of literature, and we rarely publish conventional research reports. We cannot review drafts and usually do not find query letters helpful; we prefer to read the manuscript. While your article is under review with us, we ask that you not submit it to another publication or post it on a Web site, even your own.

How to Prepare Your Manuscript. . .

- Double-space all copy and leave generous margins.
- Number all pages.
- Indicate the number of words in the manuscript, including references and figures.
- Include your name, address, phone number, fax number, and e-mail address on the cover sheet only.

Please do not single-space or otherwise crowd your pages. We prefer manuscripts that look like manuscripts, not like typeset articles from desktop publishing.

We use the reference style outlined by the American Psychological Association. Cite references in the text like this (Jones, 2000) and list them in bibliographic form at the end of the article. For other matters of style, refer to *The Chicago Manual of Style, Merriam- Webster's Collegiate Dictionary,* and the *Publication Manual of the American Psychological Association.*

Authors bear full responsibility for the accuracy of citations, quotations, figures, and facts.

How to Submit Your Manuscript

Send two copies of your manuscript. Articles will not be returned unless you include a self-addressed, stamped 9 x 12 envelope. Please do not fax or e-mail your manuscript unless requested to do so. You can expect to receive a postcard telling you that the manuscript has arrived; a letter from an editor should follow within eight weeks.

If you discover a small error after mailing your manuscript, please do not send a correction; small errors can be corrected in the editing process.

What Happens Next

If your manuscript is accepted, even provisionally, it enters the pool of manuscripts on hand for a particular theme issue (or for use as a special topic). When we assemble a particular issue, we review all manuscripts to make selections for the table of contents. We consider many factors, such as the balance of perspectives, locations, grade levels, and topics. You will be notified if your manuscript is selected for the final table of contents.

All manuscript selections are tentative until we go to press. During the editing and layout process, we may have to make last-minute space adjustments and thus, very occasionally, must omit an article we had provisionally accepted.

What to do About Computer Disks

We edit electronically, so if your manuscript is accepted, even provisionally, we will ask for an electronic version, either on disk or through e-mail. We can use IBM-compatible or Mac disks but not Apple. Write on the disk both the computer platform and the word processing program used. Be specific: Include version numbers where applicable. Please also indicate on the disk your last name and the file name of your manuscript. If your disk has a high-density format, please indicate this as well.

How to Survive the Editing Process

If your manuscript is selected for the issue's table of contents, it is assigned to a staff editor, who will shepherd it through the editing and layout process. The style requirements of Educational Leadership--as well as space limitations--often dictate heavy editing, and we appreciate collaboration with the authors in the process.

You will receive an edited version of your manuscript for your review, correction, and approval. At this time you will have a chance to correct errors, answer our queries, and update any information. Please do not retype the manuscript! Just mark your corrections directly on the manuscript, and mail or fax it back to us. If you have insertions, please type or write them on a separate piece of paper and indicate on the manuscript where to insert them.

We will ask you to certify that the article, in whole or in part, has not been previously published, in print or in electronic form, including on the Internet. When you receive the edited version of your manuscript, you will also receive a transfer of copyright form, which includes permission for ASCD to use your article online and in other electronic formats. Please sign and return the original form by first-class mail, not by fax, as soon as possible.

About Artwork and Photographs

We appreciate receiving any photographs and artwork related to your manuscript. We consider photos (color or black-and white), slides, and examples of student work for publication. Send photographs and artwork only when we request them. Send photos to us by overnight mail. We will return artwork or photos that we request.

Authors are responsible for ensuring that all persons in each photograph have given their permission for the photograph to be published; they are also responsible for attaining permission to use all other artwork, such as student work. Please include the name of the photographer or the source so that we may give proper credit; on the back of each item, tape a small piece of paper with your name and address. (Do not write directly on the back of the photo.) And please add a note to explain photos and artwork, including the name and location of the school. This information helps us when we write captions.

When Your Article Comes Out

As soon as the issue is off the press--about the first of each month of issue--we'll send your complimentary copies. Authors receive five copies; book reviewers, one copy. We'll also send an author's feedback form to gather your comments about our work. Fill out that form and return it quickly. Then it's time to arrange your autograph party!

Please send manuscripts to: Marge Scherer, Editor, Educational Leadership, ASCD, 1703 N. Beauregard St., Alexandria, VA 22311-1714

Educational Measurement: Issues and Practice

SUBMISSION PROCESS:
Postal Submission Only

<table>
<tr>
<td>

CONTACT INFORMATION:

Susan M. Brookhart, Editor
School of Education
Duquesne University
600 Forbes Avenue
Pittsburgh, PA 15282 USA

Phone:
  406-442-8257

Email:
  brookhart@duq.edu
  emip@duq.edu
  susanbrookhart@bresnan.net

Website:
  http://www.blackwellpublishing.com/jour
  nal.asp?ref=0731-1745&site=1

</td>
<td>

REVIEW PROCESS:

Type of Review:	Blind Review
No. External Reviewers:	3
No. InHouse Reviewers:	0
Acceptance Rate:	21-30%
Time to Review:	4 - 6 Months
Reviewer's Comments:	Yes
Invited Articles:	0-5%
Fees to Publish:	$0.00 US$
Fees to Review:	$0.00 US$

</td>
</tr>
<tr>
<td>

PUBLICATION GUIDELINES:

Manuscript Style:
  American Psychological Association

Manuscript Length:
  21-25

Copies Required:
  Five

</td>
<td>

CIRCULATION DATA:

Reader:
  Academics, Administrators

Frequency of Issue:
  Quarterly

Sponsor/Publisher:
  National Council of Measurement in
  Education / Blackwell Publishing, Inc.

</td>
</tr>
</table>

MANUSCRIPT TOPICS:
Tests, Measurement & Evaluation

MANUSCRIPT GUIDELINES/COMMENTS:

Statement of Editorial Policy
Educational Measurement: Issues and Practice publishes articles that illuminate issues in educational measurement and inform the practice of educational measurement. *EM:IP* is aimed at practitioners and users of tests and includes information about proven practices in testing, news of interest to the educational measurement community, and organizational news of NCME. Not as technical as *Journal of Educational Measurement*, *EM:IP* has as its primary purpose promoting a better understanding of and reasoned debate on timely measurement issues of practical importance to educators and the public.

EM:IP seeks manuscripts that deal with measurement issues of concern to practitioners and academics, applications of measurement techniques in educational settings, and exemplary practices. Examples of manuscripts appropriate for *EM:IP* include those dealing with specific measurement techniques for various educational objectives or controversial measurement issues;

surveys of practices and changes in practices; and public critiques of testing and test use. Articles on examples of good practices in educational measurement and articles presenting contrasting views concerning the educational role of testing are welcome.

Manuscript Submission and Review Procedures

Five copies of manuscripts should be submitted. Prepare four of these for "blind" reviews by removing references to author and the author's institution. Manuscripts should be consistent with the style described in the *Publication Manual of the American Psychological Association* (5th ed., 2001). Authors should be parsimonious in the use of tables, graphs, and figures. When used, one original copy suitable for high-quality reproduction as well as four photo copies should accompany the manuscript. Avoid footnotes when possible. All manuscripts [solicited or unsolicited] that are considered for publication in the Articles section are to be sent out to at least three reviewers. Submit manuscripts to the Editor, Susan M. Brookhart, School of Education, Duquesne University, 600 Forbes Avenue, Pittsburgh, PA 15282; **brookhart@duq.edu**.

Educational Perspectives

SUBMISSION PROCESS:
Postal Submission Only

CONTACT INFORMATION:	REVIEW PROCESS:	
Hunter McEwan, Editor University of Hawaii College of Education Wist Hall 113 1176 University Avenue Honolulu, HI 96822 USA	**Type of Review:**	Editorial Review
	No. External Reviewers:	
	No. InHouse Reviewers:	
	Acceptance Rate:	
	Time to Review:	1 - 2 Months
Phone: 808-956-4242	**Reviewer's Comments:**	No
	Invited Articles:	90% +
Email: epedit@hawaii.edu	**Fees to Publish:**	$0.00 US$
	Fees to Review:	$0.00 US$
Website: www.hawaii.edu/edper/		

PUBLICATION GUIDELINES:	CIRCULATION DATA:
Manuscript Style: Chicago Manual of Style	**Reader:** Academics, Practicing Teachers
Manuscript Length: 16-20	**Frequency of Issue:** 2 Times/Year
Copies Required: One	**Sponsor/Publisher:** College of Education, University of Hawaii

MANUSCRIPT TOPICS:
Curriculum Studies; Education Management / Administration; Educational Technology Systems; General Issues in Education; Health & Physical Education; Reading; School Law; Teacher Education; Tests, Measurement & Evaluation

MANUSCRIPT GUIDELINES/COMMENTS:

When preparing a manuscript for submission to *Educational Perspectives*, the following specifications should be followed:
- Length of manuscript 3,000 to 3,500 words.
- Manuscript should be typewritten, double-spaced.
- Manuscript should be submitted using two formats: 1) a computer program which can be converted into a MacIntosh Pagemaker 6.5 application; and 2) one xeroxed copy.
- Manuscript should be documented and *Chicago Manual of Style* should be followed; footnotes and bibliography included where needed.
- Subheads are desirable.
- Suitable visual material (photographs should accompany the manuscript and should be high contrast, black and white, glossy prints, 8"x10" or contact sheets with negatives. Colored slides, 2"x2" may be requested for use as front cover).

- A brief biographical sketch of manuscript's author(s).
- Reworked speeches are acceptable. Reprints from other publications are not used.

All material (manuscript, photography and biography) should be submitted to:
    The Editor; Educational Perspectives
    College of Education; University of Hawaii
    Wist Hall, Room 113
    1776 University Avenue; Honolulu HI 96822

Educational Policy

SUBMISSION PROCESS:
Electronic Submission Only **via Online Portal**
http://www.sagepub.com/journalsProdManSub.nav?prodId=Journal200936

CONTACT INFORMATION:	REVIEW PROCESS:	
Ana M. Martinez Aleman, Editor Boston College School of Education Campion Hall Chestnut Hill, MA 02467 USA	**Type of Review:**	Blind Review
	No. External Reviewers:	2
	No. InHouse Reviewers:	1
	Acceptance Rate:	19-20%
Phone:	**Time to Review:**	3 Months
617-552-1760	**Reviewer's Comments:**	Yes
	Invited Articles:	0-5%
Email:		
journal.edpolicy@bc.edu	**Fees to Publish:**	$0.00 US$
Website:	**Fees to Review:**	$0.00 US$
http://epx.sagepub.com/		

PUBLICATION GUIDELINES:	CIRCULATION DATA:
Manuscript Style: American Psychological Association	**Reader:** Academics, Administrators
Manuscript Length: 26-30	**Frequency of Issue:** 5 Times/Year
Copies Required: Electronic Only	**Sponsor/Publisher:** Sage Publications

MANUSCRIPT TOPICS:
Education Management / Administration; Education Policy; Educational Technology Systems; Elementary / Early Childhood; Teacher Education; Urban Education, Cultural / Non-Traditional

MANUSCRIPT GUIDELINES/COMMENTS:

Educational Policy provides an interdisciplinary forum for improving education in primary and secondary schools, as well as in higher education and non-school settings. *Educational Policy* blends the best of educational research with the world of practice, making it a valuable resource for educators, policy makers, administrators, researcher, teachers, and graduate students. *Educational Policy* is concerned with the practical consequences of policy decisions and alternatives. It examines the relationship between educational policy and educational practice, and sheds new light on important debates and controversies within the field. You'll find that *Educational Policy* is an insightful compilation of ideas, strategies, and analyses for improving our educational system.

A regular feature is the "Reviewing Policy" section that presents a short essay by Michael W. Apple, focusing on significant new books or documents that deserve critical attention.

Articles. Essays present thought-provoking, original - and often controversial - analyses for improving educational policy.

Special Issues. Single-theme issues provide in-depth coverage of topics of current concern.

Annual Index. Alphabetical listings of authors and titles provide quick and easy reference to valuable information and ideas.

"Educational Policy is unique among the journals in this field. The articles address genuine issues of policy and frequently succeed in doing so in an international context. It is always a pleasure and a profit to read a journal with so clear a sense of direction." Harry Judge, *University of Oxford*

"Educational Policy is one of the most important and impressive journals in the field. It is essential reading for anyone concerned with the realities of education." Michael W. Apple, *University of Wisconsin, Madison*

Submission Guidelines
Manuscripts should be typewritten, double-spaced, and on one side only of white 8 ½ x 11 paper. Leave generous margins on all four sides of the page. Article title, author's name, professional title, and institutional affiliation on a separate, removable cover sheet. Only the article title should appear on subsequent pages to facilitate blind review. Authors should closely follow the *Publication Manual of the American Psychological Association* (5th edition). Tabular material should be kept to a minimum -- three to four at most. (Authors will be asked to provide camera-ready copy for charts and graphs of articles accepted for publication.) Include a 100-word abstract, as well as a listing of a few important key words, with each article. Submit online at: **http://www.sagepub.com/ journalsProdManSub.nav?prodId=Journal200936**. Editors can be contacted at Educational Policy, School of Education, 207 Campion Hall, Boston College, Chestnut Hill, MA 02467, **journal.edpolicy@bc.edu**.

Educational Psychologist

<table>
<tr><td colspan="2" align="center">SUBMISSION PROCESS:

Electronic Submission Only
via Online Portal

www.editorialmanager.com/ep</td></tr>
</table>

CONTACT INFORMATION:

Gale M. Sinatra, Editor
University of Nevada, Las Vegas
Educational Psychology
Las Vegas, NV 89154 USA

Phone:
  702-895-2605

Email:
  sinatra@unlv.nevada.edu
  gale.sinatra@unlv.edu
  edpsy@unlv.nevada.edu

Website:
  www.editorialmanager.com/ep

REVIEW PROCESS:

Type of Review:	Blind Review
No. External Reviewers:	2
No. InHouse Reviewers:	1
Acceptance Rate:	21-30%
Time to Review:	2 - 3 Months
Reviewer's Comments:	Yes
Invited Articles:	31-50%
Fees to Publish:	$0.00 US$
Fees to Review:	$0.00 US$

PUBLICATION GUIDELINES:

Manuscript Style:
  American Psychological Association

Manuscript Length:
  30+

Copies Required:
  Electronic Only

CIRCULATION DATA:

Reader:
  Academics

Frequency of Issue:
  Quarterly

Sponsor/Publisher:
  American Psychological Association /
Taylor & Francis, Ltd.

MANUSCRIPT TOPICS:
Educational Psychology

MANUSCRIPT GUIDELINES/COMMENTS:

Editorial Scope
Educational Psychologist (*EP*) invites scholarly essays, reviews, critiques, and articles of a theoretical/conceptual nature that contribute to our understanding of the issues, problems, and research associated with the field of educational psychology. Articles representing all aspects of educational psychology are encouraged. *EP*'s Impact Index of 2.892 (according to Journal Citation Reports) ranks it second of 38 journals in the discipline and related areas. *EP* does not publish articles whose primary purpose is to report the method and results of an empirical study. *EP* uses an online submission and review system through which authors submit manuscripts and track their progress. Please visit **www.editorialmanager.com/ep** for information and instructions regarding registration and manuscript submission.

Audience. Educational Psychologists, researchers, teachers, administrators, and policymakers.

Submission of Manuscripts. Manuscripts must be prepared in accordance with the following instructions.

Follow APA Style. Authors should follow the *Publication Manual of the American Psychological Association* (5th ed.) in preparing manuscripts for submission to this journal. All manuscripts must be prefaced by an abstract of 100-150 words on a separate sheet. All manuscript pages, including reference lists and tables, must be typed double-spaced. All figures must be camera ready. Authors should comply with "Guidelines to Reduce Bias in Language" as printed in the *Publication Manual*. Manuscripts that fail to conform to APA-style guidelines will be returned to the author(s).

Prepare For Blind Peer Review. All articles appearing in *EP* are peer reviewed. Because the reviewers have agreed to participate in a blind reviewing system, authors submitting manuscripts are requested to include a cover sheet that shows the title of the manuscript, the names of the authors, the authors' institutional affiliations, the mailing address, the date the manuscript is submitted, and a running head. The first page of the manuscript should omit the authors' names and affiliations but should include the title of the manuscript and the date it is submitted. Footnotes containing information pertaining to the authors' identities or affiliations should be placed on separate pages. Every effort should be made by authors to see that the manuscript itself contains no clues to their identities.

Screen for Appropriateness. By submitting manuscripts to *Educational Psychologist*, authors are confirming that the manuscripts have not been published and are not under consideration for publication elsewhere. Prior to submission, authors should determine whether their manuscripts correspond to the journal's statement of purpose--to publish essays, critiques, and articles of a theoretical/conceptual nature that contribute to our understanding of the issues, problems, and research associated with the field of educational psychology. Articles consistent with the journal's purpose include critical, integrative reviews of educational psychology research; conceptual or theoretical syntheses or analyses of educational psychology research; scientifically documented digests of educational psychology research relevant to policy issues; and documented, scholarly essays of general interest to the educational psychology community. Consistent with the journal's mission to serve as a forum for important ideas in educational psychology, articles of varying lengths and covering all aspects of educational psychology will be considered, including articles focusing on implications for educational theory, research, practice, or policy. Articles that report mainly the results of an empirical study (e.g., would be appropriate for the *Journal of Educational Psychology*) or articles that are intended mainly as practical guides (without research documentation) are inappropriate for *EP* and will be returned to the authors. In addition to publishing regular articles, the journal publishes special issues that are devoted to important themes in educational psychology and keynote reviews with published peer commentary. Authors interested in the latter formats are requested to contact the editor prior to submitting a proposal for a special issue or keynote review.

Follow Copyright Laws. Authors are responsible for obtaining and providing written permission from copyright owners for reprinting previously published illustrations, tables, or lengthy quotes (500 or more words). Authors are responsible for the accuracy of the material in their manuscripts.

Submission of Manuscripts. EP is now using an on-line submission and review system, Editoral Manager, through which authors submit manuscripts and track their progress up until acceptance for publication. Authors will enter pertinent information into the sytem and submit the following files: (a) Cover letter file, (b) Manuscript file, containing the entire text of the article, including abstract, all text, references, footnotes, and appendices. Figures and tables may either be included at the end of this file or submitted separately, (c) Figures and tables, which may be submitted as separate files if desired. Please log on to **www.editorialmanager.com/ep** for information and instructions regarding registration and manuscript submission. After a manuscript is accepted for publication, authors are asked to submit a final version of the manuscript. Files are copyedited and typeset into page proofs. Authors are responsible for reading proofs, correcting errors and answering editors' queries.

Educational Psychology

SUBMISSION PROCESS:
Electronic Submission Preferred via EMail
ed.psych@speced.sed.mq.edu.au

CONTACT INFORMATION:	REVIEW PROCESS:	
Kevin Wheldall, Editor Macquarie University Special Education Centre Sydney, NSW 2109 Australia	**Type of Review:**	Blind Review
	No. External Reviewers: **No. InHouse Reviewers:**	2 1
Phone: +61 2 9850 9621	**Acceptance Rate:** **Time to Review:** **Reviewer's Comments:** **Invited Articles:**	45% 2 - 3 Months Yes 11-20%
Email: ed.psych@speced.sed.mq.edu.au		
Website: http://www.tandf.co.uk/journals/ 01443410	**Fees to Publish:** **Fees to Review:**	$0.00 US$ $0.00 US$

PUBLICATION GUIDELINES:	CIRCULATION DATA:
Manuscript Style: American Psychological Association	**Reader:** Academics
Manuscript Length: 11-30	**Frequency of Issue:** Bi-Monthly
Copies Required: Three or 1 Electronic	**Sponsor/Publisher:** Routledge, Taylor & Francis, Ltd.

MANUSCRIPT TOPICS:
Educational Psychology

MANUSCRIPT GUIDELINES/COMMENTS:

Aims & Scope
This journal provides an international forum for the discussion and rapid dissemination of research findings in psychology relevant to education. The journal places particular emphasis on the publishing of papers reporting applied research based on experimental and behavioural studies. Reviews of relevant areas of literature also appear from time to time. The aim of the journal is to be a primary source for articles dealing with the psychological aspects of education ranging from pre-school to tertiary provision and the education of children with special needs. The prompt publication of high-quality articles is the journal's first priority. All contributions are submitted 'blind' to at least two independent referees before acceptance for publication.

Instructions for Authors
Note to Authors. Please make sure your contact address information is clearly visible on the outside of all packages you are sending to Editors.

Papers accepted become the copyright of the Journal, unless otherwise specifically agreed.

Manuscripts, ideally between 2000 and 8000 words, should be sent electronically to the Editors at **Ed.psych@speced.sed.mq.edu.au**. Where this is not possible, 3 copies of the article, with any illustrations, should be submitted to: Professor Kevin Wheldall, Macquarie University Special Education Centre, Macquarie University, Sydney, NSW 2109, Australia. Articles supplied as hard copy should be printed on one side of the paper, double spaced, with ample margins adhering strictly to the style guide of the American Psychological Association (APA) (fifth edition). Authors should use the Oxford Dictionary as a guide for spelling.

A cover sheet should bear the title of the contribution, name(s) of the author(s) and the address where the work was carried out. A second sheet should again give the title of the piece (without the name(s) of the author(s), to facilitate 'blind' refereeing), together with an abstract of 100 - 150 words. The full postal address, email address and fax number of the author who will check proofs and receive correspondence and offprints should also be included. All pages should be numbered. Footnotes to the text should be avoided.

Statistics. Given the experimental remit of this journal, it is expected that indications of effect size will be included by authors, where possible, so as to allow readers to form a judgement as to the importance of any experimental findings reported.

To download a Word template for this journal, please visit our website at: **http://www.tandf.co.uk/journals/authors/edstyleb.dot** .

For further information on electronic submission, including information on accepted file types, visit our website at: **http://www.tandf.co.uk/journals/authors/electronic_edu.asp**.

Tables and captions to illustrations. Tables must be printed out on separate sheets and not included as part of the text. The captions to illustrations should be gathered together and also printed out on a separate sheet. Tables and figures should be numbered separately. The approximate position of tables and figures should be indicated in the manuscript. Captions should include keys to symbols.

Figures. Please supply one set of artwork in a finished form, suitable for reproduction, since figures will not normally be redrawn by the publisher.

References should be indicated in the typescript by giving the author's name, with the year of publication in parentheses, as detailed in the APA style guide. If several papers by the same author(s) and from the same year are cited, a, b, c, etc. should be put after the year of publication. The references should be listed in full at the end of the paper in standard APA format. For example:

Adams, M. J. (1990). *Beginning to read: Thinking and learning about print*. Cambridge, MA: MIT Press.

Kameenui, E. J., Simmons, D. C., Baker, S., Chard, D. J., Dickson, S. V., Gunn, B., Smith, S. B., Sprick, M., & Lin, S-J. (1998). Effective strategies in teaching beginning reading. In E. J. Kameenui & D. C. Simmons (Eds.), *Effective teaching strategies that accommodate diverse learners*. (pp. 45-70; 194-196). New Jersey: Prentice Hall.

Stanovich, K. E.(1986). Matthew effects in reading: Some consequences of individual differences in the acquisition of literacy. *Reading Research Quarterly*, 21, 360-407.

If you have any further questions about the style for this journal, please submit your questions using the Style Queries form at our website: **http://www.tandf.co.uk/journals/authors/style queries.asp**.

Acceptance. Upon acceptance of the paper for publication, authors will be required to resubmit their article to the editors on disk, in either PC or Apple Macintosh formats, preferably using the Microsoft Word program.

Proofs will be sent to authors if there is sufficient time to do so. They should be corrected and returned to the Joint Editors within three days. Major alterations to the text cannot be accepted.

Early Electronic Offprints. Corresponding authors can now receive their article by e-mail as a complete PDF. This allows the author to print up to 50 copies, free of charge, and disseminate them to colleagues. In many cases this facility will be available up to two weeks prior to publication. Or, alternatively, corresponding authors will receive the traditional 50 offprints. A copy of the journal will be sent by post to all corresponding authors after publication. Additional copies of the journal can be purchased at the author's preferential rate of £15.00/$25.00 per copy.

Copyright. It is a condition of publication that authors assign copyright or licence the publication rights in their articles, including abstracts, to Taylor & Francis. This enables us to ensure full copyright protection and to disseminate the article, and of course the Journal, to the widest possible readership in print and electronic formats as appropriate. Authors may, of course, use the article elsewhere after publication without prior permission from Taylor & Francis, provided that acknowledgement is given to the Journal as the original source of publication, and that Taylor & Francis is notified so that our records show that its use is properly authorised. Authors retain a number of other rights under the Taylor & Francis rights policies documents. These policies are referred to at **www.tandf.co.uk/journals/authorrights.pdf** for full details. Authors are themselves responsible for obtaining permission to reproduce copyright material from other sources.

Educational Psychology in Practice

SUBMISSION PROCESS:

**Postal & Electronic Submission Accepted
via EMail**

stephanie.james@highland.gov.uk

CONTACT INFORMATION:

Stephanie James, Editor
Area Principal Psychologist
Highland Council
Camaghael Hostel
Camaghael
Fort William, PH33 7ND UK

Phone:
01397 707350

Email:
stephanie.james@highland.gov.uk

Website:
http://www.tandf.co.uk/journals/titles/026
67363.asp

REVIEW PROCESS:

Type of Review:	Blind Review
No. External Reviewers:	0
No. InHouse Reviewers:	2
Acceptance Rate:	50%
Time to Review:	Over 6 Months
Reviewer's Comments:	Yes
Invited Articles:	0-5%
Fees to Publish:	$0.00 US$
Fees to Review:	$0.00 US$

PUBLICATION GUIDELINES:

Manuscript Style:
See Manuscript Guidelines

Manuscript Length:
800-6000 Words

Copies Required:
Three

CIRCULATION DATA:

Reader:
, Applied Educational Psychologists

Frequency of Issue:
Quarterly

Sponsor/Publisher:
Association of Educational
Psychologists / Taylor & Francis, Ltd.

MANUSCRIPT TOPICS:
Education Management / Administration; Educational Psychology; Elementary / Early Childhood; Gifted Children; Reading; Secondary / Adolescent Studies; Special Education

MANUSCRIPT GUIDELINES/COMMENTS:

Aims & Scope
The defining feature of *Educational Psychology in Practice* is that it aims to publish refereed articles representing theory, research and practice which is of relevance to practising educational psychologists in the UK and beyond. In its focus on applied psychology it occupies an important complementary position to those journals which emphasise the experimental work of academic psychologists. Whilst the majority of articles submitted to the journal are written by practising psychologists in the UK, submissions are welcomed from outside the profession and from outside the UK. The journal promotes an interdisciplinary approach, reflected in articles which report major pieces of research, debate issues, detail project evaluations, note research, and describe aspects of professional practice. Content also includes book and software reviews, letters, and brief resource updates. *Educational Psychology in Practice* is the major publication of the Association of

Educational Psychologists, the professional association for over 2000 educational psychologists in England, Wales and Northern Ireland.

Instructions for Authors

Note to Authors. Please make sure your contact address information is clearly visible on the **outside** of all packages you are sending to Editors.

Manuscripts. Authors are invited to submit articles which might fit one of five broad headings, although these headings should not be seen as exclusive: Research or review articles of 2,000 to 6,000 words (about 5 to 16 typewritten A4 pages); Articles reporting research in brief, 1,500 to 2,000 words (about 4 to 5 typewritten pages); Research notes of 800 to 1,000 words (about 2 to 3 typewritten pages); Practice articles of 1,500 to 2,000 words; Articles reflecting on practice, 1,500 to 2,000 words.

Manuscripts for consideration should be sent to: Stephanie James, Editor, Educational Psychology in Practice, Highland Council Psychological Service, Camaghael Hostel, Camaghael, Fort William, PH33 7ND, UK e-mail: **stephanie.james@highland.gov.uk**

All articles are refereed anonymously by two members of the editorial board. Articles should be of direct relevance to the theory, research and practice of educational psychologists. Articles should be original work, where appropriate should acknowledge any significant contribution by others, and should not have been accepted for publication elsewhere. Authors should confirm that clearance has been obtained from a relevant senior officer of the LEA if the article concerns the policies and practices of the LEA.

Books & software for review should be sent to: Dev Sharma, Book and Software Review Editor, Educational Psychology in Practice, London Borough of Newham, Educational Psychology Service, Broadway House, 322 High Street, Stratford, London E15 1AJ, UK.

Unless otherwise stated, copyright is vested in the Association of Educational Psychologists. Authors are responsible for obtaining any written permission that may be required by copyright law to quote material that has appeared or is about to appear in another publication.

Please type on one side of A4, with double spacing and adequate margins, without justifying lines on the right margin. The title should be on page 1 and not exceed 10 words (50 letters), and should be followed by a summary of not more than 100 words. Since articles are refereed anonymously, please list the name(s) of the author(s) under the title on a separate sheet of paper. To facilitate communication with readers and for receipt of proofs, please enclose a separate sheet which lists forename(s), family name(s), current role(s) and address for correspondence. The main text should be broken up into sections so that after about every 6 paragraphs there is a subheading of no more than half-a-line of print; paragraphs themselves should not be overlong.

All pages should be numbered. Footnotes to the text should be avoided wherever this is reasonably possible.

Style and Use of Language. Care must be taken to use language which is non-sexist, non-racist and non-discriminatory. On this matter, the Journal follows the *British Psychological Society Style Guide* and the *Publication Manual of the American Psychological Association*.

Electronic Submission. Authors should send the final, revised version of their articles in both hard copy paper and electronic disk forms. It is essential that the hard copy (paper) version **exactly** matches the material on disk. Please print out the hard copy from the disk you are sending. Submit the three printed copies of the final version with the disk to the journal's editorial office. Save all files on a standard 3.5-inch high-density disk. We prefer to receive disks in Microsoft work in a PC format, but can translate from most other common word-processing programs as well as Macs. Please specify which program you have used. Do not save your files as 'text only', or 'read only'.

Tables and captions to illustrations. Tables must be typed out on separate sheets and not included as part of the text. The captions to illustrations should be gathered together and also typed out on a separate sheet. Tables should be numbered by Roman numerals and figures by Arabic numerals. The approximate position of tables and figures should be indicated in the manuscript. Captions should include keys to symbols.

Figures. Please supply one set of artwork in a finished form, suitable for reproduction.

References should follow the American Psychological Association system, with the only exception that authors' names should be presented with roman letters, upper and lower case i.e. they should be indicated in the typescript by giving the author's names, with the year of publication in parentheses, e.g. Smith (1994); or if there are more than two authors - Smith, *et al.* (1994). If several papers from the same author (s) and from the same year are cited, (a), (b), (c), etc. should be listed in full alphabetically at the end of the paper on a separate sheet in the following standard form:

For article
Gale, A. (1991). The school as an organisation: new roles for psychologists in education. *Educational Psychology in Practice*, 7(2), 67-73.

For book
Conoley, J.C. & Conoley, C.W. (1992). *School Consultation: practice and training* (2nd edn). Boston, MA: Allyn & Bacon.

For chapter in edited book
Labram, A. (1992). The Educational Psychologist as consultant. In S. Wolfendale *et al.* (Eds), *The Profession and Practice of Educational Psychology: future directions*. London: Cassell.

Titles of journals should **not** be abbreviated.

If you have any further questions about the style for this journal, please submit your questions using the Style Queries form at: **http://www.tandf.co.uk/journals/authors/stylequeries.asp**.

Proofs will be sent to the authors if there is sufficient time to do so. They should be corrected and returned to the editor within three days. Major alterations to the text cannot be accepted.

Early Electronic Offprints. Corresponding authors can now receive their article by e-mail as a complete PDF. This allows the author to print up to 50 copies, free of charge, and disseminate them to colleagues. In many cases this facility will be available up to two weeks prior to publication. Or, alternatively, corresponding authors will receive the traditional 50 offprints. A copy of the journal will be sent by post to all corresponding authors after publication. Additional copies of the journal can be purchased at the author's preferential rate of £15.00/$25.00 per copy.

Copyright. It is a condition of publication that authors assign copyright or licence the publication rights in their articles, including abstracts, to the Association of Educational Psychologists. This enables us to ensure full copyright protection and to disseminate the article, and of course the Journal, to the widest possible readership in print and electronic formats as appropriate. Authors may, of course, use the article elsewhere after publication without prior permission from Taylor & Francis, provided that acknowledgement is given to the Journal as the original source of publication, and that Taylor & Francis is notified so that our records show that its use is properly authorised. Authors retain a number of other rights under the Taylor & Francis rights policies documents. These policies are referred to at **www.tandf.co.uk/journals/authorrights.pdf** for full details. Authors are themselves responsible for obtaining permission to reproduce copyright material from other sources.

Educational Psychology Review

SUBMISSION PROCESS:

Electronic Submission Only
via Online Portal

http://edpr.edmgr.com

CONTACT INFORMATION:	REVIEW PROCESS:	
Daniel H. Robinson, Editor Department of Educational Psychology University of Texas at Austin 1 University Station D5800 Austin, TX 78712-0383	**Type of Review:**	Blind Review
	No. External Reviewers: **No. InHouse Reviewers:**	3+ 0
	Acceptance Rate:	11-20%
Phone: 512-471-0683	**Time to Review:** **Reviewer's Comments:** **Invited Articles:**	1 - 2 Months Yes 21-30%
Email: dan.robinson@mail.utexas.edu	**Fees to Publish:** **Fees to Review:**	$0.00 US$ $0.00 US$
Website: http://www.springerlink.com/		

PUBLICATION GUIDELINES:	CIRCULATION DATA:
Manuscript Style: American Psychological Association	**Reader:** Academics, Educators
Manuscript Length: Any	**Frequency of Issue:** Quarterly
Copies Required: Electronic Only	**Sponsor/Publisher:** Springer

MANUSCRIPT TOPICS:
Educational Psychology; Educational Technology Systems; Learning; Motivation; Reading

MANUSCRIPT GUIDELINES/COMMENTS:

Description
Educational Psychology Review is an international forum for the publication of peer-reviewed integrative review articles, special thematic issues, reflections or comments on previous research or new research directions, replication studies, interviews, and research-based advice for practitioners - all pertaining to the field of educational psychology. All publications provide breadth of coverage appropriate to a wide readership in educational psychology and sufficient depth to inform specialists in that area.

General
In general, the journal follows the recommendations of the 2001 *Publication Manual of the American Psychological Association* (Fifth Edition), and it is suggested that contributors refer to this publication.

Manuscript Submission

Manuscripts should be submitted using the online portal: **http://edpr.edmgr.com**. Questions should be directed to the Editor: Daniel H. Robinson, Department of Educational Psychology, 1 University Station D5800, University of Texas at Austin, Austin, TX 78712-0383, **dan.robinson@ mail.utexas.edu**.

It is strongly recommended that prospective authors contact the Editor before preparing their contributions, to ensure there is no significant overlap with other manuscripts in progress and to determine appropriateness for the journal.

Copyright

Submission is a representation that the manuscript has not been published previously and is not currently under consideration for publication elsewhere. A statement transferring copyright from the authors (or their employers, if they hold the copyright) to Springer Science+Business Media, Inc. will be required before the manuscript can be accepted for publication. The Editor will supply the necessary forms for this transfer. Such a written transfer of copyright, which previously was assumed to be implicit in the act of submitting a manuscript, is necessary under the U.S. Copyright Law in order for the publisher to carry through the dissemination of research results and reviews as widely and effectively as possible.

References

List references alphabetically at the end of the paper and refer to them in the text by name and year in parentheses.

Page Charges

The journal makes no page charges. Reprints are available to authors, and order forms with the current price schedule are sent with proofs.

Educational Research and Evaluation: An Int'l Journal on Theory and Practice

SUBMISSION PROCESS:
Postal & Electronic Submission Required **via EMail** **M.P.C.van.der.werf@ppsw.rug.nl**

CONTACT INFORMATION:	REVIEW PROCESS:	

Greetje van der Werf, Editor-in-Chief
Educational Research and Evaluation
Lenderink, GION, University of Groningen
PO Box 1286
9701 BG Groningen
The Netherlands
 	
Phone:
 	
Email:
  M.P.C.van.der.werf@rug.nl
 	
Website:
  www.tandf.co.uk/journals/titles/13803611
  .asp
	Type of Review:	Blind Review

	No. External Reviewers:	2
	No. InHouse Reviewers:	1
	Acceptance Rate:	21-30%
	Time to Review:	1 - 2 Months
	Reviewer's Comments:	Yes
	Invited Articles:	11-20%
	Fees to Publish:	$0.00 US$
	Fees to Review:	$0.00 US$

PUBLICATION GUIDELINES:	CIRCULATION DATA:

Manuscript Style:
  See Manuscript Guidelines
 	
Manuscript Length:
  5000-8000 words
 	
Copies Required:
  Four
	Reader:
	  Academics
	
	Frequency of Issue:
	  6 Times/Year
	
	Sponsor/Publisher:
	  Routledge, Taylor & Francis, Ltd.

MANUSCRIPT TOPICS:

Bilingual / E.S.L.; Curriculum Studies; Education Management / Administration; Educational Psychology; Educational Technology Systems; Health & Physical Education; Higher Education; Rural Education & Small Schools; Special Education; Teacher Education; Tests, Measurement & Evaluation; Urban Education, Cultural / Non-Traditional

MANUSCRIPT GUIDELINES/COMMENTS:

Aims & Scope

Educational Research and Evaluation (*ERE*) publishes research relating to the practice of education. Its purpose is to provide an outlet for the findings of educational research from many perspectives, national contexts, and methodologies.

The journal places few limitations on content, focus or methods used in the articles, as long as they include disciplined inquiry into important issues of educational practice. *ERE* is international in content, perspectives, and readership.

ERE publishes papers on:
Fundamental research such as:
- educational and cognitive psychology,
- sociology,
- classroom management,
- instructional behaviour of teachers.

Design issues such as how to develop:
- a curriculum
- a school organization
- a textbook
- a national curriculum.

Evaluation issues such as:
- The performances of students, schools, and the system as a whole.
- Evaluation of policy and practices in education
- Research with respect to educational effectiveness

The journal invites several types of contributions on all school levels, from (pre-) primary to tertiary education: reports on research, replications of important previous work, critical, integrated theoretical and methodological contributions and review articles. The manuscripts can have different theoretical perspectives and also show different methodological approaches, quantitative as well as qualitative.

Instructions for Authors
Papers should be original. The editor prefers to receive manuscripts by email. If this is not possible, please send four copies of the complete text together with a floppy disk to the Editor-in Chief or to one of the Regional Editors: *Editor-in-Chief:* Dr. M.P.C. van der Werf, GION Groningen Institute for Educational Research, University of Groningen, Postbus 1286, 9701 BG Groningen, The Netherlands. Tel. +31 50 3636657. E-mail: **M.P.C.van.der.werf@ppsw.rug.nl**

REGIONAL EDITORS:
Australia and New Zealand: Dr. Paul W. Richardson, Associate Dean (Teaching), Director of Professional and Postgraduate Studies, Faculty of Education, Monash University, Clayton Victoria 3800, AUSTRALIA. Tel.: +61 3 9905 2771. E-mail: **paul.richardson@education.monash.edu.au**

Dr. Richardson is currently a Visiting Research Scientist at the University of Michigan. His postal address after August 1, 2004 will be (for 2 years):

Dr. Paul W. Richardson, University of Michigan, 610 East University, 4107 SEB, Ann Arbor, MI 48109-1259, USA. E-mail: **pwrichar@umich.edu**

Asia: Professor John Chi-kin Lee, c/o Department of Curriculum and Instruction, Faculty of Education, The Chinese University of Hong Kong, Shatin, New Territories, HONG KONG. E-mail: **jcklee@cuhk.edu.hk**

North America: Professor David M. Shannon, Professor & Coordinator of Educational Psychology, Educational Research Methodology, Auburn University, 4028 Haley Center, Auburn, AL 36849-5221, USA. Tel.: +1 334 844 3071. E-mail: **shanndm@auburn.edu**

Dr. Margaret Ross. Department of Educational Foundations, Leadership and Technology, Auburn University, 4036 Haley Center, Auburn, AL 36849-5221, USA. E-mail: **rossma1@auburn.edu**

Papers should normally be around 5000 words in length, but longer or shorter articles will be considered.

Manuscripts should be typed on one side of A4 paper with double spacing and a wide margin to the left. Four copies should be submitted, and a copy in Word format sent to the editors by email. In addition a copy should be retained by the authors. All pages should be numbered. To allow anonymous refereeing, all submissions must be properly formatted for reviewing (see *Publication Manual of the American Psychological Association*, 5th edition, 2001, for instructions). Authors' names and institutions should be typed on a separate sheet and submitted with the manuscript. The full postal and email address of the author who will check proofs and receive correspondence and offprints should also be included.

Each paper should be accompanied on separate sheets by an abstract of 100 to 150 words, and short note of biographical details for 'Notes on Contributors'. For further information on electronic submission, including information on accepted file types, please see **http://www.tandf.co.uk/ journals/authors/electronic_edu.asp.**

Tables and captions to illustrations. Tables must be typed out on separate sheets and not included as part of the text. The captions to illustrations should be gathered together and also typed out on a separate sheet. Tables and Figures should be numbered consecutively by Arabic numerals. The approximate position of tables and figures should be indicated in the manuscript. Captions should include keys to any symbols used.

Figures. Please supply one set of artwork in a finished form, suitable for reproduction. Figures will not normally be redrawn by the publisher.

Citations of other work should be limited to those strictly necessary for the argument. Any quotations should be brief, and accompanied by precise references.

References should be indicated in the typescript by giving the author's name, with the year of publication in parentheses, as detailed in the APA style guide. If several papers by the same author(s) and from the same year are cited, a, b, c, etc. should be put after the year of publication. The references should be listed in full at the end of the paper in standard APA format. For example:

For books
MMassey, W. R., & Jameson, W. M., Jr. (2001). *Organizational behavior and the new internet logic* (3rd ed.). New York: McGraw-Hill

For articles
Loughran, J., & Corrigan, D. (1995). Teaching portfolios: A strategy for developing learning and teaching in preservice education. *Teaching and Teacher Education*, 11, 565-577.

For chapters within books
Marzano, R. J. (1994). Commentary on literacy portfolios: Windows on potential. In S. H. Valencia, E. H. Hiebert, & P. P. E. Afflerbach (Eds.), *Authentic reading assessment: Practices and possibilities* (pp. 41-56). Newark, NJ: International Reading Association).

For online documents
Standler, R. (2000). *Plagiarism in colleges in the USA*. Retrieved August 6 2004 from www.rbs2.com/plag.htm

Titles of journals and names of publishers, etc. should not be abbreviated. Acronyms for the names of organisations, examinations, etc. should be preceded by the title in full.

If you have any further questions about the style for this journal, please submit your questions using the *Style Queries* form.

Proofs will be sent to authors by email if there is sufficient time to do so. They should be corrected and returned to the Publisher within three days. Major alterations to the text cannot be accepted.

Early Electronic Offprints. Corresponding authors can now receive their article by email as a complete PDF. This allows the author to print up to 50 copies, free of charge, and disseminate them to colleagues. In many cases this facility will be available up to two weeks prior to publication. Or, alternatively, corresponding authors will receive the traditional 50 offprints. A copy of the journal will be sent by post to all corresponding authors after publication. Additional copies of the journal can be purchased at the author's preferential rate of £15.00/$25.00 per copy.

Copyright. It is a condition of publication that authors assign copyright or licence the publication rights in their articles, including abstracts, to Taylor & Francis. This enables us to ensure full copyright protection and to disseminate the article, and of course the Journal, to the widest possible readership in print and electronic formats as appropriate. Authors may, of course, use the article elsewhere after publication without prior permission from Taylor & Francis, provided that acknowledgement is given to the Journal as the original source of publication, and that Taylor & Francis is notified so that our records show that its use is properly authorised. Authors retain a number of other rights under the Taylor & Francis rights policies documents. These policies are referred to at: **www.tandf.co.uk/journals/authorrights.pdf** for full details. Authors are themselves responsible for obtaining permission to reproduce copyright material from other sources.

Educational Review

SUBMISSION PROCESS:
Postal and Electronic Submission Accepted. **via EMail**
d.m.martin@bham.ac.uk

CONTACT INFORMATION:	REVIEW PROCESS:	
Deirdre Martin, Executive Editor University of Birmingham School of Education Edgbaston Birmingham, B15 2TT UK	**Type of Review:**	Blind Review
	No. External Reviewers:	1
	No. InHouse Reviewers:	1
	Acceptance Rate:	60%
Phone:	**Time to Review:**	2 - 3 Months
0121 414 4849	**Reviewer's Comments:**	No
	Invited Articles:	
Email:		
d.m.martin@bham.ac.uk	**Fees to Publish:**	$0.00 US$
Website:	**Fees to Review:**	$0.00 US$
http://www.tandf.co.uk/journals/titles/001 31911.asp		

PUBLICATION GUIDELINES:	CIRCULATION DATA:
Manuscript Style: See Manuscript Guidelines	**Reader:** Academics, Practicing Teachers, Researchers
Manuscript Length: 21-25	**Frequency of Issue:** Quarterly
Copies Required: Three	**Sponsor/Publisher:** Taylor & Francis, Ltd.

MANUSCRIPT TOPICS:

Adult Career & Vocational; Audiology / Speech Pathology; Bilingual / E.S.L.; Curriculum Studies; Education Management / Administration; Educational Psychology; Educational Technology Systems; Elementary / Early Childhood; Foreign Language; Health & Physical Education; Higher Education; Languages & Linguistics; Religious Education; Secondary / Adolescent Studies; Special Education; Teacher Education; Tests, Measurement & Evaluation; Urban Education, Cultural / Non-Traditional

MANUSCRIPT GUIDELINES/COMMENTS:

Aims & Scope

Educational Review is a leading journal for generic educational research and scholarship. For over half a century it has offered authoritative reviews of current national and international issues in schooling and education. It publishes peer-reviewed papers from international contributors which report research across a range of education fields including curriculum, inclusive and special education, educational psychology, policy, management and international and comparative education.

The editors welcome informed papers from new and established scholars which encourage and enhance academic debate. The journal offers editions which publish non-commissioned papers and themed issues which deal with a current topic in-depth. A regular feature of the journal is state-of-the-art reviews on issues across the educational spectrum. An extensive range of recently published books is reviewed. Readership is aimed at educationists, researchers, and policy makers.

Educational Review is pleased to announce the launch of an on-line archive, which has a database of contents listing from Issue 1(1),1948, up to the current edition.

Papers can be found by author(s), publication date or keyword. Visit *Educational Review* On-Line Archive at: **http://www.education.bham.ac.uk/webapps/edreview/**

For further information, please contact Saira Bejai, Editorial Assistant at: **S.V.Bejai@bham.ac.uk**

Instructions for Authors
Note to Authors. Please make sure your contact address information is clearly visible on the outside of all packages you are sending to Editors.

Articles submitted to *Educational Review* should not be under consideration by any other journal, or have been published elsewhere, and the letter accompanying the submission of any manuscript should contain a clear statement to this effect.

Three copies of manuscripts of c.4,000-6,000 words should be sent to the Editors, Educational Review, School of Education, University of Birmingham, Edgbaston, Birmingham B15 2TT, UK. Longer articles will be considered. They should be typed on one side of the paper, double spaced, with ample margins, and bear the title of the contribution, name(s) of the author(s) and the address where the work was carried out on one of the copies only. Each article should be accompanied by an abstract/summary of 100-150 words on a separate sheet. The full postal address of the author who will check proofs and receive correspondence and offprints should also be included, plus a telephone number. All pages should be numbered and the total word count of the article, including references, appendices, etc. given. Footnotes to the text should be avoided.

Electronic Submissions. Authors should send the final, revised version of their articles in both hard copy paper and electronic disk forms. It is essential that the hard copy (paper) version exactly matches the material on disk. Please print out the hard copy from the disk you are sending. Submit three printed copies of the final version with the disk to the journal's editorial office. Save all files on a standard 3.5 inch high-density disk. We prefer to receive disks in Microsoft Word in a PC format, but can translate from most other common word processing programs as well as Macs. Please specify which program you have used. Do not save your files as "text only" or "read only".

To download a Word template for this journal, please see: **http://www.tandf.co.uk/journals/authors/edstylea.dot**

Tables and captions to illustrations. Tables must be typed out on separate sheets and not included as part of the text. The captions to illustrations should be gathered together and also typed out on a separate sheet. Tables should be numbered by Roman numerals, and figures by Arabic numerals. The approximate position of tables and figures should be indicated in the manuscript. Captions should include keys to symbols.

Figures. Please supply one set of artwork in a finished form, suitable for reproduction. Figures will not normally be redrawn by the publisher.

References should be indicated in the typescript by giving the author's name, with the year of publication in parentheses. If several papers by the same author and from the same year are cited, a, b, c, etc. should be put after the year of publication. The references should be listed in full at the end of the paper in the following standard form:

For books
SCOTT, P. (1984) **The Crisis of the University** (London, Croom Helm).

For articles
CREMIN, L. A. (1983) The problematics of education in the 1980s: some reflections on the Oxford Workshop, **Oxford Review of Education**, 9, pp. 33-40.

For chapters within books
WILLIS, P. (1983) Cultural production and theories of reproduction, in: L. BARTON & S. WALKER (Eds) **Race, Class and Education** (London, Croom Helm).

Titles of journals should not be abbreviated.

If you have any further questions about the style for this journal, please submit your questions using the Style Queries form at: **http://www.tandf.co.uk/journals/authors/edstylea.dot**

Proofs will be sent to authors if there is sufficient time to do so. They should be corrected and returned to the Editor within three days. Major alterations to the text cannot be accepted.

Early Electronic Offprints. Corresponding authors can now receive their article by e-mail as a complete PDF. This allows the author to print up to 50 copies, free of charge, and disseminate them to colleagues. In many cases this facility will be available up to two weeks prior to publication. Or, alternatively, corresponding authors will receive the traditional 50 offprints. A copy of the journal will be sent by post to all corresponding authors after publication. Additional copies of the journal can be purchased at the author's preferential rate of £15.00/$25.00 per copy.

Copyright. It is a condition of publication that authors assign copyright or licence the publication rights in their articles, including abstracts, to the Editors of *Educational Review*. This enables us to ensure full copyright protection and to disseminate the article, and of course the Journal, to the widest possible readership in print and electronic formats as appropriate. Authors may, of course, use the article elsewhere after publication without prior permission from Taylor & Francis, provided that acknowledgement is given to the Journal as the original source of publication, and that Taylor & Francis is notified so that our records show that its use is properly authorised. Authors retain a number of other rights under the Taylor & Francis rights policies documents. These policies are referred to at **www.tandf.co.uk/journals/authorrights.pdf** for full details. Authors are themselves responsible for obtaining permission to reproduce copyright material from other sources.

Educational Studies: A Journal in Foundations of Education

<table>
<tr><td colspan="2" align="center">SUBMISSION PROCESS:

Electronic Submission Preferred
via EMail

rmartusew@emich.edu</td></tr>
<tr>
<td valign="top">

CONTACT INFORMATION:

Rebecca Martusewicz, Editor
Eastern Michigan University
College of Education
313 Porter
Yspilanti, MI 48197 USA

Phone:
  734-487-7210 ext. 2624

Email:
  rmartusew@emich.edu

Website:
  www.uakron.edu/aesa
  www.educationalstudies.org

</td>
<td valign="top">

REVIEW PROCESS:

Type of Review:	Blind Review
No. External Reviewers:	2
No. InHouse Reviewers:	1
Acceptance Rate:	11-20%
Time to Review:	2 - 3 Months
Reviewer's Comments:	Yes
Invited Articles:	11-20%
Fees to Publish:	$0.00 US$
Fees to Review:	$0.00 US$

</td>
</tr>
<tr>
<td valign="top">

PUBLICATION GUIDELINES:

Manuscript Style:
  Chicago Manual of Style

Manuscript Length:
  26-30

Copies Required:
  Three

</td>
<td valign="top">

CIRCULATION DATA:

Reader:
  Academics

Frequency of Issue:
  Bi-Monthly

Sponsor/Publisher:
  American Educational Studies
Association / Lawrence Erlbaum Associates,
Inc.

</td>
</tr>
</table>

MANUSCRIPT TOPICS:
Higher Education; Urban Education, Cultural / Non-Traditional

MANUSCRIPT GUIDELINES/COMMENTS:

Preparing a Manuscript
Submission Guidelines for Articles: Notes and References: Provide complete, formatted references, text citations, and notes according to *The Chicago Manual of Style*, fifteenth edition. Notes that contain only bibliographic material should be incorporated into the references.

Suggested length of articles is 25 to 30 pages, double-spaced. Include an abstract with your name and address, telephone number, and e-mail address. Send four copies of the manuscript and a disk formatted in Microsoft Word 2000 to the address below.

Take a few moments now to make certain that your manuscript is complete and that it complies with the editorial guidelines appearing in *The Chicago Manual of Style* (15th ed.). (*The Manual* is available from the University of Chicago Press, Direct Mail Department, 5801 South Ellis Avenue, Chicago, IL 60637; 773568 1550; www.press.uchicago.edu.) You may find it helpful to consult

The Author's Manuscript section appearing on pages 49 through 62 of *The Chicago Manual of Style*, the contributor information appearing in the journal, and/or the following summary of requirements for acceptable manuscripts. If you have any questions whatsoever, please ask for clarification.

Typing. Use 8 ½ x 11 in. non smear paper. Set all margins at 1 in. Type all components double spaced, including title page, abstract, text, acknowledgments, references, appendixes, tables, figure captions, and notes. Indent all paragraphs and make sure the entire manuscript is neat and readable. Use superscript numbers to cite notes; do not use the automatic function for notes; type all notes on a separate page (not at the bottom of the pages on which they are cited). Type all figure captions on a separate page.

Abstract. An abstract is required, consult the Editor or the journal for the limit on length.

Notes and References. Provide complete, formatted references, text citations, and notes according to *The Chicago Manual of Style* guidelines, chapters 15 and 16. For references, use the example on p. 648 as a guide. This is the humanities style, but dates immediately follow the authors' names. For text citations, use the examples on p. 641, 16.3, and p. 643,16.10. For notes, use the example on p. 530. Notes that contain only bibliographic material should be incorporated into the references.

Figures. Submit (a) high quality laser prints, professionally prepared black and white originals, or camera ready glossy reproductions; (b) photocopies of all figures; and (c) as many computer files for these figures as you have (see Preparing a Disk). Please note that figures appearing in the journal will look only as good as what you provide. Make sure lettering and details are crisp, clear, and large enough so that they will be legible upon reduction. (Figures are reduced in size to conserve space on the printed page.)

All hard copies for which we do not have computer files will be scanned electronically, so please avoid using gray shading or dot screens in graphs. Use solid black or white or diagonal lines to distinguish columns instead.

Make sure each figure is identified. Assess whether textual information appearing on a piece of artwork might be best presented as part of the caption; alter artwork and caption accordingly.

Permissions. *You* are responsible for all statements made in your work and for obtaining permission from the copyright owner(s) to reprint or adapt a table or figure or to reprint quotes from one source totaling 500 words or more. Write to original author(s) and publisher to request nonexclusive world rights in all languages to use the material in the article and in future print and online editions. Please note that you must obtain permission for any lines of poetry or song lyrics you quote as well as for prose, and that you will be liable for any licensing fees required for such use. Provide copies of all permissions and credit lines obtained. Attached to this letter are (a) a sample permission request form you can copy/ adapt and use to secure permissions and (b) sample credit lines from *The Chicago Manual of Style*.

Concordance of Elements. Make sure your manuscript is complete and internally consistent. Each reference must be cited in text at least once; each citation must have a corresponding reference. Likewise, each figure, table, and note must be cited; if a figure, table, or note is cited in text, the corresponding element must be included with the manuscript.

Preparing a Disk

Now is the time to submit the file (as well as an ASCII version) for copyediting and typesetting. Working with an electronic manuscript allows us to capture your keystrokes thereby maintaining the accuracy of your article and reducing the time between research and publication.

Shortening the production schedule involves combining the stages of author review of copyedited articles and subsequent review of typeset page proofs into a single review of proofs made from copyedited disk files via desktop publishing. With timely publication the concern of all involved, we assume you will (a) accept minor editorial changes that do not alter intended meanings and (b) alter page proofs only to correct errors, update publication information, and respond to editors' queries. As substantial alterations will not be made after manuscripts have been typeset, please take the time now to make sure that your manuscript and its file are complete and identical and that they represent your "final say."

Our first choice for format is MS word.

Macintosh and PC users. Submit on a high density disk containing a file in MS Word.

Other computer users. Please try to convert and transfer your file to an PC or Mac disk; then follow directions for PC or Mac users.

However you submit your electronic manuscript, please (a) let us know computer type (PC, Macintosh), word processor (including version number), and file name; and (b) make sure the content of the files exactly matches that of the printed, accepted, finalized manuscript.

In addition, if your figures were prepared using a computer and you can obtain files from which the hard copies were printed, please include these on your disk (or on additional disks if they are too large) too.

If you have any questions regarding disk preparation, please contact Steve Cestaro.

Preparing a Review

Book reviews in *Educational Studies* are an important scholarly contribution to the literature of education. Reviews are one way to help evaluate the quality of scholarship, to keep other scholars informed, and to examine important issues. A review should be looked at as the opportunity to critique scholarly work. In its own right, a review can be an original and creative contribution to scholarship. Emphasis should be given to the strengths, weaknesses, and possible implications of the work being reviewed. A careful analysis of the author's scholarship and the depth and breadth of the book is desirable. The reviewer should thus draw from her/his knowledge, experience, and individual style when writing a review.

Length. The desired length is 2,000 words; please provide a word count at the end of the text.

Format. Lay out the bibliographic information and reviewer's name at the top of the first page as in the following example:

> **Learning Together: A History of Coeducation in American Public Schools**. David Tyack and Elisabeth Hansot. New Haven, CT: Yale University Press, 1990. Pp. x, 369. $29.95; $XX.XX (Include The Cost Of A Paper Edition If There Is One).
>
> JANE J. JONES
> *University of California at Santa Cruz*

Deadline. Check with the editorial staff about the deadline for your submission. The editor reserves the right to edit your reviews received for publication and to reject or return for revision reviews considered wanting. You will receive one copy of the issue in which your review appears.

Taking Action

In a nutshell, now is the time for you to (a) make sure your manuscript is formatted correctly, (b) check on permissions, and (c) send the finalized manuscript printout and disk to the Editor.

We hope this letter has been informative, and we look forward to working with you. If you think of a way we can improve the production process, by all means let us know. We're here to help.

Rebecca A. Martusewicz, Editor, Educational Studies, 313 Porter, Eastern Michigan University, Yspilanti, MI 48197; (734) 487 3186; (734) 487 2101 fax; **rmartusew@emich.edu**

Tables/Figures From Other Sources

Authors are required to obtain permission to reproduce or adapt all or part of a table or figure from a copyrighted source. It is not necessary to obtain permission from Lawrence Erlbaum Associates, Inc. (LEA) to reproduce one table or figure from an LEA article provided you obtain the author's permission and give full credit to LEA as copyright holder and to the author through a complete, accurate citation. When you wish to reproduce material from sources not copyrighted by LEA, contact the copyright holders to determine their requirements. If you have any doubt about the policy of the copyright holder, you should request permission. Always enclose the letter of permission when transmitting the final version of the accepted manuscript for production.

Any reproduced table or figure must be accompanied by a source note at the bottom of the reprinted table or in the figure caption giving credit to the original author and to the copyright holder. Use the following forms for tables and figures, but omit Source: in credit lines for figures. (See Chapter 15 for more information.)

Material reprinted from a journal article
Source: Reprinted, by permission of the Copyright Owner, from Author's Full Name and Co Author's Full Name, "Title of Article," Title of Journal Volume (Year): Page Number.

Material reprinted from a book
Source: Reprinted, by permission of the Copyright Owner, from Author's Full Name and Co Author's Full Name, Title of Book, (Place of Publication: Publisher, Year), Page Number.

Educause Quarterly

SUBMISSION PROCESS:
Electronic Submission Only **via EMail** **eqeditor@educause.edu**

CONTACT INFORMATION:	REVIEW PROCESS:	
Nancy Hays, Editor Educause 4772 Walnut Street, Suite 206 Boulder, CO 80301 USA	**Type of Review:**	Blind Review
	No. External Reviewers: **No. InHouse Reviewers:**	12 1
Phone: 303-939-0321	**Acceptance Rate:** **Time to Review:** **Reviewer's Comments:**	25-30% 1 - 2 Months No
Email: eqeditor@educause.edu	**Invited Articles:**	0-5%
Website: www.educause.edu/eq/	**Fees to Publish:** **Fees to Review:**	$0.00 US$ $0.00 US$

PUBLICATION GUIDELINES:	CIRCULATION DATA:
Manuscript Style: See Manuscript Guidelines **Manuscript Length:** 21-25 **Copies Required:** Electronic Only	**Reader:** Academics, Administrators, IT Practitioners **Frequency of Issue:** Quarterly **Sponsor/Publisher:** EDUCAUSE

MANUSCRIPT TOPICS:
Education Management / Administration; Educational Technology Systems; Higher Education; Library Science / Information Resources

MANUSCRIPT GUIDELINES/COMMENTS:

About *EDUCAUSE Quarterly*
EDUCAUSE Quarterly (formerly CAUSE/EFFECT) is a practitioner's journal about managing and using information resources in higher education. It is published by EDUCAUSE four times a year. Articles published in the magazine are referenced in such national indexing and abstracting services as ERIC, Computer Literature Index, and Higher Education Abstracts.

The journal is distributed to approximately 8,500 individuals on college and university campuses, most of whom are EDUCAUSE member institutions. *EDUCAUSE Quarterly* circulates primarily to EDUCAUSE member representatives and college and university libraries. *EDUCAUSE Quarterly* readers are generally individuals who are involved in diverse areas professionally on campus, including administrative computer services, information systems development, user services, telecommunications and networking, academic computer services, institutional research and planning, database administration and data administration, and instructional technology development and coordination. Most readers are central IT organization staff, but increasingly the readership includes individuals who work in campus libraries, institutional research and planning offices, central administration and academic offices, and academic department libraries, institutional research offices, and administrative and academic offices.

EDUCAUSE Quarterly includes articles (written by professionals in the field and peer-reviewed) that relate to planning, developing, managing, using, and evaluating information resources in higher education. Information resources encompass technology, services, and information. In general, *EDUCAUSE Quarterly* articles deal with the subject of campus information resources from a management point of view. The journal offers feature articles sharing campus experiences; columns dealing with current issues (including national policy issues and campus management issues); articles in the "good ideas" department, viewpoint pieces, recommended reading; and a centerfold story focusing on an EDUCAUSE member campus's information resources organization and planning strategies.

Publication Guidelines

Higher education IT professionals and faculty (including those who are not EDUCAUSE members) may submit unsolicited manuscripts for publication consideration in *EDUCAUSE Quarterly*. Corporate representatives who feel they have material that meets the content guidelines below are encouraged to solicit authorship by campus representatives to retain the magazine's "peer-to-peer" approach and avoid promotional or commercial overtones. All material published in EDUCAUSE publications must be free from endorsement of specific hardware environments and/or proprietary software or services; corporate press releases about new products or product adoptions do not meet editorial standards. The magazine's overarching goals are to provide a vehicle for practical content on broadly innovative, nonvendor-specific IT solutions and compelling technology-related issues in higher education and to foster dialogue among campus practitioners and managers.

EQ authors receive full editorial support and gain valuable exposure and recognition in a very visible professional forum. View **http://www.educause.edu/apps/eq/testimonials.asp**.

Who Reads *EDUCAUSE Quarterly*?

EDUCAUSE is an international, nonprofit, professional association for managers and users of information resources on college and university campuses. The content of *EDUCAUSE Quarterly* relates to planning, managing, and using information resources (including technology, services, and information) in higher education -- administrative, academic, and library computing, as well as multimedia, telecommunications, and networking.

EDUCAUSE members and other subscribers are involved in many different aspects of planning for, managing, and using computing and other information resources. *EDUCAUSE Quarterly* readers are generally individuals who are involved in diverse areas professionally on campus, including administrative computer services, information systems development, user services, telecommunications and networking, academic computer services, institutional research and planning, database administration and data administration, and instructional technology development and coordination. Most readers are central IT organization staff, but increasingly the readership includes individuals who work in campus libraries, institutional research and planning offices, central administration and academic offices, and academic department libraries, institutional research offices, and administrative and academic offices.

Publication Content

EDUCAUSE publications deal with the subject of campus information resources from a planning, use, and management point of view. Areas of interest include:

- IT human resources issues
- organizational and management issues
- information technology planning and policy
- information resources policy issues
- data administration/information management/data warehouses
- managing a networked information environment

- industry and interinstitutional partnerships
- integrating voice, video, and data technologies
- scholarly communication issues
- library technology issues
- planning for and use of new technologies on campus
- hardware/software strategies and architectures
- funding information technology
- supporting use of technology in teaching and learning
- electronic classroom and multimedia management
- training and re-training of staff and users
- standards
- information services delivery models
- leveraging/value of information technology
- distributed support issues
- distance education and distributed learning challenges
- e-commerce / e-business challenges

Copyright

Once material has been accepted for publication, authors are asked to sign an author agreement form that assures EDUCAUSE that the authors have the right to publish the material and that they grant permission to EDUCAUSE to publish the material, both in print and online. The authors retain copyright of the material. Also,

- the authors retain the right to publish the material elsewhere, providing the original publication is acknowledged;
- EDUCAUSE does not pay honoraria to authors; and
- EDUCAUSE has the right to edit the material to meet the association's standards.

EDUCAUSE Quarterly Publication

EDUCAUSE Quarterly is a practitioner's journal of EDUCAUSE, published four times a year (approximately in March, June, September, and December). Articles may be contributed at any time for publication consideration. Potential articles are reviewed by members of an editorial review committee, and those published in *EDUCAUSE Quarterly* are referenced in such indexing services as ERIC, Computer Literature Index, and Higher Education Abstracts. The reviewing process usually takes from six to eight weeks; author revision and the editorial/production cycle may take up to six months.

Articles in *EDUCAUSE Quarterly* fall into several categories. A Feature is an in-depth article that may take one of the forms listed in the previous section under Publication Content. Feature articles fall in the range of 3,500 to 6,000 words. Other types of articles (800 to 3,000 words) include Current Issues, Viewpoints, and Good Ideas.

- A Current Issues article is a brief overview of a timely issue facing the profession; such an article puts the designated issue into perspective, offers insights, and may propose solutions.
- A Viewpoint article is one that expresses an author's opinion on a subject related to the field, often one about which there is some debate.
- A Good Ideas article briefly describes an application or management technique that has been successful on a campus and could be implemented by colleagues on other campuses.
- We also publish book reviews in the Recommended Reading department. Although as a rule we solicit these from members with a known expertise on the book topic, any reader may volunteer to write a review of a book that he or she would recommend for professional reading. These recommendations should not exceed 1,500 words.

Specifications for Submitting Articles for Publication Consideration

Ideally, papers should be submitted to Nancy Hays (eqeditor@educause.edu) electronically, as a word-processed file. Figures and graphics should be submitted as separate files, preferably in EPS format. EDUCAUSE can accept documents in most word-processing formats, with the preferred program being Word for Windows. Page layout and presentation software such as PageMaker, QuarkXpress, and PowerPoint are NOT acceptable. If it is not possible to send your manuscript as an e-mail attachment, EDUCAUSE can accept either 3 ½" DOS or 3 ½" Macintosh diskettes, CDs, or ZIP disks. Manuscripts should be accompanied by a letter (or e-mail message if being sent by e-mail) stating that the paper is to be considered for publication in *EDUCAUSE Quarterly*. The message should include name, title, complete address, and phone number, as well as a fax number and e-mail address, for each author. Author name(s) should appear only on the first page of the paper, as the *EDUCAUSE Quarterly* editorial procedures include blind review for feature articles.

The Editorial Review Process

Articles under consideration for publication as feature articles in *EDUCAUSE Quarterly* are sent for blind review to six or more members of an editorial review committee (the twelve members of the committee are listed on the inside front cover of each issue of the journal).

Reviewers evaluate the articles in five categories:
- overall quality of the article,
- appropriateness of the topic,
- author's knowledge and coverage of the topic (with special efforts to cover the "people" aspects of the concept or experience),
- coverage of people issues, and
- readability of the article.

They also provide comments concerning how the article could be improved, and often make specific suggestions along those lines. (Even the very well written articles are usually revised before publication.)

Following are some guidelines intended to convey what the editor and reviewers are looking for in articles submitted for publication. Here are a few questions used to help make a judgment as to whether an article should be pursued for publication. Each desirable attribute is followed by a description of things to avoid in writing for *EDUCAUSE Quarterly*:
- Is the information relevant, i.e., will readers find it practical, applicable, useful? Will it serve the needs of some segment of the readership?
  o Avoid relating an experience that is so peculiar and unique to your campus that it wouldn't work anywhere else.
- Is the information readable, i.e., is it easy to understand, clearly and cogently presented?
  o Avoid using unnecessary jargon or failing to explain the jargon you must use.
  o Avoid mixing chronological and how-to approaches, confusing the reader with inconsistent verb tenses throughout the article.
  o Avoid the passive voice and stilted language -- keep it straightforward and simple.
  o Avoid text that runs on without subdivisions or headings.
- Is the subject appropriate for *EDUCAUSE Quarterly* readers (see "Who Reads *EDUCAUSE Quarterly*?" above), and has the author taken into account the expertise and interests of CAUSE members (e.g., are the complexity, tone, and style appropriate? Has the topic been covered from a management perspective?)
  o Avoid writing about a subject that is not within the purview of EDUCAUSE.
  o Avoid relating only the technical aspects of the concepts or experience and failing to discuss the "people" and management issues.
- Is the information comprehensive, i.e., does it address the major elements of a situation or idea, or reference the literature where other major elements are addressed?
  o Avoid taking such a narrow view that your article doesn't take into account or acknowledge the experiences of others in the same area, or fails to draw on the published body of knowledge.
- Does the information advance the reader's knowledge, i.e., does it convey a new idea or deal with an old one from a fresh or innovative perspective?

o   Avoid writing on a subject that has already been covered many times before in the journal, especially if your article adds nothing new from a practical standpoint but simply re-states conventional wisdom.

When a feature-length article is essentially the presentation of a case study, it is important that the article do more than simply tell "what we did on our campus." Case study experiences must be presented in a way that makes them generalizable to others. Thus it is critical to adopt a candid attitude toward revealing not only success factors, but also problems encountered, especially from the point of view of offering lessons learned so that others can learn from your experience. It is also important to place the experience in a conceptual framework, relating it to the literature on the subject.

For any kind of feature article, a list of suggested articles, books, and other publications on the same subject is especially valuable, even if you have not used these references in the article. The EDUCAUSE style guide (**http://www.educause.edu/StyleGuide/1468**)is online for your referral.

For further information about submitting articles to *EDUCAUSE Quarterly* journal, contact the editors at the EDUCAUSE office: (303) 939-0321 or **eqeditor@educause.edu**.

e-Journal of Instructional Science and Technology

SUBMISSION PROCESS:
Electronic Submission Only via EMail **smith@usq.edu.au**

CONTACT INFORMATION:	REVIEW PROCESS:	
Alan Smith, Executive Editor	**Type of Review:**	Blind Review
Phone: +61 7 46 31 2296	**No. External Reviewers:** **No. InHouse Reviewers:**	2 1
Email: smith@usq.edu.au	**Acceptance Rate:** **Time to Review:**	21-30% 2 - 3 Months
Website: www.usq.edu.au/electpub/e-jist/	**Reviewer's Comments:** **Invited Articles:**	Yes 0-5%
	Fees to Publish: **Fees to Review:**	$0.00 US$ $0.00 US$

PUBLICATION GUIDELINES:	CIRCULATION DATA:
Manuscript Style: USC - Harvard Blue Book	**Reader:** Academics
Manuscript Length: 6-10	**Frequency of Issue:** 2 Times/Year
Copies Required: One	**Sponsor/Publisher:** The University of Southern Queensland

MANUSCRIPT TOPICS:
Education Management / Administration; Educational Psychology; Educational Technology Systems; Higher Education; Library Science / Information Resources

MANUSCRIPT GUIDELINES/COMMENTS:

About *e-JIST*
The *e-Journal of Instructional Science and Technology* (*e-JIST*) is an international peer-reviewed electronic journal. The *Journal* is a multi-faceted publication with content likely to be of interest to policy makers, managers, investors, professional staff, technical staff, and academics within education and training. The editions of *e-JIST* will adopt an evolutionary style. In the meantime, the *Journal* continues to welcome new contributions based on original work of practitioners and researchers with specific focus or implications for the design of instructional materials.

CONTRIBUTORS GUIDELINES
Papers
Presentations, in English, are solicited for consideration for publication - provided they have neither been published nor are being considered for publication, elsewhere.

314

Style
As much as possible, typescript should conform to the following:
- Word document
- Arial font
- 12 point
- Title of paper (Capitals, bold, centered), top of page
- Author's name (centered under title of paper)
- Sub-headings (left aligned, bold)

Based on an A4 page size use the following margins:
- Top 1"
- Bottom 1"
- Left 1.25"
- Right 1.25"
- Gutter 0"
- Header 0.5"
- Footer 0.5"

All figures and tables should be integrated in the typescript.

To assist you in the preparation of your submission a Microsoft Word template has been established. It has embedded in it, the layout and styles as specified above.

Abstract
An abstract of not more than 100 words should accompany each submission.

Submission of Articles
Submissions, which should normally be between 2000 and 6000 words, are to be forwarded by electronic mail to the Executive Editor, Alan Smith (**smith@usq.edu.au**)

Submission details
Authors' names, titles, affiliations, with complete mailing addresses, including e-mail, telephone and facsimile numbers should appear on the first page (if sent as a document attachment) or the first screen page (if sent as a direct email message) to ensure anonymity in reviewing.

Authors are completely responsible for the factual accuracy of their contributions and neither the Editorial Board of *e-JIST* nor the University of Southern Queensland accepts any responsibility for the assertions and opinions of contributors. Authors are responsible for obtaining permission to quote lengthy excerpts from previously-published articles.

Publications
All articles are refereed by at least two experts on the subject. The Executive Editor and the Founding Editors reserve the right to suggest changes and corrections and to decide the final acceptance and publication schedule of accepted manuscripts.

Copyright
e-JIST is published by the Distance and e-Learning Centre, University of Southern Queensland. Papers accepted for publication by *e-JIST* become the copyright of the publisher. Authors retain the right to use their own material for purely educational and research purposes. In all subsequent publications, whether in whole or part, the *Journal* must be acknowledged as the original publisher of the article. All other requests for use or re-publication in whole or part, should be addressed to the Executive Editor.

E-Journal of Organizational Learning and Leadership

SUBMISSION PROCESS:
Electronic Submission Only via EMail **flumerfe@leadingtoday.org**

CONTACT INFORMATION:	REVIEW PROCESS:	
Shannon Flumerfelt, Editor Oakland University	**Type of Review:**	Blind Review
	No. External Reviewers:	2
Phone: 248-370-3036	**No. InHouse Reviewers:**	1
	Acceptance Rate:	11-20%
Email: flumerfe@leadingtoday.org flumerfe@oakland.edu	**Time to Review:**	1 - 2 Months
	Reviewer's Comments:	Yes
	Invited Articles:	0-5%
Website: http://www.weleadinlearning.org/index.html	**Fees to Publish:**	$0.00 US$
	Fees to Review:	$0.00 US$

PUBLICATION GUIDELINES:	CIRCULATION DATA:
Manuscript Style: American Psychological Association	**Reader:** Academics, Administrators
Manuscript Length: 16-20	**Frequency of Issue:** 2-3 Times/Year
Copies Required: Electronic Only	**Sponsor/Publisher:** weLead Incorporated

MANUSCRIPT TOPICS:
Education Management / Administration; School Law

MANUSCRIPT GUIDELINES/COMMENTS:

Topics Also Include. Teacher Leadership; Leadership Development; Organizational Development.

Articles submitted to the *E-Journal of Organizational Learning and Leadership* are subject to the following review process:
Articles submitted will initially be screened by the Editor to determine the suitability of the article for the *E-Journal*.
1. If the article is suitable, it will be assigned to referees, according to its content.
2. A careful blind review by the referees will be performed. Each referee will make a recommendation to the Editor and provide comments for the author(s).
3. The Editor will appraise the reviews and make a decision regarding the outcome of the article.
4. If, in the Editor's judgment, the paper should proceed, it will be scheduled for publication.
5. If, in the Editor's judgment, the article has potential for publication, the author(s) will be invited to make revisions according to the suggestions of the reviewers and the Editor.

6. If the article is revised, the Editor will appraise the entire process to make certain that all revisions suggested by the referees and the Editor have been adequately met. If they have been adequately met, the article will be scheduled for publication.
7. If the article is determined to fail the blind review process, the author(s) will be notified that the article will not be published by the *E-Journal*.

The following are guidelines for submission:
1. Articles must be in APA format.
2. Articles should contain the following attributes as they relate to the topic of organizational learning and leadership: relevancy, practicality, usefulness, readability, clarity of expression, comprehensiveness, and value to the field of study.

English Leadership Quarterly

SUBMISSION PROCESS:

Postal Submission Only

CONTACT INFORMATION:	REVIEW PROCESS:	
Bonita L. Wilcox, Editor PO Box 142 Cambridge Springs, PA 16403 USA	**Type of Review:**	Editorial Review
	No. External Reviewers:	0-1
	No. InHouse Reviewers:	1-2
Phone: 814-398-2528	**Acceptance Rate:**	20%
	Time to Review:	2 - 3 Months
Email: blwilcox@hughes.net	**Reviewer's Comments:**	No
	Invited Articles:	0-5%
Website: www.NCTE.org	**Fees to Publish:**	$0.00 US$
	Fees to Review:	$0.00 US$

PUBLICATION GUIDELINES:	CIRCULATION DATA:
Manuscript Style: American Psychological Association	**Reader:** Administrators, Department Heads, Practicing Teachers, Student Teachers, Teacher Educators
Manuscript Length: 1-20	
	Frequency of Issue: Quarterly
Copies Required: Electronic Only	**Sponsor/Publisher:** National Council of Teachers of English (NCTE) Conference on English Leadership (CEL)

MANUSCRIPT TOPICS:
Curriculum Studies; Education Management / Administration; Educational Technology Systems; Elementary / Early Childhood; English Literature; Gifted Children; Higher Education; Languages & Linguistics; Reading; Secondary / Adolescent Studies; Teacher Education

MANUSCRIPT GUIDELINES/COMMENTS:

English Leadership Quarterly is a themed journal seeking manuscripts of interest to those in leadership positions in English education and literacy learning. Book reviews, software reviews, and Website reviews related to themes are encouraged.

ERS Spectrum

<table>
<tr><td colspan="2" align="center">

SUBMISSION PROCESS:

**Electronic Submission Preferred
via EMail**

ers@ers.org

</td></tr>
<tr><td>

CONTACT INFORMATION:

Editorial Director
Educational Research Service
1001 N. Fairfax St., Suite 500
Alexandria, VA 22314-1587 USA

Phone:
  703-243-2100

Email:
  ers@ers.org

Website:
  www.ers.org/periodicals

</td><td>

REVIEW PROCESS:

Type of Review:	Blind Review
No. External Reviewers:	2
No. InHouse Reviewers:	3
Acceptance Rate:	21-30%
Time to Review:	2 - 3 Months
Reviewer's Comments:	Yes
Invited Articles:	6-10%
Fees to Publish:	$0.00 US$
Fees to Review:	$0.00 US$

</td></tr>
<tr><td>

PUBLICATION GUIDELINES:

Manuscript Style:
  American Psychological Association
    Chicago Manual of Style

Manuscript Length:
  16-20

Copies Required:
  Two

</td><td>

CIRCULATION DATA:

Reader:
  Administrators

Frequency of Issue:
  Quarterly

Sponsor/Publisher:
  Educational Research Service

</td></tr>
</table>

MANUSCRIPT TOPICS:
Education Management / Administration

MANUSCRIPT GUIDELINES/COMMENTS:

Educational Research Service welcomes manuscripts for *ERS Spectrum* from all sources. Manuscripts from practicing school administrators dealing with research and educational programs in their local school districts are especially appropriate for publication. *Spectrum* publishes original research and information for educational leadership. Spectrum articles cover a broad range of topics, including public school management, school policy, administrative methods, finance, personnel relations, instructional programs, and related areas.

Manuscripts submitted for publication should be based on research data, practical information, or direct experience. The editors request two copies of each submitted manuscript, typed double-spaced on 8 ½ x 11" paper. Electronic submissions, sent on disk or as a Word attachement, are also welcome. Because of space limitations, manuscripts should be no longer than 25 pages.

ERS reserves the right to edit, abridge, or abstract manuscripts selected for publication. Editorial changes will be submitted to the authors for approval except when publication deadlines will not permit it. Manuscripts are accepted for publication with the understanding that they are original writings that have not been published before and are not currently under consideration for publication elsewhere.

Copyright Notice

Unless otherwise noted, ERS holds the copyright on all articles appearing in *ERS Spectrum*. Requests for permission to reprint, copy, or reproduce articles in whole or in part must be made in writing to *ERS Spectrum* at the address above.

The views, opinions, and data contained in the articles published in *ERS Spectrum* are those of the respective authors, and do not necessarily represent those of Educational Research Service or any of its sponsoring organizations.

Essays in Education

SUBMISSION PROCESS:
Electronic Submission Only **via EMail** **tlintner@usca.edu**

CONTACT INFORMATION:	REVIEW PROCESS:	
Timothy Lintner, Editor University of South Carolina, Aiken 471 University Parkway Aiken, SC 29801 USA	**Type of Review:**	Editorial Review
	No. External Reviewers:	0
	No. InHouse Reviewers:	1
Phone: 803-641-3564 **Email:**	**Acceptance Rate:**	21-30%
	Time to Review:	2 - 3 Months
	Reviewer's Comments:	Yes
	Invited Articles:	0-5%
Website: www.usca.edu/essays/	**Fees to Publish:**	$0.00 US$
	Fees to Review:	$0.00 US$

PUBLICATION GUIDELINES:	CIRCULATION DATA:
Manuscript Style: American Psychological Association	**Reader:** Academics
Manuscript Length: 11-15	**Frequency of Issue:** Quarterly
Copies Required: Electronic Only	**Sponsor/Publisher:** University of South Carolina, Aiken

MANUSCRIPT TOPICS:
Adult Career & Vocational; Art / Music; Audiology / Speech Pathology; Bilingual / E.S.L.; Counseling & Personnel Services; Curriculum Studies; Education Management / Administration; Educational Psychology; Educational Technology Systems; Elementary / Early Childhood; English Literature; Foreign Language; Gifted Children; Health & Physical Education; Higher Education; Languages & Linguistics; Library Science / Information Resources; Reading; Religious Education; Rural Education & Small Schools; School Law; Science Math & Environment; Secondary / Adolescent Studies; Social Studies / Social Science; Special Education; Teacher Education; Tests, Measurement & Evaluation; Urban Education, Cultural / Non-Traditional

MANUSCRIPT GUIDELINES/COMMENTS:

Essays in Education is an editor-reviewed electronic journal that seeks to explore the multitude of issues that impact and influence education.

In accord with its broad focus, the journal welcomes contributions that enhance the exchange of diverse theoretical and practical information among educators, practitioners, and researchers around the world.

Beyond publishing original articles, the journal's editor will consider reviews of educational software, books and pedagogical materials. However, reviews must describe the practitioner's actual experiences using such materials.

Submissions to the Journal
Authors submitting works to *Essays in Education* warrant that their works are not currently under consideration by any other publication and that any portion of the work is not subject to additional copyright regulations, unless prior required consents have been obtained.

Articles are to be submitted to the editor by electronic mail. Send articles to: **tlinter@usca.edu**

Cover Sheet, Title, Author Information and Key Words
Please provide a cover sheet indicating the title of the article, the author's name and institutional affiliation, and both electronic and standard addresses.

The title of the manuscript should appear on the first page of the text. Leave blank a single line and then list the author's name and institutional affiliation. Continue this format for multiple authors.

Abstracts
Each manuscript should be accompanied by an abstract. Abstracts should not exceed 15 lines in length.

Guidelines
Although there is no established length, scholarly articles between 15-30 pages are preferred.

Though tables and graphs are welcome, these should be used sparingly within the body of the text.

Single space all copy. Insert a blank line between paragraphs, between references in the REFERENCE section, and before and after subheadings, etc.

Use the *American Psychological Association* (APA 5th edition) format for all formatting, citation and reference issues. Please contact the editor for any format questions that are not covered in the most recent edition of the *APA Publication Manual*.

Reprints of Articles
Articles included in *Essays in Education* may be reproduced for any medium for non-commercial purposes.

Ethics and Education

SUBMISSION PROCESS:
Postal & Electronic Submission Accepted

CONTACT INFORMATION:	REVIEW PROCESS:	
Richard Smith, Editor University of Durham School of Education Leazes Road Durham, DH1 1 UK	**Type of Review:**	Blind Review
	No. External Reviewers:	2
	No. InHouse Reviewers:	1
	Acceptance Rate:	21-30%
Phone:	**Time to Review:**	2 - 3 Months
0191 334 1016	**Reviewer's Comments:**	No
	Invited Articles:	11-20%
Email:		
r.d.smith@durham.ac.uk	**Fees to Publish:**	$0.00 US$
Website:	**Fees to Review:**	$0.00 US$
http://www.tandf.co.uk/journals/titles/ 17449642		

PUBLICATION GUIDELINES:	CIRCULATION DATA:

Manuscript Style:
    See Manuscript Guidelines
	Reader:
	    Academics, Practicing Teachers,
	    Counselors

Manuscript Length:
    11-15
	Frequency of Issue:
	    2 Times/Year

Copies Required:
    One
	Sponsor/Publisher:
	    Routledge, Taylor & Francis, Ltd.

MANUSCRIPT TOPICS:
Counseling & Personnel Services; Education Management / Administration; Educational Psychology; Elementary / Early Childhood; Higher Education; Secondary / Adolescent Studies

MANUSCRIPT GUIDELINES/COMMENTS:

Aims and Scope
Ethics and Education is a new international, peer-reviewed journal which aims to stimulate discussion and debate around the ethical dimensions of education.

The journal addresses issues in both formal and informal education and upbringing, and includes within its scope relevant aspects of applied ethics, including: Bioethics; Medical ethics; Management ethics; Sex education; Ethics of therapy and counseling; Professional ethics

Ethics and Education welcomes all traditions and forms of ethical enquiry, from a wide range of philosophical and religious perspectives. As well as appealing to those with a direct interest in ethics and education, the journal will also be of interest to philosophers, educationalists, policy-makers.

Notes for Contributors
Papers should be original. Manuscripts should be sent to Professor Richard Smith, University of Durham, School of Education, Leazes Road, Durham DH1 1TA, UK. Email: **r.d.smith@ durham.ac.uk**.

Papers should normally be around 6000 words in length, but longer or shorter articles will be considered. Manuscripts should be typed on one side of A4 (or similar) paper with double spacing and a wide margin to the left. One copy should be submitted, and a copy in Word format sent to the editors by email. In addition, a copy should be retained by the authors. All pages should be numbered. Authors' names and institutions should be on a separate sheet submitted with the manuscript. The full postal and email address of the author who will check proofs and receive correspondence and offprints should also be included. Each paper should be accompanied on separate sheets by an abstract of 100 to 150 words, and a short note of biographical details for 'Notes on Contributors'.

Tables and captions to illustrations. Tables must be typed out on separate sheets and not included as part of the text. The captions to illustrations should be gathered together and also typed out on a separate sheet. Tables and Figures should be numbered consecutively by Arabic numerals. The approximate position of tables and figures should be indicated in the manuscript. Captions should include keys to any symbols used.

Figures. Please supply one set of artwork in a finished form, suitable for black-and-white reproduction. Figures will not normally be redrawn by the publisher.

Citations of other work should be limited to those strictly necessary for the argument. Any quotations should be brief, and accompanied by precise references.

Titles of journals and names of publishers, etc. should not be abbreviated. Acronyms for the names of organisations, examinations, etc. should be preceded by the title in full.

References should be indicated in the typescript by giving the author's name, with the year of publication in parentheses. If several papers by the same author(s) and from the same year are cited, a, b, c, etc. should be put after the year of publication. The references should be listed in full at the end of the paper in the following style.

For books
Norton, P. and Wiberg, K. (1998) *Teaching with technology* (Orlando, FL, Harcourt Brace).

For articles
Loughran, J. and Corrigan, D. (1995) Teaching portfolios: a strategy for developing learning and teaching in preservice education, *Teaching and Teacher Education*, 11(6), 565–577.

For chapters within books
Marzano, R. J. (1994) Commentary on literacy portfolios: windows on potential, in: S. H. Valencia, E. H. Hiebert and P. P. E. Afflerbach (Eds) *Authentic reading assessment: practices and possibilities* (Newark, NJ, International Reading Association), 41–56.

For online documents
Standler, R. (2000) *Plagiarism in colleges in the USA*. Available online at: www.rbs2.com/plag.htm (accessed 6 August 2004).

Proof corrections should be clearly identified and returned within three working days of receipt. Major alterations cannot be accepted.

324

Early Electronic Offprints. Corresponding authors can now receive their article by email as a complete PDF. This allows the author to print up to 50 copies, free of charge, and disseminate them to colleagues. In many cases this facility will be available up to two weeks prior to publication. Or, alternatively, corresponding authors will receive the traditional 50 offprints. A copy of the journal will be sent by post to all corresponding authors after publication. Additional copies of the journal can be purchased at the author's preferential rate of £15.00/$25.00 per copy.

Copyright. It is a condition of publication that authors assign copyright or licence the publication rights in their articles, including abstracts, to Taylor & Francis. This enables us to ensure full copyright protection and to disseminate the article, and of course the Journal, to the widest possible readership in print and electronic formats as appropriate. Authors may, of course, use the article elsewhere after publication without prior permission from Taylor & Francis, provided that acknowledgement is given to the Journal as the original source of publication, and that Taylor & Francis is notified so that our records show that its use is properly authorised. Authors retain a number of other rights under the Taylor & Francis rights policies documents. These policies are referred to at **http://www.tandf.co.uk/journals/authorrights.pdf** for full details. Authors are themselves responsible for obtaining permission to reproduce copyright material from other sources.

Ethnography and Education

SUBMISSION PROCESS:
Postal & Electronic Submission Accepted **via EMail** **ethnographyandeducationjournal@roehampton.ac.uk**

<table>
<tr><td colspan="2">CONTACT INFORMATION:</td><td colspan="2">REVIEW PROCESS:</td></tr>
<tr><td colspan="2">Geoff Troman, Editor
Roehampton University
Froebel College
Room QB 111 Southlands
Roehampton Lane
London, SW15 5SL UK</td><td>Type of Review:

No. External Reviewers:
No. InHouse Reviewers:

Acceptance Rate:
Time to Review:</td><td>Blind Review

2
1

50%
2 - 3 Months</td></tr>
<tr><td colspan="2">Phone:</td><td>Reviewer's Comments:
Invited Articles:</td><td>Yes
0-5%</td></tr>
<tr><td colspan="2">Email:
  g.troman@roehampton.ac.uk
Website:
  http://www.tandf.co.uk/journals/titles/
  17457823.asp</td><td>Fees to Publish:
Fees to Review:</td><td>$0.00 US$
$0.00 US$</td></tr>
<tr><td colspan="2">PUBLICATION GUIDELINES:</td><td colspan="2">CIRCULATION DATA:</td></tr>
<tr><td colspan="2">Manuscript Style:
  See Manuscript Guidelines

Manuscript Length:
  16-20

Copies Required:
  One + 1 Electronic</td><td colspan="2">Reader:
  Academics, Practicing Teachers,
  Counselors

Frequency of Issue:
  3 Times/Year

Sponsor/Publisher:
  Routledge, Taylor & Francis, Ltd.</td></tr>
</table>

MANUSCRIPT TOPICS:
Educational Psychology; Higher Education; Special Education; Teacher Education

MANUSCRIPT GUIDELINES/COMMENTS:

Aims & Scope
Ethnography and Education is an international, peer-reviewed journal that publishes articles illuminating educational practices through empirical methodologies, which prioritise the experiences and perspectives of those involved. The journal is open to a wide range of ethnographic research that emanates from the perspectives of sociology, linguistics, history, psychology and general educational studies as well as anthropology. The journal's priority is to support ethnographic research that involves long-term engagement with those studied in order to understand their cultures; uses multiple methods of generating data, and recognises the centrality of the researcher in the research process.

326

The journal welcomes substantive and methodological articles that seek to:

- explicate and challenge the effects of educational policies and practices
- interrogate and develop theories about educational structures, policies and experiences
- highlight the agency of educational actors
- provide accounts of how the everyday practices of those engaged in education are instrumental in social reproduction
- discuss new developments in ethnographic methodologies

Instructions to Authors

Note to Authors. Please make sure your contact address information is clearly visible on the outside of all packages you are sending to Editors.

Papers accepted become the copyright of the Publisher, unless otherwise specifically agreed. The journal will publish three issues a year in March, June and September. Manuscripts should ideally be between 5,000 and 8,000 words and should be sent to Ethnography and Education, Professor Geoff Troman, Reader in Education Policy, Froebel College, Roehampton University, Roehampton Lane, London, UK, SW 15 5PJ. Articles can only be considered if one complete copy of each manuscript is submitted together with one email attachment sent to: **ethnographyandeducation journal@roehampton.ac.uk**

Manuscripts, in English, should be typed on one side of the paper, double spaced, with ample margins, and bear the title of the contribution without any identification of the author(s), together with an abstract/summary of 100-150 words on a separate sheet. A short note of biographical details should also be supplied. A second separate sheet should contain the title of the article, the name(s) of the author(s), the address where the work was carried out and the full postal and e-mail address of the author who will check proofs and receive correspondence and offprints. All pages should be numbered. Footnotes to the text should be avoided wherever possible.

Contributors should bear in mind that they are addressing an international audience. Jargon should be avoided where possible and all authors should use non-discriminatory language. Rejected manuscripts will not normally be returned to contributors unless sufficient international postal coupons have been sent.

Tables, figures and captions to illustrations. Tables must be typed on separate sheets and not included as part of the text. The captions to illustrations should be gathered together and also typed out on a separate sheet. Tables and figures should be numbered by Arabic numerals. The approximate position of tables and figures should be indicated in the manuscript. Captions should include keys to symbols.

Figures. Please supply one set of artwork in a finished form, suitable for reproduction. Figures will not normally be redrawn by the publisher.

Citations of other work should be limited to those strictly necessary for the argument. Any quotations should be brief, and accompanied by precise references.

References should be indicated in the typescript by giving the author's name, with the year of publication in parentheses. If several papers by the same author and from the same year are cited, a, b, c, etc. should be put after the year of publication. The references should be listed in full, including pages, at the end of the paper in the following standard form. Please capital letters to a minimum.

For books
Woods, P., Boyle, M. and Hubbard, N. (1999) *Multicultural children in the early years: creative teaching, meaningful learning* (Clevedon, Multilingual Matters)

For articles
Stacey, J. (1988) Can there be a feminist ethnography? *Women's Studies International Forum*, 17 (4), 21-27.

For chapters within books
Pollard, A. and Filer, A. (1999) Learning policy and pupil career: issues from longtitudinal ethnography, in: M. Hammersely, (Ed.) *Researching School Experience* pp. 153-168 (London, Falmer Press).

Titles of journals and names of publishers, etc. should not be abbreviated. Acronyms for the names of organisations, examinations, etc. should be preceded by the title in full.

To download a Word template for this journal, please visit the web site.

If you have any further questions about the style for this journal, please submit your questions using the Style Queries form.

Proofs will be sent to authors if there is sufficient time to do so. They should be corrected and returned to the Editor within three days. Major alterations to the text cannot be accepted.

Early Electronic Offprints. Corresponding authors can now receive their article by e-mail as a complete PDF. This allows the author to print up to 50 copies, free of charge, and disseminate them to colleagues. In many cases this facility will be available up to two weeks prior to publication. Or, alternatively, corresponding authors will receive the traditional 50 offprints. A copy of the journal will be sent by post to all corresponding authors after publication. Additional copies of the journal can be purchased at the authors' preferential rate of £15.00/$25.00 per copy.

Copyright. It is a condition of publication that authors assign copyright or licence the publication rights in their articles, including abstracts, to Taylor & Francis. This enables us to ensure full copyright protection and to disseminate the article, and of course the Journal, to the widest possible readership in print and electronic formats as appropriate. Authors may, of course, use the article elsewhere after publication without prior permission from Taylor & Francis, provided that acknowledgement is given to the Journal as the original source of publication, and that Taylor & Francis is notified so that our records show that its use is properly authorised. Authors retain a number of other rights under the Taylor & Francis rights policies documents. These policies are referred to at **www.tandf.co.uk/journals/authorrights.pdf** for full details. Authors are themselves responsible for obtaining permission to reproduce copyright material from other sources. For further information on electronic submission, including information on accepted file types, please visit the web site.

European Journal of Education

SUBMISSION PROCESS:
Electronic Submission Only **via EMail** **gordon@dauphine.fr**

CONTACT INFORMATION:	REVIEW PROCESS:	
Jean Gordon & Jean-Pierre Jallade, Eds.	**Type of Review:**	Editorial Review
Phone:	**No. External Reviewers:** **No. InHouse Reviewers:**	2 2

Email:
  gordon@dauphine.fr
  christine.keyes@wanadoo.fr
Website:
  www.ieeps.org
	Acceptance Rate:
	Time to Review:
	Reviewer's Comments:
	Invited Articles:
	
	Fees to Publish:
	Fees to Review:
		6-10%
		1 - 2 Months
		Yes
		0-5%
		
		$0.00 US$
		$0.00 US$

PUBLICATION GUIDELINES:	**CIRCULATION DATA:**	

Manuscript Style:
  See Manuscript Guidelines
 	
Manuscript Length:
  26-30
 	
Copies Required:
  One
	Reader:
	  Academics, Administrators
	
	Frequency of Issue:
	  Quarterly
	
	Sponsor/Publisher:
	  Blackwell Publishing, Inc.	

MANUSCRIPT TOPICS:
Higher Education

MANUSCRIPT GUIDELINES/COMMENTS:

Aims and Scope
The prime aims of the *European Journal of Education* are:
- To examine, compare and assess education policies, trends, reforms and programmes of European countries in an international perspective
- To disseminate policy debates and research results to a wide audience of academics, researchers, practitioners and students of education sciences
- To contribute to the policy debate at the national and European level by providing European administrators and policy-makers in international organisations, national and local governments with comparative and up-to-date material centred on specific themes of common interest.

Each issue is organised around a particular theme, with emphasis on commissioned papers requested by the individual editor responsible for the issue and a member of the Journal's Editorial Board. Space for submitted papers is, therefore, limited. These papers are subject to anonymous peer review by independent referees.

The *Journal* gives high priority to articles which provide a comparative perspective and offer a link between academic and policy issues. It favours viewpoints from various disciplines connected with education.

Author Guidelines
All manuscripts should be sent to the following address: Joint Editors, European Journal of Education, European Institute of Education and Social Policy, Universite de Paris-Dauphine, 75116 Paris France; Email: **CHRISTINE.KEYES@wanadoo.fr**; **eje@dauphine.fr**

Exclusive Licence Form. Authors will be required to sign an Exclusive Licence Form (ELF) for all papers accepted for publication. Signature of the ELF is a condition of publication and papers will not be passed to the publisher for production unless a signed form has been received. Please note that signature of the Exclusive Licence Form does not affect ownership of copyright in the material. (Government employees need to complete the Author Warranty sections, although copyright in such cases does not need to be assigned). After submission authors will retain the right to publish their paper in various media/circumstances (please see the form for further details). To assist authors an appropriate form will be supplied by the editorial office. Alternatively, authors may like to download a copy of the form from the web site.

Evaluation and Program Planning

SUBMISSION PROCESS:
Electronic Submission Preferred **via EMail** **jamorell@jamorell.com**

CONTACT INFORMATION:	REVIEW PROCESS:	
Jonathan Morell, Editor NewVectors LLC PO Box 134001 3520 Green Court, Suite 300 Ann Arbor, MI 48113-4001 USA	**Type of Review:**	Blind Review
	No. External Reviewers:	3
	No. InHouse Reviewers:	1
	Acceptance Rate:	40%
Phone:	**Time to Review:**	2 - 3 Months
734-302-4558	**Reviewer's Comments:**	Yes
	Invited Articles:	21-30%
Email:		
jamorell@jamorell.com	**Fees to Publish:**	$0.00 US$
Website:	**Fees to Review:**	$0.00 US$
http://www.elsevier.com/		

PUBLICATION GUIDELINES:	CIRCULATION DATA:
Manuscript Style: American Psychological Association	**Reader:** Academics
Manuscript Length: 21-25	**Frequency of Issue:** Quarterly
Copies Required: Electronic Only	**Sponsor/Publisher:** Elsevier Inc.

MANUSCRIPT TOPICS:
Education Management / Administration; Tests, Measurement & Evaluation

MANUSCRIPT GUIDELINES/COMMENTS:

Purpose and Intent of the Journal
Evaluation and Program Planning is based on the principle that the techniques and methods of evaluation and planning transcend the boundaries of specific fields and that relevant contributions to these areas come from people representing many different positions, intellectual traditions, and interests. In order to further the development of evaluation and planning, we publish articles from the private and public sectors in a wide range of areas: organizational development and behavior, training, planning, human resource development, health and mental, social services, mental retardation, corrections, substance abuse, and education. The primary goals of the journal are to assist evaluators and planners to improve the practice of their professions, to develop their skills and to improve their knowledge base.

Submission of Papers
All manuscripts should be submitted to the Editor-in-Chief in triplicate. Major articles should not exceed 7,000 words and must include five copies of the abstract of no more than 150 words. All

manuscripts and suggestions for books to be reviewed must be mailed to: Jonathan A. Morell, NewVectors LLC, PO Box 134001, 3520 Green Court, Suite 300, Ann Arbor, MI 48113-4001, USA. The Editor can also be contacted via email at **jamorell@jamorell.com**.

General

It is essential to give a fax number and e-mail address when submitting a manuscript. Articles must be written in good English. Authors should also submit an electronic copy of their paper with the final version of the manuscript. The electronic copy should match the hard copy exactly. Always keep a backup copy of the electronic file for reference and safety. Full details of electronic submission and acceptable formats can be obtained from **http://authors.elsevier.com** or from Author Services at Elsevier. Submission of an article implies that the work has not been published previously (except in the form of an abstract or as part of a published lecture or academic thesis), that it is not under consideration for publication elsewhere, and that its publication is approved by all authors and tacitly or explicitly by the responsible authorities where the work was carried out, and that, if accepted, it will not be published elsewhere in the same form, in English or in any other language, without the written consent of the Publisher. Translated material which has not previously been published in English will also be considered.

Upon acceptance of an article, authors will be asked to transfer copyright (for more information on copyright see **http://authors.elsevier.com**). This transfer will ensure the widest possible dissemination of information. A letter will be sent to the corresponding author confirming receipt of the manuscript. A form facilitating transfer of copyright will be provided. If excerpts from other copyrighted works are included, the author(s) must obtain written permission from the copyright owners and credit the source(s) in the article. Elsevier has preprinted forms for use by authors in these cases: contact ES Global Rights Department, P.O. Box 800, Oxford OX5 1DX, UK; Tel: + 44 (0) 1865 843830; fax: +44 (0) 1865 853333; e-mail: **permissions@elsevier.com** To facilitate blind review by one or more readers, all indication of authorship should appear on a detachable cover page only. Please include a brief biography of each author for major articles and brief reports, to be published in the journal. The senior author's complete mailing address for reprints, and any statements of credit or research support should appear in an introductory footnote. Please supply corresponding author's telephone and FAX numbers, and E-mail address if available.

Types of Contributions

- We publish articles, "special issues" (usually a section of an issue), and book reviews. Articles are of two types: 1) reports on specific evaluation or planning efforts, and 2) dicussions of issues relevant to the conduct of evaluation and planning.
- Reports on individual evaluations should include presentation of the evaluation setting, design, analysis and results. Because of our focus and philosophy, however, we also want a specific section devoted to "lessons learned". This section should contain advice to other evaluators about how you would have acted differently if you could do it all over again. The advice may involve methodology, how the evaluation was implemented or conducted, evaluation utilization tactics, or any other wisdom that you think could benefit your colleagues. More general articles should provide information relevant to the evaluator/planner's work. This might include theories in evaluation, literature reviews, critiques of instruments, or discussions of fiscal, legislative, legal or ethical affecting evaluation or planning.
- Special issues are groups of articles which cover a particular topic in depth. They are organized by "special issue editors" who are willing to conceptualize the topic, find contributors, set up a quality control process, and deliver the material. Often several editors share responsibility for these tasks. Suggestions for special issues are encouraged.
- Book reviews cover any area of social science or public policy which may interest evaluators and planners. As the special issues, suggestions for books and book reviewers are encouraged.

MANUSCRIPT PREPARATION
General
Please write your text in good English (American or British usage is accepted, but not a mixture of these). Italics are not to be used for expressions of Latin origin, for example, in vivo, et al., per se.

Use decimal points (not commas); use a space for thousands (10 000 and above). Print the entire manuscript on one side of paper only, using double spacing and wide (3 cm) margins. (Avoid full justification, i.e., do not use a constant right-hand margin.) Ensure that each new paragraph is clearly indicated. Present tables and figure legends on separate pages at the end of the manuscript. If possible, consult a recent issue of the journal to become familiar with layout and conventions. Number all pages consecutively. Good quality print-outs with a font size of 12 or 10 pt are required.

Paper length. The recommended length for a paper is 5000-8000 words, plus illustrations; the preferred length for reviews and conference reports is 2500 words. Provide the following data on the title page (in the order given).

Title. Concise and informative. Titles are often used in information-retrieved systems. Avoid abbreviations and formulae where possible. The title should not exceed 50 characters (including spaces).

Author names and affiliations. Where the family name may be ambiguous (e.g.., a double name), please indicate this clearly. Present the author's affiliation addresses (where the actual work was done) below the names. Indicate all affiliations with a lower-case superscript letter immediately after the author's name and in front of the appropriate address. Provide the full postal address of each affiliation including the country name, and, if available, the e-mail address of each author.

Corresponding author. Clearly indicate who is willing to handle correspondence at all stages of refereeing and publication, also post-publication. Ensure the telephone and fax numbers (with country and area code) are provided in addition to the e-mail address and the complete postal address.

Present/permanent address. If an author has moved since the work described in the article was done, or was visiting at the time, a "Present address" (or "Permanent address") may be indicated as a footnote to that author's name. The address at which the author actually did the work must be retained as the main, affiliation address. Superscript Arabic numerals are used for such footnotes.

Abstract. A concise and factual abstract is required (maximum length 200 words). The abstract should state briefly the purpose of the research, the principal results and major conclusions. An abstract is often presented separate from the article, so it must be able to stand alone. References should therefore be avoided, but if essential, they must be cited in full, without reference to the reference list. Non-standard or uncommon abbreviations should be avoided, but if essential they must be defined at their first mention in the abstract itself.

N.B. Acknowledgements. Collate acknowledgements in a separate section at the end of the article and do not, therefore, include them on the title page, as footnote to the title page or otherwise.

Arrangement of the article
Subdivision of the article. Divide your article into clearly defined and numbered sections. Subsections should be numbered 1.1 (then 1.1.1., 1.1.2.), 1.2., etc, (the abstract is not included in section numbering). Use this numbering also for internal cross-referencing: do not just refer to 'the text'. Any subsections may be given a brief heading. Each heading on its own separate line.

Text. Follow this order when typing manuscripts: Title, Authors, Affiliations, Abstract, Keywords, Main text, Acknowledgements, Appendix, References, Figure Captions, Tables (and figures) should be kept separate from the rest of the manuscript (see instructions for illustrations below). The corresponding should be identified with an asterisk and footnote. All other footnotes (except table footnotes) should be identified with superscript Arabic numerals.

Appendices. If there is more than one appendix, they should be identified as A, B, etc. Formulae and equations in appendices should be given separate numbering: (Eq.A.1), (Eq.A.2), etc.: in a subsequent appendix, (Eq.B.1) and so forth.

Acknowledgements. Please acknowledgements, including information on grants received, before the references, in a separate section, and not as a footnote on the title page.

References. See separate section, below.

Figure legends, tables, figures, schemes. Present these, in this order, at the end of the article. They are described in more details below. High-resolution graphics files must always be provided separate from the main text file (see Preparation of illustrations).

References
Responsibility for the accuracy of bibliographic citations lies entirely with the authors.

Citations in the text. Please ensure that every reference cited in the text is also present in the reference list (and vice versa). Any references cited in the abstract must be given in full. Un published results and personal communications should not be in the reference list, but may be mentioned in the text. Citation of a reference as 'in press' implies that the item has been accepted for publication. In the text refer to the author's name (without initial) and year of publication, followed - if necessary - by a short reference to appropriate pages. Examples: "Since Peterson (1988) has shown that..." "This is in agreement with results obtained later (Kramer, 1989, pp. 12-16)". If reference is made in the text to a publication written by more than two authors the name of the first author should be used followed by "et al.". This indication, however, should never be used in the list of references. In this list names of first author and co-authors should be mentioned. References cited together in the text should be arranged chronologically. The list of references should be arranged alphabetically on authors' names, and chronologically per author. If an author's name in the list is also mentioned with co-authors the following order should be used: publications of the single author, arranged according to publication dates -- publications of the same author with one co-author -- publications of the author with more than one co-author. Publications by the same author(s) in the same year should be listed as 1974a, 1974b, etc

Citing and listing of web references. As a minimum, the full URL should be given. Any further information, if known (author names, dates, reference to a source publication, etc.), should also be given. Web references can be listed separately (e.g., after the reference list) under a different heading if desired, or can be included in the reference list. Use the following system for arranging your references, please note the proper position of the punctuation: In the text refer to the author's name (without initial) and year of publication, followed - if necessary - by a short reference to appropriate pages. Examples: "Since Peterson (1988) has shown that..." "This is in agreement with results obtained later (Kramer,1989, pp. 12-16)".

Reference to a journal publication: Van der Geer, J., Hanraads, J.A.J. α Lupton, R.A.(2000) . The art of writing a scientific article. J Sci Commun., 163, 51-9. Reference to a book: Strunk, Jr W. α White, E.B. (1979). The elements of style (3rd ed.). New York, Macmillan.

Reference to a chapter in an edited book: Mettam, G.R. α Adams, L.B. (1999). How to prepare an electronic version of your article. In B.S. Jones α R.Z. Smith, (Eds), Introduction to the electronic age. New York: E-Publishing Inc, p.281-304.

Note shortened form for last page number. e.g., 51-9, and that for more than 6 authors the first 6 should be listed followed by 'et al'. For further details you are referred to "Uniform Requirements for Manuscripts submitted to Biomedical Journals" (J Am Med Assoc 1997;277:927-934) (see also http://www.nejm.org/general/text/requirements/1.html)

Preparation of illustrations

Submitting your artwork in an electronic format helps us to produce your work to the best possible standards, ensuring accuracy, clarity and a high level of detail.

- Always supply high-quality printouts of your artwork, in case conversion of the electronic artwork is problematic.
- Make sure you use uniform lettering and sizing of your original artwork.
- Save text in illustrations as "graphics" or enclose the font.
- Only use the following fonts in your illustrations: Arial, Courier, Times, Symbol.
- Number the illustrations according to their sequence in the text.
- Use a logical naming convention for your artwork files, and supply a separate listing of the files and the software used.
- Provide all illustrations as separate files and as hardcopy printouts on separate sheets.
- Provide captions to illustrations separately.
- Produce images near to the desired size of the printed version.

Files can be stored on diskette, ZIP-disk or CD (either MS-DOS or Macintosh). A detailed guide on electronic artwork is available on our website: **http://authors.elsevier.com/artwork**. You are urged to visit this site; some excerpts from the detailed information are given here.

Formats

Regardless of the application used, when your electronic artwork is finalised, please "save as" or convert the images to one of the following formats (Note the resolution requirements for line drawings, halftones, and line/halftone combinations are given below.):

- EPS: Vector drawings. Embed the font or save the text as "graphics".
- TIFF: Colour or greyscale photographs (halftones): always use a minimum of 300dpi.
- TIFF: Bitmapped line drawings line drawings: use a minimum of 1000dpi.
- TIFF: Combinations bitmapped line/half-tone (colour or greyscale): a minimum of 500 dpi is required.
- DOC, XLS, or PPT: If your electronic artwork is created in any of these Microsoft Office applications please supply "as is".

Please do not:

- Supply embedded graphics in your wordprocessor (spreadsheet, presentation) documentation;
- Supply files that are optimized for screen use (like GIF, BMP, PICT, WPG); the resolution is too low;
- Supply files that are too low in resolution;
- Submit graphics that are disproportionately large for the content.

Non-electronic illustrations

Provide all illustrations as high-quality printouts, suitable for reproduction (which may include reduction) without retouching. Number illustrations consecutively in the order in which they are referred to in the text. They should accompany the manuscript, but should not be included within the text. Clearly mark all illustrations on the back (or - in case of line drawings - on the lower front side) with the figure number and the author's name and, in cases of ambiguity, the correct orientation. Mark the appropriate position of a figure in the article.

Captions

Ensure that each illustration has a caption. Supply captions on a separate sheet, not attached to the figure. A caption should compromise a brief title (**not** on the figure itself) and a description of the illustration. Keep text in the illustrations themselves to a minimum but explain all symbols and abbreviations used.

Line drawings. Supply high-quality printouts on white paper produced with black ink. The lettering and symbols, as well as other details, should have proportionate dimensions, so as to become illegible or unclear after possible reduction; in general, the figures should be designed for a reduction factor of two to three. The degree of reduction will be determined by the Publisher. Illustrations will not be enlarged. Consider the page format of the journal when designing the illustration. Photocopies are not suitable for reproduction. Do not use any type of shading on computer-generated.

Photographs (halftones). Please supply original photographs for reproduction, printed on glossy paper, very sharp and with good contrast. Remove non-essential areas of a photograph. Do not mount photographs unless they form part of a composite figure. Where necessary, insert a scale bar in the illustration (not below it), as opposed to giving a magnification factor in the legend. Note that photocopies of photographs are not acceptable.

Colour illustrations. Submit colour illustrations as original photographs, high-quality computer prints or transparencies, close to the size expected in publication, or as 35 mm slides. Polaroid colour prints are not suitable. If, together with your accepted article, you submit usable colour figures then Elsevier will ensure, at no additional charge, that these figures will appear in colour on the web (e.g., ScienceDirect and other sites) regardless of whether or not these illustrations are reproduced in colour in the printed version. For colour reproduction in print, you will receive information regarding the costs from Elsevier after receipt of your accepted article. Further information on the preparation of electronic artwork, please see **http://authors.elsevier.com /artwork**. Please note: Because of technical complications which can arise by converting colour figures to 'grey scale' (for the printed version should you not opt for colour in print) please submit in addition usable black and white prints corresponding to all the colour illustrations.

Evaluation and Research in Education

<table>
<tr><td colspan="2" align="center">

SUBMISSION PROCESS:

Electronic Submission Preferred
via EMail

info@multilingual-matters.com

</td></tr>
<tr><td>

CONTACT INFORMATION:

Keith Morrison, Editor
Multilingual Matters Ltd.
Frankfurt Lodge
Clevedon Hall
Victorial Road, Clevedon
North Somerset, BS21 7HH UK

Phone:
  +44 1275 876519

Email:
  info@multilingual-matters.com

Website:
  www.multilingual-matters.net

</td><td>

REVIEW PROCESS:

Type of Review:	Blind Review
No. External Reviewers:	2
No. InHouse Reviewers:	0
Acceptance Rate:	50%
Time to Review:	2 - 3 Months
Reviewer's Comments:	Yes
Invited Articles:	11-20%
Fees to Publish:	$0.00 US$
Fees to Review:	$0.00 US$

</td></tr>
<tr><td>

PUBLICATION GUIDELINES:

Manuscript Style:
  Multilingual Matters

Manuscript Length:
  16-20

Copies Required:
  One

</td><td>

CIRCULATION DATA:

Reader:
  Academics, Administrators, Practicing
  Teachers

Frequency of Issue:
  3 Times/Year

Sponsor/Publisher:
  Multilingual Matters Ltd.

</td></tr>
</table>

MANUSCRIPT TOPICS:
Curriculum Studies; Education Management / Administration; Tests, Measurement & Evaluation

MANUSCRIPT GUIDELINES/COMMENTS:

Evaluation & Research in Education aims to make methods of evaluation and research in education available to teachers, administrators and research workers. Papers published in the journal: (1) report evaluation and research findings; (2) treat conceptual and methodological issues; and/or (3) consider the implications of the above for action. There is a book reviews section and also occasional reports on educational materials and equipment.

Guidelines for Authors of Journal Papers
Articles should not normally exceed 7000 words. Note that it is our policy not to review papers which are currently under consideration by other journals.

They should be typed, double-spaced on A4 paper, with ample left- and right-hand margins, on one side of the paper only, and every page should be numbered consecutively. A cover page should contain only the title, thereby facilitating anonymous reviewing by two independent assessors.

Authors may also wish to take precautions to avoid textual references which would identify themselves to the referees. In such cases the authors of accepted papers will have the opportunity to include any such omitted material before the paper is published.

Submissions for Work in Progress/Readers' Response/Letters to the Editor sections should be approximately 500 words in length.

Main contact author should also appear in a separate paragraph on the title page.

An abstract should be included. This should not exceed 200 words (longer abstracts are rejected by many abstracting services).

A short version of the title (maximum 45 characters) should also be supplied for the journal's running headline.

To facilitate the production of the annual subject index, a list of key words (not more than six) should be provided, under which the paper may be indexed.

If submitting by mail, one copy and a disc must be submitted.

Footnotes should be avoided. Essential notes should be numbered in the text and grouped together at the end of the article. Diagrams and Figures, if they are considered essential, should be clearly related to the section of the text to which they refer. The original diagrams and figures should be submitted with the top copy.

References should be set out in alphabetical order of the author's name in a list at the end of the article. They should be given in standard form, as in the Appendix below.

References in the text of an article should be by the author's name and year of publication, as in these examples: Jones (1987) in a paper on ... [commonest version]; Jones and Evans (1997c: 22) state that ... [where page number is required]; Evidence is given by Smith *et al*. (1984) ... [for three or more authors]. Further exploration of this aspect may be found in many sources (e.g. Brown & Green, 1982; Jackson, 1983; White, 1981a) [note alphabetical order, use of & and semi-colons].

Once the refereeing procedures are completed, authors should if possible supply a word-processor disc containing their manuscript file(s). If presented on disc, we require files to be saved:
- on an IBM-PC compatible 3.5 inch disc (5.25 inch discs also acceptable), or
- on an Apple Mac **high-density** 3.5 inch disc.
- Text should be saved in the author's normal word-processor format. The name of the word-processor program used should also be supplied. Tables and Figures should be saved in separate files.

The author of an article accepted for publication will receive page proofs for correction, if there is sufficient time to do so. This stage must not be used as an opportunity to revise the paper. Speedy return of corrected proofs is important.

Contributions and queries should be sent to the Editors, c/o Multilingual Matters Ltd, Frankfurt Lodge, Clevedon Hall, Victoria Road, Clevedon, BS21 7HH, England.

Appendix: **References**
A very large majority of authors' proof-corrections are caused by errors in references. Authors are therefore requested to check the following points particularly carefully when submitting manuscripts:
- Are all the references in the reference list cited in the text?
- Do all the citations in the text appear in the reference list?
- Do the dates in the text and the reference list correspond?

- Do the spellings of authors' names in text and reference list correspond, and do all authors have the correct initials?
- Are journal references complete with volume and pages numbers?
- Are references to books complete with place of publication and the name of the publisher?

It is extremely helpful if references are presented as far as possible in accordance with our house style. A few more typical examples are shown below. Note, especially, use of upper & lower case in paper titles, use of capital letters and italic (underlining can be used as an alternative if italic is not available) in book and journal titles, punctuation (or lack of it) after dates, journal titles, and book titles. The inclusion of issue numbers of journals, or page numbers in books, is optional but if included should be as per the examples below.

Department of Education and Science (DES) (1985) *Education for All* (The Swann Report). London: HMSO.

Evans, N.J. and Ilbery, B.W. (1989) A conceptual framework for investigating farm-based accommodation and tourism in Britain. *Journal of Rural Studies* 5 (3), 257–266.

Evans, N.J. and Ilbery, B.W. (1992) Advertising and farm-based accommodation: A British case-study. *Tourism Management* 13 (4), 415–422.

Laufer, B. (1985) Vocabulary acquisition in a second language: The hypothesis of 'synforms'. PhD thesis, University of Edinburgh.

Mackey, W.F. (1980) The ecology of language shift. In P.H. Nelde (ed.) *Languages in Contact and in Conflict* (pp. 35–41). Wiesbaden: Steiner.

Marien, C. and Pizam, A. (1997) Implementing sustainable tourism development through citizen participation in the planning process. In S. Wahab and J. Pigram (eds) *Tourism, Development and Growth* (pp. 164–78). London: Routledge.

Morrison, D. (1980) Small group discussion project questionnaire. University of Hong Kong Language Centre (mimeo).

Zahn, C.J. and Hopper, R. (1985) The speech evaluation instrument: A user's manual (version 1.0a). Unpublished manuscript, Cleveland State University.

Zigler, E. and Balla, D. (eds) (1982) *Mental Retardation: The Developmental-Difference Controversy*. Hillsdale, NJ: Lawrence Erlbaum.

For more details, please e-mail us on **info@multilingual-matters.com**.

Exceptional Children

SUBMISSION PROCESS:
Postal Submission Only

CONTACT INFORMATION:	REVIEW PROCESS:	
Steve Graham, Editor	**Type of Review:**	Blind Review
Vanderbilt University		
Peabody College of Education	**No. External Reviewers:**	3-4
Department of Special Education	**No. InHouse Reviewers:**	1
Box 328		
Nashville, TN 37203-5701 USA	**Acceptance Rate:**	17-20%
	Time to Review:	2 - 3 Months
Phone:	**Reviewer's Comments:**	Yes
301-405-6493	**Invited Articles:**	0%
Email:	**Fees to Publish:**	$0.00 US$
sg23@umail.umd.edu	**Fees to Review:**	$0.00 US$
Website:		

PUBLICATION GUIDELINES:	CIRCULATION DATA:
Manuscript Style:	**Reader:**
American Psychological Association	Academics
Manuscript Length:	**Frequency of Issue:**
25-50	Quarterly
Copies Required:	**Sponsor/Publisher:**
Four	Council for Exceptional Children

MANUSCRIPT TOPICS:
Adult Career & Vocational; Audiology / Speech Pathology; Bilingual / E.S.L.; Elementary / Early Childhood; Gifted Children; Reading; Secondary / Adolescent Studies; Special Education; Teacher Education; Tests, Measurement & Evaluation; Urban Education, Cultural / Non-Traditional

MANUSCRIPT GUIDELINES/COMMENTS:

Purpose
Exceptional Children is the research journal of The Council for Exceptional Children. It presents research and analyses on: Education and development of exceptional infants, toddlers, children, and youth, and adults. Professional issues and policies relevant to exceptional infants, toddlers, children, youth, and adults.

The *Journal* primarily publishes five types of articles:
Research Studies report a qualitative, large-group quantitative, or single-subject design study. Effect sizes should be reported for quantitative studies.

Research Reviews involve the analysis and integration of research in one or more areas. Reviews must be comprehensive and critical. Whenever possible, effect sizes for individual studies should be reported.

Methodological Reviews systematically examine the methodological strengths and weaknesses of a specific body of literature (e.g., a methodological review of the soundness of research on teaching phonological awareness). This can include a methodological analysis of qualitative, quantitative, and single-subject design studies.

Data-Based Position Papers address an important issue (practical or theoretical) in special or gifted education. This involves analyzing and integrating the existing research literature to provide a balanced and scholarly examination of the issue.

Policy Analyses include critical analyses and research related to public policy that impact the education of exceptional infants, toddlers, children, youth, and adults.

All research that is published in *Exceptional Children* should have implications for practice, and these must be stated in the article. Manuscripts that focus on practical methods and materials for classroom use should be submitted to *Teaching Exceptional Children*, the CEC journal that is specifically for teachers of children with disabilities and children who are gifted.

Exceptional Children does not publish descriptions of instructional procedures or classroom materials, accounts of personal experiences, letters to the editor, book or test reviews, and single case studies. Nondatabased reports on innovative techniques, programs, or models as well as studies involving a pretest-posttest only design with no comparison condition are also not published in *Exceptional Children*. Investigations involving questionnaires and survey are generally not published unless the sample is representative of the population being studied.

Writing for *Exceptional Children*
While *Exceptional Children* is the research journal, its articles are read by a much broader audience than just researchers. Therefore, articles written for *Exceptional Children* need to be written for this broader audience. Articles should not be viewed as shortened versions of dissertation or technical reports, but rather as a way to inform other researchers, school administrators, state department personnel, service providers, teachers, parents, and others about your research and its implications for practice. Articles must be clear and concise. To best meet the needs of the broader audience, consider the following questions as you prepare your manuscript:

Introduction
- Why is your research needed?
- What are 2 to 3 key points the reader needs to understand before reading about what you did?
- Is the tone positive?
- Have you successfully communicated in less than 5 pages, and ideally in 2 to 3 pages?

Methodology
- Have you provided enough general information in a way that a lay reader can understand what you have done?
- Have you provided a source of further information about methodology for the researcher who wants to replicate your research?

Results
- Have you organized your results in a way that promotes the understanding of your findings?
- Have you provided the necessary details for the researcher without making it difficult for others to read?

Discussion
- What are the 2 to 3 key points that need to be made about your findings?
- What limitations are there on your research and its findings?
- What are the practical implications of your findings?
- What are the next steps to be taken?

Manuscript Requirements
Before submitting a manuscript to *Exceptional Children*, please review the Author Checklist below. This will help ensure that your manuscript is not screened out or returned before review.

- Manuscript is consistent with the purpose of the journal.
- Manuscript conforms to APA format (see *APA Publication Manual*, 5th edition, 2001) particularly:
  1. Manuscript is double spaced, with 1" margins (12 font type preferred).
  2. All pages are numbered in sequence, starting with the title page.
  3. Effect size information is provided for quantitative studies.

- All references in text are listed and in complete agreement with text citations.
- Abstract is not more than 120 words long.
- The first page of the manuscript contains the running head, title of the article, authors' names, affiliations, date of submission, address of submitting author (including street name for overnight delivery), phone number, fax number, and e-mail address. The second page duplicates the first page except that only the running head and title are included.
- An exact electronic copy of the manuscript on a 3½" disk is included and saved as either a Microsoft Word (preferred) or RTF file. The label on the disk includes an abbreviated title, the authors' names, file names, date submitted for review, and word processing program.
- All word processing codes are removed from the electronic version of the manuscript for apostrophes, quotation marks, hyphens, and so forth.
- Cover letter states that manuscript is original and not previously published, all authors have given consent to submit the manuscript to Exceptional Children, and the manuscript is not under consideration elsewhere.
- The cover letter indicates if the data from this manuscript is part of a larger study or if any part of the data has been included in another manuscript. The cover letter must provide a full explanation if either of these situations exist.

Review Process
Selection of manuscripts for publication is based on a blind peer review process. However, all manuscripts are screened first. Those manuscripts that do not meet the manuscript requirements, or that are not consistent with the purpose of the journal, are not forwarded for peer review. The author either is notified that the manuscript is not acceptable for Exceptional Children, or is requested to make changes in the manuscript so that it meets requirements. Copies of the manuscript are not returned to the author in either case.

Manuscripts that are not screened out and that are consistent with the purpose of the journal are sent out for peer review. Reviewers will not know the identity of the author.

Based on the blind reviews, the Associate editors and/or co-editors will communicate the results of that review to the author. The decision that is communicated to the author will be one of the following:
- Acceptable, with routine editing
- Acceptable, with revisions indicated by the action editor
- Revise and resubmit
- Unacceptable

When a decision is made that a manuscript is unacceptable for *Exceptional Children*, it may be recommended that it be sent to a journal of one of the CEC Divisions. This recommendation does not mean that the manuscript would be automatically accepted by a Division journal; the manuscript would have to go through the review process again.

Exceptional Parent

SUBMISSION PROCESS:

Postal Submission Only

CONTACT INFORMATION:

Jan Hollingsworth, Managing Editor
43 Miller's Cove Circle
Signal Mountain, TN 37377 USA

Phone:
814-361-3860 ext. 291

Email:
jhollingsworth@eparent.com

Website:
www.eparent.com

REVIEW PROCESS:

Type of Review:	Editorial Review
No. External Reviewers:	0
No. InHouse Reviewers:	2
Acceptance Rate:	6-10%
Time to Review:	Over 6 Months
Reviewer's Comments:	No
Invited Articles:	
Fees to Publish:	$0.00 US$
Fees to Review:	$0.00 US$

PUBLICATION GUIDELINES:

Manuscript Style:
See Manuscript Guidelines

Manuscript Length:
900-1500 words

Copies Required:
One

CIRCULATION DATA:

Reader:
Practicing Teachers, Families, Healthcare Providers

Frequency of Issue:
Monthly

Sponsor/Publisher:
EP Global Communications, Inc.

MANUSCRIPT TOPICS:
Audiology / Speech Pathology; Behavioral, Developmental Disabilities; Educational Psychology; Elementary / Early Childhood; Gifted Children; Special Education

MANUSCRIPT GUIDELINES/COMMENTS:

Exceptional Parent publishes articles on a broad scale of social, psychological, legal, political, technological, financial, and educational concerns faced by families and professionals supporting and treating children, adolescents and adults with disabilities and special needs.

Our primary audience is parents. We strive to maintain respect and consideration for both the professional and the parent who want to work together in understanding the child's disability. Therefore, our tone is "How to work together." As journalists we examine ALL sides of controversial issues.

Our tone is generally upbeat, but we also recognize that our audience is no stranger to difficulties and realities.

Exceptional Parent advises; it does not preach. We try as much as possible to avoid saying "You must..." or "You should..." Rather, we suggest, "A good way of doing this is...," or "You can."

Exceptional Parent's **Style**

We try to use language geared toward the consumer/reader who has a high-school diploma (i.e., McCall's, Woman's Day, Newsweek) as opposed to professional, medical or business journals (i.e., JAMA, Business Week, New England Journal of Medicine.) Professional Journal style-with reference to studies and imbedded footnotes--is unacceptable. Therefore, professional jargon and specialized terminology is discouraged. If there is a term parents will be coming across on a regular basis ("intervention," "aspirate" "URL," "OBRA Trust"), it needs to be "translated" into everyday or ordinary terms.

Sensitivity

Because our readers are professionals as well as parents, we write about "the child" rather than "your specific child."

We try to be as sensitive to our readers as possible. We speak of "children with disabilities" or "children with special needs" rather than "disabled children" or "handicapped children."

We avoid discussion of what could have been done to prevent a disability. Our readers are interested in what they can do now.

If you write about a child with a specific disability, it should be worded in such a way that it reaches out to all families that have children with disabilities. Think to yourself, "What information can my story contain that will be of use to other parents of any child with a disability?" Also, please give a brief description of any disabilities that are mentioned.

The approach our publication takes is
1. Parents are the best experts on their children.
2. *Exceptional Parent* offers practical information and advice that readers can use to make life easier and happier when caring for a child or young adult with special needs.
3. *Exceptional Parent* is also a valuable resource for educational and health care professionals.

Technical Hints

Disorders, diseases and disabilities are used in lower case, unless they are "named after" someone. Therefore, we capitalized Down syndrome (always lower-case syndrome) because Dr. Down is the person who identified it. We use multiple sclerosis in the lower case because it defines a condition.

Please be sure to spell-check your article before sending it to us!! Fact checking is also very important! Be sure to check all names, dates, and addresses. For example, Kodak is really referred to as Eastman Kodak. Please be as thorough as possible, the more accurate the information, the more professional the article will be.

Article lengths vary. Approximately 1200-1800 words would be appropriate. Please indicate if there is any artwork (art is: printed pictures, paper-copy illustrations, slides, and transparencies) that should accompany the article if selected for publication. It is not necessary to send artwork with the submitted manuscript, but a brief description or photocopies of the artwork are welcome.

Please remember, to include author "bio" information that will be included in total word count. This information consists of the name and pertinent background of the author. This should be no longer than three or four sentences.

Copy should be typed and double-spaced, preferably in 12 pt. type and provided on Mac disc in a Word compatible program. Copy should be sent to: Exceptional Parent, c/o Manuscript Submission, 65 East Route 4, River Edge, NJ 07661

Copy can also be e-mailed to **epedit@aol.com**. The review process can vary from six months to a year.

Photos

Pictures and illustrations should be clearly labeled with the name(s) of the person/people, the activity, or the subject-matter shown. This is so the pictures and/or illustrations can be easily captioned and fit into the story. Put names in order of appearance in pictures. For example, Brenda (right) and John (left). People should be identified by name, relationship to a child if shown, home address (city/state), age of child, and the activity they are involved in (school, vacation, play, etc.).

Please do not write directly on the back of photographs. Include on the label, the name and address of the person who is sending the pictures and the title of the article for which they are intended. Slides and transparencies should be numbered and described on a separate sheet of paper. Please note, **we cannot guarantee that art will be returned**.

A picture should be accompanied by written permission to publish. An address and phone number should also be supplied. We need the permission of everyone in a photo(s)! *Enclosed please find a permission form for you to copy.

Include with your article a list of all sources you contacted, their telephone numbers, and copies of any materials you used (i.e., an article from another magazine, a photocopy of a technical or medical definition).

We also need the addresses of all those mentioned in the article so that we may send them a copy of the magazine.

Other materials

Our emphasis is on family over clinical experience. Personal anecdotes, quotes, or sidebars are encouraged because they bring "life" to the articles. Our readers need to identify with the story and the child/young adults disability on some level. Whether it has to do with siblings, advocacy etc., it should help as many parents as possible!

Website editorial content

Exceptional Parent is fortunate to receive a voluminous amount of editorial submissions, more, in fact, than the print publication will accommodate in a given year. In the spring of 2007 *Exceptional Parent* is launching a fresh, new website (same address: **www.eparent.com**) which will contain timely and changing editorial content. Therefore, submissions will be considered for print publication and/or for the *EP* website.

Exceptionality - A Special Education Journal

SUBMISSION PROCESS:
Postal Submission Only

CONTACT INFORMATION:	REVIEW PROCESS:	
Edward J. Sabornie, Editor North Carolina State University	**Type of Review:**	Editorial Review
College of Education		
Poe Hall	**No. External Reviewers:**	3
Campus Box 7801	**No. InHouse Reviewers:**	1-2
Raleigh, NC 27695-7801 USA	**Acceptance Rate:**	20-25%
	Time to Review:	1 - 2 Months
	Reviewer's Comments:	Yes
Phone:	**Invited Articles:**	50%
919-515-1777		
	Fees to Publish:	$0.00 US$
Email:	**Fees to Review:**	$0.00 US$
edward_sabornie@ncsu.edu		
Website:		
www.erlbaum.com		

PUBLICATION GUIDELINES:	CIRCULATION DATA:
Manuscript Style: American Psychological Association	**Reader:** Academics
Manuscript Length: 26-30	**Frequency of Issue:** Quarterly
Copies Required: Five	**Sponsor/Publisher:** Lawrence Erlbaum Associates, Inc.

MANUSCRIPT TOPICS:
Adult Career & Vocational; Educational Psychology; Gifted Children; Reading; Science Math & Environment; Secondary / Adolescent Studies; Special Education; Teacher Education; Tests, Measurement & Evaluation

MANUSCRIPT GUIDELINES/COMMENTS:

Editorial Scope
The purpose of *Exceptionality* is to provide a forum for presentation of current research and professional scholarship in special education. Areas of scholarship published in the journal include quantitative, qualitative, and single-subject research designs examining students and persons with exceptionalities, as well as reviews of the literature, discussion pieces, invited works, position papers, theoretical papers, policy analyses, and research syntheses. Appropriate data-based papers include basic, experimental, applied, naturalistic, ethnographic, and historical investigations. Papers that describe assessment, diagnosis, placement, teacher education, and service delivery practices will also be included. Manuscripts accepted for publication will represent a cross section of all areas of special education and exceptionality and will attempt to further the knowledge base and improve services to individuals with disabilities and gifted and talented behavior.

The purpose of *Exceptionality* is to provide a forum for presentation of current research and professional scholarship in special education. Areas of scholarship published in the journal include quantitative, qualitative, and single-subject research designs examining students and persons with

Audience

Education researchers, education professionals interested in students at risk, developmental and school psychologists, neuropsychologists, medical personnel involved with students and persons with exceptionalities, social workers, teachers, and higher education students in education.

Instructions to Contributors

Manuscript Submission. Only manuscripts written in English will be considered. Submit five manuscript copies to the Editor, Dr. Edward J. Sabornie, North Carolina State University, College of Education and Psychology, Poe Hall, Campus Box 7801, Raleigh, NC 27695-7801. Prepare manuscripts according to the *Publication Manual of the American Psychological Association* (5th ed.). Type all components of the manuscript double-spaced, including the title page, abstract, text, quotes, acknowledgments, references, appendixes, tables, figure captions, and footnotes. An abstract of fewer than 200 words should be typed on a separate page. Authors should comply with the "Guidelines to Reduce Bias in Language," which appears on pages 61 to 76 of the APA Manual. Five photocopies of the illustrations and the original illustrations should accompany the manuscript. All manuscripts submitted will be acknowledged promptly. Authors should keep a copy of their manuscript to guard against loss.

Peer Review Policy. The editorial board evaluates manuscripts with regard to scientific rigor and importance of the implications for practice or policy. To accelerate the review process, reviewers only provide comments to authors whose manuscripts are found acceptable for publication. In this way, we are able to provide author feedback in approximately 6 weeks from the time of receipt of the manuscript. Authors who prefer that their identities and affiliations be masked are responsible for requesting blind review. Every effort should be made by the authors to see that the manuscript itself contains no clues to their identities.

Permissions. Authors are responsible for all statements made in their work and for obtaining permission from copyright owners to reprint or adapt a table or figure or to reprint a quotation of 500 words or more. Authors should write to the original author(s) and publisher to request nonexclusive world rights in all languages for use of the material in the article and in future editions. Provide copies of all permissions and credit lines obtained.

Regulations. In a cover letter, authors should state that the findings and ideas reported in the manuscript are original and have not been published previously and that the manuscript is not being simultaneously submitted elsewhere. Authors should also state that they have complied with *American Psychological Association* ethical standards in the treatment of their samples.

Production Notes. After a manuscript is accepted for publication, the author is asked to provide a computer disk containing the manuscript file. Files are copyedited and typeset into page proofs. Authors read proofs to correct errors and answer editors' queries. Authors may order reprints of their articles only when they return page proofs.

FORUM: for promoting 3-19 comprehensive education

SUBMISSION PROCESS:

Postal Submission Only

CONTACT INFORMATION:	REVIEW PROCESS:	
Clyde Chitty, Editor 19 Beaconsfield Road, Bickley Bromley, Kent, BR1 2BL UK	**Type of Review:**	Blind Review
	No. External Reviewers:	1
	No. InHouse Reviewers:	1
Phone: 0181-464 4962	**Acceptance Rate:** **Time to Review:**	75% 1 - 2 Months
Email: c.chitty@gold.ac.uk	**Reviewer's Comments:** **Invited Articles:**	Yes
Website: http://www.wwwords.co.uk/forum/index.html	**Fees to Publish:** **Fees to Review:**	$0.00 US$ $0.00 US$

PUBLICATION GUIDELINES:	CIRCULATION DATA:
Manuscript Style: See Manuscript Guidelines	**Reader:** Administrators, Governors, Parents, Practicing Teachers
Manuscript Length: 6-10	**Frequency of Issue:** 3 Times/Year
Copies Required: Two	**Sponsor/Publisher:** Symposium Journals

MANUSCRIPT TOPICS:
Education Management / Administration; Government Educational Policy

MANUSCRIPT GUIDELINES/COMMENTS:

About the Journal
FORUM has for over forty years been the pre-eminent focal point for topical and informed analysis - very often highly forthright and critical - of all aspects of United Kingom government policy as it influences the education of children from primary through to higher education. *FORUM* - a journal-cum-magazine - vigorously campaigns for the universal provision of state-provided education, and seeks to identify and expose all attempts to overturn the gains of the past thirty years. Every teacher, headteacher, administrator, parent, or governor should read this exciting publication.

Contributions are not drawn only from the familiar sources in universities and colleges, but also in large numbers from teachers, writing of their own experiences in the classroom.

That *FORUM* is an excellent means of keeping up-to-date with events within the education scene in Britain is born out by the fact that although, naturally, the vast majority of its readers are teachers within the UK, about 20% of all subscribers live outside the country.

FORUM: for promoting 3-19 comprehensive education is published three times a year in Spring, Summer and Autumn, those three issues constituting one volume. ISSN 0963-8253

Editorial correspondence, including typescript articles (1500-2000 words), contributions to discussion (800 words maximum), and books for review, should be addressed to: Professor Clyde Chitty, 19 Beaconsfield Road, Bickley, Bromley, Kent BR1 2BL, United Kingdom. Telephone: 0181-464 4962; Email: **c.chitty@gold.ac.uk**. Please send two copies and enclose a stamped addressed envelope.

Self-archiving

Authors are welcome to deposit their original/personal manuscript files 'live' in their institution's archive (ideally with a link to the final version of the article as it appears on the journals' website) but the journal asks that authors do not deposit the final typeset version (i.e. the website version) until 18 months after formal publication. Please note that all articles published within Symposium journals automatically become open access 18 months after publication, so authors are asked to respect that embargo period.

Futurist

SUBMISSION PROCESS:
Postal Submission Only

CONTACT INFORMATION:	REVIEW PROCESS:	
Cynthia G. Wagner, Managing Editor 7910 Woodmont Avenue, Suite 450 Bethesda, MD 20814 USA	**Type of Review:**	Editorial Review
	No. External Reviewers:	0
	No. InHouse Reviewers:	3
Phone: 301-656-8274	**Acceptance Rate:**	21-30%
	Time to Review:	4 - 6 Months
Email: cwagner@wfs.org	**Reviewer's Comments:**	No
	Invited Articles:	6-10%
Website: www.wfs.org	**Fees to Publish:**	$0.00 US$
	Fees to Review:	$0.00 US$

PUBLICATION GUIDELINES:	CIRCULATION DATA:
Manuscript Style: Chicago Manual of Style	**Reader:** Academics, Business Persons
Manuscript Length: 16-20	**Frequency of Issue:** Bi-Monthly
Copies Required: One	**Sponsor/Publisher:** World Future Society

MANUSCRIPT TOPICS:

Adult Career & Vocational; Educational Technology Systems; Futures Studies; General Trends; Innovations; Health & Physical Education; Higher Education; Science Math & Environment; Social Studies / Social Science

MANUSCRIPT GUIDELINES/COMMENTS:

The Futurist is constantly looking for articles to publish, both by established authorities and new authors. Articles must pass the following tests:

1. Subject Matter

The article should have something new and significant to say about the future, not merely repeat what has already been said before. For example, an article noting that increasing air pollution may damage human health is something everyone has already heard. Writers for *The Futurist* should remember that the publication focuses on the future, especially the period five to 50 years ahead.

The Futurist does not publish fiction or poetry. An exception is occasionally made for scenarios presenting fictionalized people in future situations. These scenarios are kept brief.

The Futurist covers a wide range of subject areas--virtually everything that will affect our future or will be affected by the changes the future will bring. Past articles have focused on topics ranging from technology, planning, resources, and economics, to religion; the arts, values, and health. Articles we avoid include: (A) overly technical articles that would be of little interest to the general reader; (B) opinion pieces on current government issues; (C) articles by authors with only a casual knowledge of the subject being discussed.

2. Author's Knowledge of the Subject
Authors should provide some biographical material, which should indicate their qualifications to write about a particular subject.

3. Quality of Writing
Make points clearly and in a way that holds the reader's interest. A reader should not have to struggle to guess an author's meaning or wade through lots of unnecessary words in the process. Use concrete examples and anecdotes to illustrate the points made; nothing is duller than a page of generalities unrelieved by specific examples. Keep sentences short, mostly under 25 words. Avoid the jargon of a particular trade or profession; when technical terms are necessary, be sure to explain them.

The Futurist's copyeditors use the University of Chicago Press's *A Manual of Style* and *Merriam Webster's Unabridged Dictionary* as guidelines on spelling and style.

Authors can get a feel for *The Futurist's* style by reviewing recent issues, available in many large libraries, bookstores, and newsstands. Sample copies may be purchased from the Society for $7.95 each, prepaid.

Writer's Guidelines for the Futurist
Submissions. The editors prefer to read completed manuscripts but will consider queries that include a strong thesis, detailed outline, and summary of the author's expertise on the proposed topic.

Manuscripts submitted must be typed, **double-spaced**, and accompanied by a self-addressed, stamped envelope to be considered or returned. A brief "about the author" note is recommended. E-mailed submissions are acceptable. **Do not** submit manuscripts by fax. Simultaneous queries or submissions are acceptable; please make note of this in your cover letter.

Length of Articles. Articles in *The Futurist* generally run 1,000 to 4,000 words, but both longer and shorter articles are acceptable.

Opinion pieces about the future may be submitted to "Future View," *The Futurist's* guest editorial column; these normally should be no longer than 800 words.

Photographs and Drawings. *The Futurist* is very interested in photographs, drawings, or other materials that might be used to illustrate articles. Color slides or glossy prints (either color or black and white) are acceptable, as are digital images. *The Futurist is* not responsible for damage to materials during the mailing process. All such materials must be accompanied by a self-addressed, stamped envelope or mailing tube with sufficient postage to be returned.

Response Time. The editors will make every attempt to respond to all queries and manuscript submissions as soon as possible, but please allow at least three weeks for queries and three months for manuscripts.

In certain cases, the editors of *The Futurist* may show manuscripts to the editors of other World Future Society publications, including *Futures Research Quarterly*, *Future Times*, and the *Forums* on the Society's Web site. This may further delay response, but will increase the author's opportunities for publication.

Withdrawal of Manuscript from Planned Publication. Authors may withdraw a manuscript from the publication process provided written notice is given at least seven weeks before the date of publication. At the same time, the editors reserve the right to withdraw from publication any previously accepted material.

Compensation. Authors of articles are provided 10 free copies of the issue in which their work appears and the right to purchase additional copies at the lowest multiple rate ($3 each).

The Futurist does NOT offer financial compensation for articles.

Send all submissions to: Managing Editor, The Futurist, World Future Society, 7910 Woodmont Avenue, Suite 450, Bethesda, MD 20814, U.S.A; E-mail: **cwagner@wfs.org**.

Gender and Education

<table>
<tr><td colspan="2" align="center">

SUBMISSION PROCESS:

**Electronic Submission Only
via Online Portal**

http://mc.manuscriptcentral.com/cgee

</td></tr>
<tr><td>

CONTACT INFORMATION:

Epstein, Renold & Kehily, Editors
Cardiff School of Social Sciences
Glamorgan Building
King Edward VII Avenue
Cardiff, CF10 3WT UK

Phone:
  +44 1912 226535

Email:
  genderandeducation@cf.ac.uk

Website:
  http://www.tandf.co.uk/journals/titles/095
  40253.asp

</td><td>

REVIEW PROCESS:

Type of Review:	Blind Review
No. External Reviewers:	2
No. InHouse Reviewers:	1
Acceptance Rate:	11-20%
Time to Review:	2 - 3 Months
Reviewer's Comments:	Yes
Invited Articles:	0-5%
Fees to Publish:	$0.00 US$
Fees to Review:	$0.00 US$

</td></tr>
<tr><td>

PUBLICATION GUIDELINES:

Manuscript Style:
  See Manuscript Guidelines

Manuscript Length:
  4,000-8,000 words

Copies Required:
  Four Hardcopy

</td><td>

CIRCULATION DATA:

Reader:
  Academics

Frequency of Issue:
  6 Times/Year

Sponsor/Publisher:
  Routledge, Taylor & Francis, Ltd.

</td></tr>
</table>

MANUSCRIPT TOPICS:
Educational Psychology; Gender / Education

MANUSCRIPT GUIDELINES/COMMENTS:

This journal publishes articles and shorter, more polemic 'viewpoints' from throughout the world which contribute to feminist knowledge, theory, consciousness, action and debate as well as short topical articles on 'current concerns' relevant to gender and education. All articles, current concerns and viewpoints are submitted to at least two referees before acceptance for publication.

Notes for Contributors
The Editors welcome a variety of contributions that focus on gender as a category of analysis in education and that further feminist knowledge, theory, consciousness, action and debate. Education will be interpreted in a broad sense to cover both formal and informal aspects, including nursery, primary and secondary education; youth cultures inside and outside schools; adult, community, further and higher education; vocational education and training; media education; parental education. Contributors are asked to avoid unnecessary or mystifying jargon and to use non-sexist and non-racist language.

All submissions should be made online at *Gender and Education*'s Manuscript Central site (**http://mc.manuscriptcentral.com/cgee**). New users should first create an account. Once a user is logged onto the site submissions should be made via the Author Centre.

Manuscripts may fall into one of the following categories:

- articles, ideally between 4000 and 8000 words
- viewpoints, usually up to 3000 words, that are more polemical in tone and possibly based on the life experiences, ideas and views of the writer
- comment and critique, usually up to 3000 words, about current events and policy developments in education. Such comment and critique could relate to the international stage or to a particular country

Please state clearly in your covering email and on the front page of your submission which type of contribution you intend to make (article, viewpoint, or comment and critique). All manuscripts submitted are subjected to independent refereeing. The full name, postal address and email address of the author who will check proofs and receive correspondence and offprints should also be included.

Manuscripts should not presently be under consideration for publication elsewhere.

Submissions should be double spaced, with ample margins and bear the title of the contribution plus an abstract of 100-150 words and six keywords for online searching purposes. If hard copies are sent, they must be typed on one side of the paper only. In order to protect anonymity, name(s) of the author(s) and institutional address, if any, should appear on a separate title page. The full postal address of the author who will check proofs and receive correspondence and offprints should also be included. All pages should be numbered. Footnotes to the text should be avoided wherever this is reasonably possible. The approximate total number of words should be specified on the title page.

To download a Word template for this journal, please visit the web site.

For further information on electronic submission, including information on accepted file types, please visit the web site.

Tables and captions to illustrations. Tables should be typed out on separate sheets and not included as part of the text. The captions to illustrations should be gathered together and also typed out on a separate sheet. Tables should be numbered with Roman numerals, and figures with Arabic numerals. The approximate position of tables and figures should be indicated in the manuscript. Captions should include keys to symbols.

Figures. Please supply one set of artwork in a finished form, suitable for reproduction. If this is not possible, figures will be redrawn by the publishers.

References should be indicated in the typescript by giving the author's name with the year of publication in parentheses. If several papers by the same author and from the same year are cited, a, b, c, etc., should be placed after the year of publication. References should be listed in full at the end of the paper in the following standard form:

For books
ARNOT, M. (2000) *Reproducing Gender* (London, Routledge Falmer).

For articles
BENJAMIN, S. (2000) Challenging masculinities: disability and achievement in testing times, *Gender and Education*, 13(1), pp.39-55.

For chapters within books
MAHONY, P. (1998) Girls will be girls and boys will be first, in D. Epstein, J. Elwood, V. Hey & J. Maw (Eds) *Failing Boys?* (Buckingham, Open University Press).

Titles of journals should not be abbreviated.

Proofs will be sent to authors if there is sufficient time to do so. They should be corrected and returned to the Editor within three days. Major alterations to the text cannot be accepted.

Offprints. Fifty offprints of each paper are supplied free. Additional copies may be purchased and should be ordered when the proofs are returned. Offprints, together with a complete copy of the relevant journal issue, are sent by accelerated surface post about three weeks after publication.

Copyright. It is a condition of publication that authors vest copyright in their articles, including abstracts, in Taylor & Francis Ltd. This enables us to ensure full copyright protection and to disseminate the article, and the journal, to the widest possible readership in print and electronic formats as appropriate. Authors may, of course, use the article elsewhere after publication without prior permission from Taylor & Francis, provided that acknowledgement is given to the Journal as the original source of publication, and that Taylor & Francis is notified so that our records show that its use is properly authorised. Authors are themselves responsible for obtaining permission to reproduce copyright material from other sources.

Government Union Review

SUBMISSION PROCESS:
Postal Submission Only

CONTACT INFORMATION:	REVIEW PROCESS:

<table>
<tr><td>Editor
Government Union Review
Public Service Research Foundation
320 D Maple Avenue East
Vienna, VA 22180 USA

Phone:
  703-242-3575

Email:
  info@psrf.org

Website:
  www.psrf.org</td><td>

Type of Review: Editorial Review

No. External Reviewers: 0
No. InHouse Reviewers: 2

Acceptance Rate: 70%
Time to Review: 1 - 2 Months
Reviewer's Comments: No
Invited Articles: 31-50%

Fees to Publish: $0.00 US$
Fees to Review: $0.00 US$

</td></tr>
</table>

PUBLICATION GUIDELINES:	CIRCULATION DATA:

<table>
<tr><td>

Manuscript Style:
  Chicago Manual of Style

Manuscript Length:
  21-30

Copies Required:
  Two

</td><td>

Reader:
  Academics

Frequency of Issue:
  Quarterly

Sponsor/Publisher:
  Public Service Research Foundation

</td></tr>
</table>

MANUSCRIPT TOPICS:
Education Management / Administration; Public Sector Labor Relations

MANUSCRIPT GUIDELINES/COMMENTS:

In 1980, the Foundation began publication of *Government Union Review*, a quarterly journal dedicated to providing a forum for scholarly research on the impact of unionism on government and union influence on public policy. The *Review* also provides a forum for those who are interested in developing alternatives to unionism in the public sector.

Harvard Civil Rights-Liberties Law Review

SUBMISSION PROCESS:
Postal Submission Only

CONTACT INFORMATION:	REVIEW PROCESS:	
Executive Articles Editor Publications Center, Hastings Hall Harvard Law School 1541 Massachusetts Avenue Cambridge, MA 02138 USA	Type of Review:	Editorial Review
	No. External Reviewers:	3+
	No. InHouse Reviewers:	0
	Acceptance Rate:	6-10%
Phone: 617-495-4500	Time to Review:	1 - 2 Months
	Reviewer's Comments:	Yes
	Invited Articles:	6-10%
Email: hlscrc@law.harvard.edu	Fees to Publish:	$0.00 US$
Website: http://www.law.harvard.edu/students/orgs/crcl/	Fees to Review:	$0.00 US$

PUBLICATION GUIDELINES:	CIRCULATION DATA:
Manuscript Style: USC - Harvard Blue Book	**Reader:** Academics
Manuscript Length: More than 20	**Frequency of Issue:** 2 Times/Year
Copies Required: One	**Sponsor/Publisher:** Harvard University

MANUSCRIPT TOPICS:
Civil Rights, Civil Liberties Law; School Law; Social Studies / Social Science; Urban Education, Cultural / Non-Traditional

MANUSCRIPT GUIDELINES/COMMENTS:

Submissions. The editors invite the submission of unsolicited manuscripts and consider them on a rolling basis. Submissions by mail should be typed, double-spaced, and accompanied by a diskette containing the submission in Microsoft Word. Footnotes should comply with *The Bluebook: A Uniform System of Citation* (18th ed. 2005).

Mailing address. Executive Articles Editor, Harvard Civil Rights-Civil Liberties Law Review, Publications Center, Hastings Hall, Harvard Law School, 1541 Massachusetts Avenue, Cambridge, Massachusetts 02138

Harvard Educational Review

SUBMISSION PROCESS:

Postal Submission Preferred / Elec. Sub. with Approval via EMail

hepg@harvard.edu

CONTACT INFORMATION:	REVIEW PROCESS:

CONTACT INFORMATION:

Manuscript Editor
Harvard Graduate School of Education
8 Story Street, 1st Floor
Cambridge, MA 02138 USA

Phone:
617-495-3432

Email:
hepg@harvard.edu
laura_clos@harvard.edu

Website:
http://www.harvardeducationalreview.org

REVIEW PROCESS:

Type of Review:	Blind Review
No. External Reviewers:	0
No. InHouse Reviewers:	3+
Acceptance Rate:	1-5%
Time to Review:	Over 6 Months
Reviewer's Comments:	No
Invited Articles:	31-50%
Fees to Publish:	$0.00 US$
Fees to Review:	$0.00 US$

PUBLICATION GUIDELINES:

Manuscript Style:
Chicago Manual of Style
American Psychological Association

Manuscript Length:
15,000 words

Copies Required:
Three Print + Electronic

CIRCULATION DATA:

Reader:
Academics, Researchers, Teachers, Policymakers

Frequency of Issue:
Quarterly

Sponsor/Publisher:
Harvard University Graduate School of Education

MANUSCRIPT TOPICS:
Adult Career & Vocational; Art / Music; Bilingual / E.S.L.; Education Management / Administration; Higher Education; Languages & Linguistics; Teacher Education; Tests, Measurement & Evaluation; Urban Education, Cultural / Non-Traditional

MANUSCRIPT GUIDELINES/COMMENTS:

The *Harvard Educational Review* accepts contributions from teachers, practitioners, policymakers, scholars, and researchers in education arid related fields, as well as from informed observers. In addition to discussions and reviews of research and theory, *HER* welcomes articles that reflect on teaching and practice in educational settings in the United States and abroad. Authors can elect to indicate whether they are submitting their manuscript as an article, a Voices Inside Schools article, an essay review, or a book review. *HER* has a two stage review process. Manuscripts that pass the initial stage are then considered by the full Editorial Board and receive detailed written feedback. It is the policy of the *Review* to consider for publication only articles that are not simultaneously being considered elsewhere. Please follow our guidelines in preparing your manuscript for submission (**http://hepg.org/page/20**).

1. Authors must submit **three copies** of the manuscript, including a one-page abstract. Manuscripts will be returned only if a stamped, self-addressed envelope is included at the time of submission. In addition, please include a clearly labeled 3.5-inch disk or cd-rom containing an electronic version of the manuscript in Microsoft Word format. If you do not have access to MS Word, please contact us to make other arrangements.

2. Manuscripts are considered **anonymously**. The author's name must appear *only* on the title page; any references that identify the author in the text must be deleted.

3. *HER* accepts manuscripts of **up to 15,000 words** and reserves the right to return any manuscript that exceeds that length.

4. All text must be **double-spaced**, and type size must be at least **12 point with 1" margins on both sides**.

5. Quoted material is extracted in the text when it is more than 45 words, unless the editors determine otherwise.

6. Authors should refer to *The Chicago Manual of Style* for general questions of style, grammar, punctuation, and form. Chicago should also be referred to for footnotes of theoretical, descriptive, or essay-like material.

7. For technical and research manuscripts, authors should use the *Publication Manual of the American Psychological Association* for reference and citations format.

8. *The Uniform System of Citation*, published by the *Harvard Law Review*, should be used for articles that rely heavily on legal documentation. Because this form is not easily adaptable to other sources, it is usually combined with *The Chicago Manual of Style* as necessary.

9. Authors should select the style most suitable for their manuscripts and adhere consistently to that style. The Editors reserve the right to request that authors use an alternative style if the one chosen seems inappropriate. Styles may not be combined, with the exception of legal citations.

10. **References must be in APA format**. We request that authors provide complete references, including page citations in book reviews. Authors should be certain that citations and footnotes in the text agree with those in the references.

11. As a generalist journal, *HER* discourages the use of technical jargon. We encourage authors to minimize the use of underlining, parentheses, italics, and quotation marks for emphasis in the text. Footnotes should be as few and as concise as possible. Tables and figures should be kept to a minimum.

Voices Inside Schools
The purpose of this section is to provide a forum devoted to the voices of teachers, students, and others committed to education within the school community broadly defined who interact with students and who have important knowledge and expertise about life inside schools gained through practice, reflection, and/or research. We value the writing of adults and students who have intimate and first-hand experience with teaching and learning.

Submissions for the Voices Inside Schools section are written by teachers and other professionals in the field of education about their own practice, and by students about their own educational experiences. In the past, *HER* has published articles by practitioners on a wide variety of issues: a Black educator's experiences teaching writing as a process to minority students, a literacy educator teaching women in a correctional facility, a university professor describing the content and pedagogy of her course on AIDS, and a school principal reflecting on school restructuring. Authors may choose to present their perspective through a range of formats, from data-driven to more reflective essays.

Book Reviews

HER also accepts reviews of recent publications (within the last 2 publication years) about education. Book reviews, in which the author reviews a book related to education, should be 8-12 double-spaced pages. *HER* also publishes essay reviews, in which one or more books in a particular field are analyzed and the implications for future research and practice are discussed. These essays should range from 15-20 pages.

High Ability Studies

SUBMISSION PROCESS:
Electronic Submission Preferred via EMail **heidrun.stoeger@uni-ulm.de**

CONTACT INFORMATION:	REVIEW PROCESS:	

Albert Ziegler, Editor
University of Ulm
Centre of Educational Sciences
Department of Educational Psychology
Robert-Koche-Strasse 2
D-89069,   Germany
 	
Phone:
 	
Email:
   heidrun.stoeger@uni-ulm.de
 	
Website:
   http://www.tandf.co.uk/journals/1359813
9
	Type of Review:
	
	No. External Reviewers:
	No. InHouse Reviewers:
	
	Acceptance Rate:
	Time to Review:
	Reviewer's Comments:
	Invited Articles:
	
	Fees to Publish:
	Fees to Review:
		Blind Review
		
		2
		1
		
		11-20%
		4 - 6 Months
		Yes
		0-5%
		
		$0.00 US$
		$0.00 US$

PUBLICATION GUIDELINES:	CIRCULATION DATA:

Manuscript Style:
      See Manuscript Guidelines
 	
Manuscript Length:
   11-20
 	
Copies Required:
   Three
	Reader:
	   Practicing Teachers, Academics,
	   Counselors, Managers, Policy Makers,
	   Parents
	
	Frequency of Issue:
	   2 Times/Year
	
	Sponsor/Publisher:
	   European Council for High Ability
	   (ECHA) / Routledge, Taylor & Francis, Ltd.

MANUSCRIPT TOPICS:
Educational Psychology; Gifted Children; Special Education

MANUSCRIPT GUIDELINES/COMMENTS:

Aims & Scope
High Ability Studies provides a forum for scholars in a variety of disciplines associated with the development of human abilities to their highest level. It is a medium for the promotion of high ability, whether through the communication of scientific research, theory, or the exchange of practical experience and ideas.

The contents of this journal are unique in reflecting concerns and recent developments in this area from childhood and across the whole life span in a variety of contexts. Far from being restricted to the traditional focus on high-level cognitive development, it also presents investigations into all other areas of human endeavour, including sport, technology, the arts, business, management and social relations.

The journal is concerned with aspects of development, personality, cognition, social behaviour and cross-cultural issues in relation to high ability. Theoretical modelling and measurement techniques, as well as instructional strategies and curriculum issues, are of interest. Consequently, the journal presents material which is relevant to researchers in the field, to managers who have highly able individuals employed, to policy makers who need to find frameworks by which to make the best use of high ability in society, to mentors, coaches, teachers, counsellors and parents of highly able children. Furthermore, the contents are not restricted to the study of manifest high level achievement, but include the identification and nurturance of unexercised potential.

High Ability Studies is an international refereed journal which publishes papers in English, as well as reviews of books and other relevant material. It is the official scholarly journal of the European Council for High Ability (ECHA).

Instructions for Authors
Note to Authors. Please make sure your contact address information is clearly visible on the outside of all packages you are sending to Editors.

Manuscripts submitted to *High Ability Studies* should contain original research, theory or accounts of practice, which may not have been previously published nor be simultaneously under consideration for publication elsewhere. However, conference papers included as part of conference proceedings may be considered for submission, if such papers are revised in accordance with the format accepted by this journal, updated if need be, and full acknowledgement given in regard to the conference or convention in which the paper was originally presented.

To download a Word template for this journal, please visit our website at **http://www.tandf. co.uk/journals/authors/edstylea.dot**.

For further information on **electronic submission**, including information on accepted file types, please visit our website at **http://www.tandf.co.uk/journals/authors/electronic_edu. asp**.

All submitted papers are assessed by a blind refereeing process and will be reviewed by at least two independent referees. Therefore, avoid clues in the text which might identify you as the author. Authors will receive constructive feedback on the outcome of this process. Please note that the process will take two to three months in duration. High *Ability Studies* is published twice annually.

Text
Manuscripts should be written in accordance with the publication manual of the American Psychological Association (4th Edition). For example, the following should be adhered to:

Title page
Include title of paper, name(s) of author(s), affiliation, mailing address (include postal codes, if applicable also e-mail address and fax-number) and a running headline. The title page will be removed by the Editor prior to the refereeing process to allow for a masked review.

Abstract
Should consist of a maximum 120 words on a separate sheet. The abstract must, if the result of empirical research, briefly outline theoretical basis, research question/s (in one sentence if possible), methodology and instrumentation, sample/s and pertinent characteristics (e.g. number, type, gender and age) as well as the main findings of the study (if applicable include statistical significance levels). Also, include conclusion and the implications or applications. An abstract for a review or a theoretical article should describe in no more than 100 words the topic (in one sentence), the purpose, thesis or organising structure and the scope of the article. It should outline the sources used (e.g. personal observation and/or published literature) and the conclusions.

Length
A paper submitted should not exceed 5000 words including abstract, references and illustrations.

Language

HAS is an international scholarly journal and papers must be written in English. It is recommended that non-native English speakers have their papers checked in regard to language accuracy prior to submission. British spelling, as well as American spelling is accepted.

Manuscript

Papers must be word processed, and printed or photocopied with a clear print, double-spaced and with margins of at least 4 cm (approximately 1.5 inches) on all four sides. Use one side of the page only. Carbon copies are not accepted. A4-format is recommended, but if not available in the country in which the paper originates, other and their appropriate paper sizes will be accepted. Pages should be numbered consecutively, starting with the title page.

Statistics

Are an aid to interpretation and not an end in themselves. If reporting statistics, include sufficient information to help the reader corroborate the analyses conducted (cf APA-manual).

Qualitative data

If submitting a qualitative study, be sure to include a discussion on the stringency observed whilst obtaining and analysing the data (e.g. biases, analysis model, transcription keys, validation of results and so on). Include sufficient data to help the reader, as far as possible, to corroborate the analyses conducted.

Footnotes

Should be kept to a minimum or preferably avoided completely. If used, they should be numbered consecutively with superscript Arabic numerals.

Abbreviations

Must be kept to a minimum and not followed by a full stop, for example cm (not cm.), kg (not kg.)

References should be indicated in the typescript by giving the author's name, with the year of publication in parentheses. (e.g. Smith, 1998). If several papers by the same author and from the same year are cited, a, b, c, etc. should be put after the year of publication. References should be listed in full, including pages, at the end of the paper in the following standard form:

For books
Weisberg, R. W. (1993). *Creativity: beyond the myth of genius.* (New York, W. H. Freeman & Company).

For chapters in edited books
Thompson, L. A., & Plomin, R. (1993). Genetic influence on cognitive ability. In K. A. Heller, F. J. Mönks & A. H. Passow (Eds.), *International handbook of research and development of giftedness and talent* (Oxford, UK, Pergamon Press), 103-114.

For journal articles
Van Rossum, J. H. A. and Van der Loo, H. (1997) Gifted athletes and complexity of family structure: a condition for talent development? *High Ability Studies*, 8(1), 19-30.

Illustrations

Authors should follow APA-format in designing tables and figures and consider the fact that illustrations **supplements** - not duplicates - the text. In the text, refer to every table and figure and tell the reader what to look for. Discuss only the table's highlights.

Figures

Must be computer drawn or photographed and submitted on separate pages in the manuscript; not included in the text. Note that they must also be submitted as separate computer files on disk (jpg, jpeg or gif format). Figures should be identified with Arabic numbers and an explaining text, and their approximate place in the text should be clearly indicated in the manuscript.

Tables
Should be placed on separate pages; not included in the text. Note that tables also should be submitted as separate file/s. Tables must have an Arabic number, an explaining text and a title. Their approximate place in the text should be clearly indicated in the manuscript. Observe also that templates for tables provided with most word processing software may not be used unless templates follow APA-format. Spreadsheets, while inevitable when constructing diagrams with software such as for example Microsoft Excel of SPSS, should **not** be used as basis for table construction in the paper.

If you have any further questions about the style for this journal, please submit your questions using the Style Queries form at our website: **http://www.tandf.co.uk/journals/authors/style queries.asp**.

Proofs
One proof will be sent to the author(s) to be corrected and returned—within three days of receipt—to the Editor-in-Chief. The cost of corrections in the first proof resulting from extensive alterations in the text will be charged to the author.

Early Electronic Offprints. Corresponding authors can now receive their article by e-mail as a complete PDF. This allows the author to print up to 50 copies, free of charge, and disseminate them to colleagues. In many cases this facility will be available up to two weeks prior to publication. Or, alternatively, corresponding authors will receive the traditional 50 offprints. A copy of the journal will be sent by post to all corresponding authors after publication. Additional copies of the journal can be purchased at the author's preferential rate of £15.00/$25.00 per copy.

Copyright
It is a condition of publication that authors assign copyright or licence the publication rights in their articles, including abstracts, to the European Council for High Ability. This enables us to ensure full copyright protection and to disseminate the article, and of course the Journal, to the widest possible readership in print and electronic formats as appropriate. Authors may, of course, use the article elsewhere after publication without prior permission from Taylor & Francis, provided that acknowledgement is given to the Journal as the original source of publication, and that Taylor & Francis is notified so that our records show that its use is properly authorised. Authors retain a number of other rights under the Taylor & Francis rights policies documents. These policies are referred to at **www.tandf.co.uk/journals/author rights.pdf** for full details. Authors are themselves responsible for obtaining permission to reproduce copyright material from other sources.

Delivery
For your submission, please send manuscript/s, in triplicate, which will not be returned, to the Editor-in-Chief: Professor Dr Albert Ziegler (**heidrun.stoeger@uni-ulm.de**), Editor in Chief, Centre of Educational Sciences, Department of Educational Psychology, University of Ulm, Robert-Koche-Strasse 2, D-89069, Germany.

Please observe that if a manuscript is accepted as is, or accepted with a recommendation of some revision, you must then submit the manuscript on disk (IBM compatible, and clearly marked with name and title of manuscript. Also, signify type and version of word processor used, or alternatively submit the revised manuscript by e-mail using RTF-format). Submission via e-mail for revised and final manuscripts is the preferred means of submission. Note that you must submit also, on a separate sheet of paper together with your manuscript, 8-10 lines of biographical information about each author for 'Notes on Authors' to be published with the article. Contact address/es should be included.

Higher Education

SUBMISSION PROCESS:
Electronic Submission Only **via Online Portal** **http://high.edmgr.com**

CONTACT INFORMATION:	REVIEW PROCESS:	
Publishing Editor Springer Higher Education Editorial Office PO Box 17 Dordrecht, 3300 AA The Netherlands	**Type of Review:**	Editorial Review
	No. External Reviewers:	2
	No. InHouse Reviewers:	1
	Acceptance Rate:	20%
Phone: (+31) 78 6576157	**Time to Review:**	4 - 6 Months
	Reviewer's Comments:	Yes
	Invited Articles:	Special Issues
Email: maria.jonckheere@springer.com	**Fees to Publish:**	$0.00 US$
	Fees to Review:	$0.00 US$
Website: www.springer.com		

PUBLICATION GUIDELINES:	CIRCULATION DATA:
Manuscript Style: See Manuscript Guidelines	**Reader:** Academics
Manuscript Length: 6000 words	**Frequency of Issue:** 12 Times/Year
Copies Required: Electronic Only	**Sponsor/Publisher:** Springer

MANUSCRIPT TOPICS:
Higher Education

MANUSCRIPT GUIDELINES/COMMENTS:

Aims and Scope
Higher Education is recognised as the leading international journal of Higher Education studies, publishing twelve separate numbers each year. Since its establishment in 1972, *Higher Education* has followed educational developments throughout the world in universities, polytechnics, colleges, and vocational and education institutions. It has actively endeavoured to report on developments in both public and private *Higher Education* sectors. Contributions have come from leading scholars from different countries while articles have tackled the problems of teachers as well as students, and of planners as well as administrators.

While each *Higher Education* system has its own distinctive features, common problems and issues are shared internationally by researchers, teachers and institutional leaders. *Higher Education* offers opportunities for exchange of research results, experience and insights, and provides a forum for ongoing discussion between experts.

Higher Education publishes authoritative overview articles, comparative studies and analyses of particular problems or issues. All contributions are peer reviewed.

Manuscript Submission

Springer now offers authors, editors and reviewers of *Higher Education* the option of using our fully web-enabled online manuscript submission and review system. To keep the review time as short as possible (no postal delays!), we encourage authors to submit manuscripts online to the journal's editorial office. Our online manuscript submission and review system offers authors the option to track the progress of the review process of manuscripts in real time.

The online manuscript submission and review system for *Higher Education* offers easy and straightforward log-in and submission procedures. This system supports a wide range of submission file formats: for manuscripts – Word, WordPerfect, RTF, TXT and LaTex; for figures – TIFF, GIF, JPEG, EPS, PPT, and Postscript.

Note. By using the online manuscript submission and review system, it is NOT necessary to submit the manuscript also in printout + disk. In case you encounter any difficulties while submitting your manuscript on line, please get in touch with the responsible Editorial Assistant by clicking on "CONTACT US" from the tool bar.

Manuscripts should be submitted to: **http://high.edmgr.com**

Manuscript Presentation

The journal's language is English. British English or American English spelling and terminology may be used, but either one should be followed consistently throughout the article. Manuscripts should be printed or typewritten on A4 or US Letter bond paper, one side only, leaving adequate margins on all sides to allow reviewers' remarks. Please double-space all material, including notes and references. Quotations of more than 40 words should be set off clearly, either by indenting the left-hand margin or by using a smaller typeface. Use double quotation marks for direct quotations and single quotation marks for quotations within quotations and for words or phrases used in a special sense.

Number the pages consecutively with the first page containing:
- running head (shortened title)
- title
- author(s)
- affiliation(s)
- full address for correspondence, including telephone and fax number and e-mail address

Abstract

All articles should include an abstract of 100–150 words and should normally be no longer than 6000 words including references and tables. The abstract should not contain any undefined abbreviations or unspecified references. As the abstract and key words will be used to select appropriate reviewers, it is essential to make them as informative as possible.

Key Words

Please provide 5 to 10 key words or short phrases in alphabetical order.

Figures and Tables

Submission of electronic figures. In addition to hard-copy printouts of figures, authors are requested to supply the electronic versions of figures in either Encapsulated PostScript (EPS) or TIFF format. Many other formats, e.g., Proprietary Formats, PiCT (Macintosh) and WMF (Windows), cannot be used and the hard copy will be scanned instead.

Figures should be saved in separate files without their captions, which should be included with the text of the article. Files should be named according to DOS conventions, e.g., 'figure1.eps'. For vector graphics, EPS is the preferred format. Lines should not be thinner than 0.25pts and in-fill patterns and screens should have a density of at least 10%. Font-related problems can be avoided by using standard fonts such as Times Roman and Helvetica. For bitmapped graphics, TIFF is the preferred format but EPS is also acceptable. The following resolutions are optimal: black-and-white line figures − 600 − 1200 dpi; line figures with some grey or coloured lines − 600 dpi; photographs − 300 dpi; screen dumps − leave as is. Higher resolutions will not improve output quality but will only increase file size, which may cause problems with printing; lower resolutions may compromise output quality. Please try to provide artwork that approximately fits within the typeset area of the journal. Especially screened originals, i.e. originals with grey areas, may suffer badly from reduction by more than 10−15%.

Avoiding problems with EPS graphics. Please always check whether the figures print correctly to a PostScript printer in a reasonable amount of time. If they do not, simplify your figures or use a different graphics program.

If EPS export does not produce acceptable output, try to create an EPS file with the printer driver (see below). This option is unavailable with the Microsoft driver for Windows NT, so if you run Windows NT, get the Adobe driver from the Adobe site (www.adobe.com).

If EPS export is not an option, e.g., because you rely on OLE and cannot create separate files for your graphics, it may help us if you simply provide a PostScript dump of the entire document.

How to set up for EPS and Postscript Dumps under Windows. Create a printer entry specifically for this purpose: install the printer 'Apple Laserwriter Plus' and specify 'FILE': as printer port. Each time you send something to the 'printer' you will be asked for a filename. This file will be the EPS file or PostScript dump that we can use.

The EPS export option can be found under the PostScript tab. EPS export should be used only for single-page documents. For printing a document of several pages, select 'Optimise for portability' instead. The option 'Download header with each job' should be checked.

Submission of hard-copy figures. If no electronic versions of figures are available, submit only high-quality artwork that can be reproduced as is, i.e., without any part having to be redrawn or re-typeset. The letter size of any text in the figures must be large enough to allow for reduction. Photographs should be in black-and-white on glossy paper. If a figure contains colour, make absolutely clear whether it should be printed in black-and-white or in colour. Figures that are to be printed in black-and-white should not be submitted in colour. Authors will be charged for reproducing figures in colour.

Each figure and table should be numbered and mentioned in the text. The approximate position of figures and tables should be indicated in the margin of the manuscript. On the reverse side of each figure, the name of the (first) author and the figure number should be written in pencil; the top of the figure should be clearly indicated. Figures and tables should be placed at the end of the manuscript following the Reference section. Each figure and table should be accompanied by an explanatory legend. The figure legends should be grouped and placed on a separate page. Figures are not returned to the author unless specifically requested.

In tables, footnotes are preferable to long explanatory material in either the heading or body of the table. Such explanatory footnotes, identified by superscript letters, should be placed immediately below the table.

Section Headings
First−, second−, third−, and fourth−order headings should be clearly distinguishable but not numbered.

Appendices
Supplementary material should be collected in an Appendix and placed before the Notes and Reference sections.

Notes
Please use endnotes rather than footnotes. Notes should be indicated by consecutive superscript numbers in the text and listed at the end of the article before the References. A source reference note should be indicated by means of an asterisk after the title. This note should be placed at the bottom of the first page.

Cross-Referencing
In the text, a reference identified by means of an author's name should be followed by the date of the reference in parentheses and page number(s) where appropriate. When there are more than two authors, only the first author's name should be mentioned, followed by 'et al.'. In the event that an author cited has had two or more works published during the same year, the reference, both in the text and in the reference list, should be identified by a lower case letter like 'a' and 'b' after the date to distinguish the works.

Examples:
Winograd (1986, p. 204)
(Winograd 1986a, b)
(Winograd 1986; Flores et al. 1988)
(Bullen and Bennett 1990)

Acknowledgements
Acknowledgements of people, grants, funds, etc. should be placed in a separate section before the References.

References
1. *Journal article*
Barlow, D. H. & Lehman, C. L. (1996). Advances in the psychosocial treatment of anxiety disorders. Archives of General Psychiatry, 53, 727-735

2. *Book chapter*
Cutrona, C. E. & Russell, D. (1990). Type of social support and specific stress: Towards a theory of optimum matching. (In I.G. Sarason, B. R. Sarason, & G. Pierce (Eds.), Social support: An interactional view (pp. 341-366). New York: Wiley.)

3. *Book, authored*
Capland, G. (1964). Principles of preventive psychiatry. (New York: Basic Books)

Proofs
Proofs will be sent to the corresponding author. One corrected proof, together with the original, edited manuscript, should be returned to the Publisher within three days of receipt by mail (airmail overseas).

Offprints
Fifty offprints of each article will be provided free of charge. Additional offprints can be ordered by means of an offprint order form supplied with the proofs.

Page Charges and Colour Figures
No page charges are levied on authors or their institutions. Colour figures are published at the author's expense only.

368

Copyright
Authors will be asked, upon acceptance of an article, to transfer copyright of the article to the Publisher. This will ensure the widest possible dissemination of information under copyright laws.

Permissions
It is the responsibility of the author to obtain written permission for a quotation from unpublished material, or for all quotations in excess of 250 words in one extract or 500 words in total from any work still in copyright, and for the reprinting of figures, tables or poems from unpublished or copyrighted material.

Springer Open Choice
In addition to the normal publication process (whereby an article is submitted to the journal and access to that article is granted to customers who have purchased a subscription), Springer now provides an alternative publishing option: Springer Open Choice. A Springer Open Choice article receives all the benefits of a regular subscription-based article, but in addition is made available publicly through Springer's online platform SpringerLink. To publish via Springer Open Choice, upon acceptance please click on the link below to complete the relevant order form and provide the required payment information. Payment must be received in full before publication or articles will publish as regular subscription-model articles. We regret that Springer Open Choice cannot be ordered for published articles.

Additional Information
Additional information can be obtained from: Publishing Editor Higher Education, Springer, P.O. Box 17, 3300 AA Dordrecht, The Netherlands; Tel.: +31 (0)78 6576 206; Fax: +31 (0)78 6576 254

Higher Education in Europe

SUBMISSION PROCESS:
Electronic Submission Preferred via EMail
p.wells@cepes.ro

CONTACT INFORMATION:	REVIEW PROCESS:	
Peter J. Wells, Editor Programme Specialist UNESCO-CEPES 39 Stirbei Voda Street RO-010102 Bucharest, Romania	**Type of Review:**	Peer Review
	No. External Reviewers:	Varies
	No. InHouse Reviewers:	Varies
	Acceptance Rate:	75%
	Time to Review:	1 - 2 Months
Phone:	**Reviewer's Comments:**	Yes
+40 21 313 0839	**Invited Articles:**	50% +
Email:		
d.lincoln@cepes.ro	**Fees to Publish:**	$0.00 US$
Website:	**Fees to Review:**	$0.00 US$
www.tandf.co.uk/journals www.cepes.ro		

PUBLICATION GUIDELINES:	CIRCULATION DATA:
Manuscript Style: American Psychological Association Harvard Method	**Reader:** Academics, Administrators, Grad Students, Policy Makers
Manuscript Length: 21-25 5,000 Words	**Frequency of Issue:** Quarterly
Copies Required: One	**Sponsor/Publisher:** UNESCO / Routledge, Taylor & Francis, Ltd.

MANUSCRIPT TOPICS:
Education Management / Administration; Higher Education

MANUSCRIPT GUIDELINES/COMMENTS:

Topics Also Include. All aspects of Governance, Organizational Management, and International Cooperation in Higher Education

Aims and Scope
Higher Education in Europe is a quarterly review published on behalf of UNESCO European Centre for Higher Education (CEPES). It is a scholarly publication dealing with major problems and trends in contemporary higher education. It presents information, interpretations, and criticism in regard to current developments in the field. While focusing primarily on Europe and North America within the context of the other activities of the Centre, it regularly features contributions from other regions of the world as well.

Instructions for Prospective Authors. Persons wishing to publish in the review should send their proposals to the Editor and request a copy of the guidelines for the preparation of articles.

Unsolicited articles and book review manuscripts will not be returned. All correspondence should be addressed to the Editor, UNESCO-CEPES, 39 Stirbei-Voda Street, R-70732 Bucharest, Romania; or by E-mail to **P.Wells@cepes.ro** preferably as a Word-for-Windows, Word Perfect 5.1, or rich text format attachment. Finally, texts can be sent by computer diskette, preferably in Word-for-Windows or in Word Perfect 5.1.

Articles should be typed, double-space, with normal margins and should not exceed 5000 words. Notes, references, and bibliography should be presented separately, according to the so-called Harvard or APA Method. A list of "References" appearing at the end of the text should give full names of authors, full original titles (with English, French, or Russian translation, if appropriate), publisher, place of publication, date of publication, and page numbers. Charts, diagrams, tables, and graphs can be presented in a compatible Word for Windows format or produced by hand in black ink. They should be presented on separate pages, their respective positions indicated in the text. References in the text should only indicate the author's surname, date of publication, and page number, if necessary.

UNESCO-CEPES would be grateful to receive manuscripts not only in English but accompanied by French and Russian translations if possible.

The text of an article should be preceded by an abstract of approximately 100 words. The author's name, address, and a brief biography should be given on a separate sheet of paper.

Higher Education Management and Policy

SUBMISSION PROCESS:	
Electronic Submission Preferred **via EMail** **inhe@oecd.org**	

CONTACT INFORMATION:	REVIEW PROCESS:	
Michael Shattock, Editor OECD/IMHE 2 rue Andre-Pascal 75775 Paris Cedex 16, France	**Type of Review:**	Editorial Review
	No. External Reviewers: **No. InHouse Reviewers:**	 1-2
Phone: +33 1 45 24 93 23	**Acceptance Rate:** **Time to Review:** **Reviewer's Comments:**	21-30% 1-3 Months Yes
Email: inhe@oecd.org	**Invited Articles:**	0-5%
Website: www.oecd.org/edu/higher	**Fees to Publish:** **Fees to Review:**	$0.00 US$ $0.00 US$

PUBLICATION GUIDELINES:	CIRCULATION DATA:
Manuscript Style: See Manuscript Guidelines **Manuscript Length:** 16-25 **Copies Required:** Three or Electronic	**Reader:** Administrators, Academics, Policy Makers, Inst. Leaders, Grad. Students **Frequency of Issue:** 3 Times/Year **Sponsor/Publisher:** Organisation for Economic Co-operation and Development (OECD)

MANUSCRIPT TOPICS:
Education Management / Administration; Higher Education; Policy

MANUSCRIPT GUIDELINES/COMMENTS:

About the Journal
The journal is produced in both English and French. French title: *Politiques et gestion de l'enseignement supérieur*. Abstracts are also produced in Spanish, Japanese, and often in German and in Italian. Abstracts in other languages are freely accessible on the OECD website at: **www.oecd.org**, in the online bookshop.

The opinions expressed and arguments employed in this publication are the responsibility of the authors and do not necessarily represent those of the OECD or of the national or local authorities concerned.

- A journal addressed to leaders, managers, researchers and policy makers in the field of higher education institutional management and policy.
- Covering practice and policy in the field of system and institutional management through articles and reports on research projects of wide international scope.

- First published in 1977 under the title *International Journal of Institutional Management in Higher Education*, then *Higher Education Management* from 1989 to 2001, it appears three times a year in English and French editions. Information for authors wishing to submit articles for publication appears at the end of each issue.

Articles and related correspondence should be sent directly to the Editor: Prof. Michael Shattock, Higher Education Management and Policy, OECD/IMHE, 2 rue André-Pascal, 75775 Paris Cedex 16, France ; E mail contact: **imhe@oecd.org**

To enter a subscription, send your order to: OECD Publications Service, 2, rue André-Pascal, 75775 Paris Cedex 16, France 2005 subscription (3 issues):
€ 104 US$119 £70 Y 14 000
Online bookshop: **www.oecdbookshop.org**

Information for Authors
Contributions to the *Higher Education Management and Policy Journal* should be submitted in either English or French and all articles are received on the understanding that they have not appeared in print elsewhere.

Selection criteria
The *Journal* is primarily devoted to the needs of those involved with the administration and study of institutional management in higher education. Articles should be concerned, therefore, with issues bearing on the practical working and policy direction of higher education. Contributions should, however, go beyond mere description of what is, or prescription of what ought to be, although both descriptive and prescriptive accounts are acceptable if they offer generalisations of use in contexts beyond those being described. Whilst articles devoted to the development of theory for is own sake will normally find a place in other and more academically based journals, theoretical treatments of direct use to practitioners will be considered.

Other criteria include clarity of expression and thought. Titles of articles should be as brief as possible.

Presentation
Electronic submission is preferred. Three copies of each article should be sent if the article is submitted on paper only.

Length. Should not exceed 15 pages (single spaced) including figures and references (about 5 000 words).

The first page. Before the text itself should appear centred on the page in this order the title of the article and the name(s), affiliation(s) and country/countries of the author(s).

Abstract. The main text should be preceded by an abstract of 100 to 200 words summarising the article.

Quotations. Long quotations should be single spaced and each line should be indented 7 spaces.

Footnotes. Authors should avoid using footnotes and incorporate any explanatory material in the text itself. If notes cannot be avoided, they should be endnotes, at the end of the article.

Tables and illustrations. Tabular material should bear a centred heading "Table". Presentations of non-tabular material should bear a centred heading "Figure". The source should always be cited.

Addresses of author(s), including email, should be typed at the end of the article.

References in the text. Vidal and Mora (2003) or Bleiklie *et al.* (2000) in the case of three or more authors. However, the names of all authors should appear in the bibliography at the end of the article.

Bibliography at the end of the article. References should be listed in alphabetical order under the heading "References". Examples of the reference style used in the *Journal* are:

For periodicals
Kogan, M. (2004), "Teaching and Research: Some Framework Issues", *Higher Education Management and Policy*, Vol. 16, No. 2, pp. 9-18.

For books
Helen Connell (ed.) (2004), *University Research Management – Meeting the Institutional Challenge* OECD, Paris.

The covering letter
This should give full addresses and telephone numbers and, in the case of multi-authored papers, indicate the author to whom all correspondence should be sent.

Complimentary copies
Each author will receive two complimentary copies of the Journal issue in which his article appears, in the original language.

Higher Education Quarterly

SUBMISSION PROCESS:

Postal Submission Only

CONTACT INFORMATION:	REVIEW PROCESS:	
Lee Harvey, Editor Sheffield Hallam University	**Type of Review:**	Editorial Review
Ruth Harris, Manging Editor 7 Copt Elm Road Cheltenham, GL53 8AG UK	**No. External Reviewers:** **No. InHouse Reviewers:**	2 1
	Acceptance Rate:	21-30%
	Time to Review:	4 - 6 Months
Phone:	**Reviewer's Comments:**	Yes
	Invited Articles:	11-20%
Email:	**Fees to Publish:**	$0.00 US$
	Fees to Review:	$0.00 US$
hequ.managingeditor@oxon.blackwellpublishing.com		
Website: http://www.blackwellpublishing.com/		

PUBLICATION GUIDELINES:	CIRCULATION DATA:
Manuscript Style: See Manuscript Guidelines	**Reader:** Academics, Administrators, National Policy Makers
Manuscript Length: 5000-8000 words	**Frequency of Issue:** Quarterly
Copies Required: Three	**Sponsor/Publisher:** Society for Research into Higher Education/ Blackwell Publishing, Inc.

MANUSCRIPT TOPICS:
Education Management / Administration; Education Policy; Higher Education

MANUSCRIPT GUIDELINES/COMMENTS:

Aims and Scope
Higher Education Quarterly publishes articles concerned with policy, strategic management and ideas in higher education. A substantial part of its contents is concerned with reporting research findings in ways that bring out their relevance to senior managers and policy makers at institutional and national levels, and to academics who are not necessarily specialists in the academic study of higher education.

Higher Education Quarterly also publishes papers that are not based on empirical research but give thoughtful academic analyses of significant policy, management or academic issues.

Papers from countries other than the UK, especially those from other European countries, that highlight issues of international concern are particularly welcomed.

Endnote Section. One article in each issue is published with the aim of stimulating debate and rejoinders from readers. The new Endnote section is reserved for this purpose.

Author Guidelines
Exclusive Licence Form. Authors will be required to sign an Exclusive Licence Form (ELF) for all papers accepted for publication. Signature of the ELF is a condition of publication and papers will not be passed to the publisher for production unless a signed form has been received. Please note that signature of the Exclusive Licence Form does not affect ownership of copyright in the material. (Government employees need to complete the Author Warranty sections, although copyright in such cases does not need to be assigned). After submission authors will retain the right to publish their paper in various media/circumstances (please see the form for further details). To assist authors an appropriate form will be supplied by the editorial office. Alternatively, authors may like to download a copy of the form from the web site.

Manuscripts should be sent to the Managing Editor: Ruth Harris, 7 Copt Elm Road, Cheltenham, GL53 8AG. U.K. Email: **HEQU.ManagingEditor@oxon.blackwellpublishing.com**

Authors should present one electronic copy of their manuscript - double spaced, with ample margins, bearing the title of the article, name(s) of the author(s) and the address where the work was carried out. Each article should be accompanied by an abstract of 100-150 words on a separate sheet, together with a biographical note of about 30 words. A note should appear at the end of the last page indicating the total number of words in the article (including those in the Abstract and References).

Books for review should be sent to Dr Peter W.G. Wright, 22 Sidney Square, Stepney, London E1 2EY, UK. Email: **pwright@dsl.pipex.com**

Tables and Captions to Illustrations. Tables must be typed out on separate sheets and not included as part of the text. The captions to illustrations should be numbered by Roman numerals, and figures by Arabic numerals. The approximate position of tables and figures should be indicated in the manuscript. Captions should include keys to symbols.

Figures. Figures involving line drawings will be redrawn by the publisher unless the author specifically requests that the original be used.

References. References should be indicated in the typescript by giving the author's name, with the year of publication in parenthesis. If several papers by the same author and from the same year are cited, a, b, c, etc should be put after the year of publication. The references should be listed in full at the end of the article in the following standard form:

Clark, Burton, R. (Ed.)(1985), *The School and the University: An International Perspective* (Berkeley, University of California Press).
Shinn, Christine Helen (1986), *Paying the Piper: The Development of the University Grants Committee 1919-1946* (London, Falmer Press).
Neave, Guy (1986), On Shifting Sands, Changing Priorities and Perspectives in European Higher Education from 1984 to 1986, *European Journal of Education*, pp.7-24.

Titles of journals should not be abbreviated.

Proofs will be sent to authors if there is sufficient time to do so. They should be corrected and returned to the Editorial Office within three days. Major alterations of the text cannot be accepted.

Free copies. Corresponding authors will receive a free PDF offprint of their article, which they should forward to their co-authors.

Pre-submission English-language editing. Authors for whom English is a second language may choose to have their manuscript professionally edited before submission to improve the English. A list of independent suppliers of editing services can be found at: **www.blackwellpublishing.com/ bauthor/english_language.asp.**

All services are paid for and arranged by the author, and use of one of these services does not guarantee acceptance or preference for publication.

Author Services. Online production tracking is now available for your article through Blackwell's Author Services. Author Services enables authors to track their article - once it has been accepted - through the production process to publication online and in print. Authors can check the status of their articles online and choose to receive automated e-mails at key stages of production so they don't need to contact the production editor to check on progress. Visit **http://www.blackwell publishing.com/bauthor/journal.asp** for more details on online production tracking and for a wealth of resources including FAQs and tips on article preparation, submission and more.

Higher Education Research and Development

<table>
<tr><td colspan="2" align="center">

SUBMISSION PROCESS:

Electronic Submission Only
via EMail

office@herdsa.org.au
</td></tr>
<tr><td>

CONTACT INFORMATION:

Gerlese Akerlind & Margot Pearson, Eds.

Phone:
  61 2 61250056

Email:
  gerlese.akerlind@anu.edu.au

Website:
  www.tandf.co.uk/journals/journal.asp?iss
  n=0729-4360&linktype=5
</td><td>

REVIEW PROCESS:

Type of Review:	Blind Review
No. External Reviewers:	2
No. InHouse Reviewers:	1
Acceptance Rate:	20%
Time to Review:	6 Months
Reviewer's Comments:	Yes
Invited Articles:	
Fees to Publish:	$0.00 US$
Fees to Review:	$0.00 US$
</td></tr>
<tr><td>

PUBLICATION GUIDELINES:

Manuscript Style:
  See Manuscript Guidelines

Manuscript Length:
  30+

Copies Required:
  Electronic Only
</td><td>

CIRCULATION DATA:

Reader:
  Academics, Administrators

Frequency of Issue:
  Quarterly

Sponsor/Publisher:
  Higher Education Research &
  Development Society of Australia/ Routledge,
  Taylor & Francis, Ltd.
</td></tr>
</table>

MANUSCRIPT TOPICS:
Higher Education

MANUSCRIPT GUIDELINES/COMMENTS:

Aims and Scope
Higher Education Research and Development (*HERD*) is a refereed international journal, established in 1982 as the principle learned journal of the Higher Education Research and Development Society of Australasia.

Higher Education Research and Development aims to serve the needs of teachers, researchers, students, administrators and those concerned with the present and future of higher education. The journal publishes research-based articles on the theory and practice of higher education. This includes comparative reviews and critically reflective case studies, as well as empirically-based papers. All articles are appropriately framed for an international audience, and are designed to lead to critical insights into the area being addressed.

Instructions for Authors
The journal seeks to publish research-based articles on the theory and practice of higher education. This includes comparative reviews and critically reflective case studies as well as empirically-based

papers. All articles, of whatever nature, should lead to critical insights into the area being addressed, framed within an appropriate international context.

Key topics include: higher education policy and practice; university teaching, learning and curriculum design; postgraduate education; academic leadership and management; and academic work. A range of methodological approaches -- empirical, reflective, quantitative, qualitative --are accepted.

Special issues. At least one issue each year may be a "special issue" which focuses on a specific area of educational practice or research. Those interested in preparing such an issue should contact the Editor.

The review and publication process starts with an initial screening of the manuscript by the editorial team, to ensure readiness for review. Those manuscripts which pass the screening process are sent out for review, after which they may be accepted for publication, accepted subject to minor revisions, invited to resubmit following substantial revisions or rejected. The review process normally takes six months, and publication about one year. All papers that are published will have been reviewed by at least two internationally recognised peers.

The criteria used to guide the review process are:
- The paper says something of interest to the *HERD* readership;
- The paper provides an important critical and/or analytical insight;
- The paper is succinct and coherent;
- The conclusion is well supported and persuasively argued;
- The paper demonstrates methodological soundness;
- The issue/problem is well situated in an appropriate literature;
- Overall, the paper reads well and will engage a broad higher education audience.

Style. Manuscripts should be submitted in Times New Roman 12 point font. Use no more than three levels of heading. The first page should give the title of the manuscript, and the name and institutional affiliation/s of the authors plus full postal and email address of the corresponding author. The second page should repeat the title of the manuscript, followed by an abstract of 100-150 words. The remainder of the text should follow the abstract. References should conform to the style set out in the *Publication Manual of the American Psychological Association* (fifth edition). For more details please visit **www.herdsa.org.au/HERD_style_guide-notes%20Aug%202004. pdf**

Length. The length of the manuscript should in general be 5,000 - 7,000 words. Authors should place a word count at the end of their manuscript.

Book reviews. Book reviews of approximately 800 words are invited. Reviews should be of recently published books dealing with any aspect of higher education that the reviewer considers to be inspiring or to have significant implications for future policy, research and/ or practice in higher education. They should conform to the style requirements indicated above.

Submission of manuscripts. Manuscripts should be submitted as email attachments in the form of Word (otherwise .rtf) files - to the HERDSA office: **office@herdsa.org.au**. Please send the manuscript as one file, using the surname of the first author as the title of the file. Submitted manuscripts may not have been published elsewhere (though they may be based on a prior conference presentation or the like) and should not concurrently be being considered by another journal.

For further information on electronic submission, including information on accepted file types, please visit **http://www.tandf.co.uk/journals/authors/electronic_edu.asp**

Copyright. It is a condition of publication that the authors vest copyright in their articles, in HERDSA. This enables us to ensure full copyright protection and to disseminate the article, and the journal, to the widest possible readership in print and electronic formats, as appropriate. Authors may use the article elsewhere after publication without prior permission from the publisher (Routledge, Taylor & Francis Group), provided that acknowledgment is given to the journal as the original source of publication, and that the Publisher is notified so that our records show its use is properly authorised.

Historical Studies in Education

SUBMISSION PROCESS:	
Postal & Electronic Submission Required via EMail	
hse-rhe@uwo.ca	

CONTACT INFORMATION:	REVIEW PROCESS:	
Managing Editor	**Type of Review:**	Blind Review
University of Western Ontario		
Faculty of Education	**No. External Reviewers:**	2-3
1137 Western Road	**No. InHouse Reviewers:**	1-2
London, Ontario, Canada		
	Acceptance Rate:	21-30%
	Time to Review:	2 - 3 Months
Phone:	**Reviewer's Comments:**	
519-661-2111 x 88624	**Invited Articles:**	0-5%
Email:		
hse-rhe@uwo.ca	**Fees to Publish:**	$0.00 US$
Website:	**Fees to Review:**	$0.00 US$
http://www.edu.uwo.ca/HSE/		

PUBLICATION GUIDELINES:	CIRCULATION DATA:
Manuscript Style:	**Reader:**
Chicago Manual of Style	Academics, Practicing Teachers
Manuscript Length:	**Frequency of Issue:**
26-30	2 Times/Year
Copies Required:	**Sponsor/Publisher:**
One + 1 Electronic	Canadian History of Educ Assn, Social Sciences & Humanities Research Council of Canada, UWO

MANUSCRIPT TOPICS:
Elementary / Early Childhood; Health & Physical Education; Higher Education; History of Education; Rural Education & Small Schools; Teacher Education; Urban Education, Cultural / Non-Traditional

MANUSCRIPT GUIDELINES/COMMENTS:

Mission Statement
The journal provides a forum for scholarship in the history of Canadian and international education and related subjects. We publish articles on every aspect of education, from pre-school to university education, on informal as well as formal education, and on methodological and historiographical issues. We also look forward to articles which reflect the methods and approaches of other disciplines. Articles are published in English or French, from scholars in universities and elsewhere, from Canadians and non-Canadians, from graduate students, teachers, researchers, archivists and curators of educational museums, and all those who are interested in this field.

Guidelines for Authors
Manuscripts in English should be sent to the Editors, Historical Studies in Education, 1137 Western Road, University of Western Ontario, London, Ontario, Canada N6G 1G7 (email: **hse-rhe@**

uwo.ca). Manuscripts in French should be sent to Andrée Dufour, Rédactrice, Revue d'histoire de l'éducation, Département de sciences humaines, Cégep Saint-Jean-sur Richelieu, 30, boul. du Séminaire, C.P. 1018, St-Jean-sur-Ruichelieu (Québec), Canada J3B 7B1 (courriel: **Andree. Dufour@cstjean.qc.ca**). Text and footnotes should be double-spaced. For English manuscripts, follow *Chicago Manual of Style* (15th ed.) and *Oxford Canadian Dictionary* or *Concise Oxford Dictionary* spelling. One paper copy and a copy by e-mail attachment should be submitted, and an abstract (100-150 words).

Authors whose manuscripts are accepted for publication will be asked to supply a final copy, on diskette and/or by e-mail attachment. WordPerfect, MS Word and RTF files are all acceptable.

This journal supports the elimination of sexual, racial, and ethnic stereotyping.

Submission of a manuscript implies that the work contained therein is the author's own, and that no substantial part of it has been submitted for publication or has been published elsewhere.

Historical Studies in Education/Revue d'histoire de l'éducation, published by Athabasca University Press for the Canadian History of Education Association/Association canadienne d'histoire de l'éducation, publishes work in the history of education and educational policy-making, in Canada and elsewhere. In addition to scholarly articles, the journal publishes research notes, book reviews and review essays, and a bibliography.

Format for References
1. Jean-Pierre Proulx, "L'évolution de la législation relative au système électoral scolaire québécois (1829-1989)," *Historical Studies in Education/Revue d'histoire de l'éducation* 10, 1 & 2 (1998): 20-48.

2. Neil Sutherland, *Growing Up: Childhood in English Canada from the Great War to the Age of Television* (Toronto: University of Toronto Press, 1997), 12-14.

3. Proulx, "L'évolution de la législation," 24.

4. Ibid., 25.

5. Sutherland, *Growing Up*, 106-7.

6. Ruby Heap and Alison Prentice, eds., *Gender and Education in Ontario: An Historical Reader* (Toronto: Canadian Scholars' Press, 1991).

7. University of Toronto Archives (UTA), B74-0020, Mossie May Waddington Kirkwood, transcript of her interview with Elizabeth Wilson, 27 Mar. 1973, 57.

8. Cathy L. James, "Gender, Class and Ethnicity in the Organization of Neighbourhood and Nation: The Role of Toronto's Settlement Houses in the Formation of the Canadian State, 1902 to 1914" (Ph.D. diss., University of Toronto, 1997), 115-16.

9. UTA, Office of the President (Falconer Papers), A67-0007/112, File 19, "Matriculation Conference," Gordon to Falconer, 24 Apr. 1928.

10. Elizabeth Smyth, "'A Noble Proof of Excellence': The Culture and Curriculum of a Nineteenth-Century Ontario Convent Academy," in *Gender and Education*, ed. Heap and Prentice, 273-75.

History of Education

SUBMISSION PROCESS:
Electronic Submission Only **via EMail** **joyce.goodman@winchester.ac.uk**

CONTACT INFORMATION:	REVIEW PROCESS:	
Jane Martin, Editor Institute of Education University of London	**Type of Review:**	Blind Review
Joyce Goodman, Editor University of Winchester	**No. External Reviewers:** **No. InHouse Reviewers:**	2 2
	Acceptance Rate:	
	Time to Review:	1 - 2 Months
Phone: 01962 827392	**Reviewer's Comments:** **Invited Articles:**	Yes 0-5%
Email: joyce.goodman@winchester.ac.uk j.martin@ioe.ac.uk historyofeducation@winchester.ac.uk	**Fees to Publish:** **Fees to Review:**	$0.00 US$ $0.00 US$
Website: www.tandf.co.uk/journals/journal. asp?issn=0046-760X&linktype=5		

PUBLICATION GUIDELINES:	CIRCULATION DATA:
Manuscript Style: See Manuscript Guidelines	**Reader:** Academics, Practicing Teachers, Historians
Manuscript Length: 30+	**Frequency of Issue:** 6 Times/Year
Copies Required: Three	**Sponsor/Publisher:** Routledge, Taylor & Francis, Ltd.

MANUSCRIPT TOPICS:
Adult Career & Vocational; Art / Music; Curriculum Studies; Education Management / Administration; Educational Psychology; Elementary / Early Childhood; Health & Physical Education; Higher Education; History of Education; Religious Education; Rural Education & Small Schools; School Law; Special Education; Teacher Education; Urban Education, Cultural / Non-Traditional

MANUSCRIPT GUIDELINES/COMMENTS:

Aims and Scope
History of Education has established itself as a leading, international, peer-reviewed journal, focusing on the history of education in all parts of the world. The journal is recognised as a key resource for both educationists and social historians alike.

The journal publishes original research and major reviews of books in the history of education. Papers dealing with both formal and informal education systems, comparative education, policy-making, the politics and experience of education and pedagogy are welcomed.

The journal also includes a section entitled Sources and Interpretations, which examines historical sources and debates around their interpretation in research and practice.

Special Issues have focused on:
- feminism, femininity and feminization
- the second world war
- education and economic performance
- education and national identity
- education in Wales and Scandinavia
- ways of seeing education and schooling emerging historiographies
- reforming lives? progressivism, leadership and educational change

Instructions for Authors
Note to Authors. Please make sure your contact address information is clearly visible on the outside of <u>all</u> packages you are sending to Editors.

History of Education publishes original papers, correspondence and reviews of books on the history of education in both formal institutions and informal situations.

Articles submitted to *History of Education* should not be under consideration by any other journal, or have been published elsewhere, and the letter accompanying the submission of any manuscript should contain a clear statement to this effect.

Failure to confirm to these notes for guidance may result in your paper being delayed or not being considered for publication.

Three copies of the manuscript for consideration should be submitted to the Editorial Office: **Joyce.Goodman@winchester.ac.uk**. University of Winchester, West Hill, Winchester SO22 4RN, UK. A disk version of the manuscript in Microsoft word should also be submitted.

Book reviews should be sent to: **w.b.richardson@exeter.ac.uk**, School of Education, University of Exeter, Heavitree Road, Exeter EX1 1SL, UK

Sources and Interpretations submissions should be sent to: **pjc36@cam.ac.uk**, University of Cambridge, Faculty of Education, Homerton Site, Hills Road, Cambridge CB2 2PH, UK

Articles should be original and written in a clear, straightforward style, stating objectives clearly and defining terms. Arguments should be substantiated with well-reasoned supporting evidence. For all submissions, non-discriminatory language is mandatory. Sexist or racist terms should not be used.

All pages should be numbered. To allow for anonymous refereeing, all submissions must be properly formatted for blind reviewing. Authors' names and institutions should be typed on a separate sheet and submitted with the manuscript. The full postal and email address of the author who will check proofs and receive correspondence and offprints should also be included. Endnotes should be used sparingly and listed on a separate page entitled 'Notes' at the end of the submission. Endnotes should be cited in the text by super-scribed, consecutive numbers.

Each paper should be accompanied on a separate sheets by an abstract of 50 to 100 words, and a short note of biographical details of each author for 'Notes on Contributors'.

For further information on electronic submission, including information on accepted file types, please visit **www.tandf.co.uk/journals/authors/electronic_edu.asp**

Tables, diagrams, chart and/or illustrations should be submitted on a separate piece of paper, clearly marked and referenced, with short descriptive titles. Additional information (such as legends) should be noted at the bottom of the page. Their placement in the text should be clearly marked. Black and white images or copies of photographs are permitted, provided that permission from the copyright owner has been obtained in advance by the author. Artwork should be supplied in a finished form, suitable for reproduction. Figures will not normally be redrawn by the publisher.

References should be cited using the numerical system with superscripts. They should be listed separately at the end of the paper in the order in which they appear in the text. Bibliographical references in footnotes should be precise, correct and consistent in style. *History of Education* uses the following conventions for references:

For books with a single author
Blackfoot, Emery. *Chance Encounter*s. Boston: Serendipity Press, 1987.

For chapters within books
Kaiser, Ernest. "The Literature of Harlem." In *Harlem: A Community in Transition*, edited by J. H. Clarke. New York: Citadel Press, 1964.

For articles in journals
Bellworthy, Cartright C. "Reform of Congressional Remuneration." *Political Review 7*, no. 6 (1990): 87-101.

After the first use, the reference should be given in abbreviated form as Name, Short title, pages:

Smith, *East towards Home*, 34. Jones, "Title of Article", 948

Please visit **www.tandf.co.uk/journals/authors/StyleCNotes.pdf** for the complete style guidelines.

To download the Chicago Humanities Reference Guide, visit **www.tandf.co.uk/journals/ authors/ChicagoStyleGuideHumanities.pdf**.

Citations of other work should be limited to those strictly necessary for the argument. Any quotations should be brief, and accompanied by precise references.

Titles of journals and names of publishers, etc. should not be abbreviated. Acronyms for the names of organisations, examinations, etc. should be preceded by the title in full.

Proofs are sent to each author if there is sufficient time to do so. The Editors ask that corrected proofs are returned within 48 hours of receipt. Substantial changes to articles at proof stage are not permitted.

Early Electronic Offprints. Corresponding authors can now receive their article by e-mail as a complete PDF. This allows the author to print up to 50 copies, free of charge, and disseminate them to colleagues. In many cases this facility will be available up to two weeks prior to publication. Or, alternatively, corresponding authors will receive the traditional 50 offprints. A copy of the journal will be sent by post to all corresponding authors after publication. Additional copies of the journal can be purchased at the author's preferential rate of £15.00/$25.00 per copy.

Copyright Material. It is a condition of publication that authors assign copyright or licence the publication rights in their articles, including abstracts, to Taylor & Francis. This enables us to ensure full copyright protection and to disseminate the article, and of course the Journal, to the widest possible readership in print and electronic formats as appropriate. Authors may, of course, use the article elsewhere *after* publication without prior permission from Taylor & Francis, provided that acknowledgement is given to the Journal as the original source of publication, and that Taylor & Francis is notified so that our records show that its use is properly authorised. Authors retain a number of other rights under the Taylor & Francis rights policies documents. These policies are referred to at **www.tandf.co.uk/journals/author rights.pdf** for full details.

Authors are themselves responsible for obtaining permission to reproduce copyright material from other sources.

Improving Schools

SUBMISSION PROCESS:
Electronic Submission Only **via EMail** **terry.wrigley@ed.ac.uk**

CONTACT INFORMATION:	REVIEW PROCESS:	
Terry Wrigley, Editor University of Edinburgh, UK	**Type of Review:**	Blind Review
	No. External Reviewers:	2
Phone:	**No. InHouse Reviewers:**	1
	Acceptance Rate:	21-30%
Email:	**Time to Review:**	4 - 6 Months
terry.wrigley@ed.ac.uk	**Reviewer's Comments:**	Yes
Website:	**Invited Articles:**	11-20%
hcb5@le.ac.uk	**Fees to Publish:**	$0.00 US$
	Fees to Review:	$0.00 US$

PUBLICATION GUIDELINES:	CIRCULATION DATA:
Manuscript Style: See Manuscript Guidelines	**Reader:** Academics, Administrators
Manuscript Length: 21-25	**Frequency of Issue:** 3 Times/Year
Copies Required: Electronic Only	**Sponsor/Publisher:** Sage Publications

MANUSCRIPT TOPICS:
Education Management / Administration

MANUSCRIPT GUIDELINES/COMMENTS:

Description
'*Improving Schools* is an excellent resource bringing together academics, researchers and teachers in a journal that is accessible and practical while drawing on work from leading-edge thinkers.' John MacBeath

Improving Schools is for all those engaged in school development, whether improving schools in difficulty or making successful schools even better. The journal includes contributions from across the world with an international readership including teachers, heads, academics, education authority staff, inspectors and consultants.

Improving Schools has created a forum for the exchange of ideas and experiences. Major national policies and initiatives have been evaluated, to share good practice and to highlight problems. The journal also reports on visits to successful schools in diverse contexts, and includes book reviews on a wide range of developmental issues.

Guidelines for the Submission of Manuscripts

To hasten the manuscript review and publication process, email the manuscript/article as a Word file attachment to the Editor and Co-Editor: **Terry.Wrigley@ed.ac.uk** and **Hugh.Busher@le.ac. uk**

Please do not send manuscripts/articles by post.

When submitting your article please confirm, in your email, that all authors have agreed to the submission and that the article is not currently being considered for publication by any other journal. (You will be asked to sign a formal printed agreement once your article is accepted.)

The Editors will be pleased to look at and advise on early drafts and ideas for publication.

Layout

Title Page. Title (preferably short), not capitalized or italicized or emboldened; name(s) and affiliation(s) of author(s) e.g. place of work / role; your contact details (postal address, telephone, and email. Your email will normally be shown in the journal, so that readers can contact you).

Second page. Title; an abstract of 100-150 words; up to 6 keywords (not found in the title).

Subsequent pages. Main body of text; Acknowledgements (if needed); References. Figures / tables / diagrams and the like should be numbered sequentially throughout the text but placed at the end of the article, and their intended place in the article should be clearly indicated.

Length of papers accepted. **Major articles** (refereed, marked in the journal by 'R' after the title) should normally be between 3000 and 6000 words long excluding references. Shorter items such as reports on interesting developments in schools are very welcome (e.g. 1000-2000 words, preferably with photographs).

Style. Articles must be typed, double spaced, written in English and avoid discriminatory language. They should be aimed at an international audience, using a clear style, avoiding jargon. You must therefore explain points that might only be understood within your own education system. Acronyms, abbreviations and technical terms should be defined when they are first used. UK spellings are preferred. If notes are essential only use endnotes. Do not indent at the start of a new paragraph; instead, leave one line between each paragraph and at least two lines between each (sub)section and the next.

Headings and subheadings. Only use up to three levels, including main headings and subheadings. Subheadings are helpful to the reader.

Quotations. For shorter quotations (up to 10 or so words) please use single quotation marks. Longer quotations should appear as separate paragraphs and be indented. All quotations should include page number(s) from the original source.
Final version of accepted articles and items: Should be supplied by email and as one hardcopy. It is the author's responsibility to make sure the electronic and hard versions match exactly. Figures, tables, illustrations and photographs should be supplied as camera-ready copy, or as TIFF or EPS (all fonts embedded) files, with minimum resolutions of 300 dpi for halftones and 600 dpi for line drawings.

Copyright and permissions for reproducing the work of others. On acceptance of their article, authors will be asked to assign copyright to SAGE Publications. Authors are responsible for obtaining permissions from copyright holders for reproducing any illustrations, tables, figures or lengthy quotations previously published elsewhere.

Book reviews. Books for review should be sent to the Reviews Editor, via either of the Editors.

Proofs and off-prints. Authors must comment on proofs of articles accepted for publication within two weeks of receipt from SAGE Publications. They will receive a complimentary copy of the Journal and controlled access to a pdf of their article.

References. The styles indicated below must be followed exactly by authors
- Every citation should have a reference and every reference should be cited.
- Use ampersands in multiple references (e.g. Smith, Brown & Jones), but in the text put first author et al. (e.g. Smith et al.).
- Do not use bold, underlining or quotation marks in references.
- Provide translations for non-English titles in the references.

Journal article
Smith, J. R. (2003) Choosing your style for references. *Journal of Guidelines*, 4(1), 24-9.

Books
Smith, J. R. (2003) Reference Style Guidelines. London: SAGE.

Smith, J. R. & Brown, A. P. (2003) *References for All: Choosing an Appropriate Style*. London: SAGE.

Online
Smith, J. R. (2003) Choosing a suitable layout for your quotations. *Guidance on Referencing*. Online: http:/www.sagepub.com [accessed January 2003].

Industry and Higher Education

SUBMISSION PROCESS:
Postal Submission Only

CONTACT INFORMATION:	REVIEW PROCESS:	
John Edmondson, Editor	**Type of Review:**	Blind Review
IP Publishing, LTD.		
Coleridge House	**No. External Reviewers:**	2
4-5 Coleridge Gardens	**No. InHouse Reviewers:**	1
London, NW6 3QH UK		
	Acceptance Rate:	40%
Phone:	**Time to Review:**	1 - 2 Months
44 207-372-2600	**Reviewer's Comments:**	Yes
	Invited Articles:	6-10%
Email:		
jedmondip@aol.com	**Fees to Publish:**	$0.00 US$
Website:	**Fees to Review:**	$0.00 US$
www.ippublishing.com		

PUBLICATION GUIDELINES:	CIRCULATION DATA:
Manuscript Style:	**Reader:**
See Manuscript Guidelines	Academics
Manuscript Length:	**Frequency of Issue:**
16-20	Bi-Monthly
Copies Required:	**Sponsor/Publisher:**
Three	

MANUSCRIPT TOPICS:
Adult Career & Vocational; Continuing Education; Curriculum Studies; Education Management / Administration; Technology Transfer

MANUSCRIPT GUIDELINES/COMMENTS:

Notes for authors
Please send all submissions to John Edmondson, Industry and Higher Education, IP Publishing Ltd, Coleridge House, 4-5 Coleridge Gardens, London NW6 3QH, UK. Phone: +44 20 7372 2600 Fax: +44 7372 2253. E-mail: **jedmondip@aol.com**. For more details about *Industry and Higher Education*, see **www.ippublishing.com**.

Industry and Higher Education is an international bimonthly journal. It is concerned with policy and practice in relation to all types of collaboration between business and higher education.

Type and length of contributions
The major part of the journal is taken up by papers between 4,000 and 8,000 words long. These should be analytical and evaluative in approach and not simply descriptive. Other contributions include opinion or 'viewpoint' pieces (1,500-3,000 words); case studies of specific ventures or programmes (1,500-3,000 words); brief factual summaries of reports, agency programmes, educational institutions, etc (1,000-2,000 words); and letters to the editors.

Presentation

Submissions should be double-spaced, printed on one side of the paper in one column. Two hard copies should be accompanied by an electronic version on disk (please state the software used). The *title page* should contain full names of the authors, their professional status or affiliation and the address to which they wish correspondence to be sent. There should be an *abstract* of about 100 words at the beginning of the paper. The text should be organized under appropriate *cross-headings* and where possible these should not be more than 800 words apart.

Between 3 and 6 keywords should appear below the abstract, highlighting the main topics of the paper.

References should follow the Harvard system. That is, they should be shown within the text as the author's surname (or authors' surnames) followed by a comma and the year of publication, all in round brackets: for example, (Smith, 1998). At the end of the article a bibliographical list should be supplied, organized alphabetically by author (surnames followed by initials - all authors should be named). Bibliographic information should be given in the order indicated by the following examples:

- *Articles*: Collins, Steven W. (2001), 'Academic research and regional innovation: insights from Seattle, Washington', Industry and Higher Education, Vol 15, No 3, pp 217–221.

- *Books*: Roberts, E.B., ed (1991), Entrepreneurs in High Technology, Oxford University Press, Oxford.

Notes should be numbered consecutively in the text and typed in plain text at the end of the paper (not as footnotes on text pages)

Figures and tables should be presented separately on separate sheets at the end of the text. Each figure or table must be referred to in the text - the first reference will be used to locate the figure or table in the final printed version.

Copyright

Unless otherwise indicated, articles are received on the understanding that they are original contributions, and have not been published or submitted for publication elsewhere. The editors reserve the right to edit or otherwise alter contributions, but authors will see proofs before publication. Wherever possible, authors are asked to assign copyright to IP Publishing Ltd. Relevant authors' rights are protected.

Infant Mental Health Journal

SUBMISSION PROCESS: **Electronic Submission Only via EMail** **imhj@lsuhsc.edu**	

<table>
<tr>
<td>

CONTACT INFORMATION:

Joy Osofsky, Editor
Louisiana State University
Health Science Center
Division of Psychiatry
1542 Tulane Avenue
New Orleans, LA 70112 USA

Phone:
  504-568-6004

Email:
  imhj@lsuhsc.edu

Website:

</td>
<td>

REVIEW PROCESS:

Type of Review:	Blind Review
No. External Reviewers:	2
No. InHouse Reviewers:	
Acceptance Rate:	65%
Time to Review:	2 - 3 Months
Reviewer's Comments:	Yes
Invited Articles:	0-5%
Fees to Publish:	$0.00 US$
Fees to Review:	$0.00 US$

</td>
</tr>
<tr>
<td>

PUBLICATION GUIDELINES:

Manuscript Style:
  American Psychological Association

Manuscript Length:
  30+

Copies Required:
  Electronic Only

</td>
<td>

CIRCULATION DATA:

Reader:
  Academics

Frequency of Issue:
  Bi-Monthly

Sponsor/Publisher:
  John Wiley & Sons

</td>
</tr>
</table>

MANUSCRIPT TOPICS:
Educational Psychology; Elementary / Early Childhood

MANUSCRIPT GUIDELINES/COMMENTS:

Reader. Counselors, Early Childhood Education Specialists, Nurses, Physicians, Psychologists, and Public Health Workers

The *IMHJ* publishes research articles, literature reviews, program descriptions/evaluations, clinical studies, and book reviews that focus on infant social-emotional development, care giver-infant interactions, contextual and cultural influences on infant and family development, and all conditions that place infants and/or their families at-risk for less than optimal development. The *IMHJ* is dedicated to an interdisciplinary approach to the optimal development of infants and their families, and, therefore, welcomes submissions from all disciplinary perspectives.

Manuscripts. One copy submitted via e-mail to the Editor typed, with double spacing throughout and ample margins. Blind reviewing will be used. The manuscript should include a cover sheet with the following information: Title of manuscript, name of author(s), and author(s) affiliation.

The title should appear on the abstract and on the first page of text. Information about the identity of the author(s) contained in footnotes should appear on the title page only. The title page is not included when the manuscript is sent out for review. A cover letter to the Editor should accompany the paper: it should request a review and indicate that the manuscript has not been published previously or submitted elsewhere.

An abstract of approximately 150 words must be included. Tables and figures must be sufficiently clear so that they can be photographed directly. (Black and white glossy prints are acceptable.) Letter quality or near letter-quality print must be used for computer-prepared manuscripts.

Style must conform to that described by the *American Psychological Association Publication Manual*, Fourth Edition, 1994 revision (American Psychological Association, 1200 Seventeenth Street, N.W., Washington, D.C. 20036). Authors are responsible for final preparation of manuscripts to conform to the *APA* style.

Manuscripts are reviewed by the Editor, Associate Editor(s), members of the Editorial Board, and invited reviewers with special knowledge of the topic addressed in the manuscript. The Editor retains the right to reject articles that do not conform to conventional clinical or scientific ethical standards. Normally, the review process is completed in 3 months. Nearly all manuscripts accepted for publication require some degree of revision. There is no charge for publication of papers in the *Infant Mental Health Journal*. The publisher may levy additional charges for changes in proof other than correction of printers errors. Proof will be sent to the corresponding author and must be read carefully because final responsibility for accuracy rests with the author(s). Author(s) must return corrected proof to the publisher in a timely manner. If the publisher does not receive corrected proof from the author(s), publication will still proceed as scheduled.

Additional questions with regard to style and submission of manuscripts should be directed to the Editor.

Informing Faculty

<table>
<tr>
<td colspan="2" align="center">

SUBMISSION PROCESS:

**Electronic Submission Only
via Online Portal**

http://InformingFaculty.org

</td>
</tr>
<tr>
<td valign="top">

CONTACT INFORMATION:

Grandon Gill, Editor-in-Chief
University of South Florida

Phone:
813-974-6755

Email:
ggill@coba.usf.edu
grandon@grandon.com

Website:
http://InformingFaculty.org

</td>
<td valign="top">

REVIEW PROCESS:

Type of Review:	Editorial Review
No. External Reviewers:	2
No. InHouse Reviewers:	1
Acceptance Rate:	25%
Time to Review:	1 Month or Less
Reviewer's Comments:	Yes
Invited Articles:	50% +
Fees to Publish:	$0.00 US$
Fees to Review:	$0.00 US$

</td>
</tr>
<tr>
<td valign="top">

PUBLICATION GUIDELINES:

Manuscript Style:
See Manuscript Guidelines

Manuscript Length:
16-30

Copies Required:
Electronic Only

</td>
<td valign="top">

CIRCULATION DATA:

Reader:
Academics, Administrators, Practicing Teachers

Frequency of Issue:
Yearly

Sponsor/Publisher:
Informing Science Institute

</td>
</tr>
</table>

MANUSCRIPT TOPICS:
Curriculum Studies; Education Management / Administration; Higher Education; Teacher Education

MANUSCRIPT GUIDELINES/COMMENTS:

Focus and Scope
Informing Faculty (*IF*) publishes high quality discussion cases that present real-life situations encountered by higher education faculty across all disciplines. Its particular emphasis is situations involving the use of technology in teaching and learning, but other situations that are likely to resonate with the international community of higher education faculty members will also be considered.

In addition to case studies, each volume of *Informing Faculty* may contain one or more articles from the follow categories:
- **Venue case studies**: Case studies describing venues in which *IF* cases have been used. These may take the form of either discussion case studies or research case studies.
- **Essays**: Articles, written by the editors or faculty members known for their expertise in the case method, that deal with the development or facilitation of discussion cases

- **Editors' prerogative**: From time to time, *IF* editors may choose to include submissions relating to higher education that meet two criteria: they are unusually powerful and their presentation represents a sufficient departure from traditional academic writing that they are unlikely to be suitable for any journal known to the editors.

Author Guidelines

In preparing their case study submissions, authors should use the template available on the Informing Faculty Community web site, provided in both MS-Word and HTML format (with MS-Word being strongly preferred). All submitted case studies should follow the same basic pattern (also described in the template), which is:

- **Author Names**: These may be omitted during review
- **Case Title**: A jargon-free name that describes the case
- **Introduction**: An unlabeled section, sized to fit completely on the front page of the case study, that summarizes the case situation and, more importantly, frames the decisions that must be made by the case protagonist or protagonists. Although experienced case discussants can often generate their own plausible "decisions to be made" without an explicit statement of them in the case, the audience for Informing Faculty case studies will include many individuals for whom the discussion pedagogy is novel. Therefore, any submission that does not begin with a suitable "Introduction" section will normally be returned without further review, accompanied by the instructions "Please frame the decision issues for this case".
- **Sections**: Individual sections, determined by the nature of the case itself (titles should be H2, centered). One level of subsection may also be used (subtitles should be H3, left justified).
- **References**: Any specific items referenced in the case. An APA format should be used (examples are provided in the template).
- **Exhibits**: Each beginning on a new page, exhibits should contain supporting or archival materials relating to the case. These should be numbered 1,2,3, etc. and any exhibit included must be referenced in the case.
- **References**: Any specific items referenced in the case. An APA format should be used (examples are provided in the template).
- **Biographies**: Short descriptions of each author's background, with photographs. May be omitted during review.

Although no strict length guidelines have been established for *Informing Faculty* cases, experience tells us that case studies prepared according to the template will normally end up being 8-12 pages in length, not including exhibits. Cases that are much shorter usually lack the level of detail required to convey a realistic view of the situation; cases that are much longer tend to lose the reader's interest. Should a case study reference a complex technology or pedagogy that cannot be fully explored within the case itself, authors may be encouraged to write an accompanying technical note describing the technology/approach itself in greater detail. These will not be published as part of the journal itself, but will be made available on the Informing Faculty Community web site.

Submission Preparation Checklist

1. The submission has not been previously published, nor is it before another journal for consideration (or an explanation has been provided in Comments to the Editor).
2. The submission file is in Microsoft Word format, or is an HTML file that is zipped with any included images.
3. All URL addresses in the text (e.g., **http://pkp.sfu.ca**) are activated and ready to click.
4. The text adheres to the stylistic and bibliographic requirements outlined in the Author Guidelines, which is found in About the Journal.
5. The author has consulted formatting guidelines provided at the Informing Science Community web site, and has used appropriate templates
6. The case study meets the following criteria:
    - It is based upon an actual situation, and is not fictionalized
    - It is written using language that should be understandable to readers across all disciplines

- It explains any terms that might be confusing to readers from different disciplines or cultures
- It provides background explanations of any practices likely to be specific to a given organization, discipline or culture
- It presents a situation where decisions need to be made, and identifies these decisions on the first page

Copyright Notice

Informing Faculty will retain the copyright of all published materials, whether in electronic or paper format. Permission to copy or post electronic copies of written materials for non-commercial purposes is granted. Materials posted in the secure areas of the Informing Faculty Community web site, such as teaching notes and follow-on cases, may also be copied. These materials should not be posted electronically, however, unless reasonable precautions are taken to prevent their widespread dissemination on the web (e.g., they may be placed on a limited access secure web site, such as a course management system installation, but they must not be posted on a public web site).

Privacy Statement

The names and email addresses entered in this journal site will be used exclusively for the stated purposes of this journal and will not be made available for any other purpose or to any other party.

Intelligence

<table>
<tr><td colspan="2" align="center">SUBMISSION PROCESS:

Electronic Submission Only
via Online Portal

http://ees.elsevier.com/intell/</td></tr>
<tr><td>CONTACT INFORMATION:

Douglas K. Detterman, Editor
Case Western Reserve University
Department of Psychology
10900 Euclid Avenue
Cleveland, OH 44106-7123 USA

Phone:
215-368-2681

Email:
detterman@case.edu
intelligence_journal@hotmail.com
dkd2@po.cwru.edu

Website:
http://ees.elsevier.com/intell/
www.ISIRonline.org</td><td>REVIEW PROCESS:

Type of Review: Editorial Review

No. External Reviewers: 3
No. InHouse Reviewers: 0

Acceptance Rate: 50-60%
Time to Review: 1-3 Months
Reviewer's Comments: Yes
Invited Articles: 0-5%

Fees to Publish: $0.00 US$
Fees to Review: $0.00 US$</td></tr>
<tr><td>PUBLICATION GUIDELINES:

Manuscript Style:
American Psychological Association

Manuscript Length:
21-25

Copies Required:
Electronic Only</td><td>CIRCULATION DATA:

Reader:
Academics, Researchers

Frequency of Issue:
Bi-Monthly

Sponsor/Publisher:
International Society for Intelligence Research / Elsevier Inc.</td></tr>
</table>

MANUSCRIPT TOPICS:
Art / Music; Educational Psychology; Elementary / Early Childhood; Gifted Children; Higher Education; Reading; Science Math & Environment; Secondary / Adolescent Studies; Special Education; Tests, Measurement & Evaluation; Urban Education, Cultural / Non-Traditional

MANUSCRIPT GUIDELINES/COMMENTS:

Guide for Authors
The journal *Intelligence* publishes papers reporting work that makes a substantial contribution to an understanding of the nature and function of intelligence. Varied approaches to the problem will be welcome. Theoretical and review articles will be considered if appropriate, but preference will be given to original research. In general, studies concerned with application will not be considered appropriate unless the work also makes a contribution to basic knowledge.

For submission, all papers should be submitted online in MS Word or PDF format. A blind review will be conducted upon the request of the author. The paper, in MS Word or PDF format, should be submitted at **http://ees.elsevier.com/intell/** where authors will find full instructions.

Manuscripts should conform to the conventions specified in the fifth edition (2001) of the *Publication Manual of the American Psychological Association* (750 First St. NE, Washington, DC 20002-4242) with the exceptions listed below.

1. **Preparation of Manuscript**. Please double space *all* material. Manuscripts should be typewritten on 8 ½ x 11 in. bond paper, *one side only*, ragged right margin, leaving 1-in. margins on all sides. Number pages consecutively with the title page as page 1, and include a brief abstract from 100 to 150 words as page 2. All tables and other end-of-paper matter, except art, should be numbered also.

2. **Illustrations**. Submit only clear reproductions of artwork. Authors should retain original artwork until a manuscript has been accepted in its final version. All figures must be in a camera-ready form. All artwork should be placed in the manuscript. Authors must provide high-quality figures, preferably laser printed, typeset, or professionally inked. Photographs must be black and white glossies. The largest figure that can be accommodated is 5 x 7 in., so please keep this in mind when constructing artwork. Colour Reproduction: submit colour illustrations as original photographs, high-quality computer prints or transparencies, close to the size expected in publication, or as 35 mm slides. Polaroid colour prints are not suitable. *If, together with your accepted article, you submit usable colour figures then Elsevier will ensure, at no additional charge, that these figures will appear in colour on the web (e.g., ScienceDirect and other sites) regardless of whether or not these illustrations are reproduced in colour in the printed version.* For colour reproduction in print, you will receive information regarding the costs from Elsevier after receipt of your accepted article. For further information on the preparation of electronic artwork, please see http://authors.elsevier.com/artwork.

Please note. Because of technical complications which can arise by converting colour figures to "grey scale" (for the printed version should you not opt for colour in print) please submit in addition usable black and white prints corresponding to all the colour illustrations.

3. **Numbering of Figures and Tables**. Each figure and table must be mentioned in the text and must be numbered consecutively using Arabic numerals in the order of its appearance in the text. On the reverse side of every figure *write the name of the author and the figure number*. A brief title should be typed directly above each table. Please indicate in the manuscript approximately where you wish each table or figure to be placed.

4. **Footnotes**. Footnotes should be used sparingly and indicated by consecutive numbers in the text. Material to be footnoted should be typed separately and submitted with the manuscript following the figure legends. Acknowledgments, grant numbers, an author correspondence address, E-mail, and any change of address should be given in a separate, asterisked footnote, which will appear at the end of text.

5. **References**. Contributors should refer to the *APA Publication Manual* for the correct listing of references in the text and reference list. The only exception is that unpublished references should not be treated as reference notes, but listed in the same format as published references. All references must be closely checked in text and lists to determine that dates and spellings are consistent. Please note that the names of *all* authors should be given in the list of references, and "et al." used only in the text. Examples for journals, unpublished papers, and books (in that order) are given below:

Atkinson, R. C., & Shiffrin, R. M. (1971). The control of short-term memory. *Scientific American, 225*, 82-90.

Lightburn, L. T. (1955). *The relation of critical fusion frequency to age.* Unpublished doctoral dissertation, University of New Jersey.

Riesen, A. H. (1966). Sensory deprivation. In E. Stellar & J. M. Sprague (Eds.), *Progress in physiological psychology* (pp 105-112). New York: Academic

6. **Spelling, Terminology, and Abbreviations**. American spelling, rather than British, is preferred. The Third Edition of *Webster's Unabridged Dictionary* is the standard reference work when in doubt. Please try to avoid jargon and, whenever possible, abbreviations that are not commonly accepted.

7. **Role of corresponding author**. The corresponding authors of a manuscript for *Intelligence* has the duty to ensure that all the named authors have seen and approved the original and any revised version of the paper and are in agreement with its content before it is submitted to the Editorial Office. Each author should have participated sufficiently in the work to take public responsibility for the content. The corresponding author should also ensure that all those who have contributed to the research are acknowledged appropriately either as co-author or in the Acknowledgements. In addition, the corresponding author has the prime responsibility for ensuring the paper is correctly prepared according to the Guide for Authors. Submitted manuscripts not complying with the Guide for Authors may be returned to the authors for possible revision and resubmission.

Upon acceptance of an article, authors will be asked to transfer copyright (for more information on copyright see http://authors.elsevier.com). This transfer will ensure the widest possible dissemination of information. A letter will be sent to the corresponding author confirming receipt of the manuscript. A form facilitating transfer of copyright will be provided. If excerpts from other copyrighted works are included, the author(s) must obtain written permission from the copyright owners and credit the source(s) in the article. Elsevier has preprinted forms for use by the authors in these cases: contact ELSEVIER, Global Rights Department, P.O. Box 800, Oxford, OX5 IDX, UK; phone: (444) 1865 843830, e-mail: permissions@elsevier.com

8. **Affiliation, Running Head**. Please include under your name on the title page the institutions with which you are connected, your complete mailing address, E-mail, and credits to any other institution where the work may have been done. A shortened version of your title, suitable for alternate page headings, should be typed underneath your affiliation and identified as *Running Head*.

9. **Acceptance**. Upon acceptance we request an IBM compatible disk, spell checked and stripped of all embedded graphics. Graphics should be saved in a separate eps, tiff, or ps file. The accuracy of the disk and page proofs is the author's responsibility.

10. **Offprints**. The lead author will be provided 25 free copies of his or her article.

11.**Supplementary data**. Elsevier now accepts electronic supplementary material to support and enhance your scientific research. Supplementary files offer the author additional possibilities to publish supporting applications, movies, animation sequences, high-resolution images, background datasets, sound clips and more. Supplementary files supplied will be published online alongside the electronic version of your article in Elsevier web products, including ScienceDirect: http://www.sciencedirect.com. In order to ensure that your submitted material in directly usable, please ensure that data is provided in one of our recommended file formats. Authors should submit the material in electronic format together with the article and supply a concise and descriptive caption for each file. For more detailed instructions please visit our Author Gateway at http://authors.elsevier.com.

12. **Enquiries**. Authors can keep track on the progress of their accepted article, and set up e-mail alerts, informing them of changes to their manuscript's status, by using the "track a Paper" feature of Elsevier's Author Gateway http://authors.elsevier.com. For privacy, information on each article is password protected. The author should key in the "Our References" code (which is in the letter of acknowledgement sent by the publisher on receipt of the accepted article) and the name of the corresponding author. In case of problems or questions, authors may contact the Author Service Department. E-mail: authorsupport@elsevier.com.

Interactions: UCLA Journal of Education & Information Studies

SUBMISSION PROCESS:
Electronic Submission Preferred **via EMail** **interactions@gseis.ucla.edu**

CONTACT INFORMATION:	REVIEW PROCESS:	
S Calderone, S Meeker & T Trujillo, Eds. University of California - Los Angeles Grad School of Education & Info Studies 2933 Mathematical Sciences Bldg. Box 951521 Los Angeles, CA 90095-1521 USA	**Type of Review:**	Blind Review
	No. External Reviewers:	2
	No. InHouse Reviewers:	3
	Acceptance Rate:	11-20%
	Time to Review:	1 - 2 Months
Phone: 310-825-8992	**Reviewer's Comments:**	No
	Invited Articles:	21-30%
Email: interactions@gseis.ucla.edu	**Fees to Publish:**	$0.00 US$
	Fees to Review:	$0.00 US$
Website: http://www.interactions.gseis.ucla.edu		

PUBLICATION GUIDELINES:	CIRCULATION DATA:
Manuscript Style: American Psychological Association	**Reader:** Academics, Graduate Students
Manuscript Length: 26-30	**Frequency of Issue:** 2 Times/Year
Copies Required: Four	**Sponsor/Publisher:** UCLA Grad School of Education & Info Studies / Escholarship via California Digital Library

MANUSCRIPT TOPICS:

Adult Career & Vocational; Art / Music; Audiology / Speech Pathology; Bilingual / E.S.L.; Counseling & Personnel Services; Curriculum Studies; Education Management / Administration; Educational Psychology; Educational Technology Systems; Elementary / Early Childhood; Gifted Children; Higher Education; Library Science / Information Resources; Reading; Religious Education; Rural Education & Small Schools; School Law; Science Math & Environment; Secondary / Adolescent Studies; Social Studies / Social Science; Special Education; Teacher Education; Tests, Measurement & Evaluation; Urban Education, Cultural / Non-Traditional

MANUSCRIPT GUIDELINES/COMMENTS:

Interdisciplinary Focus

Throughout the social sciences and humanities, there is a continuing trend toward interdisciplinarity. An important goal of *InterActions* is to further, in a careful and coherent way, this process of cross-fertilization. Within education, there is increasing awareness both of the connections between the various sub-disciplines in the field, as well as between education and other fields in the academy. Likewise, in information studies, scholars have begun to challenge traditional practices and suggest new and different directions for research. Currently, work in fields as diverse as legal theory, literary criticism, design, and technology studies are profoundly impacting developments in educational and information studies research. Furthermore, traditionally separate areas of research in information studies and education, such as sociology, curriculum, policy, and psychological studies are being connected by researchers in new and innovative ways. We believe that when perspectives from diverse traditions are brought together, the interests, power, and practicability of research are multiplied.

Critical Perspectives

At a time when education and the management of information have again moved to center stage in public debates, there is a great deal of controversy over the best purposes, practices, and organization of educational institutions and information systems at various institutional levels. Another important goal of *InterActions* is to offer a timely and reasoned contribution to these debates. Our aim is to provide critical commentary on current issues and to promote perspectives that aid the development of educational projects and information systems that can serve the cause of social justice. Much of the public discourse about education and information management is driven by superficial analysis and misinformation; in this regard, our goal is to offer a variety of critical interventions that will help to move discussions of both education and information studies to a more informed, creative, and politically engaged level.

Submission Guidelines

The journal cannot re-publish material that has previously been published elsewhere, and does not accept papers that are simultaneously submitted to other journals. All submissions should be completed while the author is an 'emerging scholar' (graduate student, postdoctoral fellow, practitioner, or activist). Papers co-authored with faculty members are acceptable. All articles undergo a double-blind peer-review by graduate student colleagues and/or faculty scholars in the field.

We require one electronic copy and four paper copies of your submission. All information that could identify the author should be removed from the manuscript. Papers should be in accordance with American Psychological Association (APA) Fifth Edition format and must include an abstract. Papers should not exceed 30 double-spaced pages (including references). Include author's name, address, email, institutional affiliation, and position on a cover page.

Please send an electronic version of your submission in Word or Rich Text (rtf) format to: **interactions@gseis.ucla.edu**.

In addition, send four paper copies of your submission to: UCLA - Graduate School of Education & Information Studies, InterActions: UCLA Journal of Education and Information Studies, 2933 Mathematical Sciences Building - Box 951521, Los Angeles, CA 90095-1521

InterActions Formatting Guidelines

InterActions: UCLA Journal of Education and Information Studies uses the *Publication Manual of the American Psychological Association*: Fifth Edition as its publication style guide. All in-text citations and references must abide by APA guidelines.

Text & Paragraph Formatting

Text. Margins are 1.5" on all sides. 12 pt Times New Roman font. Margins are justified.

Paragraph. Double spacing between lines. First sentence of each paragraph is indented .5".

Block quotes. 5 indentation spaces from the left margin, with the right margin of the quote the same as the right margin of the text. Block quotes are separated from the text by double spaces. Text is double-spaced, Times New Roman 11 pt font. The page number(s) of the quote appears at the end of the quote in parentheses.

Endnotes. Use endnotes instead of footnotes. Use Arabic numerals for indicating notes in the text. Endnotes should appear before the References section. This section should be titled "Notes." Heading should be centered and bold.

Acknowledgments. If included, this section should come after the Notes section. Heading should be centered and bold.

References. In-text citations include the author's last name, followed by the year of publication; e.g., (Rao, 1987). Direct quotations should include the page number as well, following the publication year.

When the name of author appears in the narrative, cite only the year of publication in parentheses; e.g., Angela Valenzuela (2004) notes…

Other
When referencing author in narrative, use first and last name on initial occasion and then last namely only thereafter.

The list of citations, in alphabetical order, appears after the Acknowledgments section. If the Acknowledgments section is not included, this section comes after the Notes section. This section should be titled "References," and the heading should be centered and bold. All citations must have a hanging indent of .5" for the second and any subsequent lines of the citation.

Examples of citations:
Book
Orfield, G. & Eaton, S. (1996). *Dismantling desegregation: The quiet reversal of Brown v. Board of Education*. New York: The New Press.

Chapter in Edited Book
Palmer, S.R. (2001). Diversity and affirmative action: Evolving principles and continuing legal battles. In G. Orfield (Ed.), *Diversity challenged: Evidence on the impact of affirmative action* (pp. 49-80). Cambridge, MA: Harvard Education Publishing Group.

Article in Journal
Wise, T. (1998). Is sisterhood conditional? White women and the rollback of affirmative action. *NWSA Journal*, 10(3), 1-25.

Document Heading Formatting
Author Information. Should be titled "Author." Heading should be centered and bold. This section should appear last in the article, after the "References" section.

Title Page Information. Title should be 10-12 words. Abstract should be no longer than 120 words. Three keywords should be supplied.

Note. When formatting the final document, it should not include a title page, author, running head, abstract or page numbers. The title, author information, running-head, title, abstract, and keywords should be separately input for each article by the publication editor into the E-scholarship system.

Headers:
1. Main Heading: centered, bold, and capitalized. For example:
   Developing Standards for Online Journal Publishing

2. Subheading: centered, italicized, and capitalized. For example:
   The Information-Seeking Behavior of Teenagers

3. Sub-subheading: left-justified, italicized, and capitalized. For example:
School Libraries

Spacing between headings:

Main heading: 2 lines spaces before heading and 1 line space after heading
Subheading: 1 line space before heading and 1 line after heading
Sub-subheading: 1 line space before heading and no line space after heading

Interactive Learning Environments

SUBMISSION PROCESS:	
Electronic Submission Only **via EMail** **rada@umbc.edu** **b.c.e.scott@cranfield.ac.uk**	

CONTACT INFORMATION:	REVIEW PROCESS:	
Roy Rada, Editor University of Maryland	**Type of Review:**	Blind Review
Bernard Scott, Editor Cranfield University	**No. External Reviewers:** **No. InHouse Reviewers:**	3 1
Phone:	**Acceptance Rate:** **Time to Review:** **Reviewer's Comments:** **Invited Articles:**	21-30% 1 - 2 Months Yes 0-5%

Email:
    rada@umbc.edu
    b.c.e.scott@cranfield.ac.uk
	Fees to Publish:
	Fees to Review:
		$0.00 US$
		$0.00 US$

Website:
    www.tandf.co.uk/journals/titles/10494820
    .asp		

PUBLICATION GUIDELINES:	CIRCULATION DATA:

Manuscript Style:
    See Manuscript Guidelines
 	
Manuscript Length:
    21-25
 	
Copies Required:
    One
	Reader:
	    Academics, Administrators, Practicing
	    Teachers
	
	Frequency of Issue:
	    3 Times/Year
	
	Sponsor/Publisher:
	    Routledge, Taylor & Francis

MANUSCRIPT TOPICS:
Education Management / Administration

MANUSCRIPT GUIDELINES/COMMENTS:

Aims and Scope
Founded in 1990, *Interactive Learning Environments* publishes peer-reviewed articles on all aspects of the design and use of interactive learning environments in the broadest sense, encompassing environments that support individual learners through to environments that support collaboration amongst groups of learners or co-workers.

Relevant domains of application include education and training at all levels, life-long learning and knowledge sharing. Relevant topics for articles include: adaptive systems, learning theory, pedagogy and learning design, the electronically-enhanced classroom, computer mediated communications of all kinds, computer aided assessment, the design and use of virtual learning environments and learning management systems, facilitating organisational change, applying standards for courseware reuse, tracking, record keeping and system interoperability, the use of learning content management systems, including workflow design and publication to a range of media, and issues associated with scaling up delivery to large cohorts of students and trainees within the corporate, educational and other public sectors.

Review and survey articles that show scholarly depth, breadth and richness are particularly welcome. The field of interactive learning environments is developing and evolving rapidly. As well as tracking changes and emerging trends, it is also important to draw lessons from the recent and not so recent past.

Specific themes the journal covers include the following:

Individual learning
- Innovative learning situations, including adaptive systems, intelligent tutoring, conversational and advisory systems
- Tools to aid learning and tools for studying and modelling learners
- Cognitive, social, developmental and motivational aspects of how learning comes about
- Principles of course design for effective learning, authoring tools
- Self-organised learning and learning to learn

Group Activity
- Informal knowledge exchange networks
- Participation in on-line discussion
- Computer supported teamwork projects
- Collaborative learning processes
- Peer tutoring and mentoring in computer mediated learning
- Self assessment and peer assessment in virtual classrooms
- Interactive video and audio technologies

Social and organisational issues
- Facilitating and managing organisational change
- Integrating e-learning with other business processes
- The interface between e-learning and knowledge management

Courseware
- Production processes
- The use of digital repositories
- Courseware sharing and reuse

Instructions for Authors
Notes for Contributors. Papers should be original. If possible, please send your manuscripts to the Editors by email. Please submit your manuscript as a PDF file to: Professor Roy Rada, Department of Information Systems, University of Maryland, Baltimore County, 1000 Hilltop Circle, Baltimore, MD 21250, USA, email: **rada@umbc.edu** or Dr Bernard Scott, Cranfield University, Defence Academy, Shrivenham, Wiltshire, SN6 8LA, UK, email: **b.c.e.scott@cranfield.ac.uk**

Papers should normally be between 2,000 and 6,000 words in length.

Follow the formatting guidelines of the *Publication Manual of the American Psychological Association*, 5th edition, 2001. Each manuscript must include an abstract of 100 to 300 words. The full postal and email address of the author who will check proofs and receive correspondence and offprints should also be included.

After acceptance for publishing, authors should send the final, revised version of their manuscripts in both hard copy paper and electronic forms to the publisher. It is essential that the hard copy (paper) version exactly matches the material on electronic file. Please print the hard copy from the electronic version. Submit one printed copy of the final version, together with the electronic version, to the publisher. Electronic material should be in PC compatible MS Word format. All pages should be numbered.

Tables and captions to illustrations. For the manuscript to be reviewed, the tables and figures should be in the body of the text. After acceptance, the manuscript should be reformatted to: 1) put the tables and figures at the end of the document on separate sheets and 2) collect the captions together on a separate sheet. Tables and Figures should be numbered consecutively by Arabic numerals. The approximate position of tables and figures should be indicated in the manuscript. Captions should include keys to any symbols used. Please supply one set of artwork in a finished form, suitable for reproduction. Figures will not normally be redrawn by the publisher.

References should be indicated in the typescript by giving the author's name, with the year of publication in parentheses, as detailed in the APA style guide. If several papers by the same author(s) and from the same year are cited, a, b, c, etc. should be put after the year of publication. The references should be listed in full at the end of the paper in standard APA format. For example:

For books
Massey, W. R., & Jameson, W. M., Jr. (2001). Organizational behavior and the new internet logic (3rd ed.). New York: McGraw-Hill.

For articles within books
Loughran, J., & Corrigan, D. (1995). Teaching portfolios: A strategy for developing learning and teaching in preservice education. Teaching and Teacher Education, 11, 565-577.

For online documents
Standler, R. (2000). Plagiarism in colleges in the USA. Retrieved August 6 2004 from www.rbs2.com/plag.htm

Titles of journals and names of publishers, etc. should not be abbreviated. Acronyms for the names of organisations, examinations, etc. should be preceded by the title in full.

Download a Word template for this journal at: **www.tandf.co.uk/journals/authors/edstyleb.dot**

If you have any further questions about the style for this journal, please submit your questions using the Style Queries form at **www.tandf.co.uk/journals/authors/stylequeries.asp**

Duality of Interest. Authors are responsible for recognizing and disclosing any duality of interest that could be perceived to bias their work, acknowledging all financial support and any other personal connections.

Proofs will be sent to authors by email if there is sufficient time to do so. They should be corrected and returned to the Publisher within three days. Major alterations to the text cannot be accepted.

Early Electronic Offprints. Corresponding authors can now receive their article by email as a complete PDF. This allows the author to print up to 50 copies, free of charge, and disseminate them to colleagues. In many cases this facility will be available up to two weeks prior to publication. Or, alternatively, corresponding authors will receive the traditional 50 offprints. A copy of the journal will be sent by post to all corresponding authors after publication. Additional copies of the journal can be purchased at the author's preferential rate of £15.00/$25.00 per copy.

For further information on electronic submission, including information on accepted file types, please visit **www.tandf.co.uk/journals/authors/electronic_edu.asp**

Taylor & Francis makes every effort to ensure the accuracy of all the information (the "Content") contained in its publications. However, Taylor & Francis and its agents and licensors make no

406

representations or warranties whatsoever as to the accuracy, completeness or suitability for any purpose of the Content and disclaim all such representations and warranties whether express or implied to the maximum extent permitted by law. Any views expressed in this publication are the views of the authors and are not the views of Taylor & Francis.

Copyright. It is a condition of publication that authors assign copyright or licence the publication rights in their articles, including abstracts, to Taylor & Francis. This enables us to ensure full copyright protection and to disseminate the article, and of course the Journal, to the widest possible readership in print and electronic formats as appropriate. Authors may, of course, use the article elsewhere after publication without prior permission from Taylor & Francis, provided that acknowledgement is given to the Journal as the original source of publication, and that Taylor & Francis is notified so that our records show that its use is properly authorised. Authors retain a number of other rights under the Taylor & Francis rights policies documents. These policies are referred to at **http://www.tandf.co.uk/journals/authorrights.pdf** for full details. Authors are themselves responsible for obtaining permission to reproduce copyright material from other sources.

Intercultural Education

SUBMISSION PROCESS:	
Postal & Electronic Submission Accepted via EMail	
francesca.gobbo@unito.it	

CONTACT INFORMATION:	REVIEW PROCESS:	
Francesca Gobbo, Editor Via G. Ferrari 9/11 10124 Torino Italy	**Type of Review:**	Editorial Review
	No. External Reviewers:	25
	No. InHouse Reviewers:	2
Phone:	**Acceptance Rate:**	35%
	Time to Review:	1 - 2 Months
	Reviewer's Comments:	Yes
Email: francesca.gobbo@unito.it	**Invited Articles:**	21-30%
Website: www.tandf.co.uk/journals/14675986	**Fees to Publish:**	$0.00 US$
	Fees to Review:	$0.00 US$

PUBLICATION GUIDELINES:	CIRCULATION DATA:
Manuscript Style: See Manuscript Guidelines	**Reader:** Academics, Counselors, Practicing Teachers, Teacher Trainers
Manuscript Length: 3000-6000 words	**Frequency of Issue:** 5 Times/Year
Copies Required: One	**Sponsor/Publisher:** Int'l Assn for Intercultural Education / Routledge, Taylor & Francis, Ltd.

MANUSCRIPT TOPICS:
Bilingual / E.S.L.; Curriculum Studies; Education Management / Administration; Higher Education; Teacher Education

MANUSCRIPT GUIDELINES/COMMENTS:

Topics Also Include. Multilingual / E.S.L.; Conflict Management; Human Rights Education; Intercultural Education; Multicultural Education; Anti-Racist Education; Pluralism; Migration & Indigeneous Minority Issues

Intercultural Education is published by Taylor & Franics for the International Association for Intercultural Education (IAIE). To view the IAIE website, please visit: **www.iaie.org**

Aims and Scope
Intercultural Education is a global forum for the analysis of issues dealing with education in plural societies. It provides educational professionals with the knowledge and information that can assist them in contributing to the critical analysis and the implementation of intercultural education. Topics covered include: terminological issues, education and multicultural society today, intercultural communication, human rights and anti-racist education, pluralism and diversity in a democratic frame work, pluralism in post-communist and in post-colonial countries, migration and

indigenous minority issues, refugee issues, language policy issues, curriculum and classroom organization, and school development.

Manuscripts

(Hard copy and a version on disk, preferably in Word format) should be sent to: Francesca Gobbo, Dip. Scienze Educazione, Via G. Ferrari 9/11, 10124 Torino, Italy or by E-mail to **francesca. gobbo@unito.it**.

All articles will be refereed by members of the editorial board, which may lead to suggestions for the improvement of the article. The author's final draft will be edited and corrected by the journal's final editor.

Main articles should be between 3,000 and 6,000 words, including a short biographical note of the author(s), and with one's address for correspondence including fax and e-mail at the end of the article. An abstract of 80-120 words, preferably in two languages, English and the author's own language, should be provided at the beginning of the article.

Books for review, originally written in English, should be addressed to Sven Sierens, Center for Intercultural Education, Sint Pietersnieuwstraat, B-9000 Ghent, Belgium

Electronic Submission

Authors should send the final, revised version of their articles in both hard copy and electronic disk form. We prefer to receive disks in Microsoft Word in a PC format. It is essential that the hard copy (paper) version **exactly** matches the material on disk. Please print out the hard copy from the disk you are sending. Submit three printed copies of the final version with the disk to the journal's editorial office. Save all files on a standard 3.5 inch high-density disk. We prefer to receive disks in Microsoft Word in a PC format, but can translate from most other common word processing programs as well as Macs. Please specify which program you have used. Do not save your files as "text only" or "read only". For further details on electronic submission, please visit our website at: **http://www.tandf.co.uk/journals/authors/electronic_edu.asp**

Tables and captions to illustrations

Tables and captions to illustrations must be typed out on separate sheets and not included as part of the text.

Figures

Please, supply one set of artwork in a finished form, suitable for reproduction.

References

These should be indicated in the typescript by giving the author's name, with the year of publication in parentheses. If several papers by the same author and from the same year are cited, a, b, c, etc. should be put after the year of publication. The references should be listed in full, including pages, at the end of the paper in the following standard form:

For books
Fryer, P. (1984) *Staying Power* (London, Pluto Press).

For articles
Haarmann, H. (1995) Multilingualism and ideology: the historical experiment of Soviet language politics, *European Journal of Intercultural Studies*, 5(3), 16-17.

For chapters within books
Lotan, R. (1997) Principles of a principled curriculum, in: E. Cohen & R. Lotan (Eds)

Working for equity in heterogeneous classrooms: sociological theory in practice (New York, Teachers College Press), 105-116.

Titles of journals and names of publishers, etc. should **not** be abbreviated. Acronyms for the names of organizations, examinations, etc. should be preceded by the title in full.

End notes should be kept to a minimum. They should be numbered consecutively throughout the article, and should immediately precede the 'References' section.

If you have any further questions about the style for this journal, please submit your questions using the Style Queries form which can be found at our website: **http://www.tandf.co.uk/ journals/authors/stylequeries.asp**

Early Electronic Offprints. Corresponding authors can now receive their article by e-mail as a complete PDF. This allows the author to print up to 50 copies, free of charge, and disseminate them to colleagues. In many cases this facility will be available up to two weeks prior to publication. Or, alternatively, corresponding authors will receive the traditional 50 offprints. A copy of the journal will be sent by post to all corresponding authors after publication. Additional copies of the journal can be purchased at the author's preferential rate of £15.00/$25.00 per copy.

Copyright. It is a condition of publication that authors vest copyright in their articles, including abstracts, in Taylor & Francis Ltd. This enables us to ensure full copyright protection and to disseminate the article, and the journal, to the widest possible readership in print and electronic formats as appropriate.

Authors may, of course, use the article elsewhere **after** publication without prior permission from Taylor & Francis, provided that acknowledgement is given to the Journal as the original source of publication, and that Taylor & Francis is notified so that our records show that its use is properly authorized. Authors retain a number of other rights under the Taylor & Francis rights policies documents. These policies are referred to at **www.tandf.co.uk/journals/authorrights.pdf** for full details. Authors are themselves responsible for obtaining permission to reproduce copyright material from other sources.

International Electronic Journal for Leadership in Learning

SUBMISSION PROCESS:	
Electronic Submission Only **via EMail** **iejll@ucalgary.ca**	

CONTACT INFORMATION:	**REVIEW PROCESS:**	
J. Kent Donlevy, Editor University of Calgary Graduate Division of Edu. Research Faculty of Education Calgary, AB Canada	**Type of Review:**	Blind Review
	No. External Reviewers:	3
	No. InHouse Reviewers:	1
	Acceptance Rate:	21-30%
Phone:	**Time to Review:**	2 - 3 Months
	Reviewer's Comments:	Yes
	Invited Articles:	0-5%
Email: iejll@ucalgary.ca donlevy@ucalgary.ca	**Fees to Publish:**	$0.00 US$
	Fees to Review:	$0.00 US$
Website: www.ucalgary.ca/~iejll		

PUBLICATION GUIDELINES:	**CIRCULATION DATA:**
Manuscript Style: American Psychological Association	**Reader:** Academics, Administrators, Practicing Teachers
Manuscript Length: 16-20	**Frequency of Issue:** 24 Times/Year
Copies Required: Electronic Only	**Sponsor/Publisher:** Univ. of Calgary Press, Assn. for Supervision & Curr. Devel, Center for Leadership in Learning

MANUSCRIPT TOPICS:
Education Management / Administration; Higher Education; Urban Education, Cultural / Non-Traditional

MANUSCRIPT GUIDELINES/COMMENTS:

Statement of Purpose
The *International Electronic Journal for Leadership in Learning* (*IEJLL*) promotes the study and discussion of substantive leadership issues that are of current concern in educational communities. Preference is given to articles and commentaries that focus upon issues with a significant impact upon life in schools.

Prospective authors should submit work that will be of interest to a broad readership, including teachers, administrators, members of governance bodies, parents, community members, department of education personnel, and academics.

The *IEJLL* is imprinted by the University of Calgary Press and is sponsored by the Centre for Leadership in Learning and the Faculty of Education at the University of Calgary.

General Guidelines

The *IEJLL* is a refereed electronic journal intended for a broad audience of persons interested in leadership in learning. Our audience includes members of government education departments, school boards, school councils, faculties of education, parent organizations, and school staffs.

Submissions can take various forms:
- articles on current quantitative or qualitative research
- reports on innovative programs
- position papers
- reflective commentaries on published submissions

The Editorial Team invites submissions related to various Leadership in Learning issues: • school culture • accountability • politics in education • shared leadership • teacher professionalism • parent leadership • school reform • the role of business in education • alternative forms of schooling • teacher development • educational finance

Formatting Requirements for Submissions

Submissions to the *IEJLL* should not exceed 5000 words excluding references. Articles may initiate electronic conversations among readers and authors. These conversations will be facilitated by e-mail links to the author and to The Change Agency Listserver. Submissions must adhere to the guidelines of the *Publication Manual of the American Psychological Association* (Fifth Edition) and IEJLL Ethical Guidelines for Authors available on the web site.

References to other electronic journals and sites should contain web site addresses (URLs).

Abstract

Include an abstract of approximately100 words identifying the essence of the submission. Abstracts will be published independently from the article for readers to "browse" before choosing an article to view/read.

Authorship Information

A brief autobiography of the author should accompany the submission in a separate file to facilitate a blind review process. Include such information as academic background, current position, professional affiliation, mailing address, area of current interest or research and other interests. E-mail addresses are expected as are WWW addresses for authors' home pages, if applicable.

Sending Your Work

The *IEJLL* is committed to making effective use of electronic delivery for timely communication. Therefore, the *IEJLL* is unable to accept paper submissions.

Acceptable Electronic Format for Submissions

Word files are preferred. Rich Text Format (RTF) is acceptable. Graphics submitted in GIF or JPEG format are preferred. Authors who are interested in including sound and/or video are encouraged to discuss such submissions with the Editor. The Editorial Committee is very interested in investigating the expanding opportunities of the electronic medium.

Sending Your Submission to *IEJLL*

Submissions can be sent to *IEJLL* through e-mail to **IEJLL@ucalgary.ca**

International Journal for Educational and Vocational Guidance

<table>
<tr><td colspan="2" align="center">SUBMISSION PROCESS:

Postal Submission Only</td></tr>
<tr>
<td>CONTACT INFORMATION:</td>
<td>REVIEW PROCESS:</td>
</tr>
</table>

SUBMISSION PROCESS: **Postal Submission Only**	

CONTACT INFORMATION:

Raoul Van Esbroeck, Editor
Vrije Universiteit Brussel
Pleinlaan 2
1050 Brussels, Belgium

Phone:

Email:
  rvesbroe@vub.ac.be

Website:
  www.springer.com/journal/10775

REVIEW PROCESS:

Type of Review:	Blind Review
No. External Reviewers:	3
No. InHouse Reviewers:	0
Acceptance Rate:	15-20%
Time to Review:	4 - 6 Months
Reviewer's Comments:	Yes
Invited Articles:	30-40%
Fees to Publish:	$0.00 US$
Fees to Review:	$0.00 US$

PUBLICATION GUIDELINES:

Manuscript Style:
  American Psychological Association

Manuscript Length:
  30+

Copies Required:
  One

CIRCULATION DATA:

Reader:
  Academics, Counselors, Practicing
  Teachers

Frequency of Issue:
  3 Times/Year

Sponsor/Publisher:
  International Assn for Educational &
  Vocational Guidance / Springer

MANUSCRIPT TOPICS:
Adult Career & Vocational; Career Guidance

MANUSCRIPT GUIDELINES/COMMENTS:

Springer requests the submission of manuscripts and figures in electronic form in addition to a hard-copy printout. The preferred storage medium for your electronic manuscript is a 3 ½ inch diskette. Please label your diskette properly, giving exact details on the name(s) of the file(s), the operating system and software used. Always save your electronic manuscript in the word processor format that you use; conversions to other formats and versions tend to be imperfect. In general, use as few formatting codes as possible. For safety's sake, you should always retain a backup copy of your file(s). After acceptance, please make absolutely sure that you send the latest (i.e., revised) version of your manuscript, both as hard-copy printout and on diskette (submission in electronic form of the final version of your article is compulsory), to the editor, Prof. Raoul Van Esbroeck.

For the purpose of reviewing, articles for publication should be submitted via e-mail, to: Prof. Raoul Van Esbroeck, Vrije Universiteit Brussel, Pleinlaan 2, 1050 Brussels, Belgium; Fax: (0)2-6292220; E-mail: **rvesbroe@vub.ac.be**

Reviewing Procedure
The *International Journal for Educational and Vocational Guidance* follows a double-blind reviewing procedure. Authors are therefore requested to place their name and affiliation on a

separate page. Self-identifying citations and references in the article text should either be avoided or left blank when manuscripts are first submitted. Authors are responsible for reinserting self-identifying citations and references when manuscripts are prepared for final submission.

Manuscript Presentation

Articles should be original and written in one of the official languages used in IAEVG: French (standard French), English (British English spelling should be used) or German. Main articles should range in length between 4000 and 6000 words. The main articles will be classified in subcategories as: effective techniques (description and assessment of theoretically-based techniques), comparative studies, theoretical studies, new directions and trends in the field, models of practice, etc. Debates should be between 750 and 1500 words and comprise a response to articles which have appeared in previous issues of the journal. Manuscripts should be printed or typewritten on A4 or US Letter bond paper, one side only, leaving adequate margins on all sides to allow reviewers' remarks. Please double-space all material, including notes and references. Quotations of more than 40 words should be set off clearly by indenting the left-hand margin. Use double quotation marks for direct quotations and for words or phrases used in a special sense. Single quotation marks are only used for quotations within quotations.

Number the pages consecutively with the first page (separate page) containing:
- title
- author(s)
- affiliation(s)
- full address for correspondence, including telephone and fax number and e-mail address

Abstract

Main articles should contain a short abstract of 60 to 100 words. The abstract should not contain any undefined abbreviations or unspecified references.

Style

A logical organisation is essential. Short headings and (where appropriate) subheadings should be used to structure the article. The ideas should flow coherently and be written in a clear, concise and straightforward style. Technical jargon and acronyms should be avoided. Authors are encouraged to avoid sexist language and to reduce bias on basis of gender, sexual orientation, social or racial or ethnic group, disability or age. References in the text and reference list should follow the APA guidelines. Only items cited in the manuscript should be listed in the reference list. Footnotes are strongly discouraged, except for an introductory footnote.

Figures and Tables

Figures and tables should be self-explanatory and used sparingly. Please do not submit more than three tables or two figures. Tables and figures should be saved as separate files.

Submission of electronic figures

In addition to hard-copy printouts of figures, authors are requested to supply the electronic versions of figures in either Encapsulated PostScript (EPS) or TIFF format. Many other formats, e.g., Microsoft Postscript, PiCT (Macintosh) and WMF (Windows), cannot be used and the hard copy will be scanned instead. Figures should be saved in separate files without their captions, which should be included with the text of the article.

Submission of hard-copy figures

If no electronic versions of figures are available, submit only high-quality artwork that can be reproduced as is, i.e., without any part having to be redrawn or re-typeset. The letter size of any text in the figures must be large enough to allow for reduction. Photographs should be in black-and-white on glossy paper. If a figure contains colour, make absolutely clear whether it should be printed in black-and-white or in colour. Figures that are to be printed in black-and-white should not be submitted in colour. Authors will be charged for reproducing figures in colour.

Each figure and table should be numbered and mentioned in the text. The approximate position of figures and tables should be indicated in the margin of the manuscript. On the reverse side of each figure, the name of the (first) author and the figure number should be written in pencil; the top of the figure should be clearly indicated. Figures and tables should be placed at the end of the manuscript following the Reference section. Each figure and table should be accompanied by an explanatory legend. The figure legends should be grouped and placed on a separate page. Figures are not returned to the author unless specifically requested.

In tables, footnotes are preferable to long explanatory material in either the heading or body of the table. Such explanatory footnotes, identified by superscript letters, should be placed immediately below the table.

Section Headings
First-, second-, third-, and fourth-order headings should be clearly distinguishable but not numbered.

Appendices
Supplementary material should be collected in an Appendix and placed before the Notes and References.

Cross-Referencing
In the text, a reference identified by means of an author's name should be followed by the date of the reference in parentheses and page number(s) where appropriate. For special cases, the APA style should be followed.

Acknowledgements
Acknowledgements of people, grants, funds, etc. should be placed in a separate section before the References.

References
Journal article
Barlow, D. H. & Lehman, C. L. (1996). Advances in the psychosocial treatment of anxiety disorders. Archives of General Psychiatry, 53, 727-735

Book chapter
Cutrona, C. E. & Russell, D. (1990). Type of social support and specific stress: Towards a theory of optimum matching. (In I.G. Sarason, B. R. Sarason, & G. Pierce (Eds.), Social support: An interactional view (pp. 341-366). New York: Wiley.)

Book, authored
Capland, G. (1964). Principles of preventive psychiatry. (New York: Basic Books)

Please visit our web site for more detailed examples.

Proofs
Proofs will be sent to the corresponding author. One corrected proof, together with the original, edited manuscript, should be returned to the Publisher within three days of receipt by mail (airmail overseas).

Offprints
Twenty-five offprints of each article will be provided free of charge. Additional offprints can be ordered by means of an offprint order form supplied with the proofs.

Page Charges and Colour Figures
No page charges are levied on authors or their institutions. Colour figures are published at the author's expense only.

Copyright
Authors will be asked, upon acceptance of an article, to transfer copyright of the article to the Publisher. This will ensure the widest possible dissemination of information under copyright laws.

Permissions
It is the responsibility of the author to obtain written permission for a quotation from unpublished material, or for all quotations in excess of 250 words in one extract or 500 words in total from any work still in copyright, and for the reprinting of figures, tables or poems from unpublished or copyrighted material.

Additional Information
Additional information can be obtained from: Springer, International Journal for Educational and Vocational Guidance, P.O. Box 17, 3300 AA Dordrecht, The Netherlands; Fax: 78-6576254; Internet: **http://www.springer.com**

International Journal of Continuing Engineering Education & Life Long Learning

<table>
<tr><td colspan="2" align="center">**SUBMISSION PROCESS:**

Postal Submission Only</td></tr>
<tr><td>

CONTACT INFORMATION:

M.A. Dorgham, Editor
IEL Editorial Office
PO Box 735
Olney
Buckinghamshire, MK46 5EL UK

Phone:
 +44 1234 240 519

Email:
 m.dorgham@inderscience.com

Website:
 www.inderscience.com

</td><td>

REVIEW PROCESS:

Type of Review:	Editorial Review
No. External Reviewers:	3
No. InHouse Reviewers:	0
Acceptance Rate:	18%
Time to Review:	2 - 3 Months
Reviewer's Comments:	Yes
Invited Articles:	10%
Fees to Publish:	$0.00 US$
Fees to Review:	$0.00 US$

</td></tr>
<tr><td>

PUBLICATION GUIDELINES:

Manuscript Style:
 See Manuscript Guidelines

Manuscript Length:
 16-20

Copies Required:
 Electronic Only

</td><td>

CIRCULATION DATA:

Reader:
 Academics, Business Persons

Frequency of Issue:
 6 Times/Year

Sponsor/Publisher:
 Inderscience Enterprises Limited

</td></tr>
</table>

MANUSCRIPT TOPICS:
Science Math & Environment; Urban Education, Cultural / Non-Traditional

MANUSCRIPT GUIDELINES/COMMENTS:

IJCEELL is the journal of continuing engineering education, lifelong learning and professional development for scientists, engineers and technologists. It deals with continuing education and the learning organisation, virtual laboratories, interactive knowledge media, new technologies for delivery of education and training, future developments in continuing engineering education; continuing engineering education and lifelong learning in the field of management, and government policies relating to continuing engineering education and lifelong learning.

Objectives
The objectives of the *IJCEELL* are to help professionals working in the field, educators, training providers and policy-makers to disseminate information and to learn from each other's work. The journal publishes original papers, case studies, technical reports, conference reports, book reviews, commentaries and news items. Commentaries on papers and reports published in the Journal are encouraged. Authors will have the opportunity to respond to a commentary on their work before the correspondence is published.

Readership
Professionals, academics, researchers, and managers.

Contents
The *IJCEELL* is a refereed, international journal that provides a forum and an authoritative source of information in the field of continuing engineering and management education, training and career development.

Subject Coverage
• Interactive knowledge media and their management • New technologies for delivery of education, such as: multimedia, CD-ROMs, videoconferencing, Internet and Intranet, satellites and other communication systems • Continuing engineering education and the learning organization • Case studies and experiences in engineering education and lifelong learning • Virtual laboratories • The nature of continuing engineering education • Government policy relating to continuing engineering education • Continuing engineering education in the field of management • Curriculum and course design • Future developments in continuing engineering education: challenges, prospects and future trends

Specific Notes for Authors
Submitted papers should not have been previously published nor be currently under consideration for publication elsewhere.

All papers are refereed through a double blind process. A guide for authors, sample copies and other relevant information for submitting papers are available on the Submission of Papers web-page.

You may send one copy in the form of an MS Word file attached to an e-mail (details of file formats in Author Guidelines) to Dr. Mohammed Dorgham with an email copy only to: IEL Editorial Office; E-mail: **ijceell@inderscience.com**

Please include in your submission the title of the Journal.

Submission of Papers
Papers, case studies, technical and conference reports, etc. are invited for submission, together with a brief abstract (100-150 words) and 1-10 keywords that reflect the content. Authors may wish to send in advance abstracts of proposed papers along with cover letters/e-mails (see requirements below). Please refer to notes for intending authors for more detailed guidance.

Please submit your manuscript with a cover letter/e-mail containing the following imperative statements:
1. Title and the central theme of the article.

2. Journal for which publication is intended.

3. Which subject/theme of the Journal the material fits.

4. Why the material is important in its field and why the material should be published in this Journal.

5. Nomination of up to four recognized experts who would be considered appropriate to review the submission. Please state:
• The names, title, addresses, phone, fax, and email addresses of these reviewers
• The expertise of each reviewer relating to your paper
• Your relationship with each of them.

6. The fact that the manuscript contains original unpublished work and is not being submitted for publication elsewhere.

Note that

Any non-English speaking author should have his/her paper proofread by a professional technical writer for grammatical and spelling corrections as well as the readability of the paper, before submitting it to the Editor.

A complete submission must include the following components in three separate MS-Word/Word for Windows files, plus hard copy with high quality black and white artwork for all figures, as indicated.

- The cover letter complying to the format of the sample letter
- The title page, including authors' full mailing, e-mail addresses and biographical details, attached to each of the hard copies
- One hard copy of the manuscript (title, abstract, keywords, article, references) without authors' names unless they are in the References section
- An electronic copy of the manuscript containing all details
- A hard copy of the Assignment of Copyright statement, duly signed.

These files should be submitted to the Editor-in-Chief.

Papers may also be sent directly to the relevant Editor, with copies to the Editorial Office, abov.e Each paper submitted to Inderscience Enterprises Limited is subject to the following review procedure:

- It is reviewed by the editor for general suitability for this publication.
- If it is judged suitable, two reviewers are selected and a double-blind review process takes place
- Based on the recommendations of the reviewers, the editor then decides whether the particular article should be acceptable as it is, revised or rejected.

NOTES FOR INTENDING AUTHORS
Formal Conditions of Acceptance
- Papers will only be published in English.
- Each typescript must be accompanied by a statement that it has not been submitted for publication elsewhere in English.
- Previous presentation at a conference, or publication in another language, should be disclosed.
- All papers are refereed, and the Editor-in-Chief reserves the right to refuse any typescript, whether on invitation or otherwise, and to make suggestions and/or modifications before publication.
- Typescripts which have been accepted become the property of the publisher. It is a condition of acceptance that copyright shall be vested in the publisher.
- The publisher shall furnish authors of accepted papers with proofs for the correction of printing errors. The proofs shall be returned within 14 calendar days of submittal. The publishers shall not be held responsible for errors which are the result of authors' oversights.

Typescript Preparation
- The original typescript should be submitted electronically in A4 size format, with double-spaced typing and a wide margin on the left, following the submission requirements described on the Journal's website.
- A final paper which would exceed 6000 words or occupy more than 15 pages of the Journal may be returned for abridgement.
- A complete typescript should include, in the following order: title, author(s), address(es), abstract, keywords, biographical notes, introduction, text, acknowledgements, references and notes, tables, figure captions, figures.

Electronic Copy
- The preferred word processing program is MS Word.
- Figures in the final accepted manuscript may be included in the electronic text file and also provided as separate files, but must also be accompanied by high-resolution hard copy printout.

International Context
- It should not be assumed that the reader is familiar with specific national institutions or corporations.
- Countries and groupings of countries should be referred to by their full title (for example, 'China', 'Europe' and 'America' are all ambiguous).
- Special attention should be paid to identifying units of currency by nationality.
- Acronyms should be translated in full into English. (See also 'Translated works' below.)

Title, Abstract, Keywords, Addresses, Biographical Notes
Please assist us by following these guidelines:
- Title . as short as possible
- Abstract. approximately 100 words, maximum 150
- Keywords . approximately 10 words or phrases
- Address . position, department, name of institution, full postal address
- Biographical notes . approximately 100 words per author, maximum 150.

References and Notes
- Inderscience journals use the Harvard system (name and date) short reference system for citations in the text with a detailed alphabetical list at the end of the paper. For example, 'Hamel (2000) suggests..' or 'Nonaka and Takeuchi (1995) found that…' or 'A study of economic change (Nelson and Winter, 1982) has shown that..'.
- Footnotes should be avoided, but any short, succinct notes making a specific point, may be placed in number order following the alphabetical list of references.
- References should be made only to works that are published, accepted for publication (not merely 'submitted'), or available through libraries or institutions. Any other source should be qualified by a note regarding availability.
- Full reference should include all authors' names and initials, year of publication, title of paper, title of publication (underlined), volume and issue number (of a journal), publisher and form (book, conference proceedings), page numbers.

Figures
- All illustrations, whether diagrams or photographs, are referred to as Figures and are numbered sequentially. Please place them at the end of the paper, rather than interspersed in text.
- Originals of line diagrams will be photographically reduced and used directly. All artwork for figures must be black and white and prepared to the highest possible standards. Bear in mind that lettering may be reduced in size by a factor of 2 or 3, and that fine lines may disappear.

Translated Works
- Difficulty often arises in translating acronyms, so it is best to spell out an acronym in English (for example, IIRP—French personal income tax).
- Similarly, labels and suffixes need careful attention where the letters refer to words which have been translated.
- The names of mathematical functions may change in translation—check against an English or American mathematical reference text.

Units of Measurement

- Inderscience journal follows the Système International for units of measurement.
- Imperial units will be converted, except where conversion would affect the meaning of a statement, or imply a greater or lesser degree of accuracy.

For further detailed instruction, please see **www.inderscience.com**.

International Journal of Distance Education Technologies

SUBMISSION PROCESS: **Postal Submission Only**	

CONTACT INFORMATION:	**REVIEW PROCESS:**
Timothy K. Shih, Co-Editor Tamkang University Department of Computer Science and Information Engineering 151, Ying-Chuan Road Tamsui, Taipei Hsien, 25137 Taiwan	**Type of Review:** Blind Review **No. External Reviewers:** 3+ **No. InHouse Reviewers:** 0 **Acceptance Rate:** 40-50% **Time to Review:** 3-6 Months **Reviewer's Comments:** Yes **Invited Articles:** 0-5%
Phone: 886 2 2621 5656 ext. 2616	
Email: tshih@cs.tku.edu.tw	**Fees to Publish:** $0.00 US$ **Fees to Review:** $0.00 US$
Website: www.idea-group.com/journals	

PUBLICATION GUIDELINES:	**CIRCULATION DATA:**

Manuscript Style:
  American Psychological Association
	Reader:
	  Academics

Manuscript Length:
  16-20
	Frequency of Issue:
	  Quarterly

Copies Required:
  One
	Sponsor/Publisher:
	  Information Resources Management
	  Association (IRMA) / Idea Group Publishing

MANUSCRIPT TOPICS:
Urban Education, Cultural / Non-Traditional

MANUSCRIPT GUIDELINES/COMMENTS:

Topics Also Include. Automatic assessment methods; Automatic FAQ reply methods; Broadband & wireless communication tools; Copyright protection & authentification mechanisms; Distance Education; Distributed systems; Effective & efficient authoring systems; Individualized distance learning; Intelligent tutoring; Mobile systems; Multimedia streaming technology; Multimedia synchronization controls; Neural network; New network infrastructures; Practical & new learning models; Quality-of Services issues; Real-time protocols; Statistical approaches to behavior analysis

Description
The *International Journal of Distance Education Technologies* (*JDET*) is a forum for researchers and practitioners to disseminate practical solutions to the automation of open and distance learning. Targeted to academic researchers and engineers who work with distance learning programs and software systems, as well as general users of distance education technologies and methods, *JDET* discusses computational methods, algorithms, implemented prototype systems, and applications of open and distance learning.

Mission

The *International Journal of Distance Education Technologies* (*JDET*) publishes original research articles of distance education four issues per year. *JDET* is a primary forum for researchers and practitioners to disseminate practical solutions to the automation of open and distance learning. The journal is targeted to academic researchers and engineers who work with distance learning programs and software systems, as well as general participants of distance education.

Coverage. Discussions of computational methods, algorithms, implemented prototype systems, and applications of open and distance learning are the focuses of this publication. Practical experiences and surveys of using distance learning systems are also welcome. Distance education technologies published in *JDET* will be divided into three categories, Communication Technologies, Intelligent Technologies, and Educational Technologies: New network infrastructures, real-time protocols, broadband and wireless communication tools, Quality-of Services issues, multimedia streaming technology, distributed systems, mobile systems, multimedia synchronization controls, intelligent tutoring, individualized distance learning, neural network or statistical approaches to behavior analysis, automatic FAQ reply methods, copyright protection and authentification mechanisms, practical and new learning models, automatic assessment methods, effective and efficient authoring systems, and other issues of distance education.

Originality

Prospective authors should note that only original and previously unpublished manuscripts will be considered. Furthermore, simultaneous submissions are not acceptable. Submission of a manuscript is interpreted as a statement of certification that no part of the manuscript is copyrighted by any other publication nor is under review by any other formal publication. It is the primary responsibility of the author to obtain proper permission for the use of any copyrighted materials in the manuscript, prior to the submission of the manuscript.

Style

Submitted manuscripts must be written in the APA (*American Psychological Association*) editorial style. References should relate only to material cited within the manuscript and be listed in alphabetical order, including the author's name, complete title of the cited work, title of the source, volume, issue, year of publication, and pages cited. Please do not include any abbreviations. See the following examples:

- **Example 1**: Single author periodical publication. Smith, A.J. (2001). Information and organizations. Management Ideology Review. 16(2), 1-15.
- **Example 2**: Multiple authors periodical publication. Smith, A.J., & Brown, CJ. (2001). Organizations and information processing. Management Source, 10(4), J1-88.
- **Example 3**: Books.

State author's name and year of publication where you use the source in the text. See the following examples:

- **Example 1**: In most organizations, information resources are considered to be a major resource (Brown, 2001; Smith, 2000).
- **Example 2**: Brown (2002) states that the value of information is recognized by most organizations.

Direct quotations of another author's work should be followed by the author's name, date of publication, and the page(s) on which the quotation appears in the original text.

- **Example 1**: Brown (2001) states that "the value of information is realized by most organizations" (p. 45).
- **Example 2**: In most organizations, information resources are considered to be a major organization asset" (Smith, 2001, pp. 35-36) and must be carefully monitored by the senior management. For more information please consult the *APA Manual* or review previous issues of the *Information Resources Management Journal*.

Review process

To ensure the high quality of published material, *JDET* utilizes a group of experts to review submitted manuscripts. Each submission is reviewed on a blind basis by at least four members of the International Editorial review Board of the Journal. Revised manuscripts will be reviewed again by the original review panel with the addition of one new reviewer. Return of a manuscript to the author(s) for revision does not guarantee acceptance of the manuscript for publication. The final decision will be based upon the comments of the reviewers and associate editors, upon their final review of the revised manuscript.

Copyright

Authors are asked to sign a warranty and copyright agreement upon acceptance of their manuscript, before the manuscript can be published. All copyrights, including translation of the published material into other languages are reserved by the publisher, Idea Group Inc. Upon transfer of the copyright to the publisher, no part of the manuscript may be reproduced in any form without written permission of the publisher, except for noncommercial, educational use such as for classroom teaching purposes.

Submission

Interested authors are asked to submit their manuscript as an attachment to an email. The manuscript must be in Word or PDF format. The cover page should contain the paper title, and the name, affiliation, address, phone number, fax number, and email address of each author. The second page should start with the paper title at the top and be immediately followed by the abstract. Except on the cover page, the authors' names and affiliations must NOT appear in the manuscript. The abstract of 100-150 words should clearly summarize the objectives and content of the manuscript. For additional information, please consult the journal website at http://www.idea-group.com/journals/

Length

The length of the submitted manuscript is not specifically limited, however, the length should be reasonable in light of the chosen topic. Discussion and analysis should be complete, but not unnecessarily long or repetitive.

Correspondence

The acknowledgment e-mail regarding the receipt of the manuscript will be promptly sent. The review process will take approximately 8-16 weeks, and the author will be notified concerning the possibility of publication of the manuscript as soon as the review process is completed. All correspondence will be directed to the first author of multi-authored manuscripts. It is the responsibility of the first author to communicate with the other author(s). Authors of accepted manuscript will be asked to provide a final copy of their manuscript in Word format (IBM) or Apple Macintosh format stored on a 3/4" disk, accompanied by a hard copy of the manuscript and the signed copy of the Warranty and Copyright Agreement The accepted manuscript will be edited by the Journal copy editor for format and style.

Book Review

JDET invites prospective book reviewers to submit their review of either textbooks or professional books for possible inclusion in the Journal. Reviewers should focus on the following guidelines when developing the book review: Book reviews must not exceed 1500 words. Reviews should summarize the book and indicate the highlights, strengths, and weaknesses of the book. Reviews should evaluate the organizational and managerial applications of the material discussed in the book relevant to information resources and technology management. Reviews should critique and constructively evaluate the author's work and not merely list the chapters' contents. The writing style, accuracy, relevance, and the need for such a work in the discipline should be analyzed. The review must include the title of the book, author, publishing company, publication date, number of pages, cost (if listed), and ISBN number. Each submission must be accompanied by a short biography of the reviewer. biography of the reviewer.

Case studies

JDET also encourages submission of case studies based on actual cases related to different issues and aspects of electronic commerce in organizations. Case studies must provide adequate information regarding the organization upon which the case is based, discussion of the issues involved, coverage of any experiments or trials of techniques or managerial approaches, and finally, discussion of any lessons learned or conclusions drawn from this study. All submissions should be submitted to: All inquiries and submissions should be sent to: Timothy K. Shih, Professor, Dept of Computer Science & Information Engineering, Tamkang University, Suite 200, 151, Ying-Chuan Road, Tamsui, Taipei Hsien, Taiwan 25137, R.O.C.; Tel: + 886 2 26215656 x2743, x2616, Fax:+ 886 2 26209749; E-Mail: **tshih@cs.tku.edu.tw**

International Journal of Doctoral Studies

SUBMISSION PROCESS:
Electronic Submission Only **via Online Portal** **http://IJDS.org**

CONTACT INFORMATION:	REVIEW PROCESS:	
Yair Levy, Editor c/o Eli Cohen, Managing Editor	**Type of Review:**	Blind Review
	No. External Reviewers:	3+
Phone:	**No. InHouse Reviewers:**	1
707-537-4925	**Acceptance Rate:**	New J
Email:	**Time to Review:**	1 - 2 Months
elicohen@informingscience.org	**Reviewer's Comments:**	Yes
editor@ijds.org	**Invited Articles:**	0-5%
levyy@nova.edu		
Website:	**Fees to Publish:**	$0.00 US$
http://IJDS.org	**Fees to Review:**	$0.00 US$

PUBLICATION GUIDELINES:	CIRCULATION DATA:
Manuscript Style: American Psychological Association	**Reader:** Academics, Administrators, Practicing Teachers
Manuscript Length: 11-30+	**Frequency of Issue:** Yearly Continuous Online
Copies Required: Electronic Only	**Sponsor/Publisher:** Informing Science Institute / Informing Science Press

MANUSCRIPT TOPICS:

Adult Career & Vocational; Curriculum Studies; Educational Technology Systems; Higher Education; Library Science / Information Resources; Teacher Education

MANUSCRIPT GUIDELINES/COMMENTS:

Authors should consult the website at **http://IJDS.org** for the most current guidelines. The mission of the *International Journal of Doctoral Studies* (*IJDS*) is to provide readers around the world with the widest possible coverage of developments in doctoral studies using the IS (Informing Science) discipline as a framework or paradigm to understand doctoral studies. IJDS especially encourages publications co-authored by doctoral students and doctoral faculty.

IJDS is an interdisciplinary forum that publishes high quality articles on theory, practice, innovation, and research that cover all aspects of doctoral studies. Book reviews are also welcome. Authors may use epistemologies from engineering, computer science, education, psychology, business, anthropology, and such. Papers that essentially cover "teaching tips" or unstructured anecdotal data are not considered for publication. *IJDS* provides those who submit manuscripts for publication with useful, timely feedback by making the review process constructive. *IJDS* will strive to be the most authoritative journal on doctoral studies.

Prior to submission, it is essential that prospective authors carefully peruse the paper "Doctoral Studies and the IS Framework." The paper identifies key aspects of doctoral studies in which the IS discipline provides a framework for conducting research on doctoral studies. Although "Doctoral Studies and the IS Framework" covers essential elements of the IS framework, prospective authors should carefully access the IS Journal and learn more about the IS discipline by perusing the paper "From Ugly Duckling to Swan".

International Journal of Education Policy and Leadership

SUBMISSION PROCESS: **Electronic Submission Preferred** **via Online Portal** **http://www.ijepl.org**	

<table>
<tr>
<td>

CONTACT INFORMATION:

Penelope M. Earley, Co-Editor
Center for Education Policy
George Mason University
Robinson A, Room 441
4400 University Drive, MS 4B3
Fairfax, VA 22030 USA

Daniel A. Laitsch, Co-Editor
Simon Fraser University

Phone:
703-993-3361
604-268-7589

Email:
ijepl@gmu.edu
dlaitsch@sfu.ca

Website:
http://www.ijepl.org

</td>
<td>

REVIEW PROCESS:

Type of Review:	Blind Review
No. External Reviewers:	3
No. InHouse Reviewers:	3
Acceptance Rate:	11-20%
Time to Review:	1 - 2 Months
Reviewer's Comments:	Yes
Invited Articles:	0-5%
Fees to Publish:	$0.00 US$
Fees to Review:	$0.00 US$

</td>
</tr>
<tr>
<td>

PUBLICATION GUIDELINES:

Manuscript Style:
See Manuscript Guidelines

Manuscript Length:
16-20

Copies Required:
Electronic Only

</td>
<td>

CIRCULATION DATA:

Reader:
Academics, Administrators

Frequency of Issue:
On Demand

Sponsor/Publisher:
Assn for Supervision & Curriculum Dev,
George Mason Univ, Simon Fraser Univ

</td>
</tr>
</table>

MANUSCRIPT TOPICS:
Education Management / Administration; Policy

MANUSCRIPT GUIDELINES/COMMENTS:

Focus and Scope
IJEPL is a refereed electronic journal dedicated to enriching the education policy and leadership knowledge base, and promoting exploration and analysis of policy alternatives. The *Journal* welcomes articles on educational policy and leadership related to a variety of disciplines and educational settings, as well as policy initiatives that emanate from various levels of government. The *Journal* seeks to build bridges between researchers, policymakers, and practitioners to help identify best practices in learning, teaching, and leadership. Individuals from each group, therefore, are encouraged to submit articles for publication. Articles should focus on studies and systematic

analyses that employ qualitative, quantitative, or mixed methodologies. The number of theoretical articles published will be limited. Because of its international scope, authors are encouraged to focus on the underlying aspects of their research that make the work relevant for the larger community of educators and policymakers. Articles should be 5,000 to 7,000 words. The opinions and conclusions of the authors do not necessarily reflect the policy of ASCD, GMU, or SFU.

Author Guidelines

The *Journal* welcomes articles on educational policy and leadership, as well as policy initiatives that emanate from various levels of government. The *Journal* seeks to build bridges between researchers, policymakers, and practitioners to help identify best practices in learning, teaching, and leadership. Individuals from each group, therefore, are encouraged to submit articles for publication. Articles should focus on studies and systematic analyses that employ qualitative, quantitative, or mixed methodologies. Because of its international scope, authors are encouraged to focus on the underlying aspects of their research that make the work relevant for the larger community of educators and policymakers. Articles should be 5,000 to 7,000 words.

Articles should use the bibliographic and formatting standards found in the *Publication Manual of the American Psychological Association*, 5th Edition, 2001. In addition to their submitted papers, authors are encouraged to include other supplementary files they feel are relevant to reviewers and readers of the journal, including data-sets, research instruments, etc.

Submission Preparation Checklist

As part of the submission process, authors are required to check off their submission's compliance with all of the following items, and submissions may be returned to authors that do not adhere to these guidelines.

1. The submission has not been previously published, nor is it before another journal for consideration (or an explanation has been provided in Comments to the Editor).
2. The submission file is in Microsoft Word, RTF, or WordPerfect document file format.
3. All URL addresses in the text (e.g., **http://www.ijepl.org**) are activated and ready to click.
4. The text is single-spaced; uses a 12-point font; employs italics, rather than underlining (except with URL addresses); and all illustrations, figures, and tables are placed within the text at the appropriate points, rather than at the end.
5. The text adheres to the stylistic and bibliographic requirements outlined in the Author Guidelines, which is found on the web site.
6. The text has had the authors' names removed. If an author is cited, "Author" and year are used in the bibliography and footnotes, instead of author's name, paper title, etc. The author's name has also been removed from the document's Properties, which in Microsoft Word is found in the File menu.
7. I have read and accept the Publishing Agreement below.

Publishing Agreement

I hereby grant and assign to the publishers of the *International Journal of Education Policy and Leadership* (*IJEPL*) the exclusive right of first publication of my work. I represent that the work is my own original work and has not been previously published in any format, including an electronic or Web version, or accepted for publication by another party. I represent that my work contains no defamatory material and does not libel or slander any person. I have full power and authority to enter into this agreement.

I agree that:
IJEPL editors have the right to edit the work for style, readability, and appropriate length.

The publishers of *IJEPL* have the full, worldwide, and exclusive right of first publication, as well as the nonexclusive right to print, publish, sell, and distribute the work in all languages, forms, and media, whether now known or hereafter invented, identifying me as the author and copyright holder.

This Work is a contribution to the education profession; I will receive no compensation.

Regarding the right of first publication:
During the first 90 days of publication and thereafter, I and any coauthors retain the right to revise, adapt, prepare derivative works, present orally, and distribute the work on a closed organizational intranet system (not the World Wide Web) for personal, noncommercial benefit.

At the conclusion of the first 90 days of publication by *IEJPL*, I may then publish the work on the World Wide Web and grant to others the right to reprint or otherwise use the work for commercial benefit so long as full and appropriate citation is given to *IJEPL* as original publisher.

Copyright Notice
Copyright for articles published in this journal is retained by the authors, with first publication rights granted to the journal. By virtue of their appearance in this open access journal, articles are free to use, with proper attribution, in educational and other non-commercial settings 90 days after initial publication.

International Journal of Education Research

SUBMISSION PROCESS:
Electronic Submission Only **via EMail** **conference@iabpad.com**

CONTACT INFORMATION:	REVIEW PROCESS:	
Abdalla Hagen, Editor	**Type of Review:**	Blind Review
Phone: 318-255-1491	**No. External Reviewers:** **No. InHouse Reviewers:**	2 0
Email: conference@iabpad.com abdallahfagenf@yahoo.com hagengrambling@yahoo.com	**Acceptance Rate:** **Time to Review:** **Reviewer's Comments:** **Invited Articles:**	New J 2 - 3 Months Yes New J
Website:	**Fees to Publish:** **Fees to Review:**	$15.00 US$ Per Page $25.00 US$

PUBLICATION GUIDELINES:	CIRCULATION DATA:
Manuscript Style: American Psychological Association **Manuscript Length:** 21-25 **Copies Required:** Electronic Only	**Reader:** Academics, Administrators, Counselors, Practicing Teachers, Practitioners **Frequency of Issue:** Yearly **Sponsor/Publisher:** International Academy of Business and Public Administration Disciplines (IABPAD) / Davis Assoc.

MANUSCRIPT TOPICS:

Adult Career & Vocational; Audiology / Speech Pathology; Business Education; Counseling & Personnel Services; Curriculum Studies; Education Management / Administration; Educational Psychology; Educational Technology Systems; Elementary / Early Childhood; Gifted Children; Health & Physical Education; Higher Education; Library Science / Information Resources; Reading; Rural Education & Small Schools; School Law; Science Math & Environment; Secondary / Adolescent Studies; Social Studies / Social Science; Special Education; Teacher Education; Tests, Measurement & Evaluation; Urban Education, Cultural / Non-Traditional

MANUSCRIPT GUIDELINES/COMMENTS:

The aim is to support and encourage research and the scope is to freely exchange ideas throughout the world. The journal website is not available at the present time. Editorial guidelines, style sheet and author's guidelines will be provided to authors and will appear at the end of the journal.

International Journal of Education through Art

SUBMISSION PROCESS:
Postal Submission Only

CONTACT INFORMATION:	REVIEW PROCESS:
Rachel Mason, Editor Roehampton University of Surrey Froebel College Roehampton Lane London, SW15 5PJ UK **Phone:** +44 (0) 208 392 3009 **Email:** r.mason@roehampton.ac.uk **Website:** http://www.intellectbooks.co.uk/journals. appx.php?issn=17435234	**Type of Review:** Blind Review **No. External Reviewers:** 2 **No. InHouse Reviewers:** 1 **Acceptance Rate:** 21-30% **Time to Review:** 2 - 3 Months **Reviewer's Comments:** Yes **Invited Articles:** 0-5% **Fees to Publish:** $0.00 US$ **Fees to Review:** $0.00 US$
PUBLICATION GUIDELINES:	**CIRCULATION DATA:**

Manuscript Style:
    See Manuscript Guidelines
 	
Manuscript Length:
    11-15
 	
Copies Required:
    Three
	Reader:
	    Academics, Practicing Teachers
	
	Frequency of Issue:
	    3 Times/Year
	
	Sponsor/Publisher:
	    International Society for Education
	through Art / Intellect

MANUSCRIPT TOPICS:
Art / Music; Curriculum Studies; Elementary / Early Childhood; Higher Education; Secondary / Adolescent Studies; Teacher Education

MANUSCRIPT GUIDELINES/COMMENTS:

Aims and Scope
The *International Journal of Education through Art* is a new English language journal that promotes relationships between art and education. Each issue, published three times a year within a single volume, will consist of refereed texts in the form of critical essays, articles, exhibition reviews and image-text features.

Particular emphasis will be placed on articles and visual materials that:
- Critically reflect on the relationship between education and art
- Propose original ways of rethinking the status of education and art education
- Address the role of teaching and learning in either formal or informal educational contexts and along side issues of age, gender and social background
- Adopt an open and inventive interpretation of research-based analysis
- Promote and experiment with visual/textual forms of representing art education activities, issues and research

The journal will be interdisciplinary in its reflection of teaching and learning contexts and also in its representation of artistic approaches and practices. It will provide a platform for those who wish to question and evaluate the ways in which art is produced, disseminated and interpreted across a diverse range of educational contexts.

Topics covered include: Art, craft and design education; Formal and informal education contexts; Pedagogy; Policy and practice; Research; Comparative education; Transcultural issues

Guidelines for Contributors

Opinion. The views expressed in the *Journal* are those of the authors, and do not necessarily coincide with those of the Editor or the Editorial Advisory Board.

Referees. The *Journal* of the International Society for Education through Art is a refereed journal. Referees are chosen for their expertise within the subject area. They are asked to comment on comprehensibility, originality and scholarly worth of the article submitted.

Length. Articles should not normally exceed 6000 words in length.

Submitting. Articles/visual texts should be original and not be under consideration by any other publication. Three hard copies must be sent to the editor, typewritten or printed on one side only, and double-spaced. If the article is accepted, it should be put on disk, with any required amendments, and this electronic version of the article as agreed for final publication should then be sent to the Editor. The electronic version should be in Word, and be submitted on a 3.5 inch disk or CD, along with a hard-copy version. The disk should be labelled with the name of the author, the title of the article, and the software used. (Formats other than Word are not encouraged, but please contact the editor for further details.) Please provide a self-addressed envelope to cover the return postage of submissions.

Language. The journal uses standard British English. The editor reserves the right to alter usage to this end. Because of the interdisciplinary nature of the readership, jargon should be kept to a minimum. Whereas articles in Spanish, Portuguese, Chinese, Greek and Japanese may be submitted for review, translation into English will be the responsibility of authors should they be accepted for publication.

Format. The journal is set with Apple Macintosh equipment and reset using QuarkXPress; it is therefore best whenever possible to supply text in Word as this crosses easily from PC to Mac systems

Visual Materials. Illustrations to articles are welcome when they assist discussion of artworks, learning activities and/or environments. Generally, only non-colour reproduction is available. All illustrations, photographs, diagrams, maps etc. should follow the same numerical sequence and be shown as Figure 1, Figure 2 etc.

Please do not send original slides, photographs and other artworks. If originals are all that is available, these will need to be supplied electronically. Visuals in proposals should initially be sent as low-res JPEG files on PC formatted floppy disk or as an email attachment. They should be accompanied by an electronic version of the original text in MS Word on either 3.5 inch PC formatted disk or a CD. If articles are selected for publication contributors will be asked to provide images to the Editor with respect to Intellect's Notes to Contributors.

Hard Copy. Hard copy text should be double-spaced and single-sided with at least a 3cm left margin.

Copyright. Copyright clearance should be indicated by the contributor and is always the responsibility of the contributor. The source has to be indicated beneath the text. When they are on a separate sheet or file, indication must be given as to where they should be placed in the text. The author has responsibility to ensure that the proper permissions/model for visual image releases are obtained.

Quotations. Paragraph quotations must be indented with an additional one-line space above and below and without quotes.

Captions. All illustrations should be accompanied by a caption, which should include the figure number and the acknowledgement to the holder of the copyright.

Other Styles. Margins should be at least one inch all round and pagination should be continuous. Foreign words and sentences inserted in the text should be italicised.

Author biography. A note on each author is required and this should include an institution or address. This should not exceed 75 words. Authors should also indicate how they wish their names to appear. The custom is without titles, one forename plus surname, but authors may vary this. The author should also provide a short sentence (of no more than sixteen words) stating their name and institutional affiliation or their identification.

Abstract. Each article should be accompanied by an abstract, which should not exceed 150 words in length and should concentrate on the significant findings. Authors may submit a second abstract in a first language other than English also where appropriate.

Notes. Notes will appear at the side of appropriate pages, but the numerical sequence runs throughout the article. These should be kept as short as possible and to a minimum, and be identified by a superscript numeral.

Please avoid the use of automatic footnoting programmes; simply append the footnotes to the end of the article.

References and Bibliography. Bibliographical references within the notes must adhere to the following models: Books: author's full name, title (italics), place of publication, publisher, year, and page reference.

Articles: author's full name, title (within single quotation marks), name of journal (italics), volume and issue numbers, date, and page reference.

A bibliography may be included if this is deemed to be a necessary addition to the sidenotes.

Reviewing. Please contact the Editor if you are interested in reviewing for this journal.

Publisher Notes for Contributors
The publisher Notes are an essential supplement to gain the full extent of what is required to submit and article, especially for final submission once an article has been accepted for publication. These can be acquired directly from the Editor.

Contributions Welcome
The Editor welcomes contributions. Any matter concerning the format and presentation of articles not covered by the above notes should be addressed to the Editor, Rachel Mason, at: Roehampton University of Surrey, Froebel College, Roehampton Lane, London SW 15 5PJ UK. Email: **r.mason@roehampton.ac.uk**; Tel: 44 (0) 2023923009/4

International Journal of Educational Management, The

SUBMISSION PROCESS:
Postal Submission Only

CONTACT INFORMATION:	REVIEW PROCESS:	

Brian Roberts, Editor
c/o Emerald Group Publishing Limited
60/62 Toller Lane
Bradford
West Yorkshire, BD8 9BY UK
 	
Phone:
  +44 1274 777700
 	
Email:
 	
Website:
  www.emeraldinsight.com/ijem.htm
	Type of Review:	Blind Review

	No. External Reviewers:	2
	No. InHouse Reviewers:	1
	Acceptance Rate:	21-30%
	Time to Review:	1 - 2 Months
	Reviewer's Comments:	No
	Invited Articles:	0-5%
	Fees to Publish:	$0.00 US$
	Fees to Review:	$0.00 US$

PUBLICATION GUIDELINES:	CIRCULATION DATA:

Manuscript Style:
  See Manuscript Guidelines
 	
Manuscript Length:
  16-30
 	
Copies Required:
  Three
	Reader:
	  Academics, Administrators, Practicing
	  Teachers
	
	Frequency of Issue:
	  7 Times/Year
	
	Sponsor/Publisher:
	  Emerald Group Publishing Limited

MANUSCRIPT TOPICS:

Curriculum Studies; Education Management / Administration; Educational Psychology; Educational Technology Systems; Higher Education; Library Science / Information Resources; Reading; Teacher Education; Tests, Measurement & Evaluation; Urban Education, Cultural / Non-Traditional

MANUSCRIPT GUIDELINES/COMMENTS:

About the journal

The International Journal of Educational Management addresses the increasingly complex role of the educational manager against a backdrop of fundamental changes in structure and philosophy, and diminishing budgets and resources. It offers essential information to professionals dedicated to maximizing resources through intelligent management strategies which respond to national and international considerations, as well as specific concerns within individual communities and educational institutions.

AUTHOR GUIDELINES
Copyright

Articles submitted to the journal should be original contributions and should not be under consideration for any other publication at the same time. Authors submitting articles for publication warrant that the work is not an infringement of any existing copyright and will indemnify the publisher against any breach of such warranty. For ease of dissemination and to ensure proper policing of use, papers and contributions become the legal copyright of the publisher unless otherwise agreed.

For details of Emerald's editorial policy on plagiarism, please see the plagiarism in depth information.

Submissions should be sent to: The Editor, Dr Brian Roberts, c/o Emerald Group Publishing Limited, 60/62 Toller Lane, Bradford, West Yorkshire BD8 9BY, UK; Tel: +44 1274 777700; Fax: +44 1274 785200/1

Editorial objectives

To provide those interested in the effective management of the educational process with a broad overview of developments and best practice in the field, with particular reference to how new ideas can be applied worldwide. The journal will seek to contain material relating to innovation in educational management across the spectrum, the development of educational delivery mechanisms, and the creation of an environment in which the management of resources provides the most efficient outputs achievable on an international basis to allow the sharing of new initiatives.

It is our intention to maintain a sound balance between theory and practice. Contributors are encouraged to spell out the practical implications of their work for those involved in the management of education. Articles based on experiences and evidence - rather than just philosophical speculation - will receive particular encouragement. A series of short articles on a linked theme appearing in successive issues would be particularly welcome.

The reviewing process

Each paper submitted is subjected to the following review procedures:
a. It is reviewed by the editor for general suitability for this publication.
b. If it is judged suitable two reviewers are selected and a double blind review process takes place.
c. Based on the recommendations of the reviewers, the editor then decides whether the particular article should be accepted as it is, revised or rejected. The process described above is a general one.

Emerald Literati Editing Service

The Literati Club can recommend the services of a number of freelance copy editors, all themselves experienced authors, to contributors who wish to improve the standard of English in their paper before submission. This is particularly useful for those whose first language is not English. (**www.emeraldinsight.com/editingservice**)

The editor, however, may, in some circumstances, vary this process.

Manuscript requirements

Three copies of the manuscript should be submitted in double line spacing with wide margins. All authors should be shown and author's details must be printed on a separate sheet and the author should not be identified anywhere else in the article.

As a guide, articles should be between 1,000 and 4,000 words in length. A title of not more than eight words should be provided. A brief autobiographical note should be supplied including full name, affiliation, e-mail address and full international contact details. Authors must supply a structured abstract set out under 4-6 sub-headings: Purpose; Methodology/Approach; Findings; Research limitations/implications (if applicable); Practical implications (if applicable); and, the Originality/value of paper. Maximum is 250 words in total. In addition provide up to six keywords which encapsulate the principal topics of the paper and categorise your paper under one of these classifications: Research paper, Viewpoint, Technical paper, Conceptual paper, Case study,

Literature review or General review. For more information and guidance on structured abstracts visit: **www.emerald insight.com/structuredabstracts**

Where there is a **methodology**, it should be clearly described under a separate heading. **Headings** must be short, clearly defined and not numbered. **Notes or Endnotes** should be used only if absolutely necessary and must be identified in the text by consecutive numbers, enclosed in square brackets and listed at the end of the article.

Figures, charts and **diagrams** should be kept to a minimum. They should be provided both electronically and as good quality originals. They must be black and white with minimum shading and numbered consecutively using Arabic numerals.

Artwork should be either copied or pasted from the origination software into a blank Microsoft Word document, or saved and imported into a blank Microsoft Word document. Artwork created in MS Powerpoint is also acceptable. Artwork may be submitted in the following standard image formats: .eps - Postscript, .pdf - Adobe Acrobat portable document, .ai - Adobe Acrobat portable document, .wmf - Windows Metafile. If it is not possible to supply graphics in the formats listed above, authors should ensure that figures supplied as .tif, .gif, .jpeg, .bmp, .pcx, .pic, .pct are supplied as files of at least 300 dpi and at least 10cm wide.

In the text the position of a figure should be shown by typing on a separate line the words "take in Figure 2". Authors should supply succinct captions.

For photographic images good quality original photographs should be submitted. If submitted electronically they should be saved as tif files of at least 300dpi and at least 10cm wide. Their position in the text should be shown by typing on a separate line the words "take in Plate 2".

Tables should be kept to a minimum. They must be numbered consecutively with roman numerals and a brief title. In the text, the position of the table should be shown by typing on a separate line the words "take in Table IV".

Photos and **illustrations** must be supplied as good quality black and white original half tones with captions. Their position should be shown in the text by typing on a separate line the words "take in Plate 2".

References to other publications should be complete and in Harvard style. They should contain full bibliographical details and journal titles should not be abbreviated. For multiple citations in the same year use a, b, c immediately following the year of publication. References should be shown within the text by giving the author's last name followed by a comma and year of publication all in round brackets, e.g. (Fox, 1994). At the end of the article should be a reference list in alphabetical order as follows:

a. *for books*
surname, initials and year of publication, title, publisher, place of publication, e.g.Casson, M. (1979), Alternatives to the Multinational Enterprise, Macmillan, London.

b. *for chapter in edited book*
surname, initials and year, "title", editor's surname, initials, title, publisher, place, pages, e.g.Bessley, M. and Wilson, P. (1984), "Public policy and small firms in Britain", in Levicki, C. (Ed.), Small Business Theory and Policy, Croom Helm, London, pp.111-26. Please note that the chapter title must be underlined.

c. *for articles*
surname, initials, year "title", journal, volume, number, pages, e.g.Fox, S. (1994) "Empowerment as a catalyst for change: an example from the food industry", Supply Chain Management, Vol 2 No 3, pp. 29-33

If there is more than one author list surnames followed by initials. All authors should be shown.

Electronic sources should include the URL of the electronic site at which they may be found, as follows:
Neuman, B.C.(1995), "Security, payment, and privacy for network commerce", IEEE Journal on Selected Areas in Communications, Vol. 13 No.8, October, pp.1523-31. Available (IEEE SEPTEMBER) http://www.research.att.com/jsac/

Notes/Endnotes should be used only if absolutely necessary. They should, however, always be used for citing Web sites. They should be identified in the text by consecutive numbers enclosed in square brackets and listed at the end of the article. Please then provide full Web site addresses in the end list.

Final submission of the article
Once accepted for publication, the final version of the manuscript must be provided, accompanied by a 3.5" disk of the same version labelled with: disk format; author name(s); title of article; journal title; file name.

Each article must be accompanied by a completed and signed Journal Article Record Form available from the Editor or on **www.emeraldinsight.com/jarform**. Authors should note that proofs are not supplied prior to publication.

The manuscript will be considered to be the definitive version of the article. The author must ensure that it is complete, grammatically correct and without spelling or typographical errors.

In preparing the disk, please use one of the following preferred formats: Word, Word Perfect, Rich text format or TeX/LaTeX.

Technical assistance is available by contacting Mike Massey at Emerald, e-mail **mmassey@ emeraldinsight.com**.

A summary of submission requirements:
* Good quality hard copy manuscript
* A labelled disk
* A brief professional biography of each author
* An abstract and keywords
* Figures, photos and graphics electronically and as good quality originals
* Harvard style references where appropriate
* A completed Journal Article Record form

International Journal of Information and Communication Technology Education

SUBMISSION PROCESS:	
Postal Submission Only	
tomei@rmu.edu	

CONTACT INFORMATION:	REVIEW PROCESS:	
Lawrence Tomei, Editor-in-Chief Robert Morris University Acad Services - PH Room 214 6001 University Blvd. Moon Twp, PA 15108 USA	**Type of Review:**	Blind Review
	No. External Reviewers:	3
	No. InHouse Reviewers:	0
	Acceptance Rate:	
Phone:	**Time to Review:**	2 - 3 Months
	Reviewer's Comments:	Yes
	Invited Articles:	0-5%
Email: tomei@rmu.edu	**Fees to Publish:**	$0.00 US$
Website: www.idea-group.com/journals	**Fees to Review:**	$0.00 US$

PUBLICATION GUIDELINES:	CIRCULATION DATA:

Manuscript Style:
   American Psychological Association
	Reader:
	   Academics

Manuscript Length:
   21-25
	Frequency of Issue:
	   Quarterly

Copies Required:
   One
	Sponsor/Publisher:
	   Idea Group Inc.

MANUSCRIPT TOPICS:
Educational Technology Systems; Information Technologies

MANUSCRIPT GUIDELINES/COMMENTS:

Mission
The *International Journal of Information and Communication Technology Education* (*IJICTE*) publishes original materials concerned with the theoretical underpinnings, successful application, and potential for advancing technology education within formal education, corporate training, higher education, professional development, and proprietary education. The primary mission of the *IJICTE* is to explore multiple perspectives of technology education and promote research, positions, and practices that advance the state-of-the-art application of technology for teaching and learning.

Coverage
The *IJICTE* will publish contributions from all disciplines of business, computer, and information technology education, educational technology, instructional systems design, teaching and learning with technology, computer science, corporate training science, and distance learning education.

In particular, the journal supports multidisciplinary research in the:

- Pedagogy and androgogy of teaching with technology, technology as a teaching strategy, technology as a learning style, making technology work in schools, early childhood technology literacy, adult learners and technology education, impact of technology on student achievement, dimensions of technological learning
- Impact of technology in society, equity issues, technology education and copyright laws, censorship, acceptable use and fair use laws, community education and public outreach using technology
- Effective planning for technology education, marketing technology education, managing classroom technology education, developing successful information technology education leadership, teacher/trainer preparation and retention
- Impact of multicultural differences on technology education, special technology education for diversity and at-risk learners
- Information technology training tools, educational/ training software evaluation, writing technology training materials, models of instructional systems design, instructional design theories
- Corporate information technology training, administrative applications of information technology education
- Assessment of technology education, technology-based learning and training outcomes, assessment of technology-based curricular objectives
- School improvement and reform, developing standards-based technology education programs, data-driven decision making, strategic technology education planning, technology education standards development.

And, all other related issues that impact the research, position, and practice of information technology education on schools, corporate entities, and society.

Originality
Prospective authors should note that only original and previously unpublished manuscripts will be considered. Submission of a manuscript implies a certification that not part of the manuscript is neither copyrighted or under review by any other publication. It is the primary responsibility of the author to see and obtain proper permission for the use of any copyrighted materials in the manuscript prior to submission.

Style
Submitted manuscripts must be prepared in the *American Psychological Association* (APA) editorial style. References should relate only to material cited within the manuscript and be listed in alphabetical order by author(s)' name, complete title of the cited work, title of the source, volume, issue, year of publication, and pages cited. Please do not include any abbreviations. See the following examples:

- Single author periodical publication.
  Example 1: Smith, A.J. (2002). Information and organizations. Management Ideology Review. 16(2), 1-15.
  Multiple authors periodical publication.
- **Example 2**: Smith, A.J., & Brown, CJ. (2001). Organizations and information processing. Management Source, 10(4), J1-88.
  Single author text (book) publication.
- **Example 3**: Brown (2002) states that the value of information is recognized by most organizations.
  Multiple authors text (book) publication.
- **Example 4**: In most organizations, information resources are considered to be a major resource (Brown, 2001; Smith, 2000).

Direct quotations of another author's work should be followed by the author's name, date of publication, and the page(s) on which the quotation appears in the original text.

- **Example 5**: Brown(2001) states that "the value of information is realized by most organizations" (p. 45).
- **Example 6**: In most organizations, information resources are considered to be a major organization asset" (Smith, 2001, pp. 35-36) and must be carefully monitored by the senior management.

For more information please consult the *APA Manual* or review previous issues of the *Information Resources Management Journal*.

Review process

To ensure the high quality of published material, the *IJICTE* provides a cadre of technology content and writing experts to review submitted manuscripts. Upon receipt of a manuscript, it is judged by the editor-in-chief for focus and format. Suitable submissions are assigned at least three reviewers selected from the Editorial Review Board based upon the particular content involved. Both the original manuscript and the editorial reviews are sent to an associate editor for final recommendation. Final selections of manuscripts for publication is the responsibility of the editor-in-chief. Manuscripts with potential for publication will be returned to the author for revision; requests for re-writes do not guarantee acceptance of the manuscript for final publication. Revised manuscripts will be reviewed again by the original review panel and one additional reviewer. Final recommendations will be based upon the quality of the revision and comments of reviewers and associate editors. Final selections of manuscripts for publication remains the responsibility of the editor-in-chief.

Copyright

Authors are asked to sign a warranty and copyright agreement upon acceptance of their manuscript, before the manuscript can be published. All copyrights, including translation of the published material into other languages are reserved by the publisher, Idea Group Inc. Upon transfer of the copyright to the publisher, no part of the manuscript may be reproduced in any form without written permission of the publisher, except for noncommercial, educational uses such as for classroom teaching.

Submission

Prospective authors are invited to submit manuscripts for consideration for publication in the *International Journal of Information and Communication Technology Education* (*IJICTE*). Accepted manuscripts will comply with the following submission guidelines.

1. Authors are requested to submit their manuscripts electronically for consideration to the editor-in-chief at **tomei@rmu.edu** as an email attachment in Microsoft Word, RTF, or Plain Text format. Hard copy submissions may be sent via surface to: Dr. Lawrence Tomei, Robert Morris University, Acad Services - PH Room 214; 6001 University Blvd., Moon Twp PA 15108, and must include a disk containing the digital version of the manuscript.

2. Submissions must be double-spaced, prepared in English and include at least a 1" margin on all sides. The cover page should contain the paper title and the name, affiliation, address, phone number, fax number, and email address of each contributing author. The cover page must also specify the focus and format of the paper (e.g., Focus: Educational Technology, Format: Practice-based Abstract). Acceptable foci for the paper include: business, computer science, and information technology education; educational technology; instructional systems design; teaching and learning with technology; corporate training science; or, distance learning education. Acceptable formats for the journal include: research synopsis, position papers, and practice-based abstracts.

3. The second page of the submission should provide the title at the top followed immediately by the focus and format and an abstract of 100-150 words (maximum) clearly summarizing the target audience, objectives, nature of the paper, and key findings/recommendations of the manuscript.

Except for the cover page, the author's name and affiliations must NOT appear anywhere in the abstract or manuscript to ensure anonymity during the refereed review process.

4. Submitted manuscripts (apart from the abstract) should normally not exceed 5000 words for position and practice manuscripts; longer research manuscripts (not to exceed 6000 words) may be considered subject to editorial revision prior to publication. Word count includes all appendices and references.

5. Submission of papers implies original content previously unpublished, free from copyright violations, and not currently under review elsewhere. Significantly extended papers previously presented at conferences and symposia may be considered. It remains the responsibility of the author to secure the proper permissions for use of any copyrighted materials in the manuscript prior to submission for consideration.

Correspondence/Communication of Review Status

An email acknowledging receipt of the manuscript will be promptly forwarded by the editor-in-chief. The review process is expected to take approximately 8-10 weeks and the author will be notified of the status of the review as soon as the review process is complete. All correspondence will be directed to the lead author of multi-authored manuscripts. It is the responsibility of the lead author to communicate the status of the review process and editorial recommendations to other contributing author(s). Authors of accepts manuscripts will be asked to provide a final copy of their manuscript in Word format on floppy or zip disk or CDROM, accompanied by a hard copy of the manuscript and signed copy of the Warranty and Copyright Agreement. Digital signatures will are not acceptable. Final manuscripts may be edited by the *Journal* copy editor for format and style.

Book Reviews (Research-based)

The *IJICTE* invites prospective book reviewers to submit their review of either textbooks or professional books pertaining to technology education for possible inclusion in the *Journal*. Reviewers should focus on the following guidelines when developing the review. Book reviews must not exceed 1500 words. Reviews should summarize the book and point out the highlights, strengths, and weaknesses of its content. Reviews should concentrate on the educational research and practical applications of the material discussed in the book as they pertain to information technology education. Reviews should critique and constructively evaluate the research base offered by the author and not merely list the contents of the chapters. The accuracy and relevance of the book to technology education, along with the quality and importance of its findings and impact on furthering the discipline should be analyzed. The review must include the title of the book, author, publisher and publication date, number of pages, cost, and ISBN number. Each submission must be accompanied by a short biography of the reviewer.

Case Studies (Practice-based)

The *IJICTE* encourages submissions of case studies based on actual scenarios related to practice-based issues and practical applications of information technology education. Case studies must not exceed 2000 words and must provide adequate information regarding the educational environment upon which the study is based, presentation of the issues involved, coverage of any experiments or techniques involved, and elaborations of the lessons learned or conclusions drawn from the study.

Position Papers (Position-based)

Finally, the *IJICTE* solicits controversial opinions, viewpoints, and personal judgments focusing on all aspects of information technology education. Papers must not exceed 1000 words and only those papers backed by research, literature, or citations of practical application will be considered.

All inquiries and submissions should be sent to: Editor-in-Chief: Lawrence A. Tomei, EdD, International Journal of Information and Communication Technology Education, Robert Morris University, Acad Services - PH Room 214; 6001 University Blvd; Moon Twp PA 15108; Phone: 412-269-3696; Fax: 412-269-3851; Email: **tomei@rmu.edu**

International Journal of Interdisciplinary Social Sciences

SUBMISSION PROCESS:
Electronic Submission Only **via Online Portal** http://www.SocialSciences-Journal.com

CONTACT INFORMATION:	REVIEW PROCESS:	
Mary Kalantzis & Bill Cope, Editors University of Illinois, Urbana-Champaign	**Type of Review:**	Blind Review
	No. External Reviewers:	2
Phone:	**No. InHouse Reviewers:**	1
	Acceptance Rate:	50%
Email:	**Time to Review:**	1 - 2 Months
support+iji@commongroundpublishing.com	**Reviewer's Comments:**	Yes
	Invited Articles:	0-5%
Website:	**Fees to Publish:**	$0.00 US$
http://www.SocialSciences-Journal.com	**Fees to Review:**	$0.00 US$

PUBLICATION GUIDELINES:	CIRCULATION DATA:
Manuscript Style: See Manuscript Guidelines	**Reader:** Academics, Practicing Teachers
Manuscript Length: 6-20	**Frequency of Issue:** 6-8 Times/Year
Copies Required: Electronic Only	**Sponsor/Publisher:** The University Press, an imprint of Common Ground Publishing

MANUSCRIPT TOPICS:
Social Studies / Social Science

MANUSCRIPT GUIDELINES/COMMENTS:

About the Journal
The *International Journal of Interdisciplinary Social Sciences* aims to examine the nature of disciplinary practices, and the interdisciplinary practices that arise in the context of 'real world' applications. It also interrogates what constitutes 'science' in a social context, and the connections between the social and other sciences.

The journal discusses the distinctive disciplinary practices within the sciences of the social, and examines examples of these practices. In order to define and exemplify disciplinarity, the journal fosters dialogue ranging from the broad and speculative to the microcosmic and empirical. In considering the varied interdisciplinary, transdisciplinary or multidisciplinary work across and between the social, natural and applied sciences, the journal showcases interdisciplinary practices in action.

The focus of papers ranges from the finely grained and empirical, to wide-ranging multi-disciplinary and transdisciplinary practices, to perspectives on knowledge and method.

Submission Guidelines
View: **http://iji.cgpublisher.com/submission_guidelines.html**

About the Submission Process
Registration in the Social Sciences Conference gives participants the opportunity to publish in an academic journal. Presenters have the option to submit their papers to the International Journal of the Interdisciplinary Social Sciences anytime before the conference and up to one month after the conference. Papers submitted for publication will be fully refereed. The publication decision is based on the referees' reports.

To submit, at least one author of each paper must be registered to attend the conference (to a maximum of one paper per registered author—which means, for instance, that two registered authors may submit two jointly authored papers). For those unable to attend the conference in person, virtual registrations are available.

All registered participants will be given online access to all papers published by the journal from the time of registration until one year after the end date of the conference.

Papers are published continuously to the journal's online bookstore, as soon as the publication process is completed for each paper (and that can be any time before the conference, and continues after the conference as papers are refereed).

It is possible to attend and present at the conference without submitting or publishing a formal written paper if you choose not to do so.

Author Guidelines—Preparing Your Paper
Formatting Requirements
- We require presenters to use our CGCreator Microsoft Word Template which can be downloaded.
- We are not able to accept papers that have not used the template.
- Papers should be approximately 2,000-5,000 words in length. They should be written as continuous expository narrative in a chapter or article style - not as lists of points or a PowerPoint presentation.
- Please remember that the papers are to be published in a fully refereed academic journal. This means that the style and structure of your text should be relatively formal. For instance, you should not submit a verbatim transcript of your oral presentation, such as 'Today I want to speak to you about ...'
- Authors are responsible for the accuracy of citations, quotations, diagrams, tables and maps.
- You may use any referencing style you choose, as long as you use it consistently and to the appropriate standards.
- Spelling can vary according to national usage, but should be internally consistent.
- Papers should be thoroughly checked and proof-read before submission, both by the author and a critical editorial friend – after you have submitted your paper you are unable to make any changes to it during the refereeing process.
- Papers will be assessed by referees against ten criteria - or fewer if some criteria do not apply to a particular kind of paper.

Illustration/Electronic Artwork Guidelines
- Figures and images must be clear and easy to view. We cannot improve the quality of images.
- Figures and tables need to be placed where they are to appear in the text. If preferred, you can also place images and tables at the end of your paper.
- Please refrain from using Word Drawing objects. Instead use images imported from a drawing program. Word Drawing objects will not be rendered in the typeset version.

Keyword Guidelines

Keywords are extremely important in search engine rankings. To achieve better exposure for your paper, please make sure your keywords are clear and accurate.

Resubmission Policy

If your paper has been rejected we will allow a maximum of TWO further resubmissions until TWO months prior to the anticipated publication date.

Editorial Quality

The refereeing process for publication in the journal is a rigorous measure of the quality of content. Authors are expected to revise to the standards required of the more negative of the referee reports they receive. For instance, if one referee recommends 'resubmit with major revisions' and another 'resubmit with minor revisions', the author is expected to resubmit with major revisions.

Furthermore, some papers may have excellent content, but may be poorly expressed in English—in the case, for instance, of authors whose first language is not English. When we receive a negative response from a referee to Criterion 10, 'Quality of Communication', we may request a complete rewrite regardless of the overall score.

The Submission Process—How and Where to Submit Your Paper for Publication

Final papers can now be submitted to Common Ground using our online conference and paper management system "CGPublisher".

The Publication Process

The publication process is as follows:

- Submit a presentation proposal to the conference (in-person or virtual) before the next deadline.
- If your proposal is accepted by the conference advisory team, complete your registration for an in-person or virtual presentation. You may submit your paper to the journal anytime between registration and one calendar month after the closing date of the conference.
- Once your paper is received, it is verified against template and submission requirements. Your identity and contact details are then removed and the paper is matched to two appropriate referees and sent for review. You can view the status of your paper at any time by logging into your CGPublisher account at www.CGPublisher.
- When referee reports are uploaded, you will be notified by email and provided with a link to view the reports (after the referees' identities have been removed).
- You will then be asked to accept the Publishing Agreement and submit a revised final copy of your paper.
- Your paper will be typeset and the proofs sent to you for final approval before publication.
- Papers are published continuously in the online bookstore. Registered conference participants will be given online access to the journal from the time of registration until one year after the conference end date. Individual papers will also be available for purchase from the journal's bookstore.

International Journal of Leadership in Education

SUBMISSION PROCESS:
Electronic Submission Only **via Online Portal** **http://mc.manuscriptcentral.com/tedl**

CONTACT INFORMATION:	REVIEW PROCESS:	
Duncan Waite, Editor Texas State University EAPS 601 University Drive San Marcos, TX 78666-4685 USA	**Type of Review:**	Blind Review
	No. External Reviewers:	3+
	No. InHouse Reviewers:	2
	Acceptance Rate:	20-25%
	Time to Review:	4 - 6 Months
Phone:	**Reviewer's Comments:**	Yes
512-245-8918	**Invited Articles:**	10%
512-245-2575		
Email:	**Fees to Publish:**	$0.00 US$
ijle@txstate.edu	**Fees to Review:**	$0.00 US$
Website: www.tandf.co.uk/journals		

PUBLICATION GUIDELINES:	CIRCULATION DATA:
Manuscript Style: See Manuscript Guidelines **Manuscript Length:** 14-30 **Copies Required:** Two	**Reader:** Academics, Administrators, Practitioners, Supervisors, Educational Laeders **Frequency of Issue:** Quarterly **Sponsor/Publisher:** Taylor & Francis, Ltd.

MANUSCRIPT TOPICS:

Adult Career & Vocational; Curriculum Studies; Education Management / Administration; Higher Education; Rural Education & Small Schools; Secondary / Adolescent Studies; Teacher Education; Urban Education, Cultural / Non-Traditional

MANUSCRIPT GUIDELINES/COMMENTS:

Topics Also Include. Educational Leadership; Leadership Education and Preparation; Organizational Leadership / Theory; Professional Development; Supervision

The Journal Presents

- Cutting-edge writing on educational leadership, instructional supervision, curriculum and teaching development, and educational administration
- An alternative voice: reports of alternative theoretical perspectives, alternative methodologies, and alternative experiences of leadership
- A broad definition of leadership, including teachers-as-leaders, shared governance, site-based decision making, and community-school collaborations
- A progressive orientation

- An international medium for the publication of theoretical and practical discussions of educational leadership. across a range of approaches, as these relate to ethical, political, epistemological and philosophical issues
- A forum for researchers, academics, policy makers and practitioners to consider conceptual, methodological, and practical issues in a range of professional and service settings and sectors.

Submission of Papers

Before preparing your submission, please visit our website for a complete style guide; contact details are given below. Manuscript submission is now done via a web-based system, accessed at: **http://mc.manuscriptcentral.com/tedl**

Two copies of papers (one full and one blind) should be uploaded at the journal's website or manuscript central. The blind copy should be in a form suitable for blind peer review, with all author identifiers removed from the text proper, and included only on a cover sheet.

Papers are accepted for consideration on condition that you will accept and warrant the following conditions. In order to ensure both the widest dissemination and protection of material published in our journal, we ask authors to assign the rights of copyright in the articles they contribute. This enables Taylor & Francis Ltd to ensure protection against infringement.

1. In consideration of the publication of your Article, you assign us with full title guarantee all rights of copyright and related rights in your Article. So that there is no doubt, this assignment includes the right to publish the Article in all forms, including electronic and digital forms, for the full legal term of the copyright and any extension or renewals. You shall retain the right to use the substance of the above work in future works, including lectures, press releases and reviews provided that you acknowledge its prior publication in the journal.

2. We shall prepare and publish your Article in the *Journal*. We reserve the right to make such editorial changes as may be necessary to make the Article suitable for publication; and we reserve the right not to proceed with publication for whatever reason. In such an instance, copyright in the Article will revert to you.

3. You hereby assert your moral rights to be identified as the author of the Article according to the UK Copyright Designs & Patents Act 1988.

4. You warrant that you have secured the necessary written permission from the appropriate copyright owner or authorities for the reproduction in the Article and the journal of any text, illustration. or other material. You warrant that, apart from any such third party copyright material included in the Article, the Article is your original work, and cannot be construed as plagiarizing any other published work, and has not been and will not be published elsewhere.

5. In addition you warrant that the Article contains no statement that is abusive, defamatory, libelous, obscene, fraudulent, nor in any way infringes the rights of others, nor is in any other way unlawful or in violation of applicable laws.

6. You warrant that any patient. client or participant mentioned in the text has given informed consent to the inclusion of material pertaining to themselves, and that they acknowledge that they cannot be identified via the text.

7. If the Article was prepared jointly with other authors, you warrant that you have been authorized by all co authors to sign this Agreement on their behalf, and to agree on their behalf the order of names in the publication of the Article.

Fifty complimentary offprints of your article will be sent to the principal or sole author of articles; book reviewers will be sent three complimentary offprints. Larger quantities may be ordered at a special discount price. An order form will accompany the proof, which must be completed and returned, irrespective of whether you require additional copies. All authors (including co-authors and book reviewers) will receive a complimentary copy of the issue in which their article appears.

Editorial Office
Duncan Waite, PhD, Editor. *International Journal of Leadership in Education*, EAPS. Texas State University. 601 University Drive. San Marcos. TX 78666, USA. Tel: +I S12 245 8918; email: **IJLE@txstate.edu**

To submit a manuscript, or to volunteer to serve as a manuscript reviewer, visit Manuscript Central at: **http://mc.manuscriptcentral.com/tedl**

Please refer to the following website for the journal style guide: **http://www.educationarena.com/**

For more information on our journals and books publishing, visit our Taylor & Francis website: **http://www.tandf.co.uk**

If you are unable to access the website please write to: Journals Editorial, Taylor & Francis Ltd. I I New Fetter Lane. London EC4P 4EE, UK

International Journal of Lifelong Education

SUBMISSION PROCESS:
Electronic Submission Preferred **via EMail** **p.jarvis@surrey.ac.uk**

CONTACT INFORMATION:	REVIEW PROCESS:	
Peter Jarvis & John Holford, Editors University of Surrey Dpt of Political, Int'l & Policy Studies Guildford, GU2 7XH UK	**Type of Review:**	Blind Review
	No. External Reviewers:	2
	No. InHouse Reviewers:	2
Phone:	**Acceptance Rate:**	21-30%
	Time to Review:	2 - 3 Months
	Reviewer's Comments:	Yes
Email:	**Invited Articles:**	0-5%
p.jarvis@surrey.ac.uk		
j.holford@surrey.ac.uk	**Fees to Publish:**	$0.00 US$
Website:	**Fees to Review:**	$0.00 US$
http://www.tandf.co.uk/journals/0260137 0		

PUBLICATION GUIDELINES:	CIRCULATION DATA:

Manuscript Style:
  See Manuscript Guidelines
	Reader:
	  Academics, Practicing Teachers

Manuscript Length:
  No Limit
	Frequency of Issue:
	  Bi-Monthly

Copies Required:
  Four
	Sponsor/Publisher:
	  Routledge, Taylor & Francis, Ltd.

MANUSCRIPT TOPICS:
Adult Career & Vocational; Higher Education; Social Studies / Social Science; Urban Education, Cultural / Non-Traditional

MANUSCRIPT GUIDELINES/COMMENTS:

Aims & Scope
The *International Journal of Lifelong Education* provides a forum for debate on the principles and practice of lifelong, adult, continuing, recurrent and initial education and learning, whether in formal, institutional or informal settings. Common themes include social purpose in lifelong education, and sociological, policy and political studies of lifelong education. The journal recognises that research into lifelong learning needs to focus on the relationships between schooling, later learning, active citizenship and personal fulfilment, as well as the relationship between schooling, employability and economic development.

With this in mind, the journal provides the context for an informed debate on the theory and practice of lifelong education in a variety of countries and settings. All papers are peer reviewed. Each issue carries a lively reviews section.

Instructions for Authors

Note to Authors. Please make sure your contact address information is clearly visible on the outside of all packages you are sending to Editors.

Submitting a paper to *International Journal of Lifelong Education*

Please read these Guidelines with care and attention: failure to follow them may result in your paper being delayed. Note especially the referencing conventions used by *International Journal of Lifelong Education* and the requirement for gender-, race-, and creed-inclusive language.

International Journal of Lifelong Education considers all manuscripts on condition they are the property (copyright) of the submitting author(s) and that copyright will be transferred to the publishers if the paper is accepted. *International Journal of Lifelong Education* considers all manuscripts on the strict condition that they have been submitted only to *International Journal of Lifelong Education*, that they have not been published already, nor are they under consideration for publication, nor in press elsewhere. Authors who fail to adhere to this condition will be charged all costs which *International Journal of Lifelong Education* incurs, and their papers will not be published.

- Please write clearly and concisely, stating your objectives clearly and defining your terms. Your arguments should be substantiated with well reasoned supporting evidence.
- For all manuscripts, gender-, race-, and creed-inclusive language is mandatory.
- Abstracts are required for all papers submitted and should precede the text of a paper; see 'Abstracts'.
- Manuscripts should be printed on one single side of A4 or 8 x 11 inch white good quality paper, double-spaced throughout, including the reference section.
- Four copies of the manuscript should be submitted, plus one electronic version, either on disk or by email to **p.jarvis@surrey.ac.uk**. MS Word format is preferred.
- Accepted manuscripts in their final, revised versions, should also be submitted as electronic word processing files on disk; please visit our website at **http://www.tandf.co.uk/journals/ authors/electronic_edu.asp** to see notes on Electronic Processing.
- Authors should include telephone and fax numbers as well as email addresses on the cover page of manuscripts.
- Bionotes should be contained on a separate sheet and be located at the beginning of a paper.

In writing your paper, you are encouraged to review articles in the area you are addressing which have been previously published in the journal, and where you feel appropriate, to reference them. This will enhance context, coherence, and continuity for our readers.

Abstracts

Structured abstracts are required for all papers, and should be submitted as detailed below, following the title and author's name and address, preceding the main text.

For papers reporting original research, state the primary objective and any hypothesis tested; describe the research design and your reasons for adopting that methodology; state the methods and procedures employed, including where appropriate tools, hardware, software, the selection and number of study areas/subjects, and the central experimental interventions; state the main outcomes and results, including relevant data; and state the conclusions that might be drawn from these data and results, including their implications for further research or application/practice.

For review essays, state the primary objective of the review; the reasoning behind your literature selection; and the way you critically analyse the literature; state the main outcomes and results of your review; and state the conclusions that might be drawn, including their implications for further research or application/practice.

Early Electronic Offprints

Corresponding authors can now receive their article by e-mail as a complete PDF. This allows the author to print up to 50 copies, free of charge, and disseminate them to colleagues. In many cases this facility will be available up to two weeks prior to publication. Or, alternatively, corresponding authors will receive the traditional 50 offprints. A copy of the journal will be sent by post to all corresponding authors after publication. Additional copies of the journal can be purchased at the author's preferential rate of £15.00/$25.00 per copy.

Notes on style

All authors are asked to take account of the diverse audience of *International Journal of Lifelong Education*. Clearly explain or avoid the use of terms that might be meaningful only to a local or national audience. However, note also that *International Journal of Lifelong Education* does not aspire to be international in the ways that McDonald's restaurants or Hilton Hotels are 'international'; we much prefer papers that, where appropriate, reflect the particularities of each higher education system.

Some specific points of style for the text of articles, research reports, case studies, reports, essay reviews, and reviews follow:

- *International Journal of Lifelong Education* prefers US to 'American', USA to 'United States', and UK to 'United Kingdom'.
- *International Journal of Lifelong Education* uses conservative British, not US, spelling, i.e. colour not color; behaviour (behavioural) not behavior; [school] programme not program; [he] practises not practices; centre not center; organization not organisation; analyse not analyze, etc.
- Single 'quotes' are used for quotations rather than double "quotes", unless the 'quote is "within" another quote'.
- Punctuation should follow the British style, e.g. 'quotes precede punctuation'.
- Punctuation of common abbreviations should follow the following conventions: e.g. i.e. cf. Note that such abbreviations are not followed by a comma or a (double) point/period.
- Dashes (M-dash) should be clearly indicated in manuscripts by way of either a clear dash (-) or a double hyphen (- -).
- *International Journal of Lifelong Education* is sparing in its use of the upper case in headings and references, e.g. only the first word in paper titles and all subheads is in upper case; titles of papers from journals in the references and other places are not in upper case.
- Apostrophes should be used sparingly. Thus, decades should be referred to as follows: 'The 1980s [not the 1980's] saw ...'. Possessives associated with acronyms (e.g. APU), should be written as follows: 'The APU's findings that ...', but, NB, the plural is APUs.
- All acronyms for national agencies, examinations, etc. should be spelled out the first time they are introduced in text or references. Thereafter the acronym can be used if appropriate, e.g. 'The work of the Assessment of Performance Unit (APU) in the early 1980s ...'. Subsequently, 'The APU studies of achievement ...', in a reference ... (Department of Education and Science [DES] 1989a).
- Brief biographical details of significant national figures should be outlined in the text unless it is quite clear that the person concerned would be known internationally. Some suggested editorial emendations to a typical text are indicated in the following with square brackets: 'From the time of H. E. Armstrong [in the 19th century] to the curriculum development work associated with the Nuffield Foundation [in the 1960s], there has been a shift from heurism to constructivism in the design of [British] science courses'.
- The preferred local (national) usage for ethnic and other minorities should be used in all papers. For the USA, African-American, Hispanic, and Native American are used, e.g. 'The African American presidential candidate, Jesse Jackson...' For the UK, African-Caribbean (not 'West Indian'), etc.
- Material to be emphasized (italicized in the printed version) should be underlined in the typescript rather than italicized. Please use such emphasis sparingly.
- n (not N), % (not per cent) should be used in typescripts.
- Numbers in text should take the following forms: 300, 3000, 30 000. Spell out numbers under 10 unless used with a unit of measure, e.g. nine pupils but 9 mm (do not introduce periods with measure). For decimals, use the form 0.05 (not .05).

Mathematics

Special care should be taken with mathematical scripts, especially subscripts and superscripts and differentiation between the letter 'ell' and the figure one, and the letter 'oh 'and the figure zero. If your keyboard does not have the characters you need, it is preferable to use longhand, in which case it is important to differentiate between capital and small letters, K, k and x and other similar groups of letters. Special symbols should be highlighted in the text and explained in the margin. In some cases it is helpful to supply annotated lists of symbols for the guidance of the sub-editor and the typesetter, and/or a 'Nomenclature' section preceding the 'Introduction'.

For simple fractions in the text, the solidus / should be used instead of a horizontal line, care being taken to insert parentheses where necessary to avoid ambiguity, for example, I $/(n\text{-}1)$. Exceptions are the proper fractions available as single type on a keyboard.

Full formulae or equations should be displayed, that is, written on a separate line. Horizontal lines are preferable to solidi, for examples please visit our web site.

The solidus is not generally used for units: ms^{-1} not m/s, but note electrons/s, counts/channel, etc.

Displayed equations referred to in the text should be numbered serially (1, 2, etc.) on the right hand side of the page. Short expressions not referred to by any number will usually be incorporated in the text.

Symbols should not be underlined to indicate fonts except for tensors, vectors and matrices, which are indicated with a wavy line in the manuscript (not with a straight arrow or arrow above) and rendered in heavy type in print: upright sans serif r (tensor), sloping serif r (vector) upright serif r (matrix).

Typographical requirements must be clearly indicated at their first occurrence, e.g. Greek, Roman, script, sans serif, bold, italic. Authors will be charged for corrections at proof stage resulting from a failure to do so.

Braces, brackets and parentheses are used in the order {[( )]}, except where mathematical convention dictates otherwise (i.e. square brackets for commutators and anticommutators)

Citations in text

- Ibid. (and the like) are not used when repeating citations. Simply repeat the original citation verbatim, e.g. (Orwell 1945).
- Citations should be included in prefatory material to quotes (wherever possible) rather than placing them at the end. Thus, for example, 'Orwell (1945: 23) reduces the principles of animalism to seven commandments, namely, ...' is preferred to 'Orwell reduced the principles of animalism to seven commandments, namely, ... (Orwell 1945: 23)'.
- Multiple citations within parentheses should be divided by a comma, not a semi-colon, and there should be no use of '&' within such multiple references. References to works published in the same year should be cited as, e.g. (Smith 1991a, b).
- Multiple citations within a text should be ordered by date, not alphabetically by author's name, e.g. (Smith 1902, Jones and Bower 1934, Brown 1955, 1958a, b, Green 1995).
- *et al.* may be used in citations within the text when a paper or book has three or more authors, but note that all names are given in the reference itself.
- Page spans in references should be given in full, e.g. 'Sedgewick (1935: 102-103; emphasis added) outlines them as follows:'

Notes on tables and figures

Artwork submitted for publication will not be returned and will be destroyed after publication, unless you request otherwise. Whilst every care is taken of artwork, neither the Editor nor Taylor &

Francis shall bear any responsibility or liability for non-return, loss, or damage of artwork, nor for any associated costs or compensation. You are strongly advised to insure appropriately.

- Tables and figures should be referred to in text as follows: figure 1, table 1, i.e. lower case. 'As seen in table [or figure] 1 ...' (not Tab., fig. or Fig).
- The place at which a table or figure is to be inserted in the printed text should be indicated clearly on a manuscript:

Insert table 2 about here

- Each table and/or figure must have a title that explains its purpose without reference to the text.
- All figures and tables must be on separate sheets and not embedded in the text. Thus tables and figures must be referred to in the text and numbered in order of appearance. Each table should have a descriptive title and each column an appropriate heading. For all figures, original copies of figures should be supplied. All figures should allow for reduction to column width (7.5 cm) or page width (16 cm). Photographs may be sent as glossy prints or negatives. The legends to any illustrations must be typed separately following the text and should be grouped together.

Author's bionote

This note should be brief (fifty words) and include the author's institutional position and affiliation and a full address for correspondence. For example:

'Nel Noddings is the Lee L. Jacks Professor of Child Education in the School of Education, Stanford University, Stanford, CA 94305-3096, USA. Her most recent books are *The Challenge of Care to Schools: Alternative Approaches to Education* (New York: Teachers College Press, 1992) and (edited with Carol Witherell) *Stories Lives Tell: Narrative and Dialogue in Education* (New York: Teachers College Press, 1991).'

Acknowledgements

Any acknowledgements authors wish to make should be included in a separate headed section at the end of the manuscript. Please do not incorporate these into the bionote or notes.

Book reviews

- The following header material should appear in all reviews in the following order (note also the punctuation): *Student Engagement and Achievement in the American Secondary School.* Edited by Fred M. Newmann (Teachers College Press, New York, 1992), 240 pp., $38.00 (hbk), ISBN 8077-3183-8, $17.95 (pbk), ISBN 8077-3182-X.
- Page references within reviews should be given as follows: (p. 337) or (pp. 36-37).

References

International Journal of Lifelong Education uses the following conventions for references:

To a book
Walkerdine, V., (1990), *Schoolgirl Fictions*, 2nd edn (London: Verso).

To a chapter in a boo
Cohen, D. K. and Spillane, J.P., (1992), Policy and practice: the relations between governance and instruction. In G. Grant (ed.), *Review of Research in Education*, 18 (Washington, DC: American Educational Research Association), pp. 3-50.

To an article in a journa
Elbaz, Freema, (1991), Research on teachers' knowledge: the evolution of a discourse. *Journal of Curriculum Studies*, 23, 1-20.

Other points to note

1. References to multi-authored books and papers should be fully spelled out in the references, i.e. *et al.* should not be used. The '&' should not be used except for publisher's names.

2. References to chapters in edited books must include the page references for any chapter being cited. Such references should include the full page span (e.g. 212-252 , NOT 212-52). Note that a single editor is indicated by (ed.) - with a point/period - and multiple editors by (eds) - without a point/period.

Copyright

It is a condition of publication that authors assign copyright or licence the publication rights in their articles, including abstracts, to Taylor & Francis. This enables us to ensure full copyright protection and to disseminate the article, and of course the Journal, to the widest possible readership in print and electronic formats as appropriate. Authors may, of course, use the article elsewhere *after* publication without prior permission from Taylor & Francis, provided that acknowledgement is given to the Journal as the original source of publication, and that Taylor & Francis is notified so that our records show that its use is properly authorised. Authors retain a number of other rights under the Taylor & Francis rights policies documents. These policies are referred to at **www.tandf.co.uk/journals/authorrights.pdf** for full details. Authors are themselves responsible for obtaining permission to reproduce copyright material from other sources.

International Journal of Management in Education

SUBMISSION PROCESS: Postal Submission Only	
CONTACT INFORMATION:	**REVIEW PROCESS:**
Binshan Lin, Editor Louisiana State University in Shreveport College of Business Administration Dept of Management & Marketing BE321 One University Place Shreveport, LA 71115 USA **Phone:** **Email:** blin@lsus.edu **Website:** www.inderscience.com/ijmie	**Type of Review:** Blind Review **No. External Reviewers:** 3 **No. InHouse Reviewers:** 0 **Acceptance Rate:** 11-20% **Time to Review:** 2 - 3 Months **Reviewer's Comments:** Yes **Invited Articles:** 0-5% **Fees to Publish:** $0.00 US$ **Fees to Review:** $0.00 US$
PUBLICATION GUIDELINES:	**CIRCULATION DATA:**
Manuscript Style: See Manuscript Guidelines **Manuscript Length:** 21-25 **Copies Required:** Three	**Reader:** Academics, Administrators, Counselors, Practicing Teachers **Frequency of Issue:** Quarterly **Sponsor/Publisher:** Inderscience Enterprises Limited

MANUSCRIPT TOPICS:
Education Management / Administration; Educational Technology Systems; Higher Education;
Secondary / Adolescent Studies

MANUSCRIPT GUIDELINES/COMMENTS:

Guide for authors and further Information and requirements, shown below , for papers submission
are available on web site : **https://www.inderscience.com/papers/about.php**
1. Author Guidelines (PDF Version)
2. Author Entitlement and Postprint Permission
3. Copyright Notice
4. Privacy Statement
5. Sample Cover Letter/E-mail
6. Author Agreement (PDF Version)

Internationalisation, growing technology and their development increasingly influence education in
society. This also increases the need for managing education and learning. The significance of
education management is becoming apparent in schools, entire education systems and other areas.
The management of education and knowledge is therefore becoming an important factor of control
in national systems and organisations in all areas of social life.

Globalisation, along with other processes, such as decentralisation, deregulation, autonomy and professionalism, open the question of the international comparability and effectiveness of education systems, the role of the state, and thereby create the demands for a new kind of organisation within schools and school systems. Accordingly, the need for effective administration and management of educational organisations, especially to achieve a greater responsiveness, flexibility and innovativeness of organisations in a rapidly changing environment – where employees represent an important resource and potential – is growing steadily.

Various studies on the success and effectiveness of schools and education systems have shown that the quality of management and organisation is the most important variable influencing the success and/or failure in schools or national education systems. By introducing new forms of school financing, new demands regarding the training and education of leadership staff and professionals in the fields of economy, law, management and business keep emerging.

Objectives
IJMIE aims to publish papers which analyse all aspects of international education, providing researchers and professionals from education with the opportunity to discuss the most demanding issues regarding the development and leadership of education at all levels and in all areas of education management. Similarly, it is interested in how international or intercultural questions can produce problems which are ethical in nature or which have ethical consequences with regard to the management in education.

Readership
Professionals, academics, researchers, managers, policy makers, and nonprofit organisations.

Contents
IJMIE publishes original and review papers, technical reports, case studies, conference reports, management reports, book reviews, and notes, commentaries, and news. Contribution may be by submission or invitation, and suggestions for special issues and publications are welcome.
- High quality papers to keep you at the forefront of the latest thinking and research on management education
- Case studies and practical applications to illustrate management education design, policy, development, and implementation

Subject Coverage
Papers are solicited that address these issues from an empirical and/or conceptual point of view. Possible topics of interest include (but are not limited to): • Analysis of political, economic, social, legal and cultural environment in which educational organisations work • Autonomy, professionalism and decision policies • Case studies from schools in different countries • Change management and education quality • Classroom management • Computers in educational administration • Differing cultural perceptions of management in education • Distance education and multimedia environments • Education economics • Educational leadership • Educational systems planning/strategic planning • Equity and education • Finance and accountability • Globalisation and education • Individual professional learning portfolio • Information systems for education and training support • Knowledge and education • Leadership in education • Lifelong learning and development of competences • Management in higher education • Management of e-education • Managing the curriculum • Marketing in education • Mobile learning: policy and management • Organisations as learning communities • Policy analysis and evaluation of institutions and study programmes • Professional development of teaching staff • Public policies management • Research methods in education • School and school system improvement • Transactional education, student and teaching mobility • Other relevant topic areas

Specific Notes for Authors

Submitted papers should not have been previously published nor be currently under consideration for publication elsewhere.

All papers are refereed through a double blind process. A guide for authors, sample copies and other relevant information for submitting papers are available on the Submission of Papers web-page.

You may send one copy in the form of an MS Word file attached to an e-mail (details of file formats in Author Guidelines) to Prof. Dr. Binshan Lin with an email copy only to: Editor-in-Chief, IEL Editorial Office, E-mail: **ijmie@inderscience.com**. Please include in your submission the title of the Journal.

Submission of Papers

Papers, case studies, technical and conference reports, etc. are invited for submission, together with a brief abstract (100-150 words) and 1-10 keywords that reflect the content. Authors may wish to send in advance abstracts of proposed papers along with cover letters/e-mails (see requirements below). Please refer to notes for intending authors for more detailed guidance.

Please submit your manuscript with a cover letter/e-mail containing the following imperative statements:
1. Title and the central theme of the article.

2. Journal for which publication is intended.

3. Which subject/theme of the Journal the material fits.

4. Why the material is important in its field and why the material should be published in this Journal.

5. Nomination of up to four recognized experts who would be considered appropriate to review the submission. Please state:
- The names, title, addresses, phone, fax, and email addresses of these reviewers
- The expertise of each reviewer relating to your paper
- Your relationship with each of them.

6. The fact that the manuscript contains original unpublished work and is not being submitted for publication elsewhere.

Note that

Any non-English speaking author should have his/her paper proofread by a professional technical writer for grammatical and spelling corrections as well as the readability of the paper, before submitting it to the Editor.

A complete submission must include the following components in three separate MS-Word/Word for Windows files, plus hard copy with high quality black and white artwork for all figures, as indicated.
- The cover letter complying to the format of the sample letter
- The title page, including authors' full mailing, e-mail addresses and biographical details, attached to each of the hard copies
- One hard copy of the manuscript (title, abstract, keywords, article, references) without authors' names unless they are in the References section
- An electronic copy of the manuscript containing all details
- A hard copy of the Assignment of Copyright statement, duly signed.

These files should be submitted to the Editor-in-Chief.

Papers may also be sent directly to the relevant Editor, with copies to the Editorial Office, above Each paper submitted to Inderscience Enterprises Limited is subject to the following review procedure:

- It is reviewed by the editor for general suitability for this publication.
- If it is judged suitable, two reviewers are selected and a double-blind review process takes place
- Based on the recommendations of the reviewers, the editor then decides whether the particular article should be acceptable as it is, revised or rejected.

NOTES FOR INTENDING AUTHORS
Formal Conditions of Acceptance

- Papers will only be published in English.
- Each typescript must be accompanied by a statement that it has not been submitted for publication elsewhere in English.
- Previous presentation at a conference, or publication in another language, should be disclosed.
- All papers are refereed, and the Editor-in-Chief reserves the right to refuse any typescript, whether on invitation or otherwise, and to make suggestions and/or modifications before publication.
- Typescripts which have been accepted become the property of the publisher. It is a condition of acceptance that copyright shall be vested in the publisher.
- The publisher shall furnish authors of accepted papers with proofs for the correction of printing errors. The proofs shall be returned within 14 calendar days of submittal. The publishers shall not be held responsible for errors which are the result of authors' oversights.

Typescript Preparation

- The original typescript should be submitted electronically in A4 size format, with double-spaced typing and a wide margin on the left, following the submission requirements described on the Journal's website.
- A final paper which would exceed 6000 words or occupy more than 15 pages of the Journal may be returned for abridgement.
- A complete typescript should include, in the following order: title, author(s), address(es), abstract, keywords, biographical notes, introduction, text, acknowledgements, references and notes, tables, figure captions, figures.

Electronic Copy

- The preferred word processing program is Microsoft's Word or Word for Windows.
- Figures in the final accepted manuscript may be included in the electronic text file and also provided as separate files, but must also be accompanied by high-resolution hard copy printout.

International Context

- It should not be assumed that the reader is familiar with specific national institutions or corporations.
- Countries and groupings of countries should be referred to by their full title (for example, 'China', 'Europe' and 'America' are all ambiguous).
- Special attention should be paid to identifying units of currency by nationality.
- Acronyms should be translated in full into English. (See also 'Translated works' below.)

Title, Abstract, Keywords, Addresses, Biographical Notes
Please assist us by following these guidelines:

- Title. as short as possible
- Abstract. approximately 100 words, maximum 150
- Keywords. approximately 10 words or phrases
- Address. position, department, name of institution, full postal address
- Biographical notes. approximately 100 words per author, maximum 150.

References and Notes

- Inderscience journals use the Harvard system (name and date) short reference system for citations in the text with a detailed alphabetical list at the end of the paper. For example, 'Hamel (2000) suggests..' or 'Nonaka and Takeuchi (1995) found that...' or 'A study of economic change (Nelson and Winter, 1982) has shown that..'.
- Footnotes should be avoided, but any short, succinct notes making a specific point, may be placed in number order following the alphabetical list of references.
- References should be made only to works that are published, accepted for publication (not merely 'submitted'), or available through libraries or institutions. Any other source should be qualified by a note regarding availability.
- Full reference should include all authors' names and initials, year of publication, title of paper, title of publication (underlined), volume and issue number (of a journal), publisher and form (book, conference proceedings), page numbers.

Figures

- All illustrations, whether diagrams or photographs, are referred to as Figures and are numbered sequentially. Please place them at the end of the paper, rather than interspersed in text.
- Originals of line diagrams will be photographically reduced and used directly. All artwork for figures must be black and white and prepared to the highest possible standards. Bear in mind that lettering may be reduced in size by a factor of 2 or 3, and that fine lines may disappear.

Translated Works

- Difficulty often arises in translating acronyms, so it is best to spell out an acronym in English (for example, IIRP—French personal income tax).
- Similarly, labels and suffixes need careful attention where the letters refer to words which have been translated.
- The names of mathematical functions may change in translation—check against an English or American mathematical reference text.

Units of Measurement

- Inderscience journal follows the Système International for units of measurement.
- Imperial units will be converted, except where conversion would affect the meaning of a statement, or imply a greater or lesser degree of accuracy.

For further detailed instructions please see **www.inderscience.com**

International Journal of Mobile Learning and Organisation

SUBMISSION PROCESS:
Postal Submission Only

CONTACT INFORMATION:		REVIEW PROCESS:	
Jason C.H. Chen, Editor Gonzaga University Graduate School of Business E. 502 Boone Avenue Spokane, WA 99258 USA		**Type of Review:**	Blind Review
		No. External Reviewers:	3
		No. InHouse Reviewers:	0
		Acceptance Rate:	11-20%
Phone:		**Time to Review:**	2 - 3 Months
		Reviewer's Comments:	Yes
		Invited Articles:	0-5%
Email:			
chen@jepson.gonzaga.edu		**Fees to Publish:**	$0.00 US$
Website:		**Fees to Review:**	$0.00 US$
www.inderscience.com/ijmlo			

PUBLICATION GUIDELINES:	CIRCULATION DATA:
Manuscript Style: See Manuscript Guidelines	**Reader:** Academics, Administrators, Counselors, Practicing Teachers
Manuscript Length: 21-25	**Frequency of Issue:** Quarterly
Copies Required: Three	**Sponsor/Publisher:** Inderscience Enterprises Limited

MANUSCRIPT TOPICS:
Educational Technology Systems; Higher Education; Mobile Learning

MANUSCRIPT GUIDELINES/COMMENTS:

As mobile devices are gradually converging into Individual Information Centres, mobile learning becomes a viable learning channel that would fit the living style of today. *IJMLO* is a refereed, multidisciplinary journal for bridging the latest advances in mobile learning and organisation. It provides a global forum for presenting authoritative references, academically rigorous research and case studies. The journal publishes well-written and academically validated manuscripts in both theoretical development and applied research.

Objectives
With constant connectivity and the volume of information new mobile devices can deliver, mobile learning will shape the new landscape for organisational training and life-long learning as well as impromptu information gathering for problem solving. *IJMLO* intends to establish an effective communication channel among decision makers and policy makers in business, government agencies, and academic and research institutions which recognise the important role mobile learning may play in organisations. Specifically, *IJMLO* aims to be an outlet for creative, innovative concepts, as well as effective research methodologies and emerging technologies.

Readership

IJMLO intends to attract professionals in business, government and technology fields to share their insight in new technologies and new applications. It will also attract researchers in the academia who work in the field of technology management, engineering and business education to disseminate information and to learn from each other's work.

Contents

IJMLO publishes original papers, review papers, technical reports, case studies, conference reports, and management reports. Occasional Special Issues devoted to important topics in Mobile Learning and Organisation will also be published.

Subject Coverage

The areas covered by *IJMLO* include, but are not limited to: Globalisation of mobile learning • Lifelong learning for a changing demographics • Assessment, authentication, and security in mobile learning • Synchronous/asynchronous m-learning, m-coaching, and m-training • Collaborative GDSS and mobile learning • Pedagogy and design methodology in mobile learning • Learning management systems (LMS) and learning content management systems (LCMS) • Decomposability and modular design of course contents • Time modularisation, time management in mobile-learning design • Mobile life • Learning and knowledge creation in a mobile organization • Virtual collaboration in the workplace • Virtual communities and universities • Value-based m-learning in commerce • Integrated mobile marketing communication • Knowledge and learning strategy in the mobile organization • Methodologies for effective learning in the mobile organization • Ubiquitous and pervasive learning • Emerging technologies for mobile learning and organization • Managing sustainable change and learning in the m-organisation • Innovative case studies in the mobile organization • Trust issues in the mobile learning and organization • Tools for mobile educational presentation and delivery • Mobile tools and devices for e-learning • Corporate universities and new approaches/models to mobile learning content diffusion • Technologies and standards for developing tools for mobile learning • Mobile tools to enhance field study • Creating learning communities for mobile learning • Efficacy and effect of mobile learning • Ethical and copyright issues in mobile learning • Cross-culture issues in mobile learning • Problems and challenges in mobile learning • Any other topics relevant to mobile learning and organisation

Specific Notes for Authors

Submitted papers should not have been previously published nor be currently under consideration for publication elsewhere. All papers are refereed through a double blind process. A guide for authors, sample copies and other relevant information for submitting papers are available on the Submission of Papers web-page.

You may send one copy in the form of an MS Word file attached to an e-mail (details of file formats in Author Guidelines) to Dr. Jason C.H. Chen (**chen@jepson.gonzaga.edu**) or Prof. Dr. P. Pete Chong (**chongp@uhd.edu**), with an email copy only to: IEL Editorial Office; E-mail: **ijmlo@inderscience.com**

Please include in your submission the title of the Journal.

Submission of Papers

Papers, case studies, technical and conference reports, etc. are invited for submission, together with a brief abstract (100-150 words) and 1-10 keywords that reflect the content. Authors may wish to send in advance abstracts of proposed papers along with cover letters/e-mails (see requirements below). Please refer to notes for intending authors for more detailed guidance.

Please submit your manuscript with a cover letter/e-mail containing the following imperative statements:
1. Title and the central theme of the article.

2. Journal for which publication is intended.

3. Which subject/theme of the Journal the material fits.

4. Why the material is important in its field and why the material should be published in this Journal.

5. Nomination of up to four recognized experts who would be considered appropriate to review the submission. Please state:
- The names, title, addresses, phone, fax, and email addresses of these reviewers
- The expertise of each reviewer relating to your paper
- Your relationship with each of them.

6. The fact that the manuscript contains original unpublished work and is not being submitted for publication elsewhere.

Note that
Any non-English speaking author should have his/her paper proofread by a professional technical writer for grammatical and spelling corrections as well as the readability of the paper, before submitting it to the Editor.

A complete submission must include the following components in three separate MS-Word/Word for Windows files, plus hard copy with high quality black and white artwork for all figures, as indicated.
- The cover letter complying to the format of the sample letter
- The title page, including authors' full mailing, e-mail addresses and biographical details, attached to each of the hard copies
- One hard copy of the manuscript (title, abstract, keywords, article, references) without authors' names unless they are in the References section
- An electronic copy of the manuscript containing all details
- A hard copy of the Assignment of Copyright statement, duly signed.

These files should be submitted to the Editor-in-Chief.

Papers may also be sent directly to the relevant Editor, with copies to the Editorial Office, abov.e Each paper submitted to Inderscience Enterprises Limited is subject to the following review procedure:
- It is reviewed by the editor for general suitability for this publication.
- If it is judged suitable, two reviewers are selected and a double-blind review process takes place
- Based on the recommendations of the reviewers, the editor then decides whether the particular article should be acceptable as it is, revised or rejected.

NOTES FOR INTENDING AUTHORS
Formal Conditions of Acceptance
- Papers will only be published in English.
- Each typescript must be accompanied by a statement that it has not been submitted for publication elsewhere in English.
- Previous presentation at a conference, or publication in another language, should be disclosed.
- All papers are refereed, and the Editor-in-Chief reserves the right to refuse any typescript, whether on invitation or otherwise, and to make suggestions and/or modifications before publication.
- Typescripts which have been accepted become the property of the publisher. It is a condition of acceptance that copyright shall be vested in the publisher.

- The publisher shall furnish authors of accepted papers with proofs for the correction of printing errors. The proofs shall be returned within 14 calendar days of submittal. The publishers shall not be held responsible for errors which are the result of authors' oversights.

Typescript Preparation
- The original typescript should be submitted electronically in A4 size format, with double-spaced typing and a wide margin on the left, following the submission requirements described on the *Journal*'s website.
- A final paper which would exceed 6000 words or occupy more than 15 pages of the *Journal* may be returned for abridgement.
- A complete typescript should include, in the following order: *title, author(s), address(es), abstract, keywords, biographical notes, introduction, text, acknowledgements, references and notes, tables, figure captions, figures.*

Electronic Copy
- The preferred word processing program is Microsoft's Word or Word for Windows.
- Figures in the final accepted manuscript may be included in the electronic text file and also provided as separate files, but must also be accompanied by high-resolution hard copy printout.

International Context
- It should not be assumed that the reader is familiar with specific national institutions or corporations.
- Countries and groupings of countries should be referred to by their full title (for example, 'China', 'Europe' and 'America' are all ambiguous).
- Special attention should be paid to identifying units of currency by nationality.
- Acronyms should be translated in full into English. (See also 'Translated works' below.)

Title, Abstract, Keywords, Addresses, Biographical Notes
Please assist us by following these guidelines:
- Title. as short as possible
- Abstract. approximately 100 words, maximum 150
- Keywords. approximately 10 words or phrases
- Address. position, department, name of institution, full postal address
- Biographical notes. approximately 100 words per author, maximum 150.

References and Notes
- Inderscience journals use the Harvard system (name and date) short reference system for citations in the text with a detailed alphabetical list at the end of the paper. For example, 'Hamel (2000) suggests..' or 'Nonaka and Takeuchi (1995) found that…' or 'A study of economic change (Nelson and Winter, 1982) has shown that..'.
- Footnotes should be avoided, but any short, succinct notes making a specific point, may be placed in number order following the alphabetical list of references.
- References should be made only to works that are published, accepted for publication (not merely 'submitted'), or available through libraries or institutions. Any other source should be qualified by a note regarding availability.
- Full reference should include *all authors' names and initials, year of publication, title of paper, title of publication* (underlined), *volume and issue number* (of a journal), *publisher and form* (book, conference proceedings), *page numbers.*

Figures
- All illustrations, whether diagrams or photographs, are referred to as Figures and are numbered sequentially. Please place them at the end of the paper, rather than interspersed in text.

- Originals of line diagrams will be photographically reduced and used directly. All artwork for figures must be black and white and prepared to the highest possible standards. Bear in mind that lettering may be reduced in size by a factor of 2 or 3, and that fine lines may disappear.

Translated Works

- Difficulty often arises in translating acronyms, so it is best to spell out an acronym in English (for example, IIRP—French personal income tax).
- Similarly, labels and suffixes need careful attention where the letters refer to words which have been translated.
- The names of mathematical functions may change in translation—check against an English or American mathematical reference text.

Units of Measurement

- Inderscience journal follows the *Système International* for units of measurement.
- Imperial units will be converted, except where conversion would affect the meaning of a statement, or imply a greater or lesser degree of accuracy.

For further detailed instructions please see **www.inderscience.com**.

SUBMISSION PROCESS:	
Electronic Submission Only via EMail	
mraeditorial@e-contentmanagement.com	

CONTACT INFORMATION:	**REVIEW PROCESS:**	
Carol Grbich, Editor-in-Chief Flinders University School of Medicine , SA 5042 Australia	**Type of Review:**	Blind Review
	No. External Reviewers:	3
	No. InHouse Reviewers:	2
Phone: +61-8-8201 3271	**Acceptance Rate:**	New J
	Time to Review:	1 - 2 Months
	Reviewer's Comments:	Yes
Email:	**Invited Articles:**	New J
carol.grich@flinders.edu.au mraeditorial@e-contentmanagement.com davidson@e-contentmanagement.com	**Fees to Publish:**	$0.00 US$
	Fees to Review:	$0.00 US$
Website: http://www.e-contentmanagement.com/ journals/multiple-research-approaches/		

PUBLICATION GUIDELINES:	**CIRCULATION DATA:**
Manuscript Style: See Manuscript Guidelines	**Reader:** Academics, Administrators, Counselors
Manuscript Length: 21-25	**Frequency of Issue:** 2 Times/Year
Copies Required: Electronic Only	**Sponsor/Publisher:** eContent Management P/L

MANUSCRIPT TOPICS:
Art / Music; Counseling & Personnel Services; Curriculum Studies; Education Management / Administration; Educational Psychology; Languages & Linguistics; Library Science / Information Resources; Social Studies / Social Science; Teacher Education; Tests, Measurement & Evaluation; Urban Education, Cultural / Non-Traditional

MANUSCRIPT GUIDELINES/COMMENTS:

Aims and Scope
The *International Journal of Multiple Research Approaches* (*JRMA*) is an international peer-reviewed journal publishing research, educational and practitioner perspectives on multiple, hybrid (outcome of unusual blending), synergistic (combined effect), integrated and cultural approaches – be these indigenous, institutional, or community based. It provides global perspectives – including from the Asian, Pacific, Latin-American and African regions as well as Europe and North America – on methodological and theoretical advances, trends, adaptations and innovations of benefit to researchers, scholars, educators, students, practitioners, policy-makers and consultants.

The focus is on combining or synergising the various theoretical frameworks, methodologies and methods most appropriate for addressing research questions and achieving research aims and objectives. *JMRA* addresses the research interests of anthropology, criminology, cultural studies, economics, education, development studies, health care, Indigenous studies, management, marketing, political science, psychology, public health and social work, as well as those of social science academics and researchers. Its forum includes:

- Multiple, hybrid, synergistic, integrated, cultural, mixed qualitative and quantitative empirical research approaches
- Theoretical and conceptual articles on methodological and ethical dilemmas and advances
- Critical perspectives and proposals for the management of technical issues (eg, software development and data handling)
- Discussion of the philosophical issues, practical problems and benefits associated with multiple, hybrid, synergistic, integrated and cultural approaches including theoretical frameworks, methodologies, data collection, management and analytic methods and the different forms of transformation and representation
- Literature reviews – including those from theses – on methodological trends
- Articles on methodology education, technologies and learning techniques
- Practitioner perspectives, experiences from the field and case applications of methodologies and results

JMRA article formats include traditional academic research articles, research design, case applications, literature reviews, approaches to teaching and learning, software advances and constraints, practitioner perspectives and advice for novice researchers.

Original articles informing multiple and mixed methodological research and practice are encouraged from a range of disciplines – including all health sciences, social and political sciences, anthropology, criminology, psychology, Indigenous and cultural studies, business or development studies, education, organisational science, geography and history, the arts and related disciplines.

Articles within the aims and scope of the journal should be written for at least two of the discipline readerships, and should be prepared and submitted as an email attachment to **MRAeditorial@e-contentmanagement.com** according to the Style Guide below.

Contributions to *JMRA*
The *International Journal of Multiple Research Approaches* (*JMRA*) invites submission of original manuscripts within its Aims and Scope. Criteria for selection for publication include academic merit, individuality and integrity. Submissions should be concise, relevant and informative papers of interest to readers of the *Journal*.
JMRA's two issues per year offer contributors the advantages of:
- Timely double blind peer review and publication;
- High calibre global editorial board;
- Professional publishing services offering high circulation due to qualified marketing;
- A forum for discussion of philosophical issues, practical problems and benefits associated with multiple, hybrid, synergistic, integrated and cultural approaches including theoretical frameworks, methodologies, data collection, management and analytic methods and the different forms of transformation and representation;
- An avenue for discussion and dissemination of: Literature reviews – including those from theses – on methodological trends; Articles on methodology education, technologies and learning techniques; Practitioner perspectives, experiences from the field and case applications of methodologies and results.

Authors are generally restricted to one article per volume, unless multiple authorship is involved. Upon publication, the Publisher provides one copy of the issue in which the article appears to the Corresponding Author and a pdf of the published article to multiple authors. There are no monetary payments for contributors.

Submissions are requested directly to the *Journal* at **MRAeditorial@e-contentmanagement.com** in accordance with Author Guidelines stipulated below. Professor Carol Grbich, JMRA Editor-in-Chief, Flinders University Bedford Park 5042 Australia; Tel: +61 (0)8-8201 3271; Fax: +61 (0)8-8201 3646; Email: **carol.grbich@flinders.edu.au**

These notes are intended as a brief guide for contributors. The editorial team is most willing to provide additional help and encouragement. Please do not hesitate to make contact.

Article Submission
The manuscript may be a research note, theoretical/empirical research article, a literature review, with a focus on issues of research design, analysis or data presentation, case application or methodology education within the aims and scope of the journal and should be approximately –

- up to 4,000 words in length for a research note
- up to 6000 for an article
- or up to 8000 for a literature review
- all exclusive of References, Appendices, Tables and Figures. However, shorter or longer articles of exceptional quality may be accepted by the Editor.

Materials should be prepared as a Microsoft Word document and submitted electronically under as an email attachment to **MRAeditorial@e-contentmanagement.com** according to the following guidelines.

It is preferred that authors are consistent in whichever style they would normally use. They are advised to consult the Style Guide below and those needing direction should view the *Journal* website at **www.IJMRA.com** and APA Journal Guidelines (5th edn) at **http://www.vanguard. edu/faculty/ddegelman/index.aspx?doc_id=796**

eContent Management Pty Ltd uses a semi-automated manuscript tracking system to receive and review articles. Manuscripts submitted for publication are subject to a double blind peer review process. Please note that manuscripts that are inappropriately prepared may be returned to the author for revision prior to submission to the full review process.

To ensure prompt review of your manuscript, and to preserve anonymity during the review process, please observe the following steps:
- In the email message covering the manuscript attachment, please:
  o List title of manuscript; author name(s), affiliation(s) (in the order they are to appear), including all co-author postal & email address details for our records;
  o Indicate Corresponding Author for multiple author submissions;
  o Include any Acknowledgments;
  o Acknowledge acceptance of warranty and copyright conditions;
  o Under 'Properties' on 'Tools' pull-down menu, please select 'Options', 'Security' and then tick 'Remove personal information from file properties on save' before sending.
- If your article is for consideration for a selected special issue, please indicate which issue.
- There should be no information in the attached manuscript that could identify authors or institutions, such as coding with initials, except where appropriate as a citation.

Author Warranties
By submission of material to the *International Journal of Multiple Research Approaches*, all authors warrant that the material is their own, original material or that copyright clearance has been acquired to reproduce other material from employers, third parties or attributed to third parties, and that the material has not been previously published and is not under consideration for publication elsewhere.

It is the responsibility of authors to secure the release of any copyright material and to provide written evidence to this effect to eContent Management Pty Ltd. It is also the author's responsibility to obtain clearance for reproduction from the organisation which commissioned the work if applicable.

Submission of material to *JMRA* also implies all authors' consent to assignment of the material's copyright to eContent Management Pty Ltd when that material is accepted for publication in the journal, for the full legal term of copyright and any renewals thereof throughout the world in all formats and in any medium of communication (see Copyright below).

By submitting material to *JMRA*, all authors of the material agree to indemnify eContent Management Pty Ltd, and its heirs and assigns in business, against any litigation or claims that may arise from the content of or opinions in the material provided.

On acceptance for publication, an agreement specifying these terms will be sent to the corresponding author for signature by all authors of that manuscript. No printers proof will be sent to the author. The hard copy provided by the author on acceptance is the version used for typesetting. The publisher reserves the right to make editing corrections.

Copyright
Copyright of published articles is held by eContent Management Pty Ltd. No limitation will be placed on the personal freedom of authors to copy or to use in subsequent work, material contained in their papers. Please contact the Publisher for clarification if you are unsure of the use of copyright material. Apart from fair dealing for the purposes of research and private study, or criticism and/or review, as permitted under the Copyright Act 1968 of Australia, this publication may only be reproduced, stored or transmitted, in any form or by any means, with the prior permission in writing of the Publishers, or in the case of reprographic reproduction, in accordance with the terms of the licence issued by the Copyright Agency Limited, Level 19, 157 Liverpool Street, Sydney NSW 2000 Australia; Tel: +61 (0)2 9394 7600; Fax: +61 (0)2 9394 7601; info@copyright.com.au; www.copyright.com.au

International Journal of Private Education

SUBMISSION PROCESS:
Electronic Submission Only **via EMail** **ijphe@yahoo.com.cn** **ijphe@163.com**

CONTACT INFORMATION:	REVIEW PROCESS:	
Editors	**Type of Review:**	Blind Review
Phone: 0086-029-88751331	**No. External Reviewers:** **No. InHouse Reviewers:**	2 2
Email: ijphe@yahoo.com.cn ijphe@163.com ijphe@sohu.com	**Acceptance Rate:** **Time to Review:** **Reviewer's Comments:** **Invited Articles:**	60% 2 - 3 Months No 0-5%
Website: http://www.xaiu.com/xaiujournal	**Fees to Publish:** **Fees to Review:**	$0.00 US$ $10.00 US$

PUBLICATION GUIDELINES:	CIRCULATION DATA:
Manuscript Style: American Psychological Association	**Reader:** Academics, Administrators, Counselors
Manuscript Length: 16-20	**Frequency of Issue:** 2 Times/Year
Copies Required: Electronic Only	**Sponsor/Publisher:** Xi'an International University / Qifang Institute of Private Education Research

MANUSCRIPT TOPICS:

Adult Career & Vocational; Counseling & Personnel Services; Curriculum Studies; Education Management / Administration; Educational Psychology; Elementary / Early Childhood; Higher Education; Private & For-profit Higher Education; Rural Education & Small Schools; School Law; Teacher Education; Tests, Measurement & Evaluation; Urban Education, Cultural / Non-Traditional

MANUSCRIPT GUIDELINES/COMMENTS:

About the Journal

International Journal of Private Education is a scholarly, online journal hosted by the Qifang Private Education Research Institute of Xi'an International University (XAIU). China. The journal seeks to provide an interdisciplinary forum for the exchange of original and culturally diverse ideas promoting discussion and debate focused on private higher education. The editors welcome articles significant to the understanding and improvement of private higher educational practices, theory and policy. Submissions may take various forms such as case studies, policy analyses, reflections on dilemmas of practice, and reports or reviews of research.

Submissions

The *International Journal of Private Education* welcomes submissions year round. All manuscripts are considered for publication through a blind peer review process.

Preparation of the Manuscript

- Submissions must be written in English.
- References are to be made using the American Psychological Association (APA) style.
- Manuscripts should be written with 12 pt., double spaced type, with one inch margins on all sides.
- Manuscripts should not exceed 40 pages exclusive of references.
- All documents must be submitted in Microsoft Word.
- Keep charts and tables to a minimum. Tables should be submitted in Microsoft Word Table Format.
- The manuscript file should be free from any information identifying the author(s).
- Manuscripts should be clearly structured with introduction, background, methodology, results, conclusions, suggestions for further research and any other applicable sections helpful to the reader.

Abstract

The author is asked to include a short abstract comprised of a maximum of 100 words. Following the abstract, please list up to ten key words for use in indexing and searching.

Title Page

Each manuscript should be accompanied by a title page including the following information for each author. Full name Brief biographical information including institutional affiliations, research interests, level of education. Contact information Including an email address, telephone number, fax, conventional mail and URL (if applicable).

Submitting Documents

Submit each manuscript as an attachment to an email message addressed to **ijphe@163.com** or **ijphe@yahoo.com.cn**

International Journal of Sustainability in Higher Education

SUBMISSION PROCESS:	
Electronic Submission Preferred **via EMail** **leal@tutech.de**	
CONTACT INFORMATION:	**REVIEW PROCESS:**
Walter Leal Filho, Editor TuTech Innovation Hamburger, Schlossstrasse 6-10 D-21079 Hamburg, Germany	**Type of Review:** Blind Review **No. External Reviewers:** 2 **No. InHouse Reviewers:** 0
Phone: +49 40 766 18059 **Email:** leal@tutech.de **Website:** www.emeraldinsight.com/ijshe.htm	**Acceptance Rate:** 60% **Time to Review:** 2 - 3 Months **Reviewer's Comments:** Yes **Invited Articles:** 6-10% **Fees to Publish:** $0.00 US$ **Fees to Review:** $0.00 US$
PUBLICATION GUIDELINES:	**CIRCULATION DATA:**
Manuscript Style: See Manuscript Guidelines **Manuscript Length:** 3000-6000 words **Copies Required:** Electronic Only	**Reader:** Academics, Administrators, Practicing Teachers **Frequency of Issue:** Quarterly Online Only **Sponsor/Publisher:** Emerald Group Publishing Limited

MANUSCRIPT TOPICS:
Education Management / Administration; Higher Education; Science Math & Environment

MANUSCRIPT GUIDELINES/COMMENTS:

About the Journal
The *International Journal of Sustainability in Higher Education* is a fully-refereed academic journal. Published in conjunction with the Association of University Leaders for a Sustainable Future (ULSF), the journal aims at addressing environmental management systems (EMS), sustainable development and Agenda 21 issues at higher education institutions, worldwide. It intends to act as an outlet for papers dealing with curriculum greening and methodological approaches to sustainability. In addition, the journal will report on initiatives aimed at environmental improvements in universities, and the increased competitiveness of self-regulatory mechanisms such as environmental auditing and maintaining EMS. *IJSHE* disseminates case studies, projects and programmes whilst still considering the market opportunities available.

Author Guidelines
Authors should note that the *International Journal of Sustainability in Higher Education* is published electronically only.

Copyright

Articles submitted to the journal should be original contributions and should not be under consideration for any other publication at the same time. Authors submitting articles for publication warrant that the work is not an infringement of any existing copyright and will indemnify the publisher against any breach of such warranty. For ease of dissemination and to ensure proper policing of use, papers and contributions become the legal copyright of the publisher unless otherwise agreed.

For full details of Emerald's editorial policy on plagiarism please view the Plagiarism in depth information on the web site.

Submissions should be sent by email to: Professor Walter Leal Filho, **leal@tutech.de** or contact the Publisher at: Claire Jones, Emerald Group Publishing Limited, 60-62 Toller Lane, Bradford, West Yorkshire, BD8 9BY, UK; **cejones@emeraldinsight.com**

Editorial Scope

IJSHE publishes original papers in the field of sustainability, including environmental management systems, curriculum greening and operational aspects of environmental improvements at higher education institutions. The *Journal* shall publish state-of-the-art papers, that reflect new concepts, ideas and changes brought about by those engaged in pursuing sustainability and working in related disciplines.

In addition to papers and articles, book reviews, news items and features will be published. For submissions other those related to papers and articles, please contact the relevant editors to discuss the format of your submission. Letters to the editor will be published on approval by the editorial board.

The Reviewing Process

Each paper submitted is subject to the following review procedure. The editor will review the paper for general suitability for the journal. Subject to the exact reviewing criteria noted below, a double blind review process will be operated.

Due to the practical nature of articles submitted for inclusion in the Practice Briefing, contributions for this section will be considered by a member of the editorial board and one external referee.

The editorial board reserves the right to suspend the above criteria in the case of special issues, any such suspension of refereeing standards being duly noted at the time of publication.

Emerald Literati Editing Service

Emerald can recommend the services of a number of freelance copy editors, all themselves experienced authors, to contributors who wish to improve the standard of English in their paper before submission. This is particularly useful for those whose first language is not English. **www.emeraldinsight.com/editingservice**

Manuscript Requirements

One copy of the manuscript should be submitted by email in double line spacing with wide margins. All authors should be shown - authors details must be on the first page and the author should not be identified anywhere else in the article.

As a guide, articles should be between **3,000 and 6,000** words in length. A title of not more than eight words should be provided. A **brief autobiographical note** should be supplied including full name, affiliation, e-mail address and full international contact details. Authors must supply a **structured abstract** set out under 4-6 sub-headings: Purpose; Methodology/Approach; Findings; Research limitations/implications (if applicable); Practical implications (if applicable); and, the Originality/value of paper. Maximum is 250 words in total. In addition provide up to six keywords which encapsulate the principal topics of the paper and categorise your paper under one of these classifications: Research paper, Viewpoint, Technical paper, Conceptual paper, Case study, Literature review or General review. For more information and guidance on structured abstracts visit: **http://www.emeraldinsight.com/structuredabstracts**

Where there is a **methodology**, it should be clearly described under a separate heading. **Headings** must be short, clearly defined and not numbered. **Notes or Endnotes** should be used only if absolutely necessary and must be identified in the text by consecutive numbers, enclosed in square brackets and listed at the end of the article.

Figures, charts and diagrams should be kept to a minimum. They should be provided both electronically and as good quality originals. They must be black and white with minimum shading and numbered consecutively using Arabic numerals.

Artwork should be either copied or pasted from the origination software into a blank Microsoft Word document, or saved and imported into a blank Microsoft Word document. Artwork created in MS Powerpoint is also acceptable. Artwork may be submitted in the following standard image formats: .eps - Postscript, .pdf - Adobe Acrobat portable document, .ai - Adobe Acrobat portable document, .wmf - Windows Metafile. If it is not possible to supply graphics in the formats listed above, authors should ensure that figures supplied as .tif, .gif, .jpeg, .bmp, .pcx, .pic, .pct are supplied as files of at least 300 dpi and at least 10cm wide.

In the text the position of a figure should be shown by typing on a separate line the words "take in Figure 2". Authors should supply succinct captions.

For photographic images good quality original **photographs** should be submitted. If submitted electronically they should be saved as tif files of at least 300dpi and at least 10cm wide. Their position in the text should be shown by typing on a separate line the words "take in Plate 2".

Tables should be kept to a minimum. They must be numbered consecutively with roman numerals and a brief title. In the text, the position of the table should be shown by typing on a separate line the words "take in Table IV".

Photos and **illustrations** must be supplied as good quality black and white original half tones with captions. Their position should be shown in the text by typing on a separate line the words "take in Plate 2".

References to other publications should be complete and in Harvard style. They should contain full bibliographical details and journal titles should not be abbreviated. For multiple citations in the same year use a, b, c immediately following the year of publication. References should be shown within the text by giving the author's last name followed by a comma and year of publication all in round brackets, e.g. (Fox, 1994). At the end of the article should be a reference list in alphabetical order as follows

for books
surname, initials and year of publication, title, publisher, place of publication, e.g.Casson, M. (1979), Alternatives to the Multinational Enterprise, Macmillan, London.

for chapter in edited book
surname, initials and year, "title", editor's surname, initials, title,publisher, place, pages, e.g. Bessley, M. and Wilson, P. (1984), "Public policy and small firms in Britain", in Levicki, C. (Ed.), Small Business Theory and Policy, Croom Helm, London, pp.111-26. Please note that the chapter title must be underlined.

for articles
surname, initials, year "title", journal, volume, number, pages, e.g.Fox, S.(1994) "Empowerment as a catalyst for change: an example from the food industry", Supply Chain Management, Vol 2 No 3, pp. 29-33

If there is more than one author list surnames followed by initials. All authors should be shown.

Electronic sources should include the URL of the electronic site at which they may be found, as follows: Neuman, B.C.(1995), "Security, payment, and privacy for network commerce", IEEE Journal on Selected Areas in Communications, Vol. 13 No.8, October,pp.1523-31. Available (IEEE SEPTEMBER)

Notes/Endnotes should be used only if absolutely necessary. They should, however, always be used for citing Web sites. They should be identified in the text by consecutive numbers enclosed in square brackets and listed at the end of the article. Please then provide full Web site addresses in the end list.

Final Submission of the Article
Once accepted for publication, the final version of the manuscript must be provided, accompanied by a 3.5" disk of the same version labelled with: disk format; author name(s); title of article; journal title; file name.

Each article must be accompanied by a completed and signed Journal Article Record Form available from the Editor or on http://www.emeraldinsight.com/jarform Authors should note that proofs are not supplied prior to publication.

The manuscript will be considered to be the definitive version of the article. The author must ensure that it is complete, grammatically correct and without spelling or typographical errors.

In preparing the disk, please use one of the following preferred formats: Word, Word Perfect, Rich text format or TeX/LaTeX.

Technical assistance is available by contacting Mike Massey at Emerald, e-mail **mmassey@emeraldinsight.com**.

A summary of submission requirements:
• Good quality hard copy manuscript
• A labelled disk
• A brief professional biography of each author
• An abstract and keywords
• Figures, photos and graphics electronically and as good quality originals
• Harvard style references where appropriate
• A completed Journal Article Record form

International Journal of Testing

SUBMISSION PROCESS:

**Electronic Submission Preferred
via EMail**

ijt@auckland.ac.nz

CONTACT INFORMATION:	REVIEW PROCESS:
John Hattie, Editor Faculty of Education University of Auckland PO Box 92019 Auckland, New Zealand **Phone:** 64 9 373 7599 ext. 82496 **Email:** ijt@auckland.ac.nz **Website:** www.leaonline.com/loi/ijt	**Type of Review:** Blind Review **No. External Reviewers:** 2 **No. InHouse Reviewers:** 0 **Acceptance Rate:** 11-20% **Time to Review:** 4 - 6 Months **Reviewer's Comments:** Yes **Invited Articles:** 11-20% **Fees to Publish:** $0.00 US$ **Fees to Review:** $0.00 US$

PUBLICATION GUIDELINES:	CIRCULATION DATA:
Manuscript Style: American Psychological Association **Manuscript Length:** 26-30 **Copies Required:** One	**Reader:** Academics **Frequency of Issue:** Quarterly **Sponsor/Publisher:** International Testing Commission / Lawrence Erlbaum Associates, Inc.

MANUSCRIPT TOPICS:
Counseling & Personnel Services; Educational Psychology; Tests, Measurement & Evaluation

MANUSCRIPT GUIDELINES/COMMENTS:

Statement of Purpose
The International Journal of Testing (IJT) is dedicated to the advancement of theory, research, and practice in the area of testing and assessment in psychology, education, counseling, organizational behavior, human resource management, and related disciplines. *IJT* publishes original articles addressing theoretical issues, methodological approaches, and empirical research as well as integrative interdisciplinary reviews of testing-related topics and reports of current testing practices.

Examples of topics appropriate for *IJT* include:
a. new perspectives in test development and validation;
b. issues concerning the qualification and training of test users and test developers;
c. recent trends in testing and measurement arising in a particular field or discipline;
d. comparisons of national/regional differences in test practices;
e. methods and procedures in adapting tests for use in new languages or cultural groups;

f.   international assessment projects or other international studies in which testing constitutes an essential element;

g.   testing culturally and/or linguistically heterogeneous populations; and

h.   internationalization of testing (e.g., personnel selection for global organizations, Internet applications, and international copyrights of tests and test adaptations).

It is important when submitting articles to *IJT* to consider the messages for international readers; to place the context of the study into an international perspective; to indicate ways that assessment or testing ideas can be adapted or generalised across borders; to focus more on the construct than on the method when discussing validation studies; to discuss applications that have universal messages; to relate to ITC guidelines for adaptation; or to discuss equitable assessment practices that transcend borders or demonstrate uniqueness within a country. Another consideration could be to include a wide profile of authors across countries. Most important is to ensure quality of the ideas and their appeal to international readers of testing issues.

In addition to regular articles, short communications of topics relevant to an international audience will be considered for publication in *IJT*. Substantive comments on articles previously published in *IJT* will also be considered and the authors of the original articles will have an opportunity to reply. Announcements of activities (e.g., conferences, symposia, and training workshops) in the area of testing and measurement are welcomed. Reviews of books and software relevant to testing and measurement as well as reviews of widely used tests are welcome. Reviews should be descriptive and evaluative; comparative reviews are encouraged.

Audience
Scholars, professionals, and graduate students interested in test development and test use. Practitioners conducting assessments in human behavior in psychology, education, counseling, organizational behavior, personnel selection, human resource management, and related disciplines.

Manuscript Preparation
Manuscripts must be prepared according to the *Publication Manual of the American Psychological Association* (5th ed.). On the first page, indicate the full title of the article, a running head (less than 50 characters), the word count of the manuscript, submission date, and the author(s) name(s), affiliations(s), and complete mailing address(es). The second page of the manuscript should omit the authors' names and affiliations but should include the title of the manuscript, running head, and submission date. Every effort should be made by authors to see that the manuscript itself contains no clues to their identities.

Manuscripts must be prefaced by an abstract of 100-150 words, as well as a maximum of six key words. All manuscript pages, including references lists and tables, must be typed double-spaced. Pages must be numbered consecutively. Define acronyms and abbreviations used in the manuscript when first mentioned. Place each figure and table on a separate page. All figures must be camera-ready. Authors should comply with "Guidelines to Reduce Bias in Language" as printed in the *Publication Manual*. Manuscripts that fail to conform to APA-style guidelines will be returned to the author(s). MSWord files are preferred. If English is not the first language of the authors, the editorial team would be pleased to assist with matters of style.

Manuscript Submission
Electronic submission is preferred. Please refer to **www.leaonline.com/loi/ijt** for more information.

Permissions
All manuscripts submitted must contain material that has not been published and is not being considered elsewhere. Authors are responsible for all statements made in their work; for obtaining consent to use tests, other instruments, and datasets used in the research; and for obtaining permission from copyright owners for reprinting or adapting tables or figures, or for reprinting a quotation of more than 500 words. Copies of all permissions must be provided prior to publication. Figures must be provided in camera-ready form.

476

Production Notes

After a manuscript has been accepted for publication, authors will be requested to send to the Editor: (a) an electronic file of the final version of the manuscript; (b) the signed publication and copyright transfer agreement form; and (c) figures in camera-ready form. Copy-edited page proofs will be sent to the authors for review and correction before publication.

International Journal of the Arts in Society

SUBMISSION PROCESS:
Electronic Submission Only **via Online Portal**
http://www.Arts-Journal.com

CONTACT INFORMATION:	REVIEW PROCESS:	
Mary Kalantzis & Bill Cope, Editors University of Illinois, Urbana-Champaign	**Type of Review:**	Blind Review
	No. External Reviewers:	2
Phone:	**No. InHouse Reviewers:**	1
	Acceptance Rate:	50%
Email:	**Time to Review:**	1 - 2 Months
	Reviewer's Comments:	Yes
	Invited Articles:	0-5%
Website:		
http://www.Arts-Journal.com	**Fees to Publish:**	$0.00 US$
	Fees to Review:	$0.00 US$

PUBLICATION GUIDELINES:	CIRCULATION DATA:

Manuscript Style:
    See Manuscript Guidelines
	Reader:
	    Academics, Practicing Teachers

Manuscript Length:
    6-20
	Frequency of Issue:
	    6-8 Times/Year

Copies Required:
    Electronic Only
	Sponsor/Publisher:
	    The University Press, an imprint of
	Common Ground Publishing

MANUSCRIPT TOPICS:
Art / Music

MANUSCRIPT GUIDELINES/COMMENTS:

About the Journal
The *International Journal of the Arts in Society* aims to create an intellectual frame of reference for the arts and arts practices, and to create an interdisciplinary conversation on the role of the arts in society. It is intended as a place for critical engagement, examination, and experimentation of ideas that connect the arts to their contexts in the world, on stage, in museums and galleries, on the streets, and in communities.

The journal is responding to trends in international arts festivals and biennales, indicating the need for critical discussion on issues in the arts, and specifically as they are situated in the present-day contexts of globalisation, and its social, economic and political artefacts of cultural homogenisation, commodification and militarisation.

Papers published in the journal will range from the expansive and philosophical to finely grained analysis based on deep familiarity and understanding of a particular area of arts knowledge or arts practice. They bring into the dialogue artists, theorists, policymakers, arts educators, and their overlapping roles.

The journal is relevant for artists, curators, writers, theorists and policymakers with an interest in, and a concern for, arts practice, arts theory and research, curatorial and museum studies, and arts education in any of its forms and in any of its sites.

Submission Guidelines
View: **http://ija.cgpublisher.com/submission_guidelines.html**

About the Submission Process
Registration in the Arts Conference gives participants the opportunity to publish in an academic journal. Presenters have the option to submit their papers to the International Journal of the Arts in Society anytime before the conference and up to one month after the conference. Papers submitted for publication will be fully refereed. The publication decision is based on the referees' reports.

To submit, at least one author of each paper must be registered to attend the conference (to a maximum of one paper per registered author—which means, for instance, that two registered authors may submit two jointly authored papers). For those unable to attend the conference in person, virtual registrations are available.

All registered participants will be given online access to all papers published by the journal from the time of registration until one year after the end date of the conference.

Papers are published continuously to the journal's online bookstore, as soon as the publication process is completed for each paper (and that can be any time before the conference, and continues after the conference as papers are refereed).

It is possible to attend and present at the conference without submitting or publishing a formal written paper if you choose not to do so.

Author Guidelines—Preparing Your Paper
Formatting Requirements
- We require presenters to use our CGCreator Microsoft Word Template which can be downloaded.
- We are not able to accept papers that have not used the template.
- Papers should be approximately 2,000-5,000 words in length. They should be written as continuous expository narrative in a chapter or article style - not as lists of points or a PowerPoint presentation.
- Please remember that the papers are to be published in a fully refereed academic journal. This means that the style and structure of your text should be relatively formal. For instance, you should not submit a verbatim transcript of your oral presentation, such as 'Today I want to speak to you about ...'.
- Authors are responsible for the accuracy of citations, quotations, diagrams, tables and maps.
- You may use any referencing style you choose, as long as you use it consistently and to the appropriate standards.
- Spelling can vary according to national usage, but should be internally consistent.
- Papers should be thoroughly checked and proof-read before submission, both by the author and a critical editorial friend – after you have submitted your paper you are unable to make any changes to it during the refereeing process.
- Papers will be assessed by referees against ten criteria - or fewer if some criteria do not apply to a particular kind of paper (see the Peer Review Process).

Illustration/Electronic Artwork Guidelines
- Figures and images must be clear and easy to view. We cannot improve the quality of images.
- Figures and tables need to be placed where they are to appear in the text. If preferred, you can also place images and tables at the end of your paper.

- Please refrain from using Word Drawing objects. Instead use images imported from a drawing program. Word Drawing objects will not be rendered in the typeset version.

Keyword Guidelines

Keywords are extremely important in search engine rankings. To achieve better exposure for your paper, please make sure your keywords are clear and accurate.

Resubmission Policy

If your paper has been rejected we will allow a maximum of TWO further resubmissions until TWO months prior to the anticipated publication date.

Editorial Quality

The refereeing process for publication in the journal is a rigorous measure of the quality of content. Authors are expected to revise to the standards required of the more negative of the referee reports they receive. For instance, if one referee recommends 'resubmit with major revisions' and another 'resubmit with minor revisions', the author is expected to resubmit with major revisions.

Furthermore, some papers may have excellent content, but may be poorly expressed in English—in the case, for instance, of authors whose first language is not English. When we receive a negative response from a referee to Criterion 10, 'Quality of Communication', we may request a complete rewrite regardless of the overall score.

The Submission Process—How and Where to Submit Your Paper for Publication

Final papers can now be submitted to Common Ground using our online conference and paper management system "CGPublisher".

The Publication Process

The publication process is as follows:

- Submit a presentation proposal to the conference (in-person or virtual) before the next deadline.
- If your proposal is accepted by the conference advisory team, complete your registration for an in-person or virtual presentation. You may submit your paper to the journal anytime between registration and one calendar month after the closing date of the conference.
- Once your paper is received, it is verified against template and submission requirements. Your identity and contact details are then removed and the paper is matched to two appropriate referees and sent for review. You can view the status of your paper at any time by logging into your CGPublisher account at www.CGPublisher.
- When referee reports are uploaded, you will be notified by email and provided with a link to view the reports (after the referees' identities have been removed).
- You will then be asked to accept the Publishing Agreement and submit a revised final copy of your paper.
- Your paper will be typeset and the proofs sent to you for final approval before publication.
- Papers are published continuously in the online bookstore. Registered conference participants will be given online access to the journal from the time of registration until one year after the conference end date. Individual papers will also be available for purchase from the journal's bookstore.

International Journal of Urban Educational Leadership

SUBMISSION PROCESS: **Electronic Submission Only** **via EMail** **james.koschoreck@uc.edu**	

CONTACT INFORMATION:	REVIEW PROCESS:	
James W. Koschoreck, Editor University of Cincinnati	**Type of Review:**	Blind Review
	No. External Reviewers:	3
Phone: 513-556-6622	**No. InHouse Reviewers:**	1
	Acceptance Rate:	80%
Email: james.koschoreck@uc.edu	**Time to Review:**	4 - 6 Months
	Reviewer's Comments:	Yes
Website:	**Invited Articles:**	0-5%
http://www.uc.edu/urbanleadership/journal.htm	**Fees to Publish:**	$0.00 US$
	Fees to Review:	$0.00 US$

PUBLICATION GUIDELINES:	CIRCULATION DATA:
Manuscript Style: American Psychological Association	**Reader:** Academics, Administrators
Manuscript Length: 21-25	**Frequency of Issue:** Yearly
Copies Required: Electronic Only	**Sponsor/Publisher:** University Council for Educational Administration / University of Cincinnati

MANUSCRIPT TOPICS:
Education Management / Administration; Urban Education, Cultural / Non-Traditional

MANUSCRIPT GUIDELINES/COMMENTS:

Editorial Statement
The aim of the *Journal* is to provide an academic forum in which to discuss issues and concerns of educational leadership as they relate to urban environments. The *International Journal of Urban Educational Leadership* (*IJUEL*) publishes research from a multiplicity of epistemological perspectives and seeks to enhance rather than limit our knowledge of the field. Given its electronic format, *IJUEL* encourages alternative, innovative approaches to representation as well as traditional scholarly manuscripts. Our mission is to explore through various modes of inquiry and discourse the complexities of urban educational leadership around the world.

Notes for Contributors
The *International Journal of Urban Educational Leadership* is a peer-reviewed electronic journal. We invite the submission of manuscripts and other multimedia representations of inquiry that contribute to the knowledge base of urban educational leadership issues.

Documents submitted for publication should be sent via electronic mail as an attachment to the Editor of the *Journal* at **james.koschoreck@uc.edu**. Accompanying information within the text of the email should include the authors name, affiliated institution, and telephone number(s). Contributing authors should also include a brief (50-75 words) biographical sketch.

All references to the author should be omitted from the document in order to ensure anonymity in the review process. Traditional manuscripts should follow the form and style set forth in the *American Psychological Association Publication Manual* (5th edition), including a 100 word abstract. Manuscripts should normally be between 5,000 and 7,000 words, excluding references.

Manuscripts and other documents submitted for inclusion in the *International Journal of Urban Educational Leadership* should not concurrently be under consideration by any other journal.

Authors are expected to grant copyright to the *International Journal of Urban Educational Leadership*. Once the document has been published electronically by *IJUEL*, however, the author may request permission from the Editor of the *Journal* to use the work elsewhere.

The submission of manuscripts from outside the United States is encouraged.

SUBMISSION PROCESS: **Electronic Submission Only** **via EMail** **pubs@aace.org**	
CONTACT INFORMATION: Gary Marks, Editor AACE PO Box 3728 Norfolk, VA 23514-3728 USA **Phone:** 757-623-7588 **Email:** pubs@aace.org **Website:** www.aace.org	**REVIEW PROCESS:** **Type of Review:** Blind Review **No. External Reviewers:** 2-4 **No. InHouse Reviewers:** 2 **Acceptance Rate:** 11-20% **Time to Review:** 2-4 Months **Reviewer's Comments:** Yes **Invited Articles:** 15-25% **Fees to Publish:** $0.00 US$ **Fees to Review:** $0.00 US$
PUBLICATION GUIDELINES: **Manuscript Style:** American Psychological Association **Manuscript Length:** 30 pgs max **Copies Required:** Electronic Only	**CIRCULATION DATA:** **Reader:** Academics **Frequency of Issue:** Quarterly **Sponsor/Publisher:** Association For the Advancement of Computing in Education (AACE)

MANUSCRIPT TOPICS:
Distance Education; Educational Technology Systems; Higher Education; Knowledge Management; On-line Learning; Science Math & Environment

MANUSCRIPT GUIDELINES/COMMENTS:

Advances in technology and the growth of e-learning to provide educators and trainers with unique opportunities to enhance learning and teaching in corporate, government, healthcare, and higher education. *IJEL* serves as a forum to facilitate the international exchange of information on the current research, development, and practice of e-learning in these sectors.

Led by an Editorial Review Board of leaders in the field of e-Learning, the *Journal* is designed for the following audiences: researchers, developers, and practitioners in corporate, government, healthcare, and higher education. *IJEL* is a peer-reviewed journal.

For complete author guidelines please visit: **http://www.aace.org**

International Migration Review

SUBMISSION PROCESS:
Postal Submission Only

CONTACT INFORMATION:	REVIEW PROCESS:	
Editor Center for Migration Studies 27 Carmine Street New York, NY 10014 USA	**Type of Review:**	Blind Review
	No. External Reviewers:	3
	No. InHouse Reviewers:	2
Phone:	**Acceptance Rate:**	11-20%
	Time to Review:	2 - 3 Months
	Reviewer's Comments:	Yes
Email: imr@cmsny.org	**Invited Articles:**	0-5%
	Fees to Publish:	$0.00 US$
Website: www.cmsny.org	**Fees to Review:**	$0.00 US$

PUBLICATION GUIDELINES:	CIRCULATION DATA:
Manuscript Style: See Manuscript Guidelines	**Reader:** Academics
Manuscript Length: 26-30	**Frequency of Issue:** Quarterly
Copies Required: Four	**Sponsor/Publisher:** Center for Migration Studies

MANUSCRIPT TOPICS:
Immigration and Refugee Studies; Social Studies / Social Science

MANUSCRIPT GUIDELINES/COMMENTS:

Editorial Procedure. In order to provide impartiality in the selection of manuscripts for publication, all papers deemed appropriate for *IMR* are sent out anonymously to readers. To protect anonymity, the author's name and affiliation should appear only on a separate cover page. *IMR* has the right to first publication of all submitted manuscripts. Manuscripts submitted to *IMR* cannot be submitted simultaneously to another publication. Submission of a manuscript to *IMR* is taken to indicate the author's commitment to publish in this *Review*. No paper known to be under jurisdiction by any other journal will be reviewed by *IMR*. Authors are not paid for accepted manuscripts. If manuscripts are accepted and published, all rights, including subsidiary rights, are owned by the Center for Migration Studies. The author retains the right to use his/her article without charge in any book of which he/she is the author or editor after it has appeared in the *Review*.

Preparation and Submission of Copy. *IMR* is moving to electronic processing of manuscripts, book reviews and related materials. Submissions, correspondence, revisions, etc. should be made, whenever possible, by electronic exchanges over the Internet.

1. Type all copy – including indented matter, footnotes, and references – double-spaced.

2. Save each table in a separate file. Insert a location note. e.g., "Table 2 about here," at the appropriate place in the text. Tables should not contain lines or more than 20 two-digit columns or the equivalent.

3. Type footnotes (double-spaced) on separate sheets. Footnotes should include grant numbers or credits but not author's affiliation.

4. Include an abstract of not more than 100 words summarizing the findings of the paper.

5. One copy of the manuscript is required and should be addressed to: Editor, International Review, Center for Migration Studies, 27 Carmine Street, New York, NY 10014. fax (212)255-1771, e-mail **imr@cmsny.org**. Manuscripts are not returned to authors. Electronic version of the manuscript (e.g. Word file) should be e-mailed to: **imr@cmsny.org**.

6. Original copies of figures are acceptable on disk as EPS files (Encapsuled PostScript File) or TIFF files (Tag Image File Format) that have been created in graphics programs such as "Adobe Illustrator" or "Aldus Free Hand"; if artworks is not available in the above formats, a PDF file (Portable Document Format) or a laser proof are acceptable; however, spreadsheets containing data from which figures are drawn are preferred (see No. 7)

7. We can read files created in most standard word processing packages; however, if you have any questions, please call (212)337-3080. Tables prepared in word processors should be exported to (saved as) ASCII, comma-delimited files. Tables can also be created in Excel. All disks should be either IBM-compatible or high-density Macintosh.

Format of References in Text. All references to monographs, articles, and statistical sources are to be identified at an appropriate point in the text by last name of author, year of publication, and pagination where appropriate, all within parentheses. Footnotes are to be used only for substantive observations. Specify subsequent citations of the same source in the same way as the first one; do not use *ibid., op cit.*, or *loc cit.*
1. When author's name is in the text: Duncan (1969). When author's name is not in the text: (Gouldner 1963).

2. Pagination follows year of publication: (Lipset, 1964:61-64).

3. For more than three authors, use *et al.* For institutional authorship, supply minimum identification from the beginning of the complete citation: (U.S. Bureau of the Census, 1963:117).

4. With more than one reference to an author in the same year, distinguish them by use of letters (*a.b*) attached to year of publication: (Levy, 1965*a*:311)

5. Enclose a series of references within a single pair of parentheses, separated by semicolon: (Johnson, 1942; Perry, 1947; Linguist, 1984).

Form of References in Appendix. List all items alphabetically by author and, within author(s), by year of publication beginning with the most recent year, in an appendix titled, "REFERENCES". For multiple author or editor listings (more than two), give authors. Use italics for titles of books and journals. For example, see text of articles published in the *Review*.

International Review of Education

SUBMISSION PROCESS:
Electronic Submission Only Hans.vanSintmaartensdijk@springer.com http://www.editorialmanager.com/revi/

CONTACT INFORMATION:	REVIEW PROCESS:	
Christopher McIntosh, Editor UNESCO Institute for Lifelong Learning Feldbrunnenstrasse 58, 201 Germany	**Type of Review:**	Blind Review
	No. External Reviewers:	2
	No. InHouse Reviewers:	0
Phone: +49-40 4480 4121	**Acceptance Rate:**	11-20%
	Time to Review:	1-6+ Months
	Reviewer's Comments:	Yes
Email: c.mcintosh@unesco.org	**Invited Articles:**	21-30%
Website: www.unesco.org/education/uie	**Fees to Publish:**	$0.00 US$
	Fees to Review:	$0.00 US$

PUBLICATION GUIDELINES:	CIRCULATION DATA:
Manuscript Style: See Manuscript Guidelines	**Reader:** Academics, Policy-Makers
Manuscript Length: 16-25	**Frequency of Issue:** 6 Times/Year
Copies Required: Electronic Only	**Sponsor/Publisher:** Springer

MANUSCRIPT TOPICS:
Adult Career & Vocational; Education Management / Administration; Educational Technology Systems; Elementary / Early Childhood; Foreign Language; Library Science / Information Resources; Rural Education & Small Schools; Teacher Education; Tests, Measurement & Evaluation; Urban Education, Cultural / Non-Traditional

MANUSCRIPT GUIDELINES/COMMENTS:

Description
... The longest running international journal on the comparative theory and practice of formal and non-formal education ...

The *International Review of Education*, first published in its present form in 1955, is the longest-running international journal for the comparative theory and practice of formal and non-formal education. The *Review* serves the needs of departments and institutes of education, teacher-training institutions, educational policy-makers and planners, and other professionals throughout the world by providing scholarly information on major educational innovations, research projects and trends in countries at all stages of development. The journal is currently in an exciting phase of its own growth. While maintaining its broad scope and academic rigour, it now addresses matters of education and learning throughout the whole of life.

Edited by the UNESCO Institute for Lifelong Learning, Hamburg, with the advice of an international Editorial Board and additional academic evaluators, each volume usually includes general issues containing essays and notes on a wide variety of educational topics, together with book reviews, and special issues, guest-edited by distinguished educationists, with contents devoted to themes of particularly contemporary relevance. Contributions are published in English, French or German, preceded by abstracts in all three languages as well as Spanish and Russian.

INSTRUCTIONS FOR AUTHORS
Online Manuscript Submission
Springer now offers authors, editors and reviewers of *International Review of Education* the option of using our fully web-enabled online manuscript submission and review system. To keep the review time as short as possible (no postal delays!), we encourage authors to submit manuscripts online to the journal's editorial office. Our online manuscript submission and review system offers authors the option to track the progress of the review process of manuscripts in real time. Manuscripts should be submitted to: **http://revi.edmgr.com**.

The online manuscript submission and review system for *International Review of Education* offers easy and straightforward log-in and submission procedures. This system supports a wide range of submission file formats: for manuscripts - Word, WordPerfect, RTF, TXT and LaTex; for figures - TIFF, GIF, JPEG, EPS, PPT, and Postscript.

NOTE: By using the online manuscript submission and review system, it is NOT necessary to submit the manuscript also in printout + disk.

In case you encounter any difficulties while submitting your manuscript on line, please get in touch with the responsible Editorial Assistant by clicking on "CONTACT US" from the tool bar.

The copyright for any submission published in the *International Review of Education* is owned by Springer.

Permission to reprint is normally granted, provided that credit, including details as to volume and issue of the journal in which the original appeared, is given. No honorarium is paid to contributors.

Rejected material is not normally returned. If the author wishes to have his submission returned, he should specify that this is the case and accompany it with an International Postal Order to cover postage.

Electronic figures. Electronic versions of your figures must be supplied. For vector graphics, EPS is the preferred format. For bitmapped graphics, TIFF is the preferred format. The following resolutions are optimal: line figures - 600 - 1200 dpi; photographs - 300 dpi; screen dumps - leave as is. Colour figures can be submitted in the RGB colour system. Font-related problems can be avoided by using standard fonts such as Times Roman, Courier and Helvetica.

Colour figures. Springer offers two options for reproducing colour illustrations in your article. Please let us know what you prefer: 1) Free online colour. The colour figure will only appear in colour on www.springer.com and not in the printed version of the journal. 2) Online and printed colour. The colour figures will appear in colour on our website and in the printed version of the journal. The charges are EUR 950/USD 1150 per article.

Language. We appreciate any efforts that you make to ensure that the language is corrected before submission. This will greatly improve the legibility of your paper if English is not your first language.

The copyright for any submission published in the *International Review of Education* is owned by Springer.

Permission to reprint is normally granted, provided that credit, including details as to volume and issue of the journal in which the original appeared, is given. No honorarium is paid to contributors.

Rejected material is not normally returned. If the author wishes to have his submission returned, he should specify that this is the case and accompany it with an International Postal Order to cover postage.

Character of Publications

The *International Review of Education* publishes original essays, studies and reports of research in the areas of comparative and international education, including lifelong learning, as well as more general discussions of educational theory and practice of interest to a worldwide readership.

Usually only original contributions are welcomed, although in exceptional cases essays that have previously been published in journals with a purely national circulation may be accepted.

Contributions are published in English, French or German. The Editorial Office is prepared to consider submissions in other languages on condition that a short summary in one of the above three languages is attached. In the case of the acceptance of such a work, the author must arrange for its competent translation.

Three types of contributions are accepted: essays and studies, notes and book reviews. Essays and studies consist of a well-rounded discussion of a topic chosen for its international significance. They should normally not exceed 6,000 words in length (10–20 pages, 12–point type, double-spaced). Notes are short, descriptive accounts of educational innovations, research results etc. Their length should normally not exceed 2,000 words (approximately 8 double-spaced pages). See the guidelines for book reviews at the end of these instructions.

Presentation of the Manuscript

All submissions should be grammatically correct and stylistically consistent in a manner reflecting the propriety and facility of a native speaker of the language in which they are composed. They should be submitted both on paper (in four copies) and on diskette (preferably in Word or WordPerfect). The text should be double-spaced throughout with wide margins on both sides and the pages numbered consecutively. The author should retain an exact copy of the material submitted so that if questions arise the Editorial Office can refer to specific pages, paragraphs or lines for clarification. Inadequately prepared texts may be returned without comment.

All material should be arranged in the following order except as otherwise noted:

Title Page (page 1)

The title should be as short as possible and capitalized. A subtitle may be used if necessary to supply greater information on the contents. The authors full name should be given below the title.

Abstract and/or Key Words (page 2)

If the submission is an essay, it must be accompanied by an abstract: a short summary (approx. 150 words) typed double-spaced on a separate sheet. Both essays and notes should be attended by a list of five key words defining the content of the text. These will help in its evaluation. In the case of acceptance the abstract will be translated by the Editorial Office into the four other languages for inclusion at the beginning of the essay.

Biographical Note (page 3)

If the submission is an essay or study, a brief biographical note of some 5–8 typewritten lines should also be included. It should give: full name, major professional qualifications, relevant past positions and present position (with dates), main field(s) of research. It must also include the authors full address and, if available, email address.

Main Text

- The title of the essay or note should appear once more at the beginning of the main text. The authors name should not appear.
- The main text should be prepared for blind review. There should be no references identifying the author in any way at all.
- The relative importance of headings and subheadings in essays should be clear.

Use of the term Introduction should be avoided. Four types of heading can be used:
- Main Heading (H1) bold.
- Second-order Heading (H2) italicized, with extra spacing above and below.
- Third-order Heading (H3) italicized, with extra spacing above and no spacing below.
- Fourth-order Heading (H4) italicized, ending with a full stop and with text following on the same line.
- The approximate location of figures and tables should be indicated in the text.
- New paragraphs should be indicated by clear indentation.
- Quoted passages longer than 3 lines should be indented throughout.
- The use of endnotes should be avoided; footnotes are not acceptable. However, if essential, endnotes should be designated by superscript numbers consecutively throughout the manuscript and placed in Notes after the main text. The endnote function of the word-processing system must be employed for this purpose.
- Italicization. Single foreign words and phrases are italicized, although authors are requested to substitute the native term for the foreign one whenever possible. A definition of the foreign term should be supplied the first time it is used.
- No other formatting should be employed.

Following the main text

- Notes (if any) should be listed in numerical order and placed after the main text.
- Appendix (if any) should follow the Notes.

Figures

All photographs, graphs and diagrams should be referred to as a 'Figure' and they should be numbered consecutively (1, 2, etc.). Multi-part figures ought to be labelled with lower case letters (a, b, etc.). Please insert keys and scale bars directly in the figures. Relatively small text and great variation in text sizes within figures should be avoided as figures are often reduced in size. Figures may be sized to fit approximately within the column(s) of the journal. Provide a detailed legend (without abbreviations) to each figure, refer to the figure in the text and note its approximate location in the margin. Please place the legends in the manuscript after the references.

Tables

Each table should be numbered consecutively (1, 2, etc.). In tables, footnotes are preferable to long explanatory material in either the heading or body of the table. Such explanatory footnotes, identified by superscript letters, should be placed immediately below the table. Please provide a caption (without abbreviations) to each table, refer to the table in the text and note its approximate location in the margin. Finally, please place the tables after the figure legends in the manuscript.

References

The References should be arranged alphabetically. They should be typed double-spaced and given in the text as: author and year of publication, for example: (Wilson 1966; Olsen 1966a, b; Stodolsky and Lesser 1993: 580). For the list of References follow the style shown below:

Essays in journals
Roberts, Peter. 1999. The Future of the University. International Review of Education 45(1): 65−85. Forrester, Keith, Nick Frost, and Keven Ward. 2000. Researching Work and Learning: A Birds Eye View. International Review of Education 46(6): 483−489.

Books
Bernardo, Allan B. I. 1998. Literacy and the Mind. The Contexts and Cognitive Consequences of Literacy Practice. Hamburg: UNESCO Institute for Education. Hill, Dave, and Mike Cole (eds.). 2001. Schooling and Equality. Fact, Concept and Policy. London: Kogan Page.

Essays in books
Jewett, Alfred E. 1987. Participant Purposes for Engaging in Physical Activity. In: Myths, Models, and Methods in Sport Pedagogy, ed. by George T. Barrette, 87−100. Champaign, IL: Human Kinetics. Dunn, Judy, and Jane Brown. 1991. Becoming American or English? Talking about the Social World in England and the United States. In: Cultural Approaches to Parenting, ed. by Marc H. Bornstein, 155−172. Hillsdale, NJ: Lawrence Erlbaum Associates.

Websites should be cited as follows
http://www.unesco.org/education/uie/publications/uiestud8 shtml, accessed August 4, 2004.

Note that first names of authors must be included along with date and place of publication and publisher for books as well as the pagination of the essay and the full name of the editor for anthologies. Titles, including those of journals, should not be abbreviated; subtitles should be included. All other cases should be treated in accordance with these examples. If there is both a list of Notes and a list of References, all bibliographical details should be included in the References and not repeated in the Notes.

Book reviews
The same rules of style and presentation apply to book reviews. Each review should be headed by the details of the book, as follows:

NASH, GARY B. 1997. History on Trial. New York: Alfred A. Knopf. 318 pp. ISBN 0−679−44687−7. Where two or more books are reviewed together the review can be commensurately longer. In length, book reviews should not exceed 800 words.

Book reviews can be in English, French or German. The books reviewed are normally in one of those languages, but books in other languages can also be considered for review on a case-by-case basis.

Offprints
Authors of essays, studies and notes will receive 50 complimentary offprints of their publication in addition to a copy of the issue of the journal in which their contribution is published. Authors of book reviews will receive a complimentary copy of the issue in which their review appears.

Springer Open Choice
In addition to the normal publication process (whereby an article is submitted to the journal and access to that article is granted to customers who have purchased a subscription), Springer now provides an alternative publishing option: Springer Open Choice. A Springer Open Choice article receives all the benefits of a regular subscription-based article, but in addition is made available publicly through Springer's online platform SpringerLink. To publish via Springer Open Choice, upon acceptance please click on the link below to complete the relevant order form and provide the required payment information. Payment must be received in full before publication or articles will publish as regular subscription-model articles. We regret that Springer Open Choice cannot be ordered for published articles.

Journal for Specialists in Group Work

<table>
<tr><td colspan="2" align="center">SUBMISSION PROCESS:

Postal Submission Only</td></tr>
<tr>
<td>
CONTACT INFORMATION:

Donald E. Ward, Editor
Pittsburg State University
Department of Psychology and Counseling
Pittsburg, KS 66762 USA

Phone:
620-235-4530

Email:
dward@pittstate.edu

Website:
http://asgw.org/jsgw/jsgw.htm
</td>
<td>
REVIEW PROCESS:

Type of Review: Blind Review

No. External Reviewers: 3
No. InHouse Reviewers: 1

Acceptance Rate: 53%
Time to Review: 2 - 3 Months
Reviewer's Comments: Yes
Invited Articles: 0-5%

Fees to Publish: $0.00 US$
Fees to Review: $0.00 US$
</td>
</tr>
<tr>
<td>
PUBLICATION GUIDELINES:

Manuscript Style:
American Psychological Association

Manuscript Length:
16-30

Copies Required:
One After Acceptance
</td>
<td>
CIRCULATION DATA:

Reader:
Academics, Group Practitioners

Frequency of Issue:
Quarterly

Sponsor/Publisher:
Association for Specialists in Group Work / Taylor & Francis, Ltd.
</td>
</tr>
</table>

MANUSCRIPT TOPICS:
Adult Career & Vocational; Art / Music; Counseling & Personnel Services; Urban Education, Cultural / Non-Traditional

MANUSCRIPT GUIDELINES/COMMENTS:

Topics Include. Career & Vocational; Children & Adults; Counseling, Therapy Guidance, Psychoeducational, Preventative, Support, Work/Task, and Process Groups; International Group Work; Group Research; Group Practice: Group Theory; Group Work Practice; Group Work Research; Group Work Theory

The Journal for Specialists in Group Work invites articles of interest to the readers and membership. To contribute to the journal, follow these guidelines. Manuscripts should be well organized and concise so the development of ideas is logical. Avoid dull, stereotyped writing and aim at the clear and interesting communication of ideas. All manuscripts should include information describing applicability of the topic to group work practitioners.

Authors are expected to submit the manuscript for review as a PC-compatible, Microsoft Word file. In addition, a hard copy is required upon acceptance.

The title of the article should appear on a separate page accompanying the manuscript. Include on this page the names of the authors followed by a paragraph that repeats the names of the authors and gives their titles and institutional affiliations and a paragraph that provides author contact information for the contact author.

Article titles and headings within the article should be concise.

Manuscripts should be submitted as PC-Compatible, Microsoft Word files in 12-point Times New Roman font.

Include a 100-word abstract of the manuscript that conveys the main message to the reader. Four or five keywords should be included at the bottom of the Abstract page to facilitate electronic access to the article.

Double-space all material, including references and extensive quotations. Allow 1" margins.

Adhere to guidelines to reduce bias in language against persons on the basis of gender, sexual orientation, racial or ethnic group, disability or age by referring to the fourth edition of the APA publication manual. Also, use terms such as client, student, or participant rather than subject.

Do not use footnotes.

References should follow the *Publication Manual of The American Psychological Association* (fifth edition). Check all references for completeness; adequate information should be given to allow the reader to retrieve the referenced material from the most available source. All references cited in text must be listed in the reference section and vice versa. Direct quotations must have page numbers cited.

Lengthy quotations (generally 300-500 cumulative words or more from one source) require written permission from the copyright holder for reproduction. Adaptation of tables and figures also requires reproduction approval from the copyrighted source. It is the author's responsibility to secure such permission, and a copy of the publisher's written permission must be provided to the journal editor immediately upon acceptance of the article for publication by AAC.

Tables should be kept to a minimum. Include only essential data and combine tables wherever possible. Each table should be on a separate page following the reference section of the article. Final placement of the tables is at the discretion of the production editor; in all cases, tables will be placed after the first reference to the table in the text. Supply figures (graphs, illustrations, Line drawings) as camera-ready art (prepared by a commercial artist on glossy or repro paper), with sans serif text no smaller than 8 points.

Never submit material that is under consideration by another publication.

For other questions of format or style, refer to the 2001 (fifth) edition of the *Publication Manual of the American Psychological Association*. Copies may be ordered from APA, 750 First St. N.E., Washington, DC 20002-4242.

Journal articles are edited within a uniform style for correctness and consistency of grammar, spelling, and punctuation. In some cases, manuscripts are reworded for conciseness or clarity of expression. Authors bear the responsibility for the accuracy of references, tables, and figures.

Journal for the Advancement of Educational Research

SUBMISSION PROCESS: Postal Submission Only	
CONTACT INFORMATION:	**REVIEW PROCESS:**
Dianne A. Wright, Editor Florida Atlantic University Davie Campus Department of Educational Leadership 2912 College Avenue, ES #235 Davie, FL 33314 USA **Phone:** 954-236-1080 **Email:** dwright@fau.edu **Website:** www.AAER.com	**Type of Review:** Blind Review **No. External Reviewers:** 0 **No. InHouse Reviewers:** 3 **Acceptance Rate:** **Time to Review:** 4 - 6 Months **Reviewer's Comments:** Yes **Invited Articles:** 0-5% **Fees to Publish:** $ US$ **Fees to Review:** $75.00 US$
PUBLICATION GUIDELINES:	**CIRCULATION DATA:**
Manuscript Style: American Psychological Association **Manuscript Length:** 15 **Copies Required:** Three	**Reader:** Academics, Educators, Practitioners **Frequency of Issue:** Yearly **Sponsor/Publisher:** The Association for the Advancement of Educational Research

MANUSCRIPT TOPICS:
Curriculum Studies; Education Management / Administration

MANUSCRIPT GUIDELINES/COMMENTS:

The Official Journal of the Association for the Advancement of Educational Research

The *Journal for the Advancement of Educational Research* (*JAER*) publishes scholarly papers, descriptive and timely reports, and continuing information and findings related to research and development in education. The Editorial Board of the *Journal* encourages submission of articles with the understanding that it is to be published exclusively in the *Journal for the Advancement of Educational Research*. All manuscripts for the journal should be submitted to: Dianne Wright, Editor, Florida Atlantic University, 2912 College Avenue, Davie, Florida 33314, E-mail **dwright@FAU.edu** Tel. 954.236.1080.

All fees must be submitted to: Merve Lynch, 59 Clear Pond Dr., Walpole, MA 02081. Phone: 508.668.5989. E-mail **Me.Lynch@Neu.edu**.

To be published in the *Journal for the Advancement of Educational Research*, the manuscript should meet the following criteria:

1. **Importance**. The manuscript should make a significant contribution to research in the field of education.

2. **Relevance to Audience**. The manuscript should be relevant to educators in diverse fields/settings.

3. **Methodological; Adequacy**. Manuscripts reporting empirical studies should have clearly described designs and methods, and clearly formulated findings/conclusions supported by valid, reliable data. Other manuscripts (on theory development or methodological issues) must be supported by appropriate documentation, reasoning, and/or examples.

4. **Manuscript**. Authors should submit an original manuscript and two blinded copies. In addition, the manuscript should be submitted on a floppy disc in Microsoft Word format.

5. **Preparation of Copy**. The manuscript (including references) should be double spaced with one inch margins and should not exceed 15 pages). A separate cover sheet should indicate the title of the article and the name(s) and full academic degrees of the author(s). Choose one author to act as the receiver of all correspondence, and include his or her name, address, position, institution, telephone number, fax number, and e-mail address (this information should only appear on the original copy and not on the blinded copies). In addition, a short one paragraph abstract should accompany manuscript submission (not to exceed 150 words).

6. **Style and References**. Manuscripts and references should follow the American Psychological Association, 5th Edition guidelines. All written material including references should be double spaced.

7. **Manuscript Acceptance**. Submissions are blind reviewed by a minimum of three members of the *JAER* editorial board. The average time for review and acceptance or rejection is three months.

8. **Due Date**. All manuscripts must be received by April 1st to be considered for publication in the *Journal*.

Journal of Academic Administration in Higher Education, The

SUBMISSION PROCESS:
Electronic Submission Only **via EMail** **JAAHE@AcademicBusinessWorld.org**

<table>
<tr>
<td>

CONTACT INFORMATION:

Edd R. Joyner, Editor
JW Press
PO Box 49
Martin, TN 38237

Phone:
 731-588-0701

Email:
 jaahe@academicbusinessworld.org
 eddjoyner@charter.net

Website:
 http://JWPress/JAAHE/JAAHE.htm

</td>
<td colspan="2">

REVIEW PROCESS:

Type of Review:	Blind Review
No. External Reviewers:	3
No. InHouse Reviewers:	0
Acceptance Rate:	11-20%
Time to Review:	1 Month or Less
Reviewer's Comments:	Yes
Invited Articles:	0-5%
Fees to Publish:	$0.00 US$
Fees to Review:	$25.00 US$

</td>
</tr>
<tr>
<td>

PUBLICATION GUIDELINES:

Manuscript Style:
 See Manuscript Guidelines

Manuscript Length:
 11-15

Copies Required:
 Electronic Only

</td>
<td colspan="2">

CIRCULATION DATA:

Reader:
 Academics, Administrators

Frequency of Issue:
 2 Times/Year

Sponsor/Publisher:
 Academic Business World / JW Press

</td>
</tr>
</table>

MANUSCRIPT TOPICS:
Academic Administration in Higher Education; Curriculum Studies; Education Management / Administration; Higher Education

MANUSCRIPT GUIDELINES/COMMENTS:

About the Journal
The Journal of Academic Administration in Higher Education is a new journal devoted to providing a venue for the distribution, discussion, and documentation of the art and science of administration of academic units in colleges and universities. A cornerstone of the philosophy that drives *JAAHE*, is that we all can learn from the research, practices, and techniques of administration in discipline-based units other than our own. The Information Systems Chair can share with and learn from the Chair of the English Department. To enhance this cross pollination, submitted manuscripts should not dwell on the disciplines involved but rather the methods, techniques, environments, etc. that make administration more or less effective or efficient.

Manuscripts that support the advancement of the administration of academic units in higher education are actively sought for publication in *The Journal of Academic Administration in Higher Education* Articles that report on innovative practices and articles that research theoretical issues in administration are equally desired. Additionally, papers that take a philosophical perspective on the state of higher education administration of yesterday, today and/or tomorrow are welcome.

Submission Information

Review Process. Papers will be blind/peer reviewed and judged as either: Accept, Revise and Accept, Revise and Resubmit, or Reject. Authors will normally be notified of the status of their paper within a month of submission.

Submission Deadline. None, all accepted manuscripts will be published in the next available edition.

Submission Fees. A submission fee of $25 must accompany all submissions. This submission fee is waived for all complete papers presented at an Academic Business World Conference, which are automatically considered for publication in *The Journal of Academic Administration in Higher Education.*

Submission fees may be forwarded online: **http://jwpress.com/JAAHE/JAAHE-Submission.htm** or by check, payable to JW Press, mailed to: The Journal of Academic Administration in Higher Education, JW Press, P.O. Box 49, Martin, TN 38237

Submission email address. Send your manuscript as an MS Word attachment to: **JAAHE@ academicbusinessworld.org**

File Format. Microsoft Word

Paper Format. All papers should be submitted via email and conform to the following guidelines:
- Page Size. 8.5"x11"
- Paper Length. Maximum of 10 single-spaced pages ($10/page charge for more than 10 pages)
- Margins. 1.5" in left, 1" all other margins
- First Page. Adjust vertical spacing so that Title, Author, and Abstract will fit completely on the 1st page, without flowing to the 2nd page.
- Font. Times New Roman
- Body. 12 pt Normal, Left Justified
- Level 1 Heading. 14 pt Bold, Centered
- Level 2 Heading. 14 pt Bold, Left
- Level 3 Heading. 14 pt Normal, Left
- References. 12 pt Normal, Hanging Indent .5" (Uses APA style for references)

Please note. While Abstracts and Presentation Outlines are acceptable for presentation at the Academic Business World conferences, they cannot be considered for publication in *The Journal of Academic Administration in Higher Education.*

Journal of Academic Ethics

SUBMISSION PROCESS:	
Electronic Submission Preferred **via EMail** **poff@unbc.ca**	

CONTACT INFORMATION:	REVIEW PROCESS:	
Deborah Poff, Editor-in-Chief University of Northern British Columbia Prince George, Canada	**Type of Review:**	Blind Review
	No. External Reviewers:	3
	No. InHouse Reviewers:	0
Phone: 250-962-8719	**Acceptance Rate:**	New J
	Time to Review:	4 - 6 Months
Email: poff@unbc.ca	**Reviewer's Comments:**	Yes
	Invited Articles:	31-50%
Website: www.springerlink.com	**Fees to Publish:**	$0.00 US$
	Fees to Review:	$0.00 US$

PUBLICATION GUIDELINES:	CIRCULATION DATA:
Manuscript Style: American Psychological Association	**Reader:** Academics, Administrators
Manuscript Length: 21-25	**Frequency of Issue:** Quarterly
Copies Required: Four	**Sponsor/Publisher:** Springer

MANUSCRIPT TOPICS:
Ethics; Higher Education

MANUSCRIPT GUIDELINES/COMMENTS:

Aims and Scope
The *Journal of Academic Ethics* is an interdisciplinary, peer reviewed journal devoted to the examination of ethical issues related to all aspects of post-secondary education, primarily within a university context. The journal will provide a forum for the publication and discussion of original research on a broad range of ethical considerations in research, teaching, administration and governance. In the presence of the rapidly changing global knowledge economy, there is a need for sustained inquiry into the values, purposes and functions of the world's principal institutions responsible for the creation and dissemination of knowledge. The Journal of Academic Ethics aims to encourage, foster and promote this inquiry.

Representative areas of investigation include ethical considerations in: Research e.g., Selection of research subjects and research methods; Treatment of human and animal subjects; Treatment of diversity regarding race, gender, class, ethnicity; Referencing and citation behaviour; Grant and funding assessments; Publication editing, refereeing processes and procedures; Conflicts of interest; Plagiarism, deception, fraud; and Graduate training versus exploitation of graduate students.

Manuscript Submission
The *Journal of Academic Ethics* prefers the submission of papers in LaTeX; however, papers submitted in AMSTeX, LAMSTeX, and software programmes such as WordPerfect, Apple Macintosh, Word for Windows, etc. can also be accepted. For the purpose of refereeing, papers for publication should initially be submitted in hard copy (4–fold) to: The Journals Editorial Office, The Journal of Academic Ethics, Springer, P.O. Box 990, 3300 AZ Dordrecht, The Netherlands. Manuscripts should be typewritten on A4 or US Letter bond paper, one side only, leaving enough margin on all sides to permit remarks by the reviewers. Please double-space all materials, including footnotes, endnotes, and references.

Manuscript Presentation
Number the pages consecutively with the first page containing the title, the authors, the affiliation, a short abstract of 100 to 250 words, and five to ten key words in alphabetical order. Since the abstract and the key words will be used to select appropriate reviewers, it is essential to make them as informative as possible. Quoted passages of more than 40 words should be typed in smaller size and set off from the text, not indented, as a block quotation.

Illustrations
Springer request electronic submission of figures. Preferred file formats are TIFF (Tagged Image File Format) and Encapsulated PostScript (resolution between 300 and 600 dpi), but figures in other electronic formats may also be used. File names should not be longer than 8 characters. A printout of ALL figures should be supplied with the hardcopy manuscript. Submit only clear reproductions of artwork. Authors should retain original artwork until a manuscript has been accepted in its final version. All figures must be in a form suitable for reproduction (reduction). Original ink drawings or laserprinter output reproduce best, but if they are not available, same-sized glossies or matt photostats are acceptable. Photographs should be in black and white on glossy paper. Computer prints are acceptable for figures only if they are done on a high quality laserprinter.

Figures and Tables
Each figure and table should be mentioned in the text and should be numbered consecutively using Arabic numbers in order of appearance in the text for figures, and Roman numbers for tables. On the reverse side of each figure, write in pencil the name of the (first) author and the figure number. Figures and tables should be placed at the end of the manuscript following the Reference section.

Section Headings
Headings should be in: capital letters.

Footnotes and References
Please use footnotes only. Do not use endnotes. Be sure you do not mix footnote text and Bibliographic information. Bibliographic information should be listed in a separate Reference section (see REFERENCE section for more information). Footnotes should be indicated by consecutive superscript numbers (use an asterisk for the first footnote referring to the title of the article) in the text. In tables, footnotes are preferable to long explanatory material in either the heading or body of the table. Such explanatory footnotes, identified by superscript letters, should be placed immediately below the table.

Cross-Referencing
Please make optimal use of the cross-referencing features of your software package. Do not cross–reference page numbers. Cross-references should refer to:
- section number of a heading
- the number of a displayed equation
- the number of a table
- the number of a figure
- the number of an enunciation
- the name / year of a reference entry

In the text, a reference already identified by the author should be followed by the date of the reference in parentheses (follow the journal style) and page number(s) where appropriate, for ex.: Winograd (1986, p. 204). Otherwise the reference should be enclosed within parentheses (follow the journal style) including the name of the author followed by the date and page number, for ex.: (Winograd, 1986; Flores et al., 1988). In the event that the author has had two or more works published during the same year, the citation and the reference should contain a lower case letter like a and b after the date to distinguish the works.

References
Journal article
Barlow, D. H. & Lehman, C. L. (1996). Advances in the psychosocial treatment of anxiety disorders. Archives of General Psychiatry, 53, 727-735

Book chapter
Cutrona, C. E. & Russell, D. (1990). Type of social support and specific stress: Towards a theory of optimum matching. (In I.G. Sarason, B. R. Sarason, & G. Pierce (Eds.), Social support: An interactional view (pp. 341-366). New York: Wiley.)

Book, authored
Capland, G. (1964). Principles of preventive psychiatry. (New York: Basic Books)

Please visit the web site for more examples.

Offprints
Twenty-five offprints of each article will be provided free of charge. Additional offprints can be ordered when proofs are returned to the publisher.

Page Charges and Color Illustrations
No page charges are levied on authors or their institutions. Color illustrations are published at the author's expense only.

Copyright
Copyright will be established in the name of Springer.

Permissions
It is the responsibility of the author to obtain written permission for a quotation from unpublished material, or for all quotations in excess of 250 words in one extract or 500 words in total from any work still in copyright, and for the reprinting of illustrations or tables or poems from unpublished or copyrighted material.

Additional Information
Additional information can be obtained from: The Journals Editorial Office, The Journal of Academic Ethics, Springer, P.O. Box 990, 3300 AZ Dordrecht, The Netherlands

More Information about Submitting Papers
We kindly refer you to page iii of the cover for instructions for the Submission of Papers in Electronic Form.

Affiliation
As the last item, the Affiliation address of the Author(s) should be inserted.

Technical Appendices
Supplementary technical material (e.g. mathematical proofs or descriptions of experimental procedures) should be collected in an Appendix which comes before the Notes and Reference sections.

Journal of Accounting Education

SUBMISSION PROCESS:
Postal Submission Only

CONTACT INFORMATION:	REVIEW PROCESS:	
James E. Rebele, Editor Robert Morris University School of Business 6001 University Boulevard Coraopolis, PA 15108	**Type of Review:**	Blind Review
	No. External Reviewers:	2
	No. InHouse Reviewers:	0
	Acceptance Rate:	11-20%
Phone:	**Time to Review:**	2 - 3 Months
412-397-4894	**Reviewer's Comments:**	Yes
	Invited Articles:	6-10%
Email:		
rebele@rmu.edu	**Fees to Publish:**	$0.00 US$
Website:	**Fees to Review:**	$0.00 US$
www.elsevier.com/locate/jaccedu		

PUBLICATION GUIDELINES:	CIRCULATION DATA:
Manuscript Style: Chicago Manual of Style	**Reader:** Academics
Manuscript Length: 11-15	**Frequency of Issue:** Quarterly
Copies Required: Four	**Sponsor/Publisher:** Elsevier Inc.

MANUSCRIPT TOPICS:
Curriculum Studies; Educational Technology Systems

MANUSCRIPT GUIDELINES/COMMENTS:

Description
The *Journal of Accounting Education* (*JAEd*) is a refereed journal dedicated to promoting excellence in teaching and stimulating research in accounting education internationally. The journal provides a forum for exchanging research results and innovative instructional materials and approaches among accounting educators from around the world. The journal is divided into three sections. Papers in the "Main Articles" section are generally empirical, and present in-depth analyses of topics. The "Teaching and Educational Notes" section is designed to provide a forum for exchanging innovative instructional approaches and materials. This section contains short papers with information of interest to *JAEd* readers. The "Case Section" provides a vehicle for dissemination of materials that faculty can use in the classroom. The case material should aid in providing a positive learning experience for both student and professor and should be available for general use. Topics covered in the *JAEd* include: faculty issues, instructional technology, innovative teaching methods, results of classroom experiments, and assurance of learning, among others. Articles written by non-accounting faculty can be published if they deal with education in general or include some relevance to accounting education.

Journal of Adult Development

SUBMISSION PROCESS:
Postal Submission Only

CONTACT INFORMATION:	REVIEW PROCESS:	
Jack Demick, Editor	**Type of Review:**	Blind Review
Butler Hospital		
Weld Building, 3rd Floor	**No. External Reviewers:**	3
345 Blackstone Blvd.	**No. InHouse Reviewers:**	1
Providence, RI 02906 USA		
	Acceptance Rate:	30%
Phone:	**Time to Review:**	6-9 Months
	Reviewer's Comments:	Yes
	Invited Articles:	0-50%
Email:		
jack_demick@brown.edu	**Fees to Publish:**	$0.00 US$
Website:	**Fees to Review:**	$0.00 US$
http://www.springer.com/		

PUBLICATION GUIDELINES:	CIRCULATION DATA:
Manuscript Style:	**Reader:**
American Psychological Association	Academics
Manuscript Length:	**Frequency of Issue:**
1-25	Quarterly
Copies Required:	**Sponsor/Publisher:**
Four	Springer

MANUSCRIPT TOPICS:
Adult Career & Vocational; All topics as related to Career Development; Counseling & Personnel Services; Education Management / Administration; Educational Psychology; Higher Education; Social Studies / Social Science; Tests, Measurement & Evaluation; Urban Education, Cultural / Non-Traditional

MANUSCRIPT GUIDELINES/COMMENTS:

Aims and Scope
Journal of Adult Development published in collaboration with the Society for Research in Adult Development, is a transdisciplinary forum for the publication of peer-reviewed, original theoretical and empirical articles on biological, psychological (cognitive, affective, valuative, behavioral), and/or sociocultural development in young, middle, or late adulthood. Working toward an integrated perspective, contributions feature developments in both basic and applied research as well as quantitative and/or qualitative approaches to inquiry. Papers focus on such issues as: the acquisition of moral ideas and principles; the development and character of the ego; the changing nature of human relationships across the life span; relationship between the ethical atmosphere of higher education institutions and the development of adults within them; ways in which clinical interventions and adult developmental characteristics promote development in a variety of settings.

General

In general, the journal follows the recommendations of the 2001 *Publication Manual of the American Psychological Association* (Fifth Edition), and it is suggested that contributors refer to this publication.

Manuscript Submission

Manuscripts, in quadruplicate and in English, should be submitted to: Jack Demick, Butler Hospital, Weld Building 3rd Floor, 345 Blackstone Blvd., Providence, RI 02906; **jack_demick@ brown.edu**. Authors should include a cover letter that states the paper's relevance to the scope of the journal and should submit the manuscript in a form appropriate to the blind review process. In addition to hard copy (manuscripts), authors are encouraged to submit disks using Word for Windows, if possible.

Publication Policies

Submission is a representation that the manuscript has not been published previously and is not currently under consideration for publication elsewhere. A statement transferring copyright from the authors (or their employers, if they hold the copyright) to Plenum Publishing Corporation will be required before the manuscript can be accepted for publication. The Editor will supply the necessary forms for this transfer. Such a written transfer of copyright, which previously was assumed to be implicit in the act of submitting a manuscript, is necessary under the U.S. Copyright Law in order for the publisher to carry through the dissemination of research results and reviews as widely and effectively as possible.

Manuscript Style

Type double-spaced on one side of 8 ½ × 11 inch white paper using generous margins on all sides, and submit the original and three copies (including, where possible, copies of all illustrations and tables).

A title page is to be provided and should include the title of the article, author's name (no degrees), author's affiliation, and suggested running head. The affiliation should comprise the department, institution (usually university or company), city, and state (or nation) and should be typed as a footnote to the author's name. The suggested running head should be less than 80 characters (including spaces) and should comprise the article title or an abbreviated version thereof. For office purposes, the title page should include the complete mailing address and telephone number of the one author designated to review proofs.

An abstract is to be provided, preferably no longer than 150 words.

A list of 4-5 key words is to be provided directly below the abstract. Key words should express the precise content of the manuscript, as they are used for indexing purposes.

Footnotes should be avoided. When their use is absolutely necessary, footnotes should be numbered consecutively using Arabic numerals and should be typed at the bottom of the page to which they refer. Place a line above the footnote, so that it is set off from the text. Use the appropriate superscript numeral for citation in the text.

References

List references alphabetically at the end of the paper and refer to them in the text by name and year in parentheses. References should include (in this order):
- last names and initials of all authors
- year published
- title of article
- name of publication
- volume number
- and inclusive pages

502

The style and punctuation of the references should conform to strict APA style - illustrated by the following examples:

Journal Article
Pilisuk, M., Montgomery, M. B., Parks, S. H., & Acredolo, C. (1993). Locus of control, life stress, and social networks: Gender differences in the health status of the elderly. Sex Roles, 28, 147—166.

Book
Hart, D. A. (1992). Becoming men: The development of aspirations, values, and adaptational styles. New York: Plenum Press.

Contribution to a Book
Haviland, J. M., & Walker–Andrews, A. S. (1992). Emotion socialization: A view from development and ethology. In V. B. Van Hasselt & M. Hersen (Eds.), Handbook of social development: A lifespan perspective (pp. 29—49). New York: Plenum Press.

Illustration Style
Illustrations (photographs, drawings, diagrams, and charts) are to be numbered in one consecutive series of Arabic numerals. The captions for illustrations should be typed on a separate sheet of paper. Photographs should be large, glossy prints, showing high contrast. Drawings should be prepared with India ink. Either the original drawings or good-quality photographic prints are acceptable. Artwork for each figure should be provided on a separate sheet of paper. Identify figures on the back with author's name and number of the illustration. Electronic artwork submitted on disk should be in the TIFF or EPS format (1200 dpi for line and 300 dpi for half-tones and gray-scale art). Color art should be in the CYMK color space. Artwork should be on a separate disk from the text, and hard copy must accompany the disk.

Tables should be numbered (with Roman numerals) and referred to by number in the text. Each table should be typed on a separate sheet of paper. Center the title above the table, and type explanatory footnotes (indicated by superscript lowercase letters) below the table.

Submission of Accepted Manuscripts
After a manuscript has been accepted for publication and after all revisions have been incorporated, manuscripts should be submitted to the Editor's Office as hard copy accompanied by electronic files on disk. Label the disk with identifying information - software, journal name, and first author's last name. The disk must be the one from which the accompanying manuscript (finalized version) was printed out. The Editor's Office cannot accept a disk without its accompanying, matching hard-copy manuscript.

Page Charges
The journal makes no page charges. Reprints are available to authors, and order forms with the current price schedule are sent with proofs.

Springer Open Choice
In addition to the normal publication process (whereby an article is submitted to the journal and access to that article is granted to customers who have purchased a subscription), Springer now provides an alternative publishing option: Springer Open Choice. A Springer Open Choice article receives all the benefits of a regular subscription-based article, but in addition is made available publicly through Springer's online platform SpringerLink. To publish via Springer Open Choice, upon acceptance please visit the link below to complete the relevant order form and provide the required payment information. Payment must be received in full before publication or articles will publish as regular subscription-model articles. We regret that Springer Open Choice cannot be ordered for published articles.

Journal of Agricultural Education

SUBMISSION PROCESS:
Postal Submission Only

CONTACT INFORMATION:	REVIEW PROCESS:	
Rama B. Radhakrishna, Editor Penn State University 323 Agricultural Administration Building University Park, PA 16802 USA	**Type of Review:**	Blind Review
	No. External Reviewers:	2
	No. InHouse Reviewers:	1
Phone: 814-863-7069	**Acceptance Rate:**	21-30%
	Time to Review:	1 - 2 Months
	Reviewer's Comments:	Yes
Email: brr100@psu.edu	**Invited Articles:**	0-5%
Website:	**Fees to Publish:**	$0.00 US$
	Fees to Review:	$0.00 US$

PUBLICATION GUIDELINES:	CIRCULATION DATA:
Manuscript Style: American Psychological Association	**Reader:** Academics, Administrators, Practicing Teachers
Manuscript Length: 21-25	**Frequency of Issue:** Quarterly
Copies Required: Four	**Sponsor/Publisher:** American Association for Agricultural Education

MANUSCRIPT TOPICS:

Adult Career & Vocational; Counseling & Personnel Services; Curriculum Studies; Education Management / Administration; Educational Psychology; Educational Technology Systems; Higher Education; Rural Education & Small Schools; Secondary / Adolescent Studies; Social Studies / Social Science; Teacher Education; Tests, Measurement & Evaluation

MANUSCRIPT GUIDELINES/COMMENTS:

Philosophy Underlying the Publication of the Journal

The *Journal* is to promote the profession of agricultural education by facilitating and expediting communication among members of the profession to the end that results of research, trends, developments, and innovations in agricultural education are widely shared. We possess a broad view of agricultural education that includes extension education, communications, leadership development, teacher education, and related areas that support the agricultural sciences.

Editorial Policy

The *Journal of Agricultural Education* is a publication of the American Association for Agricultural Education (AAAE). And is published four times a year. The *Journal* publishes blind, peer-reviewed manuscripts addressing current trends and issues, descriptions or analyses of innovations, research, philosophical concerns, and learner/program evaluation in agricultural education, including extension and international agricultural education. The submission of empirically based manuscripts that report original quantitative or qualitative research, manuscripts based on historical or philosophical research, and reviews/synthesis of empirical or theoretical literature are encouraged. The *Journal* will not consider any manuscript that has been published by or is under consideration by another journal. All or part of this issue and previous issues may be reproduced only for educational purposes.

Subscriptions

All AAAE members receive the *Journal*. Nonmember subscriptions are $120 per year, (includes library rate postage) and foreign/overseas subscriptions are $150 per year (includes airmail postage to foreign/overseas addresses). Back issues are $10 per copy when copies are available. Subscriptions and back issue requests should be addressed to the Business Manager (for address see website). Articles from the *Journal* are indexed in the Current Index to Journals of Education (CITE) and are accessible through ERIC.

Manuscript Submission

Submit manuscripts to the Editor at any time. Authors should submit:
A. A Cover letter

B. A separate title page that includes the manuscript title and the name, mailing address, phone number, facsimile number, and e-mail address for all authors.

C. Four copies of the manuscript prepared for blind review (no references to authors' names or institutional affiliation):
   1. The first page of the manuscript should include the following:
      a. Manuscript title
      b. An abstract (no more than 200 words)
      c. The introduction/theoretical base section of the manuscript should start
      d. Immediately after the abstract (on page 1).
   2. Manuscripts, including tables/figures, must be no more than twenty (20) typed, double spaced pages, including tables, figures and references. Times Roman 12 point font with one inch margins should be used. Tables and figures should be placed within the body of the manuscript as soon as feasible after their first mention in the text. Page numbers should be centered at the bottom of each page.
   3. Authors should ensure that tables, figures and references are prepared according to the guidelines in the *Publication Manual of the American Psychological Association* (5th Edition, 2001). The font size for all text in tables and figures must be at least 12 point. Patterns rather than colors should be used for the bars in bar charts and for the "pie slices" in pie charts. Authors should ensure that table notes are formatted according to the *APA Manual*. Consult the *APA Manual* for all other questions concerning manuscript style and the reporting of data analyses. Authors should report effect sizes in the manuscript and tables when reporting statistical significance.

D. The cover letter, title page and four copies of the manuscript should be mailed to the Editor at Penn State University, 323 Agricultural Administration Building, University Park, PA 16802. The lead author will receive a letter confirming that the manuscript has been received. In most cases, the lead author will be notified of the results of the review process within 3-4 months.

Journal of American College Health

SUBMISSION PROCESS:	
Electronic Submission Only via Online Portal **http://mc.manuscriptcentral.com/jach**	

CONTACT INFORMATION:	REVIEW PROCESS:	
Deanna Lowery, Managing Editor Heldref Publications, Inc. 1319 Eighteenth Street N.W. Washington, DC 20036-1802 USA	**Type of Review:**	Blind Review
	No. External Reviewers: **No. InHouse Reviewers:**	3 0
Phone: 202-296-6267 ext. 1214	**Acceptance Rate:** **Time to Review:** **Reviewer's Comments:**	2 - 3 Months Yes
Email: dlowery@heldref.org jach@heldref.org	**Invited Articles:**	0-5%
	Fees to Publish: **Fees to Review:**	$0.00 US$ $0.00 US$
Website: www.heldref.org/jach.php		

PUBLICATION GUIDELINES:	CIRCULATION DATA:
Manuscript Style: See Manuscript Guidelines **Manuscript Length:** 16-30 **Copies Required:** Electronic Only	**Reader:** Academics, Administrators, Practicing Teachers **Frequency of Issue:** Bi-Monthly **Sponsor/Publisher:** American College Health Association (ACHA) / Heldref Publications, Inc.

MANUSCRIPT TOPICS:
Education Management / Administration; Educational Psychology; Educational Technology Systems; Health & Physical Education; Higher Education; Special Education; Tests, Measurement & Evaluation

MANUSCRIPT GUIDELINES/COMMENTS:

Binge drinking, campus violence, eating disorders, sexual harassment: today's college students face challenges their parents never imagined. The *Journal of American College Health*, the only scholarly publication devoted entirely to college students' health, focuses on these issues, as well as use of tobacco and other drugs, sexual habits, psychological problems, and guns on campus. Published in cooperation with the American College Health Association, the *Journal of American College Health* is must reading for physicians, nurses, health educators, and administrators who are involved with students every day. Parents and secondary school educators will also find the journal a useful resource in preparing students for future campus life. The journal includes major research articles, clinical and program notes, practical accounts of developing prevention strategies, and lively viewpoint articles on controversial issues.

Guidelines for Authors

The *Journal of American College Health* provides information related to health in institutions of higher education. The journal publishes articles encompassing many areas of this broad field, including clinical and preventive medicine, environmental and community health and safety, health promotion and education, management and administration, mental health, nursing, pharmacy, and sports medicine.

The *Journal of American College Health* is intended for college health professionals: administrators, health educators, nurses, nurse practitioners, physicians, physician assistants, professors, psychologists, student affairs personnel, and students as peer educators, consumers, and preprofessionals.

The journal publishes (1) scientific or research articles presenting significant new data, insights, or analyses; (2) state-of-the-art reviews; (3) clinical and program notes that describe successful and innovative procedures; and (4) brief reports, viewpoints, book reviews, and letters to the editor.

Types of Articles

Major Articles. Theoretical, scientific, and research manuscripts and reviews will be considered as major articles. The preferred length is 15 to 20 double-spaced pages (15,000—20,000 words), including tables, figures, and references.

Clinical and Program Notes. Clinical and program notes report on clinical experiences, new or especially interesting ideas and services, or collaboration in clinical studies. Program notes run 5 to 7 double-spaced pages (5,000—7,000 words), including a brief abstract, but do not usually include tables or figures; references must conform to the style used in major articles.

Viewpoint. Viewpoint is a forum for opinions. Topics may be ethical, organizational, social, professional, or economic. Debate on controversial subjects is welcome. Manuscripts vary from 4 to 10 pages (4,000—10,000 words), but we prefer concise presentations. Abstracts, tables, and figures are unnecessary. References should follow the same format as that used in major articles.

Letters to the Editor in response to published articles are also welcome. They should be brief (500—1,000 words) and they may be edited.

Preparing Your Manuscript

1. Submit your manuscript, including tables, as double-spaced Word files with minimal formatting in Times. Save it as a .doc, .rtf, or .ps file. Please use simple filenames and avoid special characters. Do not use word-processing styles, forced section or page breaks, or automatic footnotes or references. Number every five lines in the document.
2. Follow the *American Medical Association Manual of Style*, 9th edition, in medical and scientific usage.
3. Abstract (when applicable) must be no longer than 150 words, be written in an unstructured AMA format, and include these words as subheadings: Objective, Participants, Method Summary, Results, and Conclusions.
4. Text in research articles must be divided into these headings: Methods, Results, and Comment (which can include the subheadings: Limitations, Conclusions, etc.).
5. Proofread carefully, double-checking all statistics, numbers, symbols, references, and tables. Authors are responsible for the accuracy of all material submitted.
6. Indicate approval of the appropriate institutional review board (IRB) for all studies involving human participants and describe how participants provided informed consent.
7. Provide written permission from publishers and authors to reprint or adapt previously published tables or figures.

Submitting Your Manuscript in Manuscript Central

When your files are ready, visit the online submission Web site: **http://mc.manuscriptcentral. com/heldref/jach**

1. First, log into the system. Register, if you have not done so before, by clicking on the Create Account button on the log-in screen and following the on-screen instructions.
2. To submit a new manuscript, go to Author Center, then click on Submit a Manuscript and follow the on-screen instructions.
3. Enter your manuscript data into the relevant fields.
4. When you upload your manuscript files via the File Upload screen, Manuscript Central will automatically create a PDF and HTML document of your main text and any figures and tables that you submit. This document will be used when your manuscript undergoes peer review.
5. Make sure you attach 1 blinded manuscript file for review, with all identifying information removed.

Editorial Process

All submissions are blind reviewed by at least 1 consulting editor or ad hoc reviewer, a statistical reviewer (when appropriate), and an executive editor. The process may take up to 4 months. The managing editor will notify authors of the decision—accept, revise, or reject. Review comments will be returned to the author.

Heldref reserves the right to edit accepted manuscripts for clarity, coherence, and felicity of style. Authors receive an edited draft to proof, answer queries, and correct errors that may have been introduced in the editing process. Extensive changes and rewriting are not permitted at this stage.

Accepted manuscripts are usually published within 1 year of acceptance. Each author will receive 2 complimentary copies of the issue in which the article appears. Additional copies are available to authors at a reduced price (minimum order 50 copies).

References

Authors should cite references consecutively in the text, using a superscript to indicate source. References are listed by number at the end of the text, with titles of journals abbreviated in the form listed in *Index Medicus*. Titles of unlisted journals should be written out in full. The following are examples of reference style.

Journals
1. Enqwal D, Hunter R, Steinberg M. Gambling and other risk behaviors on university campuses. *J Am Coll Health*. 2004; 52: 245—255.

Books
2. Bernstein TM. *The Careful Writer: A Modern Guide to English Usage*. New York: Atheneum; 1965.

Other

Citations for data on a Web site should take this form: Health Care Financing Administration. 1996 statistics at a glance. Available at: http://www.hcfa.gov/stats/stathili.htm. Accessed December 2, 1996.

References to unpublished material should be noted parenthetically in the text (eg, James Jones, personal communication, September 2002).

Quoted material must include an indication of the page on which the quoted words appeared (eg, 7(p26)).

Please use current references and use hard-copy, rather than Web, references whenever possible.

Journal of Applied Developmental Psychology

SUBMISSION PROCESS:
Electronic Submission Only **via Online Portal** **http://ees.elsevier.com/japd**

CONTACT INFORMATION:	REVIEW PROCESS:	
Ann McGillicuddy-Delisi, Editor c/o Editorial Office Manager	**Type of Review:**	Blind Review
Lafayette College Department of Psychology Easton, PA 18042-1781 USA	**No. External Reviewers:** **No. InHouse Reviewers:**	2 0
	Acceptance Rate:	
Phone:	**Time to Review:**	2 - 3 Months
610-330-5859	**Reviewer's Comments:**	Yes
	Invited Articles:	0-5%
Email:		
jadp@lafayette.edu	**Fees to Publish:**	$0.00 US$
Website:	**Fees to Review:**	$0.00 US$
http://www.sciencedirect.com		

PUBLICATION GUIDELINES:	CIRCULATION DATA:
Manuscript Style: American Psychological Association	**Reader:** Academics, Counselors
Manuscript Length: 30+	**Frequency of Issue:** Bi-Monthly
Copies Required: Electronic Only	**Sponsor/Publisher:** Elsevier Inc.

MANUSCRIPT TOPICS:
Developmental Psychology; Educational Psychology; Elementary / Early Childhood

MANUSCRIPT GUIDELINES/COMMENTS:

Description
The *Journal of Applied Developmental Psychology* provides a forum for the presentation of conceptual, methodological, policy, and research studies involved in the application of behavioral science research in developmental and life span psychology. The *Journal* publishes quality papers from an interdisciplinary perspective focusing on a broad array of social issues. The *Journal of Applied Developmental Psychology* focuses on two key concepts: human development, which refers to the psychological transformations and modifications that occur during the life cycle and influence an individual's behavior within the social milieu; and application of knowledge, which is derived from investigating variables in the developmental process. Its contributions cover research that deals with traditional life span markets (age, social roles, biological status, environmental variables) and broadens the scopes of study to include variables that promote understanding of psychological processes and their onset and development within the life span. Most importantly, the Journal demonstrates how knowledge gained from research can be applied to policy making and to educational, clinical, and social settings.

Guide for Authors

The *Journal of Applied Developmental Psychology* is intended as a forum for communication about empirical research with a bearing on human development. Articles describing empirical research from social and behavioral disciplines with application to life-span developmental issues are appropriate. Conceptual and methodological reviews and position papers that facilitate the application of research results to social, educational, clinical, and other settings are also welcome. Discussion of intervention or policy issues or recommendations are appropriate when data based.

Review of manuscripts. To prepare for blind review, authors should remove any identifying information from the manuscript. All information pertaining to identification, title, institutional affiliation, etc. should be on a cover page and only the title of the manuscript should appear on the first page of the manuscript.

Articles submitted must contain original material that has not been published and that is not being considered for publication elsewhere. Papers accepted by the journal may not be published elsewhere in any language without the consent of the Publisher. Authors should indicate that the research presented has been approved by their local institutional human subjects review board.

Submission to the journal prior to acceptance

Authors should submit their articles electronically via the Elsevier Editorial System (EES) page of this journal **http://ees.elsevier.com/jadp**. The system automatically converts source files to a single Adobe Acrobat PDF version of the article, which is used in the peer-review process. Please note that even though manuscript source files are converted to PDF at submission for the review process, these source files are needed for further processing after acceptance. All correspondence, including notification of the Editor's decision and requests for revision, takes place by e-mail and via the Author's homepage at the EES website removing the need for a hard-copy paper trail. Questions about the appropriateness of a manuscript for the *Journal of Applied Developmental Psychology* should be directed (prior to submission) to Editors Ann McGillicuddy-De Lisi and Merry Bullock at **jadp@lafayette.edu**

Arrangement of the manuscript

Cover Page. Provide the following data on the Cover Page only (in the order given).

Title. Concise and informative. Titles are often used in information-retrieval systems. Avoid abbreviations and formulae where possible.

Author names and affiliations. Where the family name may be ambiguous (e.g., a double name), please indicate this clearly. Present the authors' affiliation addresses (where the actual work was done) below the names. Indicate all affiliations with a lower-case superscript letter immediately after the author's name and in front of the appropriate address. Provide the full postal address of each affiliation, including the country name, and, if available, the e-mail address of each author.

Corresponding author. Clearly indicate who is willing to handle correspondence at all stages of refereeing and publication, also post-publication. **Ensure that telephone and fax numbers (with country and area code) are provided in addition to the e-mail address and the complete postal address**.

Present/permanent address. If an author has moved since the work described in the article was done, or was visiting at the time, a 'Present address' (or 'Permanent address') may be indicated as a footnote to that author's name. The address at which the author actually did the work must be retained as the main, affiliation address. Superscript Arabic numerals are used for such footnotes.

Title Page. Provide the Title, followed by:
Abstract. A concise and factual abstract is required (100 - 175 words). The abstract should state briefly the purpose of the research, the principal results and major conclusions. An abstract is often

presented separate from the article, so it must be able to stand alone. References should therefore be avoided, but if essential, they must be cited in full, without reference to the reference list.

Keywords. Immediately after the abstract, provide a maximum of 6 keywords. These keywords will be used for indexing purposes.

Presentation of manuscript

Please write your text in clear English (American or British usage is accepted, but not a mixture of these). Italics are not to be used for expressions of Latin origin, for example, in vivo, et al., per se. Use decimal points (not commas); use a space for thousands (10 000 and above). Use clear heading and paragraph markings. The usual headings (which may include subheadings) are Introduction, Method, Results and Discussion.

Please avoid full justification, i.e., do not use a constant right-hand margin. Ensure that each new paragraph is clearly indicated. Present tables and figure legends on separate pages at the end of the manuscript. If possible, consult a recent issue of the journal to become familiar with layout and conventions. Number all pages consecutively.

Presentation. The manuscript should be double-spaced, including quotations, footnotes, references, and tables.

Abbreviations. Define abbreviations that are not standard in this field at their first occurrence in the article: in the abstract but also in the main text after it. Ensure consistency of abbreviations throughout the article.

N.B. Acknowledgements. Collate acknowledgements, including grant and other support for the research, in a separate section that follows the text of the article and precedes the references. Do **not**, therefore, include them on the title page, as a footnote to the title or otherwise.

Tables, Figure legends, figures, schemes. Present these, in this order, at the end of the article, following the references. They are described in more detail below. High-resolution graphics files must always be provided separate from the main text file (see Electronic Illustrations).

Specific remarks

Use of 'gender' vs. 'sex'. 'Gender' is a term to refer to social categories and is referenced by the terms masculine and feminine. 'Sex' is a term to refer to a differentiation based on male-female. Therefore comparisons between males and females (or boys and girls) should be refereed to with the term "sex" unless their masculine and feminine traits are part of the classification.

Terms denoting ethnicity. When describing race/ethnic group we request that authors use terms designating ethnicity (e.g., African-American, African-Caribbean, Anglo-American, Hispanic-American, Asian-American, Chinese-American) instead of terms designating race (e.g., White, Black) to refer to participants in your own study and in studies reported in your paper whenever feasible. We recognize that in describing procedures and results, authors will need to use the terms that they used in their studies so references to skin color (White, Black) may remain.

Tables. Number tables consecutively in accordance with their appearance in the text. Place footnotes to tables below the table body and indicate them with superscript lowercase letters. Avoid vertical rules. Be sparing in the use of tables and ensure that the data presented in tables do not duplicate results described elsewhere in the article.

Preparation of supplementary data. Elsevier now accepts electronic supplementary material to support and enhance your scientific research. Supplementary files offer the author additional possibilities to publish supporting applications, movies, animation sequences, high-resolution images, background datasets, sound clips and more. Supplementary files supplied will be published online alongside the electronic version of your article in Elsevier web products, including

ScienceDirect: **http://www.sciencedirect.com**. In order to ensure that your submitted material is directly usable, please ensure that the material provided is in one of our recommended file formats. Authors should submit the material in electronic format together with the article and supply a concise and descriptive caption for each file. For more detailed instructions please visit our Author Gateway at **http://authors.elsevier.com**. Files can be stored on 3? inch diskette, ZIP-disk or CD (either MS-DOS or Macintosh).

Citations in the text. Please ensure that every reference cited in the text is also present in the reference list (and vice versa). Any references cited in the abstract must be given in full. Unpublished results and personal communications should not be in the reference list, but may be mentioned in the text. Citation of a reference as 'in press' implies that the item has been accepted for publication. Citations in the text should follow the referencing style used by the American Psychological Association. You are referred to the *Publication Manual of the American Psychological Association*, Fifth Edition, ISBN 1-55798-790-4, copies of which may be ordered from http://www.apa.org/books/4200061.html or APA Order Dept., P.O.B. 2710, Hyattsville, MD 20784, USA or APA, 3 Henrietta Street, London, WC3E 8LU, UK. Details concerning this referencing style can also be found at http://linguistics.byu.edu/faculty/henrichsenl/apa/apa01.html

Citing and listing of web references. As a minimum, the full URL should be given. Any further information, if known (author names, dates, reference to a source publication, etc.), should also be given. Web references can be listed separately (e.g., after the reference list) under a different heading if desired, or can be included in the reference list.

References. Follow APA style. Responsibility for the accuracy of bibliographic citations lies entirely with the authors

List. References should be arranged first alphabetically and then further sorted chronologically if necessary. More than one reference from the same author(s) in the same year must be identified by the letters "a", "b", "c", etc., placed after the year of publication.

Examples
Reference to a journal publication
Van der Geer, J., Hanraads, J. A. J., and Lupton R. A. (2000). The art of writing a scientific article. *Journal of Scientific Communications*, 163, 51-59.

Reference to a book
Strunk, W., Jr., and White, E. B. (1979). *The elements of style*. (3rd ed.). New York: Macmillan, (Chapter 4).

Reference to a chapter in an edited book
Mettam, G. R., and Adams, L. B. (1994). How to prepare an electronic version of your article. In B. S. Jones, and R. Z. Smith (Eds.), *Introduction to the electronic age* (pp. 281-304). New York: E-Publishing Inc.

Note that journal names are not to be abbreviated.

Electronic illustrations
Submitting your artwork in an electronic format helps us to produce your work to the best possible standards, ensuring accuracy, clarity and a high level of detail. General points:
- Always supply high-quality printouts of your artwork, in case conversion of the electronic artwork is problematic.
- Make sure you use uniform lettering and sizing of your original artwork.
- Save text in illustrations as "graphics" or enclose the font.
- Only use the following fonts in your illustrations: Arial, Courier, Helvetica, Times, Symbol.
- Number the illustrations according to their sequence in the text.

- Use a logical naming convention for your artwork files, and supply a separate listing of the files and the software used.
- Provide all illustrations as separate files and as hardcopy printouts on separate sheets.
- Provide captions to illustrations separately.
- Produce images near to the desired size of the printed version.

A detailed guide on electronic artwork is available on our website: **http://authors.elsevier.com/ artwork**. You are urged to visit this site; excerpts from the detailed information are given here.

Formats

Regardless of the application used, when your electronic artwork is finalised, please "save as" or convert the images to one of the following formats (Note the resolution requirements for line drawings, halftones, and line/halftone combinations given below.):

- EPS: Vector drawings. Embed the font or save the text as "graphics".
- TIFF: Colour or greyscale photographs (halftones): always use a minimum of 300 dpi.
- TIFF: Bitmapped line drawings: use a minimum of 1000 dpi.
- TIFF: Combinations bitmapped line/half-tone (colour or greyscale): a minimum of 500 dpi is required.
- DOC, XLS or PPT: If your electronic artwork is created in any of these Microsoft Office applications please supply "as is".

Line drawings

Supply high-quality printouts on white paper produced with black ink. The lettering and symbols, as well as other details, should have proportionate dimensions, so as not to become illegible or unclear after possible reduction; in general, the figures should be designed for a reduction factor of two to three. The degree of reduction will be determined by the Publisher. Illustrations will not be enlarged. Consider the page format of the journal when designing the illustrations. Photocopies are not suitable for reproduction. Do not use any type of shading on computer-generated illustrations.

Photographs (halftones)

Please supply original photographs for reproduction, printed on glossy paper, very sharp and with good contrast. Remove non-essential areas of a photograph. Do not mount photographs unless they form part of a composite figure. Where necessary, insert a scale bar in the illustration (not below it), as opposed to giving a magnification factor in the legend. Note that photocopies of photographs are not acceptable.

Copyright

Upon acceptance of an article, authors will be asked to transfer copyright (for more information on copyright see **http://authors.elsevier.com**). This transfer will ensure the widest possible dissemination of information. A letter will be sent to the corresponding author confirming receipt of the manuscript. A form facilitating transfer of copyright will be provided. If excerpts from other copyrighted works are included, the author(s) must obtain written permission from the copyright owners and credit the source(s) in the article. Elsevier has forms for use by authors in these cases available at **www.elsevier.com/locate/permissions** phone: (+44) 1865 843830, fax: (+44) 1865 853333, e-mail: **permissions@elsevier.com**

Proofs

When your manuscript is received by the Publisher it is considered to be in its final form. Proofs are not to be regarded as 'drafts'. One set of page proofs will be sent to the corresponding author, to be checked for typesetting/editing. No changes in, or additions to, the accepted (and subsequently edited) manuscript will be allowed at this stage. Proofreading is solely your responsibility. The Publisher reserves the right to proceed with publication if corrections are not communicated. Return corrections within 3 days of receipt of the proofs. Should there be no corrections, please confirm this.

Offprints

Twenty-five offprints will be supplied free of charge. Additional offprints and copies of the issue can be ordered at a specially reduced rate using the order form sent to the corresponding author after the manuscript has been accepted. Orders for reprints (produced after publication of an article) will incur a 50% surcharge.

Journal of Applied Psychology

SUBMISSION PROCESS: **Electronic Submission Only** **via Online Portal** **http://www.apa.org/journals/apl**	

CONTACT INFORMATION:	REVIEW PROCESS:
Sheldon Zedeck, Editor University of California Department of Psychology Berkeley, CA 94720-1650 USA	**Type of Review:** Blind Review **No. External Reviewers:** 2 **No. InHouse Reviewers:** 0
Phone: 510-642-5292 **Email:** zedeck@socrates.berkeley.edu **Website:** www.apa.org/apl	**Acceptance Rate:** 11-20% **Time to Review:** 2 - 3 Months **Reviewer's Comments:** Yes **Invited Articles:** 0-5% **Fees to Publish:** $0.00 US$ **Fees to Review:** $0.00 US$
PUBLICATION GUIDELINES:	**CIRCULATION DATA:**
Manuscript Style: American Psychological Association **Manuscript Length:** 26-30 **Copies Required:** Four	**Reader:** Academics, Clinical, Government **Frequency of Issue:** Bi-Monthly **Sponsor/Publisher:** American Psychological Association

MANUSCRIPT TOPICS:
Tests, Measurement & Evaluation

MANUSCRIPT GUIDELINES/COMMENTS:

The *Journal of Applied Psychology* is devoted primarily to original investigations that contribute new knowledge and understanding to fields of applied psychology other than clinical and applied experimental or human factors. The journal considers quantitative investigations of interest to psychologists doing research or working in such settings as universities, industry, government, urban affairs, police and correctional systems, health and educational institutions, transportation and defense systems, labor unions, and consumer affairs. A theoretical or review article may be accepted if it represents a special contribution to an applied field. Topics appropriate for the *Journal of Applied Psychology* include personnel selection, performance measurement, training, work motivation, job attitudes, eyewitness accuracy, leadership, drug and alcohol abuse, career development, the conflict between job and family demands, work behavior, work stress, organizational design and interventions, technology, polygraph use, the utility of organizational interventions, consumer buying behavior, and cross-cultural differences in work behavior and attitudes. The specific topics addressed, however, change as a function of societal and organizational change; studies of human behavior in novel situations are also encouraged.

Submission. All efforts should be undertaken to submit manuscripts electronically to the editor. Files can be sent in Microsoft word, in WordPerfect, or as a PDF file. The version sent should be consistent with the complete APA-style printed version. Authors without Internet access should submit a disk copy of the manuscript to: Sheldon Zedeck, Editor, Journal of Applied Psychology, Department of Psychology, University of California, Berkeley, CA 94720-1650

The journal will accept submissions in masked (blind) review format only. Each copy of a manuscript should include a separate title page with author names and affiliations, and these should not appear anywhere else on the manuscript. Furthermore, author identification notes should be typed on the title page (see *Manual*). Authors should make every reasonable effort to see that the manuscript itself contains no clues to their identities. Manuscripts not in masked format will not be reviewed.

Articles submitted for publication in the *Journal of Applied Psychology* are evaluated according to the following criteria: (a) significance of contribution, (b) technical adequacy, (c) appropriateness for the journal, and (d) clarity of presentation. In addition, articles must be clearly written in concise and unambiguous language and must be logically organized. The goal of APA primary journals is to publish useful information that is accurate and clear.

Authors should prepare manuscripts according to the *Publication Manual of the American Psychological Association* (5th ed.). Articles not prepared according to the guidelines of the *Manual* will not be reviewed. All manuscripts must include an abstract containing a maximum of 180 words typed on a separate sheet of paper. Typing instructions (all copy must be double-spaced) and instructions on preparing tables, figures, references, metrics, and abstracts appear in the *Manual*. Also, all manuscripts are copyedited for bias-free language (see chap. 2 of the *Publication Manual*). Original color figures can be printed in color provided the author agrees to pay half of the associated production costs.

The journal will publish both regular articles, or Feature Articles, and Research Reports. Authors can refer to recent issues of the journal for approximate length of Feature Articles. (Total manuscript pages divided by 4 provides an estimate of total printed pages.) Longer articles will be considered for publication, but the contribution they make must justify the number of journal pages needed to present the research. Research Reports feature shorter manuscripts that make a distinct but relatively narrow contribution, such as important replications or studies that discuss specific applications of psychology. Authors may request Research Report status at the time of submission, or the editor may suggest that a regular-length submission be pared down to Research Report length. Research Reports are limited to no more than 17 pages of text proper; these limits do not include the title page, abstract, references, tables, or figures. Different printers, fonts, spacing, margins, and so forth can substantially alter the amount of text that can be fit on a page. In determining the length limits of Research Reports, authors should count 25–26 lines of text (60 characters per line) as the equivalent of one page.

Authors are required to obtain and provide to APA all necessary permissions to reproduce any copyrighted work, including, for example, test instruments and other test materials or portions thereof.

APA policy prohibits an author from submitting the same manuscript for concurrent consideration by two or more publications. In addition, it is a violation of APA Ethical Principles to publish "as original data, data that have been previously published" (Standard 6.24). As this journal is a primary journal that publishes original material only, APA policy prohibits as well publication of any manuscript that has already been published in whole or substantial part elsewhere. Authors have an obligation to consult journal editors concerning prior publication of any data upon which their article depends.

In addition, APA Ethical Principles specify that "after research results are published, psychologists do not withhold the data on which their conclusions are based from other competent professionals who seek to verify the substantive claims through reanalysis and who intend to use such data only for that purpose, provided that the confidentiality of the participants can be protected and unless legal rights concerning proprietary data preclude their release" (Standard 6.25). APA expects authors submitting to this journal to adhere to these standards. Specifically, authors of manuscripts submitted to APA journals are expected to have their data available throughout the editorial review process and for at least 5 years after the date of publication.

Authors will be required to state in writing that they have complied with APA ethical standards in the treatment of their sample, human or animal, or to describe the details of treatment. A copy of the APA Ethical Principles may be obtained by writing the APA Ethics Office, 750 First Street, NE, Washington, DC 20002-4242 (or see "Ethical Principles," December 1992, *American Psychologist,* Vol. 47, pp. 1597-1611).

APA requires authors to reveal any possible conflict of interest in the conduct and reporting of research (e.g., financial interests in a test procedure, funding by pharmaceutical companies for drug research).

Journal of Applied Research in the Community College

SUBMISSION PROCESS:	
Electronic Submission Only **via EMail** **serban.andreea.mihaela@gmail.com**	

CONTACT INFORMATION:	REVIEW PROCESS:	
Andreea Serban, Editor	**Type of Review:**	Blind Review
Phone:	**No. External Reviewers:**	2
	No. InHouse Reviewers:	2
Email: serban.andreea.mihaela@gmail.com	**Acceptance Rate:**	50%
	Time to Review:	2 - 3 Months
Website: www.ncccrp.org	**Reviewer's Comments:**	Yes
	Invited Articles:	6-10%
	Fees to Publish:	$0.00 US$
	Fees to Review:	$0.00 US$

PUBLICATION GUIDELINES:	CIRCULATION DATA:
Manuscript Style: American Psychological Association	**Reader:** Academics, Administrators, Institutional Researchers
Manuscript Length: 16-20	**Frequency of Issue:** 2 Times/Year
Copies Required: Electronic Only	**Sponsor/Publisher:** National Community College Council for Research and Planning (NCCCRP) / New Forums Press

MANUSCRIPT TOPICS:
Education Management / Administration; Higher Education; Tests, Measurement & Evaluation

MANUSCRIPT GUIDELINES/COMMENTS:

The *Journal of Applied Research in the Community College* is a refereed journal sponsored by the National Community College Council of Research and Planning (NCCCRP), an affiliated council of the American Association of Community Colleges. The purpose of the biannual journal is to serve the needs and interests of institutional researchers and planners in the community college as well as those of administrators, faculty, policy makers and others with an interest in the community college.

The *Journal of Applied Research in the Community College* publishes applied research articles as well as those that describe innovative approaches and models for use in planning and assessment in community colleges. *JARCC* is also interested in "toolbox" articles, those that describe in some detail a specific technique (e.g., a data collection instrument or approach, an analytic technique, a way to communicate data to decision makers, etc.) that can improve research, planning and assessment practices in community colleges; special essays where the author(s) take a particular point of view; and book reviews.

518

Manuscripts should generally be 10-20 pages in length (double-spaced) and should be sent to the Executive Editor in a Word document by e-mail. Each manuscript should be accompanied by an abstract of 150 words or less, along with the address, phone number, e-mail address and FAX number for the lead author. Each table and figure should be saved as a Word document in a separate file with an indication in the article of about where each should be placed. Images created in pdf must be converted to jpg or tif and Excel tables must be converted to Word. Manuscripts submitted to the journal must not be under consideration by other publishers. All manuscripts should conform to the guidelines as outlined in the *APA Style Manual*, 5th Edition.

Articles are screened initially by one of the editors for appropriateness with the purposes of *JARCC* and overall quality. If the screening is positive, then the article is sent out for blind peer review to two members of the Editorial Advisory Board (see listing). The criteria used in the review process include the following: makes a significant contribution to administration, policy making and/or the practice of institutional research at community colleges; generates reader interest; represents a timely topic; clearly defines and states the problem; makes a clear link to previous literature; uses appropriate design and methodology; logically organizes the presentation; writes clearly, and provides conclusions/implications/recommendations substantiated by the content presented. If, after review, the article is accepted for publication, the Executive Editor will assign an Associate Editor to work with the author(s) on any revisions that are requested.

If you have presented at a local, regional or national conference and are wondering if your work might be appropriate for consideration by *JARCC*, we encourage you to contact the Executive Editor via e-mail. An important purpose of the journal is to encourage more community college institutional researchers, planners and assessment specialists to consider sharing their good work through formal publication.

Send manuscripts to Andreea M. Serban, Executive Editor: **serban.andreea.mihaela@gmail.com**

Journal of Applied School Psychology

SUBMISSION PROCESS:
Postal Submission Only

CONTACT INFORMATION:	REVIEW PROCESS:	
Charles A. Maher, Editor Rutgers University Graduate School of Applied and Professional Psychology 152 Frelinghusyen Road Piscataway, NJ 08854 USA	**Type of Review:**	Blind Review
	No. External Reviewers:	3
	No. InHouse Reviewers:	1
	Acceptance Rate:	21-30%
	Time to Review:	4 - 6 Months
Phone: 732-445-2000 ext.103	**Reviewer's Comments:**	Yes
	Invited Articles:	11-20%
Email: camaher@rci.rutgers.edu	**Fees to Publish:**	$0.00 US$
	Fees to Review:	$0.00 US$
Website: www.haworthpressinc.com		

PUBLICATION GUIDELINES:	CIRCULATION DATA:
Manuscript Style: American Psychological Association	**Reader:** Academics, Applied Researchers, Psychology Practitioners
Manuscript Length: 26-30	**Frequency of Issue:** 2 Times/Year
Copies Required: Four	**Sponsor/Publisher:** Haworth Press, Inc.

MANUSCRIPT TOPICS:
Counseling & Personnel Services; Educational Psychology; Secondary / Adolescent Studies; Special Education

MANUSCRIPT GUIDELINES/COMMENTS:

About the Journal
A biannual journal with an applied focus, the *Journal of Applied School Psychology* includes up-to-the-minute, practical information that assists practicing school psychologists and related professionals in performing the wide range of service delivery tasks for which they are responsible and for which they must coordinate their efforts, in areas of assessment, instruction, counseling, staff development, and organizational development.

Informative and instructive articles are aimed at school psychologists, social workers, other special service providers, school supervisors, directors, and administrators. All of these groups will find topics of interest, such as
- reviews of applied educational research and relevant literature
- descriptions of successful programs
- policy perspectives on current and future issues and trends
- guidelines for designing, implementing, and evaluating special service programs

520

This invaluable professional resource helps readers
- assess individual pupils and groups to determine their special educational needs
- design individualized and group programs
- assist regular and special classroom teachers in fostering academic achievement and functional living of special students
- enhance the social and emotional development of pupils through preventive and remedial approaches
- help school administrators to develop smoothly functioning organizational systems
- foster the physical well-being of special students
- involve parents and families in special programs
- educate and train school staff to more effectively educate special needs students

About the Editor

Charles A. Maher, PsyD. is Professor of Psychology at the Graduate School of Applied and Professional Psychology at Rutgers University where he served eight years as Chairperson of the Department of Applied Psychology. He is actively involved, both nationally and internationally, as a consultant to schools, private corporations, government agencies, and professional sports organizations. His consultation programs and services encompass a broad area including educational planning, professional self management, enhancement of the psychoeducational performance of individuals and groups, and sport psychology. He is a recipient of the 1991 Capital Award of the National Leadership Council for principled leadership, business professionalism, and success achievement. He is a fellow of the American Psychological Association, American Psychological Society, and the American Association of Applied Preventive Psychology.

1. **Original articles only**. Submission of a manuscript to this *Journal* represents a certification on the part of the author(s) that it is an original work and that neither this manuscript nor a version of it has been published elsewhere nor is being considered for publication elsewhere.

2. **Manuscript length**. Your manuscript may be approximately 20 typed pages double-spaced (including references and abstract). Lengthier manuscripts may be considered, but only at the discretion of the Editor. Sometimes, lengthier manuscripts may be considered if they can be divided up into sections for publication in successive *Journal* issues.

3. **Manuscript style**. References, citations, and general style of manuscripts for this *Journal* should follow the Chicago style (as outlined in the latest edition of the *Manual of Style* of the University of Chicago Press). References should be double-spaced and placed in alphabetical order.

If an author wishes to submit a paper that has been already prepared in another style, he or she may do so. However, if the paper is accepted (with or without reviewer's alterations), the author is fully responsible for retyping the manuscript in the correct style as indicated above. Neither the Editor nor the Publisher is responsible for re-preparing manuscript copy to adhere to the *Journal*'s style.

4. **Manuscript preparation**.
Margins: leave at least a one-inch margin on all four sides.
Paper: use clean white, 8-1/2" x 11" bond paper.
Number of copies: 3 (the original plus two photocopies).
Cover page: Important-staple a cover page to the manuscript indicating only the article title (this is used for anonymous refereeing).
Second "title page": enclose a regular title page but do not staple it to the manuscript. Include the title again, plus:
- Full authorship
- An ABSTRACT of about 100 words. (Below the abstract provide 3-10 key words for index purposes).
- An introductory footnote with authors' academic degrees, professional titles, affiliations, mailing addresses, and any desired acknowledgment of research support or other credit.

5. **Return envelopes**. When you submit your three manuscript copies, also include:
- A 9" x 12" envelope, self-addressed and stamped (with sufficient postage to ensure return of your manuscript);
- A regular envelope, stamped and self-addressed. This is for the Editor to send you an "acknowledgement of receipt" letter.

6. **Spelling, grammar, and punctuation**. You are responsible for preparing manuscript copy which is clearly written in acceptable scholarly English, and which contains no errors of spelling grammar, or punctuation. Neither the Editor nor the Publisher is responsible for correcting errors of spelling and grammar: the manuscript, after acceptance by the Editor, must be immediately ready for typesetting as it is finally submitted by the author(s). Check your paper for the following common errors:
- Dangling modifiers
- Misplaced modifiers
- Unclear antecedents
- Incorrect or inconsistent abbreviations Also, check the accuracy of all arithmetic calculations, statistics, numerical data, text citations, and references.

7. **Inconsistencies must be avoided**. Be sure you are consistent in your use of abbreviations terminology, and in citing references, from one part of your paper to another.

8. **Preparation of tables, figures, and illustrations**. All tables, figures, illustrations, etc. must be "camera-ready." That is, they must be cleanly typed or artistically prepared so that they can be used either exactly as they are or else used after a photographic reduction in size. Figures, tables, and illustrations must be prepared on separate sheets of paper. Always use black ink and professional drawing instruments. On the back of these items, write your article title and the journal title lightly in pencil, so they do not get misplaced. In text, skip extra lines and indicate where these figures and tables are to be placed (please do not write on face of art). Photographs are considered part of the acceptable manuscript and remain with Publisher for use in additional printings.

9. **Alterations Required By Referees And Reviewers**. Many times a paper is accepted by the Editor contingent upon changes that are mandated by anonymous specialist referees and members of the Editorial Board. If the Editor returns your manuscript for revisions, you are responsible for retyping any sections of the paper to incorporate these revisions (if applicable, revisions should also be put on disk).

10. **Typesetting**. You will not be receiving galley proofs of your article. Editorial revisions, if any, must therefore be made while your article is still in manuscript. The final version of the manuscript will be the version you see published. Typesetter's errors will be corrected by the production staff of The Haworth Press. Authors are expected to submit manuscripts, disks, and art that are free from error.

11. **Electronic media**. Haworth's in-house type-setting unit will now be able to utilize your final manuscript material as prepared on most personal computers and word processors. This will minimize typographical errors and decrease overall production timelag.

A. Please continue to send your first draft and final draft copies of your manuscript to the journal Editor in print format for his/her final review and approval;

B. Only after the journal editor has approved your final manuscript, you may submit the final approved version both on:
- Printed format ("hard copy")
- Floppy diskette

C. Please make sure that the disk version and the hard copy (printed cony) are exactly the same.

D. Wrap your floppy diskettes in a strong diskette wrapper or holder, and write on the outside of the package:
- The brand name of your computer or word processor
- The word-processing program that you used to create your article, book chapter, or book
- File name

The benefits of this procedure are many with speed and accuracy being the most obvious. We look forward to working with you on this, knowing we will be able to serve you more efficiently in the future.

12. **Reprints**. The senior author will receive one copy of the journal issue and 10 complimentary reprints of his or her article. The junior author will receive one copy of the issue. These are sent several weeks after the journal issue is published and in circulation. An order form for the purchase of additional reprints will also be sent to all authors at this time. (Approximately 4-6 weeks is necessary for the preparation of reprints.) Please do not query the *Journal*'s Editor about reprints. ALI such questions should be sent directly to The Haworth Press, Inc., Production Department, 21 East Broad Street, West Hazleton, PA 18201. To order additional reprints (minimum: 50 copies), please contact The Haworth Document Delivery Center, 10 Alice Street, Binghamton, New York 13904-1580 (607) 722-5857.

13. **Copyright**. Copyright ownership of your manuscript must be transferred officially to The Haworth Press, Inc. before we can begin the peer-review process. The Editor's letter acknowledging receipt of the manuscript will be accompanied by a form fully explaining this. All authors must sign the form and return the original to the Editor as soon as possible. Failure to return the copyright form in a timely fashion will result in delay in review and subsequent publication.

Journal of Behavioral Education

<table>
<tr><td colspan="2" align="center">

SUBMISSION PROCESS:

Electronic Submission Only
via Online Portal

https://www.editorialmanager.com/jobe/
</td></tr>
<tr><td>

CONTACT INFORMATION:
</td><td>

REVIEW PROCESS:
</td></tr>
<tr><td>

George H. Noell, Editor
Department of Psychology
233 Audubon Hall
Louisiana State University
Baton Rouge, LA 70803 USA

Phone:
  225-578-4119

Email:
  gnoell@lsu.edu

Website:
  https://www.editorialmanager.com/ jobe/
</td><td>

Type of Review:	Blind Review
No. External Reviewers:	0-1
No. InHouse Reviewers:	2-3
Acceptance Rate:	21-30%
Time to Review:	1 - 2 Months
Reviewer's Comments:	Yes
Invited Articles:	11-20%
Fees to Publish:	$0.00 US$
Fees to Review:	$0.00 US$
</td></tr>
<tr><td>

PUBLICATION GUIDELINES:

Manuscript Style:
  American Psychological Association

Manuscript Length:
  21-25

Copies Required:
  Electronic Only
</td><td>

CIRCULATION DATA:

Reader:
  Academics

Frequency of Issue:
  Quarterly

Sponsor/Publisher:
  Springer
</td></tr>
</table>

MANUSCRIPT TOPICS:
Elementary / Early Childhood; Languages & Linguistics; Reading; Science Math & Environment; Secondary / Adolescent Studies; Social Studies / Social Science; Special Education

MANUSCRIPT GUIDELINES/COMMENTS:

Aims and Scope
Journal of Behavioral Education provides the first single-source forum for the publication of research on the application of behavioral principles and technology to education. This international journal publishes original empirical research and brief reports covering behavioral education in regular, special, and adult education settings. Subject populations include handicapped, at-risk, and non-handicapped students of all ages.

General
In general, the journal follows the recommendations of the 1994 *Publication Manual of the American Psychological Association* (Fourth Edition), and it is suggested that contributors refer to this publication. The research described in the manuscripts should be consistent with generally accepted standards of ethical practice.

Manuscript Submission

Manuscripts should be submitted to the Co−Editor: George Noell, Journal of Behavioral Education, Department of Psychology, 233 Audubon Hall, Louisiana State University, Baton Rouge, LA 70803; Email: **gnoell@lsu.edu** (together with a letter requesting review and possible publication) and should be checked for content and style (correct spelling, punctuation, and grammar; accuracy and consistency in the citation of figures, tables, and references; stylistic uniformity of entries in the References section; etc.), as the typesetter is instructed to follow (accepted) manuscripts as presented. Page proofs are sent to the designated author for proofreading and checking. Typographical errors are corrected; authors' alterations are not allowed.

Publication Policies

Submission is a representation that the manuscript has not been published previously and is not currently under consideration for publication elsewhere. A statement transferring copyright from the authors (or their employers, if they hold the copyright) to Springer Science+Business Media, Inc. will be required before the manuscript can be accepted for publication. The Co-Editor will supply the necessary forms for this transfer. Such a written transfer of copyright, which previously was assumed to be implicit in the act of submitting a manuscript, is necessary under the U.S. Copyright Law in order for the publisher to carry through the dissemination of research results and reviews as widely and effectively as possible.

Manuscript Style

Type double-spaced on one side of 8 ½ × 11 inch white paper using generous margins on all sides, and submit the original and four copies (including copies of all illustrations and tables).

Title Page

A title page is to be provided and should include:
- the title of the article
- author's name (with degree)
- author's affiliation
- and suggested running head.

The affiliation should comprise:
- the department
- institution (usually university or company)
- city
- and state (or nation)

and should be typed as a numbered footnote to the author's name. The suggested running head should be less than 80 characters (including spaces) and should comprise the article title or an abbreviated version thereof. The title page should also include
- the complete mailing address
- telephone number
- fax number
- and e-mail address of the one author designated to review proofs.

Abstract

An abstract is to be provided, preferably no longer than 200 words. The abstract should be concise and complete in itself without reference to the body of the paper, and should contain a brief summary of the paper's purpose, method, major findings, and educational significance.

Key Words

A list of 5 key words is to be provided directly below the abstract. Key words should express the precise content of the manuscript, as they are used for indexing purposes.

References

List references alphabetically at the end of the paper and refer to them in the text by name and year in parentheses. References should include (in this order):

- last names and initials of all authors
- year published
- title of article
- name of publication
- volume number
- and inclusive pages

The style and punctuation of the references should conform to strict APA style – illustrated by the following examples:

Journal Article. Duckwall, J. M., Arnold, L., & Hayes, J. (1991). Approaches to learning by undergraduate students: A longitudinal study. Research in Higher Education, 32, 1–13.

Book. Strain, P. S. (1981). The utilization of classroom peers as behavior change agents. New York: Plenum Press.

Contribution to a Book. Matson, J. L., & Schaughency, E. A. (1988). Mild and moderate mental retardation. In J. C. Witt, S. N. Elliott, & F. M. Gresham (Eds.), Handbook of behavior therapy in education (pp. 631–651). New York: Plenum Press.

Footnotes

Footnotes should be avoided. When their use is absolutely necessary, footnotes should be numbered consecutively using Arabic numerals and should be typed at the bottom of the page to which they refer. Place a line above the footnote, so that it is set off from the text. Use the appropriate superscript numeral for citation in the text.

Illustration Style

- Illustrations (photographs, drawings, diagrams, and charts) are to be numbered in one consecutive series of Arabic numerals. The captions for illustrations should be typed on a separate sheet of paper. Photographs should be large, glossy prints, showing high contrast. Drawings should be high-quality laser prints or should be prepared with India ink. Either the original drawings or good-quality photographic prints are acceptable. Artwork for each figure should be provided on a separate sheet of paper. Identify figures on the back with author's name and number of the illustration. Electronic artwork submitted on disk should be in the TIFF or EPS format (1200 dpi for line and 300 dpi for halftones and gray-scale art). Color art should be in the CYMK color space. Artwork should be on a separate disk from the text, and hard copy must accompany the disk.
- Tables should be numbered and referred to by number in the text. Each table should be typed on a separate sheet of paper. Center the title above the table, and type explanatory footnotes (indicated by superscript lowercase letters) below the table.

Submission of Accepted Manuscripts

After a manuscript has been accepted for publication and after all revisions have been incorporated, manuscripts should be submitted to the Editor's Office as hard copy accompanied by electronic files on disk. Label the disk with identifying Information – software, journal name, and first author's last name. The disk must be the one from which the accompanying manuscript (finalized version) was printed out. The Editor's Office cannot accept a disk without its accompanying, matching hard-copy manuscript.

Page Charges

The journal makes no page charges. Reprints are available to authors, and order forms with the current price schedule are sent with proofs.

Journal of Broadcasting & Electronic Media

SUBMISSION PROCESS: Postal Submission Only	
CONTACT INFORMATION:	**REVIEW PROCESS:**
Donald G. Godfrey, Editor Arizona State University Walter Cronkite School of Journalism and Mass Communications P O Box 851304 Tempe, AZ 85287-1305 USA	**Type of Review:** Blind Review **No. External Reviewers:** 3 **No. InHouse Reviewers:** 0 **Acceptance Rate:** 11-20% **Time to Review:** 2 - 3 Months
Phone: 480-965-8661	**Reviewer's Comments:** Yes **Invited Articles:** 0-5%
Email: don.godfrey@asu.edu	**Fees to Publish:** $0.00 US$ **Fees to Review:** $0.00 US$
Website: www.beaweb.org	
PUBLICATION GUIDELINES:	**CIRCULATION DATA:**
Manuscript Style: American Psychological Association	**Reader:** Academics, Administrators, Professionals
Manuscript Length: 15-30	**Frequency of Issue:** Quarterly
Copies Required: Four	**Sponsor/Publisher:** Broadcast Education Association

MANUSCRIPT TOPICS:

Broadcasting and electronic media; Criticism; History; Law; Research; Social Studies / Social Science

MANUSCRIPT GUIDELINES/COMMENTS:

The *Journal of Broadcasting & Electronic Media* is an international quarterly devoted to advancing, research, knowledge, and understanding of communication and the electronic media. The *Journal* invites submissions of original research that examine a broad range of issues concerning the electronic media, including their historical, technological, economic, policy, cultural, and social dimensions. Scholarship that extends a historiography, tests theory, or that fosters innovative perspectives on topics of importance to the field, is particularly encouraged. The *Journal* is open to a diversity of theoretic paradigms and methodologies.

Submitted work is evaluated according to the quality of its conceptualization; the importance of the topic to scholars, policy makers, and practitioners; the lasting contribution it will make to electronic media studies; and the research execution. Key considerations of research execution include the research design, soundness of the research procedure, and the clarity of presentation. The Editor reserves the right not to send manuscripts out for review that fall outside the scope of the *Journal* or make an insignificant contribution to the field.

1. It is assumed that only the original work of the author will be submitted for *Journal* consideration. Any manuscript submitted must not be under consideration by another publication. Papers presented first at conferences or symposia should be carefully revised prior to submission for publication in the *Journal*.

2. Four copies of the manuscript should be submitted. The author should retain the original. Manuscripts will not be returned.

3. The published journal follows APA style, but manuscripts may be submitted in APA, MLA or *The Chicago Manual of Style*. Upon acceptance manuscripts must be prepared by the author in strict accordance with the current edition of the *Publication Manual of the American Psychological Association*. Nonsexist language should be used.

4. Because manuscripts are reviewed blindly, author identification should be on the title page only. The title page should include the following: the complete title; author name(s); corresponding postal addresses, electronic mail addresses, and telephone numbers; and any necessary credits. Any further references that might identify the author(s) should be removed from the manuscript.

5. The second page of the manuscript should consist of an abstract of 75 to 100 words. The text of the manuscript (including its title) should begin on the next page, with the remaining pages numbered consecutively with running heads.

6. Notes and references should be double-spaced on pages following the text of the manuscript, and follow the formats of the current edition of the *Publication Manual of the American Psychological Association*. Notes should be kept to a minimum. Complete citations for references should be supplied.

7. Clear, economical, and orderly expression is expected of submissions to the *Journal*. Most *Journal* submissions should be circa 25 pages, including references and tables. Brevity is encouraged.

8. The number of tables should be kept to a minimum. No table should be included if the equivalent information can be communicated in a few sentences in the text. If the author wishes to offer large or esoteric tables for interested readers, their availability from the author should be indicated in a text note. Graphic material, other than tables, should be submitted in camera ready form if the manuscript is accepted for publication.

9. Authors normally will have an editorial decision within 3–4 months. Because manuscripts are sent to expert referees for evaluation, the consideration time may vary.

10. The Editor reserves the right to make minor changes in any accepted manuscript that do not alter the substantial meaning or results of the article or the expressed views of the author. Authors will be given the opportunity to approve all such changes and can withdraw their manuscript from consideration at any time.

11. The Broadcast Education Association holds copyright to all issues of the *Journal of Broadcasting & Electronic Media*. The Executive Director of the Association must grant permission for reproduction in any form of any of the contents of the *Journal*. The address is: Executive Director, Broadcast Education Association, 1771 N Street, NW, Washington, D. C., 20036.

12. Research manuscripts and correspondence should be addressed to: Donald G. Godfrey, Editor, Journal of Broadcasting & Electronic Media, Walter Cronkite School of Journalism & Mass Communications, Arizona State University, Box 871305, Tempe, AZ 85287-1305.

Inquiries and correspondence about book/video/electronic-media reviews or critical essays should be addressed to: Michael D. Murray, Review and Criticism Editor, Journal of Broadcasting & Electronic Media, School of Journalism, 4505 Maryland Parkway, Las Vegas, NV 89154-5007.

Journal of Business and Training Education

SUBMISSION PROCESS:	
Electronic Submission Only	
via EMail	
betty.kleen@nicholls.edu	

CONTACT INFORMATION:	REVIEW PROCESS:	
Betty A. Kleen, Editor Nicholls State University Accounting & Information Systems Dept. PO Box 2015 Thibodaux, LA 70310 USA	**Type of Review:**	Blind Review
	No. External Reviewers:	3
	No. InHouse Reviewers:	0
	Acceptance Rate:	21-30%
Phone:	**Time to Review:**	4 - 6 Months
985-448-4191	**Reviewer's Comments:**	Yes
	Invited Articles:	0-5%
Email:		
betty.kleen@nicholls.edu	**Fees to Publish:**	$0.00 US$
Website:	**Fees to Review:**	$0.00 US$

PUBLICATION GUIDELINES:	CIRCULATION DATA:
Manuscript Style: American Psychological Association	**Reader:** Academics, Practicing Teachers, Trainers
Manuscript Length: 11-15	**Frequency of Issue:** Yearly
Copies Required: Electronic Only	**Sponsor/Publisher:** Louisiana Association of Business Educators

MANUSCRIPT TOPICS:
Adult Career & Vocational; Teacher Education

MANUSCRIPT GUIDELINES/COMMENTS:

Manuscripts should deal with topics of interest to business educators (at both the secondary and post-secondary levels) and to trainers in business and industry. Manuscripts dealing with practical topics are encouraged, as are research based or theoretical papers. Books reviews are accepted. Occasionally, invited authors' papers will be published.

Manuscripts will be selected through a blind review process and should not have been published or be under current consideration for publication by another journal. Remove all personal and institutional identification from the body and title of the paper. Title page should include the title of the manuscript, a 50-100 word abstract, a list of keywords, and a running header. Email accompanying the manuscript should include: title of manuscript; and each author's full name, position title, place of employment, city, state, zip code, telephone numbers, and e-mail address.

Journal of Business Communication

SUBMISSION PROCESS:

Electronic Submission Preferred
via EMail

mgraham@iastate.edu

CONTACT INFORMATION:	REVIEW PROCESS:
Margaret Baker Graham, Editor Iowa State University 445 Ross Hall Ames, IA 50011 USA **Phone:** 515-294-5203 **Email:** mgraham@iastate.edu **Website:** http://www.sagepub.com/	**Type of Review:** No. External Reviewers: 3 No. InHouse Reviewers: 2 Acceptance Rate: 11-20% Time to Review: 2 - 3 Months Reviewer's Comments: Yes Invited Articles: 0-5% Fees to Publish: $0.00 US$ Fees to Review: $0.00 US$
PUBLICATION GUIDELINES:	**CIRCULATION DATA:**
Manuscript Style: American Psychological Association **Manuscript Length:** Average 30 **Copies Required:** Four or 1 Electronic	**Reader:** Academics **Frequency of Issue:** Quarterly **Sponsor/Publisher:** Association for Business Communication

MANUSCRIPT TOPICS:

Adult Career & Vocational; Education Management / Administration; Higher Education; Social Studies / Social Science; Tests, Measurement & Evaluation

MANUSCRIPT GUIDELINES/COMMENTS:

Aims and Scope

The Journal of Business Communication (*JBC*) publishes manuscripts that contribute to the knowledge and theory of business communication as a distinct, multifaceted field approached through the administrative disciplines, the liberal arts, and the social sciences. Accordingly, *JBC* seeks manuscripts that address all areas of business communication including but not limited to business composition/technical writing, information systems, international business communication, management communication, and organizational and corporate communication. In addition, *JBC* welcomes submissions concerning the role of written, oral, nonverbal and electronic communication in the creation, maintenance, and performance of profit and not for profit business. *JBC* accepts all rigorous research methods, including but not limited to qualitative, quantitative, and critical. *JBC* conducts masked reviews in which the Editor, an Associate Editor, and at least two subject-matter experts examine submitted manuscripts.

Types of Manuscripts Published

- Traditional scholarly studies of 15-35 double-spaced pages, excluding references, notes, and appendices.
- Commentaries of 10-14 pages, excluding references, notes, and appendices.
- Forums consisting of 2-4 articles organized around a unifying theme. Manuscripts comprising forums typically resemble commentaries rather than traditional research submissions. Forums might also have an introduction written by a guest editor.
- Book reviews. Contact the Book Review Editor to inquire about reviewing a book.
- Quantitative and Qualitative Guidelines
- Quantitative manuscripts must report estimates of reliability for all dependent measures, variance accounted for in tests of significance, and power estimates when tests fail to achieve significance.
- Content analysis employing quantitative measures should note intercoder reliability.
- Survey research should describe the sampling frame (relevant population), sampling method, sample unit, and response rate.
- Qualitative research must note standards used to ensure the quality and verification of the presented interpretation.

Submitting Manuscripts

Electronic submission of manuscripts is STRONGLY ENCOURAGED. Electronic submission to the Editor will greatly expedite the review of your manuscript. Title your e-mail: <YourName.JBC>. Include your name and contact information in the e-mail message. Attach two documents: the cover page and the complete manuscript (consult instructions that follow). Save the manuscript and cover page as a Microsoft Word file or a rich text file. Save any figures, tables, or charts in a PDF document.

For traditional submission, submit 2 copies of the cover page and 4 complete copies of the manuscript to the Editor.

Manuscript Preparation

Write the manuscript in English, following the format specified in *the Publication Manual of the American Psychological Association* (5th edition). You may use either U.S. or British spelling, but use U.S. punctuation.

Remove all personal and institutional identification from the body of the manuscript.

The cover page should include:
- Manuscript title.
- Name, institutional affiliation, mailing address, e-mail address, and telephone and fax numbers for the corresponding author.
- Name, institutional affiliation, and e-mail address for all other authors.
- One to two sentences for each author's biography.
- A statement that the manuscript is original and is not under consideration or published elsewhere.

Submit the manuscript as a separate attachment.
- On the first page of the manuscript, include 1) the title, 2) an abstract of 150 words or fewer, 3) five keywords for online searchability.
- Start the body of the paper on the second page.
- Check the paper and references for accuracy.
- Write clearly and concisely using inclusive language.
- To hide your identity during the review process, refer to your own previously published research by using the word AUTHOR rather than your name.

Submit figures, tables, and charts as a PDF document. Such visuals are often lost when sent in a Word document. Indicate on the manuscript where each visual should be placed.

If your article is accepted, you might be asked to provide:
- Some additional text formatting.
- An electronic copy of the article (if not originally submitted electronically).
- A camera-ready copy of any images.
- Author notes (e.g., acknowledgments and manuscript history) .
- A statement showing that you have complied with the principles outlined in Appendix C (Ethical Standards for the Reporting and Publishing of Scientific Information) of the APA, 5th edition.

Editor. Margaret Baker Graham, Journal of Business Communication, Iowa State University, 445 Ross Hall, Ames, IA 50011; Phone: 515-294-5203; E-mail: **mgraham@iastate.edu**

Book Review Editor. Melinda Knight, Journal of Business Communication, The George Washington University, Rome Hall 562, 801 22nd St. NW, Washington, DC 20052; Phone: 202-994-2429; E-mail: **maknight@gwu.edu**

Editorial Assistant. Alzire Messenger; E-mail: **alzire@iastate.edu**

Cabell Publishing, Inc.
also publishes:

Education:
Educational Curriculum and Methods
Educational Psychology and Administration
Educational Technology and Library Science

Psychology:
Psychology and Psychiatry

Business:
Accounting
Economics and Finance
Management
Marketing

Visit our website for the latest editions and information!
www.cabells.com

All directories available electronically!

If you know of a journal that you feel should be included in:

Cabell's Directories

Please submit through our website:
www.cabells.com

Also, feel free to let us know if the current information in a journal entry requires updating.

WITHDRAWAL